THE WIDE WORLD
ALL AROUND

Longman English and Humanities Series

Series Editor: Lee A. Jacobus
University of Connecticut, Storrs

THE WIDE WORLD ALL AROUND

An Anthology of Children's Literature

Francelia Butler

Anne Devereaux Jordan

Richard Rotert

Longman
New York & London

To my great-grandson Mathew Derek Wandell
FB

For Bob and David and, of course, for my mother
ADJ

Executive Editor: Gordon T. R. Anderson
Senior Production Editor: Ronni Strell
Text Design: Angela Foote
Cover Illustration: Gail E. Haley
Production Supervisor: Judi Stern
Compositor: The Clarinda Company
Printer and Binder: The Murray Printing Company

The Wide World All Around

Longman Inc., 95 Church Street, White Plains, N.Y. 10601

Associated companies: Longman Group Ltd., London; Longman Cheshire Pty., Melbourne; Longman Paul Pty., Auckland; Copp Clark Pitman, Toronto; Pitman Publishing Inc., New York

Library of Congress Cataloging-in-Publication Data

The Wide world all around.

(Longman English and humanities series)
Summary: A collection of poetry, fiction, folklore, fables, myths, and rhymes arranged in three sections that reflect a child's discovery of the world. The sections are titled ''The Primary World: Family,'' ''The Created World: The Country and the City,'' and ''The Natural World.''
   1. Children's literature. (1. Literature—Collections)
I. Butler, Francelia, 1913– . II. Jordan, Anne Devereaux. III. Rotert, Richard, 1948– .
IV. Series.
PZ5.W6344 1987   808.8'99282   86-7480
ISBN 0-582-28601-8

87   88   89   90   9 8 7 6 5 4 3 2 1

Acknowledgments

pp.11, 52: ''Hector and Andromache'' and ''Perseus,'' from *Mythology,* by Edith Hamilton. Copyright 1942 by Edith Hamilton; copyright © renewed 1969 by Dorian Fielding Reid and Doris Fielding Reid, Executrix of the will of Edith Hamilton.

p. 21: ''The Huckabuck Family and How They Raised Pop Corn in Nebraska and Quit and Came Back,'' from *Rootabaga Stories,* by Carl Sandburg, copyright 1922, 1923 by Harcourt Brace Jovanovich, Inc.; renewed 1950, 1951 by Carl Sandburg. Reprinted by permission of the publisher.

p. 40: Excerpt from *A Parcel of Patterns,* by Jill Paton Walsh. Copyright © 1983 by Jill Paton Walsh. Reprinted by permission of Farrar, Straus and Giroux, Inc.

p. 45: ''Absolute Zero'' from *A Wrinkle in Time,* by Madeleine L'Engle. Copyright © 1962 by Madeleine L'Engle. Reprinted by permission of Farrar, Straus and Giroux, Inc.

p.51: ''The Raven and His Young,'' from *Fable and Fairy Tales,* by Leo Tolstoy, translated by Ann Dunnigan. Copyright © 1962 by Ann Dunnigan. Reprinted by arrangement with New American Library, New York, New York.

p. 62: ''Matryona's Home,'' by Alexander Solzhenitsyn, from *Halfway to the Moon,* by Patricia Blake and Max Hayward. Copyright 1985 by Patricia Blake. Reprinted by permission of the author.

p. 72: From *My Mother Is the Most Beautiful Woman in the World,* by Becky Reyher. Copyright © 1945, 1973 by Becky Reyher and Ruth Gannett. By permission of Lothrop, Lee & Shepard Books (A Division of William Morrow and Company), illustrations by Ruth Gannett.

p. 75: ''Mummy Slept Late and Daddy Fixed Breakfast,'' from *You Read to Me, I'll Read to You,* by John Ciardi, illustrated by Edward Gorey (J. B. Lippincott). Copyright © 1962 by John Ciardi. Reprinted by permission of Harper & Row, Publisher, Inc.

p. 76: ''Father's Day,'' from *Mom, the Wolf Man and Me,* by Norma Klein. Copyright © 1972 by Norma Klein. Reprinted by permission of Pantheon Books, a division of Random House, Inc.

p. 81: ''The Cyclone,'' Illustration by Evelyn Copelman (based on W. W. Denslow's original illustration), reprinted by permission of Grosset & Dunlap from *The Wizard of Oz,* by L. Frank Baum.

p. 82: ''The Hunter Brings Home a Baby,'' from *The Animal Family,* by Randall Jarrell. Copyright © 1965 by Random House, Inc.

p. 92: ''The Firebird,'' from *Russian Fairy Tales,* collected by Aleksandr Afanas'ev, translated by Norbert Guterman. Copyright 1945 by Pantheon Books, Inc., and renewed 1973 by Random House, Inc. Reprinted by permission of the publisher. Illustration from *The Twelve Dancing Princesses and Other Fairy Tales,* by Alfred and Mary Elizabeth David and illustrated by Sheila Greenwald. Illustrations © 1964 by New American Library. Reprinted by arrangement with New American Library, New York, New York.

p. 99: ''Baba Yaga,'' from *Russian Fairy Tales,* collected by Aleksandr Afanas'ev, translated by Norbert Guterman. Copyright 1945 by Pantheon Books, Inc., and renewed 1973 by Random House, Inc. Reprinted by permission of the publisher.

p. 103: ''The Little Match Girl,'' © Oxford University Press, 1961. Reprinted from *Hans Andersen's Fairy Tales,* translated by L. W. Kingsland (1961), by permission of Oxford University Press. Line illustration, © 1961 by E. H. Shepard, reproduced by permission of Curtis Brown Ltd., London.

p. 114: ''Muddy Duddy,'' by Brother Blue (Hugh Morgan Hill). Reprinted by permission of the author.

p. 115: Cynthia Voigt, excerpted from *Homecoming.* Copyright © 1981 Cynthia Voigt. Reprinted by permission of Atheneum Publishers, Inc.

p. 123: ''The Cat That Walked by Himself,'' by Rudyard Kipling, from *Just So Stories.* Copyright 1902 by Rudyard Kipling. Reprinted by permission of Doubleday & Company, Inc.

p. 129: ''Pig and Pepper,'' from *Alice's Adventures in Wonderland,* by Lewis Carroll, illustrated by Willy Pogany. Copyright 1929 by E. P. Dutton, renewed 1957 by Mrs. Willy Pogany. Reproduced by permission of the publisher, E. P. Dutton, a division of New American Library.

p. 134: Text and art from pp. 10–17 of *Pierre: A Cautionary Tale in Five Chapters and a Prologue,* by Maurice Sendak. Copyright © 1962, by Maurice Sendak. Reprinted by permission of Harper & Row, Publisher, Inc.

p. 146: ''The Founding of Mexico City,'' from Carlton Beals, *Stories Told by the Aztecs before the Spaniards Came.* Permission granted by Bertha Klausner International Literary Agency, Inc.

p. 152: ''The Old House,'' from Hans Christian Andersen, *The Complete Fairy Tales and Stories,* translated by Erik Christian Haugaard. Copyright © 1974 by Eric Christian Haugaard. Reprinted by permission of Doubldday & Company, Inc.

p. 156: ''The Happy Prince,'' from *The Complete Works of Oscar Wilde,* ed. J. B. Foreman. Wm. Collins Sons & Co., Ltd. Reprinted with permission.

p. 161: ''The Snow in Chelm,'' from *Zlateh the Goat: And Other Stories,* by Isaac Bashevis Singer. Translated from Yiddish by the author and Elizabeth Shub. Pictures by Maurice Sendak. Text copyright © 1966 by Isaac Bashevis Singer. Pictures copyright © 1966 by Maurice Sendak. Reprinted by permission of Harper & Row, Publishers, Inc.

p. 165: ''The Clock,'' from *Nursery Friends from France,* Olive Beaupré Miller, trans. Copyright 1927 by the Book House for Children. Reprinted with permission.

p. 165: ''Parliament Hill,'' by H. H. Bashford, from *Songs Out of School.* Reprinted by permission of Constable Publishers.

pp. 166, 167: ''City,'' ''Juke Box Love Song,'' by Langston Hughes,

v

reprinted by permission of Harold Ober Associates Incorporated. Copyright © 1958 by Langston Hughes. Copyright renewed 1986 by George Houston Bass.

p. 166: "Skyscrapers," reprinted with permission of Macmillan Publishing Company from *Poems,* by Rachel Field (New York: Macmillan, 1957).

p. 166: "Manhole Covers," copyright © 1967 by Karl Shapiro. Reprinted from *Collected Poems 1940–1978,* by Karl Shapiro, by permission of Random House, Inc.

p. 167: "Thaw in the City," copyright © 1967 by Lou Lipsitz. Reprinted from *Cold Water* by permission of Wesleyan University Press.

p. 167: "In a Station of the Metro," by Ezra Pound, from *Personae.* Copyright 1926 by Ezra Pound. Reprinted by permission of New Directions Publishing Corp.

p. 168: "Of Kings and Things," by Lillian Morrison, from *The Ghosts of Jersey City and Other Poems.* Reprinted by permission of the author.

p. 168: "Rain," from *I Think I Saw a Snail,* Lee Bennett Hopkins, ed. Reprinted by permission of the author.

p. 169: E. L. Konigsburg, Chapter 5 and illustrations from *From the Mixed-Up Files of Mrs. Basil E. Frankweiler.* Copyright © 1967 E. L. Konigsburg. Reprinted with the permission of Atheneum Publishers, Inc.

p. 176: From *Paddington Goes to Town* by Michael Bond. Copyright © 1968 by Michael Bond. Reprinted by permission of Houghton Mifflin Company.

p. 183: "Telipinu," by Theodor H. Gaster, from *The Oldest Stories in the World,* edited and translated by Theodor H. Gaster. Reprinted by permission of Viking Penguin Inc.

p. 185: "Earth and Its Seeds," by Carlton Beals, from *Stories Told by the Aztecs before the Spaniards Came.* Permission granted by Bertha Klausner International Literary Agency, Inc.

p. 191: "The Boggart and the Farmer," from *Round About and Long Ago,* by Eileen Colwell. Text copyright © Eileen Colwell 1972. Reprinted by permission of Houghton Mifflin Company. Two illustrations by Anthony Colbert from *Round About and Long Ago: Tales from the English Counties,* retold by Anthony Colbert (Longman Young Books, 1972), pp. 57, 59; illustrations copyright © 1972 by Longman Young Books.

p. 193: "The Winning of Kwelanga," from *Behind the Back of the Mountain,* by Verna Aardema, Dial Press ©.

p. 195: "The Kingdom of the Lazy People," from Dov Noy, *Folktales of Israel,* trans. by Gene Baharav, 1963:104-6. The University of Chicago Press.

p. 197: From *The Great Big Enormous Turnip,* by Alexei Tolstoy and Helen Oxenbury. Copyright © 1968 by Helen Oxenbury.

p. 198: "Hens to Sell," from *Nursery Friends from France,* Olive Beaupré Miller, trans. Copyright 1927 by the Book House for Children. Reprinted with permission.

pp. 198, 199: "Klumperty and His Wife," "Bim, Bam, Beggs," from *Tales Told in Holland.* Reprinted by permission of Book House for Children.

p. 200: "Paper Boats," by Rabindranath Tagore, reprinted with permission of Macmillan Publishing Company from *Collected Poems and Plays* by Rabindranath Tagore. Copyright 1913 by Macmillan Publishing Company, renewed 1941 by Rabindranath Tagore.

p. 200: "The Pasture," by Robert Frost, from *The Poetry of Robert Frost* edited by Edward Connery Lathem. Copyright 1939 © 1969 by Holt, Rinehart & Winston. Reprinted by permission of Holt, Rinehart & Winston Publishers.

p. 200: Haiku, by Kenneth Rexroth, reprinted by permission of New Direction Publishing Corporation.

p. 201: "After Snow," by Walter Clark, from *View from Mt. Paugus.* Reprinted by permission of the author.

p. 201: "He Was," by Richard Wilbur, from *Ceremony and Other Poems,* copyright 1950, 1978 by Richard Wilbur. Reprinted by permission of Hancourt Brace Jovanovich, Inc.

p. 201: "The Farm," by Vassar Miller, copyright © 1968 by Vassar Miller. Reprinted from *Onions and Roses* by permission of Wesleyan University Press.

p. 202: "I Never Saw a Moor," by Emily Dickinson, reprinted by permission of the publishers from *The Poems of Emily Dickinson,* edited by Thomas H. Johnson, Cambridge, Mass.: The Belknap Press of Harvard University Press, Copyright 1951, © 1955, 1979, 1983 by the President and Fellows of Harvard College.

p. 202: From *Farmer Boy,* by Laura Ingalls Wilder. Text copyright 1933 by Harper & Row, Publishers, Inc.; renewed 1961 by Roger L. MacBride.

p. 205: "Stairstep Farm," reprinted by permission of Curtis Brown, Ltd.

p. 211: From *Rabbit Hill,* by Robert Lawson. Copyright 1944 by Robert Lawson, renewed © 1972 by John W. Boyd. Reprinted by permission of Viking Penguin, Inc.

p. 216: "The Shepherd at Court," from *Italian Folktales,* by Italo Calvino, copyright © 1956 by Giulio Einaudi editore, s.p.a.; English translation copyright © 1980 by Harcourt Brace Jovanovich, Inc. Reprinted by permission of Harcourt Brace Jovanovich, Inc.

p. 219: "The Shepherd Who Laughed Last," by Ralph Steele Boggs and Mary Gould Davis. Reprinted with permission from *Three Golden Oranges and Other Spanish Folktales,* by Ralph Steele Boggs any Mary Gould Davis, copyright 1936. Published by David McKay Company, Inc.

p. 220: "The Mermaid of Edam," from *Tales Told in Holland.* Reprinted by permission of Book House for Children.

p. 223: "Elsie Piddock Skips in Her Sleep," by Eleanor Farjeon. Reprinted by permission of Harold Ober Associates Incorporated. Copyright © 1937 by Eleanor Farjeon. Copyright renewed 1965 by Eleanor Farjeon.

p. 230: "Two Skyscrapers Who Decided to Have a Child," by Carl Sandburg, from *Rootabaga Stories,* by Carl Sandburg, copyright 1922, 1923 by Harcourt Brace Jovanovich, Inc.; renewed 1950, 1951 by Carl Sandburg. Reprinted by permission of the publisher.

p. 233: "The Story of the Little Market Woman," illustrations by Pauline Baynes from *The Puffin Book of Nursery Rhymes,* gathered by Iona and Peter Opie (Puffin Books, 1963), pp. 142–143. Illustrations copyright © Penguin Books, 1963. Reprinted by permission of Penguin Books Ltd.

p. 234: "The Tropics in New York," by Claude McKay, from *The Selected Poems of Claude McKay.* Copyright © 1953 by Twayne Publishers.

p. 234: "In the City," by Lois Lenski, reprinted by permission of the Lois Lenski Covey Foundation.

p. 235: "Rudolph Is Tired of the City," by Gwendolyn Brooks, from *Selected Poems,* 1960. Reprinted by permission of Gwendolyn Brooks.

p. 235: "Ellis Park," by Helen Hoyt. Originally appeared in *Poetry.* Copyright © 1913 by the Modern Poetry Association. Reprinted by permission of the editor of *Poetry.*

p. 235: "Afternoon on a Hill," from *Collected Poems,* Harper & Row. Copyright 1917, 1945 by Edna St. Vincent Millay.

p. 236: "Population Drifts," by Carl Sandburg, from *Chicago*

Contents

The Fragmented Family   *51*

Children Alone   *84*

The Country   *182*

City versus Country   **215**

THE NATURAL WORLD 265

Water and the Sea 268

Trees and Hills   308

Preface

The Wide World All Around enables the educator, librarian, student, and parent to follow children through their journey of discovery of the world. As children develop, their world also grows, and the readings in *The Wide World All Around* reflect this expansion and exploration. The selections are grouped under three main headings—''The Primary World: the Family''; ''The Created World: City and Country''; and ''The Natural World.''

Children first begin to know the world through the family. They come to understand the structure of their family and their place within it. However, trips to the grocery store and day-care centers, vacations, and encounters with other families soon show children that outside their small family group is another world entirely. This larger world is more complex, but children readily learn that they also have a place in this created world of human communities. They learn about their own community, whether in the city or the country, and what communities other than their own are like. They gain a knowledge of their own heritage and an appreciation of different cultures. The world of children also expands to include the natural world; and the trees and hills, water and seas, and animals become a part of the child's universe. Through experience and through reading, the child journeys and finds a place in ''the wide world all around.''

The book is arranged so as to parallel the child's journey into the world. This enables the adult reader to re-experience, through literature, his or her own discovery of the world or to present literature to children in a way that will aid them in their first ventures into the world. *The Wide World All Around* is an application of literature to life itself.

For flexibility in presentation, each section is also divided according to genre. Should a reader wish to focus on the folktale, for example, selections in this genre are presented and discussed in each section. Thus a reader can follow various themes and, at the same time, experience the richness that the forms of literature offer.

At the end of each of the three major sections, ''Explorations,'' or suggested activities, are included to permit the reader to delve more deeply into the material of the theme that excites him or her the most. Similarly, suggestions for further reading for both children and adults are listed. In choosing selections for *The Wide World All Around*, we were faced with a surplus of material. We made our selections on the basis of what was representative of the various genres, appropriate to the overall themes of the book, and, of course, on the basis of what delighted or enthralled us. Because of the necessity of limiting the number of selections, further reading is encouraged in the ''References for Children'' and the ''References for Adults.''

The Wide World All Around is meant to be an experience. It is meant to be an enjoyable voyage for children and adults through the myriad facets of life, a journey whose destination is simply the world.

We wish to acknowledge the intelligent assistance (far beyond that which was required) of Ellen Embardo in Special Collections, Homer Babbidge Library, The University of Connecticut, and also Robert Vrecenak, Head of the Inter-Library Loan Department in that library. We are also greatly indebted to Regina H. Patroski, from the children's department of the Willimantic Public Library, and to Dr. Barbara Kasper, head of that department. Elizabeth Moody of Windham Center gave us the benefit of her lifetime of experience with children's books. In New York, Michael Patrick Hearn contributed invaluable assistance, emanating from his extensive research and writing in the field of children's literature. May Cutler, publisher of Tundra Books in Montreal, not only gave advice but arranged for us to reprint pages from her award-winning publications *A Prairie Boy's Summer* and *A Prairie Boy's Winter*.

Francelia Butler
Anne Devereaux Jordan
Richard Rotert

Introduction

Infants are the center of their own universe. The moon and stars circle around them, and all whom they encounter are there to do their bidding. For infants and toddlers, the universe is chiefly peopled with family, and books for this age group reflect this egocentric, limited view. These books may portray outside objects and actions, but they focus emotionally on this small cosmos. As children grow, their attention expands and their interest is centered more and more on the larger world beyond the family. All is theirs to explore: cities and towns, the countryside, the entire planet. This anthology follows the footsteps of children as they move in ever-widening circles from discovery of self within the family to exploration of "the wide world all around."

The selections included in *The Wide World All Around* reflect these ever-widening circles as transmitted through literature. At a very early age the child learns the most striking features of his or her small world: "Mommy and Daddy take care of me," "The city is different from the country," "A butterfly is pretty." As children grow, they gradually learn and understand the complexities and interrelationships within and among these spheres of experience. While *The Wide World All Around* is divided into three main sections, with representative literature depicting each, it is important to keep in mind that these divisions are for convenience only; in reality, children experience all three areas concurrently as they grow. For this reason, many of the selections would fit equally well in any of the three sections.

The primary world of the child is the family unit. Circling around and moving out from the family is the larger world of the human community of city and country, the created world. Simultaneous with these two spheres of experience is the natural world. Even when very young, a child senses and comes to realize that he or she has a relationship with the world beyond mankind.

Selections within each section cover a wide range of ages—picture books, for small children; folktales and stories, for the middle years (really, for everyone); and fiction, some of it for teenagers. The book is organized as follows:

   I. The Primary World: The Family
      1. The Traditional Family
      2. The Fragmented Family
      3. Children Alone
  II. The Created World: City and Country
      1. The City
      2. The Country
      3. City versus Country

III. The Natural World
   1. Water and the Sea
   2. Trees and Hills
   3. Birds and Animals

To date, anthologies of children's literature have presented a broad spectrum of selections. The stress has been more on the literature itself than on its intended audience. This anthology, however, attempts to keep in mind the child's need to become part of the world through books. In this journey through literature, the editors serve as guides to explain the ways in which an author reveals the world so that children can better understand themselves, their experiences, and the wonders all around them. In addition, *The Wide World All Around* should enable adults to retrace and understand the long path they have already traveled so that they can be companions to young readers.

The Wide World All Around is intended to be used in college classes in children's literature and by parents, librarians, and educators—anyone wishing to explore with children the world at large and the world of children's books. For this reason, the thematic arrangement follows the child's natural progression outward into the world. Within each section, the selections are arranged according to genre to enable both adult and child to experience the variety of forms that literature can assume.

Many forms of literature were originally transmitted orally from person to person and age to age and were recited, acted out, or sung. Today, we often tend to forget that what is frozen on a page was once alive and dynamic, capable of change. But for the prereading child such pieces—the folk rhymes, fables, myths and legends, and folktales—are still dynamic, because like earlier peoples, children often receive them orally and re-create them in their own imaginations. In exploring the world of literature a child's development parallels that of literature itself, moving from the oral to the written.

Because of their apparent simplicity, fables are often presented to very young children. Fables are one of the earliest literary forms and, in Western cultures, are often associated with Aesop. They are brief stories, usually with animals as characters, that end with a moral. It is thought that one purpose of Aesop's fables was to comment on the political structure of the time. Regardless of their initial intent the stories have an innate appeal that caused them to spread in their original form or in variant form to many countries outside Greece. Many of the verse-fables of the seventeenth-century French poet Jean de La Fontaine can be traced back to Aesop.

While fables communicate an earthy common sense, at least on one level, the ancients' myths and legends transmitted those peoples' views of history, religious beliefs, and explanations of natural phenomena. At the time of their currency, myths and legends were thought to be true, although some (such as those in Ovid's *Metamorphoses*) were known by their audience to be fictional and written purely for entertainment. The myths and legends that have survived through the ages appeal greatly to children and adults because of the grandeur of the deeds described and the halcyon glow surrounding the heroes and heroines, gods and goddesses of the tales. They inform us of the past and entertain us in the present.

Folktales and folk rhymes also inform and entertain but are disconnected, for the most part, from any religious credo. The original authorship of these tales and rhymes is usually unknown, but even if a source can be identified, the rhyme or tale is considered folklore if it has been adopted by a particular people and spread among them. Folktales are simple in structure and use recurring motifs, archetypes, and story patterns (see Stith Thompson's *Motif-Index of Folk Literature*). Most civilizations, for example, have a version of the Cinderella tale using the motif of the cruel stepmother. These tales are rich in plot, and they tell us a bit about the cultural beliefs of the people among whom they originated.

Folk rhymes—including nursery rhymes, counting-out rhymes and skip-rope rhymes—also tell us something of the society in which they developed but, in addition, they are the stuff of childhood. The small stories the rhymes tell, their bouncy, addictive rhythm, the silliness of many of the scenes they present and words they use have enchanted children for generations and continue to do so. Folk rhymes not only entertain children but also start them on the road to the appreciation of more sophisticated poetry.

Much early poetry was transmitted orally, and the ballads and narrative poems of earlier ages are appealing ways to initiate the child or the adult into the realm of "adult" poetry. A wide variety of poetry has been included in this anthology, from the rollicking *Diverting History of John Gilpin* or the pensive sonnets of William Wordsworth to the free verse of such contemporary poets as Vassar Miller. The rhythmic resonance of poetry, together with the feeling it can convey in just a few lines, make it especially enticing to children.

When the art of printing was introduced to the world, people were able to create and record their stories and poems. In many cases, they continued to use traditional oral forms in much of their popular literature. The literary folktale, for example, follows the structure of the traditional or inherited folktale and uses many of the motifs and archetypes indigenous to the folktale but has a known author and is shared through the printed rather than the spoken word. Both the older, traditional folklore and the more recent literary folktale form part of the foundation on which modern and contemporary works for children have been built.

Modern fiction and fantasy go a step beyond folklore and the literary folktale. An outgrowth of both the folktale and the romance (a tale of exciting adventures in marvelous lands, in verse or prose form), fantasy makes the impossible possible and believable. New worlds are created, animals speak, magic can be practiced successfully, new creatures can people this planet or any other world within the writer's imagination. Fantasy is the product of imagination, fantasy literature can show children what their own imaginations are capable of. Fiction, on the other hand, entertainingly re-creates reality. It may partake of some of the elements of fantasy but usually deals with problems and concerns that are closer to our own world than to worlds created by pure imagination.

Fiction and fantasy are but two genres that the author of picture books uses to introduce very young children to the world of literature. Picture books are a means of visual storytelling. In the best picture books, illustrations and text unite to create a harmony of sight and sound that can entrance and captivate a young audience—and older readers too. Text and pictures complement and explain each other and in 32 pages create a believable world or make the existing world more understandable.

The Wide World All Around explores the world thematically but also explores the world of literature. As the child expands the circles of his or her world outward from the family to the community and into the natural world, so too, through literature does he or she come to know the various forms that inhabit the world of books.

The intent of this anthology is to progress through the successive worlds that the child encounters. The themes, however, are so closely enmeshed that a selection can be relevant to more than one theme and, in many instances, can be discussed or transferred freely. One theme grows naturally out of the preceding ones and into the next, the editors have worked together closely to achieve this interrelationship. Since such a wide choice of literature is available, the editors have considered not only literature that has received general critical acceptance but also stories and poems that they personally think are delightful. Sometimes, well-known and easily available selections have been passed over for worthy but less-known ones. Sometimes, it has been essential to include famous selections because they are so appropriate. In making selections for the section dealing with the natural world, an attempt has been made to select books that deal with that world in a realistic rather than an anthropomorphic manner so that both adult and child can view the world as it is. In the majority of books dealing with the natural world, however, particularly those for the very young, a certain amount of anthropomorphism seems to be unavoidable.

Beginning with the stories of the child's first world, the family, *The Wide World All Around* proceeds through the various genres and various realms of a child's experience. Each section ends with ''Explorations'' which suggest ways in which the literature can be used creatively. Finally, each section features bibliographies to extend learning for both the child and adult reader. The hope is that the learning process will not stop with this book but will be applied to the reader's experience of fields that the book covers—the family, the country and the city, and the world at large.

That such absorption of literature can have a powerful and beneficial influence is not a fantasy. Teachers who have taught children's literature for any length of time have experienced the gratification of having students return some years later who have been so influenced by the disarming complexity of children's stories that they have followed this interest in their careers or in their reading, continuing to read books ''for children.''

As with so many people exposed to the field, the editors themselves have been irresistibly attracted by its magic and mystery. All three have been fascinated by children's literature for years. Francelia Butler, professor of English at the University of Connecticut, is founder and editor-in-chief of the annual *Children's Literature* (Yale University Press). She cofounded with Glenn Edward Sadler the Division on Children's Literature of the Modern Language Association, and she conducted the first two Institutes on Children's Literature for the National Endowment for the Humanities. Anne Devereaux Jordan, who teaches at the University of Hartford, is founder of the Children's Literature Association and also managing editor of *The Magazine of Fantasy and Science Fiction*. In addition, she has reviewed children's books for the *New York Times* and other publications. She has published a number of articles on such topics as baby books and illustration in children's books. Richard Rotert, coeditor of *Reflections on Literature for Children* (Library Professional Publications, 1984), has done considerable editorial work in the field for such publications as *200 Selected Film Classics for Children of All Ages* (Charles C Thomas, 1984). He has represented a number of publications on children's literature at international conferences, including the International Children's Book Fair at Bologna, Italy (1983), the International Board of Books for Young People at Cyprus (1984), and the International Research Society in Montreal (1985).

The Wide World All Around developed out of a unanimous realization on the part of the editors that all people—children and adults alike—thirst for literature of quality that they can read and share, tell and teach. It also grew from a belief that literature can be enjoyed to a greater degree when both young and old can share a path into the world at large and into the world of books.

More than ever, there is now great interest in expanding the child's horizons. Because children observe the world as fresh and new and view it with delight, the selections included here attempt to bring this world to the child to enrich his or her experience. This book is for the child, focusing on the child and the child's need to become part of "the world all around."

THE PRIMARY WORLD:
THE FAMILY

The family is the most basic of human organizations and exerts a profound influence over growing children. As children begin to experience the world, it is the family that they first encounter and it is the family's views of the world that they adopt. The family shapes the child's acceptance or nonacceptance of phenomena human and natural. At the same time, the family is perhaps the most complex unit of organization because of the diversity of forms it can take.

Everyone has a family of one sort or another. A family may consist of mother, father, brothers, and sisters, or it may be made up of a group of totally unrelated people. Regardless of its composition, however, the *ideal* goals of any family are to offer love, encouragement, and support to its members and to provide a home—the place where, when you go there, they have to take you in.

For more than 20 years, we have taught children's literature and each semester, we have assigned students to write essays on "the sounds, touch, taste, smell, and sight of home." What has emerged from 20 years of essays, 600 a year, is a portrait of the family that is amazingly diverse. There are all sorts of families, yet we have never read an essay that is wholly negative about the family. In most, there is a heartwarming feeling of closeness and pride in the family, whether there are one, two—or even more—parents and stepparents.

Similarly, this pride and love of family are consistent underlying themes in much of the literature that deals with the family. In *The Swiss Family Robinson,* for example, all the members of the family work together to promote their survival, and despite passing disagreements, they love one another clearly and strongly. Similarly, in Randall Jarrell's *The Animal Family,* the members form a family that is cohesive and affectionate, even though they are not related in any way.

Though the child's life is centered in the family and home, the child has an awareness of the world beyond. He or she ventures out to explore the larger human communities of the city and country and the realm of nature and then returns to the family. And the family encourages these forays. It is heartening to the child to know that, regardless of Thomas Wolfe, one can, at least literally, "go home again" and there find refuge and support. This feeling comes across clearly in such works as *The Diverting History of John Gilpin*. In this lively story-poem, John Gilpin attempts to ride a horse. To say he does this ineptly is a vast understatement, but throughout this masterpiece of droll humor his family worries about him and at the end is consoling and comforting. The message about the role of the family is subtle yet unmistakable. Most children's literature conveys a similar sense of closeness and affection in the family, whether the family is complete in the traditional sense—with two parents, children, and perhaps other relatives living together—or fragmented, with one or more members missing.

The fragmented family is also a traditional motif in children's literature, particularly in folktales. Folktales express the feelings and experiences of our ancestors and often depict the family as incomplete, in some ways reflecting the hardships endured at the time the tales evolved. In many of the folktales, a wise old man or woman or a faithful animal may supplant or represent the missing family member. In *The Firebird,* for example, Ivan is accompanied on his quest by his companion, the gray wolf, who provides support and protection similar to that which a parent might give a child.

The very incompleteness of the family, too, may stimulate the child to seek completeness, to attempt a worthy task or perform a brave deed. In Madeleine L'Engle's *A Wrinkle In Time,* a selection of which is included in this section, Meg must attempt what seems to her to be the impossible—to save both her father and her brother, Charles Wallace, and to find a certain maturity for herself. She is motivated by this need for completeness and supported in her task by the love her family gives her and the love she herself has for her family. Similarly, Louisa May Alcott's *Little Women* tells the story of a warm, close-knit family that deals with the joys and sorrows of everyday life. The fact that the father is temporarily gone from the family draws the others even closer together in an attempt to find wholeness.

But what of the child without a family, the child alone? We tend to think of such a child as a poignant, tragic figure, and in many cases this is so. The children in Cynthia Voigt's *Homecoming* are alone and searching for a home. *Homecoming* is a tale of loneliness, but it is also a tale of the children's courage and self-sufficiency. The children band together to form a family made up only of themselves, with Dicey, the main character and eldest sister, assuming the maternal role. Similarly, Dorothy, in *The Wizard of Oz,* creates a temporary family with the Lion, the Scarecrow, and the Tin Woodsman. These children have built families where one was lacking, showing the universal need for a family, although they still long for their true families.

Sometimes, however, children, like adults, want to be alone. They want to explore on their own, to seek and discover different worlds by themselves, to show that they are capable of caring for themselves. Lewis Carroll's Alice in *Alice in Wonderland* revels in the discovery of the surrealistic world down a rabbit's hole, and Maurice Sendak's Pierre wishes to stand on his own two feet. His "I don't care!" is an exuberant yell for autonomy in a world of interfering grown-ups. As in everything, there are both negative and positive sides to the image of the child alone.

Similarly, there are negative and positive aspects to old age. No book dealing with the family would be complete without considering the older members of a family, for they too people the child's primary world. It has often been said that youth and age go hand in hand, but in our culture and era children often don't have the opportunity to interact with their grandparents or other older people. Often, older people are shunted aside and children are denied the sense of continuity that the elderly can teach them. Literature for children can present the viewpoint of the old and communicate the warmth and wisdom of years. In *The Traveling Musicians,* the old animals have been sadly disregarded because of their age and they band together to form an artificial family. The poignancy of the casting out of the old is captured in this tale, as is a sense of the cleverness, wit, and warmth born of experience. No book can take the place of experience, but such stories as *The Traveling Musicians* can help children realize some of the nuances of situations they might not actually have the opportunity, particularly today, to experience.

Ultimately, this is the intention of this section: to show the child and remind the adult of the various kinds of families that exist in the world and to show that, despite their differences, the goals of each family are, at bottom, the same. Leo Tolstoy wrote, in his novel *Anna Karenina,* ''All happy families resemble one another, every unhappy family is unhappy in its own fashion.'' But happy or unhappy, the family provides the child a center from which he or she can go forth to discover ''the wide world all around.''

The Traditional Family

FABLES, MYTHS, AND LEGENDS

The Belly and the Other Members

Aesop

In this fable by Aesop, the body is considered as if it were a family or a political state in which, to be most effective, the members must cooperate.

Aesop, a slave who became ambassador from Lydia to Greece, is considered the originator of the fable form. His name is possibly derived from the Greek adjective aithops, *or "dark," or the noun* Aithiops, *or "Ethiopian," and one version of the life of Aesop describes him as black and Ethiopian. He is said to have lived in the sixth century B.C.*

Aesop's fables typically embody a moral message and consist of simple situations, concretely conceived and presented. Fables invariably enter culture for political reasons, and Aesop used them for political purposes. At Corinth, he warned his listeners against mob law in the fable "The Frogs Desiring a King," which Socrates later used. Having a log for a king, the frogs asked Zeus, king of the gods, for a stronger ruler, so he sent them a stork, who gobbled them up. The moral is that a change in rulers may not be for the better.

Aesop told his fables at the time of the Greek tyrants. He was arrested at Delphi on a trumped-up charge and was hurled to his death from a high cliff.

The adult may want to tell this fable to a child in an idiom suitable to the child's age.

IT IS SAID that in former times the various members of the human body did not work together as amicably as they do now. On one occasion the members began to be critical of the belly for spending an idle life of luxury while they had to spend all their time laboring for its support and ministering to its wants and pleasures.

The members went so far as to decide to cut off the belly's supplies for the future.

From *Aesop's Fables* (New York: Grosset & Dunlap, 1947).

The hands were no longer to carry food to the mouth, nor the mouth to receive, nor the teeth to chew it.

But, lo and behold, it was only a short time after they had agreed upon this course of starving the belly into subjection when they all began, one by one, to fail and flop and the whole body to waste away. In the end the members became convinced that the belly also, cumbersome and useless as it seemed, had an important function of its own, and that they could no more exist without it than it could do without them.

Application:
AS IN THE BODY, SO IN THE STATE,
EACH MEMBER IN HIS PROPER SPHERE
MUST WORK FOR THE COMMON GOOD.

Hector and Andromache

Edith Hamilton

Sometimes, a great poet needs only a few lines to convey the essence of a human relationship. Homer gives us a brief glimpse of Hector's farewell to his wife, Andromache, and his little son, Astyanax, but it is enough to let us know how deep their love was for one another, to realize that more than 2000 years ago, some families were as devoted to one another as families are today. Edith Hamilton's account, taken from Homer's Iliad, *explains how Hector, as a loyal Trojan, felt that it was his duty to defend his city. Andromache had a premonition about how the fighting would end.*

At this crisis a brother of Hector's, wise in discerning the will of the gods, urged Hector to go with all speed to the city and tell the Queen, his mother, to offer to Athena the most beautiful robe she owned and pray her to have mercy. Hector felt the wisdom of the advice and sped through the gates to the palace, where his mother did all as he said. She took a robe so precious that it shone like a star, and laying it on the goddess's knees she besought her: "Lady Athena, spare the city and the wives of the Trojans and the little children." But Pallas Athena denied the prayer.

As Hector went back to the battle he turned aside to see once more, perhaps for the last time, the wife he tenderly loved, Andromache, and his son Astyanax. He met her on the wall where she had gone in terror to watch the fighting when she heard the Trojans were in retreat. With her was a hand-maid carrying the little boy. Hector smiled and looked at them silently, but Andromache took his hand in hers and wept. "My dear lord," she said, "you who are father and mother and brother unto me as well as husband, stay here with us. Do not make me a widow and your child an orphan." He refused her gently. He could not be a coward, he said. It was for him to fight always in the forefront of the battle. Yet she could know that he never forgot what her anguish would be when he died. That was the thought that troubled him above all else, more than his many other cares. He turned to leave her, but first he held out his arms to his son. Terrified the little boy shrank back, afraid of the helmet and its fierce nodding crest. Hector laughed and took the shining helmet from his head. Then holding the child in his arms he caressed him and prayed, "O Zeus, in after years may men say of this my son when he

From Edith Hamilton, *Mythology* (Boston: Little, Brown, 1942).

returns from battle, 'Far greater is he than his father was.' "

So he laid the boy in his wife's arms and she took him, smiling, yet with tears. And Hector pitied her and touched her tenderly with his hand and spoke to her: "Dear one, be not so sorrowful. That which is fated must come to pass, but against my fate no man can kill me." Then taking up his helmet he left her and she went to her house, often looking back at him and weeping bitterly.

Once again on the battlefield he was eager for the fight, and better fortune for a time lay before him. Zeus had by now remembered his promise to Thetis to avenge Achilles' wrong. He ordered all the other immortals to stay in Olympus; he himself went down to earth to help the Trojans. Then it went hard with the Greeks. Their great champion was far away. Achilles sat alone in his tent, brooding over his wrongs. The great Trojan champion had never before shown himself so brilliant and so brave. Hector seemed irresistible. Tamer of horses, the Trojans always called him, and he drove his car through the Greek ranks as if the same spirit animated steeds and driver. His glancing helm was everywhere and one gallant warrior after another fell beneath his terrible bronze spear. When evening ended the battle, the Trojans had driven the Greeks back almost to their ships.

There was rejoicing in Troy that night, but grief and despair in the Greek camp. Agamemnon himself was all for giving up and sailing back to Greece. Nestor, however, who was the oldest among the chieftains and therefore the wisest, wiser even than the shrewd Odysseus, spoke out boldly and told Agamemnon that if he had not angered Achilles they would not have been defeated. "Try to find some way of appeasing him," he said, "instead of going home disgraced." All applauded the advice and Agamemnon confessed that he had acted like a fool. He would send Briseis back, he promised them, and with her many other splendid gifts, and he begged Odysseus to take his offer to Achilles.

Odysseus and the two chieftains chosen to accompany him found the hero with his friend Patroclus, who of all men on earth

was dearest to him. Achilles welcomed them courteously and set food and drink before them, but when they told him why they had come and all the rich gifts that would be his if he would yield, and begged him to have pity on his hard-pressed countrymen, they received an absolute refusal. Not all the treasures of Egypt could buy him, he told them. He was sailing home and they would be wise to do the same.

But all rejected that counsel when Odysseus brought back the answer. The next day they went into battle with the desperate courage of brave men cornered. Again they were driven back, until they stood fighting on the beach where their ships were drawn up. But help was at hand. Hera had laid her plans. She saw Zeus sitting on Mount Ida watching the Trojans conquer, and she thought how she detested him. But she knew well that she could get the better of him only in one way. She must go to him looking so lovely that he could not resist her. When he took her in his arms she would pour sweet sleep upon him and he would forget the Trojans. So she did. She went to her chamber and used every art she knew to make herself beautiful beyond compare. Last of all she borrowed Aphrodite's girdle wherein were all her enchantments, and with this added charm she appeared before Zeus. As he saw her, love overcame his heart so that he thought no more of his promise to Thetis.

At once the battle turned in favor of the Greeks. Ajax hurled Hector to the ground, although before he could wound him Aeneas lifted him and bore him away. With Hector gone, the Greeks were able to drive the Trojans far back from the ships and Troy might have been sacked that very day if Zeus had not awakened. He leaped up and saw the Trojans in flight and Hector lying gasping on the plain. All was clear to him and he turned fiercely to Hera. This was her doing, he said, her crafty, crooked ways. He was half-minded to give her then and there a beating. When it came to that kind of fighting Hera knew she was helpless. She promptly denied that she had had anything to do with the Trojans' defeat. It was all Poseidon, she said, and indeed the Sea-god had been helping the

Greeks contrary to Zeus's orders, but only because she had begged him. However, Zeus was glad enough of an excuse not to lay hands on her. He sent her back to Olympus and summoned Iris, the rainbow messenger, to carry his command to Poseidon to withdraw from the field. Sullenly the Sea-god obeyed and once more the tide of battle turned against the Greeks.

Apollo had revived the fainting Hector and breathed into him surpassing power. Before the two, the god and the hero, the Greeks were like a flock of frightened sheep driven by mountain lions. They fled in confusion to the ships, and the wall they had built to defend them went down like a sand wall children heap up on the shore and then scatter in their play. The Trojans were almost near enough to set the ships on fire. The Greeks, hopeless, thought only of dying bravely.

Patroclus, Achilles' beloved friend, saw the rout with horror. Not even for Achilles' sake could he stay longer away from the battle. "You can keep your wrath while your countrymen go down in ruin," he cried to Achilles. "I cannot. Give me your armor. If they think I am you, the Trojans may pause and the worn-out Greeks have a breathing space. You and I are fresh. We might yet drive back the enemy. But if you will sit nursing your anger, at least let me have the armor." As he spoke one of the Greek ships burst into flame. "That way they can cut off the Army's retreat," Achilles said. "Go. Take my armor, my men too, and defend the ships. I cannot go. I am a man dishonored. For my own ships, if the battle comes near them, I will fight. I will not fight for men who have disgraced me."

So Patroclus put on the splendid armor all the Trojans knew and feared, and led the Myrmidons, Achilles' men, to the battle. At the first onset of this new band of warriors the Trojans wavered; they thought Achilles led them on. And indeed for a time Patroclus fought as gloriously as that great hero himself could have done. But at last he met Hector face to face and his doom was sealed as surely as a boar is doomed when he faces a lion. Hector's spear gave him a mortal wound and his soul fled from his body down to the house of Hades. Then Hector stripped his armor from him and casting his own aside, put it on. It seemed as though he had taken on, too, Achilles' strength, and no man of the Greeks could stand before him.

Evening came that puts an end to battle. Achilles sat by his tent waiting for Patroclus to return. But instead he saw old Nestor's son running toward him, fleet-footed Antilochus. He was weeping hot tears as he ran. "Bitter tidings," he cried out. "Patroclus is fallen and Hector has his armor." Grief took hold of Achilles, so black that those around him feared for his life. Down in the sea caves his mother knew his sorrow and came up to try to comfort him. "I will no longer live among men," he told her, "if I do not make Hector pay with his death for Patroclus dead." Then Thetis weeping bade him remember that he himself was fated to die straightway after Hector. "So may I do," Achilles answered, "I who did not help my comrade in his sore need. I will kill the destroyer of him I loved; then I will accept death when it comes."

Thetis did not attempt to hold him back. "Only wait until morning," she said, "and you will not go unarmed to battle. I will bring you arms fashioned by the divine armorer, the god Hephaestus himself."

Marvelous arms they were when Thetis brought them, worthy of their maker, such as no man on earth had ever borne. The Myrmidons gazed at them with awe and a flame of fierce joy blazed in Achilles' eyes as he put them on. Then at last he left the tent in which he had sat so long, and went down to where the Greeks were gathered, a wretched company, Diomedes grievously wounded, Odysseus, Agamemnon, and many another. He felt shame before them and he told them he saw his own exceeding folly in allowing the loss of a mere girl to make him forget everything else. But that was over; he was ready to lead them as before. Let them prepare at once for the battle. The chieftains applauded joyfully, but Odysseus spoke for all when he said they must first take their fill of food and wine, for fasting men made poor fighters. "Our comrades lie dead on the field and you call to food," Achilles answered scornfully. "Down my throat shall go neither bite nor sup until my dear comrade is avenged." And to himself he said, "O dearest of friends, for want of you I cannot eat, I cannot drink."

When the others had satisfied their hunger he led the attack. This was the last fight between the two great champions, as all the immortals knew. They also knew how it would turn out. Father Zeus hung his golden balances and set in one the lot of Hector's death and in the other that of Achilles. Hector's lot sank down. It was appointed that he should die.

Nevertheless, the victory was long in doubt. The Trojans under Hector fought as brave men fight before the walls of their home. Even the great river of Troy, which the gods call Xanthus and men Scamander, took part and strove to drown Achilles as he crossed its waters. In vain, for nothing could check him as he rushed on slaughtering all in his path and seeking everywhere for Hector. The gods by now were fighting, too, as hotly as the men, and Zeus sitting apart in Olympus laughed pleasantly to himself when he saw god matched against god: Athena felling Ares to the ground; Hera seizing the bow of Artemis from her shoulders and boxing her ears with it this way and that; Poseidon provoking Apollo with taunting words to strike him first. The Sun-god refused the challenge. He knew it was of no use now to fight for Hector.

By this time the gates, the great Scaean gates of Troy, had been flung wide, for the Trojans at last were in full flight and were crowding into the town. Only Hector stood immovable before the wall. From the gates old Priam, his father, and his mother Hecuba cried to him to come within and save himself, but he did not heed. He was thinking, "I led the Trojans. Their defeat is my fault. Then am I to spare myself? And yet — what if I were to lay down shield and spear and go tell Achilles that we will give Helen back and half of Troy's treasures with her? Useless. He would but kill me unarmed as if I were a woman. Better to join battle with him now even if I die."

On came Achilles, glorious as the sun when he rises. Beside him was Athena, but Hector was alone. Apollo had left him to his fate. As the pair drew near he turned and fled. Three times around the wall of Troy pursued and pursuer ran with flying feet. It was Athena who made Hector halt. She appeared beside him in the shape of his brother, Deiphobus, and with this ally as he thought, Hector faced Achilles. He cried out to him, "If I kill you I will give back your body to your friends and do you do the same to me." But Achilles answered, "Madman. There are no covenants between sheep and wolves, nor between you and me." So saying he hurled his spear. It missed its aim, but Athena brought it back. Then Hector struck with a true aim; the spear hit the center of Achilles' shield. But to what good? That armor was magical and could not be pierced. He turned quickly to Deiphobus to get his spear, but he was not there. Then Hector knew the truth. Athena had tricked him and there was no way of escape. "The gods have summoned me to death," he thought. "At least I will not die without a struggle, but in some great deed of arms which men yet to be born will tell each other." He drew his sword, his only weapon now, and rushed upon his enemy. But Achillles had a spear, the one Athena had recovered for him. Before Hector could approach, he who knew well that armor taken by Hector from the dead Patroclus aimed at an opening in it near the throat, and drove the spearpoint in. Hector fell, dying at last. With his last breath he prayed, "Give back my body to my father and my mother." "No prayers from you to me, you dog," Achilles answered. "I would that I could make myself devour raw your flesh for the evil you have brought upon me." Then Hector's soul flew forth from his body and was gone to Hades, bewailing his fate, leaving vigor and youth behind.

Achilles stripped the bloody armor from the corpse while the Greeks ran up to wonder how tall he was as he lay there and how noble to look upon. But Achilles' mind was on other matters. He pierced the feet of the dead man and fastened them with thongs to the back of his chariot, letting the head trail. Then he lashed his horses and round and round the walls of Troy he dragged all that was left of glorious Hector.

FOLKTALES—
INHERITED AND LITERARY

Momotaro

Children, as well as adults, like to hear stories about diminutive human beings who are nevertheless very clever and strong. In Japan, storytellers still sometimes wander from place to place telling the story of Momotaro's "Peach Boy," or "Strong Boy." They carry a set of cardboard pictures of the events in the story, a segment of the text written on the back of each. Thus, by showing a set of these large pictures in sequence, they can entertain the children. Similarly, in India, storytellers carry blanket-sized cloths on which pictures of the adventures of religious figures may appear, one after the other, cartoon fashion. Indeed, the stories told by cartoons or comics are related to this style of narration, as are the puppet shows in Turkey, Greece, Indonesia, and many other places, where puppets depict each action as the story progresses. Films have derived from this art, too.

In this story Momotaro is born out of a peach. His adventures may recall those of Tom Thumb to Western readers. In old cultures such as Japan's folktales and real life are still quite close together, so that children almost half-believe the stories.

Long, long ago there lived an old man and an old woman; they were peasants, and had to work hard to earn their daily rice. The old man used to go and cut grass for the farmers around, and while he was gone the old woman, his wife, did the work of the house and worked in their own little rice field.

One day the old man went to the hills as usual to cut grass and the old woman took some clothes to the river to wash.

It was nearly summer, and the country was very beautiful to see in its fresh greenness as the two old people went on their way to work. The grass on the banks of the river looked like emerald velvet, and the pussy willows along the edge of the water were shaking out their soft tassels.

The breezes blew and ruffled the smooth surface of the water into wavelets, and passing on touched the cheeks of the old couple who, for some reason they could not explain, felt very happy that morning.

The old woman at last found a nice spot by the river bank and put her basket down. Then she set to work to wash the clothes; she took them one by one out of the basket and washed them in the river and rubbed them on the stones. The water was as clear as crystal, and she could see the tiny fish swimming to and fro, and the pebbles at the bottom.

As she was busy washing her clothes a great peach came bumping down the stream. The old woman looked up from her work and saw this large peach. She was sixty years of age, yet in all her life she had never seen such a big peach as this.

"How delicious that peach must be!" she said to herself. "I must certainly get it and take it home to my old man."

She stretched out her arm to try and get it, but it was quite out of her reach. She looked about for a stick, but there was not one to be seen, and if she went to look for one she would lose the peach.

From Yei Theodora Ozaki, ed., *Japanese Fairy Tales* (New York: A. L. Burt, 1903).

Stopping a moment to think what she would do, she remembered an old charm-verse. Now she began to clap her hands to keep time to the rolling of the peach down stream, and while she clapped she sang this song:

> "Distant water is bitter,
> The near water is sweet;
> Pass by the distant water
> And come into the sweet."

Strange to say, as soon as she began to repeat this little song the peach began to come nearer and nearer the bank where the old woman was standing, till at last it stopped just in front of her so that she was able to take it up in her hands. The old woman was delighted. She could not go on with her work, so happy and excited was she, so she put all the clothes back in her bamboo basket, and with the basket on her back and the peach in her hand she hurried homewards.

It seemed a very long time to her to wait till her husband returned. The old man at last came back as the sun was setting, with a big bundle of grass on his back—so big that he was almost hidden and she could hardly see him. He seemed very tired and used the scythe for a walking stick, leaning on it as he walked along.

As soon as the old woman saw him she called out:

"*O Fii San!* (old man) I have been waiting for you to come home for such a long time to-day!"

"What is the matter? Why are you so impatient?" asked the old man, wondering at her unusual eagerness. "Has anything happened while I have been away?"

"Oh, no!" answered the old woman, "nothing has happened, only I have found a nice present for you!"

"That is good," said the old man. He then washed his feet in a basin of water and stepped up to the veranda.

The old woman now ran into the little room and brought out from the cupboard the big peach. It felt even heavier than before. She held it up to him, saying:

"Just look at this! Did you ever see such a large peach in all your life?"

When the old man looked at the peach he was greatly astonished and said:

"This is indeed the largest peach I have ever seen! Wherever did you buy it?"

"I did not buy it," answered the old woman. "I found it in the river where I was washing." and she told him the whole story.

"I am very glad that you have found it. Let us eat it now, for I am hungry," said the *O Fii San*.

He brought out the kitchen knife, and, placing the peach on a board, was about to cut it when, wonderful to tell, the peach split in two of itself and a clear voice said:

"Wait a bit, old man!" and out stepped a beautiful little child.

The old man and his wife were both so astonished at what they saw that they fell to the ground. The child spoke again:

"Don't be afraid. I am no demon or fairy. I will tell you the truth. Heaven has had compassion on you. Every day and every

The Peach split open of itself and out stepped a beautiful little child.

night you have lamented that you had no child. Your cry has been heard and I am sent to be the son of your old age!''

On hearing this the old man and his wife were very happy. They had cried night and day for sorrow at having no child to help them in their lonely old age, and now that their prayer was answered they were so lost with joy that they did not know where to put their hands or their feet. First the old man took the child up in his arms, and then the old woman did the same; and they named him *Momotaro*, or *Son of a Peach*, because he had come out of a peach.

The years passed quickly by and the child grew to be fifteen years of age. He was taller and far stronger than any other boys of his own age, he had a handsome face and a heart full of courage, and he was very wise for his years. The old couple's pleasure was very great when they looked at him, for he was just what they thought a hero ought to be like.

One day Momotaro came to his foster-father and said solemnly:

''Father, by a strange chance we have become father and son. Your goodness to me has been higher than the mountain grasses which it was your daily work to cut, and deeper than the river where my mother washes the clothes. I do not know how to thank you enough.''

''Why,'' answered the old man, ''it is a matter of course that a father should bring up his son. When you are older it will be your turn to take care of us, so after all there will be no profit or loss between us—all will be equal. Indeed, I am rather surprised that you should thank me in this way!'' and the old man looked bothered.

''I hope you will be patient with me,'' said Momotaro; ''but before I begin to pay back your goodness to me I have a request to make which I hope you will grant me above everything else.''

''I will let you do whatever you wish, for you are quite different from all other boys!''

''Then let me go away at once!''

''What do you say? Do you wish to leave your old father and mother and go away from your old home?''

''I will surely come back again, if you let me go now!''

''Where are you going?''

''You must think it strange that I want to go away,'' said Momotaro, ''because I have not yet told you my reason. Far away from here to the northeast of Japan there is an island in the sea. This island is the stronghold of a band of devils. I have often heard how they invade this land, kill and rob the people, and carry off all they can find. They are not only very wicked but they are disloyal to our Emperor and disobey his laws. They are also cannibals, for they kill and eat some of the poor people who are so unfortunate as to fall into their hands. These devils are very hateful beings. I must go and conquer them and bring back all the plunder of which they have robbed this land. It is for this reason that I want to go away for a short time!''

The old man was much surprised at hearing all this from a mere boy of fifteen. He thought it best to let the boy go. He was strong and fearless, and besides all this, the old man knew he was no common child, for he had been sent to them as a gift from Heaven, and he felt quite sure that the devils would be powerless to harm him.

''All you say is very interesting, Momotaro,'' said the old man. ''I will not hinder you in your determination. You may go if you wish. Go to the island as soon as ever you like and destroy the demons and bring peace to the land.''

''Thank you, for all your kindness,'' said Momotaro, who began to get ready to go that very day. He was full of courage and did not know what fear was.

The old man and woman at once set to work to pound rice in the kitchen mortar to make cakes for Momotaro to take with him on his journey.

At last the cakes were made and Momotaro ready to start on his long journey.

Parting is always sad. So it was now. The eyes of the two old people were filled with tears and their voices trembled as they said:

''Go with all care and speed. We expect you back victorious!''

Momotaro was very sorry to leave his old parents (though he knew he was coming back as soon as he could), for he thought of how lonely they would be while he was away. But he said "Good-by!" quite bravely.

"I am going now. Take good care of yourselves while I am away. Good-by!" And he stepped quickly out of the house. In silence the eyes of Momotaro and his parents met in farewell.

Momotaro now hurried on his way till it was midday. He began to feel hungry, so he opened his bag and took out one of the rice-cakes and sat down under a tree by the side of the road to eat it. While he was thus having his lunch a dog almost as large as a colt came running out from the high grass. He made straight for Momotaro, and showing his teeth, said in a fierce way:

"You are a rude man to pass my field without asking permission first. If you leave me all the cakes you have in your bag you may go; otherwise I will bite you till I kill you!"

Momotaro only laughed scornfully:

"What is that you are saying? Do you know who I am? I am Momotaro, and I am on my way to subdue the devils in their island stronghold in the northeast of Japan. If you try to stop me on my way there I will cut you in two from the head downwards!"

The dog's manner at once changed. His tail dropped between his legs, and coming near he bowed so low that his forehead touched the ground.

"What do I hear? The name of Momotaro? Are you indeed Momotaro? I have often heard of your great strength. Not knowing who you were I have behaved in a very stupid way. Will you please pardon my rudeness? Are you indeed on your way to invade the Island of Devils? If you will take such a rude fellow with you as one of your followers, I shall be very grateful to you."

"I think I can take you with me if you wish to go," said Momotaro.

"Thank you!" said the dog. "By the way, I am very very hungry. Will you give me one of the cakes you are carrying?"

"This is the best kind of cake there is in Japan," said Momotaro. "I cannot spare you a whole one; I will give you half of one."

"Thank you very much," said the dog, taking the piece thrown to him.

Then Momotaro got up and the dog followed. For a long time they walked over the hills and through the valleys. As they were going along an animal came down from a tree a little ahead of them. The creature soon came up to Momotaro and said:

"Good morning, Momotaro! You are welcome in this part of the country. Will you allow me to go with you?"

The dog answered jealously:

"Momotaro already has a dog to accompany him. Of what use is a monkey like you in battle? We are on our way to fight the devils! Get away!"

The dog and the monkey began to quarrel and bite, for these two animals always hate each other.

"Now, don't quarrel!" said Momotaro, putting himself between them. "Wait a moment, dog!"

"It is not at all dignified for you to have such a creature as that following you!" said the dog.

"What do you know about it?" asked Momotaro; and pushing aside the dog, he spoke to the monkey:

"Who are you?"

"I am a monkey living in these hills," replied the monkey. "I heard of your expedition to the Island of Devils, and I have come to go with you. Nothing will please me more than to follow you!"

"Do you really wish to go the the Island of Devils and fight with me?"

"Yes, sir," replied the monkey.

"I admire your courage," said Momotaro. "Here is a piece of one of my fine rice-cakes. Come along!"

So the monkey joined Momotaro. The dog and the monkey did not get on well together. They were always snapping at each other as they went along, and always wanting to have a fight. This made Momotaro very cross, and at last he sent the dog on ahead with a flag and put the monkey behind with a sword, and he placed himself between them with a war-fan, which is made of iron.

By and by they came to a large field. Here a bird flew down and alighted on the ground just in front of the little party. It was the most beautiful bird Momotaro had ever seen. On its body were five different robes of feathers and its head was covered with a scarlet cap.

The dog at once ran at the bird and tried to seize and kill it. But the bird struck out its spurs and flew at the dog's tail, and the fight went hard with both.

Momotaro, as he looked on, could not help admiring the bird; it showed so much spirit in the fight. It would certainly make a good fighter.

Momotaro went up to the two combatants, and holding the dog back, said to the bird:

"You rascal! you are hindering my journey. Surrender at once, and I will take you with me. If you don't I will set this dog to bite your head off!"

Then the bird surrendered at once, and begged to be taken into Momotaro's company.

"I do not know what excuse to offer for quarreling with the dog, your servant, but I did not see you. I am a miserable bird called a pheasant. It is very generous of you to pardon my rudeness and to take me with you. Please allow me to follow you behind the dog and the monkey!"

"I congratulate you on surrendering so soon," said Momotaro, smiling. "Come and join us in our raid on the devils."

"Are you going to take this bird with you also?" asked the dog, interrupting.

"Why do you ask such an unnecessary question? Didn't you hear what I said? I take the bird with me because I wish to!"

"Humph!" said the dog.

Then Momotaro stood and gave this order:

"Now all of you must listen to me. The first thing necessary in an army is harmony. It is a wise saying which says that 'Advantage on earth is better than advantage in Heaven!' Union amongst ourselves is better than any earthly gain. When we are not at peace amongst ourselves it is no easy thing to subdue an enemy. From now, you three, the dog, the monkey and the pheasant, must be friends and one mind. The one who first begins a quarrel will be discharged on the spot!"

All the three promised not to quarrel. The pheasant was now made a member of Momotaro's suite, and received half a cake.

Momotaro's influence was so great that the three became good friends, and hurried onwards with him as their leader.

Hurrying on day after day they at last came out upon the shore of the North-Eastern Sea. There was nothing to be seen as far as the horizon—not a sign of any island. All that broke the stillness was the rolling of the waves upon the shore.

Now, the dog and the monkey and the pheasant had come very bravely all the way through the long valleys and over the hills, but they had never seen the sea before, and for the first time since they set out they were bewildered and gazed at each other in silence. How were they to cross the water and get to the Island of Devils?

Momotaro soon saw that they were daunted by the sight of the sea, and to try them he spoke loudly and roughly:

"Why do you hesitate? Are you afraid of the sea? Oh! what cowards you are! It is impossible to take such weak creatures as you with me to fight the demons. It will be far better for me to go alone. I discharge you all at once!"

The three animals were taken aback at this sharp reproof, and clung to Momotaro's sleeve, begging him not to send them away.

"Please, Momotaro!" said the dog.

"We have come thus far!" said the monkey.

"It is inhuman to leave us here!" said the pheasant.

"We are not at all afraid of the sea," said the monkey again.

"Please do take us with you," said the pheasant.

"Do please," said the dog.

They had now gained a little courage, so Momotaro said:

"Well, then, I will take you with me, but be careful!"

Momotaro now got a small ship, and they all got on board. The wind and weather were fair, and the ship went like an arrow over the sea. It was the first time they had ever been on the water, and so at first the dog, the monkey and the pheasant were frightened at the waves and the rolling of the vessel, but by degrees they grew accustomed to the water and were quite happy again. Every day they paced the deck of their little ship, eagerly looking out for the demons' island.

When they grew tired of this, they told each other stories of all their exploits of which they were proud, and then played games together; and Momotaro found much to amuse him in listening to the three animals and watching their antics, and in this way he forgot that the way was long and that he was tired of the voyage and of doing nothing. He longed to be at work killing the monsters who had done so much harm in his country.

As the wind blew in their favor and they met no storms the ship made a quick voyage, and one day when the sun was shining brightly a sight of land rewarded the four watchers at the bow.

Momotaro knew at once that what they saw was the devils' stronghold. On the top of the precipitous shore, looking out to sea, was a large castle. Now that his enterprise was close at hand, he was deep in thought with his head leaning on his hands, wondering how he should begin the attack. His three followers watched him, waiting for orders. At last he called to the pheasant:

"It is a great advantage for us to have you with us," said Momotaro to the bird, "for you have good wings. Fly at once to the castle and engage the demons to fight. We will follow you."

The pheasant at once obeyed. He flew off from the ship beating the air gladly with his wings. The bird soon reached the island and took up his position on the roof in the middle of the castle, calling out loudly:

"All you devils listen to me! The great Japanese general Momotaro has come to fight you and to take your stronghold from you. If you wish to save your lives surrender at once, and in token of your submission you must break off the horns that grow on your forehead. If you do not surrender at once, but make up your mind to fight, we, the pheasant, the dog and the monkey, will kill you all by biting and tearing you to death!"

The horned demons looking up and only seeing a pheasant, laughed and said:

"A wild pheasant, indeed! It is ridiculous to hear such words from a mean thing like you. Wait till you get a blow from one of our iron bars!"

Very angry, indeed, were the devils. They shook their horns and their shocks of red hair fiercely, and rushed to put on tiger skin trousers to make themselves look more terrible. They then brought out great iron bars and ran to where the pheasant perched over their heads, and tried to knock him down. The pheasant flew to one side to escape the blow, and then attacked the head of first one and then another demon. He flew round and round them, beating the air with his wings so fiercely and ceaselessly, that the devils began to wonder whether they had to fight one or many more birds.

In the meantime, Momotaro had brought his ship to land. As they had approached, he saw that the shore was like a precipice, and that the large castle was surrounded by high walls and large iron gates and was strongly fortified.

Momotaro landed, and with the hope of finding some way of entrance, walked up the path towards the top, followed by the monkey and the dog. They soon came upon two beautiful damsels washing clothes in a stream. Momotaro saw that the clothes were blood-stained, and that as the two maidens washed, the tears were falling fast down their cheeks. He stopped and spoke to them:

"Who are you, and why do you weep?"

"We are captives of the Demon King. We were carried away from our homes to this island, and though we are the daughters of Daimios (Lords), we are obliged to be his servants, and one day he will kill us"—and the maidens held up the blood-stained clothes—"and eat us, and there is no one to help us!"

And their tears burst out afresh at this horrible thought.

"I will rescue you," said Momotaro. "Do not weep any more, only show me how I may get into the castle."

Then the two ladies led the way and showed Momotaro a little back door in the lowest part of the castle wall—so small that Momotaro could hardly crawl in.

The pheasant, who was all this time fighting hard, saw Momotaro and his little band rush in at the back.

Momotaro's onslaught was so furious that the devils could not stand against him. At first their foe had been a single bird, the pheasant, but now that Momotaro and the dog and the monkey had arrived they were bewildered, for the four enemies fought like a hundred, so strong were they. Some of the devils fell off the parapet of the castle and were dashed to pieces on the rocks beneath; others fell into the sea and were drowned; many were beaten to death by the three animals.

The chief of the devils at last was the only one left. He made up his mind to surrender, for he knew that his enemy was stronger than mortal man.

He came up humbly to Momotaro and threw down his iron bar, and kneeling down at the victor's feet he broke off the horns on his head in token of submission, for they were the sign of his strength and power.

"I am afraid of you," he said meekly. "I cannot stand against you. I will give you all the treasure hidden in this castle if you will spare my life!"

Momotaro laughed.

"It is not like you, big devil, to beg for mercy, is it? I cannot spare your wicked life, however much you beg, for you have killed and tortured many people and robbed our country for many years."

Then Momotaro tied the devil chief up and gave him into the monkey's charge. Having done this, he went into all the rooms of the castle and set the prisoners free and gathered together all the treasure he found.

The dog and the pheasant carried home the plunder, and thus Momotaro returned triumphantly to his home, taking with him the devil chief as a captive.

The two poor damsels, daughters of Daimios, and others whom the wicked demon had carried off to be his slaves, were taken safely to their own homes and delivered to their parents.

The whole country made a hero of Momotaro on his triumphant return, and rejoiced that the country was now freed from the robber devils who had been a terror of the land for a long time.

The old couple's joy was greater than ever, and the treasure Momotaro had brought home with him enabled them to live in peace and plenty to the end of their days.

The Huckabuck Family and How They Raised Pop Corn in Nebraska and Quit and Came Back

Carl Sandburg

The Huckabuck popcorn wouldn't stop popping. A Chinese silver slipper buckle is the magical element in this story (it seems there is always magic involved when human efforts go out of control). But the Huckabucks stick together—although they never raise popcorn again.

Jonas Jonas Huckabuck was a farmer in Nebraska with a wife, Mama Mama Huckabuck, and a daughter, Pony Pony Huckabuck.

"Your father gave you two names the same in front," people had said to him.

And he answered, "Yes, two names are easier to remember. If you call me by my first name Jonas and I don't hear you then when you call me by my second name Jonas maybe I will."

"And," he went on, "I call my pony-face girl Pony Pony because if she doesn't hear me the first time she always does the second."

And so they lived on a farm where they raised pop corn, these three, Jonas Jonas Huckabuck, his wife, Mama Mama Hucka-

From Carl Sandburg, *Rootabaga Stories* (Orlando, Fla.: Harcourt Brace Jovanovich, 1951).

buck, and their pony-face daughter, Pony Pony Huckabuck.

After they harvested the crop one year they had the barns, the cribs, the sheds, the shacks, and all the cracks and corners of the farm, all filled with pop corn.

"We came out to Nebraska to raise pop corn," said Jonas Jonas, "and I guess we got nearly enough pop corn this year for the pop corn poppers and all the friends and relations of all the pop corn poppers in these United States."

And this was the year Pony Pony was going to bake her first squash pie all by herself. In one corner of the corn crib, all covered over with pop corn, she had a secret, a big round squash, a fat yellow squash, a rich squash all spotted with spots of gold.

She carried the squash into the kitchen, took a long sharp shining knife, and then she cut the squash in the middle till she had two big half squashes. And inside just like out-

She carried the squash into the kitchen.

side it was rich yellow spotted with spots of gold.

And there was a shine of silver. And Pony Pony wondered why silver should be in a squash. She picked and plunged with her fingers till she pulled it out.

"It's a buckle," she said, "a silver buckle, a Chinese silver slipper buckle."

She ran with it to her father and said, "Look what I found when I cut open the golden yellow squash spotted with gold spots—it is a Chinese silver slipper buckle."

"It means our luck is going to change, and we don't know whether it will be good luck or bad luck," said Jonas Jonas to his daughter, Pony Pony Huckabuck.

Then she ran with it to her mother and said, "Look what I found when I cut open the yellow squash spotted with spots of gold—it is a Chinese silver slipper buckle."

"It means our luck is going to change, and we don't know whether it will be good luck or bad luck," said Mama Mama Huckabuck.

And that night a fire started in the barns, crib, sheds, shacks, cracks, and corners, where the pop corn harvest was kept. All night long the pop corn popped. In the morning the ground all around the farm house and the barn was covered with white pop corn so it looked like a heavy fall of snow.

All the next day the fire kept on and the pop corn popped till it was up to the shoulders of Pony Pony when she tried to walk from the house to the barn. And that night in all the barns, cribs, sheds, shacks, cracks and corners of the farm, the pop corn went on popping.

In the morning when Jonas Jonas Huckabuck looked out of the upstairs window he saw the pop corn popping and coming higher and higher. It was nearly up to the window. Before evening and dark of that day, Jonas Jonas Huckabuck, and his wife Mama Mama Huckabuck, and their daughter Pony Pony Huckabuck, all went away from the farm saying, "We came to Nebraska to raise pop corn, but this is too much. We will not come back till the wind blows away the pop corn. We will not come back till we get a sign and a signal."

They went to Oskaloosa, Iowa. And the

next year Pony Pony Huckabuck was very proud because when she stood on the sidewalks in the street she could see her father sitting high on the seat of a coal wagon, driving two big spanking horses hitched with shining brass harness in front of the coal wagon. And though Pony Pony and Jonas Jonas were proud, very proud all that year, there never came a sign, a signal.

The next year again was a proud year, exactly as proud a year as they spent in Oskaloosa. They went to Paducah, Kentucky, to Defiance, Ohio; Peoria, Illinois; Indianapolis, Indiana; Walla Walla, Washington. And in all these places Pony Pony Huckabuck saw her father, Jonas Jonas Huckabuck, standing in rubber boots deep down in a ditch with a shining steel shovel shoveling yellow clay and black mud from down in the ditch high and high up over his shoulders. And though it was a proud year they got no sign, no signal.

The next year came. It was the proudest of all. This was the year Jonas Jonas Huckabuck and his family lived in Elgin, Illinois, and Jonas Jonas was a watchman in a watch factory watching the watches.

"I know where you have been," Mama Mama Huckabuck would say of an evening to Pony Pony Huckabuck. "You have been down to the watch factory watching your father watch the watches."

"Yes," said Pony Pony. "Yes, and this evening when I was watching father watch the watches in the watch factory, I looked over my left shoulder and I saw a policeman with a star and brass buttons and he was watching me to see if I was watching father watch the watches in the watch factory."

It was a proud year. Pony Pony saved her money. Thanksgiving came. Pony Pony said, "I am going to get a squash to make a squash pie." She hunted from one grocery to another; she kept her eyes on the farm wagons coming into Elgin with squashes.

She found what she wanted, the yellow squash spotted with gold spots. She took it home, cut it open, and saw the inside was like the outside, all rich yellow spotted with gold spots.

There was a shine like silver. She picked and plunged with her fingers and pulled and pulled till at last she pulled out the shine of silver.

"It's a sign; it is a signal," she said. "It is a buckle, a slipper buckle, a Chinese silver slipper buckle. It is the mate to the other buckle. Our luck is going to change. Yoo hoo! Yoo hoo!"

She told her father and mother about the buckle. They went back to the farm in Nebraska. The wind by this time had been blowing and blowing for three years, and all the pop corn was blown away.

"Now we are going to be farmers again," said Jonas Jonas Huckabuck to Mama Mama Huckabuck and to Pony Pony Huckabuck. "And we are going to raise cabbages, beets and turnips; we are going to raise squash, rutabaga, pumpkins and peppers for pickling. We are going to raise wheat, oats, barley, rye. We are going to raise corn such as Indian corn and kaffir corn—but we are *not* going to raise any pop corn for the pop corn poppers to be popping."

And the pony-face daughter, Pony Pony Huckabuck, was proud because she had on new black slippers, and around her ankles, holding the slippers on the left foot and the right foot, she had two buckles, silver buckles, Chinese silver slipper buckles. They were mates.

Sometimes on Thanksgiving Day and Christmas and New Year's, she tells her friends to be careful when they open a squash.

"Squashes make your luck change good to bad and bad to good," says Pony Pony.

FOLK RHYMES AND POETRY

Folk Rhymes

Even in the best of families, there is anger over the arrival and subsequent behavior of siblings. The turning rope creates an invisible world around the skipper's body, within which problems can be worked out privately, as in this American rhyme.

> Johnnie over the ocean,
> Johnnie over the sea.
> Johnnie broke a milk bottle
> And blamed it on me.
> I told Ma,
> Ma told Pa,
> Johnnie got a lickin'—
> Ha! Ha! Ha!*

Most children soon become aware of death, either through the death of pets or of family members. Following is a French children's rhyme about the cycle of life, death, and rebirth.

> Grandmama is buried
> In a field of chicory.
> When the chicory begins to sprout,
> Grandmama will come out.

The inevitability of death is also grimly stated in a philosophical rhyme from the United States.

> Mother, mother,
> I am ill.
> Call for the doctor
> Over the hill.
> Doctor, doctor,
> Will I die?
>
> Yes, my dear,
> And so will I.

Rhymes of romance are also common everywhere, including the family. A little

girl skipped to this one in Mesopotamia, Ohio, in the late nineteenth century.

> I love my Papa, that I do,
> And Mama says she loves him, too,
> But Papa says she fears some day,
> With some bad man I'll run away.*

A pleasant family rhyme comes from Russia, where a child imaginatively recalls a visit to Grandmother's house.

> Where will you go?
> Granny's.
> What will you eat?
> Grits.
> What will you drink?
> Home brew.
> Grandmother is very kind
> And her food is buttery.
> We laughed.
> We got ready—
> Cuckoo! We went off!

*From Francelia Butler, ed., and Gail E. Haley, illustrator, *The Skip Rope Book* (New York: Dial Press, 1963).

The Diverting History of John Gilpin
SHOWING HOW HE WENT FARTHER THAN HE INTENDED, AND CAME SAFE HOME AGAIN.

William Cowper

Sometimes, sad people are particularly adept at seeking out and expressing the humorous side of life. William Cowper (1731–1800) was hurt by the death of his mother when he was six. His father then put him in a school where he was severely bullied. He was mentally ill, off and on throughout most of his life. His poem about John Gilpin has always been a favorite among children, and its popularity increased after the publication of an edition that featured the lively illustrations of Randolph Caldecott, a famous picture-book artist of the nineteenth century (after whom the Caldecott Medal is named). In the 1920s, a wallpaper design with the Caldecott illustrations and Cowper text decorated the walls of many nurseries; it never bored the occupants.

John Gilpin was a citizen
    Of credit and renown,
A train-band captain eke was he,
    Of famous London town.

John Gilpin's spouse said to her dear,
    "Though wedded we have been
These twice ten tedious years, yet we
    No holiday have seen.

"To-morrow is our wedding-day,
    And we will then repair
Unto the 'Bell' at Edmonton,
    All in a chaise and pair.

"My sister, and my sister's child,
    Myself, and children three,
Will fill the chaise; so you must ride
    On horseback after we."

He soon replied, "I do admire
    Of womankind but one,
And you are she, my dearest dear,
    Therefore it shall be done.

"I am a linendraper bold,
    As all the world doth know,
And my good friend the calender
    Will lend his horse to go."

Quoth Mrs. Gilpin, "That's well said;
    And for that wine is dear,
We will be furnished with our own,
    Which is both bright and clear."

John Gilpin kissed his loving wife;
    O'erjoyed was he to find,
That though on pleasure she was bent,
    She had a frugal mind.

The morning came, the chaise was
    brought,
    But yet was not allowed
To drive up to the door, lest all
    Should say that she was proud.

So three doors off the chaise was stayed,
    Where they did all get in;
Six precious souls, and all agog
    To dash through thick and thin.

Smack went the whip, round went the
    wheels,
    Were never folks so glad!
The stones did rattle underneath,
    As if Cheapside were mad.

John Gilpin at his horse's side
    Seized fast the flowing mane,
And up he got, in haste to ride,
    But soon came down again;

From Samuel Cowper, "The Diverting History of John Gilpin," *R. Caldecott's Picture Book (London: Frederick Warne.)*

For saddletree scarce reached had he,
    His journey to begin,
When, turning round his head, he saw
    Three customers come in.

So down he came; for loss of time,
    Although it grieved him sore,
Yet loss of pence, full well he knew,
    Would trouble him much more.

'Twas long before the customers
    Were suited to their mind,
When Betty screaming came downstairs,
    "The wine is left behind!"

"Good lack!" quoth he, "yet bring it me,
    My leathern belt likewise,
In which I bear my trusty sword
    When I do exercise."

Now Mistress Gilpin (careful soul!)
    Had two stone bottles found,
To hold the liquor that she loved,
    And keep it safe and sound.

Each bottle had a curling ear,
    Through which the belt he drew,
And hung a bottle on each side,
    To make his balance true.

Then over all, that he might be
    Equipped from top to toe,
His long red cloak, well brushed and
      neat,
    He manfully did throw.

Now see him mounted once again
    Upon his nimble steed,
Full slowly pacing o'er the stones,
    With caution and good heed.

But finding soon a smoother road
    Beneath his well-shod feet,
The snorting beast began to trot,
    Which galled him in his seat.

"So, fair and softly!" John he cried,
    But John he cried in vain;
That trot became a gallop soon,
    In spite of curb and rein.

So stooping down, as needs he must
    Who cannot sit upright,
He grasped the mane with both his
      hands,
    And eke with all his might.

His horse, who never in that sort
    Had handled been before,
What thing upon his back had got,
    Did wonder more and more.

Away went Gilpin, neck or nought;
    Away went hat and wig;
He little dreamt, when he set out,
    Of running such a rig.

The wind did blow, the cloak did fly
    Like streamer long and gay,
Till, loop and button failing both,
    At last it flew away.

Then might all people well discern
    The bottles he had slung;
A bottle swinging at each side,
    As hath been said or sung.

The dogs did bark, the children screamed,
    Up flew the windows all;
And every soul cried out, "Well done!"
    As loud as he could bawl.

Away went Gilpin—who but he?
    His fame soon spread around;
"He carries weight! he rides a race!
    'Tis for a thousand pound!"

And still as fast as he drew near,
    'Twas wonderful to view
How in a trice the turnpike-men
    Their gates wide open threw.

And now, as he went bowing down
    His reeking head full low,
The bottles twain behind his back
    Were shattered at a blow.

Down ran the wine into the road,
    Most piteous to be seen,
Which made the horse's flanks to
      smoke,
    As they had basted been.

But still he seemed to carry weight.
    With leathern girdle braced;
For all might see the bottle-necks
    Still dangling at his waist.

Thus all through merry Islington
    These gambols he did play,
Until he came unto the Wash
    Of Edmonton so gay:

And there he threw the wash about
    On both sides of the way,
Just like unto a trundling mop,
    Or a wild goose at play.

At Edmonton his loving wife
    From the balcony spied
Her tender husband, wondering much
    To see how he did ride.

"Stop, stop, John Gilpin!—Here's the
    house!"
    They all at once did cry;
"The dinner waits, and we are tired;"
    Said Gilpin—"So am I!"

But yet his horse was not a whit
    Inclined to tarry there;
For why?—his owner had a house
    Full ten miles off at Ware.

So like an arrow swift he flew,
    Shot by an archer strong;
So did he fly—which brings me to
    The middle of my song.

Away went Gilpin, out of breath,
    And sore against his will,
Till at his friend the calender's
    His horse at last stood still.

The calender, amazed to see
    His neighbour in such trim,
Laid down his pipe, flew to the gate,
    And thus accosted him:

"What news? what news? your tidings
    tell;
    Tell me you must and shall—
Say why bareheaded you are come,
    Or why you come at all?"

Now Gilpin had a pleasant wit,
    And loved a timely joke;
And thus unto the calender
    In merry guise he spoke:

"I came because your horse would
    come:
    And, if I well forebode,
My hat and wig will soon be here,
    They are upon the road."

The calender, right glad to find
    His friend in merry pin,
Returned him not a single word,
    But to the house went in;

Whence straight he came with hat and
    wig,
    A wig that flowed behind,
A hat not much the worse for wear,
    Each comely in its kind.

He held them up, and in his turn
    Thus showed his ready wit:
"My head is twice as big as yours,
    They therefore needs must fit."

"But let me scrape the dirt away,
    That hangs upon your face;
And stop and eat, for well you may
    Be in a hungry case."

Said John, "It is my wedding-day,
　　And all the world would stare
If wife should dine at Edmonton,
　　And I should dine at Ware."

So turning to his horse, he said
　　"I am in haste to dine:
'Twas for your pleasure you came here,
　　You shall go back for mine."

Ah! luckless speech, and bootless boast!
　　For which he paid full dear;
For while he spake, a braying ass
　　Did sing most loud and clear;

Whereat his horse did snort, as he
　　Had heard a lion roar,
And galloped off with all his might,
　　As he had done before.

Away went Gilpin, and away
　　Went Gilpin's hat and wig;
He lost them sooner than at first,
　　For why?—they were too big.

Now Mistress Gilpin, when she saw
　　Her husband posting down
Into the country far away,
　　She pulled out half-a-crown;

And thus unto the youth she said
　　That drove them to the "Bell,"
"This shall be yours when you bring
　　back
　　My husband safe and well."

The youth did ride, and soon did meet
　　John coming back amain;
Whom in a trice he tried to stop,
　　By catching at his rein.

But not performing what he meant,
　　And gladly would have done,
The frighted steed he frighted more,
　　And made him faster run.

Away went Gilpin, and away
　　Went postboy at his heels,
The postboy's horse right glad to miss
　　The lumbering of the wheels.

Six gentlemen upon the road,
　　Thus seeing Gilpin fly,
With postboy scampering in the rear,
　　They raised the hue and cry.

"Stop thief! stop thief! a highwayman!"
　　Not one of them was mute;
And all and each that passed that way
　　Did join in the pursuit

And now the turnpike-gates again
　　Flew open in short space;
The toll-man thinking, as before,
　　That Gilpin rode a race.

And so he did, and won it too,
　　For he got first to town;
Nor stopped till where he had got up,
　　He did again get down.

Now let us sing, Long live the King,
　　And Gilpin, long live he;
And when he next doth ride abroad,
　　May I be there to see.

FICTION

Swiss Family Robinson
The Tree-House

Johann David Wyss

Daniel Defoe (1660-1731) wrote two books that inspired children's books, two of which are excerpted here. Defoe's A Journal of the Plague Year *inspired Jill Paton Walsh to write* A Parcel of Patterns, *and his* Robinson Crusoe *gave rise to hundreds of books on the theme of being shipwrecked on a deserted island. One of the most popular of these is* The Swiss Family Robinson, *by Johann David Wyss (1743–1818), which tells the story of a family shipwrecked together.*

The prayers of the family were answered, and those who desired it finally reached home. Part of the family, though, decided to remain on the island and found a colony there. The story is an enjoyable one for children and adults not only because of the lively narrative, but also because it encourages self-reliance and inventiveness.

From a literary point of view, the book has defects. But, in spite of critics, it lives on.

When dinner was over, I prepared our night quarters. I first slung our hammocks from the roots of the tree, which, meeting above us, formed an arched roof, then covering the whole with sailcloth, we made a temporary tent, which would at least keep off the night damps and noxious insects.

Leaving my wife engaged in making a set of harness for the ass and cow, whose strength I intended to employ the following day in drawing the beams up to our tree, I walked down with Fritz and Ernest to the beach to look for wood suitable for building our new abode, and also to discover, if possible, some light rods to form a ladder.

For some time we hunted in vain. Nothing but rough driftwood was to be seen, utterly unfit for our purpose. Ernest at length pointed out a quantity of bamboos, half buried in the sand. These were exactly what I wanted, and stripping them of their leaves I cut them into lengths of about five feet each. I bound them in bundles to carry to the tree, and then began to look about for some slight reeds to serve as arrows.

I presently saw what I required in a copse at a little distance. We advanced cautiously lest the thicket should contain some wild beast or venomous serpent. Juno rushed ahead. As she did so a flock of flamingos, which had been quietly feeding, rose in the air. Fritz, instantly firing, brought a couple of birds to the ground, the rest of the squadron sailing away in perfect order, their plumages continually changing, as they flew, from beautiful rose to pure white, as alternately their snowy wings and rosy breasts were visible. One of those which fell was perfectly dead, but the other appeared only slightly wounded in the wings, for it made

Johann David Wyss, *The Swiss Family Robinson* (New York: Grosset & Dunlap, 1949).

off across the swampy ground. I attempted to follow, but soon found that progress was impossible on the marsh. Juno, however, chased the bird and, seizing it, speedily brought it to my feet. Fritz and Ernest were delighted at the sight of our prize.

"What a handsome bird!" exclaimed they. "It is much hurt? Let us tame it and let it run about with the fowls."

Fritz and Ernest then carried the birds and bamboos to the trees, while I proceeded to cut my reeds. I chose those which had flowered, knowing that they were harder, and having cut a sufficient quantity of these, I selected one or two of the tallest canes I could find to assist me in measuring the height of the tree. I then bound them together and returned to my family.

"Do you mean to keep this great hungry bird Fritz has brought?" said my wife. "It is another mouth to feed, remember, and provisions are still scarce."

"Luckily," I replied, "the flamingo will not eat grain like our poultry, but will be quite satisfied with insects, fish, and little crabs, which it will pick up for itself. Pray reassure yourself, there, and let me see to the poor bird's wound."

I procured some wine and butter and anointed the wing, which though hurt was not broken. I bound it up, and then took the bird to the stream, where I fastened it by a long cord to a stake and left if to shift for itself. In a few days the wound was healed, and the bird, subdued by kind treatment, became rapidly tame.

While I was thus employed my sons were endeavoring to ascertain the height of the lowest branch of the tree from the ground. They had fastened together the long reeds I had brought, and were trying to measure the distance with them, but in vain; they soon found that were the rods ten times their length they could not touch the branch.

"Hullo, my boys," I said, when I discovered what they were about, "that is not the way to set to work. Geometry will simplify the operation considerably; with its help the altitude of the highest mountains are ascertained. We may, therefore, easily find the height of the branch."

So saying, I measured out a certain distance from the base of the tree and marked the spot, and then by means of a rod whose length I knew, and imaginary lines, I calculated the angle subtended by the trunk of the tree from the ground to the root of the branch. This done, I was able to discover the height required and, to the astonishment of the younger children, announced that we should henceforth live thirty feet above the ground. This I wanted to know, that I might construct a ladder of necessary length.

Telling Fritz to collect all our cord, and the others to roll all the twine into a ball, I sat down and, taking the reeds, speedily manufactured half a dozen arrows and feathered them from the dead flamingo. I then took a strong bamboo, bent it, and strung it so as to form a bow. When the boys saw what I had done they were delighted, and begged to have the pleasure of firing the first shot.

"No, no!" said I. "I did not make this for mere pleasure, nor is it even intended as a weapon, the arrows are pointless. Elizabeth," I continued to my wife, "can you supply me with a ball of stout thread from your wonderful bag?''

"Certainly," replied she, "I think a ball of thread was the first thing to enter the bag," and diving her hand deep in, she drew out the very thing I wanted.

"Now, boys," I said, "I am going to fire the first shot." I fastened one end of the thread to one of my arrows and aimed at a large branch above me. The arrow flew upward, bore the thread over the branch, and fell at our feet. Thus was the first step in our undertaking accomplished. Now for the rope ladder!

Fritz had obtained two coils of cord, each about forty feet in length; these we stretched on the ground side by side. Then Fritz cut the bamboos into pieces of two feet for the steps of the ladder, and as he handed them to me, I passed them through knots which I had prepared in the ropes, while Jack fixed each end with a nail driven through the wood. When the ladder was finished, I carried over the bough a rope by which it might be hauled up. This done, I fixed the lower end of the ladder firmly to the ground by means of stakes, and was all ready for an ascent. The boys, who had been watching me with intense interest, were each eager to be first.

"Jack shall have the honor," said I, "as he is the lightest. So up with you, my boy, and do not break your neck."

Jack, who was as active as a monkey, sprang up the ladder and quickly gained the top.

"Three cheers for the nest!" he exclaimed, waving his cap. "Hurrah, hurrah, hurrah for our jolly nest! What a grand house we will have up here. Come along, Fritz!"

His brother was soon by his side, and with a hammer and nails fastened the ladder yet more securely. I followed with an ax, and took a survey of the tree. It was admirably suited to our purpose. The branches were very strong and so closely interwoven that no beams would be required to form a flooring, but when some of the boughs were lopped and cleared away, a few planks would be quite sufficient.

I now called for a pulley, which my wife fastened to the cord hanging beside the ladder. I hauled it up, and finding the boys rather in my way, told them to go down, while I proceeded to fasten the pulley to a stout branch above me, that we might be able to haul up the beams we should require the next day. I then made other preparations, that there might be no delay on the morrow, and a bright moon having arisen, I by its light continued working until I was quite worn out, and then at length descended to have our supper.

On a cloth spread out upon the grass were arranged a roast shoulder of porcupine, a delicious bowl of soup made from a piece of the same animal, cheese, butter, and biscuits, forming a most tempting repast. Having done this ample justice, we collected our cattle, and the pigeons and fowls having retired to roost on the neighboring trees and on the steps of our ladder, we made up a glorious fire to keep off any prowling wild beasts, and ourselves lay down.

The children, in spite of the novelty of the hammocks, were quickly asleep. In vain I tried to follow their example. A thousand anxious thoughts presented themselves, and as quickly as I dispelled them others rose in their place. The night wore on, and I was still awake. The fire burned low, and I rose and replenished it with dry fuel. Then again I climbed into my hammock, and toward morning fell asleep.

Early next morning we were astir, and dispersed to our various occupations. My wife milked the goats and cow, while we gave the animals their food, after which we went down to the beach to collect more wood for our building operations. To the larger beams we harnessed the cow and ass, while we ourselves dragged up the remainder.

Fritz and I then ascended the tree, and finished the preparations I had begun the night before. All useless boughs we lopped off, leaving a few about six feet from the floor, from which we might sling our hammocks, and others still higher, to support a temporary roof of sailcloth. My wife made fast the planks to a rope passed through the block I had fixed to the boughs above us, and by this means Fritz and I hauled them up. These we arranged side by side on the foundation of boughs, so as to form a smooth solid floor, and round this platform built a bulwark of planks, and then throwing the sailcloth over the higher branches, we drew it down and firmly nailed it.

Our house was thus enclosed on three sides, for behind the great trunk protected us, while the front was left open to admit the fresh sea breeze which blew directly in. We then hauled up our hammocks and bedding and slung them from the branches we had left for that purpose. A few hours of daylight still remaining, we cleared the floor of leaves and chips, and then descended to fashion a table and a few benches from the remainder of the wood. After working like slaves all day, Fritz and I flung ourselves on the grass, while my wife arranged supper on the table we had made.

"Come," said she at length, "come and taste flamingo stew, and tell me how you like it. Ernest assured me that it would be much better stewed than roasted, and I have been following his directions."

Laughing at the idea of Ernest turning scientific cook, we sat down. The fowls gathered round us to pick up the crumbs, and the tame flamingo joined them, while Master Knips skipped about from one to the other, chattering and mimicking our gestures continually. To my wife's joy, the sow appeared shortly after, and was presented with all the milk that remained from the day's stock that she might be persuaded to return every night.

"For," said my wife, "this surplus milk is really of no use to us, as it will be sour before the morning in this hot climate."

"You are quite right," I explained, "but we must contrive to make it of use. The next time Fritz and I return to the wreck we will bring off a churn among the other things we require."

"Must you really go again to that dreadful wreck?" said my wife, shuddering. "You have no idea how anxious I am when you are away there."

"Go we must, I am afraid," I replied, "but not for a day or two yet. Come, it is getting late. We and the chickens must go to roost."

We lit our watch fires and, leaving the dogs on guard below, ascended the ladder. Fritz, Ernest, and Jack were up in a moment. Their mother followed very cautiously, for though she had originated the idea of building a nest, she yet hesitated to entrust herself at such a terrific height from the ground. When she was safely landed in the house, taking little Franz on my back, I let go the fastenings which secured the lower end of the ladder to the ground, and swinging to and fro, slowly ascended.

Then for the first time we stood all together in our new home. I drew up the ladder and, with a greater sense of security than I had enjoyed since we landed on the island, offered up our evening prayer and retired for the night.

Little Women
OR MEG, JO, BETH, AND AMY
Playing Pilgrims

Louisa May Alcott

Many perceptive studies have been written about this classic. One of the best is Anne Hollander's essay "Reflections on Little Women," *which appeared in* Children's Literature, *an annual published by Yale University Press (vol. 9, 1981). Hollander observes, "The novel, like many great children's books, must*

From Louisa May Alcott, *Little Women, or Meg, Jo, Beth, and Amy* (New York: A. L. Burt, 1868).

serve as a pattern and a model, a mold for goals and aspirations rather than an accurate mirror of known experience.''

Though the father in this story is away in the Civil War, he is there in spirit, and the family is psychologically complete. The warm relationship among family members, present and absent, is something that many families aspire to and many attain.

The immediate family in Little Women *has no boys in it, but the neighbor boy, Laurie, plays an important role and most children —of both sexes—enjoy the story. It is rich in both joy and sorrow—the loves of Meg and Mr. Brooke, Amy and Laurie, Jo and Mr. Bhaer, and the death of the fourth sister, Beth.*

"Christmas won't be Christmas without any presents," grumbled Jo, lying on the rug.

"It's so dreadful to be poor!" sighed Meg, looking down at her old dress.

"I don't think it's fair for some girls to have plenty of pretty things, and other girls nothing at all," added little Amy, with an injured sniff.

"We've got father and mother and each other," said Beth contentedly, from her corner.

The four young faces on which the firelight shone brightened at the cheerful words, but darkened again as Jo said sadly,—

"We haven't got father, and shall not have him for a long time." She didn't say "perhaps never," but each silently added it, thinking of father far away, where the fighting was.

Nobody spoke for a minute; then Meg said in an altered tone,—

"You know the reason mother proposed not having any presents this Christmas was because it is going to be a hard winter for every one; and she thinks we ought not to spend money for pleasure, when our men are suffering so in the army. We can't do much, but we can make our little sacrifices, and ought to do it gladly. But I am afraid I don't;" and Meg shook her head, as she thought regretfully of all the pretty things she wanted.

"But I don't think the little we should spend would do any good. We've each got a dollar, and the army wouldn't be much helped by our giving that. I agree not to expect anything from mother or you, but I do want to buy Undine and Sintram for myself;

I've wanted it *so* long," said Jo, who was a bookworm.

"I planned to spend mine in new music," said Beth, with a little sigh, which no one heard but the hearth-brush and kettleholder.

"I shall get a nice box of Faber's drawing-pencils; I really need them," said Amy decidedly.

"Mother didn't say anything about our money, and she won't wish us to give up everything. Let's each buy what we want, and have a little fun; I'm sure we work hard enough to earn it," cried Jo, examining the heels of her shoes in a gentlemanly manner.

"I know *I* do,—teaching those tiresome children nearly all day, when I'm longing to enjoy myself at home," began Meg, in the complaining tone again.

"You don't have half such a hard time as I do," said Jo. "How would you like to be shut up for hours with a nervous, fussy old lady, who keeps you trotting, is never satisfied, and worries you till you're ready to fly out the window or cry?"

"It's naughty to fret; but I do think washing dishes and keeping things tidy is the worst work in the world. It makes me cross; and my hands get so stiff, I can't practise well at all;" and Beth looked at her rough hands with a sigh that any one could hear that time.

"I don't believe any of you suffer as *I* do," cried Amy; "for you don't have to go to school with impertinent girls, who plague you if you don't know your lessons, and laugh at your dresses, and label your father if he isn't rich, and insult you when your nose isn't nice."

"If you mean *libel,* I'd say so, and not talk about *labels,* as if papa was a pickle-bottle,'' advised Jo, laughing.

"I know what I mean, and you needn't be *statirical* about it. It's proper to use good words, and improve your *vocabilary,*'' returned Amy, with dignity.

"Don't peck at one another, children. Don't you wish we had the money papa lost when we were little, Jo? Dear me! how happy and good we'd be, if we had no worries!'' said Meg, who could remember better times.

"You said, the other day, you thought we were a deal happier than the King children, for they were fighting and fretting all the time, in spite of their money.''

"So I did, Beth. Well, I think we are; for, though we do have to work, we make fun for ourselves, and are a pretty jolly set, as Jo would say.''

"Jo does use such slang words!'' observed Amy, with a reproving look at the long figure stretched on the rug. Jo immediately sat up, put her hands in her pockets, and began to whistle.

"Don't, Jo; it's so boyish!''

"That's why I do it.''

"I detest rude, unlady-like girls!''

"I hate affected, niminy-piminy chits!''

" 'Birds in their little nests agree,' '' sang Beth, the peacemaker, with such a funny face that both sharp voices softened to a laugh, and the "pecking'' ended for that time.

"Really, girls, you are both to be blamed,'' said Meg, beginning to lecture in her elder-sisterly fashion. "You are old enough to leave off boyish tricks, and to behave better, Josephine. It didn't matter so much when you were a little girl; but now you are so tall, and turn up your hair, you should remember that you are a young lady.''

"I'm not! and if turning up my hair makes me one, I'll wear it in two tails till I'm twenty,'' cried Jo, pulling off her net, and shaking down a chestnut mane. "I hate to think I've got to grow up, and be Miss March, and wear long gowns, and look as prim as a China-aster! It's bad enough to be a girl, anyway, when I like boys' games and work

and manners! I can't get over my disappointment in not being a boy; and it's worse than ever now, for I'm dying to go and fight with papa, and I can only stay at home and knit, like a poky old woman!'' And Jo shook the blue army-sock till the needles rattled like castanets, and her ball bounded across the room.

"Poor Jo! It's too bad, but it can't be helped; so you must try to be contented with making your name boyish, and playing brother to us girls,'' said Beth, stroking the rough head at her knee with a hand that all the dish-washing and dusting in the world could not make ungentle in its touch.

"As for you, Amy,'' continued Meg, "you are altogether too particular and prim. Your airs are funny now; but you'll grow up an affected little goose, if you don't take care. I like your nice manners and refined ways of speaking, when you don't try to be elegant; but your absurd words are as bad as Jo's slang.''

"If Jo is a tom-boy and Amy a goose, what am I, please?'' asked Beth, ready to share the lecture.

"You're a dear, and nothing else,'' answered Meg warmly; and no one contradicted her, for the "Mouse'' was the pet of the family.

As young readers like to know "how people look,'' we will take this moment to give them a little sketch of the four sisters, who sat knitting away in the twilight, while the December snow fell quietly without, and the fire crackled cheerfully within. It was a comfortable old room, though the carpet was faded and the furniture very plain; for a good picture or two hung on the walls, books filled the recesses, chrysanthemums and Christmas roses bloomed in the windows, and a pleasant atmosphere of home-peace pervaded it.

Margaret, the eldest of the four, was sixteen, and very pretty, being plump and fair, with large eyes, plenty of soft, brown hair, a sweet mouth, and white hands, of which she was rather vain. Fifteen-year-old Jo was very tall, thin, and brown, and reminded one of a colt; for she never seemed to know what to do with her long limbs, which were very much in her way. She had a decided mouth, a comical nose, and sharp, gray eyes, which appeared to see everything, and were by turns fierce, funny or thoughtful. Her long, thick hair was her one beauty; but it was usually bundled into a net, to be out of her way. Round shoulders had Jo, big hands and feet, a fly-away look to her clothes, and the uncomfortable appearance of a girl who was rapidly shooting up into a woman, and didn't like it. Elizabeth—or Beth, as everyone called her—was a rosy, smooth-haired, bright-eyed girl of thirteen, with a shy manner, a timid voice, and a peaceful expression, which was seldom disturbed. Her father called her "Little Tranquility," and the name suited her excellently; for she seemed to live in a happy world of her own, only venturing out to meet the few whom she trusted and loved. Amy, though the youngest, was a most important person,—in her own opinion at least. A regular snow-maiden, with blue eyes, and yellow hair, curling on her shoulders, pale and slender, and always carrying herself like a young lady mindful of her manners. What the characters of the four sisters were we will leave to be found out.

The clock struck six; and having swept up the hearth, Beth put a pair of slippers down to warm. Somehow the sight of the old shoes had a good effect upon the girls; for mother was coming, and every one brightened to welcome her. Meg stopped lecturing, and lighted the lamp, Amy got out of the easy-chair without being asked, and Jo forgot how tired she was as she sat up to hold the slippers nearer to the blaze.

"They are quite worn out; Marmee must have a new pair."

"I thought I'd get her some with my dollar," said Beth.

"No, I shall!" cried Amy.

"I'm the oldest," began Meg, but Jo cut in with a decided—

"I'm the man of the family now papa is away, and I shall provide the slippers, for he told me to take special care of mother while he was gone."

"I'll tell you what we'll do," said Beth; "let's each get her something for Christmas, and not get anything for ourselves."

"That's like you, dear! What will we get?" exclaimed Jo.

Every one thought soberly for a minute; then Meg announced, as if the idea was suggested by the sight of her own pretty hands, "I shall give her a nice pair of gloves."

"Army shoes, best to be had," cried Jo.

"Some handkerchiefs, all hemmed," said Beth.

"I'll get a little bottle of cologne; she likes it, and it won't cost much, so I'll have some left to buy my pencils," added Amy.

"How will we give the things?" asked Meg.

"Put them on the table, and bring her in and see her open the bundles. Don't you remember how we used to do on our birthdays?" answered Jo.

"I used to be *so* frightened when it was my turn to sit in the big chair with the crown on, and see you all come marching round to give the presents, with a kiss. I liked the things and the kisses, but it was dreadful to have you sit looking at me while I opened the bundles," said Beth, who was toasting her face and the bread for tea, at the same time.

"Let Marmee think we are getting things for ourselves, and then surprise her. We must go shopping to-morrow afternoon, Meg; there is so much to do about the play for Christmas night," said Jo, marching up and down, with her hands behind her back and her nose in the air.

"I don't mean to act any more after this time; I'm getting too old for such things," observed Meg, who was as much a child as ever about "dressing up" frolics.

"You won't stop, I know, as long as you can trail round in a white gown with your hair down, and wear gold-paper jewelry. You are the best actress we've got, and there'll be an end of everything if you quit the boards," said Jo. "We ought to rehearse to-night. Come here, Amy, and do the fainting scene, for you are as stiff as a poker in that."

"I can't help it; I never saw any one faint, and I don't choose to make myself all black and blue, tumbling flat as you do. If I can go down easily, I'll drop; if I can't, I shall fall into a chair and be graceful; I don't care if Hugo does come at me with a pistol," returned Amy, who was not gifted with dramatic power, but was chosen because she was small enough to be borne out shrieking by the villain of the piece.

"Do it this way; clasp your hands so, and stagger across the room, crying frantically, 'Roderigo! save me! save me!' " and away went Jo, with a melodramatic scream which was truly thrilling.

Amy followed, but she poked her hands out stiffly before her, and jerked herself along as if she went by machinery; and her "Ow!" was more suggestive of pins being run into her than of fear and anguish. Jo gave a despairing groan, and Meg laughed outright, while Beth let her bread burn as she watched the fun, with interest.

"It's no use! Do the best you can when the time comes, and if the audience laugh, don't blame me. Come on, Meg."

Then things went smoothly, for Don Pedro defied the world in a speech of two pages without a single break; Hagar, the witch, chanted an awful incantation over her kettleful of simmering toads, with weird effect; Roderigo rent his chains asunder manfully, and Hugo died in agonies of remorse and arsenic, with a wild "Ha! ha!"

"It's the best we've had yet," said Meg, as the dead villain sat up and rubbed his elbows.

"I don't see how you can write and act such splendid things, Jo, You're a regular Shakespeare!" exclaimed Beth, who firmly believed that her sisters were gifted with wonderful genius in all things.

"Not quite," replied Jo modestly. "I do think, 'The Witch's Curse, an Operatic Tragedy,' is rather a nice thing; but I'd like to try Macbeth, if we only had a trap-door for Banquo. I always wanted to do the killing part. 'Is that a dagger that I see before me?' " muttered Jo, rolling her eyes and clutching at the air, as she had seen a famous tragedian do.

"No, it's the toasting fork, with mother's shoe on it instead of the bread. Beth's stagestruck!" cried Meg, and the rehearsal ended in a general burst of laughter.

"Glad to find you so merry, my girls," said a cheery voice at the door, and actors and audience turned to welcome a tall, motherly lady, with a "can-I-help-you" look about her which was truly delightful. She was not elegantly dressed, but a noble-looking woman, and the girls thought the gray cloak and unfashionable bonnet covered the most splendid mother in the world.

"Well, dearies, how have you got on to-day? There was so much to do, getting the boxes ready to go to-morrow, that I didn't come home to dinner. Has any one called, Beth? How is your cold, Meg? Jo, you look tired to death. Come and kiss me, baby."

While making these maternal inquiries, Mrs. March got her wet things off, her warm slippers on, and sitting down in the easy-chair, drew Amy to her lap, preparing to enjoy the happiest hour of her busy day. The girls flew about, trying to make things comfortable, each in her own way. Meg arranged the tea-table; Jo brought wood and set chairs, dropping, overturning, and clattering everything she touched; Beth trotted to and fro between parlor and kitchen, quiet and busy; while Amy gave directions to every one, as she sat with her hands folded.

As they gathered about the table, Mrs. March said, with a particularly happy face, "I've got a treat for you after supper."

A quick, bright smile went round like a streak of sunshine. Beth clapped her hands, regardless of the biscuit she held, and Jo tossed up her napkin, crying, "A letter! a letter! Three cheers for father!"

"Yes, a nice long letter. He is well, and thinks he shall get through the cold season better than we feared. He sends all sorts of loving wishes for Christmas, and an especial message to you girls," said Mrs. March, patting her pocket as if she had got a treasure there.

"Hurry and get done! Don't stop to quirk your little finger, and simper over your plate, Amy," cried Jo, choking in her tea, and dropping her bread, butter side down, on the carpet, in her haste to get at the treat.

Beth ate no more, but crept away, to sit in her shadowy corner and brood over the delight to come, till the others were ready.

"I think it was so splendid in father to go as a chaplain when he was too old to be drafted, and not strong enough for a soldier,'' said Meg warmly.

"Don't I wish I could go as a drummer, a *vivan*—what's its name? or a nurse, so I could be near him and help him,'' explained Jo, with a groan.

"It must be very disagreeable to sleep in a tent, and eat all sorts of bad-tasting things, and drink out of a tin mug,'' sighed Amy.

"When will he come home, Marmee?'' asked Beth, with a little quiver in her voice.

"Not for many months, dear, unless he is sick. He will stay and do his work faithfully as long as he can, and we won't ask for him back a minute sooner than he can be spared. Now come and hear the letter.''

They all drew to the fire, mother in the big chair with Beth at her feet, Meg and Amy perched on either arm of the chair, and Jo leaning on the back, where no one would see any sign of emotion if the letter should happen to be touching. Very few letters were written in those hard times that were not touching, especially those which fathers sent home. In this one little was said of the hardships endured, the dangers faced, or the homesickness conquered; it was a cheerful, hopeful letter, full of lively descriptions of camp life, marches, and military news; and only at the end did the writer's heart overflow with fatherly love and longing for the little girls at home.

"Give them all my dear love and a kiss. Tell them I think of them by day, pray for them by night, and find my best comfort in their affection at all times. A year seems very long to wait before I see them, but remind them that while we wait we may all work, so that these hard days need not be wasted. I know they will remember all I said to them, that they will be loving children to you, will do their duty faithfully, fight their bosom enemies bravely, and conquer themselves so beautifully, that when I come back to them I may be fonder and prouder than ever of my little women.''

Everybody sniffed when they came to that part; Jo wasn't ashamed of the great tear that dropped off the end of her nose, and Amy never minded the rumpling of her curls as she hid her face on her mother's shoulder and sobbed out, "I *am* a selfish girl! but I'll

truly try to be better, so he mayn't be disappointed in me by and by.''

"We all will!'' cried Meg. "I think too much of my looks, and hate to work, but won't any more, if I can help it.''

"I'll try and be what he loves to call me, 'a little woman,' and not be rough and wild; but do my duty here instead of wanting to be somewhere else,'' said Jo, thinking that keeping her temper at home was a much harder task than facing a rebel or two down South.

Beth said nothing, but wiped away her tears with the blue army-sock, and began to knit with all her might, losing no time in doing the duty that lay nearest her, while she resolved in her quiet little soul to be all that father hoped to find her when the year brought round the happy coming home.

Mrs. March broke the silence that followed Jo's words, by saying in her cheery voice, "Do you remember how you used to play Pilgrim's Progress when you were little things? Nothing delighted you more than to have me tie my piece-bags on your backs for burdens, give you hats and sticks and rolls of paper, and let you travel through the house from the cellar, which was the City of Destruction, up, up, to the house-top, where you had all the lovely things you could collect to make a Celestial City.''

"What fun it was, especially going by the lions, fighting Apollyon, and passing through the Valley where the hob-goblins were!'' said Jo.

"I liked the place where the bundles fell off and tumbled downstairs,'' said Meg.

"My favorite part was when we came out on the flat roof where our flowers and arbors and pretty things were, and all stood and sung for joy up there in the sunshine,'' said Beth, smiling, as if that pleasant moment had come back to her.

"I don't remember much about it, except that I was afraid of the cellar and the dark entry, and always liked the cake and milk we had up at the top. If I wasn't too old for such things, I'd rather like to play it over again,'' said Amy, who began to talk of renouncing childish things at the mature age of twelve.

"We never are too old for this, my dear,

because it is a play we are playing all the time in one way or another. Our burdens are here, our road is before us, and the longing for goodness and happiness is the guide that leads us through many troubles and mistakes to the peace which is a true Celestial City. Now, my little pilgrims, suppose you begin again, not in play, but in earnest, and see how far on you can get before father comes home."

"Really, mother? Where are our bundles?" asked Amy, who was a very literal young lady.

"Each of you told what your burden was just now, except Beth; I rather think she hasn't got any," said her mother.

"Yes, I have; mine is dishes and dusters, and envying girls with nice pianos, and being afraid of people."

Beth's bundle was such a funny one that everybody wanted to laugh; but nobody did, for it would have hurt her feelings very much.

"Let us do it," said Meg thoughtfully. "It is only another name for trying to be good, and the story may help us; for though we do want to be good, it's hard work, and we forget, and don't do our best."

"We were in the Slough of Despond tonight, and mother came and pulled us out as Help did in the book. We ought to have our roll of directions, like Christian. What shall we do about that?" asked Jo, delighted with the fancy which lent a little romance to the very dull task of doing her duty.

"Look under your pillows, Christmas morning, and you will find your guidebook," replied Mrs. March.

They talked over the new plan while old Hannah cleared the table; then out came the four little work-baskets, and the needles flew as the girls made sheets for Aunt March. It was uninteresting sewing, but to-night no one grumbled. They adopted Jo's plan of dividing the long seams into four parts, and calling the quarters Europe, Asia, Africa, and America, and in that way got on capitally, especially when they talked about the different countries as they stitched their way through them.

At nine they stopped work, and sung, as usual, before they went to bed. No one but Beth could get much music out of the old piano; but she had a way of softly touching the yellow keys, and making a pleasant accompaniment to the simple songs they sung. Meg had a voice like a flute, and she and her mother led the little choir. Amy chirped like a cricket, and Jo wandered through the airs at her own sweet will, always coming out at the wrong place with a croak or a quaver that spoilt the most pensive tune. They had always done this from the time they could lisp

"Crinkle, crinkle, 'ittle 'tar,"

and it had become a household custom, for the mother was a born singer. The first sound in the morning was her voice, as she went about the house singing like a lark; and the last sound at night was the same cheery sound, for the girls never grew too old for that familiar lullaby.

Mother Carey's Chickens
Mother Carey Herself

Kate Douglas Wiggin

This story, by the author of the better-known Rebecca of Sunnybrook Farm, *is a romantic and idealized turn-of-the-century picture of motherhood. The image of the "good" mother has changed in some respects, but the story still holds charm for some children in the primary grades and even older. "Mother Carey's*

From Kate Douglas Wiggin, *Mother Carey's Chickens* (Boston: Houghton Mifflin, 1910).

*chickens'' are the birds, the petrels, who warn sailors of approaching storms.
Beginning with the father, Captain Carey, who is in the navy, nautical references
and images are used throughout the story.*

'By and by there came along a flock of petrels, who are Mother Carey's own chickens. . . . They flitted along like a flock of swallows, hopping and skipping from wave to wave, lifting their little feet behind them so daintily that Tom fell in love with them at once.'

Nancy stopped reading and laid down the copy of 'Water Babies' on the sitting-room table. 'No more just now, Peter-bird,' she said; 'I hear mother coming.'

It was a cold, dreary day in late October, with an east wind and a chill of early winter in the air. The cab stood in front of Captain Carey's house, with a trunk beside the driver and a general air of expectancy on the part of neighbors at the opposite window.

Mrs. Carey came down the front stairway followed by Gilbert and Kathleen; Gilbert with his mother's small bag and travelling cloak, Kathleen with her umbrella; while little Peter flew to the foot of the stairs with a small box of sandwiches pressed to his bosom.

Mrs. Carey did not wear her usual look of sweet serenity, but nothing could wholly mar the gracious dignity of her face and presence. As she came down the stairs with her quick, firm tread, her flock following her, she looked the ideal mother. Her fine height, her splendid carriage, her deep chest, her bright eye and fresh color all bespoke the happy, contented, active woman, though something in the way of transient anxiety lurked in the eyes and lips.

'The carriage is too early,' she said; 'let us come into the sitting-room for five minutes. I have said my good-byes and kissed you all a dozen times, but I shall never be done until I am out of your sight.'

'O mother, mother, how can we let you go!' wailed Kathleen.

'Kitty! how can you!' exclaimed Nancy. 'What does it matter about us when mother has the long journey and father is so ill?'

'It will not be for very long—it can't be,' said Mrs. Carey wistfully. 'The telegram only said "symptoms of typhoid"; but these low fevers sometimes last a good while and are very weakening, so I may not be able to bring father back for two or three weeks; I ought to be in Fortress Monroe day after tomorrow; you must take turns in writing to me, children!'

'Every single day, mother!'

'Every single thing that happens.'

'A fat letter every morning,' they promised in chorus.

'If there is any real trouble remember to telegraph your Uncle Allan—did you write down his address, 11 Broad Street, New York? Don't bother him about little things, for he is not well, you know.'

Gilbert displayed a note-book filled with memoranda and addresses.

'And in any small difficulty send for Cousin Ann,' Mrs. Carey went on.

'The mere thought of her coming will make me toe the mark, I can tell you that!' was Gilbert's rejoinder.

'Better than any ogre or bug-a-boo, Cousin Ann is, even for Peter!' said Nancy.

'And will my Peter-bird be good and make Nancy no trouble?' said his mother, lifting him to her lap for one last hug.

'I'll be an angel boy pretty near all the time,' he asserted between mouthfuls of apple, 'or most pretty near,' he added prudently, as if unwilling to promise anything superhuman in the way of behavior. As a matter of fact it required only a tolerable show of virtue for Peter to win encomiums at any time. He would brush his curly mop of hair away from his forehead, lift his eyes, part his lips, showing a row of tiny white teeth; then a dimple would appear in each cheek and a seraphic expression (wholly at variance with the facts) would overspread the baby face, whereupon the beholder—Mother Carey, his sisters, the cook or the chambermaid, everybody indeed but Cousin Ann, who could never be wheedled—would cry

'Angel boy!' and kiss him. He was even kissed now, though he had done nothing at all but exist and be an enchanting personage, which is one of the injustices of a world where a large number of virtuous and well-behaved people go unkissed to their graves!

'I know Joanna and Ellen will take good care of the housekeeping,' continued Mrs. Carey, 'and you will be in school from nine to two, so that the time won't go heavily. For the rest I make Nancy responsible. If she is young, you must remember that you are all younger still, and I trust you to her.'

'The last time you did it, it didn't work very well!' And Gilbert gave Nancy a sly wink to recall a little matter of family history when there had been a delinquency on somebody's part.

Nancy's face crimsoned and her lips parted for a quick retort, and none too pleasant a one, apparently.

Her mother intervened quietly. 'We'll never speak of "last time," Gilly, or where would any of us be! We'll always think of "next" times. I shall trust Nancy next time, and next time and next time, and keep on trusting till I can trust her forever!'

Nancy's face lighted up with a passion of love and loyalty. She responded to the touch of her mother's faith as a harp to the favoring wind, but she said nothing; she only glowed and breathed hard and put her trembling hand about her mother's neck and under her chin.

'Now it's time! One more kiss all around. Remember you are Mother Carey's own chickens! There may be gales while I am away, but you must ride over the crests of the billows as merry as so many flying fish! Good-by! Good-by! Oh, my littlest Peter-bird, how can mother leave you?'

'I opened the lunch box to see what Ellen gave you, but I only broke off two teenty, weenty corners of sandwiches and one little new-moon bite out of a cookie,' said Peter, creating a diversion according to his wont.

Ellen and Joanna came to the front door and the children flocked down the frozen pathway to the gate after their mother, getting a touch of her wherever and whenever they could and jumping up and down between whiles to keep warm. Gilbert closed the door of the carriage, and it turned to go down the street. One window was open, and there was a last glimpse of the beloved face framed in the dark blue velvet bonnet, one last wave of a hand in a brown muff.

'Oh! she is beautiful!' sobbed Kathleen, 'her bonnet is just the color of her eyes; and she was crying!'

'There never was anybody like mother!' said Nancy, leaning on the gate, shivering with cold and emotion. 'There never was, and there never will be! We can try and try, Kathleen, and we *must* try, all of us; but mother wouldn't have to try; mother must have been partly born so!'

A Parcel of Patterns

Jill Paton Walsh

The villain of this story—the plague—has been humanity's enemy for 1500 years. The plague was a greater conqueror than Napoleon, more destructive than any war up until the present time, the most mysterious menace the world has ever known. Small wonder that in the seventeenth century, when this story takes place, there were many conjectures as to what caused the disease and these speculations shaped the behavior of the characters. The deeper drama of the story lies in the fact that the reader recognizes that even though the cause of the plague is now known, our conduct in the face of such a threat is still shaped by our beliefs.

From Jill Paton Walsh, *A Parcel of Patterns* (New York: Farrar, Straus & Giroux, 1983).

The book paints a vivid picture of the various ways in which human beings react to tragedy. At the end, the protagonist, Mall, now a bride, leaves England with her husband, Francis, for New England and a new beginning.

The tailor exclaimed in annoyance over the parcel. He tutted and clucked so loudly that Mistress Cooper stepped through from her kitchen to ask what ailed, and he prayed her for a knife to cut through the twine round the sodden bale of goods. 'He would not set his scissors to the twine, though they were even in his hand at the moment,' said Mistress Cooper, telling the tale to my mother. A knife being brought him, Goodman Vicars undid his patterns. They were a set of fancy shapes in sackcloth, or coarse canvas, and the rain had got into the parcel and wet it right through. The tailor put a line across the room, and hung up the patterns before the fire to dry. The rain pelted the little window panes from without, and soon they sweated and ran within from the mist of the drying cloth. Steam wisps rose faintly off the canvas, and Mistress Cooper went back to her breadmaking, leaving the tailor sitting on the floor, staring at his drying-line, putting the pieces together, as she supposed in his mind, figuring out how the outlandish dress was to be made.

He sat on till supper-time, and later, sewing–Mistress Cooper thought but languidly–at a collar that he had to finish, and staring at the homespun patterns. When Mistress Cooper lit her candle to go up to bed, he still sat, fingering his needle. She offered him a ladle of milk, and he would not have it, but only water. Everything in the room was moist, everything sweating with the steamy air from the drying out of the cloth, and there was a stale and dirty smell given off by the stuff. Even the tailor's brow was beaded with damp, and he sat so still that there was not stir enough in the room to fright the rats from creeping about the floor. They fled away at Mistress Cooper's heavy tread, bringing the water. She counselled him to sleep presently, and he thanked her for his care. It seemed to her that the stench from the parcel had filled up all the house, so she threw open the casement in the room where she and her sons slept, and the sound of the rain outside kept her long wakeful. She did not hear the tailor come up the stairs to his garret.

When she arose in the morning, Mistress Cooper found the fire burning merrily, so that it was clear it had been but lately mended, and the patterns were all bone dry and folded neatly, lying in a pile upon the tailor's chest in the window-corner. The drying-line was coiled upon its hook, and the room all set to rights, so that she thought nothing amiss and went about her errands. The tailor did not rise up and set to work at his usual time, but she thought he was oversleeping the late hour of the last evening. And she was bound to Bakewell that day, taking her sons with her, for she was seeking an apprenticeship for Edward, he being now about fourteen, and he had an uncle in Bakewell, a saddler, who might set him on.

It was five o'clock when they came back from Bakewell, and she was now much struck that the tailor was not sitting in his usual place, plying his needle. So going up to the loft below the eaves where he slept, she found him lying very sick, and parched for water. As night came on his fever worsened, and taking pity on him, though he was not kin of hers, Mistress Cooper called upon Goody Trickett, who came and left a pinch of herbs to make a tea to give him to drink.

Though it had cost her a groat it did little good, for on the morrow the poor goodman was worse. A hideous huge swelling had grown up upon his neck, that pushed his head crooked on his pallet, and grievously pained him. His words were wild and he knew not where he was, nor could he remember Mistress Cooper's name, but wildly gave some wench's name from long ago.

Hearing that he was sick, Mistress Momphesson came to visit him, and climbed the narrow steps to his room, and when he saw her his senses returned a moment, for he said, 'Alas, my girl, your London dress . . . '

'Be of good courage, Master Vicars,' said she. 'I shall wear it yet!'

'No! No!' cried he, starting up, and falling again upon the bed.

'I fetch forth my husband to pray with thee,' she said; and once she was gone he howled for Mistress Cooper, and implored her to burn the patterns. His words were furious as he tore at the bedding with frantic hands; and she could make not head nor tail of the half of what he said so wildly, but she understood clear enough that she should burn the patterns, and that in haste. They could not with safety be put upon the hearth, so she took them into the garden, and her two sons set fire to them with a hot coal and stood over the smoking pile till all was consumed to ashes; the sick man would have no peace till she could tell him it was done.

Parson Momphesson came in the evening, but the tailor would not hear him, and swore and blasphemed fearfully. The parson said calmly that it was but the fever speaking and not the man's soul. He gave a blessing, and spoke a prayer from the bed-foot, and was gone. The tailor howled and moaned piteously for half the night, and then was quiet. When Parson Stanley came to visit him, secretly, at first light, he was found dead.

All this I know because it was much on Mistress Cooper's mind, both then and later, and she told it all over both in the gross and in the detail to any that would hear her patiently; and my poor mother was one of those who would. I have sat spinning, and heard it all told time and again, to the dew on the windows, and on the tailor's brow.

It was a sorry tale, and we had some grief of it. Many Eyam folk brought the late flowers from their garths to cover the bare earth of the grave. The church was full, and there were many to follow the corpse to the grave in the far churchyard corner, to join in prayer for him. But he had been a stranger in the village, and had not dwelt long among us. All but Mistress Cooper put him very soon out of mind. What special cause for fear she might have had she did not speak of to any at that time.

It was the sixth of September, the year of Our Lord 1665, that George Vicars died. He was buried on the seventh. Buried, and forgotten for a fortnight.

Right well do I remember the season when George Vicars was buried. The weather was soft and sweet; the hills still held the warmth of the long summer's heat, but the rainfall had cleansed and sweetened the land. The streams all ran again, and there was good drinking for men and sheep, and the new grass was springing everywhere in so marvellous a bright green our common hills might have been lawns in paradise. Yet though the grass looked spring-like, the golden blaze of autumn had come early upon the trees, and in Eyam none remembered any September like it, for a fair season.

That time I was meeting Thomas with the flocks each and every day; and as soon as our tending was done we would find a quiet spot and sit down together, and I would bring out my slate from my apron pocket and set to teach him his letters, with a stub of chalk, and our two heads leaning down together over the little slate. There was a way to sit very close, side by side, and even for me to take his hand in mine, and push it round a making of 'O' or 'M' and no harm thought of. I taught him 'Thomas' and I taught him 'Blessed are the Meek' and I taught him 'I am the Good Shepard', and he learned these teasing me all the while with asking to be shown 'Mouse' and 'Mall' and 'I love thee, my sweetheart'.

'Fie, Thomas,' I rebuked him, 'what will Parson Stanley say if he find thou canst write nought but "I love thee, sweet, Mouse"?'

'It is not for Parson Stanley that I bend my wits to this, Mall,' he said, smiling, 'but for thee.'

'Tush, tush,' I said.

'But soberly, though,' he said, one of his moments of gravity coming suddenly upon his face. 'For writing, I have little mind; but I can see that a man would do well to read. Forget the slate, Mouse, and bring to me a book, and I will be thy most diligent apprentice!'

And so full early one morning, on a day brilliant with dew in the bright sunrise, I walked down the street and to the door of the Coopers' cottage. Young Edward opened the door to me, with a cup of milk in his hand, and his collar unfastened, and he blushed a little to see me, which made me to fix my face very sad for fear of laughing at him, for he was a good lad, and though he did trail after me and make occasion to speak to me, I was not minded to mock him. My mother said while the great lads mooned after maids older in years than they, there was no need to worry; it was when they went after the younger ones it was time they should be close watched!

I would not step in, but stood on the doorstep in the sun; and when Edward brought his mother to me I asked her that I might borrow the little Bible, printed small, that had been in the tailor's box and of which she had spoken. I undertook she should have it again by nightfall. My father's Bible was as big as a flagstone step, and half as heavy. Saying, 'Have a care of it, Mall, for it is not mine,' she lent it me, and I went on my way. Edward came with me a step or two, smiling, and promising to bring me cakes and comfits when he came home from Bakewell next.

At the head of the town I took leave of him and went running upon my way, burning with eagerness to be with Thomas on the hills. I would hitch up my heavy skirts with my shepherd's crook, and free my feet for running and leaping across rocky ground. So I came up to Thomas, as always, out of breath.

We sat by a little fresh running spring, under a windstunted hawthorn all bright with haws, while the sheep bleated round us and the bell-wether ding-donged. First we bent our minds upon the Bible, and letter by letter we spelt out the tally of blesseds: blessed are the poor in spirit, and they that mourn, and the meek, and they which do hunger and thirst after righteousness . . . and then Thomas played an air upon his pipe.

When the sun was high overhead and the patch of shade we sat in was shrunk to a kerchief size, we heard voices near by. I was ill pleased at any company, but Thomas stood up and hailed them, and there were Emmot and her Roland, he with a basket on his arm,

come to seek us. They had brought bread and cheese and a jar of ale, and we all sat down together and ate heartily. Roland held Emmot by the hand, which made Thomas bold to take mine also. Emmot looked at Roland sideways with such a shine upon her face as made me smile to see. Roland Torre was but a man; of medium stature, plain features and dark hair. She looked upon him as if he had been a London gallant, or at least an angel; but he was not handsome, except when he looked at her.

When we had eaten, Thomas piped and Roland and Emmot danced. Then as we set down again together Thomas had a tale to tell. He said as he came across the sheep-walks that morning, he had met a stranger upon the road—a fat man in a dusty cloak, covered with twigs and burrs as if he had slept in a bush—who asked him for a draught of water from his flagon. Thomas had given of it gladly enough, and the stranger then set forth a bushel of talking, all dark and hard to Thomas, but of which he understood this much, that the stranger bade him seek to see the world by inner light, which should shine very bright and clear, and show him all he would ever need to know or see.

'What answer didst thou make, cousin?' Roland asked.

'Why, I told him a shepherd on the hills had always light enough to see by,' Thomas said. 'How even in the storm when the great clouds roll above, the sun puts fingers through, and how when the sky is clear our hills are lit as though they were at the gates of paradise. And shortly, that I looked to see well enough by God's own daylight!'

'What answered he again?' asked Roland.

'He told me that a man must have inner light to see the outer by, and a good deal more Sunday talk. So I told him cheerily to-day was Thursday, and took my road!'

Roland laughed and challenged Thomas to race him to the ridge, which race Thomas won easily, while Emmot and I looked on. Then he and she parted from Thomas and me, and we sat a while alone, with little said but much contentment in our quiet. In a while Thomas said, 'I mean to have you, Mall. I would rather die, else. When may I ask thy father?'

'Patience, Thomas, love,' I said. 'Thou shalt have me, anon.'

'What if he marry you to some richer man?' said Thomas, turning his head away.

'He does not think of it, yet. And he would find he could not; I would not consent. My mother is our friend in this, love. She will see all well in time.'

'I would not tarry much longer, love,' he said.

I went home in a purple dusk, pricked out in stars, like a meadow in buttercups. The streamlets murmured, and the birds of evening sang. A scatter of windows, of candlelight, or lantern-light, like a broken string of golden beads, showed me my town below me. I stepped down past half the houses to my own door. As on my deathbed, in my mind I shall walk home that evening, I shall never forget the walking, and the coming to my door, for that it was the last time ever I was light of heart, or of good hope and courage, or safe in my own place. I stood a moment with my hand upon the latch, thinking of Thomas and smiling in the darkness, and then went in.

My father was within alone, sitting by the light of one taper and the dim glow from the untended fire.

'Is that thee, Mall?' he said, looking up.

'Yes, Father,' I answered, propping my crook by the door and coming to his side. He rose up, and put his arm around me. 'Thou art well, lass? Naught amiss?'

'Why, what should be amiss, father?' I said. 'I am well, Let me put supper on the fire. Where has my mother gone?'

'She is comforting Widow Cooper, Mall. Young Edward Cooper is dead!'

'Oh, no, father, no, he cannot be!' I cried. 'He was well and laughing this very morn, and walked a way with me!'

'He is fallen sick, and was dead within the hour, Mall, believe me.'

'Oh, No! Oh, no, dear God!' I said. 'I must go down at once, I must bring some help . . . I must go!'

'No, daughter. Thy mother bade me prevent thee. There is danger enough to her in going to help the Coopers, and that peril

she would not have thee share. It was the Plague, Mall. The boy died with the plague-tokens on him, and, it now seems, the tailor had them also. Now God have mercy on us all; and most solemnly I do forbid thee, Mall, to enter the Cooper's cottage, or go near any of that kin.'

'I have this day borrowed a Bible of her, father, that I must return . . .'

'Mall, thou art our only child. Do as I have asked. I will take back the Bible for thee . . . there, now, do not weep . . . I will bring supper to the table, do not mind . . .'

So I sat down at the hearth, and watched my father putting the pot to the fire, and bringing the bread, and such tasks as he never set his hand to before, as far as I could remember. I thought of the poor callow boy who had blushed, and doted, and promised me Bakewell pies, and come glowing with youth and health with me up the street in the morning . . . I could have afforded him a little kindness . . . I was shaking from head to foot, as though I had been dropped into cold water, and weeping so fast my cheeks burned, and the firelight smeared and wavered as though I had seen it through water.

In a while my father put a shawl round me, and led me to my bed.

It was not named abroad for many days. Though my father had called it Plague that struck down poor Edward Cooper, though my mother and Mistress Cooper had seen upon the tailor and upon Edward's body that which they knew it by, they said nothing of what they knew, but hoped in God's mercy it would quickly pass. So it was called 'the sickness'. And it was nothing wonderful to have a sickness in the town; there are many sicknesses, and never a year in which a sickness does not carry men, women and children to God. There is a winter sickness that makes the gaffer and gamma cough and die, however careful of their safety their children and grandchildren are; there is a summer sickness that comes with a spotted face and burning fever, and takes off the children from one day to the next. There is a sickness from drinking foul water, and one from eating foul meats, and on, and on–only Goody Trickett could name them all over for you, and offer remedies for some, though for others help is there none to be given. There is neither an apothecary nor a surgeon in Eyam; so for what Goody Trickett and her garden of herbs cannot heal we trust to God. Except that the farrier can set a broken bone on man or horse.

FANTASY

A Wrinkle in Time
Absolute Zero

Madeleine L'Engle

Imaginative writers—including Bulwer Lytton, who predicted the discovery of radium in his novel The Coming Race, *and Jules Verne, who predicted the development of submarines and space travel—sometimes foretell future scientific discoveries.*

Science fiction in particular often speculates on things that later become reality. The science fiction idea that one can "tesser"—that is, go through a wrinkle in time and arrive almost instantly on another planet—is explored by Madeleine L'Engle, who imagines a whole family having this experience. The adventure is at times frightening, but because the characters watch out for one another, Mr. and Mrs. Murry, Meg, and Charles Wallace (with the help of Mrs. Whatsit, Mrs. Who, and Mrs. Which) are reunited.

The first sign of returning consciousness was cold. Then sound. She was aware of voices that seemed to be traveling through her across an arctic waste. Slowly the icy sounds cleared and she realized that the voices belonged to her father and Calvin. She did not hear Charles Wallace. She tried to open her eyes but the lids would not move. She tried to sit up, but she could not stir. She struggled to turn over, to move her hands, her feet, but nothing happened. She knew that she had a body, but it was as lifeless as marble.

She heard Calvin's frozen voice: "Her heart is beating so slowly—"

Her father's voice: "But it's beating. She's alive."

"Barely."

"We couldn't find a heartbeat at all at first. We thought she was dead."

From Madeleine L'Engle, *A Wrinkle in Time* (New York: Farrar, Straus & Giroux, 1962).

"Yes."

"And then we could feel her heart, very faintly, the beats very far apart. And then it got stronger. So all we have to do is wait." Her father's words sounded brittle in her ears, as though they were being chipped out of ice.

Calvin: "Yes. You're right, sir."

She wanted to call out to them. "I'm alive! I'm very much alive! Only I've been turned to stone."

But she could not call out any more than she could move.

Calvin's voice again. "Anyhow you got her away from IT. You got us both away and we couldn't have gone on holding out. IT's so much more powerful and strong than— How *did* we stay out, sir? How did we manage as long as we did?"

Her father: "Because IT's completely unused to being refused. That's the only reason I could keep from being absorbed, too. No mind has tried to hold out against IT for so many thousands of centuries that certain centers have become soft and atrophied through lack of use. If you hadn't come to me when you did I'm not sure how much longer I would have lasted. I was on the point of giving in."

Calvin: "Oh, no, sir—"

Her father: "Yes. Nothing seemed important any more but rest, and of course IT offered me complete rest. I had almost come to the conclusion that I was wrong to fight, that IT was right after all, and everything I believed in most passionately was nothing but a madman's dream. But then you and Meg came in to me, broke through my prison, and hope and faith returned."

Calvin: "Sir, why were you on Camazotz at all? Was there a particular reason for going there?"

Her father, with a frigid laugh: "Going to Camazotz was a complete accident. I never intended even to leave our own solar system. I was heading for Mars. Tessering is even more complicated than we had expected."

Calvin: "Sir, how was IT able to get Charles Wallace before it got Meg and me?"

Her father: "From what you've told me it's because Charles Wallace thought he could deliberately go into IT and return. He trusted too much to his own strength —listen!—I think the heartbeat is getting stronger!"

His words no longer sounded to her quite as frozen. Was it his words that were ice, or her ears? Why did she hear only her father and Calvin? Why didn't Charles Wallace speak?

Silence. A long silence. Then Calvin's voice again: "Can't we do anything? Can't we look for help? Do we just have to go on waiting?"

Her father: "We can't leave her. And we must stay together. We must *not* be afraid to take time."

Calvin: "You mean we were? We rushed into things on Camazotz too fast, and Charles Wallace rushed in too fast, and that's why he got caught?"

"Maybe. I'm not sure. I don't know enough yet. Time is different on Camazotz, anyhow. Our time, inadequate though it is, at least is straightforward. It may not be even fully one-dimensional, because it can't move back and forth on its line, only ahead; but at least it's consistent in its direction. Time on Camazotz seems to be inverted, turned in on itself. So I have no idea whether I was imprisoned in that column for centuries or only for minutes." Silence for a moment. Then her father's voice again. "I think I feel a pulse in her wrist now."

Meg could not feel his fingers against her wrist. She could not feel her wrist at all. Her body was still stone, but her mind was beginning to be capable of movement. She tried desperately to make some kind of a sound, a signal to them, but nothing happened.

Their voices started again. Calvin: "About your project, sir. Were you on it alone?"

Her father: "Oh, no. There were half a dozen of us working on it and I daresay a number of others we don't know about. Certainly we weren't the only nation to investigate along that line. It's not really a new idea. But we did try very hard not to let it be known abroad that we were trying to make it practicable."

"Did you come to Camazotz alone? Or were there others with you?"

"I came alone. You see, Calvin, there was no way to try it out ahead with rats or monkeys or dogs. And we had no idea whether it would really work or whether it would be complete bodily disintegration. Playing with time and space is a dangerous game."

"But why you, sir?"

"I wasn't the first. We drew straws, and I was second."

"What happened to the first man?"

"We don't—look! Did her eyelids move?" Silence. Then: "No. It was only a shadow."

But I *did* blink, Meg tried to tell them. I'm sure I did. And I can hear you! *Do* something!

But there was only another long silence, during which perhaps they were looking at her, watching for another shadow, another flicker. Then she heard her father's voice again, quiet, a little warmer, more like his own voice. "We drew straws, and I was second. We know Hank went. We saw him go. We saw him vanish right in front of the rest of us. He was there and then he wasn't. We were to wait for a year for his return or for some message. We waited. Nothing."

Calvin, his voice cracking: "Jeepers, sir. You must have been in sort of a flap."

Her father: "Yes. It's a frightening as well as an exciting thing to discover that matter and energy *are* the same thing, that size is an illusion, and that time is a material substance. We can know this, but it's far more than we can understand with our puny little brains. I think you will be able to comprehend far more than I. And Charles Wallace even more than you."

"Yes, but what happened, please, sir, after the first man?"

Meg could hear her father sigh. "Then it was my turn. I went. And here I am. A wiser and a humbler man. I'm sure I haven't been gone two years. Now that you've come I have some hope that I may be able to return in time. One thing I have to tell the others is that we know nothing."

Calvin: "What do you mean, sir?"

Her father: "Just what I say. We're children playing with dynamite. In our mad rush we've plunged into this before—"

With a desperate effort Meg made a sound. It wasn't a very loud sound, but it was a sound. Mr. Murry stopped. "Hush. Listen."

Meg made a strange, croaking noise. She found that she could pull open her eyelids. They felt heavier than marble but she managed to raise them. Her father and Calvin were hovering over her. She did not see Charles Wallace. Where was he?

She was lying in an open field of what looked like rusty, stubby grass. She blinked, slowly, and with difficulty.

"Meg," her father said. "Meg. Are you all right?"

Her tongue felt like a stone tongue in her mouth, but she managed to croak, "I can't move."

"Try," Calvin urged. He sounded now as though he were very angry with her. "Wiggle your toes. Wiggle your fingers."

"I can't. Where's Charles Wallace?" Her words were blunted by the stone tongue. Perhaps they could not understand her, for there was no answer.

"We were knocked out for a minute, too," Calvin was saying. "You'll be all right, Meg. Don't get panicky." He was crouched over her, and though his voice continued to sound cross he was peering at her with anxious eyes. She knew that she must still have her glasses on because she could see him clearly, his freckles, his stubby black lashes, the bright blue of his eyes.

Her father was kneeling on her other side. The round lenses of Mrs. Who's glasses still blurred his eyes. He took one of her hands and rubbed it between his. "Can you feel my fingers?" He sounded quite calm, as though there were nothing extraordinary in having her completely paralyzed. At the quiet of his voice she felt calmer. Then she saw that there were great drops of sweat standing out on his forehead, and she noticed vaguely that the gentle breeze that touched her cheeks was cool. At first his words had been frozen and now the wind was mild: was it icy cold here or warm? "Can you feel my fingers?" he asked again.

Yes, now she could feel a pressure against her wrist, but she could not nod. "Where's

Charles Wallace?'' Her words were a little less blurred. Her tongue, her lips were beginning to feel cold and numb, as though she had been given a massive dose of novocaine at the dentist's. She realized with a start that her body and limbs were cold, that not only was she not warm, she was frozen from head to toe, and it was this that had made her father's words seem like ice, that had paralyzed her.

"I'm frozen—" she said faintly. Camazotz hadn't been this cold, a cold that cut deeper than the wind on the bitterest of winter days at home. She was away from IT, but this unexplained iciness was almost as bad. Her father had not saved her.

Now she was able to look around a little, and everything she could see was rusty and gray. There were trees edging the field in which she lay, and their leaves were the same brown as the grass. There were plants that might have been flowers, except that they were dull and gray. In contrast to the drabness of color, to the cold that numbed her, the air was filled with a delicate, spring-like fragrance, almost imperceptible as it blew softly against her face. She looked at her father and Calvin. They were both in their shirt sleeves and they looked perfectly comfortable. It was she, wrapped in their clothes, who was frozen too solid even to shiver.

"Why am I so cold?" she asked. "Where's Charles Wallace?" They did not answer. "Father, where are we?"

Mr. Murry looked at her soberly. "I don't know, Meg. I don't tesser very well. I must have overshot, somehow. We're not on Camazotz. I don't know where we are. I think you're so cold because we went through the Black Thing, and I thought for a moment it was going to tear you away from me."

"Is this a dark planet?" Slowly her tongue was beginning to thaw; her words were less blurred.

"I don't think so," Mr. Murray said, "but I know so little about anything that I can't be sure."

"You shouldn't have tried to tesser,

then." She had never spoken to her father in this way before. The words seemed hardly to be hers.

Calvin looked at her, shaking his head. "It was the only thing to do. At least it got us off Camazotz."

"Why did we go without Charles Wallace? Did we just leave him there?" The words that were not really hers came out cold and accusing.

"We didn't 'just leave him,' " her father said. "Remember that the human brain is a very delicate organism, and it can be easily damaged."

"See, Meg," Calvin crouched over her, tense and worried, "if your father had tried to yank Charles away when he tessered us, and if IT had kept grabbing hold of Charles, it might have been too much for him, and we'd have lost him forever. And we had to do something right then."

"Why?"

"IT was taking us. You and I were slipping, and if your father had gone on trying to help us he wouldn't have been able to hold out much longer, either."

"*You* told him to tesser," Meg charged Calvin.

"There isn't any question of blame," Mr. Murry cut in severely. "Can you move yet?"

All Meg's faults were uppermost in her now, and they were no longer helping her. "No! And you'd better take me back to Camazotz and Charles Wallace quickly. You're supposed to be able to help!'' Disappointment was as dark and corrosive in her as the Black Thing. The ugly words tumbled from her cold lips even as she herself could not believe that it was to her father, her beloved, longed-for father, that she was talking to in this way. If her tears had not still been frozen they would have gushed from her eyes.

She had found her father and he had not made everything all right. Everything kept getting worse and worse. If the long search for her father was ended, and he wasn't able to overcome all their difficulties, there was nothing to guarantee that it would all come out right in the end. There was nothing left to hope for. She was frozen, and Charles Wallace was being devoured by IT, and her omnipotent father was doing nothing. She teetered on the seesaw of love and hate, and the Black Thing pushed her down into hate. "You don't even know where we are!" she cried out at her father. "We'll never see Mother or the twins again! We don't know where earth is! Or even where Camazotz is! We're lost out in space! What are you going to *do!*" She did not realize that she was as much in the power of the Black Thing as Charles Wallace.

Mr. Murry bent over her, massaging her cold fingers. She could not see his face. "My daughter, I am not a Mrs. Whatsit, a Mrs. Who, or a Mrs. Which. Yes, Calvin has told me everything he could. I am a human being, and a very fallible one. But I agree with Calvin. We were sent here for something. And we know that all things work together for good to them that love God, to them who are the called according to his purpose."

"The Black Thing!" Meg cried out at him. "Why did you let it almost get me?"

"You've never tessered as well as the rest of us," Calvin reminded her. "It never bothered Charles and me as much as it did you."

"He shouldn't have taken me, then," Meg said. "until he learned to do it better."

Neither her father nor Calvin spoke. Her father continued his gentle massage. Her fingers came back to life with tingling pain. "You're hurting me!"

"Then you're feeling again," her father said quietly. "I'm afraid it *is* going to hurt, Meg."

The piercing pain moved slowly up her arms, began in her toes and legs. She started to cry out against her father when Calvin exclaimed, "Look!"

Coming toward them, moving in silence across the brown grass, were three figures.

What were they?

On Uriel there had been the magnificent creatures. On Camazotz the inhabitants had at least resembled people. What were these three strange things approaching?

They were the same dull gray color as the flowers. If they hadn't walked upright they would have seemed like animals. They moved directly toward the three human beings. They had four arms and far more than five fingers, to each hand, and the fingers were not fingers, but long waving tentacles. They had heads, and they had faces. But where the faces of the creatures on Uriel had seemed far more than human faces, these seemed far less. Where the features would normally be there were several indentations, and in place of ears and hair were more tentacles. They were tall, Meg realized as they came closer, far taller than any man. They had no eyes. Just soft indentations.

Meg's rigid, frozen body tried to shudder with terror, but instead of the shudder all that came was pain. She moaned.

The Things stood over them. They appeared to be looking down at them, except that they had no eyes with which to see. Mr. Murray continued to kneel by Meg, massaging her.

He's killed us, bringing us here, Meg thought. I'll never see Charles Wallace again, or Mother, or the twins. . . .

Calvin rose to his feet. He bowed to the beasts as though they could see him. He said, "How do you do, sir—ma'am—?"

"Who are you?" the tallest of the beasts said. His voice was neither hostile nor welcoming, and it came not from the mouthlike indentation in the furry face, but from the waving tentacles.

—They'll eat us, Meg thought wildly.— They're making me hurt. My toes—my fingers—I hurt. . . .

Calvin answered the beast's question. "We're—we're from earth. I'm not sure how we got here. We've had an accident. Meg— this girl—is—is paralyzed. She can't move. She's terribly cold. We think that's why she can't move."

One of them came up to Meg and squatted down on its huge haunches beside her, and she felt utter loathing and revulsion as it reached out a tentacle to touch her face.

But with the tentacle came the same delicate fragrance that moved across her with the breeze, and she felt a soft, tingling warmth go all through her that momentarily assuaged her pain. She felt suddenly sleepy.

I must look as strange to it as it looks to me, she thought drowsily, and then realized with a shock that of course the beast couldn't see her at all. Nevertheless a reassuring sense of safety flowed through her with the warmth which continued to seep deep into her as the beast touched her. Then it picked her up, cradling her in two of its four arms.

Mr. Murry stood up quickly. "What are you doing?"

"Taking the child."

The Fragmented Family

FABLES, MYTHS, AND LEGENDS

The Raven and His Young

Leo Tolstoy

Most older students will enjoy reading the life of Count Leo Tolstoy. (See References for Adults, p. 140.) When Tolstoy and his friends were small boys, they organized what they called ''The Ant Brotherhood.'' They would all sit under chairs and think about the secrets supposedly known to Tolstoy's brother—how all men could be happy and how there would be no disease or war. His brother said he had written this on a green stick and buried it in a certain place. When Tolstoy died, he asked to be buried in that place, and his family carried out his wishes.

Tolstoy was a great humanist. He wrote some of his children's stories to benefit the victims of an anti-Jewish pogrom.

Should one expect gratitude from one's offspring? This is the question that confronted Shakespeare's King Lear and faces the raven in this story. Each answers that question in different ways.

Professor Gareth Matthews, who has written two books on philosophy and the young child, has observed that children think as clearly as—sometimes more clearly than—adults. This fable might make a good ''thought experiment'' to be used with children to discuss the subject of loyalty. If necessary, it can be retold by the adult in a way suitable to the age of the listeners.

The raven built his nest on an island, and when his young were hatched he began carrying them from the island to the mainland. He took the first one up in his claws and flew with him across the sea.

When he reached the middle of the ocean he grew tired, and his wings beat more slowly.

"Now I am strong and he is weak, and I am carrying him across the sea," he thought, "but when he grows great and powerful and I am old and weak, will he remember my toil

From Leo Tolstoy, *Fables and Tales* (New York: New American Library, 1962).

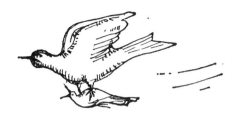

and carry me from one place to another?'' And the old raven asked the young one: "When I am weak and you are strong, will you carry me? Tell me the truth!''

The young raven was afraid that his father might drop him into the ocean, and he said: "I will!''

But the old raven did not believe his son, and he opened his claws and let him fall. He dropped like a lump and drowned in the sea. The old raven flew back to his island.

Then he took his second son in his claws and flew with him across the sea. Again he grew tired, and again he asked his son whether he would carry him from place to place when he was old. The young raven,

afraid of being dropped into the ocean, said: "I will!''

The father did not believe this son either, and he let him fall into the sea.

When the old raven flew back to his nest there remained only one young raven. He took his last son and flew with him across the sea. When he came to the middle of the ocean and grew tired he asked: "Will you feed me and carry me from place to place in my old age?''

"No, I will not,'' the young raven replied.

"Why not?'' asked the father.

"When you are old and I am grown I shall have my own nest and my own young to feed and carry.''

"He speaks the truth,'' thought the old raven. "I shall exert myself and carry him across the sea.''

And the old raven did not drop the young one, but beat his wings with his last remaining strength in order to carry him to the mainland so that he could build his nest and raise his young.

Perseus

Edith Hamilton

Perseus had a father who was a philanderer and a grandfather who wanted to see him dead. Fortunately, he had a warm and protective mother, and he grew up to marry Andromeda and live happily ever after.

King Acrisius of Argos had only one child, a daughter, Danaë. She was beautiful above all the other women of the land, but this was small comfort to the King for not having a son. He journeyed to Delphi to ask the god if there was any hope that some day he would be the father of a boy. The priestess told him no, and added what was far worse: that his daughter would have a son who would kill him.

The only sure way to escape that fate was for the King to have Danaë instantly put to death—taking no chances, but seeing to it himself. This Acrisius would not do. His fatherly affection was not strong, as events proved, but his fear of the gods was. They visited with terrible punishments those who shed the blood of kindred. Acrisius did not dare slay his daughter. Instead, he had a house built all of bronze and sunk under-

From Edith Hamilton, *Mythology* (Boston: Little, Brown, 1942).

ground, but with part of the roof open to the sky so that light and air could come through. Here he shut her up and guarded her. . . .

As she sat there through the long days and hours with nothing to do, nothing to see except the clouds moving by overhead, a mysterious thing happened, a shower of gold fell from the sky and filled her chamber. How it was revealed to her that it was Zeus who had visited her in this shape we are not told, but she knew that the child she bore was his son.

For a time she kept his birth secret from her father, but it became increasingly difficult to do so in the narrow limits of that bronze house and finally one day the little boy—his name was Perseus—was discovered by his grandfather. "Your child!" Acrisius cried in great anger. "Who is his father?" But when Danaë answered proudly, "Zeus," he would not believe her. One thing only he was sure of, that the boy's life was a terrible danger to his own. He was afraid to kill him for the same reason that had kept him from killing her, fear of Zeus and the Furies who pursue such murderers. But if he could not kill them outright, he could put them in the way of tolerably certain death. He had a great chest made, and the two placed in it. Then it was taken out to sea and cast into the water.

In that strange boat Danaë sat with her little son. The daylight faded and she was alone on the sea. . . .

Through the night in the tossing chest she listened to the waters that seemed always about to wash over them. The dawn came, but with no comfort to her for she could not see it. Neither could she see that around them there were islands rising high above the sea, many islands. All she knew was that presently a wave seemed to lift them and carry them swiftly on and then, retreating, leave them on something solid and motionless. They had made land; they were safe from the sea, but they were still in the chest with no way to get out.

Fate willed it—or perhaps Zeus, who up to now had done little for his love and his child—that they should be discovered by a good man, a fisherman named Dictys. He came upon the great box and broke it open

and took the pitiful cargo home to his wife who was as kind as he. They had no children and they cared for Danaë and Perseus as if they were their own. The two lived there many years, Danaë content to let her son follow the fisherman's humble trade, out of harm's way. But in the end more trouble came. Polydectes, the ruler of the little island, was the brother of Dictys, but he was a cruel and ruthless man. He seems to have taken no notice of the mother and son for a long time, but at last Danaë attracted his attention. She was still radiantly beautiful even though Perseus by now was full grown, and Polydectes fell in love with her. He wanted her, but he did not want her son, and he set himself to think out a way of getting rid of him.

There were some fearsome monsters called Gorgons who lived on an island and were known far and wide because of their deadly power. Polydectes evidently talked to Perseus about them; he probably told him that he would rather have the head of one of them than anything else in the world. This seems practically certain from the plan he devised for killing Perseus. He announced that he was about to be married and he called his friends together for a celebration, including Perseus in the invitation. Each guest, as was customary, brought a gift for the bride-to-be, except Perseus alone. He had nothing he could give. He was young and proud and keenly mortified. He stood up before them all and did exactly what the King had hoped he would do, declared that he would give him a present better than any there. He would go off and kill Medusa and bring back her head as his gift. Nothing could have suited the King better. No one in his senses would have made such a proposal. Medusa was one of the Gorgons,

And they are three, the Gorgons, each
  with wings
And snaky hair, most horrible to mortals.
Whom no man shall behold and draw
  again
The breath of life,

for the reason that whoever looked at them was turned instantly into stone. It seemed that Perseus had been led by his angry pride into making an empty boast. No man unaided could kill Medusa.

But Perseus was saved from his folly. Two great gods were watching over him. He took ship as soon as he left the King's hall, not daring to see his mother first and tell her what he intended, and he sailed to Greece to learn where the three monsters were to be found. He went to Delphi, but all the priestess would say was to bid him seek the land where men eat not Demeter's golden grain, but only acorns. So he went to Dodona, in the land of oak trees, where the talking oaks were which declared Zeus's will and where the Selli lived who made their bread from acorns. They could tell him, however, no more than this, that he was under the protection of the gods. They did not know where the Gorgons lived.

When and how Hermes and Athena came to his help is not told in any story, but he must have known despair before they did so. At last, however, as he wandered on, he met a strange and beautiful person. We know what he looked like from many a poem, a young man with the first down upon his cheek when youth is loveliest, carrying, as no other young man ever did, a wand of gold with wings at one end, wearing a winged hat, too, and winged sandals. At sight of him hope must have entered Perseus' heart, for he would know that this could be none other than Hermes, the guide and the giver of good.

This radiant personage told him that before he attacked Medusa he must first be properly equipped, and that what he needed was in the possession of the nymphs of the North. To find the nymphs' abode, they must go to the Gray Women who alone could tell them the way. These women dwelt in a land where all was dim and shrouded in twilight. No ray of sun looked ever on that country, nor the moon by night. In that gray place the three women lived, all gray themselves and withered as in extreme old age. They were strange creatures, indeed, most of all because they had but one eye for the three, which it was their custom to take turns with, each removing it from her forehead when she had had it for a time and handing it to another.

All this Hermes told Perseus and then he unfolded his plan. He would himself guide Perseus to them. Once there Perseus must keep hidden until he saw one of them take the eye out of her forehead to pass it on. At that moment, when none of the three could see, he must rush forward and seize the eye and refuse to give it back until they told him how to reach the nymphs of the North.

He himself, Hermes said, would give him a sword to attack Medusa with—which could not be bent or broken by the Gorgon's scales, no matter how hard they were. This was a wonderful gift, no doubt, and yet of what use was a sword when the creature to be struck by it could turn the swordsman into stone before he was within striking distance? But another great deity was at hand to help. Pallas Athena stood beside Perseus. She took off the shield of polished bronze which covered her breast and held it out to him. "Look into this when you attack the Gorgon," she said. "You will be able to see her in it as in a mirror, and so avoid her deadly power."

Now, indeed, Perseus had good reason to hope. The journey to the twilight land was long, over the stream of Ocean and on to the very border of the black country where the Cimmerians dwell, but Hermes was his guide and he could not go astray. They found the Gray Women at last, looking in the wavering light like gray birds, for they had the shape of swans. But their heads were human and beneath their wings they had arms and hands. Perseus did just as Hermes had said, he held back until he saw one of them take the eye out of her forehead. Then before she could give it to her sister, he snatched it out of her hand. It was a moment or two before the three realized they had lost it. Each thought one of the others had it. But Perseus spoke out and told them he had taken it and that it would be theirs again only when they showed him how to find the nymphs of the North. They gave him full directions at once; they would have done anything to get their eye back. He returned it to them and went on the way they had pointed out to him. He was bound, although he did not know it, to the blessed country of the Hyperboreans, at the back of the North Wind, of which it is said: "Neither by ship nor yet by land shall one find the wondrous road to the gathering place of the Hyperboreans." But Perseus had Hermes with him, so that the road lay open to him, and he reached that host of happy people who are always banqueting and holding joyful revelry. They showed him great kindness: they welcomed him to their feast, and the maidens dancing to the sound of flute and lyre paused to get for him the gifts he sought. These were three: winged sandals, a magic wallet which would always become the right size for whatever was to be carried in it, and, most important of all, a cap which made the wearer invisible. With these and Athena's shield and Hermes' sword Perseus was ready for the Gorgons. Hermes knew where they lived, and leaving the happy land the two flew back across Ocean and over the sea to the Terrible Sisters' island.

By great good fortune they were all asleep when Perseus found them. In the mirror of the bright shield he could see them clearly, creatures with great wings and bodies covered with golden scales and hair a mass of twisting snakes. Athena was beside him now as well as Hermes. They told him which one was Medusa and that was important, for she alone of the three could be killed; the other two were immortal. Perseus on his winged sandals hovered above them, looking, however, only at the shield. Then he aimed a stroke down at Medusa's throat and Athena guided his hand. With a single sweep of his sword he cut through her neck and, his eyes still fixed on the shield with never a glance at her, he swooped low enough to seize the head. He dropped it into the wallet which closed around it. He had nothing to fear from it now. But the two other Gorgons had awakened and, horrified at the sight of their sister slain, tried to pursue the slayer. Perseus was safe; he had on the cap of darkness and they could not find him.

FOLKTALES— INHERITED AND LITERARY

The Traveling Musicians

Jacob and Wilhelm Grimm

This wonderful German story of old animals banding together for companionship and survival has a descendant in a "Jack" tale of the American South. It is a good story for children to hear and for old people to heed.

An honest farmer had once an ass, that had been a faithful servant to him a great many years, but was now growing old and every day more and more unfit for work. His master therefore was tired of keeping him and began to think of putting an end to him; but

From Jacob and Wilhelm Grimm, *German Popular Stories*, trans. Edgar Taylor (Menston, England: Scolar Press, 1971. Reprinted from the original English edition of 1823).

the ass, who saw that some mischief was in the wind, took himself slyly off, and began his journey towards the great city, "for there," thought he, "I may turn musician."

After he had travelled a little way, he spied a dog lying by the road-side and panting as if he were very tired. "What makes you pant so, my friend?" said the ass. "Alas!" said the dog, "my master was going to knock me on the head, because I am old and weak, and can no longer make myself useful to him in hunting; so I ran away: but what can I do to earn my livelihood?" "Hark ye!" said the ass, "I am going to the great city to turn musician: suppose you go with me, and try what you can do in the same way?" The dog said he was willing, and they jogged on together.

They had not gone far before they saw a cat sitting in the middle of the road and making a most rueful face. "Pray, my good lady," said the ass, "what's the matter with you? you look quite out of spirits!" "Ah me!" said the cat, "how can one be in good spirits when one's life is in danger? Because I am beginning to grow old, and had rather lie at my ease by the fire than run about the house after the mice, my mistress laid hold of me, and was going to drown me; and though I have been lucky enough to get away from her, I do not know what I am to live upon." "O!" said the ass, "by all means go with us to the great city; you are a good night singer, and may make your fortune as a musician." The cat was pleased with the thought, and joined the party.

Soon afterwards, as they were passing by a farm-yard, they saw a cock perched upon a gate, and screaming out with all his might and main. "Bravo!" said the ass; "upon my word you make a famous noise; pray what is all this about?" "Why," said the cock, "I was just now saying that we should have fine weather for our washing-day, and yet my mistress and the cook don't thank me for my pains, but threaten to cut off my head tomorrow, and make broth of me for the guests that are coming on Sunday!" "Heaven forbid!" said the ass; "come with us, Master Chanticleer; it will be better, at any rate, than staying here to have your head cut off!

Besides, who knows? If we take care to sing in tune, we may get up some kind of a concert; so come along with us." "With all my heart," said the cock: so they all four went on jollily together.

They could not, however, reach the great city the first day; so when night came on, they went into a wood to sleep. The ass and the dog laid themselves down under a great tree, and the cat climbed up into the branches; while the cock, thinking that the higher he sat the safer he should be, flew up to the very top of the tree, and then, according to his custom, before he went to sleep, looked out on all sides of him to see that every thing was well. In doing this, he saw afar off something bright and shining; and calling to his companions said, "There must be a house no great way off, for I see a light." "If that be the case," said the ass, "we had better change our quarters, for our lodging is not the best in the world!" "Besides," added the dog, "I should not be the worse for a bone or two, or a bit of meat." So they walked off together towards the spot where Chanticleer had seen the light; and as they drew near, it became larger and brighter, till they at last came close to a house in which a gang of robbers lived.

The ass, being the tallest of the company, marched up to the window and peeped in. "Well, Donkey," said Chanticleer, "what do you see?" "What do I see?" replied the ass, "why I see a table spread with all kinds of good things, and robbers sitting round it making merry." "That would be a noble lodging for us," said the cock. "Yes," said the ass, "if we could only get in:" so they consulted together how they should contrive to get the robbers out; and at last they hit upon a plan. The ass placed himself upright on his hind-legs, with his fore-feet resting against the window; the dog got upon his back; the cat scrambled up to the dog's shoulders, and the cock flew up and sat upon the cat's head. When all was ready, a signal was given, and they began their music. The ass brayed, the dog barked, the cat mewed, and the cock screamed; and they all broke through the window at once, and came tumbling into the room, amongst the broken glass, with a most hideous clatter! The robbers, who had been not a little frightened by the opening concert, had now no doubt that some frightful hobgoblin had broken in upon them, and scampered away as fast as they could.

The coast once clear, our travellers soon sat down, and dispatched what the robbers had left, with as much eagerness as if they had not expected to eat again for a month. As soon as they had satisfied themselves, they put out the lights, and each once more sought out a resting-place to his own liking. The donkey laid himself down upon a heap of straw in the yard; the dog stretched himself upon a mat behind the door; the cat rolled herself up on the hearth before the warm ashes; and the cock perched upon a beam on the top of the house; and, as they were all rather tired with their journey, they soon fell asleep.

But about midnight, when the robbers saw from afar that the lights were out and that all seemed quiet, they began to think that they had been in too great a hurry to run away; and one of them, who was bolder than the rest, went to see what was going on. Finding every thing still, he marched into the kitchen, and groped about till he found a match in order to light a candle; and then, espying the glittering fiery eyes of the cat, he mistook them for live coals, and held the match to them to light it. But the cat, not understanding this joke, sprung at his face, and spit, and scratched at him. This frightened him dreadfully, and away he to the back door; but there the dog jumped up and bit him in the leg; and as he was crossing over the yard the ass kicked him; and the cock, who had been awakened by the noise, crowed with all his might. At this the robber ran back as fast as he could to his comrades, and told the captain "how a horrid witch had got into the house, and had spit at him and scratched his face with her long bony fingers; how a man with a knife in his hand had hidden himself behind the door, and stabbed him in the leg; how a black monster stood in the yard and struck him with a club, and how the devil sat upon the top of the house and cried out, 'Throw the rascal up here!'" After this the robbers never dared to go back to the house: but the musicians were so pleased with their quarters, that they took up their abode there; and there they are, I dare say, at this very day.

The Juniper Tree

Jacob and Wilhelm Grimm

Though this story may seen extremely violent on first reading, the reader will notice that at a certain point, it jumps from reality into fantasy, as most folktales do, and that all comes out well in the end. Evil is punished, and the good and loving people are reunited. In other words, the story is far more comforting than it would be if it occurred in real life and were covered by the media. It is thus an antidote to the horrors children hear about all the time.

This was all a long time ago, two thousand years or more.

There was a rich man who had a good and beautiful wife. They loved each other very dearly but they had no children, although they wished for them very much. The wife prayed for them day and night but still they had none.

In front of their house there was a courtyard where there stood a juniper tree. The

From Jacob and Wilhelm Grimm, *German Popular Stories,* trans. Edgar Taylor (Menston, England: Scolar Press, 1971. Reprinted from the original English edition of 1823).

wife was standing beneath it one winter's day, peeling herself an apple, and as she peeled it she cut her finger and the blood dripped on to the snow.

'Oh dear,' said the wife, sighing deeply as she stared at the blood. She was most unhappy, saying: 'If only I had a child as red as blood and as white as snow!'

As she said this her spirits grew lighter and she felt as if it were going to come true. Then she went indoors.

A month went by and the snow disappeared; two months and all was green; then three months, and the flowers sprang out of the earth. After four months the trees of the forest burgeoned and the green boughs were all entwined. The birds sang until the woods resounded and the blossoms dropped from the trees. When the fifth month had passed, she was standing under the juniper tree, which smelt so sweetly that her heart leapt with delight, and she fell on her knees and was overcome with joy. When six months had gone by, the fruit was round and firm and the wife was quite calm. In the seventh month she seized the juniper berries and ate them greedily and then grew sick and sorrowful. When the eighth month was past she called her husband and said to him, weeping:

'If I die, bury me under the juniper tree.'

Then she was quite comforted, and continued until the next month was over, when she had a child as white as snow and as red as blood. When she saw it, she was so overjoyed that she died.

Her husband buried her under the juniper tree and he fell to weeping bitterly. After a time he grew calmer, and although he still shed tears he was able to bear it. After a longer time he took another wife.

By the second wife he had a daughter, but the child of his first wife was a little son, as red as blood and as white as snow. When the woman looked at her daughter, she loved her deeply: but then she looked at the little boy, and it stabbed her to the heart, for it seemed to her that he would always stand in their way. She was always thinking how to get all the inheritance for her daughter. The devil inspired her so that she was quite angry with the little boy and pushed him about from corner to corner, striking him here and

cuffing him there, until the poor child went in continual fear. When he came out of school he never had any peace.

One day when the woman had gone up to her room, her little daughter came up and said:

'Mother, give me an apple.'

'Yes, my child,' said the woman, and gave her a beautiful apple out of the chest. This chest had a great, heavy lid with a big, sharp, iron lock.

'Mother,' said her little daughter, 'may not my brother have an apple too?' This angered the woman, but she said:

'Yes, when he comes home from school.'

As she looked out of the window and saw him coming, it was as if the devil entered into her, and she snatched the apple back from her daughter, saying: 'You shall not have one before your brother.' She tossed the apple back into the chest and shut the lid. The little boy came in at the door and she was driven by the devil to say to him kindly:

'My son, would you like an apple?' and she looked at him fixedly.

'Oh! Mother,' said the little boy, 'how dreadfully you stare at me! Yes, give me an apple.'

Then she felt compelled to speak to him.

'Come with me,' she said, opening the chest, 'and pick out an apple.'

As the little boy stooped inside, the devil prompted her and she flung the lid down—Crash!—so that his head flew off amongst the rosy apples. Then she was overcome with terror and thought to herself, 'How can I turn away suspicion?' She went up to her room and took out of the top drawer of her chest a white scarf. She set the head on its neck again, and bound it with the scarf so that nothing could be seen, seated him on a chair in front of the door, and placed an apple in his hand.

After this Marlenekin came to her mother in the kitchen. The woman was standing by the fire before a pan of water which she stirred continually.

'Mother,' said Marlenekin, 'my brother is sitting at the door with an apple in his hand and looks quite white. I asked him to give me the apple but he did not answer me and I was frightened.'

'Go back to him,' said her mother, 'and if he will not answer you, give him a box on the ear.'

So Marlenekin went out and said: 'Brother, give me the apple.' But he was silent, so she gave him a box on the ear and his head fell off. She was terrified and ran to her mother crying and screaming.

'Oh, Mother, I have knocked off my brother's head,' she said, and she cried and cried and would not be comforted.

'Marlenekin, what have you done?' said her mother. 'Keep quiet so that nobody knows. It cannot be helped now. We will make him into a stew.'

But Marlenekin stood there weeping and wailing, and her tears fell into the pot so that there was no need of salt. Then the father came home and sat down to table and asked: 'Where is my son?'

The mother served up a great big dish of stew and Marlenekin cried and would not stop. The father asked again:

'Where is my son?'

'Oh, he has gone across the country,' said the mother, 'to see his mother's great uncle, and he wants to stay there.'

'What is he doing there? He didn't even say good-bye to me.'

'Oh, he wanted to go very much, and asked me if he could stay six weeks. He is well cared for there.'

'I am most uneasy,' said the man, 'for fear there is something wrong. He should have said good-bye to me.'

With these words he began to eat.

'Marlenekin,' he said, 'why are you crying? Your brother is sure to come home again. Wife,' he said, 'how good this food is! Give me some more!'

The more he ate, the more he wanted, saying, 'Give me more. You shall have none, it surely all belongs to me,' and he went on eating, throwing all the bones under the table, until he had finished it. But Marlenekin went to her cupboard and took her best silk shawl from the bottom shelf. She gathered up all the bones from under the table, wrapped them in her silk shawl and took them out of doors, weeping tears of blood. There she laid them on the green grass under the juniper tree, and when she had left them

there her heart was lighter and she cried no more. Then the juniper tree began to move, and the branches parted asunder and closed together again like one rejoicing and clapping hands. At the same time a mist seemed to rise from the tree, and in the midst of it burned a fire, and out of the fire flew a beautiful bird, singing gloriously as it flew high into the air. When it had flown away, the juniper tree was just as it had been before and the shawl full of bones was gone. Marlenekin was now as glad and contented as if her brother was still alive. She went happily indoors and sat down to her dinner.

The bird flew away and perched on the roof of a goldsmith's house, where he began to sing:

'My mother made a stew of me,
My father ate it all.
My little sister wept to see,
Marlene, my sister small,
Then gathered my bones in her silken
    shawl,
And laid them under the Juniper tree.
    Sing, hey! What a beautiful bird am I!'

The goldsmith was sitting in his workshop making a golden chain when he heard the bird which sat and sang upon his roof. He thought it a beautiful song. He got up, and as he crossed the threshold he lost one of his slippers, but he went out, up the street, with one slipper on and one stockinged-foot. He was wearing his apron, and in one hand he had the golden chain and in the other the pincers. The sun was shining brightly on the street. He went on, then stood still and looked at the bird.

'Bird,' said he, 'how beautifully you sing! Sing me that song again!'

'No, I will not sing twice for nothing,' said the bird. 'Give me the golden chain and then I will sing it again for you.'

'There!' said the goldsmith, 'there is the golden chain. Now sing to me once more.'

The bird came and took the golden chain in its right claw, then sat before the goldsmith and sang:

'My mother made a stew of me,
My father ate it all.
My little sister wept to see,

Marlene, my sister small,
Then gathered my bones in her silken
    shawl,
And laid them under the Juniper tree.
    Sing, hey! What a beautiful bird am I!'

Then the bird flew away and sat on a shoemaker's roof, singing:

'My mother made a stew of me,
My father ate it all.
My little sister wept to see,
Marlene, my sister small,
Then gathered my bones in her silken
    shawl,
And laid them under the Juniper tree.
    Sing, hey! What a beautiful bird am I!'

The shoemaker heard it and ran out of doors in his shirt sleeves. He looked up to the roof, shading his eyes with his hand, for the sun dazzled him.

'Bird,' said he, 'how rarely you sing!' He called into the house. 'Wife, come outside, here's a fine bird—just look at it! How well he can sing!'

Then he called his daughter and children and apprentices, boys and girls, and they all came along the street, gazing at the bird and admiring it with its beautiful red and green feathers. Its neck looked like pure gold and its eyes shone in its head like stars.

'Bird,' said the shoemaker, 'sing me that song again.'

'No, I will not sing twice for nothing,' said the bird. 'You must give me something.'

'Wife,' said the man, 'go up to the loft. On the topmost shelf stands a pair of red shoes—bring them down.'

So the wife went away and brought the shoes.

'There, bird,' said the man, 'now sing me that song again.'

The bird came and picked up the shoes in its left claw, flew up on to the roof again and sang:

'My mother made a stew of me,
My father ate it all.
My little sister wept to see,
Marlene, my sister small,
Then gathered my bones in her silken
    shawl,

And laid them under the Juniper tree.
    Sing, hey! What a beautiful bird am I!'

When his song was done he flew away, holding the chain in his right claw and the shoes in his left. He flew far away to a mill. The mill was going klip-klap—klip-klap—klip-klap. Inside the mill were twenty miller's men at work hewing a stone. As they were cutting, hick-hack, hick-hack, hick-hack, the mill went klip-klap, klip-klap, klip-klap. The bird flew up into a linden tree which stood beside the mill.

'My mother made a stew of me.'

he sang, and one man stopped work:

'My father ate it all.'

and two more men stopped working and listened:

'My little sister wept to see,
'Marlene, my sister small,'

then four more men stopped:

'Then gathered my bones in her silken
    shawl,'

now only eight men were working:

'And laid them under—'

now only five,

               'the Juniper tree,'

and now only one:

    'Sing, hey! What a beautiful bird am I!'

and the last man stopped too and listened to the last words.

'Bird, how well you sing!' said he. 'Let me hear it too; sing it again for me!'

'No, I will not sing twice for nothing,' said the bird. 'Give me the millstone and I will sing it again for you.'

'Yes, if it were mine alone,' said the man, 'you should have it.'

'Yes, he shall have it,' said the others, 'if he will only sing again.'

Then the bird came down and all the twenty miller's men lifted the stone up with a beam, heave-ho, heave-ho, heave-ho. Then the bird put its head through the hole and wore the stone as a collar. He flew up to the tree again and sang:

'My mother made a stew of me,
My father ate it all.
My little sister wept to see,
Marlene, my sister small,
Then gathered my bones in her silken
    shawl,
And laid them under the Juniper tree.
    Sing, hey! What a beautiful bird am I!'

When his song was done he spread his wings, and with the chain in his right claw, the shoes in his left, and the millstone round his neck, he flew far away to his father's house.

Inside the house the father, mother and Marlenekin were sitting at table. His father said:

'How my heart grows lighter! I feel quite cheerful.'

'Not I,' said the mother. 'I feel afraid, as though a heavy storm were coming on.'

Marlenekin sat there crying all the time. Then the bird flew up, and as it perched on the roof, the father said:

'I am so happy, and the sun is shining brightly out of doors. I feel as though I were about to see an old acquaintance again.'

'Not I,' said the wife. 'I feel so nervous that my teeth are chattering, and there's fire in my veins,' and she unloosed her stays.

But Marlenekin sat in the corner and wept, holding a plate before her face so that it was wet with tears. The bird sat in the juniper tree and sang:

'My mother made a stew of me,'—

At that the mother covered her ears and eyes, for she wished neither to see nor hear. There was a roaring in her ears like a terrible storm and her eyes were burning and flashing like lightning.

'My father ate it all.'—

'Oh, Mother,' said the man, 'there's a beautiful bird! He sings so sweetly, and the sun is so warm, and there's a scent just like cinnamon.'

'My little sister wept to see,
Marlene, my sister small,'—

At that Marlenekin laid her head on her knees and cried without ceasing, but the man said:

'I am going out. I must see the bird closer.'

'Oh! don't go out,' cried the wife. 'I feel as if the whole house were trembling and on fire.'

But the man went out and gazed at the bird.

'Then gathered my bones in her silken
    shawl,
And laid them under the juniper tree.
    Sing, hey! What a beautiful bird am I!'

With these words the bird dropped the golden chain, and it fell on the man's neck so that it fitted him exactly. He went inside and said:

'See what a fine bird this is, and how lovely to see! He has given me a fine golden chain.'

In her fear the woman fell full length on the floor, and her cap fell off her head. The bird began again:

'My mother made a stew of me,'—

'Oh, if I were a thousand feet under the ground,' said she, 'that I might not hear it!'

'My father ate it all,'—

the woman lay on the ground.

'My little sister wept to see,
Marlene, my sister small,'—

'I will go out too,' said Marlenekin, 'and see if the bird will give me something.' So out she went.

'Then gathered my bones in her silken
    shawl,'—

and with that he dropped the shoes:

'And laid them under the Juniper tree.
    Sing, hey! What a beautiful bird am I!'

Marlenekin grew light-hearted and gay. She put on the new red shoes and danced and skipped into the house.

'I was so sad,' said she, 'when I went out, and now I am happy. This is a fine bird indeed, he has given me a pair of red shoes.'

The woman started up, her hair standing on end like flames of fire.

'It feels like the end of the world: I must go out too and see if my heart feels lighter.'

And as she went out of the door, Crash! the bird dropped the millstone on to her head and it crushed her utterly. The father and Marlenekin heard it and ran out. Smoke and flames of fire rose from the place, and when they died down, there stood the little brother. He took his father and Marlenekin by the hand, and all three were glad at heart, went indoors, and sat down to dinner.

Matryona's Home

Alexander Solzhenitsyn

This story is well loved by the Russian people. Every country has old people in it like Matryona: her husband has gone and her children have died, but she somehow manages to survive and even to show her love for others. Without thought of personal gain, Matryona helps her neighbors with their ploughing and nurses them when they are ill. She has a surrogate family member in her boarder, the schoolteacher, but even he does not fully appreciate her role in the life of those around her until after she is dead.

Like much of Solzhenitsyn's work, the story has political overtones. Earlier in the story, Matryona takes coal from the state supply to bring warmth to an ailing neighbor. In this way, Solzhenitsyn demonstrated the importance of the individual.

There was no overhead light in our big room with its forest of rubber plants. The table lamp cast a ring of light round my exercise books, and when I tore my eyes from it the rest of the room seemed to be half-dark and faintly tinged with pink. I thought I could see the same pinkish glow in her usually sallow cheeks.

'He was the first one who came courting me, before Yefim did . . . he was his brother . . . the older one . . . I was nineteen and Faddei was twenty-three . . . They lived in this very same house. Their house it was. Their father built it.'

I looked round the room automatically. Instead of the old grey house rotting under the faded green skin of wallpaper where the mice had their playground, I suddenly saw new timbers, freshly trimmed, and not yet discoloured, and caught the cheerful smell of pine-tar.

'Well, and what happened then?'

'That summer we went to sit in the coppice together,' she whispered. 'There used to be a coppice where the stableyard is now. They chopped it down . . . I was just going to marry him, Ignatich. Then the German war started. They took Faddei in the army.'

She let fall these few words—and suddenly the blue and white and yellow July of the year 1914 burst into flower before my eyes: the sky still peaceful, the floating clouds, the people sweating to get the ripe corn in. I imagined them side by side, the black-haired Hercules with a scythe over his shoulder, and the red-faced girl clasping a sheaf. And there was singing out under the open sky, such

From Patricia Blake and Max Hayward, eds., H. T. Willets, trans., *Half-Way to the Moon* (New York: Holt, Rinehart and Winston, 1964). Copyright 1985, Patricia Blake.

songs as nobody can sing nowadays, with all the machines in the fields.

'He went to the war—and vanished. For three years I kept to myself and waited. Never a sign of life did he give . . .'

Matryona's round face looked out at me from an elderly threadbare head-scarf. As she stood there in the gentle reflected light from my lamp her face seemed to lose its slovenly workaday covering of wrinkles and she was a scared young girl again with a frightening decision to make.

Yes . . . I could see it . . . The trees shed their leaves, the snow fell and melted. They ploughed and sowed and reaped again. Again the trees shed their leaves, and snow fell. There was a revolution. Then another revolution. And the whole world was turned upside down.

'Their mother died and Yefim came to court me. You wanted to come to our house, he says, so come. He was a year younger than me, Yefim was. It's a saying with us— sensible girls get married after Michaelmas, and silly ones at midsummer. They were short-handed. I got married . . . The wedding was on St Peter's day, and then about St Nicolas' day in the winter he came back . . . Faddei, I mean, from being a prisoner in Hungary.'

Matryona covered her eyes.

I said nothing.

She turned towards the door as though somebody were standing there. 'He stood there at the door. What a scream I let out! I wanted to throw myself at his feet! . . . but I couldn't. If it wasn't my own brother, he says, I'd take my axe to the both of you.'

I shuddered. Matryona's despair or her terror, conjured up a vivid picture of him standing in the dark doorway and raising his axe to her.

But she quieted down and went on with her story in a sing-song voice, leaning on a chair-back, 'Oh dear, dear me, the poor dear man! There were so many girls in the village—but he wouldn't marry. I'll look for one with the same name as you, a second Matryona, he said. And that's what he did—fetched himself a Matryona from Lipovka. They built themselves a house of

their own and they're still living in it. You pass their place every day on your way to school.'

So that was it. I realized that I had seen the other Matryona quite often. I didn't like her. She was always coming to my Matryona to complain about her husband—he beat her, he was stingy, he was working her to death. She would weep and weep, and her voice always had a tearful note in it. As it turned out, my Matryona had nothing to regret, with Faddei beating his Matryona every day of his life and being so tight-fisted.

'Mine never beat me once,' said Matryona of Yefim. 'He'd pitch into another man in the street, but me he never hit once . . . Well, there was one time . . . I quarrelled with my sister-in-law and he cracked me on the forehead with a spoon. I jumped up from the table and shouted at them, "Hope it sticks in your gullets, you idle lot of beggars, hope you choke!" I said. And off I went into the woods. He never touched me any more.'

Faddei didn't seem to have any cause for regret either. The other Matryona had borne him six children (my Antoshka was one of them, the littlest, the runt) and they had all lived, whereas the children of Matryona and Yefim had died, every one of them, before they reached the age of three months, without any illness.

'One daughter, Elena, was born and was alive when they washed her, and then she died right after . . . My wedding was on St Peter's day, and it was St Peter's day I buried my sixth, Alexander.'

The whole village decided that there was a curse on Matryona.

Matryona still nodded emphatic belief when she talked about it. 'There was a *course* on me. They took me to a woman as used to be a nun to get cured, she set me off coughing and waited for the *course* to jump out of me like a frog. Only nothing jumped out . . .'

And the years had run by like running water . . . In 1941 they didn't take Faddei into the army because of his poor sight, but they took Yefim. And what had happened to the elder brother in the First World War happened to the younger in the Second . . . he vanished without trace. Only he never came back at all. The once noisy cottage was deserted, it became old and rotten, and Matryona, all alone in the world, grew old in it.

So she begged from the other Matryona, the cruelly beaten Matryona, a child of her womb (or was it a spot of Faddei's blood?), the youngest daughter, Kira.

For ten years she brought the girl up in her own house, in place of the children who had not lived. Then, not long before I arrived, she had married her off to a young engine-driver from Cherusti. The only help she got from anywhere came in dribs and drabs from Cherusti: a bit of sugar from time to time, or some of the fat when they killed a pig.

Sick and suffering, and feeling that death was not far off, Matryona had made known her will: the top room, which was a separate frame joined by tie-beams to the rest of the house, should go to Kira when she died. She said nothing about the house itself. Her three sisters had their eyes on it too.

That evening Matryona opened her heart to me. And, as often happens, no sooner were the hidden springs of her life revealed to me than I saw them in motion.

Kira arrived from Cherusti. Old Faddei was very worried. To get and keep a plot of land in Cherusti the young couple had to put up some sort of building. Matryona's top-room would do very well. There was nothing else they could put up, because there was no timber to be had anywhere. It wasn't Kira herself so much, and it wasn't her husband, but old Faddei who was consumed with eagerness for them to get their hands on the plot at Cherusti.

He became a frequent visitor, laying down the law to Matryona and insisting that she should hand over the top room right away, before she died. On these occasions I saw a different Faddei. He was no longer an old man propped up by a stick, whom a push or a harsh word would bowl over. Although he was slightly bent by back-ache, he was still a fine figure; he had kept the virgorous black hair of a young man in his sixties; he was hot and urgent.

Matryona had not slept for two nights. It wasn't easy for her to make up her mind. She didn't grudge them the top room, which was standing there idle, any more than she ever grudged her labour or her belongings. And the top room was willed to Kira in any case. But the thought of breaking up the roof she had lived under for forty years was torture to her. Even I, a mere lodger, found it painful to think of them stripping away boards and wrenching out beams. For Matryona it was the end of everything.

But the people who were so insistent knew that she would let them break up her house before she died.

So Faddei and his sons and sons-in-law came along one February morning, the blows of five axes were heard and boards creaked and cracked as they were wrenched out. Faddei's eyes twinkled busily. Although his back wasn't quite straight yet he scrambled nimbly up under the rafters and bustled about down below, shouting at his assistants. He and his father had built this house when he was a lad, a long time ago. The top room had been put up for him, the oldest son, to move in with his bride. And now he was furiously taking it apart, board by board, to carry it out of somebody else's yard.

After numbering the beam-ends and the ceiling boards they dismantled the top room and the store-room underneath it. The living-room, and what was left of the landing, they boarded up with a thin wall of deal. They did nothing about the cracks in the wall. It was plain to see that they were wreckers, not builders, and that they did not expect Matryona to be living there very long.

While the men were busy wrecking, the women were getting the drink ready for moving day—vodka would cost a lot too much. Kira brought forty pounds of sugar from Moscow region, and Matryona carried the sugar and some bottles to the distiller under cover of night.

The timbers were carried out and stacked in front of the gates, and the engine-driver son-in-law went off to Cherusti for the tractor.

But the very same day a blizzard, or 'a blower' as Matryona called it, began. It howled and whirled for two days and nights and buried the road under enormous drifts. Then, no sooner had they made the road passable and a couple of lorries gone by, than it got suddenly warmer. Within a day everything was thawing out, damp mist hung in the air and rivulets gurgled as they burrowed into the snow, and you could get struck up to the top of your knee-boots.

Two weeks passed before the tractor could get at the dismantled top room. All this time Matryona went around like someone lost. What particularly upset her was that her three sisters came and with one voice called her a fool for giving the top room away, said they didn't want to see her any more, and went off. At about the same time the lame cat strayed and was seen no more. It was just one thing after another. This was another blow to Matryona.

At last the frost got a grip on the slushy road. A sunny day came along and everybody felt more cheerful. Matryona had had a lucky dream the night before. In the morning she heard that I wanted to take a photograph of somebody at an old-fashioned hand-loom. (There were looms still standing in two cottages in the village; they wove coarse rugs on them.) She smiled shyly and said, 'You just wait a day or two, Ignatich, I'll just send the top room there off and I'll put my loom up, I've still got it, you know, and then you can snap me. Honest to God!'

She was obviously attracted by the idea of posing in an old-fashioned setting. The red, frosty sun tinged the window of the curtailed passageway with a faint pink, and this reflected light warmed Matryona's face. People who are at ease with their consciences always have nice faces.

Coming back from school before dusk I saw some movement near our house. A big new tractor-drawn sledge was already fully loaded, and there was no room for a lot of the timbers, so old Faddei's family and the helpers they had called in had nearly finished knocking together another home-made sledge. They were all working like madmen, in the frenzy that comes upon people when there is

a smell of good money in the air or when they are looking forward to some treat. They were shouting at one another and arguing.

They could not agree whether the sledges should be hauled separately or both together. One of Faddei's sons (the lame one) and the engine-driver son-in-law reasoned that the sledges couldn't both be taken at once because the tractor wouldn't be able to pull them. The man in charge of the tractor, a hefty fat-faced fellow who was very sure of himself, said hoarsely that he knew best, he was the driver, and he would take both at once. His motives were obvious: according to the agreement the engine-driver was paying him for the removal of the upper room not for the number of trips he had to make. He could never have made two trips in a night—twenty-five kilometres each way, and one return journey. And by morning he had to get the tractor back in the garage from which he had sneaked it out for this job on the side.

Old Faddei was impatient to get the top room moved that day, and at a nod from him his lads gave in. To the stout sledge in front they hitched the one which they had knocked together in such a hurry.

Matryona was running about amongst the men, fussing and helping them to heave the beams on to the sledge. Suddenly I noticed that she was wearing my jerkin and dirtied the sleeves on the frozen mud round the beams. I was annoyed, and told her so. That jerkin held memories for me: it had kept me warm in the bad years.

This was the first time that I was ever angry with Matryona Vasilyevna.

Matryona was taken aback. 'Oh dear, dear me,' she said. 'My poor head. I picked it up in a rush, you see, and never thought about it being yours. I'm sorry, Ignatich.'

And she took it off and hung it up to dry.

The loading was finished, and all the men who had been working, about ten of them, clattered past my table and dived under the curtain into the kitchen. I could hear the muffled rattle of glasses and, from time to time, the clink of a bottle, the voices got louder and louder, the boasting more reckless. The biggest braggart was the tractor-driver. The stench of hooch floated in to me. But they didn't go on drinking long. It was getting dark and they had to hurry. They began to leave. The tractor-driver came out first, looking pleased with himself and fierce. The engine-driver son-in-law, Faddei's lame son and one of his nephews were going to Cherusti. The others went off home. Faddei was flourishing his stick, trying to overtake somebody and put him right about something. The lame son paused at my table to light up and suddenly started telling me how he loved Aunt Matryona, and that he had got married not long ago, and his wife had just had a son. Then they shouted for him and he went out. The tractor set up a roar outside.

After all the others had gone Matryona dashed out from behind the screen. She looked after them, anxiously shaking her head. She had put on her jerkin and her head-scarf. As she was going through the door she said to me, 'Why ever couldn't they hire two? If one tractor had cracked up the other would have pulled them. What'll happen now, God only knows!'

She ran out after the others.

After the booze-up and the arguments and all the coming and going it was quieter than ever in the deserted cottage, and very chilly because the door had been opened so many times. I got into my jerkin and sat down to mark exercise books. The noise of the tractor died away in the distance.

An hour went by. And another. And a third. Matryona still hadn't come back, but I wasn't surprised. When she had seen the sledge off she must have gone round to her friend Masha.

Another hour went by. And yet another. Darkness and with it a deep silence had descended on the village. I couldn't understand at the time why it was so quiet. Later I found out that it was because all evening not a single train had gone along the line five hundred yards from the house. No sound was coming from my radio and I noticed that the mice were wilder than ever. Their scampering and scratching and squeaking behind the wallpaper was getting noisier and more defiant all the time.

I woke up. It was 1 o'clock in the morning and Matryona still hadn't come home.

Suddenly I heard several people talking loudly. They were still a long way off, but something told me that they were coming to our house. And sure enough I heard soon afterwards a heavy knock at the gate. A commanding voice, strange to me, yelled out an order to open up. I went out into the pitch darkness with a torch. The whole village was asleep, there was no light in the windows, and the snow had started melting in the last week so that it gave no reflected light. I turned the catch and let them in. Four men in greatcoats went on towards the house. It's a very unpleasant thing to be visited at night by noisy people in greatcoats.

When we got into the light though, I saw that two of them were wearing railway uniforms. The older of the two, a fat man with the same sort of face as the tractor-driver, asked, 'Where's the woman of the house?'

'I don't know.'

'This is the place the tractor with a sledge came from?'

'This is it.'

'Had they been drinking before they left?'

All four of them were looking around them, screwing up their eyes in the dim light from the table-lamp. I realized that they had either made an arrest or wanted to make one.

'What's happened then?'

'Answer the question!'

'But . . .'

'Were they drunk when they went?'

'Were they drinking here?'

Had there been a murder? Or hadn't they been able to move the top room? The men in greatcoats had me off balance. But one thing was certain: Matryona could do time for making hooch.

I stepped back to stand between them and the kitchen door. 'I honestly didn't notice. I didn't see anything.' (I really hadn't seen anything—only heard.) I made what was supposed to be a helpless gesture drawing attention to the state of the cottage: a table-lamp shining peacefully on books and exercises, a crowd of frightened rubber plants, the austere couch of a recluse, not a sign of debauchery.

They had already seen for themselves, to their annoyance, that there had been no drinking in that room. They turned to leave, telling each other this wasn't where the drinking had been then, but it would be a good thing to put in that it was. I saw them out and tried to discover what had happened. It was only at the gate that one of them growled. 'They've all been cut to bits. Can't find all the pieces.'

'That's a detail. The 9 o'clock express nearly went off the rails. That would have been something.' And they walked briskly away.

I went back to the hut in a daze. Who were 'they'? What did 'all of them' mean? And where was Matryona?

I moved the curtain aside and went into the kitchen. The stink of hooch rose and hit me. It was a deserted battlefield: a huddle of stools and benches, empty bottles lying around, one bottle half-full, glasses, the remains of pickled herring, onion, and sliced fat pork.

Everything was deathly still. Just cockroaches creeping unperturbed about the field of battle.

They had said something about the 9 o'clock express. Why? Perhaps I should have shown them all this? I began to wonder whether I had done right. But what a damnable way to behave—keeping their explanations for official persons only.

Suddenly the small gate creaked. I hurried out on to the landing. 'Matryona Vasilyevna?'

The yard door opened, and Matryona's friend Masha came in, swaying and wringing her hands. 'Matryona . . . our Matryona, Ignatich . . .'

I sat her down and through her tears she told me the story.

The approach to the crossing was a steep rise. There was no barrier. The tractor and the first sledge went over, but the tow-rope broke and the second sledge, the home-made

one, got stuck on the crossing and started falling apart—the wood Faddei had given them to make the second sledge was no good. They towed the first sledge out of the way and went back for the second. They were fixing the tow-rope—the tractor-driver and Faddei's lame son, and Matryona, heaven knows what brought her there, was with them, between the tractor and the sledge. What help did she think she could be to the men? She was for ever meddling in men's work. Hadn't a bolting horse nearly tipped her into the lake once, through a hole in the ice?

Why did she have to go to the damned crossing? She had handed over the top room, and owed nothing to anybody . . . The engine-driver kept a look-out in case the train from Cherusti rushed up on them. Its headlamps would be visible a long way off. But two engines coupled together came from the other direction, from our station, backing without lights. Why they were without lights nobody knows. When an engine is backing, coal-dust blows into the driver's eyes from the tender and he can't see very well. The two engines flew into them and crushed the three people between the tractor and the sledge to pulp. The tractor was wrecked, the sledge was matchwood, the rails were buckled, and both engines turned over.

'But how was it they didn't hear the engines coming?'

'The tractor engine was making such a din.'

'What about the bodies?'

'They won't let anybody in. They've roped them off.'

'What was that somebody was telling me about the express?'

The 9 o'clock express goes through our station at a good speed and on to the crossing. But the two drivers weren't hurt when their engines crashed, they jumped out and ran back along the line waving their hands and they managed to stop the train . . . The nephew was hurt by a beam as well. He's hiding at Klavka's now so that they won't know he was at the crossing. If they find out they'll drag him in as a witness . . . 'Don't know lies up, and do know gets tied up. Kira's husband didn't get a scratch. He tried to hang himself, they had to cut him down. It's all because of me, he says my aunty's killed and my brother. Now he's gone and given himself up. But the mad-house is where he'll be going, not prison. Oh, Matryona, my dearest Matryona . . . '

Matryona was gone. Someone close to me had been killed. And on her last day I had scolded her for wearing my jerkin.

The lovingly-drawn red and yellow woman in the book advertisement smiled happily on.

Old Masha sat there weeping a little longer. Then she got up to go. And suddenly she asked me, 'Ignatich, you remember, Matryona had a grey shawl. She meant it to go to my Tanya when she died, didn't she?'

She looked at me hopefully in the half-darkness . . . surely I hadn't forgotten.

No, I remembered. 'She said so, yes.'

'Well, listen, maybe you could let me take it with me now. The family will be swarming in tomorrow and I'll never get it then.' And she gave me another hopeful, imploring look. She had been Matryona's friend for half a century, the only one in the village who truly loved her.

No doubt she was right.

'Of course . . . take it.'

She opened the chest, took out the shawl, tucked it under her coat and went out.

The mice had gone mad. They were running furiously up and down the walls, and you could almost see the green wallpaper rippling and rolling over their backs.

In the morning I had to go to school. The time was 3 o'clock. The only thing to do was to lock up and go to bed.

Lock up, because Matryona would not be coming.

I lay down, leaving the light on. The mice were squeaking, almost moaning, racing and running. My mind was weary and wandering, and I couldn't rid myself of an uneasy feeling that an invisible Matryona was flitting about and saying good-bye to her home.

And suddenly I imagined Faddei standing there, young and black-haired, in the dark patch by the door, with his axe uplifted. 'If it wasn't my own brother I'd chop the both of you to bits.'

The threat had lain around for forty years, like an old broad-sword in a corner, and in the end it had struck its blow.

When it was light the women went to the crossing and brought back all that was left of Matryona on a hand-sledge with a dirty sack over it. They threw off the sack to wash her. There was just a mess . . . no feet, only half a body, no left hand. One woman said, 'The Lord has left her her right hand. She'll be able to say her prayers where she's going . . . '

Then the whole crowd of rubber plants was carried out of the cottage . . . these plants that Matryona had loved so much that once when smoke woke her up in the night she didn't rush to save her house but to tip the plants on to the floor in case they were suffocated. The women swept the floor clean. They hung a wide towel of old home-spun over Matryona's dim mirror. They took down the jolly posters. They moved my table out of the way. Under the icons, near the windows, they stood a rough unadorned coffin on a row of stools.

In the coffin lay Matryona. Her body, mangled and lifeless, was covered with a clean sheet. Her head was swathed in a white kerchief. Her face was almost undamaged, peaceful, more alive than dead.

The villagers came to pay their last respects. The women even brought their small children to take a look at the dead. And if anyone raised a lament, all the women, even those who had looked in out of idle curiosity, always joined in, wailing where they stood by the door or the wall, as though they were providing a choral accompaniment. The men stood stiff and silent with their caps off.

The formal lamentation had to be performed by the women of Matryona's family. I observed that the lament followed a coldly calculated age-old ritual. The more distant relatives went up to the coffin for a short while and made low wailing noises over it. Those who considered themselves closer kin to the dead woman began their lament in the doorway and when they got as far as the coffin, bowed down and roared out their grief right in the face of the departed. Every lamenter made up her own melody. And expressed her own thoughts and feelings.

I realized that a lament for the dead is not just a lament, but a kind of politics. Matryona's three sisters swooped, took possession of the cottage, the goat, and the stove, locked up the chest, ripped the 200 roubles for the funeral out of the coat lining, and drummed it into everybody who came that only they were near relatives. Their lament over the coffin went like this, *Oh, nanny! nanny! Oh nan-nan!* All we had in the world was you! You could have lived in peace and quiet, you could. And we should always have been kind and loving to you. Now your top room's been the death of you. Finished you off it has, the cursed thing! Oh why did you have to take it down? Why didn't you listen to us?'

Thus the sisters' laments were indictments of Matryona's husband's family: they shouldn't have made her take the top room down. (There was an underlying meaning too: you've taken the top room all right but we won't let you have the house itself!)

Matryona's huband's family, her sisters-in-law, Yehim and Faddei's sisters, and various nieces lamented like this, *'Oh poor auntie, poor auntie!* Why didn't you take better care of yourself! Now they're angry with us for sure. Our own dear Matryona you were, and it's your own fault! The top room is nothing to do with it. Oh why did you go where death was waiting for you? Nobody asked you to go there. And what a way to die! Oh why didn't you listen to us?' (Their answer to the others showed through these laments: we are not to blame for her death, and the house we'll talk about later.)

But the 'second' Matryona, a coarse, broad-faced woman, the substitute Matryona whom Faddei had married so long ago for the sake of her name, got out of step with family policy, wailing and sobbing over the coffin in her simplicity, *'Oh my poor dear sister!* You won't be angry with me, will you

now? Oh-oh-oh! How we used to talk and talk, you and me! Forgive a poor miserable woman! You've gone to be with your dear mother, and you'll come for me some day for sure! Oh-oh-oh-oh! . . . '

At every 'oh-oh-oh' it was as though she were giving up the ghost. She writhed and gasped, with her breast against the side of the coffin. When her lament went beyond the ritual prescription the women, as though acknowledging its success, all started saying, 'Come away now, come away.'

Matryona came away, but back she went again, sobbing with even greater abandon. Then an ancient woman came out of a corner, put her hand on Matryona's shoulder, and said, 'There are two riddles in this world: how I was born I don't remember, how I shall die I don't know!'

And Matryona fell silent at once, and all the others were silent, so that there was an unbroken hush.

But the old woman herself, who was much older than all the other old women there and didn't seem to belong to Matryona at all, after a while started wailing, 'Oh, my poor sick Matryona! Oh my poor Vasilyevna! Oh what a weary thing it is to be seeing you into your grave!'

There was one who didn't follow the ritual, but wept straightforwardly, in the fashion of our age, which has had plenty of practice at it. This was Matryona's unfortunate foster-daughter, Kira, from Cherusti, for whom the top room had been taken down and moved. Her ringlets were pitifully out of curl. Her eyes looked red and bloodshot. She didn't notice that her headscarf was slipping off out in the frosty air and that her arm hadn't found the sleeve of her coat. She walked in a stupor from her foster-mother's coffin in one house to her brother's in another. They were afraid she would lose her mind, because her husband had to go for trial as well.

It looked as if her husband was doubly at fault; not only had he been moving the top room, but as an engine-driver he knew the regulations about unprotected crossings, and should have gone down to the station to warn them about the tractor. There were a thousand people on the Urals express that night, peacefully sleeping in the upper and lower berths of their dimly-lit carriages, and all those lives were nearly cut short. All because of a few greedy people, wanting to get their hands on a plot of land, or not wanting to make a second trip with a tractor.

All because of the top room, which had been under a curse ever since Faddei's hands had started itching to take it down.

The tractor-driver was already beyond human justice. And the railway authorities were also at fault, both because a busy crossing was unguarded and because the coupled engines were travelling without lights. That was why they had tried at first to blame it all on the drink, and then to keep the case out of court.

The rails and the track were so twisted and torn that for three days, while the coffins were still in the house, no trains ran—they were diverted on to another line. All Friday, Saturday, and Sunday, from the end of the investigation until the funeral, the work of repairing the line went on day and night. The repair gang was frozen, and they made fires to warm themselves and to light their work at night, using the boards and beams from the second sledge which were there for the taking, scattered around the crossing.

The first sledge just stood there, undamaged and still loaded, a little way beyond the crossing.

One sledge, tantalizingly ready to be towed away, and the other perhaps still to be plucked from the flames—that was what harrowed the soul of black-bearded Faddei all day Friday and all day Saturday. His daughter was going out of her mind, his son-in-law had a criminal charge hanging over him, in his own house lay the son he had killed, and along the street the woman he had killed and whom he had once loved. But Faddei stood by the coffins clutching his beard only for a short time, and went away again. His tall brow was clouded by painful thoughts, but what he was thinking about was how to save the timbers of the top room from the flames and from Matryona's scheming sisters.

Going over the people of Talnovo in my mind I realized that Faddei was not the only one like that.

Property, the people's property, or my property, is strangely called our 'goods'. If you lose your goods, people think you disgrace yourself and make yourself look foolish.

Faddei dashed about, never stopping to sit down, from the settlement to the station, from one official to another, stood there with his bent back, leaning heavily on his stick, and begged them all to take pity on an old man and give him permission to recover the top room.

Somebody gave permission. And Faddei gathered together his surviving sons, sons-in-law and nephews, got horses from the kolkhoz and from the other side of the wrecked crossing, by a roundabout way that led through three villages, brought the remnants of the top room home to his yard. He finished the job in the early hours of Sunday morning.

On Sunday afternoon they were buried. The two coffins met in the middle of the village, and the relatives argued about which of them should go first. Then they put them side by side on an open sledge, the aunt and the nephew, and carried the dead over the damp snow, with a gloomy February sky above, to the churchyard two villages away. There was an unkind wind, so the priest and the deacon waited inside the church and didn't come out to Talnovo to meet them.

A crowd of people walked slowly behind the coffins, singing in chorus. Outside the village they fell back.

When Sunday came the women were still fussing around the house. An old woman mumbled psalms by the coffin, Matryona's sisters flitted about, popping things into the oven, and the air round the mouth of the stove trembled with the heat of red-hot peats, those which Matryona had carried in a sack from a distant bog. They were making unappetizing pies with poor flour.

When the funeral was over and it was already getting on towards evening, they gathered for the wake. Tables were put together to make a long one, which hid the place where the coffin had stood in the morning. To start with they all stood round the table, and an old man, the husband of a sister-in-law, said the Lord's Prayer. Then they poured everybody a little honey and warm water, just enough to cover the bottom of the bowl. We spooned it up without bread or anything, in memory of the dead. Then we ate something and drank vodka and the conversation became more animated. Before the jelly they all stood up and sang 'Eternal remembrance' (they explained to me that it had to be sung before the jelly.) There was more drinking. By now they were talking louder than ever, and not about Matryona at all. The sister-in-law's husband started boasting, 'Did you notice, brother Christians, that they took the funeral service slowly today? That's because Father Mikhail noticed me. He knows I know the service. Other times it's saints defend us, homeward wend us, and that's all.

At last the supper was over. They all rose again. They sang 'Worthy is she'. Then again, with a triple repetition of 'Eternal remembrance.' But the voices were hoarse and out of tune, their faces drunken, and nobody put any feeling into this 'eternal memory'.

Then the main guests went away, and only the near relatives were left. They pulled out their cigarettes and lit up, there were jokes and laughter. There was some mention of Matryona's husband and his disappearance. The sister-in-law's husband, striking himself on the chest, assured me and the cobbler who was married to one of Matryona's sisters, 'He was dead, Yefim was dead! What could stop him coming back if he wasn't? If I knew they were going to hang me when I got to the old country I'd come back just the same!'

The cobbler nodded in agreement. He was a deserter and had never left the old country. All through the war he was hiding in his mother's cellar.

The stern and silent old woman who was more ancient than all the ancients was staying the night and sat high up on the stove. She looked down in mute disapproval on the indecently animated youngsters of fifty and sixty.

But the unhappy foster-daughter, who had grown up within these walls, went away behind the kitchen screen to cry.

Faddei didn't come to Matryona's wake—perhaps because he was holding a wake for his son. But twice in the next few days he walked angrily into the house for discussions with Matryona's sisters and the deserting cobbler.

The argument was about the house. Should it go to one of the sisters or to the foster-daughter? They were on the verge of taking it to court, but they made peace because they realized that the court would hand over the house to neither side, but to the Rural District Council. A bargain was struck. One sister took the goat, the cobbler and his wife got the house, and to make up Faddei's share, since he had 'nursed every bit of timber here in his arms', in addition to the top room which had already been carried away, they let him have the shed which had housed the goat, and the whole of the inner fence between the yard and the garden.

Once again the insatiable old man got the better of sickness and pain and became young and active. Once again he gathered together his surviving sons and sons-in-law, and they dismantled the shed and the fence, and he hauled the timbers himself, sledge by sledge, and only towards the end did he have Antoshka of 8-D, who didn't slack this time, to help him.

They boarded Matryona's house up till the spring, and I moved in with one of her sisters-in-law, not far away. This sister-in-law on several occasions came out with some recollection of Matryona, and made me see the dead woman in a new light. 'Yefim didn't love her. He used to say, 'I like to dress in an educated way, but she dresses any old way, like they do in the country.' Well then, he thinks, if she doesn't want anything, he might as well drink whatever's to spare. One time I went with him to the town to work, and he got himself a madam there and never wanted to come back to Matryona.'

Everything she said about Matryona was disapproving. She was slovenly, she made no effort to get a few things about her. She wasn't the saving kind. She didn't even keep a pig, because she didn't like fattening them up for some reason. And the silly woman helped other people without payment. (What brought Matryona to mind this time was that the garden needed ploughing and she couldn't find enough helpers to pull the plough.)

Matryona's sister-in-law admitted that she was warmhearted and straightforward, but pitied and despised her for it.

It was only then, after these disapproving comments from her sister-in-law, that a true likeness of Matyrona formed itself before my eyes, and I understood her as I never had when I lived side by side with her.

Of course! Every house in the village kept a pig. But she didn't. What can be easier than fattening a greedy piglet that cares for nothing in the world but food! You warm his swill three times a day, you live for him—then you cut his throat and you have some fat.

But she had none . . .

She made no effort to get things round her . . . She didn't struggle and strain to buy things and then care for them more than life itself.

She didn't go all out after fine clothes. Clothes, that beautify what is ugly and evil.

She was misunderstood and abandoned even by her husband. She had lost six children, but not her sociable ways. She was a stranger to her sisters and sisters-in-law, a ridiculous creature who stupidly worked for others without pay. She didn't accumulate property against the day she died. A dirty-white goat, a gammy-legged cat, some rubber plants . . .

We had all lived side by side with her and never understood that she was that righteous one without whom, as the proverb says, no village can stand.

Nor any city.

Nor our whole land.

My Mother Is the Most Beautiful Woman in the World

Becky Reyher

This old folktale has been retold in a literary version with a Ukrainian country setting. While working in the fields, the little girl is separated from her mother— not a pretty woman, but "the most beautiful woman in the world" to her daughter, who describes her thus to those who are helping to find her. The solution is simple—the child sees with her heart.

Varya peered into the next row of wheat which was not yet cut. There it was cool and pleasant and the sun did not bear down with its almost unbearable heat. Varya moved in just a little further to surround herself with that blessed coolness. "How lucky I am!" she thought, "to be able to hide away from the hot sun. I will do this for just a few minutes. Surely Mamochka will not mind if I do not help her all the day."

Soon Varya grew sleepy, for in so cool a place, one could curl up and be very quiet and comfortable.

When Varya woke, she jumped to her feet and started to run toward her mother. But her mother was nowhere in sight.

From Becky Reyher, *My Mother Is the Most Beautiful Woman in the World* (New York: Lothrop, Lee & Shepard, 1945). Pictures by Ruth Gannett.

Varya called, "Mama," "Mama," "Mamochka," but there was no answer.

Sometimes her mother got ahead of her and was so busy with her work she did not hear.

"Maybe if I run along the row, I will catch up with her," Varya thought.

She ran and ran, and soon she was out of breath, but nowhere could she see her mother.

"Maybe I have gone in the wrong direction," she said to herself. So she ran the other way. But here, too, there was no trace of her mother.

Varya was alone in the wheat fields, where she could see nothing but tall pyramids of wheat towering above her. When she called out, her voice brought no response, no help. Overhead the sun was not so bright as it had been. Varya knew that soon it would be night and that she must find her mother.

Varya cut through the last of the wheat that had not yet been cut, breaking her own pathway, which bent and hurt the wheat. She would not have done this, had she not been frightened.

When it was almost dark, Varya stumbled into a clearing where several men and women had paused to gossip after the day's work. It took her only a second to see that these were strangers, and that neither her mother nor father was among them.

The little girl stared ahead of her, not knowing what to do. One of the men spied her and said in a booming voice which he thought was friendly. "Look what we have here!"

Everyone turned to Varya. She was sorry that with so many strangers looking at her, she had her hair caught back in a tiny braid with a bit of string, and that she was wearing only her oldest, most faded dress. Surely, too, by now her face and hands must be as streaked with dirt as were her legs and dress. This made her burst into tears.

"Poor little thing," cried one of the women, putting her arms around Varya, "she is lost!" But this sympathy, and the strange voices made Varya want her mother all the more. She could not help crying.

"We must know her name, and the name of her mother and father. Then we can unite them," said the women.

"Little girl, little girl," they said, "what is your name? What is your mother's and father's name?" But Varya was too unhappy to speak.

Finally because her longing for her mother was so great, she sobbed out:

"My mother is the most beautiful woman in the world!"

All the men and women smiled. The tallest man, Kolya, clapped his hands and laughingly said, "Now we have something to go on."

This was long, long ago, when there were no telephones and no automobiles. If people wanted to see each other, or carry a message, they went on their two feet.

From every direction, friendly, good-hearted boys ran to village homes with orders to bring back the beautiful women.

"Bring Katya, Manya, Vyera, Nadya," the tall man, Kolya, called to one boy.

"Ay, but don't forget the beauty, Lisa," he called to still another boy.

The women came running. These were orders from Kolya, the village leader. Also the mothers, who had left the fields early to get supper for their families, thought perhaps this was indeed their child who was lost.

As each beautiful woman came rushing up, blushing and proud that she had been so chosen, Kolya would say to her: "We have a little lost one here. Stand back, everyone, while the little one tells us if this is her mother!"

The mothers laughed and pushed, and called to Kolya: "You big tease! What about asking each mother if this is her child? We know our children!"

To Varya this was very serious, for she was lost and she was desperate without her mother. As she looked at each strange woman, Varya shook her head in disappointment and sobbed harder. Soon every known beauty from far and near, from distances much further than a child could have strayed, had come and gone. Not one of them was Varya's mother.

The villagers were really worried. They shook their heads. Koyla spoke for them. "One of us will have to take the little one home for the night. Tomorrow may bring fresh wisdom to guide us!"

Just then a breathless, excited woman came puffing up to the crowd. Her face was big and broad, and her body even larger. Her eyes were little pale slits between a great lump of a nose. The mouth was almost toothless. Even as a young girl everyone had said, "A homely girl like Marfa is lucky to get a good husband like Ivan."

"Varyachka!" cried this woman.

"Mamochka!" cried the little girl, and they fell into each other's arms. The two of them beamed upon each other. Varya cuddled into that ample and familiar bosom. The smile Varya had longed for was once again shining upon her.

All of the villagers smiled thankfully when Varya looked up from her mother's shoulder and said with joy:

"This is my mother! I told you my mother is the most beautiful woman in the world!"

The group of friends and neighbors, too, beamed upon each other, as Kolya repeated the proverb so well known to them, a proverb which little Varya had just proved: *"We do not love people because they are beautiful, but they seem beautiful to us because we love them."*

FOLK RHYMES AND POETRY

Folk Rhymes

During the Troubles in Ireland in 1973, families were often crowded too closely together; the effect was divisive. Houses were boarded up so that they resembled small forts. On a playground in Belfast, we heard children skipping rhymes. The Irish have many old skipping rhymes, but the children chose these derisive and disrespectful ones which express irritation.

My Aunt Nellie has a boil on her belly.
She rubs it up and down.
She sells pigs' feet at the bottom of the
  street.
And a policeman knocked her down.

My Sister Fanny walks very canny,
For she isn't very steady on her feet.
She spends all her money
Drinking with her honey
At the pub at the corner of the street.

In South Vietnam, children were under considerable agony and stress. In Saigon (now called Ho Chi Minh City), shortly before its fall in 1975, we heard the following skip-rope rhymes chanted in the street by the children of Lynette Quang Ti, an American nurse married to a Vietnamese school teacher.

Hamburgers! Meat balls!
Your maternal grandfather bows down
  to me.

Your father runs around, your mother's
crazy.

Oh, Second Brother, your wife is
pregnant.
Don't pucker up like fresh dried fruit.
Uncle Charlot went to ride his cyclo.

Seventh Brother, the Indian, went to sell
curry.
Your wife went to dance sexy dances.

*"Second Brother" is the name by which the
oldest child in a family is called by his
younger siblings and cousins. There is no
First Brother or Sister, as one so called
would be in danger from evil spirits.*

Illustration by Edward Gorey.

Mummy Slept Late and Daddy Fixed Breakfast

John Ciardi

*John Ciardi's poems have been amusing
children and adults for decades. With the
feminist movement and packaged frozen
waffles, fathers have now learned to prepare
better breakfasts than this poem might
suggest. The idea is still funny, though.*

Daddy fixed the breakfast
He made us each a waffle.
It looked like gravel pudding.
It tasted something awful.

From John Ciardi, *I'll Read to You, You Read to Me*
(Philadelphia: Lippincott, 1962).

"Ha, ha," he said, "I'll try again.
This time I'll get it right."
But what *I* got was in between
Bituminous and anthracite.

"A little too well done? Oh well,
I'll have to start all over."
That time what landed on my plate
Looked like a manhole cover.

I tried to cut it with a fork:
The fork gave off a spark.
I tried a knife and twisted it
Into a question mark.

I tried it with a hack-saw.
I tried it with a torch.
It didn't even make a dent.
It didn't even scorch.

The next time Dad gets breakfast
When Mummy's sleeping late,
I think I'll skip the waffles.
I'd sooner eat the plate!

FICTION

Mom, the Wolf Man and Me
Father's Day

Norma Klein

In Mom, the Wolf Man and Me, *the child, Brett, tells the story. Deborah, her mother, is a photographer for a magazine. She is a warm and understanding parent, so not having a father to produce at school for Father's Day is not a major crisis for Brett. Rather, the prospect of having a father worries her until she becomes acquainted with Theo, whom she calls "The Wolf Man" because of his Irish wolfhound.*

"Where's your father? Did he have to go to work or something?"

It was Father's Day at school and Mary Jane Wakowski was eyeing me with this funny expression. Her father, a sort of fat man with glasses, was off in the corner talking to Mrs. Darling. I gave her a kind of steady, blank look and just said, "No."

"So, where is he?"

"I don't have a father." You've got to say this just the right way and, in fact, I was out of practice, because for years I'd always gone to the same school and everybody knew and didn't ask. I don't really mind if they do, but if they haven't for a long time, you tend not to think of good, quick answers. Evelyn, this girl who lives in my building, says it's the same with her birthmark. She has a birthmark on her leg, a brown spot, and she says there are months and months when practically everyone she meets says, "What's that *thing* on your leg?" or "Did you fall and hit yourself?" (Once she said some little boy asked, "Did a dog go against your leg?") So she has to think of something to say that will sort of put the person in his place or make him feel a little dumb for asking. But then, she says, there are months when nobody asks

about it and she forgets it's there. Then, when somebody mentions it again, she's forgotten all her good remarks. That's the way it is with me.

Mary Jane's got a wise expression. She thinks she's very smart because her father, who's a teacher, is always teaching her things at home like algebra so she knows them before anyone at school. "Oh, your parents are divorced, I guess," she said.

"Nope," I said.

Her eyes got bigger. "What do you mean? What are they, then?"

"They aren't divorced," I said. "They were never married."

Some days I kind of like going through this routine, even though it might be easier to say, "They're divorced," since it wouldn't really matter. But I like seeing that expression on people's faces—*sometimes* I like it.

"They have to have been married," she said, almost mad. "You couldn't have been born otherwise."

I smiled.

"Everybody has a mother and a father," she went on. "That's how people get born."

"Is it?" I said.

"A mommy can't do it all by herself,"

From Norma Klein, *Mom, the Wolf Man and Me* (New York: Pantheon Books, 1972).

Mary Jane said. "She can't sit on an egg or something."

"Gee, can't she?" I said, looking as bland as vanilla pudding, I hoped.

"You *know* she can't," said Mary Jane, ruffled.

"All I said was, they didn't get married," I said. "I didn't say she sat on an *egg*."

Maybe the light was beginning to dawn in Mary Jane's head, but she still kept looking at me in this funny, puzzled way. Finally, she said, "I never heard of anything like *that*."

Mary Jane is the type who if she never heard of it, thinks it should never have happened. "Live and learn," I said and walked over to the corner to play.

That's the trouble with starting in a new school. The reason I did was that we moved to a different part of New York, and we were in a different district. I was sorry we moved anyway. We used to live in the Village on this little street with trees, where it was quiet most of the time. But Mom said they were going to raise our rent, and she heard of an apartment in a new building uptown right near "a very good school." I guess the school is good, but I don't like the apartment building. It's *too* new. The doorman asks everyone who comes up who they are and that makes a lot of people nervous. He even asks people who've been there before. Mom doesn't like that either. She's always telling him just to let people up if they want to visit us, but he always says, "That's my job, Mrs. Levin."

Mom doesn't mind being called Mrs. Levin, even if she's not married. She says it's a convenience. I guess she doesn't like explaining all the time either. But the people at work call her Miss Levin. When they call up, they ask for her by that name or sometimes just by her first name, Deborah. She's a photographer for a magazine. She takes pictures, mostly of actors and actresses, sometimes of criminals and people along the street and things like that. When I was a baby, and even now, she took hundreds of pictures of me. If I'm just sitting there reading, I'll look up and there's Mom, sneaking up on me with her camera. Sometimes she

lets me look through it, and she said that for my next birthday, when I'm twelve, she'll let me have my own camera. Then she says we can go to Africa together and take pictures of wild animals. That's something Mom has always wanted to do and I'd like to do it, too, since I love animals.

The only part that I really mind about Mom not being married is when people ask questions. Otherwise we have a good time, better in some ways than lots of my friends who have mothers *and* fathers. Like, when I visit Andrew, who was my best friend from my old school, everything has to be done at just a certain time. First we have to do our homework, then we can play, and at just a certain time, we have to have dinner. "Don't you see what time it is?" Andrew's mother keeps saying. In our house we hardly even have clocks. Mom never cares what time it is or when we eat. She says I have to go to bed more or less on time but if I don't, she doesn't really care. Maybe it's because her schedule is so odd. She works at night lots of times, developing pictures in our little back room. Sometimes she works all night and then just leaves me breakfast. I eat it by myself and go off to school by myself, too. Sometimes—which seems funny to some people—she's just getting up when I come home from school. Once she was just having breakfast when Andrew and I came in. "How come your mother is in her pajamas?" he said. "Is she sick?"

I felt funny then. I guess I wanted her to be like Andrew's mother, who is always dressed up and greets us at the door with sandwiches or cookies. So I said she was sick and when Andrew went home, I told Mom she shouldn't just be in pajamas at three in the afternoon. The good thing about Mom is that you can tell her these things. She never gets mad, but she doesn't always do them either. But after that, she tried sleeping in her blue jeans and shirt so that, even if she was just getting up, my friends wouldn't know. I thought that was okay, even though not that many mothers wear blue jeans either. But Mom is just sort of like that. She wears her hair in a pony tail, too, and she never gets dressed up like Evelyn's mother and never puts on makeup. Evelyn and I sometimes watch her mother get dressed up for dates and it takes her hours. She sits in front of this big mirror, that makes her face look gigantic, like a pumpkin. Then she puts on all sorts of stuff and lets us try some, too—moon drops and blushers and eye makeup and perfume. Mom never uses that stuff. If she goes out, she just washes her hair and maybe puts on something different, but not that different from what she was wearing already. She's just that way. Even Andrew says mothers are just a certain way, whatever that way is, and it's silly to think they will ever change. But on the whole, I like Mom the way she is and don't especially mind not having a father.

Andrew's father, for instance, isn't nice at all. He never wants to play with him and he's always telling Andrew he isn't good at things. So mainly he makes Andrew feel worse than he would if he never had a father. There are lots of fathers like that, so I'd rather have none than one of those. Of course, it would be nice to have a great one. Sometimes I pretend Wally, this man that Mom works with, is my real father. (I know he isn't, because Mom said my real father lives in some other city and doesn't even know he's my real father, or that I was even born.) Wally has a wife, actually, but he doesn't like her. Mom says she doesn't like her either. But even though I like Wally, I don't know if I'd want him for a father all the time. He has a funny face, which is one thing I like—it's very round, like a moon, with a long dark moustache that he always pulls on when he's thinking. He always says to me, "Hi kid. What's new?" He never calls me by my real name, Brett. What I like best is that sometimes, as a special treat, he brings over his movie projector and on Sunday nights, which is the time he has his children visit him (he has Nicky who is two years younger than me and Marshall who's just three), he shows us all movies and we have pizza sent up and it's a lot of fun. If he lived with us, though, we'd do that every week, and it might not be so much fun. Also, I couldn't do as many things with

Mom the way I do now. Most mothers and fathers go off together and leave their children with a babysitter, but Mom lets me come along if I want. If I had a father, maybe she wouldn't.

It's funny. Evelyn, whose parents are divorced, really wants a father. Her mother spends practically all her time going out on dates. Once Evelyn said to me, "That's her work."

"Going out on dates isn't work," I said.

"It *is*," said Evelyn. "She does it to find a father. She doesn't even like it, but she knows she has to."

"Why does she have to?" I said. "Mine doesn't."

"She has to. She goes to look them all over. If she finds a good one, she'll pick him."

There must be a lot of bad ones, because Evelyn's mother has been going on dates for years. Whenever Evelyn and I play, she usually thinks of some game about fathers. Or she'll say, "Wouldn't it be great to have Pat as a father?"

Pat is one of the doormen in our building and he's always joking and telling Evelyn that her uncle's dog, Miffy, this poodle, is in a wooden box that is in the lobby. "I've got him in there. Should I let him out?" He always says that and I don't think it's so funny anymore, but Evelyn really likes him. He always gives Miffy a biscuit, but he makes her dance around on her hind legs, even though she's quite old. Evelyn says Miffy likes that, but I think it's cruel.

"What would be so good about having a father who was a doorman?" I'd say.

"Oh, you'd see him all the time," Evelyn said. "If you came home from school, he'd be right there. And you could play in the lobby if you wanted."

"I guess so."

Personally I can think of things I'd rather do than play in the lobby of our building all afternoon, but Evelyn is like that. She'd give almost anything to have a father. Whenever we go places where you can make a wish, you know she's always wishing about that. Once I even used my wish to wish it for her, but later, when it didn't happen, I was sorry that I threw the wish away. I don't think it ever works if you use your wish up on someone else.

This day they had Father's Day at school, not all of the fathers came. Melinda's mother is divorced and so is Kenneth's, and some of the fathers work, so I didn't feel funny about it. I just don't feel funny about being the only one not to do things. I guess it's my personality. People like my teacher at my old school think I'm pretending about that. I can tell that sometimes they feel sorry for me and they even say I'm being "brave," even if the thing has nothing to do with being brave. It's funny. But, even if all the fathers had come on Father's Day, I wouldn't have minded so much. It's just that they all didn't. But when I came home from school and was having a snack with Mom, I could see she was worried about it.

"Oh, there weren't so many fathers," I said. I even made it seem like there were hardly any so she wouldn't worry about it.

"I could've had Wally come," she said. "He had today off."

"Mom, it didn't matter," I said. "Anyway, Wally's not my father and so it's silly to make things up."

Mom sort of sighed and cut another brownie. "I just hate these rituals!" she said. "All these holidays!"

"I don't," I said. "Some of them are nice."

"It's such a waste of time," she said.

"It's funny," I said. "They don't have a *Mother's* Day at school."

Mom frowned. "Ya, Scratcher, that is funny. Why don't they? . . . I guess it's because some mothers are at the school all the time. They have nothing better to do."

"I guess that's it," I said. I wish Mom wouldn't worry so much about this stuff, but she's that way. Unlike me, she really cares if she's the only one doing something a certain way. And the trouble is, usually she *is* the only one. That's the funny part.

FANTASY

The Wizard of Oz
The Cyclone

L. Frank Baum

In volume 10 of Children's Literature *(Yale University Press) Margaret Hamilton, who played the Wicked Witch of the West in the 1939 film version of* The Wizard of Oz, *wrote a brief essay on the importance of home in the book. She commented*

From L. Frank Baum, *The Wizard of Oz* (New York: Grosset & Dunlap, 1946. Originally published in 1900).

on the lesson Dorothy says she has learned about feeling she has lost her home. Dorothy concludes, "If I have lost something and I look all over for it and can't find it, it means I really never lost it in the first place." According to Hamilton, "If you can't find it, it is still there somewhere—you still have it." That is, its spiritual essence is with you forever, even if the structure itself is destroyed.

In her several lectures at the University of Connecticut with Michael Patrick Hearn, author of The Annotated Wizard of Oz, *Hamilton often stressed the importance of family to Dorothy. Since Dorothy's father and mother were dead, her family consisted of her aunt and uncle. Up in Oz, she developed a substitute family of the Scarecrow, the Tin Man, and the Cowardly Lion, but still she longed to be back in Kansas. When Glinda the Good told her, "All you have to do is to knock the heels together and command the shoes to carry you wherever you wish to go," Dorothy quickly complied, and a few minutes later, she was surrounded by those she loved.*

Dorothy lived in the midst of the great Kansas prairies, with Uncle Henry, who was a farmer, and Aunt Em, who was the farmer's wife. Their house was small, for the lumber to build it had to be carried by wagon many miles. There were four walls, a floor and a roof, which made one room; and this room contained a rusty-looking cooking stove, a cupboard for the dishes, a table, three or four chairs, and the beds. Uncle Henry and Aunt Em had a big bed in one corner and Dorothy a little bed in another corner. There was no garret at all, and no cellar—except a small hole dug in the ground, called a cyclone cellar, where the family could go in case one of those great whirlwinds arose, mighty enough to crush any building in its path. It was reached by a trap door in the middle of the floor, from which a ladder led down into the small, dark hole.

When Dorothy stood in the doorway and looked around, she could see nothing but the great gray prairie on every side. Not a tree nor a house broke the broad sweep of flat country that reached to the edge of the sky in all directions. The sun had baked the plowed land into a gray mass, with little cracks running through it. Even the grass was not green, for the sun had burned the tops of the long blades until they were the same gray color to be seen everywhere. Once the house had been painted, but the sun blistered the paint and the rains washed it away, and now the house was as dull and gray as everything else.

When Aunt Em came there to live she was a young, pretty wife. The sun and wind had changed her, too. They had taken the sparkle from her eyes and left them a sober gray; they had taken the red from her cheeks and lips, and they were gray also. She was thin and gaunt, and never smiled now. When Dorothy, who was an orphan, first came to her, Aunt Em had been so startled by the child's laughter that she would scream and and press her hand upon her heart whenever Dorothy's merry voice reached her ears; and she still looked at the little girl with wonder that she could find anything to laugh at.

Uncle Henry never laughed. He worked hard from morning till night and did not know what joy was. He was gray also, from his long beard to his rough boots, and he looked stern and solemn, and rarely spoke.

It was Toto that made Dorothy laugh, and saved her from growing as gray as her other surroundings. Toto was not gray; he was a little black dog, with long silky hair and small black eyes that twinkled merrily on either side of his funny, wee nose. Toto played all day long, and Dorothy played with him, and loved him dearly.

Today, however, they were not playing. Uncle Henry sat upon the doorstep and looked anxiously at the sky, which was even grayer than usual. Dorothy stood in the door with Toto in her arms, and looked at the sky too. Aunt Em was washing the dishes.

From the far north they heard a low wail of the wind, and Uncle Henry and Dorothy could see where the long grass bowed in waves before the coming storm. There now came a sharp whistling in the air from the south, and as they turned their eyes that way they saw ripples in the grass coming from that direction also.

Suddenly Uncle Henry stood up.

"There's a cyclone coming, Em," he called to his wife. "I'll go look after the stock." Then he ran toward the sheds where the cows and horses were kept.

Aunt Em dropped her work and came to the door. One glance told her of the danger close at hand.

"Quick, Dorothy!" she screamed. "Run for the cellar!"

Toto jumped out of Dorothy's arms and hid under the bed, and the girl started to get him. Aunt Em, badly frightened, threw open the trap door in the floor and climbed down the ladder in the small, dark hole. Dorothy caught Toto at last and started to follow her aunt. When she was halfway across the room there came a great shriek from the wind, and the house shook so hard that she lost her

The house rose slowly through the air.
Illustration by Evelyn Copelman, adapted from W. W. Denslow.

footing and sat down suddenly upon the floor.

Then a strange thing happened.

The house whirled around two or three times and rose slowly through the air. Dorothy felt as if she were going up in a balloon.

The north and south winds met where the house stood, and made it the exact center of the cyclone. In the middle of a cyclone the air is generally still, but the great pressure of the wind on every side of the house raised it up higher, and higher, until it was at the very top of the cyclone; and there it remained and was carried miles and miles away as easily as you could carry a feather.

It was very dark, and the wind howled horribly around her, but Dorothy found she was riding quite easily. After the first few whirls around, and one other time when the house tipped badly, she felt as if she were being rocked gently, like a baby in a cradle.

Toto did not like it. He ran about the room, now here, now there, barking loudly; but Dorothy sat quite still on the floor and waited to see what would happen.

Once Toto got too near the open trap door, and fell in; and at first the little girl thought she had lost him. But soon she saw one of his ears sticking up through the hole, for the strong pressure of the air was keeping him up so that he could not fall. She crept to the hole, caught Toto by the ear, and dragged him into the room again, afterward closing the trap door so that no more accidents could happen.

Hour after hour passed away, and slowly Dorothy got over her fright; but she felt quite lonely, and the wind shrieked so loudly all about her that she nearly became deaf. At first she had wondered if she would be dashed to pieces when the house fell again; but as the hours passed and nothing terrible happened, she stopped worrying and resolved to wait calmly and see what the future would bring. At last she crawled over the swaying floor to her bed, and lay down upon it; and Toto followed and lay down beside her.

In spite of the swaying of the house and the wailing of the wind, Dorothy soon closed her eyes and fell fast asleep.

The Animal Family
The Hunter Brings Home a Baby

Randall Jarrell

Randall Jarrell (1914–1965) was a poet and his children's stories read like poetry. In this excerpt, the hunter and the mermaid adopt a bear cub. The hunter is scratched and clawed in bringing it home, almost as if he had given birth to it. But this was not the first of the adopted children, and he goes on to bring home a lynx. Finally, the lynx and the bear bring home a baby boy they find lying beside his dead mother in a boat at the mouth of the river. It was as if the boy had been with them always. The fragmented family is now whole.

*Jerome Griswold (see Bibliography) who has made a long and thorough study of Jarrell's children's books—*The Gingerbread Rabbit, The Bat Poet, Fly by Night, *and* The Animal Family*—finds the story a sequel, in a sense, to Kipling's* Jungle Books *and Burroughs's* Tarzan of the Apes. *The hunter is "a kind of Robinson Crusoe without a Friday, an Adam in Eden with no Eve" until the mermaid appears. She is "an emigré from Hans Andersen's tales." He applies Otto Rank's observation on the detachment of the growing individual from the authority of the parents as part of human evolution and notes that it can be traced in the characters of the mermaid, the hunter, and the child in* The Animal Family.

But after the hunter and the mermaid had lived together a long time, the hunter began to have a dream. He would say in the morning to the mermaid, with a troubled look: "I had my dream."

"I'm sorry," she would answer. "It was the same as ever," the hunter went on, looking out into the air as though the dream were still there for him to see. "My father was standing by the fire and he was double, like a man and his shadow—I was his shadow. And my mother sat there singing, and she was double too, like a woman and her shadow; and when I looked at it you were her shadow. But when I looked over to where I used to lie on the floor by the fire, there was nothing, not even a shadow; the place was empty. And the empty place got dark, and the fire went out, and I woke."

"It's a bad dream," the mermaid said, frowning.

The hunter said, "I hope I never dream it again." Every few weeks, though, he would dream it. Finally the mermaid said to him: "I know what your dream means. It means you want a boy to live with us. Then you'll be your father's shadow, and I'll be your mother's, and the boy will be yourself the way you used to be—it will all be the way it used to be."

The hunter thought for a moment. Then he nodded; he could see that what she said was so. But there was nothing he could do about it: they had no child themselves, and out in the wilderness there were no human beings from whom they could beg or borrow or steal a child.

One day the man was hunting. The night came and he hadn't come home—it got later and later, darker and darker, and he still hadn't come. The mermaid would go outside and look up toward the forest and the moun-

From Randall Jarrell, *The Animal Family* (New York: Random House, 1965).

tains, but she could see nothing. It began to rain. The big drops beat on the roof and against the window, and the wind roared in the trees outside; but finally the rain and clouds blew out to sea, the stars came out, and the wet black night was silent except for the sound of the waves. The mermaid lay in the windowseat half awake and half asleep . . . All at once there were footsteps, the door opened, and the hunter staggered in with something in his arms. He said to the mermaid, laughing: "I've a boy for us."

"What's happened to you! What's happened to you!" the mermaid cried. There were three long cuts down the side of the hunter's face, and the blood had dripped from them onto his wet, naked shoulder; there were terrible bruises all along his back and chest; and he held in his arms, smothered inside his wet deerskin shirt, something that struggled to get free, and snapped up at the man's face, and made a queer angry miserable sound, half a whine and half a growl. The mermaid looked at its brown furry head and its big teeth and shining eyes, and saw that it was a bear cub.

"If I hadn't had an arrow out I'd never have got home to you," the hunter answered. "It was getting dark and I was going through some bushes full of berries when I heard that sound a bear makes to her cubs, and before I could take two steps she was on me—I'd come between her and *him*.

"I shot her from so close the arrow went half through her. She was so near I couldn't run, I couldn't dodge, even; her claws came here—" he touched the side of his face— "she hugged me to her so hard I thought my back would break, and then I drove my knife in her from behind. I had my left arm in front of my face, and I could feel her teeth going into it through the leather. She shook me the way a grown-up shakes a child, I

thought, 'I'm done for,' and then she went limp all over and fell down on top of me and never moved again. And for a while I couldn't move myself, I just lay there. Look where her teeth went in my arm." He held out his left arm—the right was still hugging the cub in the shirt—and halfway between the wrist and the elbow she could see the regular, bloody pattern of the bear's teeth.

The hunter plopped the bundle of wet leather and bear cub down onto the bearskin of the bed; and while the mermaid washed the hunter's face and arm and shoulder, the cub struggled out of the shirt, crawled back into the farthest corner of the bed, and growled and growled at them. "He was in a tree," the hunter said. "If he'd been a month older I could never have got him down. Oh, he was hard to get home! He snapped and wriggled the whole way."

When the hunter was dressed and dry they had their dinner. It felt like a holiday to them, somehow; they laughed as they ate. As he smelled the food the cub came out to the center of the bearskin, and the hunter threw him a piece of meat. The little bear growled and backed away, but then sidled up to the meat, hit it with his paw, and began to shake it. When he had gulped it down the mermaid threw him another piece, and another; finally she held some out in her hand, and he came to the edge of the bed and reached for it. The hunter said with a peaceful smile: "In a couple of days he'll be eating at the table."

That night they put deerskins and sealskins on the bed and let the cub sleep on the bearskin, in the corner. Sometimes he would wake and cry for a while, and then huddle in the corner with his face pushed into the bearskin, and go back to sleep. And in two days he was sitting on the floor by the table when they ate, eating with them; in a week it was as if he had lived with them always.

Children Alone

FABLES, MYTHS, AND LEGENDS

The Dog and the Shadow*

Aesop

When people jockey for power, nobody wins, because all are one: evil boomerangs. The dog's shadow also reflects his greed.

It happened that a Dog had got a piece of meat and was carrying it home in his mouth to eat it in peace. Now on his way home he had to cross a plank lying across a running brook. As he crossed, he looked down and saw his own shadow reflected in the water beneath. Thinking it was another dog with another piece of meat, he made up his mind to have that also. So he made a snap at the shadow in the water, but as he opened his mouth the piece of meat fell out, dropped into the water and was never seen more.

BEWARE LEST YOU LOSE THE SUBSTANCE
BY GRASPING AT THE SHADOW.

A Wonder Book for Boys and Girls†
The Paradise of Children

Nathaniel Hawthorne

The Greek myth of Pandora's box is very much like the story of Adam and Eve and the forbidden apple; it is an attempt to explain how troubles came into the world. Similar stories exist in other cultures. Nathaniel Hawthorne called his version of this legend, which is included here, ''The Paradise of Children.''

*From Joseph Jacobs, ed., *The Fables of Aesop* (New York: Schocken Books, 1966. First published 1894).

†From Nathaniel Hawthorne, *A Wonder Book for Boys and Girls* (Boston: Houghton Mifflin, 1887).

Long, long ago, when this old world was in its tender infancy, there was a child, named Epimetheus, who never had either father or mother; and, that he might not be lonely, another child, fatherless and motherless like himself, was sent from a far country, to live with him, and be his playfellow and helpmate. Her name was Pandora.

The first thing that Pandora saw, when she entered the cottage where Epimetheus dwelt, was a great box. And almost the first question which she put to him, after crossing the threshold, was this,—

"Epimetheus, what have you in that box?"

"My dear little Pandora," answered Epimetheus, "that is a secret, and you must be kind enough not to ask any questions about it. The box was left here to be kept safely, and I do not myself know what it contains."

"But who gave it to you?" asked Pandora. "And where did it come from?"

"That is a secret, too," replied Epimetheus.

"How provoking!" exclaimed Pandora, pouting her lip. "I wish the great ugly box were out of the way!"

"Oh come, don't think of it any more," cried Epimetheus. "Let us run out of doors, and have some nice play with the other children."

It is thousands of years since Epimetheus and Pandora were alive; and the world, nowadays, is a very different sort of thing from what it was in their time. Then, everybody was a child. There needed no fathers and mothers to take care of the children, because there was not danger, nor trouble of any kind, and no clothes to be mended, and there was always plenty to eat and drink. Whenever a child wanted his dinner, he found it growing on a tree; and, if he looked at the trees in the morning, he could see the expanding blossom of that night's supper; or, at eventide, he saw the tender bud of to-morrow's breakfast. It was a very pleasant life indeed. No labor to be done, no tasks to be studied; nothing but sports and dances, and sweet voices of children talking, or carolling like birds, or gushing out in merry laughter, throughout the livelong day.

What was most wonderful of all, the children never quarrelled among themselves; neither had they any crying fits; nor, since time first began, had a single one of these little mortals ever gone apart into a corner, and sulked. Oh, what a good time was that to be alive in! The truth is, those ugly little winged monsters, called Troubles, which are now almost as numerous as mosquitoes, had never yet been seen on the earth. It is probable that the very greatest disquietude which a child had ever experienced was Pandora's vexation at not being able to discover the secret of the mysterious box.

This was at first only the faint shadow of a Trouble; but, every day, it grew more and more substantial, until, before a great while, the cottage of Epimetheus and Pandora was less sunshiny than those of the other children.

"Whence can the box have come?" Pandora continually kept saying to herself and to Epimetheus. "And what in the world can be inside of it?"

"Always talking about this box!" said Epimetheus, at last; for he had grown extremely tired of the subject. "I wish, dear Pandora, you would try to talk of something else. Come, let us go and gather some ripe figs, and eat them under the trees, for our supper. And I know a vine that has the sweetest and juiciest grapes you ever tasted."

"Always talking about grapes and figs!" cried Pandora, pettishly.

"Well, then," said Epimetheus, who was a very good-tempered child, like a multitude of children in those days, "let us run out and have a merry time with our playmates."

"I am tired of merry times, and don't care if I never have any more!" answered our pettish little Pandora. "And, besides, I never do have any. This ugly box! I am so taken up with thinking about it all the time. I insist upon your telling me what is inside of it."

"As I have already said, fifty times over, I do not know!" replied Epimetheus, getting a little vexed. "How, then, can I tell you what is inside?"

"You might open it," said Pandora, looking sideways at Epimetheus, "and then we could see for ourselves."

"Pandora, what are you thinking of?" exclaimed Epimetheus.

And his face expressed so much horror at the idea of looking into a box, which had been confided to him on the condition of his never opening it, that Pandora thought it best not to suggest it any more. Still, however, she could not help thinking and talking about the box.

"At least," said she, "you can tell me how it came here."

"It was left at the door," replied Epimetheus, "just before you came, by a person who looked very smiling and intelligent, and who could hardly forbear laughing as he put it down. He was dressed in an odd kind of a cloak, and had on a cap that seemed to be made partly of feathers, so that it looked almost as if it had wings."

"What sort of a staff had he?" asked Pandora.

"Oh, the most curious staff you ever saw!" cried Epimetheus. "It was like two serpents twisting around a stick, and was carved so naturally that I, at first, thought the serpents were alive."

"I know him," said Pandora, thoughtfully. "Nobody else has such a staff. It was Quicksilver; and he brought me hither, as well as the box. No doubt he intended it for me; and, most probably, it contains pretty dresses for me to wear, or toys for you and me to play with, or something very nice for us both to eat!"

"Perhaps so," answered Epimetheus, turning away. "But until Quicksilver comes back and tells us so, we have neither of us any right to lift the lid of the box."

"What a dull boy he is!" muttered Pandora, as Epimetheus left the cottage. "I do wish he had a little more enterprise!"

For the first time since her arrival, Epimetheus had gone out without asking Pandora to accompany him. He went to gather figs and grapes by himself, or to seek whatever amusement he could find, in other society than his little playfellow's. He was tired to death of hearing about the box, and heartily wished that Quicksilver, or whatever was the messenger's name, had left it at some other child's door, where Pandora would never have set eyes on it. So perseveringly as she did babble about this one thing!

The box, the box, and nothing but the box! It seemed as if the box were bewitched, and as if the cottage were not big enough to hold it, without Pandora's continually stumbling over it, and making Epimetheus stumble over it likewise, and bruising all four of their shins.

Well, it was really hard that poor Epimetheus should have a box in his ears from morning till night; especially as the little people of the earth were so unaccustomed to vexations, in those happy days, that they knew not how to deal with them. Thus, a small vexation made as much disturbance then, as a far bigger one would in our own times.

After Epimetheus was gone, Pandora stood gazing at the box. She had called it ugly, above a hundred times; but, in spite of all that she had said against it, it was positively a very handsome article of furniture, and would have been quite an ornament to any room in which it should be placed. It was made of a beautiful kind of wood, with dark and rich veins spreading over its surface, which was so highly polished that little Pandora could see her face in it. As the child had no other looking-glass, it is odd that she did not value the box merely on this account.

The edges and corners of the box were carved with most wonderful skill. Around the margin there were figures of graceful men and women, and the prettiest children ever seen, reclining or sporting amid a profusion of flowers and foliage; and these various objects were so exquisitely represented, and were wrought together in such harmony, that flowers, foliage, and human beings seemed to combine into a wreath of mingled beauty. But here and there, peeping forth from behind the carved foliage, Pandora once or twice fancied that she saw a face not so lovely, or someting or other that was disagreeable, and which stole the beauty out of all the rest. Nevertheless, on looking more closely, and touching the spot with her finger, she could discover nothing of the kind. Some face, that was really beautiful, had been made to look ugly by her catching a sideway glimpse at it.

The most beautiful face of all was done in what is called high relief, in the centre of the lid. There was nothing else, save the dark, smooth richness of the polished wood, and this one face in the centre, with a garland of flowers about its brow. Pandora had looked at this face a great many times, and imagined that the mouth could smile if it liked, or be grave when it chose, the same as any living mouth. The features, indeed, all wore a very lively and rather mischievous expression, which looked almost as if it needs must burst out of the carved lips, and utter itself in words.

Had the mouth spoken, it would probably have been something like this:—

"Do not be afraid, Pandora! What harm can there be in opening the box? Never mind that poor, simple Epimetheus! You are wiser than he, and have ten times as much spirit. Open the box, and see if you do not find something very pretty!"

The box, I had almost forgotten to say, was fastened; not by a lock, nor by any other such contrivance, but by a very intricate knot of gold cord. There appeared to be no end to this knot, and no beginning. Never was a knot so cunningly twisted, nor with so many ins and outs, which roguishly defied the skilfullest fingers to disentangle them. And yet, by the very difficulty that there was in it, Pandora was the more tempted to examine the knot, and just see how it was made. Two or three times, already, she had stooped over the box, and taken the knot between her thumb and forefinger, but without positively trying to undo it.

"I really believe," said she to herself, "that I begin to see how it was done. Nay, perhaps I could tie it up again after undoing it. There would be no harm in that, surely. Even Epimetheus would not blame me for that. I need not open the box, and should not, of course, without the foolish boy's consent, even if the knot were untied."

It might have been better for Pandora if she had had a little work to do, or anything to employ her mind upon, so as not to be so constantly thinking of this one subject. But children led so easy a life, before any Troubles came into the world, that they had really a great deal too much leisure. They could not be forever playing at hide-and-seek among the flower-shrubs, or at blind-man's-bluff with garlands over their eyes, or at whatever other games had been found out, while Mother Earth was in her babyhood. When life is all sport, toil is the real play. There was absolutely nothing to do. A little sweeping and dusting about the cottage, I suppose, and the gathering of fresh flowers (which were only too abundant everywhere), and arranging them in vases,—and poor little Pandora's day's work was over. And then, for the rest of the day, there was the box!

After all, I am not quite sure that the box was not a blessing to her in its way. It supplied her with such a variety of ideas to think of, and to talk about, whenever she had anybody to listen! When she was in good-humor, she could admire the bright polish of its sides, and the rich border of beautiful faces and foliage that ran all around it. Or, if she chanced to be ill-tempered, she could give it a push, or kick it with her naughty little foot. And many a kick did the box—(but it was a mischievous box, as we shall see, and deserved all it got)—many a kick did it receive. But, certain it is, if it had not been for the box, our active-minded little Pandora would not have known half so well how to spend her time as she now did.

For it was really an endless employment to guess what was inside. What could it be, indeed? Just imagine, my little hearers, how busy your wits would be, if there were a great box in the house, which, as you might have reason to suppose, contained something new and pretty for your Christmas or New Year's gifts. Do you think that you should be less curious than Pandora? If you were left alone with the box, might you not feel a little tempted to lift the lid? But you would not do it. Oh, fie! No, no! Only, if you thought there were toys in it, it would be so very hard to let slip an opportunity of taking just one peep! I know not whether Pandora expected any toys; for none had yet begun to be made, probably, in those days, when the world itself was one great plaything for the children that dwelt upon it. But Pandora was convinced that there was something very beautiful and valuable in the box; and therefore she felt just as anxious to take a peep as any of these little girls, here around me, would have felt. And, possibly, a little more so; but of that I am not quite so certain.

On this particular day, however, which we have so long been talking about, her curiosity grew so much greater than it usually was, that, at last, she approached the box. She was more than half determined to open it, if she could. Ah, naughty Pandora!

First, however, she tried to lift it. It was heavy; quite too heavy for the slender strength of a child, like Pandora. She raised one end of the box a few inches from the floor, and let it fall again, with a pretty loud thump. A moment afterwards, she almost fancied that she heard something stir inside of the box. She applied her ear as closely as possible, and listened. Positively, there did seem to be a kind of stifled murmur, within! Or was it merely the singing in Pandora's ears? Or could it be the beating of her heart? The child could not quite satisfy herself whether she had heard anything or no. But, at all events, her curiosity was stronger than ever.

As she drew back her head, her eyes fell upon the knot of gold cord.

"It must have been a very ingenious person who tied this knot," said Pandora to herself. "But I think I could untie it nevertheless. I am resolved, at least, to find the two ends of the cord."

So she took the golden knot in her fingers, and pried into its intricacies as sharply as she could. Almost without intending it, or quite knowing what she was about, she was soon busily engaged in attempting to undo it. Meanwhile, the bright sunshine came through the open window; as did likewise the merry voices of the children playing at a distance, and perhaps the voice of Epimetheus among them. Pandora stopped to listen. What a beautiful day it was! Would it not be wiser, if she were to let the troublesome knot alone, and think no more about the box, but run and join her little playfellows, and be happy?

All this time, however, her fingers were half unconsciously busy with the knot; and happening to glance at the flower-wreathed face on the lid of the enchanted box, she seemed to perceive it slyly grinning at her.

"That face looks very mischievous," thought Pandora. "I wonder whether it smiles because I am doing wrong! I have the greatest mind in the world to run away!"

But just then, by the merest accident, she gave the knot a kind of a twist, which produced a wonderful result. The gold cord untwined itself as if by magic, and left the box without a fastening.

"This is the strangest thing I ever knew!" said Pandora. "What will Epimetheus say? And how can I possibly tie it up again?"

She made one or two attempts to restore the knot, but soon found it quite beyond her skill. It had disentangled itself so suddenly that she could not in the least remember how the strings had been doubled into one another; and when she tried to recollect the shape and appearance of the knot, it seemd to have gone entirely out of her mind. Nothing was to be done, therefore, but to let the box remain as it was until Epimetheus should come in.

"But," said Pandora, "when he finds the knot untied, he will know that I have done it. How shall I make him believe that I have not looked into the box?"

And then the thought came into her naughty little heart, that, since she would be suspected of having looked into the box, she might just as well do so at once. Oh, very naughty and very foolish Pandora! You should have thought only of doing what was right and of leaving undone what was wrong, and not of what your playfellow Epimetheus would have said or believed. And so perhaps she might, if the enchanted face on the lid of the box had not looked so bewitchingly persuasive at her, and if she had not seemed to hear, more distinctly than before, the murmur of small voices within. She could not tell whether it was fancy or not; but there was quite a little tumult of whispers in her ear,—or else it was her curiosity that whispered,—

"Let us out, dear Pandora,—pray let us out! We will be such nice pretty playfellows for you! Only let us out!"

"What can it be?" thought Pandora. "Is there something alive in the box? Well!— yes!—I am resolved to take just one peep! Only one peep; and then the lid shall be shut

down as safely as ever! There cannot possibly be any harm in just one little peep!''

But it is now time for us to see what Epimetheus was doing.

This was the first time, since his little playmate had come to dwell with him, that he had attempted to enjoy any pleasure in which she did not partake. But nothing went right; nor was he nearly so happy as on other days. He could not find a sweet grape or a ripe fig (if Epimetheus had a fault, it was a little too much fondness for figs); or, if ripe at all, they were over-ripe, and so sweet as to be cloying. There was no mirth in his heart, such as usually made his voice gush out, of its own accord, and swell the merriment of his companions. In short, he grew so uneasy and discontented, that the other children could not imagine what was the matter with Epimetheus. Neither did he himself know what ailed him any better than they did. For you must recollect that, at the time we are speaking of, it was everybody's nature, and constant habit, to be happy. The world had not yet learned to be otherwise. Not a single soul or body, since these children were first sent to enjoy themselves on the beautiful earth, had never been sick or out of sorts.

At length, discovering that, somehow or other, he put a stop to all the play, Epimetheus judged it best to go back to Pandora, who was in a humor better suited to his own. But, with a hope of giving her pleasure, he gathered some flowers, and made them into a wreath, which he meant to put upon her head. The flowers were very lovely,—roses, and lilies, and orange-blossoms, and a great many more, which left a trail of fragrance behind, as Epimetheus carried them along; and the wreath was put together with as much skill as could reasonably be expected of a boy. The fingers of little girls, it has always appeared to me, are the fittest to twine flower-wreaths; but boys could do it, in those days, rather better than they can now.

And here I must mention that a great black cloud had been gathering in the sky for some time past, although it had not yet overspread the sun. But, just as Epimetheus reached the cottage door, this cloud began to intercept the sunshine, and thus to make a sudden and sad obscurity.

He entered softly; for he meant, if possible, to steal behind Pandora, and fling the wreath of flowers over her head, before she should be aware of his approach. But, as it happened, there was no need for his treading so very lightly. He might have trod as heavily as he pleased,—as heavily as a grown man,—as heavily, I was going to say, as an elephant,—without much probability of Pandora's hearing his footsteps. She was too intent upon her purpose. At the moment of his entering the cottage, the naughty child had put her hand to the lid, and was on the point of opening the mysterious box. Epimetheus beheld her. If he had cried out, Pandora would probably have withdrawn her hand, and the fatal mystery of the box might never have been known.

But Epimetheus himself, although he said very little about it, had his own share of curiosity to know what was inside. Perceiving that Pandora was resolved to find out the secret, he determined that his playfellow should not be the only wise person in the cottage. And if there were anything pretty or valuable in the box, he meant to take half of it to himself. Thus, after all his sage speeches to Pandora about restraining her curiosity, Epimetheus turned out to be quite as foolish, and nearly as much in fault, as she. So, whenever we blame Pandora for what happened, we must not forget to shake our heads at Epimetheus likewise.

As Pandora raised the lid, the cottage grew very dark and dismal; for the black cloud had now swept quite over the sun, and seemed to have buried it alive. There had, for a little while past, been a growling and muttering, which all at once broke into a heavy peal of thunder. But Pandora, heeding nothing of all this, lifted the lid nearly upright, and looked inside. It seemed as if a sudden swarm of winged creatures brushed past her, taking flight out of the box, while, at the same instant, she heard the voice of Epimetheus, with a lamentable tone, as if he were in pain.

"Oh, I am stung!" cried he. "I am stung! Naughty Pandora! why have you opened this wicked box?"

Pandora let fall the lid, and, starting up, looked about her, to see what had befallen Epimetheus. The thunder-cloud had so darkened the room that she could not very clearly discern what was in it. But she heard a disagreeable buzzing, as if a great many huge flies, or gigantic mosquitoes, or those insects which we call dor-bugs, and pinching-dogs, were darting about. And, as her eyes grew more accustomed to the imperfect light, she saw a crowd of ugly little shapes, with bats' wings looking abominably spiteful, and armed with terribly long stings in their tails. It was one of these that had stung Epimetheus. Nor was it a great while before Pandora herself began to scream, in no less pain and affright than her playfellow, and making a vast deal more hubbub about it. An odious little monster had settled on her forehead, and would have stung her I know not how deeply, if Epimetheus had not run and brushed it away.

Now, if you wish to know what these ugly things might be, which had made their escape out of the box, I must tell you that they were the whole family of earthly Troubles. There were evil Passions; there were a great many species of Cares; there were more than a hundred and fifty Sorrows; there were Diseases, in a vast number of miserable and painful shapes; there were more kinds of Naughtiness than it would be of any use to talk about. In short, everything that has since afflicted the souls and bodies of mankind had been shut up in the mysterious box, and given to Epimetheus and Pandora to be kept

safely, in order that the happy children of the world might never be molested by them. Had they been faithful to their trust, all would have gone well. No grown person would ever have been sad, nor any child have had cause to shed a single tear, from that hour until this moment.

But—and you may see by this how a wrong act of any one mortal is a calamity to the whole world—by Pandora's lifting the lid of that miserable box, and by the fault of Epimetheus, too, in not preventing her, these Troubles have obtained a foothold among us, and do not seem very likely to be driven away in a hurry. For it was impossible, as you will easily guess, that the two children should keep the ugly swarm in their own little cottage. On the contrary, the first thing that they did was to fling open the doors and windows, in hopes of getting rid of them; and, sure enough, away flew the winged Troubles all abroad, and so pestered and tormented the small people, everywhere about, that none of them so much as smiled for many days afterwards. And, what was very singular, all the flowers and dewy blossoms on earth, not one of which had hitherto faded, now began to droop and shed their leaves, after a day or two. The children, moreover, who before seemed immortal in their childhood, now grew older, day by day, and came soon to be youths and maidens, and men and women by and by, and aged people, before they dreamed of such a thing.

Meanwhile, the naughty Pandora, and hardly less naughty Epimetheus, remained in their cottage. Both of them had been grievously stung, and were in a good deal of pain, which seemed the more intolerable to them, because it was the very first pain that had ever been felt since the world began. Of course, they were entirely unaccustomed to it, and could have no idea what it meant. Besides all this, they were in exceedingly bad humor, both with themselves and with one another. In order to indulge it to the utmost, Epimetheus sat down sullenly in a corner with his back towards Pandora; while Pandora flung herself upon the floor and rested her head on the fatal and abominable box. She was crying bitterly, and sobbing as if her heart would break.

Suddenly there was a gentle little tap on the inside of the lid.

"What can that be?" cried Pandora, lifting her head.

But either Epimetheus had not heard the tap, or was too much out of humor to notice it. At any rate, he made no answer.

"You are very unkind," said Pandora, sobbing anew, "not to speak to me!"

Again the tap! It sounded like the tiny knuckles of a fairy's hand, knocking lightly and playfully on the inside of the box.

"Who are you?" asked Pandora, with a little of her former curiosity. "Who are you, inside of this naughty box?"

A sweet little voice spoke from within,—

"Only lift the lid, and you shall see."

"No, no," answered Pandora, again beginning to sob; "I have had enough of lifting the lid! You are inside of the box, naughty creature, and there you shall stay! There are plenty of your ugly brothers and sisters already flying about the world. You need never think that I shall be so foolish as to let you out!"

She looked towards Epimetheus, as she spoke, perhaps expecting that he would commend her for her wisdom. But the sullen boy only muttered that she was wise a little too late.

"Ah," said the sweet little voice again, "you had much better let me out. I am not like those naughty creatures that have stings in their tails. They are not brothers and sisters of mine, as you would see at once, if you were only to get a glimpse of me. Come, come, my pretty Pandora! I am sure you will let me out!"

And, indeed, there was a kind of cheerful witchery in the tone, that made it almost impossible to refuse anything which this little voice asked. Pandora's heart had insensibly grown lighter at every word that came from within the box. Epimetheus, too, though still in the corner, had turned half round, and seemed to be in rather better spirits than before.

"My dear Epimetheus," cried Pandora, "have you heard this little voice?"

"Yes, to be sure I have," answered he, but in no very good-humor as yet. "And what of it?"

"Shall I lift the lid again?" asked Pandora.

"Just as you please," said Epimetheus. "You have done so much mischief already, that perhaps you may as well do a little more. One other Trouble, in such a swarm as you have set adrift about the world, can make no very great difference."

"You might speak a little more kindly!" murmured Pandora, wiping her eyes.

"Ah, naughty boy!" cried the little voice within the box, in an arch and laughing tone. " He knows he is longing to see me. Come, my dear Pandora, lift up the lid. I am in a great hurry to comfort you. Only let me have some fresh air, and you shall soon see that matters are not quite so dismal as you think them!"

"Epimetheus," exclaimed Pandora, "come what may, I am resolved to open the box!"

"And, as the lid seems very heavy," cried Epimetheus, running across the room, "I will help you!"

So, with one consent, the two children again lifted the lid. Out flew a sunny and smiling little personage, and hovered about the room, throwing a light wherever she went. Have you never made the sunshine dance into dark corners, by reflecting it from a bit of looking-glass? Well, so looked the winged cheerfulness of this fairy-like stranger, amid the gloom of the cottage. She flew to Epimetheus, and laid the least touch of her finger on the inflamed spot where the Trouble had stung him, and immediately the anguish of it was gone. Then she kissed Pandora on the forehead, and her hurt was cured likewise.

After performing these good offices, the bright stranger fluttered sportively over the children's heads, and looked so sweetly at them, that they both began to think it not so very much amiss to have opened the box, since, otherwise, their cheery guest must have been kept a prisoner among those naughty imps with stings in their tails.

"Pray, who are you, beautiful creature?" inquired Pandora.

"I am to be called Hope!" answered the sunshiny figure. "And because I am such a cheery little body, I was packed into the box, to make amends to the human race for that swarm of ugly Troubles which was destined to be let loose among them. Never fear! we shall do pretty well in spite of them all.''

''Your wings are colored like the rainbow!'' exclaimed Pandora. ''How very beautiful!''

''Yes, they are like the rainbow,'' said Hope, ''because, glad as my nature is, I am partly made of tears as well as smiles.''

''And will you stay with us,'' asked Epimetheus, ''forever and ever?''

''As long as you need me,'' said Hope, with her pleasant smile,— ''and that will be as long as you live in the world,—I promise never to desert you. There may come times and seasons, now and then, when you will think that I have utterly vanished. But again, and again, and again, when perhaps you least dream of it, you shall see the glimmer of my wings on the ceiling of your cottage. Yes, my dear children, and I know something very good and beautiful that is to be given you hereafter!''

''Oh, tell us,'' they exclaimed,—''tell us what it is!''

''Do not ask me,'' replied Hope, putting her fingers on her rosy mouth. ''But do not despair, even if it should never happen while you live on this earth. Trust in my promise, for it is true.''

''We do trust you!'' cried Epimetheus and Pandora, both in one breath.

And so they did; and not only they, but so had everybody trusted Hope, that has since been alive. And to tell you the truth, I cannot help being glad—(though, to be sure, it was an uncommonly naughty thing for her to do)—but I cannot help being glad that our foolish Pandora peeped into the box. No doubt—no doubt—the Troubles are still flying about the world, and have increased in multitude, rather than lessened, and are a very ugly set of imps, and carry most venomous stings in their tails. I have felt them already, and expect to feel them more, as I grow older. But then that lovely and lightsome little figure of Hope! What in the world could we do without her? Hope spiritualizes the earth; Hope makes it always new; and, even in the earth's best and brightest aspect, Hope shows it to be only the shadow of an infinite bliss hereafter!

FOLKTALES—
INHERITED AND LITERARY

The Firebird

The subject of a ballet by Igor Stravinsky, the gleaming firebird glows in the human imagination, leading the reader to a wonderful conclusion. Since the story deserves repetition, it can be told again and again. Ivan, a simple, good,

From Aleksandr Nikolaevich Afanas'ev, ed., *Russian Fairy Tales,* trans. Norbert Guterman (New York: Pantheon Books, 1945).

*and intuitive fellow, has a gray wolf as a spiritual reinforcement. When Ivan is
cut to bits by envious brothers, the wolf sends a raven to fetch the water of life,
which he sprinkles on Ivan. Ivan rises, stretches his arms, and says, "I have slept
long." (Stravinsky's* Firebird Suite *is available on RCA stereo record LSC 2725
and on other recordings.)*

In a certain land in a certain kingdom there lived a king called Vyslav Andronovich. He had three sons: the first was Prince Dimitri, the second Prince Vasily, and the third Prince Ivan. King Vyslav Andronovich had a garden so rich that there was no finer one in any kingdom. In this garden there grew all kinds of precious trees, with and without fruit; one special apple tree was the king's favorite, for all the apples it bore were golden.

The firebird took to visiting King Vyslav's garden; her wings were golden and her eyes were like Oriental crystals. Every night she flew into the garden, perched on King Vyslav's favorite apple tree, picked several golden apples from it, and then flew away. King Vyslav Andronovich was greatly distressed that the firebird had taken so many apples from his golden apple tree. So he summoned his three sons to him and said: "My beloved children, which of you can catch the firebird in my garden? To him who captures her alive I will give half my kingdom during my life, and all of it upon my death!" His sons, the princes, answered in one voice: "Your Majesty, gracious sovereign, little father, with great joy will we try to take the firebird alive!"

The first night Prince Dimitri went to keep watch in the garden. He sat under the apple tree from which the firebird had been picking apples, fell asleep, and did not hear her come, though she picked much golden fruit. Next morning King Vyslav Andronovich summoned his son Prince Dimitri to him and asked: "Well, my beloved son, did you see the firebird or not?" The prince answered: "No, gracious sovereign, little father! She did not come last night!"

The next night Prince Vasily went to keep watch in the garden. He sat under the same apple tree; he stayed one hour, then another hour, and finally fell so sound asleep that he did not hear the firebird come, though she picked many apples. In the morning King Vyslav summoned his son to him and asked: "Well, my beloved son, did you see the firebird or not?" "Gracious sovereign, little father, she did not come last night!"

The third night Prince Ivan went to keep watch in the garden and sat under the same apple tree; he sat one hour, a second hour, and a third—then suddenly the whole garden was illumined as if by many lights. The firebird had come; she perched on the apple tree and began to pick apples. Prince Ivan stole up to her so softly that he was able to seize her tail. But he could not hold the firebird herself; she tore herself from his grasp and flew away. In Prince Ivan's hand there remained only one feather of her tail, to which he held very fast. In the morning, as soon as King Vyslav awoke from his sleep, Prince Ivan went to him and gave him the feather of the firebird. King Vyslav was greatly pleased that his youngest son had succeeded in getting at least one feather of the firebird. This feather was so marvelously bright that when it was placed in a dark room it made the whole room shine as if it were lit

Illustration by Sheila Greenwald.

up by many candles. King Vyslav put the feather in his study as a keepsake, to be treasured forever. From that moment the firebird stopped visiting the garden.

Once again King Vyslav summoned his sons and said: "My beloved children, set out. I give you my blessing. Find the firebird and bring her to me alive, and that which I promised before will go to him who brings me the firebird." At this time Princes Dimitri and Vasily bore a grudge against their youngest brother, Ivan, because he had succeeded in tearing a feather from the firebird's tail; they accepted their father's blessing and together went forth to seek the firebird. But Prince Ivan too began to beg for his father's blessing that he might go forth. King Vyslav said to him: "My beloved son, my dear child, you are still young and unused to such long and hard journeys; why should you depart from my house? Your brothers have gone; what if you too leave me, and all three of you do not return for a long time? I am old now and I walk in the shadow of the Lord; if during your absence the Lord takes my life, who will rule the kingdom in my place? A rebellion might break out, or dissension among the people, and there would be no one to pacify them; or an enemy might approach our land, and there would be not one to command our troops." But no matter how King Vyslav tried to hold Prince Ivan back, he finally had to yield to his son's insistent prayer. Prince Ivan received his father's blessing, chose a horse, and set out on his way; and he rode on and on, himself not knowing whither.

He rode near and far, high and low, along bypaths and byways—for speedily a tale is spun, but with less speed a deed is done—until he came to a wide, open field, a green meadow. And there in the field stood a pillar, and on the pillar these words were written: "Whosoever goes from this pillar on the road straight before him will be cold and hungry. Whosoever goes to the right side will be safe and sound, but his horse will be killed. And whosoever goes to the left side will be killed himself, but his horse will be safe and sound." Price Ivan read this inscription and went to the right, thinking that

although his horse might be killed, he himself would remain alive and would in time get another horse.

He rode one day, then a second day, then a third. Suddenly an enormous gray wolf came toward him and said: "Ah, so it's you, young lad, Prince Ivan! You saw the inscription on the pillar that said that your horse would be killed if you came this way. Why, then, have you come hither?" When he had said these words, he tore Prince Ivan's horse in twain and ran off to one side.

Prince Ivan was sorely grieved for his horse; he shed bitter tears and then continued on foot. He walked a whole day and was utterly exhausted. He was about to sit down and rest for a while when all at once the gray wolf caught up with him and said: "I am sorry for you, Prince Ivan, because you are exhausted from walking; I am also sorry that I ate your good horse. Therefore mount me, the gray wolf, and tell me whither to carry you and for what purpose." Prince Ivan told the gray wolf what errand he had come on; and the gray wolf darted off with him more swiftly than a horse and after some time, just at nightfall, reached a low stone wall. There he stopped and said: "Now, Prince Ivan, climb down from me, the gray wolf, and climb over that stone wall; behind the wall you will find a garden, and in the garden the firebird is sitting in a golden cage. Take the firebird, but touch not the golden cage; if you take the cage, you will not escape, you will be caught at once!"

Prince Ivan climbed over the stone wall into the garden, saw the firebird in the golden cage, and was utterly charmed by the beauty of the cage. He took the bird out and started back across the garden, but on his way he changed his mind and said to himself: "Why have I taken the firebird without her cage—where will I put her?" He returned, and the moment he took down the golden cage a thunderous noise resounded through the whole garden, for there were strings tied to the cage. The guards woke up at once, rushed into the garden, caught Prince Ivan with the firebird, and led him before their king, whose name was Dolmat. King Dolmat was furious at Prince Ivan and cried in a loud and angry voice: "How now! Are you not ashamed to steal, young lad! Who are you, from what land do you come, what is your father's name, and what is your own name?"

Prince Ivan answered: "I am from Vyslav's kingdom. I am the son of King Vyslav Andronovich, and my name is Prince Ivan. Your firebird took to visiting our garden night after night; she plucked golden apples from my father's favorite apple tree and spoiled almost the whole tree. For that reason my father sent me to find the firebird and bring her to him."

"Oh, young lad, Prince Ivan," said King Dolmat, "is it fitting to do what you have done? If you had come to me, I would have given you the firebird with honor. But now, will you like it if I send to all the kingdoms to proclaim how dishonorably you have acted in my kingdom? However, listen, Prince Ivan! If you will do me a service, if you go beyond thirty lands, to the thirtieth kingdom, and get for me the horse with the golden mane from the realm of King Afron, I will forgive you your offense and hand the firebird over to you with great honor. But if you do not perform this service, I shall let it be known in all the kingdoms that you are a dishonorable thief." Prince Ivan left King Dolmat in great distress, promising to get for him the horse with the golden mane.

He came to the gray wolf and told him everything that King Dolmat had said. "Oh, young lad, Prince Ivan," said the gray wolf, "why did you not heed my words, why did you take the golden cage?" "It is true, I am guilty before you," answered Prince Ivan. "Well, let it be so," said the gray wolf. "Sit on me, the gray wolf; I will carry you where you have to go."

Prince Ivan mounted to the gray wolf's back, and the wolf ran fast as an arrow. He ran till nightfall, a short distance or a long one, until he came to King Afron's kingdom. And reaching the white-walled royal stables, the gray wolf said to Prince Ivan: "Go, Prince Ivan, into those white-walled stables—all the stableboys on guard are now sleeping soundly—and take the horse with the golden mane. However, on the wall there

hangs a golden bridle; do not take it, otherwise there will be trouble!"

Prince Ivan entered the white-walled stables, took the steed, and began to retrace his steps; but he noticed the golden bridle on the wall, and was so charmed with it that he removed it from its nail. And he had no sooner removed it than a thunderous clatter and noise resounded through all the stables, for there were strings tied to that bridle. The stableboys on guard woke up at once, rushed in, caught Prince Ivan, and brought him before King Afron. King Afron began to question him. "Young lad," he said, "tell me from what kingdom you are come, whose son your are, and what your name may be." Prince Ivan answered: "I am from Vyslav's kingdom. I am King Vyslav Andronovich's son, and I am called Prince Ivan."

"Oh, young lad, Prince Ivan" said King Afron, "is the deed you have done befitting an honorable knight? If you had come to me I would have given you the horse with the golden mane in all honor. But now, will you like it if I send to all the kingdoms to proclaim how dishonorably you have behaved in my kingdom? However, listen, Prince Ivan! If you do me a service, if you go beyond the thrice ninth land, to the thrice tenth kingdom, and get for me Princess Elena the Fair, with whom I have been in love, heart and soul, for long years, but whom I cannot win for my bride, I will forgive you your offense and give you the horse with the golden mane in all honor. But if you do not perform this service for me, I shall let it be known in all the kingdoms that you are a dishonorable thief and will put down in writing how badly you have behaved in my kingdom." Then Prince Ivan promised King Afron to get Princess Elena the Fair for him and left the palace, weeping bitterly.

He came to the gray wolf and told him everything that had happened to him. "Oh, young lad, Prince Ivan," said the gray wolf, "why did you not heed my words, why did you take the golden bridle?" "It is true, I am guilty before you," answered Prince Ivan. "Well, let it be so," said the gray wolf. "Sit on me, the gray wolf; I will carry you where you have to go."

Prince Ivan mounted to the gray wolf's back, and the wolf ran fast as an arrow; he ran as beasts run in fairy tales so that in a very short time he arrived in the kingdom of Elena the Fair. And reaching the golden fence that surrounded the wonderful garden, the wolf said to Prince Ivan: "Now, Prince Ivan, climb down from me, the gray wolf, and go back along the same road that we took to come here, and wait for me in the open field under the green oak."

Prince Ivan went where he was bid. But the gray wolf sat near the golden fence and waited till Princes Elena the Fair should come to take her walk in the garden. Toward evening, when the sun began to set in the west and the air became cool, Princess Elena the Fair went to walk in the garden with her governesses and ladies-in-waiting. She entered the garden, and when she came near the place where the gray wolf was sitting behind the fence, he quickly jumped across the fence into the garden, caught the princess, jumped back again, and ran with all his strength and power. He came to the green oak in the open field where Prince Ivan was waiting for him and said: "Prince Ivan, quickly seat yourself on me, the gray wolf!" Prince Ivan seated himself and the gray wolf darted off with him and the princess toward King Afron's kingdom.

The nurses and governesses and ladies-in-waiting who had been walking in the garden with the beautiful Princess Elena ran at once to the palace and sent men-at-arms to pursue the gray wolf; but no matter how fast they ran, they could not overtake him, and so they turned back.

Sitting on the gray wolf with the beautiful Princess Elena, Prince Ivan came to love her with all his heart, and she to love Prince Ivan. And when the gray wolf came to King Afron's kingdom and Prince Ivan had to lead the beautiful princess to the palace and give her to King Afron, he grew extremely sad and began to weep bitter tears. The gray wolf asked him: "Why are you weeping, Prince Ivan?" And Prince Ivan answered: "Gray wolf, my friend, why should I not weep and grieve? I have come to love the beautiful Princess Elena with all my heart, and now I

Illustration by Sheila Greenwald.

must give her to King Afron in return for the horse with the golden mane; if I do not give her to him, he will dishonor me in all the kingdoms."

"I have served you much, Prince Ivan," said the gray wolf, "and I will do you this service too. Listen to me, Prince Ivan! I will turn myself into the beautiful Princess Elena, and do you lead me to King Afron and take from him the horse with the golden mane; he will think me the real princess. And later, when you have mounted the horse with the golden mane and gone far away, I shall ask King Afron to let me walk in the open field. And when he lets me go with the nurses and governesses and ladies-in-waiting, and I am with them in the open field, remember me, and once again I shall be with you." The gray wolf said these words, struck himelf against the damp earth, and turned into Princess Elena the Fair so that there was no way of knowing that he was not the princess. Prince Ivan took the gray wolf, went to King Afron's palace, and told the real Princess Elena to wait for him outside the town.

When Prince Ivan came to King Afron with the false Elena the Fair, the king was greatly rejoiced to receive the treasure that he had so long desired. He accepted the false princess and gave Prince Ivan the horse with the golden mane.

Prince Ivan mounted the horse and rode out of the town; he had seated Princess Elena the Fair behind him, and they set out in the direction of King Dolmat's kingdom. As for the gray wolf, he lived with King Afron one day, a second day, and a third, in the place of Elena the Fair; and on the fourth he went to King Afron and asked his permission to take a walk in the open field to dispel the cruel sadness and grief that lay on him. And King Afron said to him: "Ah, my beautiful Princess Elena! For you I will do anything; I will even let you go to walk in the open field!" And at once he commanded the governesses and nurses and all the ladies-in-waiting to walk with the beautiful princess in the open field.

Meanwhile Prince Ivan rode along byways and bypaths with Elena the Fair, conversed with her, and forgot about the gray wolf. But then he remembered. "Ah," he said, "where is my gray wolf?" Suddenly, as though he had come from nowhere, the gray wolf stood before Prince Ivan and said: "Prince Ivan, sit on me, the gray wolf, and let the beautiful princess ride on the horse with the golden mane."

Prince Ivan sat on the gray wolf and they set out for King Dolmat's kingdom. They traveled a long time or a short time, and having come to the kingdom, stopped three versts from the town. Prince Ivan began to implore the gray wolf, saying: "Listen to me, gray wolf, my dear friend! You have done many a service for me; do me this last one. Could you not turn yourself into a horse with a golden mane instead of this one? For I long to have myself a horse with a golden mane."

Suddenly the wolf struck himself against the damp earth and turned into a horse with a golden mane; Prince Ivan left Princess Elena the Fair in the green meadow, bestrode the gray wolf, and went to the palace of King Dolmat. And when King Dolmat saw Prince Ivan riding on the horse with the golden mane, he was overjoyed and at once came out of his apartment, met the prince in the great courtyard, kissed him on his sweet lips, took him by the right hand, and led him into the white-walled palace hall. In honor of this joyous occasion King Dolmat gave a great feast, and the guests sat at oaken tables

with checked tablecloths; they ate, drank, laughed, and enjoyed themselves for exactly two days. And on the third day King Dolmat handed to Prince Ivan the firebird in the golden cage. The prince took the firebird, went outside the town, mounted the golden-maned horse together with Princess Elena the Fair, and set out for his native land, the kingdom of King Vyslav Andronovich.

As for King Dolmat, he decided on the next day to break in his golden-maned horse in the open field; he had the horse saddled, then mounted him and rode off; but as soon as he began to spur the beast, it threw him, and turning back into the gray wolf, darted off and overtook Prince Ivan. "Prince Ivan," said he, "mount me, the gray wolf, and let Princess Elena the Fair ride on the horse with the golden mane."

Prince Ivan sat on the gray wolf and they continued on their way. The moment the gray wolf brought Prince Ivan to the place where he had torn the horse asunder, he stopped and said: "Well, Prince Ivan, I have served you long enough in faith and in truth. Upon this spot I tore your horse in twain, and to this spot I have brought you back safe and sound. Climb down from me, the gray wolf; now you have a horse with a golden mane; mount him and go wherever you have to go; I am no longer your servant." After he had said these words the gray wolf ran off, and Prince Ivan wept bitterly and set out on his way with the beautiful princess.

He rode with Princess Elena for a long time or a short time; when they were still about twenty versts from his own land, he stopped, dismounted from his horse, and lay down with the beautiful princess to rest under a tree from the heat of the sun; he tied the horse with the golden mane to the same tree and put the cage with the firebird by his side. The two lovers lay on the soft grass, spoke amorous words to each other, and fell fast asleep.

At that very moment Prince Ivan's brothers, Prince Dimitri and Prince Vasily, having traveled through various kingdoms and having failed to find the firebird, were on their way back to their native land; they were returning empty handed. They chanced to come upon their brother, Prince Ivan, lying asleep beside Princess Elena the Fair. Seeing the golden-maned horse on the grass and the firebird in the golden cage, they were sorely tempted and decided to slay their brother. Prince Dimitri drew his sword from its scabbard, stabbed Prince Ivan, and cut him in little pieces; then he awakened Princess Elena the Fair and began to question her. "Lovely maiden," he said, "from what kingdom have you come, who is your father, and what is your name?"

The beautiful Princess Elena, seeing Prince Ivan dead, was terribly frightened and began to weep bitter tears, and amid her tears she said: "I am Princess Elena the Fair; I was carried off by Prince Ivan, whom you have brought to an evil end. If you were valiant knights you would have gone with him into the open field and conquered him in fair combat; but you slew him while he was asleep, and what praise will that get you? A sleeping man is the same as a dead man!"

The Prince Dimitri put his sword to the heart of Princess Elena and said to her: "Listen to me, Elena the Fair! You are now in our hands; we shall take you to our father, King Vyslav Andronovich, and you must tell him that we captured you as well as the firebird and the horse with the golden mane. If you do not promise to say this, I shall put you to death at once!" The beautiful Princess Elena was frightened by the threat of death; she promised them and swore by everything sacred that she would speak as they commanded. Then Prince Dimitri and Prince Vasily cast lots to see who should get Princess Elena and who the horse with the golden mane. And it fell out that the beautiful princess went to Prince Vasily and the horse with the golden mane to Prince Dimitri. Then Prince Vasily took the beautiful Princess Elena and seated her on his good horse, and Prince Dimitri mounted the horse with the golden mane and took the firebird to give to his father, King Vyslav Andronovich, and they all set out on their way.

Prince Ivan lay dead on that spot exactly thirty days; then the gray wolf came upon him and knew him by his odor. He wanted to help the prince, to revive him, but he did not know how to do it. At that moment the gray wolf saw a raven with two young ravens flying above the body, making ready to swoop down and eat the flesh of Prince Ivan. The gray wolf hid behind a bush; and as soon as the young ravens lighted on the ground and began to eat the body of Prince Ivan, he leaped from behind the bush, caught one young raven, and prepared to tear him in twain. Then the raven flew to the ground, sat at some distance from the gray wolf, and said to him: "O gray wolf, do not touch my young child; he has done nothing to you."

"Listen to me, raven," said the gray wolf; "I shall not touch your child and will let him go safe and sound if you will do me a service. Fly beyond the thrice ninth land, to the thrice tenth kingdom, and bring me the water of death and the water of life." Thereupon the raven said to the gray wolf: "I will do this service for you, but touch not my son." Having said these words, the raven took wing and was soon out of sight. On the third day the raven came back carrying two vials, one containing the water of life, the other the water of death, and she gave these vials to the gray wolf.

The gray wolf took the vials, tore the young raven in twain, sprinkled him with the water of death, and the young raven's body grew together; he sprinkled him with the water of life, and the young raven shook his wings and flew away. Then the gray wolf sprinkled Prince Ivan with the water of death, and his body grew together; he sprinkled him with the water of life, and Prince Ivan stood up and said: "Ah, I have slept very long!"

The gray wolf answered him: "Yes, Prince Ivan, you would have slept forever had it not been for me; your brothers cut you in pieces and carried off the beautiful Princess Elena and the horse with the golden mane and the firebird. Now hasten as fast as you can to your native land; your brother Prince Vasily is this very day to marry your bride, Princess Elena the Fair. And in order to get there quickly, you had better sit on me, the gray wolf." Prince Ivan mounted the gray wolf; the wolf ran with him to King Vyslav Andronovich's kingdom and after a short time or a long time reached the town.

Prince Ivan dismounted from the gray

wolf, walked into the town, and having arrived at the palace, found that his brother Prince Vasily was indeed wedding the beautiful Princess Elena that very day; he had returned with her from the ceremony, and was already sitting at the feast. Prince Ivan entered the palace, and no sooner did Elena the Fair see him than she sprang up from the table, began to kiss his sweet lips, and cried out: "This is my beloved bridegroom, Prince Ivan—not the evildoer who sits here at the table!"

Then King Vyslav Andronovich arose from his place and began to question Princess Elena. "What is the meaning of the words you have spoken?" he demanded. Elena the Fair told him the whole truth about that had happened—how Prince Ivan had won her, the horse with the golden mane, and the firebird, how his older brothers had killed him in his sleep, and how they had forced her under threat of death to say that they had won all this. King Vyslav grew terribly angry at Prince Dimitri and Prince Vasily and threw them into a dungeon; but Prince Ivan married Princess Elena the Fair and began to live with her in such true friendship and love that neither of them could spend a single minute without the other's company.

Baba Yaga

In this fascinating tale, Baba Yaga belongs to the pantheon of ancient Russian gods—before Christianity and before communism. She is a witch but an ambivalent one, for there is both good and evil in her nature. In this respect, she combines the good and bad traits of mothers—the good mother and the wicked stepmother. She is both a hindrance and a help to the orphan girl, but she destroys the unpleasant daughter of the evil stepmother. Baba Yaga lives in a curious house on chicken legs, for she is an elemental life force, like the egg-laying hen.

A certain peasant and his wife had a daughter. The wife died; the husband married another woman, and had a daughter with her also. His wife conceived a dislike for her stepdaughter and the orphan had a hard time. Our peasant thought and thought, and finally took his daughter to the woods. As he drove in the woods, he beheld a little hut standing on chicken legs. The peasant said: "Little hut, little hut, stand with your back to the woods, and your front to me!" The hut turned around. The peasant entered it and found Baba Yaga: her head was in front, her right leg was in one corner, and her left leg in the other corner. "I smell a Russian smell!" said Yaga. The peasant bowed to her and said: "Baba Yaga the Bony-legged One, I have brought you my daughter to be your servant." "Very well, serve me, serve me!" said Yaga to the girl. "I will reward you for it." The father said farewell and returned home.

Baba Yaga gave the girl a basketful of yarn to spin, told her to make a fire in the stove, and to prepare everything for dinner. Then she went out. The girl busied herself at the stove and wept bitterly. The mice ran out and said to her: "Maiden, maiden, why are you weeping? Give us some gruel: we shall return your kindness." She gave them some gruel. "And now," they said, "stretch one thread on each spindle." Baba Yaga came back. "Well," she said, "have you prepared everything?" The girl had everything ready.

From Aleksandr Nikolaevich Afanas'ev, ed., *Russian Fairy Tales*, trans. Norbert Guterman (New York: Pantheon Books, 1945).

"And now wash me in the bath!" said her mistress. She praised the maiden and gave her several beautiful dresses.

Again Yaga went out, having set even more difficult tasks for her servant. Again the girl wept. The mice ran out. "Lovely maiden," they said, "why are you weeping? Give us some gruel: we shall return your kindness." She gave them gruel, and again they told her what to do and how. Baba Yaga upon her return again praised the maiden and gave her even more beautiful dresses.

One day the stepmother sent her husband to see whether his daughter was still alive. The peasant drove into the woods; when he came to the house on chicken legs, he saw that his daughter had become very prosperous. Yaga was not at home, so he took the maiden with him. As they approached their village, the peasant's dog began to bark: "Bow! wow! wow! A young lady is coming, a young lady is coming!" The stepmother ran out and struck the dog with a rolling pin. "You're lying!" she said. "You should bark, 'Bones are rattling in the basket!'" But the dog kept barking the same thing as be-fore. The peasant and his daughter arrived. The stepmother began to press her husband to take her daughter to Baba Yaga. He took her.

Baba Yaga set a task for her and went out. The girl was beside herself with spite, and wept. The mice ran out: "Maiden, maiden," they said, "why are you weeping?" But she did not even let them speak; she struck them with a rolling pin and scolded them roundly and did not do her work. Yaga came back and became angry. Another time the same thing happened. Then Yaga broke her in pieces and put her bones in a basket.

Now the stepmother sent her husband for his daughter. The father went and brought back only her bones. As he approached his village, his dog barked on the porch: "Bow! wow! wow! Bones are rattling in the basket!" The stepmother came running out with a rolling pin: "You're lying!" she said. "You should bark, 'A young lady is com-ing!'" The husband arrived; and then the wife moaned and groaned.

There's a tale for you, and a crock of butter for me.

Catskin

As Joseph Jacobs, who collected this English folktale in the nineteenth century, noted, it was originally a story of incest. In early seventeenth-century Italy, Basile told the same tale as "The She-Bear," in which the father's incestuous longings for his daughter force her to leave home. Basile's story reads like a female version of the Frog Prince—a handsome Prince in the woods is about to shoot a bear, thinks better of it, and takes the animal home. He lets it sleep outside his door, then at the foot of his bed, and then in his bed; and lo and behold, it turns into a beautiful princess! Another similar version of the story, called "The Thousand Furs," is told by the Brothers Grimm. To escape her father-tormentor, the beleaguered girl in this story asks for coats of the sun, moon, and stars, and finally a coat of fur from a thousand animals of the forest. She, too, ends up with a handsome prince. The stories suggest that children can have traumatic experiences at home and still go on to lead wholesome and happy adult lives. Good stories in themselves, they also contain, in Bruno Bettelheim's phrase, "the uses of enchantment," that is, they can be psychologically healing. The early Cinderella stories suggest the incest theme; in them, the girl is disguised with ashes to conceal her identity from her father. If children are to have a wholesome literary experience, the incest theme, here treated tastefully and symbolically, should not be avoided.

From Joseph Jacobs, *More English Fairy Tales* (New York: Schocken Books, 1968. First published 1894).

Well, there was once a gentleman who had fine lands and houses, and he very much wanted to have a son to be heir to them. So when his wife brought him a daughter, bonny as bonny could be, he cared naught for her, and said, "Let me never see her face."

So she grew up a bonny girl, though her father never set eyes on her till she was fifteen years old and was ready to be married. But her father said, "Let her marry the first that comes to her." And when this was known, who should be first but a nasty rough old man. So she didn't know what to do, and went to the henwife and asked her advice. The henwife said, "Say you will not take him unless they give you a coat of silver cloth." Well, they gave her a coat of silver cloth, but she wouldn't take him for all that, but went again to the henwife, who said, "Say you will not take him unless they give you a coat of beaten gold." Well, they gave her a coat of beaten gold, but still she would not take him, but went to the henwife, who said, "Say you will not take him unless they give you a coat made of the feathers of all the birds of the air." So they sent a man with a great heap of pease; and the man cried to all the birds of the air, "Each bird take a pea and put down a feather." So each bird took a pea and put down one of its feathers: and they took all the feathers and made a coat of them and gave it to her; but still she would not, but asked the henwife once again, who said, "Say they must first make you a coat of catskin." So they made her a coat of catskin; and she put it on, and tied up her other coats, and ran away into the woods.

So she went along and went along and went along, till she came to the end of the wood, and saw a fine castle. So there she hid her fine dresses, and went up to the castle gates, and asked for work. The lady of the castle saw her, and told her, "I'm sorry I have no better place, but if you like you may be our scullion." So down she went into the kitchen, and they called her Catskin, because of her dress. But the cook was very cruel to her and led her a sad life.

Well, it happened soon after that the young lord of the castle was coming home, and there was to be a grand ball in honour of

the occasion. And when they were speaking about it among the servants, "Dear me, Mrs. Cook," said Catskin, "how much I should like to go."

"What! you dirty impudent slut," said the cook, "you go among all the fine lords and ladies with your filthy catskin? a fine figure you'd cut!" and with that she took a basin of water and dashed it into Catksin's face. But she only briskly shook her ears, and said nothing.

When the day of the ball arrived, Catskin slipped out of the house and went to the edge of the forest where she had hidden her dresses. So she bathed herself in a crystal waterfall, and then put on her coat of silver cloth, and hastened away to the ball. As soon as she entered all were overcome by her beauty and grace, while the young lord at once lost his heart to her. He asked her to be his partner for the first dance, and he would dance with none other the livelong night.

When it came to parting time, the young lord said, "Pray tell me, fair maid, where you live." But Catskin curtsied and said:

"Kind sir, if the truth I must tell,
At the sign of the 'Basin of Water' I
    dwell."

Then she flew from the castle and donned her catskin robe again, and slipped into the scullery again, unbeknown to the cook.

The young lord went the very next day to his mother, the lady of the castle, and declared he would wed none other but the lady of the silver dress, and would never rest till he had found her. So another ball was soon arranged for in hope that the beautiful maid would appear again. So Catskin said to the cook, "Oh, how I should like to go!" Whereupon the cook screamed out in a rage, "What, you, you dirty impudent slut! you would cut a fine figure among all the fine lords and ladies." And with that she up with a ladle and broke it across Catskin's back. But she only shook her ears, and ran off to the forest, where she first of all bathed, and then put on her coat of beaten gold, and off she went to the ball-room.

As soon as she entered all eyes were upon

her; and the young lord recognised her as the lady of the "Basin of Water," and claimed her hand for the first dance, and did not leave her till the last. When that came, he again asked her where she lived. But all that she would say was:

"Kind sir, if the truth I must tell,
At the sign of the 'Broken Ladle' I
   dwell;"

and with that she curtsied, and flew from the ball, off with her golden robe, on with her catskin, and into the scullery without the cook's knowing.

Next day when the young lord could not find where the sign of the "Basin of Water," or of the "Broken Ladle," he begged his mother to have another grand ball, so that he might meet the beautiful maid once more.

All happened as before. Catskin told the cook how much she would like to go to the ball, the cook called her "a dirty slut," and broke the skimmer across her head. But she only shook her ears, and went off to the forest, where she first bathed in the crystal spring, and then donned her coat of feathers, and so off to the ball-room.

When she entered every one was surprised at so beautiful a face and form dressed in so rich and rare a dress; but the young lord soon recognised his beautiful sweetheart, and would dance with none but her the whole evening. When the ball came to an end, he pressed her to tell him where she lived, but all she would answer was:

"Kind sir, if the truth I must tell
At the sign of the 'Broken Skimmer' I
   dwell;"

and with that she curtsied, and was off to the forest. But this time the young lord followed her, and watched her change her fine dress of feathers for her catskin dress, and then he knew her for his own scullery-maid.

Next day he went to his mother, the lady of the castle, and told her that he wished to marry the scullery-maid, Catskin. "Never," said the lady, and rushed from the room.

Well, the young lord was so grieved at that, that he took to his bed and was very ill. The doctor tried to cure him, but he would not take any medicine unless from the hands of Catskin. So the doctor went to the lady of the castle, and told her her son would die if she did not consent to his marriage with Catskin. So she had to give way, and summoned Catskin to her. But she put on her coat of beaten gold, and went to the lady, who soon was glad to wed her son to so beautiful a maid.

Well, so they were married, and after a time a dear little son came to them, and grew up a bonny lad; and one day, when he was four years old, a beggar woman came to the door, so Lady Catskin gave some money to the little lord and told him to go and give it to the beggar woman. So he went and gave it, but put it into the hand of the woman's child, who leant forward and kissed the little lord. Now the wicked old cook—why hadn't she been sent away?—was looking on, so she said, "Only see how beggars' brats take to one another." This insult went to Catskin's heart, so she went to her husband, the young lord, and told him all about her father, and begged he would go and find out what had become of her parents. So they set out in the lord's grand coach, and travelled through the forest till they came to Catskin's father's house, and put up at an inn near, where Catskin stopped, while her husband went to see if her father would own her.

Now her father had never had any other child, and his wife had died; so he was all alone in the world and sat moping and miserable. When the young lord came in he hardly looked up, till he saw a chair close up to him, and asked him, "Pray, sir, had you not once a young daughter whom you would never see or own?"

The old gentlemen said, "It is true; I am a hardened sinner. But I would give all my worldly goods if I could but see her once before I die." Then the young lord told him what had happened to Catskin, and took him to the inn, and brought his father-in-law to his own castle, where they lived happy ever afterwards.

The Little Match Girl

Hans Christian Andersen

Though Hans Christian Andersen wrote this story more than a hundred years ago, the topic, unfortunately, is not outdated today. Children still starve in many parts of the world, and readers young and old will empathize with the neglected child in this tale.

It was so dreadfully cold! It was snowing, and the evening was beginning to darken. It was the last evening of the year, too—New Year's Eve. Through the cold and the dark, a poor little girl with bare head and naked feet was wandering along the road. She had, indeed, had a pair of slippers on when she left home: but what was the good of that! They were very big slippers—her mother had worn them last, they were so big—and the little child had lost them hurrying across the road as two carts rattled dangerously past. One slipper could not be found, and a boy ran off with the other—he said he could use it as a cradle when he had children of his own.

So the little girl wandered along with her naked little feet red and blue with cold. She was carrying a great pile of matches in an apron and she held one bundle in her hand as she walked. No one had bought a thing from her the whole day; no one had given her a halfpenny; hungry and frozen, she went her way, looking so woe-begone, poor little thing! The snow-flakes fell upon her long fair hair that curled so prettily about the nape of her neck, but she certainly wasn't thinking of how nice she looked. Lights were shining from all the windows, and there was a lovely smell of roast goose all down the street, for it was indeed New Year's Eve—yes, and that's what she was thinking about.

Over in a corner between two houses, where one jutted a little farther out into the street than the other, she sat down and huddled together; she had drawn her little legs up under her, but she felt more frozen than ever, and she dared not go home, for she had sold no matches and hadn't got a single penny, and her father would beat her. Besides, it was cold at home, too: there was only the roof over them, and the wind whistled in, although the biggest cracks had been stopped up with straw and rags. Her little hands were almost dead with cold. Ah, a little match might do some good! If she only dared pull one out of the bundle, strike it on the wall, and warm her fingers! She drew one out—Whoosh!—How it spluttered! How it burnt! It gave a warm bright flame, just like a little candle, when she held her hand round it. It was a wonderful light: the little girl thought she was sitting in front of a great iron stove with polished brass knobs and fittings; the fire was burning so cheerfully and its warmth was so comforting—oh, what was that! The little girl had just stretched her feet out to warm them, too, when—the fire went out! The stove disappeared—and she was sitting there with the little stump of a burnt-out match in her hand. Another match was struck; it burnt and flared, and where the light fell upon it, the wall became transparent like gauze; she could see right into the room where the table stood covered with a shining white cloth and set with fine china, and there was a roast goose, stuffed with prunes and apples, steaming deliciously—but what was

From *Hans Andersen's Fairy Tales*, trans. L. W. Kingsland. Illustrated by Ernest H. Shepard. 1959 and 1961, Oxford University Press.

more gorgeous still, the goose jumped off the dish, waddled across the floor with knife and fork in its back, and went straight over to the poor girl. Then the match went out, and there was nothing to see but the thick cold wall.

She struck yet another. And then she was sitting beneath the loveliest Christmas-tree; it was even bigger and more beautifully decorated than the one she had seen this last Christmas through the glass doors of the wealthy grocer's shop. Thousands of candles were burning on its green branches, and gaily coloured pictures, like those that had

decorated the shop-windows, were looking down at her. The little girl stretched out both her hands—and then the match went out; the multitude of Christmas-candles rose higher and higher, and now she saw they were the bright stars—one of them fell and made a long streak of fire across the sky.

'Someone's now dying!' said the little girl, for her old granny, who was the only one that had been kind to her, but who was now dead, had said that when a star falls a soul goes up to God.

Once more she struck a match on the wall. It lit up the darkness round about her, and in its radiance stood old granny, so bright and shining, so wonderfully kind.

'Granny!' cried the little girl. 'Oh, take me with you! I know you'll go away just like the warm stove and the lovely roast goose and the wonderful big Christmas-tree!'—And she hastily struck all the rest of the matches in the bundle, for she wanted to keep her granny there, and the matches shone with such brilliance that it was brighter than daylight. Granny had never before been so tall and beautiful; she lifted the little girl up on her arm, and they flew away in splendour and joy, high, high up towards heaven. And there was no more cold and no more hunger and no more fear—they were with God.

But in the corner by the house, in the cold of the early morning, the little girl sat, with red cheeks and a smile upon her lips—dead, frozen to death on the last evening of the old year. The morning of the New Year rose over the little dead body sitting there with her matches, one bundle nearly all burnt out. She wanted to keep herself warm, they said; but no one knew what beautiful things she had seen, nor in what radiance she had gone with her old granny into the joy of the New Year.

FOLK RHYMES AND POETRY

Folk Rhymes

*In the following rhymes from Luxembourg,
the parents' very absence speaks to the
loneliness of a child whose only friend is a
skip rope.*

> Little rope, little rope, oh, my little rope,
> Unwind yourself from the round ball.
> Twirl round and round and high.
> Take me outdoors to the air and the sun,
> Out of the room, out of the house, the
>   narrow house,
> Nobody can catch us!
> Little rope, little rope, oh my little rope,
> Unwind yourself from the ball.

*The following rhyme was skipped in such a
dangerous neighborhood in Belfast,
Northern Ireland, that we were asked to
pocket a skip rope with red, white, and blue
handles, because parents, watching from
windows, might think we were asking their
children to skip to the colors of the British
flag. The children were skipping to the
traditional rhymes, but the political situation
might have influenced the ones they chose. In
one, for instance, a Belfast boy has decided
to strike out on his own.*

> My mother said
> I never should
> Play with gypsies
> In the wood.
>
> The wood was dark,
> The grass was green.
> In came Sally
> With a tambourine.
>
> I went to the sea—
> No ship to get across.
> I paid ten dollars
> For a blind white horse.

> I was up on his back
> And gone in a crack.
>
> Sally told my mother
> I would never come back.

*The blind horse of the passions will not find
its way at first, but ultimately, the rider,
Reason, will prevail and Sally will get word
back to his mother that her son will never
return to the old emotional dependency.*

*Here is a sad, romantic rhyme from
Belfast—a girl's fear for the well-being of
her lover:*

> The wind, the wind, the wind blows high
> The rain keeps falling from the sky
> _____ thinks she'll die,
> If she doesn't get a man with a rosy eye.
>
> He is handsome, he is pretty.
> He is a lad from Belfast City.
> A knock at the door
> A ring of the bell
> Oh, my true love, are you well?

*Thousands of miles away, in Penang,
Malaysia, where many merchants are
Chinese, there is a popular game a child can
play on a swing.*

> If I swing high and reach the rooftop,
> Before my teeth grow, I can read a book.
> If I swing high and reach the tree top,
> I can buy new clothes at a Chinese shop.

*In a Vietnamese orphanage, ragged nuns
were pounding rotten vegetable scraps on the
ground and mixing them with filthy water
from a nearby vat. This was supper for 400
children. Here, a girl of about 11 was
skipping to a rhyme that she had apparently
made up.*

105

Two animals
Their hearts beat as one,
And now they have made friends
With one another.

*In such an environment as hers, she must
have felt like an animal, and she was
fantasizing closeness to a boy she liked.*

*Each day in Saigon, children were
deposited at the doors of large orphanages
by loving families who could not feed them
and who hoped that the children would find
enough food in the orphanage to subsist.
One little boy made up and tried to skip to
the following rhyme.*

A boy who is thinking about his family
Is going out to sell newspapers
To make some money to help his family.

*Children take a lonely journey toward
maturity. Rites of passage, stages in growth
toward maturity—in this instance, going on a
journey away from home—are worked out
imaginatively and forecast in this rhyme,
which a skipper chanted in Kenya, near the
Tanzanian border.*

Brave Omari!
Made a journey.
Yoho! Yoho!

On the journey
Defeated dangers.
Yoho! Yoho!

Omari's mother
Got the news.
She said, "Brave, my son!"
Yoho! Yoho!

*The youth has passed safely through places
where lions were savagely protecting their
cubs and wildebeests and poisonous snakes
lurked in the overgrowth.*

Lord Ullin's Daughter

Thomas Campbell

*In the early nineteenth century, the ballads
of Thomas Campbell and Sir Walter Scott
were very popular. This sentimental ballad,
"Lord Ullin's Daughter," is great fun
because almost every line of it can be
pantomined, so a family or a class can
perform it. Certain props help—plaid
blankets or kilts as costumes for the
chieftain, the boatman, and the lover, a lace
or net curtain for the head of the lovely
bride, a washtub for a rather tight-fitting
boat for the four of them, and, perhaps, a
broom as an oar, aluminum foil to make
thunder, and white sheets to be raised
gradually higher and higher until the
passengers in the boat are submerged. All
gestures should be elaborate, in nineteenth-
century fashion.*

A chieftain to the Highlands bound,
Cries, "Boatmen, do not tarry!
And I'll give thee a silver pound,
To row us o'er the ferry,"—

"Now who be ye, would cross Lochgyle,
This dark and stormy water!"—
"Oh I'm the chief of Ulva's isle,
And this Lord Ullin's daughter.—

"And fast before her father's men
Three days we've fled together,
For should he find us in the glen,
My blood would stain the heather.

"His horsemen hard behind us ride;
Should they our steps discover,
Then who will cheer my bonny bride
When they have slain her lover?"

From *The Poetical Works of Thomas Campbell* (Philadelphia: J. Crissy & J. Grigg, 1835).

Outspoke the hardy Highland wight,
"I'll go, my chief—I'm ready:—
It is not for your silver bright,
But for your winsome lady:

"And by my word! the bonny bird
In danger shall not tarry;
So, though the waves are raging white,
I'll row you o'er the ferry."

By this the storm grew loud apace,
The water wraith was shrieking;*
And in the scowl of heav'n each face
Grew dark as they were speaking.

But still as wilder blew the wind,
And as the night grew drearer,
Adown the glen rode armed men,
Their trampling sounded nearer.—

"O haste thee, haste!" the lady cries,
"Though tempests round us gather;
I'll meet the raging of the skies:
But not an angry father."

The boat has left a stormy land,
A stormy sea before her,—
When oh! too strong for human hand,
The tempest gathered o'er her.—

And still they rowed amidst the roar
Of waters fast prevailing:
Lord Ullin reached that fatal shore,
His wrath was changed to wailing.—

For sore dismayed, through storm and shade
His child he did discover:
One lovely hand she stretched for aid,
And one was round her lover.

"Come back! come back!" he cried in
  grief,
Across this stormy water:
"And I'll forgive your Highland chief,
My daughter!—oh my daughter!"—

'Twas vain: the loud waves lashed the shore
Return or aid preventing:—
The waters wild went o'er his child—
And he was left lamenting.

We Are Seven

William Wordsworth

*To the little girl in this poem, the family still
consists of seven children, even though two
are dead.*

—A SIMPLE Child,
That lightly draws its breath,
And feels its life in every limb,
What should it know of death?

I met a little cottage Girl:
She was eight years old, she said;
Her hair was thick with many a curl
That clustered round her head.

She had a rustic, woodland air,
And she was wildly clad:
Her eyes were fair, and very fair;
—Her beauty made me glad.

"Sisters and brothers, little Maid,
How many may you be?"
"How many? Seven in all," she said,
And wondering looked at me.

"And where are they? I pray you tell."
She answered, "Seven are we;
And two of us at Conway dwell,
And two are gone to sea.

"Two of us in the church-yard lie,
My sister and my brother;
And, in the church-yard cottage, I
Dwell near them with my mother."

"You say that two at Conway dwell,
And two are gone to sea,
Yet ye are seven!—I pray you tell,
Sweet Maid, how this may be."

Then did the little Maid reply,
"Seven boys and girls are we;
Two of us in the church-yard lie,
Beneath the church-yard tree."

From William Wordsworth, *The Poetical Works of
Wordsworth* (New York: Crowell, 1877).

*The evil spirit of the waters.

"You run about, my little Maid,
Your limbs they are alive;
If two are in the church-yard laid,
Then ye are only five."

"Their graves are green, they may be
    seen,"
The little Maid replied,
"Twelve steps or more from my mother's
    door,
And they are side by side.

"My stockings there I often knit,
My kerchief there I hem;
And there upon the ground I sit,
And sing a song to them.

"And often after sunset, Sir,
When it is light and fair,
I take my little porringer,
And eat my supper there.

"The first that died was sister Jane;
In bed she moaning lay,
Till God released her of her pain;
And then she went away.

"So in the church-yard she was laid;
And, when the grass was dry,
Together round her grave we played,
My brother John and I.

"And when the ground was white with
    snow,
And I could run and slide,
My brother John was forced to go,
And he lies by her side."

"How many are you, then," said I,
"If they two are in heaven?"
Quick was the little Maid's reply,
"O Master! we are seven."

"But they are dead; those two are dead!
Their spirits are in heaven!"
'Twas throwing words away; for still
The little Maid would have her will,
And said, "Nay, we are seven!"

The School Boy

William Blake

*Jean-Jacques Rousseau, an eighteenth-
century French philosopher, had a point in
believing that formal education at an early
age was bad for a child. A repressive
education can stifle a child's imagination.
The child in this poem tries to explain the
danger of such constraints to the parents.
William Blake (1757-1827) is best known for
his mystical poems, which often have a
childlike quality.*

I love to rise in a summer morn
When the birds sing on every tree;
The distant huntsman winds his horn,
And the sky-lark sings with me.
Oh! what sweet company.

But to go to school in a summer
    morn,
O! it drives all joy away;
Under a cruel eye outworn,
The little ones spend the day
In sighing and dismay.

Ah! then at times I drooping sit,
And spend many an anxious hour,
Nor in my book can I take delight,
Nor sit in learning's bower,
Worn thro' with the dreary shower.

How can the bird that is born for joy
Sit in a cage and sing?
How can a child, when fears annoy,
But droop his tender wing,
And forget his youthful spring?

O! father & mother, if buds are nip'd
And blossoms blown away,
And if the tender plants are strip'd
Of their joy in the springing day,
By sorrow and care's dismay,

William Blake, *Songs of Innocence*, 1789.

How shall the summer arise in joy,
Or the summer fruits appear?
Or how shall we gather what griefs destroy,
Or bless the mellowing year,
When the blasts of winter appear?

The Pied Piper of Hamelin

Robert Browning

In this narrative poem, the village of Hamelin is essentially a family, and the adults are responsible for what happens to the children. Bernard Queenan, director of the media center of Concordia University, Montreal, has spent a decade studying the legend on which the poem is based (see "References for Adults"). He theorizes that (1) the Great Plague, engendered by rats, killed off all the children; or (2) the children were part of the hundreds who joined the Children's Crusade and were sold into slavery in North America; or (3) the children danced away because of the "dancing madness," a disease stemming from ergot, a fungus that grows in improperly stored grain and persists in fresh-baked bread; or (4) the "piper" was an immigration agent sent by Rudolph von Hapsburg to round up the children while their parents worked in the fields and to disperse the children by promising them "pie in the sky" if they left immediately; or (5) the children were actually teenagers who went on a military expedition and all were killed.

I

Hamelin Town's in Brunswick,
By famous Hanover city;
  The river Weser, deep and wide,
  Washes its wall on the southern side;
  A pleasanter spot you never spied;
But, when begins my ditty,
  Almost five hundred years ago,
  To see the townsfolk suffer so
    From vermin, was a pity.

II

Rats!
They fought the dogs and killed the cats,
  And bit the babies in the cradles,
And ate the cheese out of the vats,
  And licked the soup from the cooks'
    own ladles,
Split open the kegs of salted sprats,
Made nests inside men's Sunday hats,
And even spoiled the women's chats
  By drowning their speaking
  With shrieking and squeaking
In fifty different sharps and flats.

III

At last the people in a body
  To the Town Hall came flocking:
" 'T is clear," cried they, "our Mayor's a
  noddy;
  And as for our Corporation—shocking
To think we buy gowns lined with ermine
For dolts that can't or won't determine
What's best to rid us of our vermin!
You hope, because you're old and obese,
To find in the furry civic robe ease?
Rouse up, sirs! Give your brains a racking
To find the remedy we're lacking,
Or, sure as fate, we'll send you packing!"
At this the Mayor and Corporation
Quaked with a mighty consternation.

IV

An hour they sat in council;
  At length the Mayor broke silence:
"For a guilder I'd my ermine gown sell,
  I wish I were a mile hence!
It's easy to bid one rack one's brain—
I'm sure my poor head aches again,
I've scratched it so, and all in vain.
Oh for a trap, a trap, a trap!"
Just as he said this, what should hap
At the chamber-door but a gentle tap?
"Bless us," cried the Mayor, "what's
    that?"
(With the Corporation as he sat,
Looking little though wondrous fat;
Nor brighter was his eye, nor moister

From *The Complete Poetic and Dramatic Works of Robert Browning* (Boston: Houghton Mifflin, 1896).

Than a too-long-opened oyster,
Save when at noon his paunch grew
        mutinous
For a plate of turtle green and glutinous)
"Only a scraping of shoes on the mat?
Anything like the sound of a rat
Makes my heart go pit-a-pat!"

V

"Come in!"—the Mayor cried, looking
        bigger:
And in did come the strangest figure!
His queer long coat from heel to head
Was half of yellow and half of red,
And he himself was tall and thin,
With sharp blue eyes, each like a pin,
And light loose hair, yet swarthy skin,
No tuft on cheek nor beard on chin,
But lips where smiles went out and in;
There was no guessing his kith and kin:
And nobody could enough admire
The tall man and his quaint attire.
Quoth one: "It's as my great-grandsire
Starting up at the Trump of Doom's tone,
Had walked this way from his painted
        tombstone!"

VI

He advanced to the council-table: And,
"Please your honors," said he, "I'm able,
By means of a secret charm, to draw
All creatures living beneath the sun,
That creep or swim or fly or run,
After me so as you never saw!
And I chiefly use my charm
On creatures that do people harm,
The mole and toad and newt and viper;
And people call me the Pied Piper."
(And here they noticed round his neck
A scarf of red and yellow stripe,
To match with his coat of the self-same
        cheque;
And at the scarf's end hung a pipe;
And his fingers, they noticed, were ever
        straying
As if impatient to be playing
Upon this pipe, as low it dangled
Over his vesture so old-fangled.)
"Yet," said he, "poor piper as I am,

In Tartary I freed the Cham,
Last June, from his huge swarms of gnats;
I eased in Asia the Nizam
Of a monstrous brood of vampire-bats:
And as for what your brain bewilders,
If I can rid your town of rats
Will you give me a thousand guilders?"
"One? fifty thousand!"—was the
        exclamation
Of the astonished Mayor and Corporation.

VII

Into the street the Piper stept,
    Smiling first a little smile,
As if he knew what magic slept
    In his quiet pipe the while;
Then, like a musical adept,
To blow the pipe his lips he wrinkled,
And green and blue his sharp eyes twinkled
Like a candle-flame where salt is sprinkled;
And ere three shrill notes the pipe uttered,
You heard as if an army muttered;
And the muttering grew to a grumbling;
And the grumbling grew to a mighty
        rumbling;
And out of the houses the rats came
        tumbling.
Great rats, small rats, lean rats, brawny
        rats,
Brown rats, black rats, gray rats, tawny
        rats.
Grave old plodders, gay young friskers,
    Fathers, mothers, uncles, cousins,
Cocking tails and pricking whiskers,
    Families by tens and dozens,
Brothers, sisters, husbands, wives—
Followed the Piper for their lives.
From street to street he piped advancing,
And step for step they followed dancing,
Until they came to the river Weser,
Wherein all plunged and perished!
—Save one who, stout as Julius Caesar,
Swam across and lived to carry
(As he, the manuscript he cherished)
To Rat-land home his commentary:
Which was, "At the first shrill notes of
        the pipe,
I heard a sound as of scraping tripe,
And putting apples, wondrous ripe,
Into a cider-press's gripe:

And a moving away of pickle-tub-boards,
And a leaving ajar of conserve-cupboards,
And a drawing the corks of train-oil-flasks,
And a breaking the hoops of butter-casks:
And it seemed as if a voice
(Sweeter far than by harp or by psaltery
Is breathed) called out, 'Oh rats, rejoice!
The world is grown to one vast drysaltery!
So munch on, crunch on, take your
        nuncheon,
Breakfast, supper, dinner, luncheon!'
And just as a bulky sugar-puncheon,
All ready staved, like a great sun shone
Glorious scarce an inch before me,
Just as methought it said, 'Come, bore
        me!'
—I found the Weser rolling o'er me.''

VIII

You should have heard the Hamelin people
Ringing the bells till they rocked the
        steeple.
"Go,'' cried the Mayor, "and get long
        poles,
Poke out the nests and block up the holes!
Consult with carpenters and builders,
And leave in our town not even a trace
Of the rats!''—when suddenly, up the face
Of the Piper perked in the market-place,
With a, "First, if you please, my
        thousand guilders!''

IX

A thousand guilders! The Mayor looked
        blue;
So did the Corporation too.
For council dinners made rare havoc
With Claret, Moselle, Vin-de-Grave, Hock;
And half the money would replenish
Their cellar's biggest butt with Rhenish.
To pay this sum to a wandering fellow
With a gypsy coat of red and yellow!
"Beside,'' quoth the Mayor with a
        knowing wink,
"Our business was done at the river's brink;
We saw with our eyes the vermin sink,
And what's dead can't come to life, I think.
So, friend, we're not the folks to shrink
From the duty of giving you something
        for drink,

And a matter of money to put in your poke;
But as for the guilders, what we spoke
Of them, as you very well know, was in
        joke.
Beside, our losses have made us thrifty.
A thousand guilders! Come, take fifty!''

X

The Piper's face fell, and he cried,
"No trifling! I can't wait, beside!
I've promised to visit by dinner time
Bagdat, and accept the prime
Of the Head-Cook's pottage, all he's rich
        in,
For having left, in the Caliph's kitchen,
Of a nest of scorpions no survivor:
With him I proved no bargain-driver
With you, don't think I'll bate a stiver!
And folks who put me in a passion
May find me pipe after another fashion.''

XI

"How?'' cried the Mayor, "d'ye think I
        brook
Being worse treated than a Cook?
Insulted by a lazy ribald
With idle pipe and vesture piebald?
You threaten us, fellow? Do your worst,
Blow your pipe there till you burst!''

XII

Once more he stept into the street,
        And to his lips again
Laid his long pipe of smooth straight cane;
        And ere he blew three notes (such sweet
Soft notes as yet musician's cunning
        Never gave the enraptured air)
There was a rustling that seemed like a
        bustling
Of merry crowds justling at pitching and
        hustling;
Small feet were pattering, wooden shoes
        clattering,
Little hands clapping and little tongues
        chattering,
And, like fowls in a farm-yard when
        barley is scattering,
Out came the children running.
All the little boys and girls,
With rosy cheeks and flaxen curls,

And sparkling eyes and teeth like pearls,
Tripping and skipping, ran merrily after
The wonderful music with shouting and
    laughter.

XIII

The Mayor was dumb, and the Council
    stood
As if they were changed into blocks of
    wood,
Unable to move a step, or cry
To the children merrily skipping by,
—Could only follow with the eye
That joyous crowd at the Piper's back.
But how the Mayor was on the rack,
And the wretched Council's bosoms beat,
As the Piper turned from the High Street
To where the Weser rolled its waters
Right in the way of their sons and
    daughters!
However, he turned from South to West,
And to Koppelberg Hill his steps addressed,
And after him the children pressed;
Great was the joy in every breast.
"He never can cross that mighty top!
He's forced to let the piping drop,
And we shall see our children stop!"
When, lo, as they reached the mountain-
    side,
A wondrous portal opened wide,
As if a cavern was suddenly hollowed;
And the Piper advanced and the children
    followed,
And when all were in to the very last,
The door in the mountain-side shut fast.
Did I say, all? No! One was lame,
And could not dance the whole of the way;
And in after years, if you would blame
His sadness, he was used to say,—
"It's dull in our town since my playmates
    left!
I can't forget that I'm bereft
Of all the pleasant sights they see,
Which the Piper also promised me.
For he led us, he said, to a joyous land,
Joining the town and just at hand,
Where waters gushed and fruit-trees grew
And flowers put forth a fairer hue,
And everything was strange and new;

The sparrows were brighter than peacocks
    here,
And their dogs outran our fallow deer,
And honey-bees had lost their stings,
And horses were born with eagle's wings:
And just as I became assured
My lame foot would be speedily cured,
The music stopped and I stood still,
And found myself outside the hill,
Left alone against my will,
To go now limping as before,
And never hear of that country more!''

XIV

Alas, alas for Hamelin!
  There came into many a burgher's pate
  A text which says that heaven's gate
  Opes to the rich at as easy rate
As the needle's eye takes a camel in!
The Mayor sent East, West, North and
    South,
To offer the Piper, by word of mouth,
  Wherever it was men's lot to find him,
Silver and gold to his heart's content,
If he'd only return the way he went,
  And bring the children behind him.
But when they saw 'twas a lost endeavor,
And Piper and dancers were gone forever,
They made a decree that lawyers never
  Should think their records dated duly
If, after the day of the month and year,
These words did not as well appear,
"And so long after what happened here
  On the Twenty-second of July,
Thirteen hundred and seventy-six:"
And the better in memory to fix
The place of the children's last retreat,
They called it, the Pied Piper's Street—
Where any one playing on pipe or tabor
Was sure for the future to lose his labor.
Nor suffered they hostelry or tavern
  To shock with mirth a street so solemn;
But opposite the place of the cavern
  They wrote the story on a column.
And on the great church-window painted
The same, to make the world acquainted
How their children were stolen away,
And there it stands to this very day.
And I must not omit to say

That in Transylvania there's a tribe
Of alien people who ascribe
The outlandish ways of dress
On which their neighbors lay such stress,
To their fathers and mothers having risen
Out of some subterranean prison
Into which they were trepanned
Long time ago in a mighty band
Out of Hamelin town in Brunswick land,
But how or why, they don't understand.

XV

So, Willy, let me and you be wipers
Of scores out with all men—especially
    pipers!
And, whether they pipe us free from rats
    or from mice,
If we've promised them aught, let us keep
    our promise!

In School-Days

John Greenleaf Whittier

*In this poem by Whittier, a Quaker
abolitionist, the school is a family for the
little boy and girl, who are in love. At the
time this poem was written, girls were
trained to downplay their own intelligence,
to defer to the male sex. The little girl
regrets that she has not done so.*

Still sits the school-house by the road,
  A ragged beggar sleeping;
Around it still the sumachs grow,
  And blackberry-vines are creeping.

Within, the master's desk is seen,
  Deep scarred by raps official;
The warping floor, the battered seats,
  The jack-knife's carved initial;

The charcoal frescoes on its wall;
  Its door's worn sill, betraying
The feet that, creeping slow to school,
  Went storming out to playing!

Long years ago a winter sun
  Shone over it at setting;
Lit up its western window-panes,
  And low eaves' icy fretting.

It touched the tangled golden curls,
  And brown eyes full of grieving,
Of one who still her steps delayed
  When all the school were leaving.

For near her stood the little boy
  Her childish favor singled:
His cap pulled low upon a face
  Where pride and shame were mingled.

Pushing with restless feet the snow
  To right and left, he lingered;—
As restlessly her tiny hands
  The blue-checked apron fingered.

He saw her lift her eyes; he felt
  The soft hand's light caressing,
And heard the tremble of her voice,
  As if a fault confessing.

"I'm sorry that I spelt the word:
  I hate to go above you,
Because,"—the brown eyes lower fell,—
  "Because, you see, I love you!"

Still memory to a gray-haired man
  That sweet child-face is showing.
Dear girl! the grasses on her grave
  Have forty years been growing!

He lives to learn, in life's hard school,
  How few who pass above him
Lament their triumph and his loss,
  Like her,—because they love him.

From *The Complete Poetical Works of John Greenleaf Whittier* (Boston: Houghton Mifflin, 1904).

FICTION

Muddy Duddy

Brother Blue (Dr. Hugh Morgan Hill)

Brother Blue is a famous black American storyteller and actor. He has appeared on stage as Gower in Shakespeare's Pericles, *and as Merlin in a film about a modern-day King Arthur. He has told stories to audiences all over the world— sidewalk gatherings, university classes, convicts in prison. His stories are often poignant, with hidden meanings that surface toward the end with powerful impact. An article, by John Cech, frequently praised by critics is about Brother Blue's career. It appears in* Reflections on Literature for Children *(Library Professional Publications, 1984).*

Once upon a muddy day, in the muddy month of May, a boy was born. Everybody called him Muddy Duddy because he was the color of mud and he loved to play in the mud. He thought mud was beautiful. He always had mud on his fingers, mud on his ways had mud on his fingers, mud on his toes, mud on his nose, on his clothes—he was a study in muddy.

Muddy Duddy was alone most of the time. His only friends were the mud and an earthworm called Muddy Buddy. They played in the mud together. Muddy Duddy

This is an abbreviated version of a much longer original unpublished story by Dr. Hugh Morgan Hill ("Brother Blue"), storyteller.

used his fingers to plant sweet seeds in the mud. And everything he planted grew.

Muddy Duddy went to school, but all he really liked to do was play in the mud. Once, on the way to school he filled his pockets with dust. The clouds gathered over him, and the rain came, and the dust turned to mud. And Muddy Duddy leaped and danced with joy. He opened his mouth and drank the rain. When he got to school, he took off his shoes and stockings, put mud on his toes and danced. Then he began to fingerpaint with the mud. The teacher sent him home with a note to his Mamma. His Mamma sent him to bed with no supper.

The next day Muddy Duddy made a mouse out of mud and put it on his pillow. But his Mamma say, "Take that mud mouse out of the house." Mammas don't like mouses in their houses. She shooed Muddy Duddy outside and he lay down on the ground with the mud mouse, and listened to the sounds the earth made.

Muddy Duddy made a bird out of mud one morning, and the bird began to sing. The people were astonished. He made many birds of mud for the people, and everyone could hear them sing. Muddy Duddy became famous.

Then his Mamma died. He stood by his Mamma's grave. The minister said, "Dust to dust," Muddy Duddy's tears fell and mixed with the dust, and it became "mud to mud."

Then Muddy Duddy died, and joined the greatest Muddy Duddy of them all, the one who made the mud and the stars. And Muddy Duddy played and sang in the earth with his friend Muddy Buddy the earthworm.

The people all knelt down and listened to the music coming from the ground. They named their village Mud Town. They had found out the ground is holy.

We are all dust and when the rain falls, it's mud to mud. Once we're in the ground, we all become the color of earth. God made the ground, Muddy Duddy, the earthworm, and all the muddy mystery of the stars.

The earth is holy. There's no such thing as "common" ground; it's sacred, though it's all around.

Homecoming

Cynthia Voigt

Dicey, 13 years old, has a premonition that something is wrong when her mother, out of work and deserted by her husband, has the four children, Dicey, her sister, and her two brothers, pack in the middle of the night to go to a new home. Momma leaves them in a parked car in a shopping center. They are abandoned. Then Dicey takes over and she and her brothers and sister go on a journey in search of a home.

The motor rumbled like hunger in the belly of the bus. The fumes that floated in through the open windows were swollen with heat. They were on their way. Again.

Dicey leaned back in her seat and tried to make herself relax. They had until evening, when Cousin Eunice got home. Unless the camps wondered why all the Tillermans were absent and called Cousin Eunice at work. She didn't think that was likely.

James leaned towards Dicey. They were the only people sitting in the back of the bus.

From Cynthia Voigt, *Homecoming* (New York: Atheneum, 1981).

Nobody would hear them over the sound of the motor.

"It's like a prison break, isn't it?"

Dicey knew what he meant. Even so, "That's not fair," she said. "Cousin Eunice wasn't a jailer."

James shrugged. "Whadda you think?" he asked out of the corner of his mouth. "I think, if we can get to New York without being caught—we'll be home free."

Home, Dicey thought. She remembered the inscription on the tombstone: *Home is the sailor, home is the hunter.* Until she died, Dicey wouldn't expect any place to be home. Home was with Momma—and Momma was in a hospital where the doctors said she'd always stay. There could be no home for the Tillermans. Home free—Dicey would settle for a place to stay. Stay free.

Cousin Eunice's house wasn't free; it was expensive. The price was always remembering to be grateful. And there was danger to Sammy and Maybeth, of being sent to foster homes or special schools; danger to Dicey and James of forgetting and saying what they thought before wondering if it would sound ungrateful. At Cousin Eunice's house, they were kept busy so they wouldn't be a bother, couldn't get in trouble.

Dicey had lowered her sights. She no longer hoped for a home. Now she wanted only a place where the Tillermans could be themselves and do what was good for them. Home was out of the question. Stay might be possible, if this grandmother could be persuaded. . . .

Dicey stopped thinking. She wanted to keep it simple. Get to Crisfield and see, that was her plan. That was all of it.

"Anyway, they know where we're going." Dicey told James.

"How could they know that?"

"I said so in the note I left."

"Dicey! Why'd you do that?"

"I don't think it would be fair to leave her to worry."

"She'll worry anyway. She likes worrying."

"I can't help that, James. I can't help what she's like. I can only help what I'm like."

"You've ruined it," James went on. "We can't be running away if they know where we're going."

"We're not running away—we never were running away," Dicey said. "We're just going to see."

James shook his head. "I'm running away. Before—we were always the ones who were run away from. This time I want us to do it. What's your plan?"

Dicey didn't answer.

The road flowed under the wheels. They were back on Route 1. Maybe it was her doom, always to get back on Route 1. She squeezed Maybeth's fingers. "Maybeth? What's the matter? You scared?"

Maybeth looked at Dicey and nodded.

"So am I, a little," Dicey said. "We'll just wait and see. That's all we can do."

"I don't want to go back." Maybeth spoke in a small voice.

"I thought you liked it," Dicey said. "The church, the pretty dress you wore there, all the attention."

"I did," Maybeth said.

Dicey decided to tell the truth, now. "We might have to go back. Do you know that?"

Maybeth nodded.

Well, Dicey thought. She had underestimated Maybeth. She'd been fooled, like the nuns were fooled and Maybeth's teachers. She'd been fooled into thinking Maybeth wasn't who she knew Maybeth was.

"Look, Maybeth," Dicey said, "if we do have to go back I'll go with you to church, and we'll both talk to the nuns. To Sister Berenice. I won't leave you alone so much."

Maybeth smiled, a tenuous little smile, and turned back to the window.

Smog made the air seem thick, like light, yellowed fog. In the heavy traffic the bus stopped and started, stopped and started. Buildings soared up higher than Dicey could see out the window. She twisted her head down to see their tops.

The bus turned onto a new street and headed east. Dicey felt as if they were in a maze and would never make their way out. Cars honked. Lights changed. They traveled down a narrow channel over which other roads crossed on high bridges. All the traffic, all the people, the tall buildings—Dicey felt scared, and exhilarated. There was so much life, all here in one place, teeming, whirling about her. More than at the crowded summer beaches in Provincetown. It was like a pot of vegetable soup boiling on a stove, everything moving. A restlessness and excitement came into Dicey with the air she breathed. Anything can happen, she thought.

At last the bus turned off into a huge warehouse. It followed a ramp, up and around, then fitted itself into a slot before a wall of glass doors. It became one of a row of buses.

The Tillermans stood up. Dicey led them to the front of the bus and down the steps, one after another, onto the sidewalk before the doors. Everyone was hurrying. Everyone acted as if he or she or they knew exactly where to go.

"What now Dicey?" asked James.

"An information booth," she answered briskly. "Then bathrooms, and maybe something to eat."

They entered a huge, hollow hall lined with benches and ticket windows. Emptiness hung high over their heads although the room was crowded with people. The information booth was in the center of this hall. Dicey stationed her family by a water fountain and went up to stand in line.

When her turn finally came, she couldn't think straight. The girl behind the glass window spoke without looking at Dicey: "Next? Little boy?"

Dicey gulped. "When's the next bus to Wilmington, Delaware?"

Without speaking, the girl handed her a schedule.

"Where are the bathrooms?" Dicey asked.

"Lower level, on the street side."

"Where can I buy a ticket?"

"Upper level, any window with a yellow or green light."

Dicey fled, dragging her suitcase.

"She thought I was a boy," she said to James.

"So did Louis and Edie," he answered.

Dicey put the suitcase down and opened the schedule. They had forty minutes to wait. She would play it safe. "OK, listen James. Take this money"—she gave him a ten dollar bill—"and go get two tickets for Wilmington. That ticket window over there with a green light.

"Why not four?"

"Just in case," Dicey answered. "Two and two is not the same as four."

James looked at her.

"Not in this case," Dicey said. "In this case, it is but it isn't."

"You can say so," James said. "And I'll do it. And I see what you mean. But you're wrong. Two and two is always four."

When they had all four tickets, Dicey started walking along the concourse. She found the escalators leading down. "Now we go to the bathroom."

The women's room could have held Cousin Eunice's house in it and had room to spare. Lines of women waited before each closed door, old, young, medium, some alone, some with friends, some with children, one with a tiny baby that rode in a pouch on her chest. The air smelled of perfume and cleanser. Maybeth and Dicey entered the cubicle together, because Maybeth didn't want to go in alone. Dicey protested, "But you're nine." Maybeth just shook her head.

They took turns, Maybeth first. Dicey set the suitcase on the floor and opened it. She took out shorts and a shirt for Maybeth and her shoebox of money. She put twenty more dollars in her pocket. As they left the room, they tossed Maybeth's rolled-up dress into the trash.

When they emerged from the women's room, Dicey could not see James and Sammy. People hurried past, some carrying suitcases, some shopping bags, some just purses or newspapers. You could get lost here in this crowded station. You could get swept away. Or grabbed by somebody.

"Maybeth? If we get separated—" Maybeth caught Dicey's free hand. "Just in case," Dicey said. "We'll meet back by that information booth I went to first. Remember it?"

James and Sammy joined them. They had a hot dog apiece, standing up at a counter, and a glass of orange drink. Dicey looked at a clock—only ten minutes until the bus left. The air hummed with voices, distant motors, and the muffled droning of the loud-speaker announcing what buses were leaving for what cities. If they could get on the bus all right, and out of the city, then they were on their way. And they might make it.

James and Sammy went onto the bus first. Dicey dawdled by the gate, with Maybeth beside her. Maybeth went first up into the bus. Dicey followed, pulling their two tickets out of her pocket and handing them to the driver.

He looked at her with a grimace. "What is this, kids' day out?"

Dicey tried to look as if she didn't know what he was talking about.

"Never mind. But I'll tell you what I told them. We've got a long drive and I don't stand any horsing around."

"We won't," she said.

"I know, I know. You're angels from heaven. Go on back."

After a few minutes, the driver closed the door and turned on the engine. He backed out of the parking slot. With every turn of the wheel, Dicey felt her stomach loosen and her muscles relax. By the time the bus entered a tunnel, a smile was beginning to turn up the corners of her mouth. She felt her back relaxing into the back of the seat. Beside her, Maybeth hummed softly. The bus zoomed out of the tunnel and into the light. Dicey stretched, smiled, yawned—and fell asleep.

When Dicey opened her eyes, she saw the sleek, straight lines of the rectangular interior of the bus. Out the windows, on both sides, lay farmlands. Fields of corn ripened under a bright sun. The corn swayed in the wind, like dancers with scarves.

Dicey wasn't tired any more. She was relaxed inside and out. She felt lazy and unworried. The bus rolled along.

It was as if, during that nap, Dicey had traveled days away from Cousin Eunice's house in Bridgeport. That time now felt like a distant memory, something so far behind them that they didn't have to concern themselves with it, not any more.

She looked past Maybeth's head, out the window. Fields, farmhouses, trees, sky with clouds; her eyes roamed lazily over them all. Her thoughts roamed lazily too, over memories and ideas. She rode outside of time and place.

She thought about Momma, and it seemed

to her that she almost understood why all of this had happened to them, to the Tillermans, all this sadness and running away. She thought about the long walk from Peewauket to New Haven, and the grandfather who had tipped them two dollars and Stewart with his blue-gray eyes; then her mind switched to the journey ahead of them, as if the future were a road stretching ahead, twisting and turning. What did it matter where they were going, as long as they were going?

Sammy was asleep on James' shoulder. Dicey leaned over to ask softly where they were. James told her the last stop had been Trenton.

Dicey took a map out of her suitcase. She unfolded it halfway, to show Wilmington and the Chesapeake Bay. Beneath her, the wheels rumbled on the road.

Sammy woke up. He punched James. James hit him back. Dicey quelled them with a glance and instructed them to play odds-and-evens while she thought. "But I'm hungry," Sammy argued.

"I can't do anything about that," Dicey answered.

"Why not?"

"Because I'm not a hot dog tree," Dicey said.

"Why not?"

"Because if I were, then you'd be one too because you're my brother. Only you'd be a pickle tree," Dicey said, turning back to her map. "Pickle tree," Sammy repeated, trying to repress his giggles, not wanting to laugh at Dicey's joke.

Dicey studied the map. Just below Wilmington, the Chesapeake Bay drove up like a wedge between two sections of land. The eastern shore of Maryland, where Crisfield was, was on the land between the Bay and the ocean. It looked about two hundred miles from Wilmington to Crisfield. So it might be a lot farther. Maybe as much as thirty days of walking. Too far. But there were some cities that must have buses running to them: Salisbury, Cambridge, Easton.

They'd already spent too much on bus tickets. Money was always the problem. Dicey wanted to have money left over, so they could get back to Bridgeport, if they had to. She figured they'd have to walk part of the way anyway, and she wanted to have some tools for camping. A jackknife, one with a can opener on it. A pan of some kind. Ponchos, for when it rained. She let her mind wander on briefly to other things, to a backpack and bedrolls, to a portable stove. No, those would be silly but fishing line and hooks would be useful. There was a lot of water around, so there must be fishing.

They had another choice: they could go down the western shore, to Baltimore or Annapolis—it would have to be Annapolis because that was near the only bridge over the Bay. That would leave them about half of the distance to Crisfield still to cover. Maybe two weeks of walking.

They would have to get over the bridge if they did that. The map said Toll Bridge, so they probably couldn't walk over it. They might hitchhike, but Dicey didn't like that idea. She didn't like being in somebody's car and not able to run away. Besides, who would pick up four kids. They might have to take another bus.

Definitely, then, the eastern shore was better. At Wilmington they would get on a bus going south. How far they went would depend on how much it cost. That was easy enough. She folded up the map and returned it to her suitcase.

The bus made its way through Philadelphia and then south through more farmland, more small cities. After another hour, after a bridge like a section of roller coaster, they came into Wilmington.

The Wilmington Bus Depot was a one-story building, a single room with wooden benches, a lunch counter, lockers where you could store your suitcases, six windows where tickets could be purchased and at its center an information booth with a clock on top of it. Three forty-five. Dicey told James to stay with Maybeth and Sammy by the door. Only one bus stood waiting, now that the one they had ridden on had gone on to Baltimore. That bus, she saw by the sign above its front window, was going to Annapolis.

Inside, Dicey picked out a schedule from the assortment at the information booth. The first thing she did was to see if Crisfield was there, at the bottom of the list of towns. It

was. After Salisbury, Eden and Princess Anne, came Crisfield.

Her eye went back up to the top of the list, found Wilmington and traced the buses leaving for the eastern shore. There were several, but most went no further than Cambridge. Only one went down to Crisfield, a morning bus.

Then Dicey saw that the last afternoon bus heading south to Cambridge left Wilmington at two-thirty. The only bus after that didn't leave until nine at night.

Nine. By nine, Cousin Eunice would have been home for almost three hours. By nine, she could call Father Joseph. By nine, they might be able to trace the Tillermans, and maybe find them, and stop them. She didn't know Dicey had money, did she? She might think the Tillermans were walking. But Dicey couldn't count on that. She couldn't count on anything. She rushed up to the information booth and asked when the bus for Annapolis was leaving. The man put his hand over the microphone and told her, "Five minutes."

Five minutes, how could she think it through in five minutes? Dicey hurried over to a ticket window and bought four tickets to Annapolis. They couldn't just sit around the bus station for five hours, waiting to be recognized. Cousin Eunice would have to do something to find them; she would think it was her responsibility.

Dicey joined her family. "We missed the last bus until nine."

"Tonight? We better stay here," James said.

"No," Dicey said. "We can't. We'll go to Annapolis. It's the only bus."

"But Dicey—"

"Do as I say James."

She wasn't thinking, she knew that. She wasn't thinking clearly. She hurried her family onto the bus just as the driver was closing the door. They sat at the back. Dicey chewed on her lip.

"Nobody will expect us to go to Annapolis," James said. "It was good luck that we missed the bus."

"I don't know about that," Dicey said.

The bus left Wilmington and headed south. This bus was air conditioned, and you couldn't open the windows. The windows were smeared with grime, so you couldn't see out. The hour and a half to Baltimore seemed endless. At Baltimore, a lot of dressed-up people got on, commuters, Dicey guessed, going home from work. The bus grew crowded.

The circuitous route from Baltimore to Annapolis, where they kept getting on and off the same road to stop at little huts by the road and let off passengers, took another hour and a half. Dicey tried to control her impatience by reminding herself that if they had been walking it would have taken days and days. This was slow, but it was faster than walking. They'd be walking soon enough.

At last, the bus turned into a parking lot before a low brick building. The bus driver turned around and called, "Annapolis. End of the line."

The Tillermans hopped up and joined the few people waiting to get off the bus. Dicey just followed in the direction the majority took, turning left down a sidewalk, away from the bus station. Behind her, the sun lowered, so they were walking on their own shadows, heading east.

"Where we going?"

"We'll find a place to sit down and think," Dicey said. "I'm looking for a park."

They passed a drugstore and a finance company and three banks. They saw bookshops and card stores, clothing stores and a wine-and-cheese store. The road they walked along came up to a traffic circle. Cars and trucks whirled around it, circling a church that stood at its center.

Dicey led them around the circle. Streets led off, but none promised to go to a park, although one said it went to the hospital. At the top of one street, Dicey looked down and saw blue water with sails on it. She stood, staring.

It looked like the painted backdrop to a movie, not like anything real. The long main street went downhill and then fetched up at the water. On the blue water, boats sailed or motored as if they were in an entirely different world, and it wasn't clear, in the bright August light, where water ended and sky began.

They headed down the hill to the water, passing stores and shops and more banks. The street was crowded: parked cars lined both sides, while moving vehicles crawled bumper to bumper uphill and the sidewalks were crowded with people. At the foot of the street was another circle, around which cars traveled slowly, with a steady chorus of horns and many near collisions. Across this circle, a quiet finger of water, hemmed in by concrete, marked the corner of a narrow area where people thronged, eating, talking, sitting and watching one another. Dicey moved through the milling crowd and along beside the water. They passed boats crowded as closely together as the cars in a parking lot, motor boats, sailboats and old, worn fishing boats.

At the waterfront, beyond a huge parking lot jammed with cars, they found a public park. It had no grass, just trees in wooden boxes. The ground was covered by wooden flooring. Benches, however, there were in plenty. The benches right at the water were all full, but one beneath a sparsely leaved young tree was empty. The Tillermans sat on that.

"It's hot," James said. His face was red. Sweat plastered his hair to his neck. The air hung moist and heavy over the park. A slight ripple of a breeze came off the water, but that did little to relieve them. Everybody seemed slowed down by heat. Nobody walked briskly, everybody sauntered. A lot of people were licking ice cream cones. Dicey's mouth watered.

"What time's it?" James asked. Without waiting for an answer, he hopped up and asked the same question of a man moving by, who held his suit jacket over his shoulder. "It's seven-thirty," James reported. "Time for supper."

"How about ice cream for supper?" Dicey asked. She didn't know just how much money she had in her pocket, not enough for a real dinner.

"We passed a hamburger joint," James countered.

"Ice cream," Sammy said.

"Hamburgers," James said.

Sammy stuck his jaw out.

"Ice cream's cheaper," Dicey said. "Double dip?"

"Can I have seconds?" James asked.

"We'll see how hungry you are," Dicey said.

James agreed.

"But first I've got to figure out a couple of things, OK?"

"Like what?" James asked.

"Like where to sleep, and how to find an Army-Navy surplus store. And how to get across the bay."

"Get across the bay? Why?"

Dicey pulled out the map again and showed him where they were. Then she pointed out Crisfield.

"Oh, Dicey. What are we doing on this side?"

"I told you, we missed the last bus."

"Yeah but—" James caught a glimpse of Dicey's face and stopped speaking.

"I know. I know. But if we can just get across, we'll be much nearer."

"How can we do that? OK, we're here. We need a place to sleep tonight, right?"

"I guess. The Army-Navy store will be closed, wherever it is."

"If there is one."

"I'm sorry, James," Dicey said. "I panicked. When I found out we'd missed the last bus—"

"It's OK, Dicey. I just thought you had it all planned."

"I did. For me to go."

"Are you angry at us?" Sammy asked this. It sounded like the beginning of a quarrel.

"No. Well, yes, a little, but that doesn't matter. I'd rather be all together. Really, I would. I'm just confused still because I didn't have any plan for all of us. Can you understand that?"

Sammy didn't answer.

"I was going to come back," Dicey said to him.

He looked at her, with the question in his hazel eyes. "Really?"

"Really. Really and truly. Don't you trust me, Sammy?"

"You said you didn't trust anyone."

"I didn't mean any of us. I didn't mean you. Would you leave me behind? Or James or Maybeth?"

"No!"

"Well I wouldn't leave you, either. I feel the same way."

"But you were going to leave us behind," Sammy said stubbornly. Dicey sighed.

They rose to find the ice cream store. James got a double-dip chocolate nut cone, explaining that nuts and chocolate were both rich and filling. Dicey got a scoop of chocolate and a scoop of butter almond. She noticed a pile of maps of Annapolis on the counter top and took one. Maybeth wanted pink sherbet and green, but Dicey told her to get real ice cream because of the milk. She chose two scoops of strawberry. Sammy asked for strawberry ripple ice cream topped with peanut butter ice cream. "Ugh," Dicey said, listening to his order. He grinned at her.

They sat at a small table to eat. The ice cream tasted rich and smooth and cold. You could tell that it was made from real cream, it was that rich. Dicey studied her map while her tongue made valleys in the ice cream and then smoothed them out. The cone was crunchy and sweet.

"There's a college," Dicey said. "Let's try that, OK?"

James had a single-dip cone for seconds, another scoop of chocolate-nut. They walked out and onto the crowded sidewalk. What were all these people doing? It was like a carnival.

The college lay in summer twilight, set back from the road by a long, sloping lawn. It was brick and very old. Everything looked old about it, old and tended, the smooth brick sidewalks, the many-paned windows, the little dome on top of the main building. It had trees—huge, tall trees, with branches too high for climbing—all about on its lawn. There were plenty of people. Students lay scattered about, reading. Watchmen wandered around on the brick paths. Families were eating picnic suppers. Children ran everywhere.

The Tillermans stood on the sidewalk, separated by a brier hedge from this scene.

"No good," Dicey said. "Too many people."

She did not move on, however. It looked—so quiet and solid; the air over it was lavender in the evening light, and mysterious. She wished . . . she didn't know what she wished.

Resolutely, she turned away.

Her map showed only something called the Historic District. They had walked through some of it. All the houses crowded up onto the sidewalk, close to one another.

Dicey moved on. The suitcase weighed heavy on her shoulder muscle and banged against her legs. The map showed the Naval Academy in one direction, closed in by a wall that ran all around it. She turned the other way and led them back toward the first circle they had seen. She chose the road leading to the hospital, and they walked on, past that large building.

The houses were bigger here and had front lawns. A residential area. A rich residential area.

She walked on.

They saw one vacant lot that had no cover to conceal them from the surrounding houses.

She walked on.

The air grew darker, gray-violet now. The heat did not abate. Sweat ran down her back.

She walked on.

On her left, she saw a long, narrow stretch of grass in the middle of a kind of courtyard of houses. On both sides of the stretch ran roads, and houses stood facing one another across the grass. At the end of this stretch, with all its many windows dark, stood a house larger than any other on the street. Dicey headed down towards it.

They walked down the middle of the grass. There was one broad clump of bushes the little kids could hide in, if it came to that.

When they stood before the large house, Dicey noticed oddly shaped piles. Old radiators had been dropped here and pipes and slate shingles from the roof and even a bathroom sink. They were piled up right by the front porch.

"Let's go around back," she said quietly. "I think it's empty. It looks like somebody's fixing it up. If anybody calls out, don't run. Tell them we're looking for Prince George Street. Tell them we're lost. Don't look guilty."

Their feet silent on the unmown grass, they stepped around the side of the house.

A silver pool of water glimmered at the end of the long lawn. The back of the house was as dark as the front, and Dicey breathed easy. She put her suitcase beside one of the overgrown bushes that grew by the screened porch, and they all walked down to the water.

A long-fingered willow swept the top of the grass at the water's edge. Two towering pines stood silent guard. On the silver pool, which was part of a river, some sailboats floated.

There was a bulkhead at the end of the lawn made out of railroad ties. They sat on that and dangled their feet over the water.

Dicey's stomach had butterflies of excitement in it. "Remember that first house?" she asked James.

"Yeah. Think it's empty?"

"I think so. Let's risk it."

No other houses were visible, although patches of light from windows showed through high hedges or trees. It was a private lawn.

"No fires," Dicey said.

A sailboat, its sails down, motored up the river. It made little waves that streaked the silver with black and lapped gently against the bulkheading.

Dicey turned to look at the house behind her. Its windows were comfortingly blank.

"We'll have to be quiet and get out early," she said.

Her family watched out over the water with dream-dazed eyes. They nodded. The river was narrow enough to swim easily. Across it houses looked back at them.

Dicey smiled. Sammy drummed at the wood with his heels, quietly. James lay back and looked at the sky. Maybeth hummed, a tune Dicey half-recognized. "What song is that?" she asked.

"Stewart's song," Maybeth said. "'Oft I sing for my friends,'" she sang softly. "Remember?"

Dicey shook her head. "We can't sing—but I sure feel like it," she said. "I don't really know why."

"Yes, you do," James said, but said no more. He was watching the first stars emerge in the gray sky.

And Dicey did. They had money and a good place to sleep. She had a map. They were together alone again, themselves again. The night air was warm, and the willow whispered behind her, and the water whispered before her.

"OK," she said, rousing them, rousing herself, "Let's go up and get to sleep."

FANTASY

Just So Stories
The Cat That Walked by Himself

Rudyard Kipling

This is a story of how the dog and the horse and the cow became part of the human family, but the cat always remained somewhat aloof. The aloneness of the cat is charmingly portrayed in the accompanying illustration drawn by Rudyard Kipling himself.

In his essay "On Preparing to Read Kipling" (1961), the poet Randall Jarrell, author of The Animal Family, *which is excerpted in this volume (p. 82), observed that "to Kipling the world was a dark forest full of families" and that families "have so predominant a place in no other writer." Clifton Fadiman noted that many critics failed to recognize that Kipling was essentially a children's writer.*

Kipling (1865–1936) was born in Bombay, India, and lived there until he was 6 years old. He later returned to India as the editor of a journal. His style frequently reflects the blend of his English and Indian upbringing.

Hear and attend and listen; for this befell and behappened and became and was, O my Best Beloved, when the Tame animals were wild. The Dog was wild, and the Horse was wild, and the Cow was wild, and the Sheep was wild, and the Pig was wild — as wild as wild could be — and they walked in the Wet Wild Woods by their wild lones. But the wildest of all the wild animals was the Cat. He walked by himself, and all places were alike to him.

Of course the Man was wild too. He was

Rudyard Kipling, *Just So Stories* (New York: Doubleday, 1926).

dreadfully wild. He didn't even begin to be tame till he met the Woman, and she told him that she did not like living in his wild ways. She picked out a nice dry Cave, instead of a heap of wet leaves, to lie down in; and she strewed clean sand on the floor; and she lit a nice fire of wood at the back of the Cave; and she hung a dried wild-horse skin, tail-down, across the opening of the Cave; and she said, "Wipe your feet, dear, when you come in, and now we'll keep house."

That night, Best Beloved, they ate wild sheep roasted on the hot stones, and flavoured with wild garlic and wild pepper; and wild duck stuffed with wild rice and wild fenugreek and wild coriander; and marrow-bones of wild oxen; and wild cherries, and wild grenadillas. Then the Man went to sleep in front of the fire ever so happy; but the Woman sat up, combing her hair. She took the bone of the shoulder of mutton — the big fat blade-bone — and she looked at the wonderful marks on it, and she threw more wood on the fire, and she made a Magic. She made the First Singing Magic in the world.

Out in the Wet Wild Woods all the wild animals gathered together where they could see the light of the fire a long way off, and they wondered what it meant.

Then Wild Horse stamped with his wild foot and said, "O my Friends and O my Enemies, why have the Man and the Woman made that great light in that great Cave, and what harm will it do us?

Wild Dog lifted up his wild nose and smelled the smell of roast mutton, and said, "I will go up and see and look, and say; for I think it is good. Cat, come with me."

"Nenni!" said the Cat. "I am the Cat who walks by himself, and all places are alike to me. I will not come."

"Then we can never be friends again," said Wild Dog, and he trotted off to the Cave. But when he had gone a little way the Cat said to himself, "All places are alike to me. Why should I not go too and see and look and come away at my own liking." So he slipped after Wild Dog softly, very softly, and hid himself where he could hear everything.

When Wild Dog reached the mouth of the Cave he lifted up the dried horse-skin with his nose and sniffed the beautiful smell of the roast mutton, and the Woman, looking at the blade-bone, heard him, and laughed, and said, "Here comes the first. Wild Thing out of the Wild Woods, what do you want?"

Wild Dog said, "O my Enemy and Wife of my Enemy, what is this that smells so good in the Wild Woods?"

Then the Woman picked up a roasted mutton-bone and threw it to Wild Dog, and said, "Wild Thing out of the Wild Woods, taste and try." Wild Dog gnawed the bone and it was more delicious than anything he had ever tasted, and he said, "O my Enemy and Wife of my Enemy, give me another."

The Woman said, "Wild Thing out of the Wild Woods, help my Man to hunt through the day and guard this Cave at night, and I will give you as many roast bones as you need."

"Ah!" said the Cat, listening. This is a very wise Woman, but she is not so wise as I am."

Wild Dog crawled into the Cave and laid his head on the Woman's lap, and said, "O my Friend and Wife of my Friend, I will help your Man to hunt through the day, and at night I will guard your Cave."

"Ah!" said the Cat, listening. "That is a very foolish Dog." And he went back through the Wet Wild Woods waving his wild tail, and walking by his wild lone. But he never told anybody.

When the Man waked up he said, "What is Wild Dog doing here?" And the Woman said, "His name is not wild Dog any more, but the First Friend, because he will be our friend for always and always and always. Take him with you when you go hunting."

Next night the Woman cut great green armfuls of fresh grass from the water-meadows, and dried it before the fire, so that it smelt like new-mown hay, and she sat at the mouth of the Cave and plaited a halter out of horse-hide, and she looked at the shoulder of mutton-bone — at the big broad blade-bone — and she made a Magic. She made the Second Singing Magic in the world.

Out in the Wild Woods all the wild animals wondered what had happened to Wild Dog, and at last Wild Horse stamped with his foot and said, "I will go and see and say why Wild Dog has not returned. Cat, come with me."

"Nenni!" said the Cat. "I am the Cat who walks by himself, and all places are alike to me. I will not come." But all the same he followed Wild Horse softly, very softly, and hid himself where he could hear everything.

When the Woman heard Wild Horse tripping and stumbling on his long mane, she laughed and said, "Here comes the second. Wild Thing out of the Wild Woods what do you want?"

Wild Horse said, "O my Enemy and Wife of my Enemy, where is Wild Dog?"

The Woman laughed, and picked up the blade-bone and looked at it, and said, "Wild Thing out of the Wild Woods, you did not come here for Wild Dog, but for the sake of this good grass."

And Wild Horse, tripping and stumbling on his long mane, said, "That is true; give it me to eat."

The Woman said, "Wild Thing out of the Wild Woods, bend your wild head and wear what I give you, and you shall eat the wonderful grass three times a day."

"Ah," said the Cat, listening, "this is a clever Woman, but she is not so clever as I am."

Wild Horse bent his wild head, and the Woman slipped the plaited hide halter over it, and Wild Horse breathed on the woman's feet and said, "O my Mistress, and Wife of my Master, I will be your servant for the sake of the wonderful grass."

"Ah," said the Cat, listening, "that is a very foolish Horse." And he went back through the Wet Wild Woods, waving his wild tail and walking by his wild lone. But he never told anybody.

When the Man and the Dog came back from hunting, the Man said. "What is Wild Horse doing here?" and the Woman said, "His name is not Wild Horse any more, but the First Servant, because he will carry us from place to place for always and always and always. Ride on his back when you go hunting."

Next day, holding her wild head high that her wild horns should not catch in the wild trees, Wild Cow came up to the Cave, and

This is the picture of the Cat that Walked by Himself, walking by his wild lone through the Wet Wild Woods and waving his wild tail. There is nothing else in the picture except some toadstools. They had to grow there because the woods were so wet. The lumpy thing on the low branch isn't a bird. It is moss that grew there because the Wild Woods were so wet.

the Cat followed, and hid himself just the same as before; and everything happened just the same as before; and the Cat said the same things as before, and when Wild Cow had promised to give her milk to the Woman every day in exchange for the wonderful grass, the Cat went back through the Wet Wild Woods waving his wild tail and walking by his wild lone, just the same as before. But he never told anybody. And when the Man and the Horse and the Dog came home from hunting and asked the same questions same as before, the Woman said, "Her name is not Wild Cow any more, but the Giver of Good Food. She will give us the warm white milk for always and always and always, and I will take care of her while you and the First Friend and the First Servant go hunting."

Next day the Cat waited to see if any other Wild thing would go up to the Cave, but no one moved in the Wet Wild Woods, so the Cat walked there by himself; and he saw the Woman milking the Cow, and he saw the light of the fire in the Cave, and he smelt the smell of the warm white milk.

Cat said, "O my Enemy and Wife of my Enemy, where did Wild Cow go?"

The Woman laughed and said, "Wild Thing out of the Wild Woods, go back to the Woods again, for I have braided up my hair, and I have put away the magic blade-bone, and we have no more need of either friends or servants in our Cave."

Cat said, "I am not a friend, and I am not a servant. I am the Cat who walks by himself, and I wish to come into your cave."

Woman said, "Then why did you not come with First Friend on the first night?"

Cat grew very angry and said, "Has Wild Dog told tales of me?"

Then the Woman laughed and said, "You are the Cat who walks by himself, and all places are alike to you. You are neither a friend nor a servant. You have said it yourself. Go away and walk by yourself in all places alike."

Then Cat pretended to be sorry and said, "Must I never come into the Cave? Must I never sit by the warm fire? Must I never drink the warm white milk? You are very wise and very beautiful. You should not be cruel even to a Cat."

Woman said, "I knew I was wise, but I did not know I was beautiful. So I will make a bargain with you. If ever I say one word in your praise you may come into the Cave."

"And if you say two words in my praise?" said the Cat.

"I never shall," said the Woman, "but if I say two words in your praise, you may sit by the fire in the Cave."

"And if you say three words?" said the Cat.

"I never shall," said the Woman, "but if I say three words in your praise, you may drink the warm white milk three times a day for always and always and always."

Then the Cat arched his back and said, "Now let the Curtain at the mouth of the Cave, and the Fire at the back of the Cave, and the Milk-pots that stand beside the Fire, remember what my Enemy and the Wife of my Enemy has said." And he went away through the Wet Wild Woods waving his wild tail and walking by his wild lone.

That night when the Man and the Horse and the Dog came home from hunting, the Woman did not tell them of the bargain that she had made with the Cat, because she was afraid that they might not like it.

Cat went far and far away and hid himself in the Wet Wild Woods by his wild lone for a long time till the Woman forgot all about him. Only the Bat — the little upside-down Bat — that hung inside the Cave, knew where Cat hid; and every evening Bat would fly to Cat with news of what was happening.

One evening Bat said, "There is a Baby in the Cave. He is new and pink and fat and small, and the woman is very fond of him."

"Ah," said the Cat, listening, "but what is the Baby fond of?"

"He is fond of things that are soft and tickle," said the Bat. "He is fond of warm things to hold in his arms when he goes to sleep. He is fond of being played with. He is fond of all those things."

"Ah," said the Cat, listening, "then my time has come."

Next night Cat walked through the Wet Wild Woods and hid very near the Cave till morning-time, and Man and Dog and Horse went hunting. The Woman was busy cooking that morning, and the Baby cried and interrupted. So she carried him outside the Cave and gave him a handful of pebbles to play with. But still the Baby cried.

Then the Cat put out his paddy paw and patted the Baby on the cheek, and it cooed; and the Cat rubbed against its fat knees and tickled it under its fat chin with his tail. And the Baby laughed; and the Woman heard him and smiled.

Then the Bat—the little upside-down Bat—that hung in the mouth of the Cave said, "O my Hostess and Wife of my Host and Mother of my Host's Son, a Wild Thing from the Wild Woods is most beautifully playing with your Baby."

"A blessing on that Wild Thing whoever he may be," said the Woman, straightening her back, "for I was a busy woman this morning and he has done me a service."

That very minute and second Best Beloved, the dried horse-skin Curtain that was stretched tail-down at the mouth of the Cave fell down—woosh!—because it remembered the bargain she had made with the Cat, and when the Woman went to pick it up—lo and behold!—the Cat was sitting quite comfy inside the Cave.

"O my Enemy and Wife of my Enemy and Mother of my Enemy," said the Cat, "it is I: for you have spoken a word in my praise, and now I can sit within the Cave for always and always and always. But still I am the Cat who walks by himself, and all places are alike to me."

The Woman was very angry, and shut her lips tight and took up her spinning-wheel and began to spin.

But the Baby cried because the Cat had gone away, and the Woman could not hush it, for it struggled and kicked and grew black in the face.

"O my Enemy and Wife of my Enemy and Mother of my Enemy," said the Cat, "take a strand of the wire that you are spinning and tie it to your spinning-whorl and drag it along the floor, and I will show you a magic that shall make your Baby laugh as loudly as he is now crying."

"I will do so," said the Woman, "because I am at my wits' end; but I will not thank you for it."

She tied the thread to the little clay spindle-whorl and drew it across the floor, and the Cat ran after it and patted it with his paws and rolled head over heels, and tossed it backward over his shoulder and chased it between his hind-legs and pretended to lose it, and pounced down upon it again, till the Baby laughed as loudly as it had been crying, and scrambled after the Cat and frolicked all over the Cave till it grew tired and settled down to sleep with the Cat in its arms.

"Now," said the Cat, "I will sing the Baby a song that shall keep him asleep for an hour." And he began to purr, loud and low, low and loud, till the Baby fell fast asleep. The Woman smiled as she looked down upon the two of them and said, "That was wonderfully done. No question but you are very clever, O Cat."

That very minute and second, Best Beloved, the smoke of the fire at the back of the Cave came down in clouds from the roof—puff!—because it remembered the bargain she had made with the Cat, and when it had cleared away—lo and behold!—the Cat was sitting quite comfy close to the fire.

"O my Enemy and Wife of my Enemy and Mother of my Enemy," said the Cat, "it is I, for you have spoken a second word in my praise, and now I can sit by the warm fire at the back of the Cave for always and always and always. But still I am the Cat who walks by himself, and all places are alike to me."

Then the Woman was very very angry, and let down her hair and put more wood on the fire and brought out the broad blade-bone of the shoulder of mutton and began to make a Magic that should prevent her from saying a third word in praise of the Cat. It was not a Singing Magic, Best Beloved, it was a Still Magic; and by and by the Cave grew so still that a little wee-wee mouse crept out of a corner and ran across the floor.

"O my Enemy and Wife of my Enemy and Mother of my Enemy," said the Cat, "is that little mouse part of your magic?"

"Ouh! Chee! No indeed!" said the Woman, and she dropped the blade-bone and jumped upon the footstool in front of the fire and braided up her hair very quick for fear that the mouse should run up it.

"Ah," said the Cat, watching, "then the mouse will do me no harm if I eat it?"

"No," said the Woman, braiding up her hair, "eat it quickly and I will ever be grateful to you."

Cat made one jump and caught the little mouse, and the Woman said, "A hundred thanks. Even the First Friend is not quick enough to catch little mice as you have done. You must be very wise."

That very moment and second, O Best

Beloved, the Milk-pot that stood by the fire cracked in two pieces—*ffft*—because it remembered the bargain she had made with the Cat, and when the Woman jumped down from the footstood—lo and behold!—the Cat was lapping up the warm white milk that lay in one of the broken pieces.

"O my Enemy and Wife of my Enemy and Mother of my Enemy," said the Cat, "it is I: for you have spoken three words in my praise, and now I can drink the warm white milk three times a day for always and always and always. But *still* I am the Cat who walks by himself, and all places are alike to me."

Then the Woman laughed and set the Cat a bowl of the warm white milk and said, "O Cat, you are as clever as a man, but remember that your bargain was not made with the Man or the Dog, and I do not know what they will do when they come home."

"What is that to me?" said the Cat. "If I have my place in the Cave by the fire and my warm white milk three times a day I do not care what the Man or the Dog can do."

That evening when the Man and the Dog came into the Cave, the Woman told them all the story of the bargain while the Cat sat by the fire and smiled. Then the Man said, "Yes, but he has not made a bargain with *me* or with all proper Men after me." Then he took off his two leather boots and he took up his little stone axe (that makes three) and he fetched a piece of wood and a hatchet (that is five altogether), and he set them out in a row and he said, "Now we will make *our* bargain. If you do not catch mice when you are in the Cave for always and always and always, I will throw these five things at you whenever I see you, and so shall all proper Men do after me."

"Ah," said the Woman, listening, "this is a very clever Cat, but he is not so clever as my Man."

The Cat counted the five things (and they looked very knobby) and he said, "I will catch mice when I am in the Cave for always and always and always; but *still* I am the Cat who walks by himself, and all places are alike to me."

"Not when I am near," said the Man. "If you had not said that last I would have put all these things away for always and always and always; but I am now going to throw my two boots and my little stone axe (that makes three) at you whenever I meet you. And so shall all proper Men do after me!"

Then the Dog said, "Wait a minute. He has not made a bargain with *me* or with all proper Dogs after me." And he showed his teeth and said, "If you are not kind to the Baby while I am in the Cave for always and always and always, I will hunt you till I catch you, and when I catch you I will bite you. And so shall all proper Dogs do after me."

"Ah," said the Woman, listening, "this is a very clever Cat, but he is not so clever as the Dog."

Cat counted the Dog's teeth (and they looked very pointed) and he said, "I will be kind to the Baby while I am in the Cave, as long as he does not pull my tail too hard, for always and always and always. But *still* I am the Cat that walks by himself, and all places are alike to me."

"Not when I am near," said the Dog. "If you had not said that last I would have shut my mouth for always and always and always; but *now* I am going to hunt you up a tree whenever I meet you. And so shall all proper Dogs do after me."

Then the Man threw his two boots and his little stone axe (that makes three) at the Cat, and the Cat ran out of the Cave and the Dog chased him up a tree; and from that day to this, Best Beloved, three proper Men out of five will always throw things at a Cat whenever they meet him, and all proper Dogs will chase him up a tree. But the Cat keeps his side of the bargain too. He will kill mice and he will be kind to Babies when he is in the house, just as long as they do not pull his tail too hard. But when he has done that, and between times, and when the moon gets up and night comes, he is the Cat that walks by himself, and all places are alike to him. Then he goes out to the Wet Wild Woods or up the Wet Wild Trees or on the Wet Wild Roofs, waving his wild tail and walking by his wild lone.

Alice in Wonderland
Pig and Pepper

Lewis Carroll

*Alice in Wonderland is so important, so rich in meaning, that it must be included
in any anthology of children's literature. In a sense, the underground world is
Alice's extended family—as mad as the aboveground world, but in different ways.
All concepts are altered—space (Alice puts a marmalade jar back on a shelf as
she is falling); language (a history book is used to dry tears as it is the driest
thing around); time (it is always teatime); size (Alice's size varies extraordinarily
from tiny to gigantic); the hierarchy of human beings, animals, and things (a
deck of cards rules the underground world and animals, such as the rabbit, are
rude to Alice). In the trial of the Knave of Hearts, Carroll implies that in a world
where there is no justice, any trial at a court of law is a pointless formality. (See
Donald Rackin's essay, listed under "References for Adults.")*

*In the selection featured here, one cannot be sure of identities. A family scene
becomes a nightmare. An abused child turns out to be an abused piglet. And a cat
evaporates into a grin.*

*Two illustrations of the Duchess and the pig/baby are included: one by the
original illustrator, John Tenniel (1865); and one by Willy Pogany for a 1929
edition of* Alice. *Pogany's drawing reflects the aesthetic sensibility of the
"flapper" generation of the 1920s.*

For a minute or two she stood looking at the house, and wondering what to do next, when suddenly a footman in livery came running out of the wood—(she considered him to be a footman because he was in livery: otherwise, judging by his face only, she would have called him a fish)—and rapped loudly at the door with his knuckles. It was opened by another footman in livery, with a round face and large eyes like a frog; and both footmen, Alice noticed, had powdered hair that curled all over their heads. She felt very curious to know what it was all about, and crept a little way out of the wood to listen.

The Fish-Footman began by producing from under his arm a great letter, nearly as large as himself, and this he handed over to the other, saying in a solemn tone, "For the Duchess. An invitation from the Queen to play croquet." The Frog-Footman repeated, in the same solemn tone, "From the Queen. An invitation for the Duchess to play croquet."

Then they both bowed low, and their curls got entangled together.

Alice laughed so much at this that she had to run back into the wood for fear of their hearing her, and when she next peeped out the Fish-Footman was gone, and the other was sitting on the ground near the door, staring stupidly up into the sky.

Alice went timidly up to the door, and knocked.

"There's no sort of use in knocking," said the Footman, "and that for two reasons. First, because I'm on the same side of the door as you are; secondly, because they're making such a noise inside, no one could

Lewis Carroll, *Alice in Wonderland* and *Through the Looking Glass* (Philadelphia: Henry Altemus, 1895). Illustration "Pig and Pepper" by Willy Pogany. From Lewis Carroll, *Alice's Adventures in Wonderland* (New York: Dutton, 1929).

possibly hear you.'' And certainly there *was* a most extraordinary noise going on within—a constant howling and sneezing, and every now and then a great crash, as if a dish or a kettle had been broken to pieces.

"Please, then," said Alice, "how am I to get in?"

"There might be some sense in your knocking," the Footman went on without attending to her, "if we had the door between us. For instance, if you were *inside,* you might knock, and I could let you out, you know." He was looking up into the sky all the time he was speaking, and this Alice thought decidedly uncivil. "But perhaps he can't help it," she said to herself; "his eyes are so *very* nearly at the top of his head. But at any rate he might answer questions—How am I to get in?" she repeated, aloud.

"I shall sit here," the Footman remarked, "till to-morrow——"

At this moment the door of the house opened, and a large plate came skimming out, straight at the Footman's head: it just grazed his nose, and broke to pieces against one of the trees behind him.

"——or next day, maybe," the Footman continued in the same tone, exactly as if nothing had happened.

"How am I to get in?" Alice asked again in a louder tone.

"*Are* you to get in at all?" said the Footman. "That's the first question, you know."

It was, no doubt: only Alice did not like to be told so. "It's really dreadful," she muttered to herself, "the way all the creatures argue. It's enough to drive one crazy!"

The Footman seemed to think this a good opportunity for repeating his remark, with variations. "I shall sit here," he said, "on and off, for days and days."

"But what am *I* to do?" said Alice.

"Anything you like," said the Footman, and began whistling.

"Oh, there's no use in talking to him," said Alice desperately: "he's perfectly idiotic!" And she opened the door and went in.

The door led right into a large kitchen, which was full of smoke from one end to the other: the Duchess was sitting on a three-legged stool in the middle, nursing a baby; the cook was leaning over the fire, stirring a large cauldron which seemed to be full of soup.

"There's certainly too much pepper in that soup!" Alice said to herself, as well as she could for sneezing.

There was certainly too much of it in the air. Even the Duchess sneezed occasionally; and as for the baby, it was sneezing and howling alternately without a moment's pause. The only two creatures in the kitchen that did not sneeze, were the cook, and a large cat which was sitting on the hearth and grinning from ear to ear.

"Please, would you tell me," said Alice, a little timidly, for she was not quite sure whether it was good manners for her to speak first, "why your cat grins like that?"

"It's a Cheshire cat," said the Duchess, "and that's why. Pig."

She said the last word with such sudden violence that Alice quite jumped; but she saw in another moment that it was addressed to the baby, and not to her, so she took courage, and went on again:

"I didn't know that Cheshire cats always grinned; in fact, I didn't know that cats *could* grin."

"They all can," said the Duchess; "and most of 'em do."

"I don't know of any that do," Alice said very politely, feeling quite pleased to have got into a conversation.

"You don't know much," said the Duchess; "and that's a fact."

Alice did not at all like the tone of this remark, and thought it would be as well to introduce some other subject of conversation. While she was trying to fix on one, the cook took the cauldron of soup off the fire, and at once set to work throwing everything within her reach at the Duchess and the baby—the fire-irons came first; then followed a shower of saucepans, plates, and dishes. The Duchess took no notice of them, even when they hit her; and the baby was howling so much already, that it was quite impossible to say whether the blows hurt it or not.

"Oh *please* mind what you're doing!" cried Alice, jumping up and down in an agony of terror. "Oh, there goes his *precious* nose!" as an unusually large saucepan flew close by it, and very nearly carried it off.

"If everybody minded their own business," said the Duchess in a hoarse growl, "the world would go round a deal faster than it does."

"Which would *not* be an advantage," said Alice, who felt very glad to get an opportunity of showing off a little of her knowledge. "Just think what work it would make with the day and night! You see the earth takes twenty-four hours to turn on its axis—"

"Talking of axes," said the Duchess, "chop off her head!"

Alice glanced rather anxiously at the cook, to see if she meant to take the hint; but the cook was busily stirring the soup, and seemed not to be listening, so she went on again: "Twenty-four hours, I *think;* or is it twelve? I——"

"Oh, don't bother *me,*" said the Duchess; "I never could abide figures." And with that she began nursing her child again, singing a sort of lullaby to it as she did so, and giving it a violent shake at the end of every line:—

"Speak roughly to your little boy,
   And beat him when he sneezes;
He only does it to annoy,
   Because he knows it teases."

CHORUS

(in which the cook and the baby joined):—

"Wow! wow! wow!"

While the Duchess sang the second verse of the song, she kept tossing the baby violently up and down, and the poor little thing howled so, that Alice could hardly hear the words:—

"I speak severely to my boy,
   I beat him when he sneezes;
For he can thorougly enjoy
   The pepper when he pleases!"

CHORUS

"Wow! wow! wow!"

"Here! you may nurse it a bit, if you like!" said the Duchess to Alice, flinging the baby at her as she spoke. "I must go and get ready to play croquet with the Queen," and she hurried out of the room. The cook threw a frying pan after her as she went, but it just missed her.

Alice caught the baby with some difficulty, as it was a queer-shaped little creature, and held out its arms and legs in all directions, "just like a star-fish," thought Alice. The poor little thing was snorting like a steam-engine when she caught it, and kept doubling itself up and straightening itself out again, so that altogether, for the first minute or two, it was as much as she could do to hold it.

As soon as she had made out the proper way of nursing it, (which was to twist it up into a sort of knot, and then keep tight hold of its right ear and left foot, so as to prevent

willy Pogany

its undoing itself,) she carried it out into the open air. "If I don't take this child away with me," thought Alice, "they're sure to kill it in a day or two: wouldn't it be murder to leave it behind?" She said the last words out loud, and the little thing grunted in reply (it had left off sneezing by this time). "Don't grunt," said Alice: "that's not at all a proper way of expressing yourself."

The baby grunted again, and Alice looked very anxiously into its face to see what was the matter with it. There could be no doubt that it had a *very* turn-up nose, much more like a snout than a real nose; also its eyes were getting extremely small, for a baby: altogether Alice did not like the look of the thing at all, "—but perhaps it was only sobbing," she thought, and looked into its eyes again, to see if there were any tears.

No, there were no tears. "If you're going to turn into a pig, my dear," said Alice, seriously, "I'll have nothing more to do with you. Mind now!" The poor little thing sobbed again, (or grunted, it was impossible to say which,) and they went on for some while in silence.

Alice was just beginning to think to herself, "Now, what am I to do with this creature when I get it home?" when it grunted again, so violently, that she looked down into its face in some alarm. This time there could be *no* mistake about it: it was neither more nor less than a pig, and she felt that it would be quite absurd for her to carry it any further.

So she set the little creature down, and felt quite relieved to see it trot away quietly into the wood. "If it had grown up," she said to herself, "it would have been a dreadfully ugly child: but it makes rather a handsome pig, I think." And she began thinking over other children she knew, who might do very well as pigs, and was just saying to herself, "if one only knew the right way to change them——" when she was a little startled by seeing the Cheshire Cat sitting on a bough of a tree a few yards off.

The Cat only grinned when it saw Alice. It looked goodnatured, she thought: still it had *very* long claws and a great many teeth, so she felt it ought to be treated with respect.

"Cheshire Puss," she began, rather timidly, as she did not at all know whether it would like the name: however, it only grinned a little wider. "Come, it's pleased so far," thought Alice, and she went on, "Would you tell, me, please, which way I ought to walk from here?"

"That depends a good deal on where you want to get to," said the Cat.

"I don't much care where——" said Alice.

"Then it doesn't matter which way you walk," said the Cat.

"——so long as I get *somewhere,*" Alice added as an explanation.

"Oh, you're sure to do that," said the Cat, "if you only walk long enough."

Alice felt that this could not be denied, so she tried another question. "What sort of people live about here?"

"In *that* direction," the Cat said, waving its right paw round, "lives a Hatter: and in *that* direction," waving the other paw, "lives a March Hare. Visit either you like: they're both mad."

"But I don't want to go among mad people," Alice remarked.

"Oh, you can't help that," said the Cat, "we're all mad here. I'm mad. You're mad."

"How do you know I'm mad?" said Alice.

"You must be," said the Cat, "or you wouldn't have come here."

Alice didn't think that proved it at all; however, she went on: "and how do you know that you're mad?"

"To begin with," said the Cat, "a dog's not mad. You grant that?"

"I suppose so," said Alice.

"Well then," the Cat went on, "you see a dog growls when it's angry, and wags its tail when it's pleased. Now *I* growl when I'm pleased, and wag my tail when I'm angry. Therefore I'm mad."

"*I* call it purring, not growling," said Alice.

"Call it what you like," said the Cat. "Do you play croquet with the Queen today?"

"I should like it very much," said Alice, "but I haven't been invited yet."

"You'll see me there," said the Cat, and vanished.

Alice was not much surprised at this, she was getting so well used to queer things happening. While she was still looking at the place where it had been, it suddenly appeared again.

"By-the-bye, what became of the baby?" said the Cat. "I'd nearly forgotten to ask."

"It turned into a pig," Alice answered very quietly, just as if the Cat had come back in a natural way.

"I thought it would," said the Cat, and vanished again.

Alice waited a little, half expecting to see it again, but it did not appear, and after a minute or two she walked on in the direction in which the March Hare was said to live. "I've seen hatters before," she said to herself: "the March Hare will be much the most interesting, and perhaps as this is May it won't be raving mad—at least not so mad as it was in March." As she said this, she looked up, and there was the Cat again, sitting on a branch of a tree.

"Did you say pig, or fig?" said the Cat.

"I said pig," replied Alice; "and I wish you wouldn't keep appearing and vanishing so suddenly: you make one quite giddy."

"All right," said the Cat; and this time it vanished quite slowly, beginning with the end of the tail, and ending with the grin, which remained some time after the rest of it had gone.

"Well! I've often seen a cat without a grin," thought Alice, "but a grin without a cat! It's the most curious thing I ever saw in all my life!"

She had not gone much farther before she came in sight of the house of the March Hare; she thought it must be the right house, because the chimneys were shaped like ears and the roof was thatched with fur. It was so large a house, that she did not like to go nearer till she had nibbled some more of the left-hand bit of mushroom, and raised herself to about two feet high: even then she walked up towards it rather timidly, saying to herself, "Suppose it should be raving mad after all! I almost with I'd gone to see the Hatter instead!"

PICTURE BOOK

Pierre

Maurice Sendak

According to the old proverb, "Those who live to themselves are finally left to themselves." Pierre learns the truth of this saying at an early age.

PROLOGUE
*There once was a boy
named Pierre
who only would say,
"I don't care!"
Read his story,
my friend,
for you'll find
at the end
that a suitable
moral lies there.*

From Maurice Sendak, *Pierre: A Cautionary Tale* (New York: Harper & Row, 1962).

One day
his mother said
when Pierre
climbed out of bed,
"Good morning,
darling boy,
you are
my only joy."
Pierre said,
"*I don't care!*"

"What would you
like to eat?"
"*I don't care!*"
"Some lovely
cream of wheat?"
"*I don't care!*"
"Don't sit backwards
on your chair."
"*I don't care!*"
"Or pour syrup
on your hair."
"*I don't care!*"

"You are acting
like a clown."
"I don't care!"
"And we have
to go to town."
"I don't care!"
"Don't you want
to come, my dear?"
"I don't care!"
"Would you rather
stay right here?"
"I don't care!"

So his mother
left him there.

Explorations

1. Try telling the story of the Huckabuck family to a group of people (both children and adults enjoy hearing it). Don't memorize the story, but read it often enough so that you know it thoroughly. Then memorize a few key phrases in it to give it its special style, such as " 'It's a buckle,' she said, 'a silver buckle, a Chinese silver slipper buckle.' " But don't tell this story or any other story unless you really like it and enjoy repeating it. Otherwise, the audience is sure to sense your boredom.

2. After reading the folk rhymes in any section of this book, go to a playground and listen to the rhymes the children are chanting and skipping to. You can write these down, collect them in a book, and reproduce and sell them to benefit your school or for some other purpose. If you want to copyright your book—an easy process—simply phone or write the Copyright Office of the Library of Congress, and you will be sent the necessary information. Fill out the simple form, send back a modest fee and two copies of the book with the copyright notice included. The copyright notice indicates that the material is your property and that no one can print the material without your permission; your rights of authorship are thus protected by law. The copyrighting process is an interesting learning experience for both children and adults.

3. If the equipment is available, you might want to make a videotape of children skipping rope in a playground. Try to get a variety of ethnic groups to skip. If you give advance notice, some of them might even come in costume.

4. An individual, a class, or a group can convert a folktale into a play. (Folktales are easy to use because, when orally presented, they are in the public domain and no copyright infringement occurs.) Six or so brief plays can be produced in an hour's time. Prizes can be given to the best playwright, best actor, best actress, best "cheesecake" (the prize could be a cheesecake), best "ham" (a ham), and so on. You can call the prizes "Emmy awards," or you can choose some other name for them, and you could have a formal ceremony to present them. T-shirts make good prizes, or you can use your imagination.

5. The chief gamemaker for a famous game company once told a class that before any game is approved by his company, a board meets to decides on its merits: Does it entertain everyone around the board, even when some players are waiting a turn? Does it teach how to win, how to lose, and how to deal with failure? Does it teach decision making? Try converting a folktale in this or another section of the book into an indoor or outdoor game. The gamemakers can display and explain the games, and a prize can be awarded for the best game. One benefit to be derived from gamemaking is that it exercises the imagination—a story must be transformed from one medium to another.

For instance, if "The Juniper Tree" is chosen, the tree can be in the center of the board and the dice can be thrown and pieces moved to mark the progression of each player from the goldsmith's to the shoemaker's to the stonemason's to the tree. Or, for "The Firebird," an outdoor ring-toss game can be developed in which each player tries to "capture," in turn, a bird in a cage, a horse, and a beautiful maiden.

6. Write a brief (one-page) essay on one case of child abuse you have observed or suspected. Then discuss various kinds of child abuse, such as that in "The Little Match Girl."

7. Democritus (460–370 B.C.), Giordano Bruno (1548–1600), and Gottfried Wilhelm von Leibniz (1646–1716) believed that every material object—person, animal, plant, or stone—gives off a spiritual aura that remains changeless and eternal. According to this theory, every human life and the family that surrounds it live forever in the cosmic consciousness.

Whether or not you agree with this theory, you can preserve the history of your family for generations by making a "Family Folklore Book." The book can start with a family tree, in which is recorded the birth, marriage, place of residence, and so on of as many family members and generations as possible. (It is surprising how fast such information is forgotten unless it is recorded.) The tree can be followed by five brief essays on the sounds, touch, taste, sight, and smell of your home at this point in time. Stories told around the kitchen table, funny anecdotes about family happenings, what the family members do for a living—these could be included in an essay on the "sounds of home." Swatches of fabric and descriptions of various rooms could be put in the section on the "touch of home." Favorite recipes might be written down under "taste of home." Actual pictures and verbal descriptions of the exterior and interior of the house would make up the section on "sights of home." And the smells, good and bad, could be the final chapter: the fragrances of fresh laundry, furniture polish, and favorite perfumes or after-shave lotions, along with memories of musty attics, moldy cellars, and burned food. Such a book with a family tree (even if you can only draw a few branches) makes a good holiday gift for relatives.

8. Write a rhyme of your own and try skipping to it. Such rhymes are not so simple as some people think. Often, they are a subtle mixture of various poetic meters, and sometimes they have a haunting quality—which may explain why such supposedly simple rhymes are remembered long after more sophisticated poetry is forgotten.

9. Several selections in this section deal with old age—"The Traveling Musicians," "Matryona's Home," and the rhyme "Grandmama Is Buried." Do some research on how old people are represented in contemporary children's literature, and write a short paper or hold a group discussion about it. For instance, compare the rhyme "Grandmama Is Buried," in this Family section, with Richard Wilbur's poem "He Was," in the Country and City section. Note the resemblances and differences. Depictions of old people as crotchety, or other stereotypical treatments, can be discussed in connection with the Almsuncle in *Heidi* or the Earl in the story of *Little Lord Fauntleroy*.

According to Professor Glenn Edward Sadler, an authority on the stories of George MacDonald, MacDonald uses the condition of old age in its spiritual or psychological sense, rather than its chronological sense. His glamorous wise woman in *The Golden Key*, for example, is actually thousands of years old. Age is cyclical, and Mossy and Tangle are as young at the end of their lives as they are at the beginning. In "Little Bright Eyes," the princess, who is under a spell, is sometimes an old woman until a handsome prince lifts the spell by kissing her during her "old" phase.

In Ernest Hemingway's *The Old Man and the Sea,* a little boy understands the struggle of the old man better than adults do. Old age and how it relates to the family can be explored in the fiction of more recent works, including Judy Blume's *Are You There, God? It's Me, Margaret.*

10. In connection with the traditional and fragmented families and the child alone, you might like to see some classical films, including *Little Women,* starring Katharine Hepburn; E. Nesbit's *The Railway Children;* James M. Barrie's *Peter Pan;* and Charles Dickens's *Oliver Twist* and *David Copperfield.* Information on how these may be obtained can be found in *200 Selected Film Classics for Children of All Ages,* published by Charles C Thomas, Springfield, Illinois.

References for Children

Blos, Joan W. *A Gathering of Days. A New England Girls' Journal,* 1830–32. New York; Scribner, 1979. (A winner of the John Newbery Award.)

Burton, Hester. *Kate Ryder.* Illustrated by Victor G. Ambrus. New York: Crowell, 1974.

Butler, Francelia. *Indira Gandhi.* New York: Chelsea House, 1986.

Calvino, Italo. *Italian Folktales.* Orlando, Fla: Harcourt Brace Jovanovich, 1950. (Also for adults.)

Cleaver, Vera and Bill. *Where the Lilies Bloom.* Philadelphia: Lippincott, 1969. (Also available in paperback.)

Estes, Eleanor. *The Middle Moffat.* Illustrated by Louis Slobodkin. Orlando, Fla.: Harcourt Brace Jovanovich, 1942.

Farber, Norma. *How Does It Feel To Be Old?* New York: Dutton, 1979.

Forrester, Helen. *Twopence to Cross the Mersey.* Glasgow: Fontana/Collins, 1981.

Genesis. "Joseph and His Brothers." Chapters 37–47.

Gripe, Maria. *Julia's House.* Illustrated by Harold Gripe; translated from Swedish by Gerry Bothmen. New York: Delacorte Press, 1971.

Laskay, Kathryn. *The Night Journey.* Illustrated by Trina Schart Hyman. New York: Frederick Warne, 1981. (A winner of the National Jewish Book Award.)

MacLachlan, Patricia. *Sarah, Plain and Tall.* New York: Harper & Row, 1985.

Marzollo, Jean. *Close Your Eyes.* Illustrated by Susan Jeffers. New York: Dial Press, 1978.

Nehru, Jawaharlal. *Letters of a Father to His Daughter.* London: Oxford University Press, 1969.

Nesbit, E. *The Railway Children.* New York: Macmillan, 1906. (Also available in paperback.)
Many British children still stand at railroad stations and make notes of the numbers of passing trains. In fact, booklets are sold at newsstands just for this purpose.

Norton, Mary. *The Borrowers.* Illustrated by Beth and Joe Krush. Orlando, Fla: Harcourt Brace Jovanovich, 1953. (Also available in paperback.)

Opie, Iona and Peter. *The Oxford Nursery Rhyme Book.* Oxford University Press, New York, 1955.

Preston, Edna Mitchell. *Where Did My Mother Go?* Illustrated by Chris Conover. New York: Four Winds Press, 1978.

Sebestyen, Ouida. *Words By Heart.* Boston: Little, Brown, 1979. (Also available in paperback.)

Voigt, Cynthia. *Dicey's Song.* New York: Atheneum, 1982. (The sequel to *Homecoming,* this book won the John Newbery Award in 1983.)

Walsh, Jill Paton. *Gaffer Samson's Luck.* Illustrated by Brock Cole. New York: Farrar, Straus & Giroux, 1984.

Yep, Lawrence. *Dragonwings*. New York: Harper & Row, 1975.

> *A good example of the child alone. An eight-year-old Chinese boy, Moon Shadow, joins his father in America.*

References for Adults

Bettelheim, Bruno. *The Uses of Enchantment: The Meaning and Importance of Fairy Tales*. New York: Knopf, 1976.

Brunvand, Jan Harold. *Readings in American Folklore*. New York: Norton, 1979.

Butler, Dorothy. *Babies Need Books*. New York: Atheneum, 1980.

Butler, Francelia, *Sharing the Literature with Children*. New York: Longman, 1977.

———. *Masterworks of Children's Literature, 1550–1739*. 2 vols. New York: Chelsea House, 1984.

———. *The Lucky Piece*. New York: Avon Books, 1986. (An adult novel on child abuse.)

———, ed. *Children's Literature* [Annual]. New Haven, Conn.: Yale University Press.

Butler, Francelia, and Richard Rotert. *Reflections on Literature for Children*. Hamden, Conn.: Library Professional Publications, 1984.

———. *The Triumph of the Spirit in Children's Literature*. Hamden, Conn.: Library Professional Publications, 1986.

Cameron, Eleanor. *The Green and Burning Tree*. Boston: Little, Brown, 1969. (Criticism.)

Chesterton, G.K., "The Ethics of Elfland," in *Orthodoxy*. New York: Dodd, 1957. (First published 1909.)

Coveney, Peter. *The Child in Literature*. London: Rockliff, 1957.

deAlonso, Joan Evans. "E. Nesbit's Well Hall, 1915–1921: A Memoir," *Children's Literature*, 3(1974):147–168.

Dundes, Alan. *Cinderella, A Folklore Book*. New York: Garland Press, 1982.

Egoff, Sheila, G. T. Stubbs, and L. P. Ashley, eds. *Only Connect: Readings on Children's Literature*. New York: Oxford University Press, 1969.

Griswold, Jerome. *Randall Jarrell's Children's Books: An Appreciation*. Athens, Ga: University of Georgia Press, 1987.

Hearne, Betsy, and Marilyn Kaye. *Celebrating Children's Books*. New York: Lothrop, Lee & Shepard, 1981.

Koch, Kenneth. *Rose, where did you get that red?* New York: Random House, 1973.

Meek, Margaret. *Learning to Read*. London: Bodley Head, 1982.

Plotz, Helen, ed. *Life Hungers to Abound: Poems of the Family*. New York: Greenwillow Books, 1978. (Many of these poems recount fragmented and unpleasant relationships.)

Queenan, Bernard, "The Evolution of the Pied Piper." *Reflections on Literature for Children*. Hamden, Conn.: Library Professional Publications, 1984.

Rackin, Donald. "Alice's Adventures to the End of Night." *Publications of the Modern Language Association*, October 1966.

Rudman, Masha Kabakow. *Children's Literature: An Issues Approach*. Lexington, Mass.: Heath, 1976.

Russell, William I. *Classics to Read Aloud to Your Children*. New York: Crown, 1984.

Sleeman, Phillip J., Bernard Queenan, and Francelia Butler. *200 Selected Film Classics for Children of All Ages*. Springfield, Ill. Thomas, 1984.

Smith, Barbara. "The Expression of Social Values in the Writing of E. Nesbit." *Children's Literature* (1974), 153–164.

Troyat, Henri. *Tolstoy*. Translated by Nancy Amphorix. New York: Doubleday, 1967.

Von Franz, Marie Louise. *Interpretation of Fairytales*. New York: Spring Publications, 1970.

Zipes, Jack, *Fairy Tales and the Art of Subversions*. New York: Wildman Press, 1983.

THE CREATED WORLD: CITY AND COUNTRY

A small boy approached his father one day and asked, "Daddy, where did I come from?" The father, somewhat startled, launched into a complicated explanation of human reproduction, only to be interrupted by his son. "No, no, Daddy. Tommy comes from New Jersey; where did *I* come from?" Humor usually contains an element of truth and this story is no exception. Children seek to know the world and their place within it. They want to know, need to know, "Where did I come from?"

Children first explore the primary world of the family and come to understand themselves in relation to those closest to them. When they come to understand their place within the family, all seems right with the world. After trips to the grocery store, to daycare, to Grandma and Grandpa's house, and on vacations, however, children discover that an entire universe lies outside the family and the home. They move beyond the immediate family to form friendships, to understand their place within the world, and to accept the differences between themselves and others.

By meeting others and experiencing places far and near, either in reality or vicariously through books, children gain an understanding of the social system and culture in which they live. They also develop knowledge and appreciation of and empathy with people in other communities and cultures. Suddenly such questions as "Where did I come from?" "What's a city?" or "What do people do on a farm?" become important. They are all part of the larger question "Who am I?" and form the basis of the process by which children get to know themselves and their world.

As children grow, they begin to ask other questions. Both children and adults ask someone they meet for the first time, "Where are you from?" The answer helps to form at least part of a picture of what this new acquaintance is like. Often this one brushstroke of the total picture is stereotypic. We expect someone from the country to be more in tune with nature and simpler in habits and tastes than a person from the city; we expect a city person to be more "street-smart," more sophisticated, and more in tune with current trends and fashions. These stereotypes are both reinforced and negated by the literature that children read.

The country and nature have often been idealized in literature, going as far back, in the Judeo-Christian world, as the story of Adam and Eve in the Garden of Eden. The Bible describes Paradise as a garden, and, as is pointed out by Dov

Noy, collector of the tale "The Kingdom of the Lazy People," which is included in this section, Noah is the Jewish traditional culture hero who teaches people how to till the land. In both Christian and non-Christian literature, there is the pervasive sense that people are closer to the divine when they work the soil. There is wealth, both figurative and literal, to be gained from farming and country life. Aesop's "The Farmer and His Sons" stresses the literal wealth to be gained from the soil; Robert Lawson's *Rabbit Hill* and Emily Dickinson's "I Never Saw a Moor," among others featured here, emphasize the spiritual riches that the land holds.

The literature of the country also stresses a sense of aesthetic satisfaction that grows from a close relationship with the land. The pastoral life holds a significant position in literature. It stresses the aesthetic side of country life and glorifies even its most humble aspects. Robert Frost's "The Pasture," Vassar Miller's "The Farm," and Kenneth Rexroth's haiku all seek to communicate an idealized view of the country.

In contrast to the idealizations of the country and country life are portraits of actual, everyday life in the country. "The Gander Bites" by Anne Pellowski and *Farmer Boy* by Laura Ingalls Wilder are excellent pictures of actual farm life—its hardships, joys, and the ways in which such a life can bestow strength of character on those who pursue it. But whether one is viewing the country and country life ideally or realistically, the view is usually pleasing. As Edward Everett said in an address at Buffalo, New York, on October 9, 1857, "As a work of art, I know few things more pleasing to the eye, or more capable of affording scope and gratification to a taste for the beautiful, than a well-situated, well-cultivated farm."

Similarly, the city can be both idealized and viewed realistically. When idealized, the city is a bright and shining, glittering thing. It is a place of opportunity and learning, the seat of important events. Varro (116–27 B.C.) wrote, "Divine nature gave the field, human art built the cities." Cities are often viewed as the epitome of human art and aspiration, and their rise and fall are often believed to trace the rise and fall of human hopes. People preserve the legends of great cities, and these legends are surrounded by a magical aura. "The City of Troy," retold here by Rex Warner, and "The Founding of Mexico City," the Aztec legend retold by Carleton Beals, illustrate how cities are preserved and glorified by legend. According to these myths, both Troy and Mexico City were founded with help from the gods and grew to be centers of civilization.

Although cities do have a certain glamour attached to them, realistically, they are bustling places of commerce. City dwellers go about their daily lives much as people elsewhere, the difference being that representatives of many different ethnic, religious, and cultural backgrounds live together closely rather than far apart, as in the country. E. L. Konigsburg's *From the Mixed-up Files of Mrs. Basil E. Frankweiler* presents the opportunities a city can offer, even to two runaway children.

When a child reads of both city life and country life, a tension between city and country begins to emerge, and this tension, too, is reflected, helping to form stereotypes. The child is told in different stories and fables that "the country is better" or "the city is better." Many of the selections included here under the headings of "city" and "country" could just as easily have been designated "city versus country." Literature for children tends to instruct, but that instruction is often biased toward one viewpoint or another. The tale, "Elsie Piddock Skips in Her Sleep" is a striking example of this. In addition to being a charming story, it strongly advocates the simple country life and condemns cities and urban life, as do Gwendolyn Brooks's "Rudolph Is Tired of the City" and Carl Sandburg's "Population Drifts."

Ultimately, it is the child, as he or she reads and grows, who must decide where he or she wishes to live as an adult. In this respect, a book such as Holly Wilson's *Snowbound in Hidden Valley* is helpful. It presents the life of a child who lives in town and details her reactions when she is forced by circumstances to live for a time in the country; it shows how those who live in cities and those who live in the country can have misconceptions about one another. Such a book enables the child to become familiar and comfortable with both city and country. Thus, when the child becomes an adult, he or she can make a more reasoned decision. Such a book considers the child and his or her need to know the world. And this is as it should be, for, as Ralph Waldo Emerson pointed out, "The true test of civilization is not the census, nor the size of cities, nor the crop—no, but the kind of man the country turns out."

The City

FABLES, MYTHS, AND LEGENDS

The Man and His Piece of Cloth*

Adapted by P. V. Ramaswami Raju

How do cities become established? In this Indian fable, adapted by P. V. Ramaswami Raju, we learn that small beginnings can have large results. Necessity can dictate the establishment of a town or city.

A man in the East, where they do not require as much clothing as in colder climates, gave up all worldly concerns and retired to a wood, where he built a hut and lived in it.

His only clothing was a piece of cloth which he wore round his waist. But, as ill-luck would have it, rats were plentiful in the wood, so he had to keep a cat. The cat required milk to keep it, so a cow had to be kept. The cow required tending, so a cow-boy was employed. The boy required a house to live in, so a house was built for him. To look after the house a maid had to be engaged. To provide company for the maid a few more houses had to be built, and people invited to live in them. In this manner a little township sprang up,

The man said, *"The further we seek to go from the world and its cares, the more they multiply!"*

The City of Troy[†]

Rex Warner

Certain cities, both real and mythological, live on in stories and in the imagination even after they are dust. The great walled city of Troy was such a

*From P. V. Ramaswami Raju, "The Man and His Piece of Cloth," in Eva March Tappan, ed., *Folk Stories and Fables* (Boston: Houghton Mifflin, 1907).
†From Rex Warner, *The Stories of the Greeks* (London: Macgibbon and Kee).

144

city. "The City of Troy," from The Stories of the Greeks, *has as its source the* Iliad *of Homer. It gives an account of the mythic origin of Troy and some of its turbulent history.*

Rex Warner was a distinguished novelist, poet, and translator. He taught both Greek and Latin and served for a time as the director of the British Institute in Athens.

Not far from the sea coast in the north of Asia Minor once stood the city of Troy. Here was fought the great war between the Greeks and the Trojans, a war in which Achilles and Hector and so many other heroes lost their lives but won eternal fame. The gods also took part in the war, some on the side of the Trojans and some on the side of the Greeks. For ten years the struggle was undecided and the rivers of Troy, the Scamander and the Simois, ran red with blood. In the end the city was destroyed but of the Greeks many who had escaped the battle died on their homeward voyage, or wandered for long years in stormy seas along inhospitable coasts, or at their return found murder and treachery waiting for them in their own homes. It is said that the war was for a woman's sake, the sake of Helen, the wife of Menelaus. Yet the rivalry of the gods, the folly and ambition of men played their part also.

The great walls of Troy were built by the gods. Once Apollo was banished from heaven by Zeus, the King of the Gods. There are many stories of Apollo's doings on earth, but what concerns us here is that he, with Poseidon, the god of the sea, built the high walls of Troy for the Trojan King Laomedon. This treacherous and ungrateful king, in spite of the kindness he had received, refused, when the work was done, to pay the reward which he had promised. Then Apollo sent a pestilence among the people of Laomedon, and Poseidon sent from the sea a great monster which ravaged the crops and easily destroyed the warriors who were sent against it. In the distress of his people Laomedon consulted the oracle and was told that the gods' anger could not be appeased except by the sacrifice each year of a Trojan

maiden to the monster. So each year a maiden was chosen by lot and then, in spite of her tears and the tears of her parents and her friends, was taken to the sea shore and left there to be devoured by the great beast that came out of the sea.

For five years the city paid this terrible penalty for the treachery of its king, and in the sixth year the daughter of the king himself, Hesione, was chosen to be sacrificed. Now indeed Laomedon and his wife wished that greater respect had been paid to the gods, and that the promise had been fulfilled. Yet the gods were merciful, and in their misery help was at hand.

At this time the great hero Herakles with a band of his companions was returning from his expedition against the Queen of the Amazons, whose girdle he had taken from her by the orders of his cowardly master, King Eurystheus. As his ship put in to Troy he saw on the beach the sad procession which was accompanying Hesione to her doom, and he asked the reason for the black clothes and the wailing and the lamentation. King Laomedon told him of the danger in which his daughter stood and Herakles undertook to fight with the monster on the condition that, if he was successful, the king would give him a number of his fine horses, swift as the wind, great spirited animals that raced over the plains of Troy. Laomedon gladly and willingly agreed, and Herakles threw aside his lion skin cloak, gripped his club in his strong hands and made ready for battle.

Soon, at a great distance from the shore, one could see the blue water churned white as the beast approached. Its great head towered above the waves and through its rows of enormous teeth it belched out the foam. Herakles stood firm and indeed stepped forward to the shore, meeting the monstrous animal in the shallow water. With one blow of his club he stunned it; then, thrusting his sword into its heart he stained all the water scarlet with its blood.

Hesione was saved and now one would have thought that Laomedon, in gratitude for his daughter's safety and warned already by the previous punishment for his treachery, would ungrudgingly have given the hero his reward. It seems however that many people are unable to learn from experience. Once again Laomedon refused to carry out his part of the bargain. Herakles then, with his companions, attacked the city of Troy, took it by storm, killed King Laomedon and took the whole of his family prisoner. He gave Hesione to his follower Telamon who by her had a son, Teucer, who later was to fight with the Greeks against his mother's country in the great Trojan War. As for the other descendants of King Laomedon, only one was allowed to remain. This was the young boy Priam who was to become the last and the greatest of the Trojan kings. Herakles, before he sailed away, accepted a ransom for this boy and placed him on his father's throne.

So for many years, under the rule of King Priam and his Queen Hecuba, Troy grew ever richer, stronger and more prosperous. Priam made alliances with the neighbouring princes; he strengthened the vast fortifications of his city; ships that passed along the coast paid tribute to his officers; his kingdom became one of the mightiest in the world.

Priam and Hecuba had nineteen children who, when they grew up, became famous princes and princesses. Among them none was more famous than Hector both for his strength and skill in war and for his goodness of heart and loyalty to his friends. In these qualities he had no rival unless it was Priam's nephew Aeneas, whom Aphrodite loved, since he was her son. For she, the goddess of love, had fallen in love herself with the young Prince Anchises of the Trojan royal house. Anchises was feeding his sheep along the slopes of Mount Ida, the mountain that towers above the city of Troy, when the goddess, charmed by his beauty, visited him and by him became the mother of Aeneas, the hero who long afterwards and after many adventures was to found the great race of the Romans.

With such princes and warriors, with so many allies, such wealth and such magnificence, it might have seemed that the city of Troy was securely fixed in power and happiness and that it would last forever, standing proudly in the plain below Mount Ida, with the holy rivers Simois and Scamander crossing the plain, tall and mighty with its towers, its huge walls and its tremendous gates. But this was not the will of the gods.

The Founding of Mexico City

Carleton Beals

Here are two versions of the founding of Tenochtitlán, or present-day Mexico City, by the Aztecs. Throughout history, cities that have attained glory and fame have had their origins attributed to divine intervention. The walls of the great city

From Carleton Beals, *Stories Told by the Aztecs before the Spaniards Came* (New York: Abelard-Schuman, 1970).

*of Troy were supposedly built by Apollo and Poseidon, and, in the second version
of the founding of Mexico City, the Aztecs are guided to the spot by Tlaloc, the
rain god. In the first version, they are led to the spot by a hummingbird after they
have traveled, like the tribes of Israel, for countless generations.*

The Aztecs had halted in many places. Old people had died, grandchildren were born, grew old and died. Great-great-grandchildren grew up, grew old and died. And the Hummingbird had kept saying, "Go on, go on."

Now they wandered among the desolate swamps. Some settled on a little island in Lake Texcoco, Place-of-Sands. The rest, under their chief priest, Tenocha, Thorn-Cactus-on-a-Stone, entered deeper among the reeds, using poles to vault across the worst places, until they came to a large hummock that was deserted except for frogs and snakes, ducks and eagles, birds and butterflies. It was a little island called Tlatlcocomulco, where a spring of beautiful clear water bubbled forth between two white rocks surrounded by white willows. The Aztecs were marveling at this when white frogs emerged one from another. The meadows about seemed white, and the sheen on the emerald lake about was dazzling white.

The Hummingbird appeared, saying: "Now you will be satisfied. Remember: I sent you to kill Copil, evil son of the sorceress, and to throw his heart among the canebrakes of this lake. His heart fell upon a stone, from which sprang forth a cactus, a cactus so large and beautiful that an eagle lives on it. There he stretches, a serpent in his mouth, his wide powerful wings receiving the warmth of the sun and the freshness of the mornings. All about him you will find green, blue, red, yellow and white feathers of the beautiful birds this eagle has captured. That Place-Where-you-Find-the-Eagle-on-the-Cactus you will call Tenochtitlán, Place-of-the-Cactus-on-a-Stone."

Everybody prostrated himself to give thanks. Dividing into groups, they entered the dense growth of the lake, and true enough, an eagle on a cactus, its wings spread toward the sun, held a splendid snake with gleaming scales. All about was a carpet of bright feathers.

They made reverence to the eagle. "Why," they cried, "do we merit such a blessing as this? Thanks be to our lord and creator, Huitzilopochtli! We have found the home for our city." They danced with delight, and the priests performed many ceremonies.

The Aztecs told still another story. Two high priests, Axolohua and Cuauhcóatl, went among cypresses, junipers and reeds to seek the great eagle. Vaulting over the pools on long poles, on dry ground they came upon the cactus and the eagle. All around the spot, green water sparkled like emeralds.

Axolohua suddenly sank out of sight in the water. His companion waited in vain for him to reappear.

Twenty-four hours later Axolohua presented himself safe and sound. Seized by an occult force, he had been carried to the bottom of the lake. There he had met Tlaloc, the Rain God, who said: "Welcome to my dear Huitzilopochtli and to his people. Say to all the Aztecs that this is the place where you are to establish the seat of your power, where your descendants shall be glorified."

The jubilant people hurried to prepare the foundations of the future Queen City of Anáhuac. First they constructed a humble chapel for the god, then drove in poles on which to build cane huts with reed roofs. The small settlement was divided into four clans. *This was in 1324 or 1325.*

In due time a larger sanctuary was built. Finally the great stone pyramids rose within the enormous snake-wall compound where the magic fountain still flowed.

So was founded Tenochtitlán—Mexico—the Place-of-Cactus-Stone, the Belly Button-of-the-Maguey, the birth-scar of a mighty valley—the city which was to gain mastery not only of the lake but the whole of Anáhuac and of Mexico even as the god had promised.

FOLKTALES— INHERITED AND LITERARY

Whittington and His Cat

Adapted by Joseph Jacobs

*The city is a place of opportunity for many, and rags-to-riches stories abound.
"Whittington and His Cat" is one of the few such stories to be based on fact. It
tells of a young boy who comes to the city and does indeed find his fortune.*

In the reign of the famous King Edward III there was a little boy called Dick Whittington, whose father and mother died when he was very young. As poor Dick was not old enough to work, he was very badly off; he got but little for his dinner, and sometimes nothing at all for his breakfast; for the people who lived in the village were very poor indeed, and could not spare him much more than the parings of potatoes, and now and then a hard crust of bread.

Now Dick had heard many, many very strange things about the great city called London; for the country people at that time thought that folks in London were all fine gentlemen and ladies; and that there was singing and music there all day long; and that the streets were all paved with gold.

One day a large wagon and eight horses, all with bells at their heads, drove through the village while Dick was standing by the sign-post. He thought that this wagon must be going to the fine town of London; so he took courage, and asked the wagoner to let him walk with him by the side of the wagon. As soon as the wagoner heard that poor Dick had no father or mother, and saw by his ragged clothes that he could not be worse off than he was, he told him he might go if he would so off they set together.

So Dick got safe to London, and was in such a hurry to see the fine streets paved all over with gold that he did not even stay to thank the kind wagoner; but ran off as fast as his legs would carry him, through many of the streets, thinking every moment to come to those that were paved with gold; for Dick had seen a guinea three times in his own little village, and remembered what a deal of money it brought in change; so he thought he had nothing to do but to take up some little bits of the pavement, and should then have as much money as he could wish for.

Poor Dick ran till he was tired, and had quite forgot his friend the wagoner; but at last, finding it grow dark, and that every way he turned he saw nothing but dirt instead of gold, he sat down in a dark corner and cried himself to sleep.

Little Dick was all night in the streets; and next morning, being very hungry, he got up and walked about, and asked everybody he met to give him a halfpenny to keep him from starving; but nobody stayed to answer

From Joseph Jacobs, "Whittington and His Cat," in Eva March Tappan, ed., *Folk Stories and Fables* (Boston: Houghton Mifflin, 1907).

him, and only two or three gave him a half-penny; so that the poor boy was soon quite weak and faint for the want of victuals.

In this distress he asked charity of several people, and one of them said crossly, "Go to work for an idle rogue." "That I will," said Dick; "I will go to work for you, if you will let me." But the man only cursed at him and went on.

At last a good-natured-looking gentleman saw how hungry he looked. "Why don't you go to work, my lad?" said he to Dick. "That I would, but I do not know how to get any," answered Dick. "If you are willing, come along with me," said the gentleman, and took him to a hayfield, where Dick worked briskly, and lived merrily till the hay was made.

After this he found himself as badly off as before; and being almost starved again, he laid himself down at the door of Mr. Fitzwarren, a rich merchant. Here he was soon seen by the cook-maid, who was an ill-tempered creature, and happened just then to be very busy dressing dinner for her master and mistress; so she called out to poor Dick: "What business have you there, you lazy rogue?" there is nothing else but beggars; if you do not take yourself away, we will see how you will like a sousing of some dish-water; I have some here hot enough to make you jump."

Just at that time Mr. Fitzwarren himself came home to dinner; and when he saw a dirty ragged boy lying at the door, he said to him: "Why do you lie there, my boy? You seem old enough to work; I am afraid you are inclined to be lazy."

"No, indeed, sir," said Dick to him: "that is not the case, for I would work with all my heart, but I do not know anybody, and I believe I am very sick for the want of food."

"Poor fellow, get up; let me see what ails you."

Dick now tried to rise, but was obliged to lie down again, being too weak to stand, for he had not eaten any food for three days, and was no longer able to run about and beg a halfpenny of people in the street. So the kind merchant ordered him to be taken into the house, and have a good dinner given him, and be kept to do what work he was able to do for the cook.

Little Dick would have lived very happy in this good family if it had not been for the ill-natured cook. She used to say, "You are under me, so look sharp; clean the spit and the dripping-pan, make the fires, wind up the jack, and do all the scullery work nimbly, or"—and she would shake the ladle at him. Besides, she was so fond of basting that, when she had no meat to baste, she would baste poor Dick's head and shoulders with a broom, or anything else that happened to fall in her way. At last her ill-usage of him was told to Alice, Mr. Fitzwarren's daughter, who told the cook she should be turned away if she did not treat him kinder.

The behavior of the cook was now a little better; but besides this, Dick had another hardship to get over. His bed stood in a garret, where there were so many holes in the floor and the walls that every night he was tormented with rats and mice. A gentleman having given Dick a penny for cleaning his shoes, he thought he would buy a cat with it. The next day he saw a girl with a cat, and asked her, "Will you let me have that cat for a penny?" The girl said, "Yes, that I will, master, though she is an excellent mouser."

Dick hid his cat in the garret, and always took care to carry a part of his dinner to her; and in a short time he had no more trouble with the rats and mice, but slept quite sound every night.

Soon after this his master had a ship ready to sail; and, as it was the custom that all his servants should have some chance for good fortune as well as himself he called them all into the parlor and asked them what they would send out.

They all had something that they were willing to venture except poor Dick, who had neither money nor goods, and therefore could send nothing. For this reason he did not come into the parlor with the rest; but Miss Alice guessed what was the matter, and ordered him to be called in. She then said, "I will lay down some money for him, from my own purse;'' but her father told her, ''This will not do, for it must be something of his own.''

When poor Dick heard this, he said, ''I have nothing but a cat which I bought for a penny some time since of a little girl.''

''Fetch your cat, then, my lad,'' said Mr. Fitzwarren, ''and let her go.''

Dick went upstairs and brought down poor puss, with tears in his eyes, and gave her to the captain. ''For,'' he said, ''I shall now be kept awake all night by the rats and mice.'' All the company laughed at Dick's odd venture; and Miss Alice, who felt pity for him, gave him some money to buy another cat.

This, and many other marks of kindness shown him by Miss Alice, made the ill-tempered cook jealous of poor Dick, and she began to use him more cruelly than ever, and always made game of him for sending his cat to sea. She asked him, ''Do you think your cat will sell for as much money as would buy a stick to beat you?''

At last poor Dick could not bear this usage any longer, and he thought he would run away from his place; so he packed up his few things, and started very early in the morning, on All-hallows Day, the first of November. He walked as far as Halloway; and there sat down on a stone, which to this day is called ''Whittington's Stone,'' and began to think to himself which road he should take.

While he was thinking what he should do, the Bells of Bow Church, which at that time were only six, began to ring, and at their sound seemed to say to him:

''Turn again, Whittington,
Thrice Lord Mayor of London.''

''Lord Mayor of London!'' said he to himself. ''Why, to be sure, I would put up with almost anything now, to be Lord Mayor of London, and ride in a fine coach, when I grow to be a man! Well, I will go back, and think nothing of the cuffing and scolding of the old cook, if I am to be Lord Mayor of London at last.''

Dick went back, and was lucky enough to get into the house, and set about his work, before the cook came downstairs.

We must now follow Miss Puss to the coast of Africa. The ship with the cat on board was a long time at sea; and was at last driven by the winds on a part of the coast of Barbary, where the only people were the Moors, unknown to the English. The people came in great numbers to see the sailors, because they were of different color to themselves, and treated them civilly, and when they became better acquainted were very eager to buy the fine things that the ship was loaded with.

When the captain saw this, he sent patterns of the best things he had to the king of the country, who was so much pleased with them that he sent for the captain to the palace. Here they were placed, as is the custom of the country, on rich carpets flowered with gold and silver. The king and queen were seated at the upper end of the room, and a number of dishes were brought in for dinner. They had not sat long, when a vast number of rats and mice rushed in, and devoured all the meat in an instant. The captain wondered at this, and asked if these vermin were not unpleasant.

''Oh, yes,'' said they, ''very offensive; and the king would give half his treasure to be freed of them, for they not only destroy his dinner, as you see, but they assault him in his chamber, and even in bed, so that he is obliged to be watched while he is sleeping, for fear of them.''

The captain jumped for joy; he remembered poor Whittington and his cat, and told the king he had a creature on board the ship that would despatch all these vermin immediately. The king jumped so high at the joy which the news gave him that his turban dropped off his head. ''Bring this creature to me,'' says he; ''vermin are dreadful in a court, and if she will perform what you say, I will load your ship with gold and jewels in exchange for her.''

The captain, who knew his business, took this opportunity to set forth the merits of Mrs. Puss. He told his majesty: ''It is not very convenient to part with her, as when she is gone the rats and mice may destroy the goods in the ship—but to oblige your majesty, I will fetch her.''

"Run, run!" said the queen; "I am impatient to see the dear creature."

Away went the captain to the ship, while another dinner was got ready. He put Puss under his arm, and arrived at the palace just in time to see the table full of rats. When the cat saw them, she did not wait for bidding, but jumped out of the captain's arms, and in a few minutes laid almost all the rats and mice dead at her feet. The rest of them in their fright scampered away to their holes.

The king was quite charmed to get rid so easily of such plagues, and the queen desired that the creature who had done them so great a kindness might be brought to her, that she might look at her. Upon which the captain called, "Pussy, pussy, pussy!" and she came to him. He then presented her to the queen, who started back, and was afraid to touch a creature that had made such a havoc among the rats and mice. However, when the captain stroked the cat and called, "Pussy, pussy," the queen also touched her and cried, "Putty, Putty," for she had not learned English. He then put her down on the queen's lap, where she purred and played with her majesty's hand, and then purred herself to sleep.

The king, having seen the exploits of Mrs. Puss, and being informed that her kittens would stock the whole country, and keep it free from rats, bargained with the captain for the whole ship's cargo, and then gave him ten times as much for the cat as all the rest amounted to.

The captain then took leave of the royal party, and set sail with a fair wind for England, and after a happy voyage arrived safe in London.

One morning early, Mr. Fitzwarren had just come to his counting-house and seated himself at the desk, to count over the cash, and settle the business for the day, when somebody came, tap, tap, at the door. "Who's there?" said Mr. Fitzwarren. "A friend," answered the other. "I come to bring you good news of your ship Unicorn." The merchant, bustling up in such a hurry that he forgot his gout, opened the door, and whom should he see waiting but the captain and factor, with a cabinet of jewels and a bill

of lading. When he looked at this the merchant lifted up his eyes and thanked Heaven for sending him such a prosperous voyage.

They then told the story of the cat, and showed the rich present that the king and queen had sent for her to poor Dick. As soon as the merchant heard this, he called out to his servants,—

"Go send him in, and tell him of his fame;
Pray call him Mr. Whittington by name."

Mr. Fitzwarren now showed himself to be a good man; for when some of his servants said so great a treasure was too much for Dick, he answered, "God forbid I should deprive him of the value of a single penny; it is his own, and he shall have it to a farthing."

He then sent for Dick, who at that time was scouring pots for the cook, and was quite dirty. He would have excused himself from coming into the counting-house, saying, "The room is swept, and my shoes are dirty and full of hob-nails." But the merchant ordered him to come in.

Mr. Fitzwarren ordered a chair to be set for him, and so he began to think they were making game of him, and at the same time said to them, "Do not play tricks with a poor simple boy, but let me go down again, if you please, to my work."

"Indeed, Mr. Whittington," said the merchant, "we are all quite in earnest with you, and I most heartily rejoice in the news that these gentlemen have brought you; for the captain has sold your cat to the King of Barbary, and brought you in return for her more riches than I possess in the whole world; and I wish you may long enjoy them!"

Mr. Fitzwarren then told the men to open the great treasure they had brought with them, and said, "Mr. Whittington has nothing to do but to put it in some place of safety."

Poor Dick hardly knew how to behave himself for joy. He begged his master to take what part of it he pleased, since he owed it all to his kindness. "No, no," answered Mr. Fitzwarren, "this is all your own: and I have no doubt but you will use it well."

Dick next asked his mistress, and then

Miss Alice, to accept a part of his good fortune; but they would not, and at the same time told him they felt great joy at his good success. But this poor fellow was too kindhearted to keep it all to himself; so he made a present to the captain, the mate, and the rest of Mr. Fitzwarren's servants, and even to the ill-natured old cook.

After this Mr. Fitzwarren advised him to send for a proper tailor, and get himself dressed like a gentleman; and told him he was welcome to live in his house till he could provide himself with a better.

When Whittington's face was washed, his hair curled, his hat cocked, and he was dressed in a nice suit of clothes, he was as handsome and genteel as any young man who visited at Mr. Fitzwarren's; so that Miss Alice, who had once been so kind to him, and thought of him with pity, now looked upon him as fit to be her sweetheart; and the more so, no doubt, because Whittington was now always thinking what he could do to oblige her, and making her the prettiest presents that could be.

Mr. Fitzwarren soon saw their love for each other, and proposed to join them in marriage; and to this they both readily agreed. A day for the wedding was soon fixed; and they were attended to church by the Lord Mayor, the court of aldermen, the sheriffs and a great number of the richest merchants in London, whom they afterwards treated with a very rich feast.

History tells us that Mr. Whittington and his lady lived in great splendor, and were very happy. They had several children. He was sheriff of London, thrice Lord Mayor, and received the honor of knighthood by Henry V.

He entertained this King and his Queen at dinner, after his conquest of France, so grandly, that the King said, "Never had prince such a subject;" when Sir Richard heard this, he said, "Never had subject such a prince."

The figure of Sir Richard Whittington with his cat in his arms, carved in stone, was to be seen till the year 1780 over the archway of the old prison at Newgate which he built for criminals.

The Old House

Hans Christian Andersen

The city harbors numerous places where the past lives on. Areas of a city fall out of fashion and their buildings and houses fall into disrepair, their time of glory only a memory. For a child like the little boy in "The Old House," such places and houses provide a link with the past and an understanding of change and the loneliness change can bring at times. The tales of Hans Christian Andersen (1805–1875), unlike traditional folktales, abound with furniture and houses— inanimate objects—as characters, all of which are uniquely individual.

Once upon a time there stood in a street a very old house; it was nearly three hundred years old. You could tell what year it had been built by reading the date cut into one of the beams: all around it tulips and curling hop vines had been carved. Right above the entrance a whole verse had been inscribed, and above each window appeared a grinning face. The second story protruded over the first. The lead gutters, which hung under the roof, were shaped like dragons, with the monster's head at either end. The water was

From Hans Christian Andersen, *Hans Andersen: His Classic Fairy Tales.* Translated by Erik Christian Haugaard (Garden City, NY: Doubleday, 1974).

supposed to spout out of their mouths, but it didn't; the gutter was filled with holes and the water ran out of the dragon's stomachs.

All the other houses in the street were new and well kept, their walls were straight and smooth, and they had large windows. It was quite reasonable that they should feel themselves superior to the old house. Had they been able to speak they probably would have said: "How long are we to tolerate that old ruin? Bow windows are out of fashion and, besides, they obstruct our view. It must believe itself to be a castle, judging from the size of the steps leading up to the entrance, and that iron railing makes one think of funerals; not to speak of the brass knobs. It's embarrassing!"

Right across from the old house stood a new house; it was of the same opinion as all the other houses in the street. But behind one of its windows sat a little boy, a little red-cheeked child with bright, shining eyes who preferred the old house, and that both in the daytime when the sun shone and at night in the moonlight. When he looked at the walls of the old house, with its cracks and bare spots where the mortar had fallen off, then he could imagine how the street once had looked; in olden times, when all the houses had had broad steps leading up to their doors, and bay windows, and gables with tall pointed roofs. He could see the soldiers marching through the streets armed with halberds. Oh, he found the old house worth looking at and dreaming about.

Its owner was an old man who wore the strangest old-fashioned breeches, a coat with brass buttons, and a wig that you could see was a wig. Every morning an old servant arrived to clean and run errands for the old gentleman; otherwise, he was all alone. Sometimes he came to the window and looked out into the street; then the little boy nodded to him and the old man nodded back. In this manner they became acquainted; no, more than that, they were friends, although they had never spoken to each other.

The little boy heard his parents say, "Our neighbor, across the street, must be terribly lonely."

Next Sunday the boy made a little package and, when he saw the servant going by in the street, he hurried down and gave it to him. "Would you please give this to your master?" he asked. "I have two tin soldiers, and I would like your master to have one of them, for I have heard that he is so terribly lonely."

The old servant smiled and nodded and took the little package, with the tin soldier inside it, to his master. Later that day a message arrived, inviting the boy to come and visit the old man. The child's parents gave their permission; and thus he finally entered the old house.

The brass knobs on the iron railing seemed to shine so brightly that one might believe that they had been newly polished in honour of the boy's visit. The little carved trumpeters in the oak doorway seemed to be blowing especially hard on their instruments, for their cheeks were all puffed up. It was a fanfare! "Tra . . . tra . . trattalala! The boy is coming! Tra . . . tra . . trattalala!" The door was opened and he stood in the hall. All the walls were covered with paintings portraying ladies in long silk gowns and knights in armour. The boy thought that he could hear the silk gowns rustle and the armour clang. Then there were the stairs; first they went up a goodish way, and then down a little bit, and ended in a balcony. It was wooden and a bit rickety, grass and weeds grew out of every crack, making it look more like a garden than a balcony. Antique flowerpots with human faces and donkey ears stood ranged in a row; the plants grew to suit themselves. One of them was filled with carnations that spread out over the rim in all directions; that is, the green leaves and the stems, the flowers hadn't come yet. One could almost hear the plant saying: "The breeze has caressed me and the sun has kissed me and promised me a flower next Sunday, a little flower next Sunday."

The old servant led the boy into a chamber where the walls did not have paper on them; no, they were covered with leather, which had gilded flowers stamped upon it.

"Gilding fades all too fast.
Leather, that is meant to last,"

said the walls.

In the room were high-backed armchairs

with carvings all over them. "Sit down, sit down!" they cried. And when you sat down in them they mumbled. "Ugh, how it cracks inside me! I think I've got rheumatism like the old cabinet. Ugh, how it creaks and cracks."

At last the little boy entered the room with the bow windows. Here the old master of the house greeted him. "Thank you for the tin soldier, my little friend," said he. "And thank you for coming."

"Thanks, thanks," said all the furniture, although it sounded a little more like: "Crack . . . Crack." There were so many chairs, tables, and cabinets in the room that they stood in each other's way, for they all wanted to see the little boy at once.

In the centre of one of the walls hung a picture of a beautiful young girl. She was laughing and dressed in clothes from a bygone time. She did not say "thank you" or "crack" as the furniture had, but she looked down so kindly at the little boy that he could not help asking, "Where did you get her?"

"From the pawnbroker's," replied the old gentleman. "His shop is filled with pictures that no one cares about any more. The people they portray have been dead so long that no one remembers them. But though she has been dead and gone for fifty years, I knew her once."

Under the portrait hung a bouquet of faded flowers, carefully preserved behind glass. They looked old enough to have been picked half a century ago. The pendulum of the grandfather clock swung back and forth, and the hands moved slowly around, telling everything in the room that time was passing and that they were getting older; but that did not disturb the furniture.

"My parents say that you are terribly lonely," said the little boy.

"Oh," the old man smiled, "that is not altogether true. Old thoughts, old dreams, old memories come and visit me and now you are here. I am not unhappy."

Then from a shelf he took down a book that was filled with wonderful pictures. There were processions in which there were golden carriages, knights, and kings who looked like the ones in a deck of cards; and

then came the citizens carrying the banners of their trades: the tailor's emblem was a pair of scissors held by a lion; the shoemakers had an eagle with two heads above their banner—for, as you know, shoemakers do everything in pairs. What a picture book that was!

The old man left for a moment to fetch some comfits, apples, and nuts; it was certainly nice to be visiting the old house.

"But I can't stand it here!" wailed the tin soldier, who was standing on the lid of a chest. "It is so lonely and sad here; once you have lived with a family you cannot get accustomed to being alone. I can't stand it! The days are so long and the evenings feel even longer. It is not the same here as in your home, where your parents talked so pleasantly and you sweet children made such a lot of lovely noise. No, that poor old man really is lonely. Do you think anybody ever gives him a kiss? Or looks kindly at him? Here there is no Christmas tree ever, or gifts! The only thing he will ever get will be a funeral! . . . I can't stand it!"

"You mustn't take it so to heart," said the little boy. "I think it is very nice here. All the old thoughts and dreams come to visit him, so he said."

"I see none of them and I don't want to either," screamed the tin soldier. "I can't stand it!"

"You will have to," said the little boy just as the old man returned with the comfits, apples, and nuts; and at the sight of them the boy forgot all about the soldier.

Happy and content, the little boy returned home. Days and weeks went by. The boy nodded to the old man from his window, and from the funny bow window of the old house the greeting was returned. Finally the little boy was asked to come visiting again.

The carved trumpeters blew, "Tra . . . tra . . . tratralala. . . . The boy is here! . . . Tra tra!" The knights in armour clanged with their swords and the silk gowns of the ladies rustled, the leather on the wall said its little verse, and the old chairs that had rheumatism creaked. Nothing had changed, for in the old house every day and hour were exactly alike.

"I can't stand it!" screamed the tin soldier as soon as he saw the boy. "I have wept tin tears! It is much too mournful and sad here. Please, let me go to the wars and lose my arms and legs, that at least will be a change. I can't stand it, for I know what it is like to have old thoughts and old memories come visiting. Mine have been here and that is not amusing. Why, I almost jumped right off the lid of the chest. I saw all of you and my own home as plainly as if I had been there. It was Sunday morning and all you children were standing around the big table singing hymns, as you always do on Sunday. Your parents were nearby, looking solemn. Suddenly the door opened and little Maria, who is only two years old, entered. She always dances whenever she hears music, and she tried to dance to the tune you were singing, but hymns are not made for dancing they are too slow. She stood first on one leg and flung her head forward, and then on the other and flung her head forward, but it didn't work out. You looked grave, all of you, but I found it too difficult not to laugh—at least inside myself. I laughed so hard that I fell off the table and hit my head so hard that I got a lump on it. I know it was wrong of me to laugh and the lump was punishment for it. That is what the old man meant by old thoughts and memories: everything that has ever happened to you comes back inside you. . . . Tell me, do you still sing your hymns on Sunday? Tell me something about little Maria and about my comrade, the other tin soldier. He must be happy. Oh, I can't stand it!"

"I have given you away," said the little boy. "You will have to stay, can't you understand that?"

The old man brought him a drawer in which lay many wonderful things. There were old playing cards with gilded edges, a little silver piggy bank, and a fish with a wiggly tail. Other drawers were opened and all the curiosities were looked at and examined. Finally the old man opened the harpsichord; on the side of the lid was a painting of a landscape. The instrument was out of tune but the old man played on it anyway, and hummed a melody.

"Ah yes, she used to sing that," he sighed, and looked towards the painting he had bought from the pawnbroker and his eyes shone like a young man's.

"I am going to the wars! I am going to the wars!" screamed the tin soldier as loudly as he could, and fell off the chest.

"What could have happened to him?" said the old man. Together he and the boy were searching for the little soldier on the floor. "Never mind, I will find him later," said the old man, but he never did. There were so many cracks in the floor and the tin soldier had fallen right down through one of them; there he lay buried alive.

The day passed and the little boy returned home. Many weeks went by, winter had come. All the windows were frozen over. The little boy had to breathe on the glass until he could thaw a little hole so that he could see out. Across the street the old house looked quite deserted; the snow lay in drifts on the steps. They had not been swept; one would think no one was at home. And no one was. The kind old man had died.

That evening a hearse drew up in front of the old house and a coffin was carried down the steps. The old man was not to be buried in the town cemetery but somewhere out in the country, where he had been born. The hearse drove away. No one followed it, for all his friends and family had died long ago. The little boy kissed his fingers and threw a kiss after the hearse as it disappeared down the street.

A few days afterwards an auction was held; the furniture in the old house was sold. The boy watched from the window. He saw the knights in armour and the ladies with their silken gowns being carried out of the house. The old high-backed chairs, the funny flowerpots with faces and donkey ears were bought by strangers. Only the portrait of the lady found no buyer; it was returned to the pawnbroker. There it hung; no one remembered her and no one cared for the old picture.

Next spring the house itself was torn down, "It was a monstrosity," said the people as they went by. One could see right into the room with the leather-covered walls; the leather was torn and hung flapping like banners in the wind. The grass and weeds on the balcony clung tenaciously to the broken beams. But at last all was cleared away.

"That was good," said the neighbouring houses.

A new house was built, with straight walls and big windows but not quite where the old house had stood; it was a little farther back from the street. On the site of the old house a little garden was planted, and up the walls of the houses on either side grew vines. A fine iron fence with a gate enclosed it, and people would stop in the street to look in, for it was most attractive. The sparrows would sit in the vines and talk and talk as sparrows do, but not about the old house, for they were too young to remember it.

Years went by and the little boy had become a grown man, a good and clever man of whom his parents could be justly proud. He had just got married and had moved into the new house. His young wife was planting a little wild flower in the front garden. He was watching her with a smile. Just as she finished, and was patting the earth around the little plant, she pricked her little hand. Something sharp was sticking out of the soft earth. What could it be?

It was —imagine it!—the tin soldier! The one that had fallen off the chest and down through a crack in the flooring. It had survived the wrecking of the old house, falling hither and thither as beams and floors disappeared, until at last it had been buried in the earth and there it had lain for many years.

The young woman cleaned the soldier off with a green leaf and then with her own handkerchief. It had perfume on it and smelled so delicious that the soldier felt as though he were awakening from a deep sleep.

"Let me have a look at him," said the young man; then he laughed and shook his head. "I don't believe it can be him, but he reminds me of a tin soldier that I once had." Then he told his wife about the old house and its old master and about the tin soldier that he had sent over to keep the old man company, when he had been a boy, because he had known that the old man was so terribly alone.

He told the story so well that his young wife's eyes filled with tears as she heard about the old house and the old man. "It could be the same soldier," she said. "I will keep it so that I shall not forget the story you have told me. But you must show me the old man's grave."

"I do not know where it is," her husband replied. "No one does; all those who knew him were dead. You must remember that I was a very small boy then."

"How terribly lonely he must have been," sighed the young woman.

"Yes, terribly lonely," echoed the tin soldier. "But it is truly good to find that one is not forgotten."

"Good," croaked something nearby in so weak a voice that only the tin soldier heard it. It was a little piece of leather from the walls of the old house. The gilding had gone long ago, and it looked like a little clod of wet earth. But it still had an opinion, and it expressed it.

"Gilding fades all too fast,
But leather, that is meant to last."

But the tin soldier did not believe that.

The Happy Prince

Oscar Wilde

Often, we think of cities as impersonal and uncaring. "The Happy Prince," by Oscar Wilde (1854–1900), refutes this idea and makes cities and, in particular,

From Oscar Wilde, *The Complete Works of Oscar Wilde* (London: Collins, 1966).

the objects characteristic of cities, such as statues, into caring, feeling entities.
Wilde's writing is full of the color and music of poetry, and this is never more
apparent than in the following tale.

High above the city, on a tall column, stood the statue of the Happy Prince. He was gilded all over with thin leaves of fine gold, for eyes he had two bright sapphires, and a large red ruby glowed on his sword-hilt.

He was very much admired indeed. "He is as beautiful as a weathercock," remarked one of the Town Councillors who wished to gain a reputation for having artistic tastes; "only not quite so useful," he added, fearing lest people should think him unpractical, which he really was not.

"Why can't you be like the Happy Prince?" asked a sensible mother of her little boy who was crying for the moon. "The Happy Prince never dreams of crying for anything."

"I am glad there is some one in the world who is quite happy," muttered a disappointed man as he gazed at the wonderful statue.

"He looks just like an angel," said the Charity Children as they came out of the cathedral in their bright scarlet cloaks and their clean white pinafores.

"How do you know?" said the Mathematical Master, "you have never seen one."

"Ah! but we have, in our dreams," answered the children; and the Mathematical Master frowned and looked very severe, for he did not approve of children dreaming.

One night there flew over the city a little Swallow. His friends had gone away to Egypt six weeks before, but he had stayed behind, for he was in love with the most beautiful Reed. He had met her early in the spring as he was flying down the river after a big yellow moth, and had been so attracted by her slender waist that he had stopped to talk to her.

"Shall I love you?" said the Swallow, who liked to come to the point at once, and the Reed made him a low bow. So he flew round and round her, touching the water with his wings, and making silver ripples. This was his courtship, and it lasted all through the summer.

"It is a ridiculous attachment," twittered the other Swallows; "she has no money, and far too many relations;" and indeed the river was quite full of Reeds. Then, when the autumn came they all flew away.

After they had gone he felt lonely, and began to tire of his ladylove. "She has no conversation," he said, "and I am afraid that she is a coquette, for she is always flirting with the wind." And certainly, whenever the wind blew, the Reed made the most graceful curtseys. "I admit that she is domestic," he continued, "but I love travelling, and my wife, consequently, should love travelling also."

"Will you come away with me?" he said finally to her, but the Reed shook her head, she was so attached to her home.

"You have been trifling with me," he cried. "I am off to the Pyramids. Goodbye!" and he flew away.

All day long he flew, and at night-time he arrived at the city. "Where shall I put up?" he said; "I hope the town has made preparations."

Then he saw the statue on the tall column.

"I will put up there," he cried; "it is a fine position, with plenty of fresh air." So he alighted just between the feet of the Happy Prince.

"I have a golden bedroom," he said softly to himself as he looked round, and he prepared to go to sleep; but just as he was putting his head under his wing a large drop of water fell on him. "What a curious thing!" he cried; "there is not a single cloud in the sky, the stars are quite clear and bright, and yet it is raining. The climate in the north of Europe is really dreadful. The Reed used to like the rain, but that was merely her selfishness."

Then another drop fell.

"What is the use of a statue if it cannot keep the rain off?" he said; "I must look for a good chimney-pot," and he determined to fly away.

But before he had opened his wings, a third drop fell, and he looked up, and saw——Ah! what did he see?

The eyes of the Happy Prince were filled with tears, and tears were running down his golden cheeks. His face was so beautiful in the moonlight that the little Swallow was filled with pity.

"Who are you?" he said.

"I am the Happy Prince."

"Why are you weeping then?" asked the Swallow; "you have quite drenched me."

"When I was alive and had a human heart," answered the statue, "I did not know what tears were, for I lived in the Palace of Sans-Souci, where sorrow is not allowed to enter. In the daytime I played with my companions in the garden, and in the evening I led the dance in the Great Hall. Round the garden ran a very lofty wall, but I never cared to ask what lay beyond it, everything about me was so beautiful. My courtiers called me the Happy Prince, and happy indeed I was, if pleasure be happiness. So I lived, and so I died. And now that I am dead they have set me up here so high that I can see all the ugliness and all the misery of my city, and though my heart is made of lead yet I cannot choose but weep."

"What! is he not solid gold?" said the Swallow to himself. He was too polite to make any personal remarks out loud.

"Far away," continued the statue in a low musical voice, "far away in a little street there is a poor house. One of the windows is open, and through it I can see a woman seated at a table. Her face is thin and worn, and she has coarse, red hands, all pricked by the needle, for she is a seamstress. She is embroidering passion-flowers on a satin gown for the loveliest of the Queen's maids-of-honour to wear at the next Court-ball. In a bed in the corner of the room her little boy is lying ill. He has a fever, and is asking for oranges. His mother has nothing to give him but river water, so he is crying. Swallow, Swallow, little Swallow, will you not bring her the ruby out of my sword-hilt? My feet are fastened to this pedestal and I cannot move."

"I am waited for in Egypt," said the Swallow. "My friends are flying up and down the Nile, and talking to the large lotus-flowers. Soon they will go to sleep in the tomb of the great King. The King is there himself in his painted coffin. He is wrapped in yellow linen, and embalmed with spices. Round his neck is a chain of pale green jade, and his hands are like withered leaves."

"Swallow, Swallow, little Swallow," said the Prince, "will you not stay with me for one night, and be my messenger? The boy is so thirsty, and the mother so sad."

"I don't think I like boys," answered the Swallow. "Last summer, when I was staying on the river, there were two rude boys, the miller's sons, who were always throwing stones at me. They never hit me, of course; we swallows fly far too well for that, and besides, I come of a family famous for its agility; but still, it was a mark of disrespect."

But the Happy Prince looked so sad that the little Swallow was sorry. "It is very cold here," he said; "but I will stay with you for one night, and be your messenger."

"Thank you, little Swallow," said the Prince.

So the Swallow picked out the great ruby from the Prince's sword, and flew away with it in his beak over the roofs of the town.

He passed by the cathedral tower, where the white marble angels were sculptured. He passed by the palace and heard the sound of dancing. A beautiful girl came out on the balcony with her lover. "How wonderful the stars are," he said to her, "and how wonderful is the power of love!"

"I hope my dress will be ready in time for the State-ball," she answered; "I have ordered passion-flowers to be embroidered on it; but the seamstresses are so lazy."

He passed over the river, and saw the lanterns hanging to the masts of the ships. He passed over the Ghetto, and saw the old Jews bargaining with each other, and weighing out money in copper scales. At last he came to the poor house and looked in. The boy was tossing feverishly on his bed, and the mother had fallen asleep, she was so tired. In he hopped, and laid the great ruby on the table beside the woman's thimble. Then he flew gently round the bed, fanning the boy's forehead with his wings. "How cool I feel!" said the boy, "I must be getting better:" and he sank into a delicious slumber.

Then the Swallow flew back to the Happy Prince, and told him what he had done. "It is curious," he remarked, "but I feel quite warm now, although it is so cold."

"That is because you have done a good action," said the Prince. And the little Swallow began to think, and then he fell asleep. Thinking always made him sleepy.

When day broke he flew down to the river and had a bath. "What a remarkable phenomenon!" said the Professor of Ornithology as he was passing over the bridge. "A swallow in winter!" And he wrote a long letter about it to the local newspaper. Every one quoted it, it was full of so many words that they could not understand.

"To-night I go to Egypt," said the Swallow, and he was in high spirits at the prospect. He visited all the public monuments, and sat a long time on top of the church steeple. Wherever he went the Sparrows chirruped, and said to each other, "What a distinguished stranger!" so he enjoyed himself very much.

When the moon rose he flew back to the Happy Prince. "Have you any commissions for Egypt?" he cried; "I am just starting."

"Swallow, Swallow, little Swallow," said the Prince, "will you not stay with me one night longer?"

"I am waited for in Egypt," answered the Swallow. "To-morrow my friends will fly up to the Second Cataract. The river-horse couches there among the bulrushes, and on a great granite house sits the God Memnon. All night long he watches the stars, and when the morning star shines he utters one cry of joy, and then he is silent. At noon the yellow lions come down to the water's edge to drink. They have eyes like green beryls, and their roar is louder than the roar of the cataract."

"Swallow, Swallow, little Swallow," said the Prince, "far away across the city I see a young man in a garret. He is leaning over a desk covered with papers, and in a tumbler by his side there is a bunch of withered violets. His hair is brown and crisp, and his lips are red as a pomegranate, and he has large and dreamy eyes. He is trying to finish a play for the Director of the Theatre, but he is too cold to write any more. There is no fire in the grate, and hunger has made him faint."

"I will wait with you one night longer," said the Swallow, who really had a good heart. "Shall I take him another ruby?"

"Alas! I have no ruby now," said the Prince; "my eyes are all that I have left. They are made of rare sapphires, which were brought out of India a thousand years ago. Pluck out one of them and take it to him. He will sell it to the jeweller, and buy firewood, and finish his play."

"Dear Prince," said the Swallow, "I cannot do that"; and he began to weep.

"Swallow, Swallow, little Swallow," said the Prince, "do as I command you."

So the Swallow plucked out the Prince's eye, and flew away to the student's garret. It was easy enough to get in, as there was a hole in the roof. Through this he darted, and came into the room. The young man had his head buried in his hands, so he did not hear the flutter of the bird's wings, and when he looked up he found the beautiful sapphire lying on the withered violets.

"I am beginning to be appreciated," he cried; "this is from some great admirer. Now I can finish my play," and he looked quite happy.

The next day the Swallow flew down to the harbour. He sat on the mast of a large vessel and watched the sailors hauling big chests out of the hold with ropes. "Heave ahoy!" they shouted as each chest came up. "I am going to Egypt!" cried the Swallow, but nobody minded, and when the moon rose he flew back to the Happy Prince.

"I am come to bid you good-bye," he cried.

"Swallow, Swallow, little Swallow," said the Prince, "will you not stay with me one night longer?"

"It is winter," answered the Swallow, "and the chill snow will soon be here. In Egypt the sun is warm on the green palm-trees, and the crocodiles lie in the mud and look lazily about them. My companions are building a nest in the Temple of Baalbee, and the pink and white doves are watching them, cooing to each other. Dear Prince, I must leave you, but I will never forget you, and next spring I will bring you back two beautiful jewels in place of those you have given away. The ruby shall be redder than a red rose, and the sapphire shall be as blue as the great sea.''

"In the square below,'' said the Happy Prince, ''there stands a little match-girl. She has let her matches fall in the gutter, and they are all spoiled. Her father will beat her if she does not bring home some money, and she is crying. She has no shoes or stockings, and her little head is bare. Pluck out my other eye, and give it to her, and her father will not beat her.''

"I will stay with you one night longer,'' said the swallow, ''but I cannot pluck out your eye. You would be quite blind then.''

"Swallow, Swallow, little Swallow,'' said the Prince, '' do as I command you.''

So he plucked out the Prince's other eye, and darted down with it. He swooped past the match-girl, and slipped the jewel into the palm of her hand. ''What a lovely bit of glass!'' cried the little girl; and she ran home laughing.

Then the Swallow came back to the Prince. ''You are blind now,'' he said, ''so I will stay with you always.''

"No, little Swallow,'' said the poor prince, ''you must go away to Egypt.''

"I will stay with you always,'' said the Swallow, and he slept at the Prince's feet.

All the next day he sat on the Prince's shoulder, and told him stories of what he had seen in strange lands. He told him of the red ibises, who stand in long rows on the banks of the Nile, and catch goldfish in their beaks; of the Sphinx, who is as old as the world itself, and lives in the desert, and knows everything; of the merchants, who walk slowly by the side of their camels and carry amber beads in their hands; of the King of the Mountains of the Moon, who is as black as ebony, and worships a large crystal; of the great green snake that sleeps in a palm-tree, and has twenty priests to feed it with honey-cakes; and of the pygmies who sail over a big lake on the large flat leaves, and are always at war with the butterflies.

"Dear little Swallow,'' said the Prince, ''you tell me of marvellous things, but more marvellous than anything is the suffering of men and of women. There is no Mystery so great as Misery. Fly over my city, little Swallow, and tell me what you see there.''

So the Swallow flew over the great city, and saw the rich making merry in their beautiful houses, while the beggars were sitting at the gates. He flew into dark lanes, and saw the white faces of starving children looking out listlessly at the black streets. Under the archway of a bridge two little boys were lying in one another's arms to try and keep themselves warm. ''How hungry we are!'' they said. ''You must not lie here,'' shouted the watchman, and they wandered out into the rain.

Then he flew back and told the Prince what he had seen.

"I am covered with fine gold,'' said the Prince, ''you must take it off, leaf by leaf, and give it to my poor; the living always think that gold can make them happy.''

Leaf after leaf of the fine gold the Swallow picked off, till the Happy Prince looked quite dull and grey. Leaf after leaf of the fine gold he brought to the poor, and the children's faces grew rosier, and they laughed and played games in the street. ''We have bread now!'' they cried.

Then the snow came, and after the snow came the frost. The streets looked as if they were made of silver, they were so bright and glistening; long icicles like crystal daggers hung down from the eaves of the houses, everybody went about in furs, and the little boys wore scarlet caps and skated on the ice.

The poor little Swallow grew colder and colder, but he would not leave the Prince, he loved him too well. He picked up crumbs outside the baker's door when the baker was not looking, and tried to keep himself warm by flapping his wings.

But at last he knew that he was going to die. He had just enough strength to fly up to the Prince's shoulder once more. ''Good-bye, dear Prince!'' he murmured, ''will you let me kiss your hand?''

"I am glad that you are going to Egypt at last, little Swallow," said the Prince, "you have stayed too long here; but you must kiss me on the lips, for I love you."

"It is not to Egypt that I am going," said the Swallow. "I am going to the House of Death. Death is the brother of Sleep, is he not?"

And he kissed the Happy Prince on the lips, and fell down dead at his feet.

At that moment a curious crack sounded inside the statue, as if something had broken. The fact is that the leaden heart had snapped right in two. It certainly was a dreadfully hard frost.

Early the next morning the Mayor was walking in the square below in company with the Town Councillors. As they passed the column he looked up at the statue: "Dear me! how shabby the Happy Prince looks!" he said.

"How shabby, indeed!" cried the Town Councillors, who always agreed with the Mayor; and they went up to look at it.

"The ruby has fallen out of his sword, his eyes are gone, and he is golden no longer," said the Mayor; "in fact, he is little better than a beggar!"

"Little better than a begger," said the Town Councillors.

"And here is actually a dead bird at his feet!" continued the Mayor. "We must really issue a proclamation that birds are not to be allowed to die here." And the Town Clerk made a note of the suggestion.

So they pulled down the statue of the Happy Prince. "As he is no longer beautiful he is no longer useful," said the Art Professor at the University.

Then they melted the statue in a furnace, and the Mayor held a meeting of the Corporation to decide what was to be done with the metal. "We must have another statue, of course," he said, "and it shall be a statue of myself."

"Of myself," said each of the Town Councillors, and they quarrelled. When I last heard of them they were quarrelling still.

"What a strange thing!" said the overseer of the workmen at the foundry. "This broken lead heart will not melt in the furnace. We must throw it away." So they threw it on a dust-heap where the dead Swallow was also lying.

"Bring me the two most precious things in the city," said God to one of His Angels; and the Angel brought Him the leaden heart and the dead bird.

"You have rightly chosen," said God, "for in my garden of Paradise this little bird shall sing for evermore, and in my city of gold the Happy Prince shall praise me."

The Snow in Chelm

Isaac Bashevis Singer

Here is a story of a village of silly people who want their town to become a city and think they have the means by which to accomplish this. "The Snow in Chelm" has its origins in the Middle European Jewish folklore and legends that Isaac Bashevis Singer (1904–) was raised with. This tale amply illustrates the unique combination of fantasy, warmth, wit, and insight for which Singer's writings have become known.

Chelm was a village of fools, fools young and old. One night someone spied the moon reflected in a barrel of water. The people of Chelm imagined it had fallen in. They sealed

From Isaac Bashevis Singer, "The Snow in Chelm," *Zlateh the Goat and Other Stories* (New York: Harper & Row, 1966). Illustrations by Maurice Sendak.

the barrel so that the moon would not escape. When the barrel was opened in the morning and the moon wasn't there, the villagers decided it had been stolen. They sent for the police, and when the thief couldn't be found, the fools of Chelm cried and moaned.

Of all the fools of Chelm, the most famous were its seven Elders. Because they were the village's oldest and greatest fools, they ruled in Chelm. They had white beards and high foreheads from too much thinking.

Once, on a Hanukkah night, the snow fell all evening. It covered all of Chelm like a silver tablecloth. The moon shone; the stars twinkled; the snow shimmered like pearls and diamonds.

That evening the seven Elders were sitting and pondering, wrinkling their foreheads. The village was in need of money, and they did not know where to get it. Suddenly the oldest of them all, Gronam the Great Fool, exclaimed, "The snow is silver!"

"I see pearls in the snow!" another shouted.

Each one took hold of a leg.

"And I see diamonds!" a third called out.

It became clear to the Elders of Chelm that a treasure had fallen from the sky.

But soon they began to worry. The people of Chelm liked to go walking, and they would most certainly trample the treasure. What was to be done? Silly Tudras had an idea.

"Let's send a messenger to knock on all the windows and let the people know that they must remain in their houses until all the silver, all the pearls, and all the diamonds are safely gathered up.

For a while the Elders were satisfied. They rubbed their hands in approval of the clever idea. But then Dopey Lekisch called out in consternation, "The messenger himself will trample the treasure."

The Elders realized that Lekisch was right, and again they wrinkled their high foreheads in an effort to solve the problem.

"I've got it!" exclaimed Shmerel the Ox.

"Tell us, tell us," pleaded the Elders.

"The messenger must not go on foot. He must be carried on a table so that his feet will not tread on the precious snow."

Everybody was delighted with Shmerel the Ox's solution; and the Elders, clapping their hands, admired their own wisdom.

The Elders immediately sent to the kitchen for Gimpel the errand boy and stood him on a table. Now who was going to carry the table? It was lucky that in the kitchen there were Treitle the cook, Berel the potato peeler, Yukel the salad mixer, and Yontel, who was in charge of the community goat. All four were ordered to lift up the table on which Gimpel stood. Each one took hold of a leg. On top stood Gimpel, grasping a wooden hammer with which to tap on the villagers' windows. Off they went.

At each window Gimpel knocked with the hammer and called out, "No one leaves the house tonight. A treasure has fallen from the sky, and it is forbidden to step on it."

The people of Chelm obeyed the Elders and remained in their houses all night. Meanwhile the Elders themselves sat up trying to figure out how to make the best use of the treasure once it had been gathered up.

Silly Tudras proposed that they sell it and buy a goose which lays golden eggs. Thus the community would be provided with a steady income.

Dopey Lekisch had another idea. Why not buy eyeglasses that make things look bigger for all the inhabitants of Chelm? Then the houses, the streets, the stores would all look bigger, and of course if Chelm *looked* bigger, then it *would be* bigger. It would no longer be a village, but a big city.

There were other, equally clever ideas. But while the Elders were weighing their various plans, morning came and the sun rose. They looked out of the window, and, alas, they saw the snow had been trampled. The heavy boots of the table carriers had destroyed the treasure.

The Elders of Chelm clutched at their white beards and admitted to one another that they had made a mistake. Perhaps, they reasoned, four others should have carried the four men who had carried the table that held Gimpel the errand boy?

After long deliberations the Elders decided that if next Hanukkah a treasure would again fall down from the sky, that is exactly what they would do.

Although the villagers remained without a treasure, they were full of hope for the next year and praised their Elders, who they knew could always be counted on to find a way, no matter how difficult the problem.

FOLK RHYMES AND POETRY

Mother Goose Rhymes

Seasonal changes are noted even in the city. In this small rhyme, spring is heralded by the appearance of daffodils.

Daffy-down-Dilly has come up to town,
In a yellow petticoat and a green gown.

Entrepreneurship is the heart's blood of a city, and many rhymes about city life deal with buying and selling.

Tommy kept a chandler's shop,
Richard went to buy a mop,
Tommy gave him such a whop,
That sent him out of his chandler's shop.

Tommy kept a chandler's shop.

To market, to market, a gallop, a trot,
To buy some meat to put in the pot;
Threepence a quarter, fourpence a side,
If it hadn't been killed it must have died.

*Little Blue Betty is a name that appears in
a number of rhymes, as does the variant Old
Betty Blue. This particular rhyme presents
the seamier side of urban entrepreneurship.
It is thought that Betty is depicted here as a
prostitute and this occupation leads to her
fall.*

Little Blue Betty lived in a lane,
She sold good ale to gentlemen:
Gentlemen came every day,
And Little Blue Betty hopped away;
She hopped upstairs to make her bed,
And she tumbled down,
    and broke her head.

*This rhyme is one to which children would
play a game and is similar to one that would
be told to amuse infants:*

> My mother and your mother
>   Went over the way;
> Said my mother to your mother,
>   It's chop-a-nose day.

*On the last line the child's nose is held
between finger and thumb and "chopped
off" with the other hand.*

Margery Mutton-pie, and Johnny Bo-peep,
They met together in Gracechurch Street;
In and out, in and out, over the way,
Oh! says Johnny, 'tis Chop-nose Day.

*This skipping rhyme shows the
rambunctious play of city children.*

Girls and Boys,
Come out to play,
The Moon does shine,
As bright as Day,
Come with a Hoop,
Come with a Call,
Come with a good will,
Or not at all.
Loose your supper,
And loose your Sleep,
Come to your Play fellows
In the Street,
Up the Ladder
And down the Wall,
A halfpenny Loaf
Will serve us all.
You find milk
And I'll find flour,
And we'll have a pudding
In half an hour.

Oranges and Lemons

*Until recently, a city's church bells played
an important role. They told the time and
heralded events of significant joy or sadness.
If you visited all the churches mentioned in
the poem, you would make a complete tour
of the city of London.*

Gay go up and gay go down
To ring the bells of London Town.

Bulls' eyes and targets,
Say the bells of St. Marg'et's.

Brickbats and tiles,
Say the bells of St. Giles'.

Ha'pence and farthings,
Say the bells of St. Martin's.

Oranges and lemons,
Say the bells of St. Clement's.

Pancakes and fritters,
Say the bells of St. Peter's.

Two sticks and an apple,
Say the bells of Whitechapel.

Old father Baldpate,
Say the slow bells of Aldgate.

Pokers and tongs,
Say the bells of St. John's.

Kettles and pans,
Say the bells of St. Anne's.

The Clock

Olive Beaupré Miller (trans.)

Like "Oranges and Lemons," this French rhyme illustrates the important part that bells performed in the daily life of the city.

Ding dong! I am the clock!
The castle clock am I!
Ding dong! Ding dong! Tick tock!
Up in the tower so high!

From height of thy tall tower,
Thy bell, O clock, now ring,
And tell us, pray, the hour
With thy Ding dong! Ding! Ding!

From Olive Beaupré Miller, trans. *Nursery Friends from France* (Chicago: Book House for Children, 1927).

Upon Westminster Bridge

William Wordsworth

A city can have a beauty akin to that of nature. Wordsworth wrote this sonnet while

From William Wordsworth, *The Poetical Works of Wordsworth* (New York: Crowell, 1877).

he and his sister, Dorothy, were leaving London to travel to Calais, France. Both were struck by the majesty of the city. Dorothy wrote, "We mounted the Dover coach at Charing Cross. It was a beautiful morning. The city, St. Paul's, with the river, and a multitude of little boats, made a most beautiful sight as we crossed Westminster Bridge. . . . The sun shone so brightly, with such a fierce light that there was something like the purity of one of nature's grandest spectacles."

Earth has not anything to show more fair:
Dull would he be of soul who could pass by
  A sight so touching in its majesty:
This City now doth like a garment wear
The beauty of the morning; silent, bare,
  Ships, towers, domes, theatres, and
    temples lie
Open unto the fields, and to the sky;
All bright and glittering in the smokeless air.
Never did sun more beautifully steep
  In his first splendour valley, rock, or hill;
Ne'er saw I, never felt, a calm so deep!
  The river glideth at his own sweet will:
Dear God! the very houses seem asleep;
  And all that mighty heart is lying still!

Parliament Hill

H. H. Bashford

The city can be a fearful, confusing place for a child. In this poem, however, the child has an island of warmth and light that makes the rest of the city a welcome place. Children need to know that there is a place of safety for them, whether in a city or in the country.

Have you seen the lights of London how they
  twinkle, twinkle, twinkle,
Yellow lights, and silver lights, and crimson
  lights, and blue?

From H. H. Bashford, *Songs Out of School* (London: Constable Publishers).

And there among the other lights is Daddy's
  little lantern-light,
Bending like a finger-tip, beckoning to you.

Never was so tall a hill for tiny feet to
  scramble up,
Never was so strange a world to baffle
  little eyes,
Half of it as black as ink with ghostly feet
  to fall on it,
And half of it all filled with lamps and
  cheerful sounds and cries.

Lamps in golden palaces, and station-
  lamps, and steamer-lamps,
Very nearly all the lamps that Mother ever
  knew,
And there among the other lamps is Daddy's
  little lantern lamp
Bending like a finger-tip, and beckoning to
  you.

City

Langston Hughes

*In this short lyric, Langston Hughes captures
the essence of the city. Many cultures believe
that inanimate objects can possess an anima,
or soul. If a city were to have a soul, it might
perhaps be perceived in this way.*

In the morning the city
Spreads its wings
Making a song
In stone that sings.

In the evening the city
Goes to bed
Hanging lights
About its head.

From Langston Hughes, *The Langston Hughes Reader*
(New York: Braziller, 1958). Reprinted by permission of
Harold Ober Associates.

Skyscrapers

Rachel Field

*Rachel Field (1894–1942) is perhaps best
known for her book* Hitty, Her First Hundred
Years, *which received the Newbery Award in
1930. She was an author, playwright, and
poet. In this poem, she has turned her
considerable talent to viewing the city
through a child's eyes and asks the questions
a child might ask of skyscrapers. Carl
Sandburg's "The Two Skyscrapers Who
Decided to Have a Child" seems to answer
many of the questions posed in this poem.*

Do skyscrapers ever grow tired
  Of holding themselves up high?
Do they ever shiver on frosty nights
  With their tops against the sky?

Do they feel lonely sometimes,
  Because they have grown so tall?
Do they ever wish they could lie right down
  And never get up at all?

From Rachel Field, *Collected Poems* (New York: Macmillan, 1930).

Manhole Covers

Karl Shapiro

*Karl Shapiro received the Pulitzer Prize in
1944 and the Bollingen Prize in 1968 for his
poetry. Many of his poems deal with the
relationship between the individual and
society. "Manhole Covers" shows that there
can be beauty in even a small detail of city
life.*

The beauty of manhole covers—what of that?
Like medals struck by a great savage khan,

From Karl Shapiro, *Collected Poems, 1940–1978* (New
York: Random House, 1978).

Like Mayan calendar stones, unliftable,
   indecipherable,
Not like the old electrum, chased and scored,
Mottoed and sculptured to a turn,
But notched and whelked and pocked and
   smashed
With the great company names
(Gentle Bethlehem, smiling United States).
This rustproof artifact of my street,
Long after roads are melted away will lie
Sidewise in the grave of the iron-old world,
Bitten at the edges,
Strong with its cryptic American,
Its dated beauty.

Thaw in the City

Lou Lipsitz

As was seen in the simple rhyme "Daffy-down-Dilly," spring can be a cause for celebration even in the city. In this poem, Lou Lipsitz captures the dreariness of winter and the heightening of the senses and feeling of joy that spring can bring.

Now my legs begin to walk,
The filthy piles of snow are melting.
Pavements are wet.

What clear, tiny streams!
Suddenly I feel the blood flowing in the
   veins
in the backs of my hands.

And I hear a voice—a wonderful voice—
as if someone I loved had lifted a window
and called my name.

The streets wash over me like waves.
I sail in a boat of factories and sparrows
out of sight.

From Lou Lipsitz, *Cold Water* (Middletown, Conn.: Wesleyan University Press, 1967).

In a Station of the Métro

Ezra Pound

This haikulike poem reflects the influence that Chinese and Japanese poetry had on Ezra Pound and also the influence of the imagist movement, which advocated conciseness and the evocation of images in hard, clear poetry. As X. J. Kennedy notes in his Introduction to Literature, *"Haiku written in English frequently ignores [the traditional] pattern [three lines of 5, 7, 5] and . . . may be rhymed or unrhymed as the poet prefers."*

The apparition of these faces in the crowd;
Petals on a wet, black bough.

From Ezra Pound, *Selected Poems of Ezra Pound* (New York: New Directions, 1957).

Juke Box Love Song

Langston Hughes

Cities are diverse collections of people, each with its own traditions, music, and customs. Langston Hughes's poetry often uses black jazz and folk rhythms to convey his message. "Juke Box Love Song" is no exception; it captures the rhythm and flair of Harlem, in New York City, with its imagery and beat.

I could take the Harlem night
and wrap around you,
Take the neon lights and make a crown,
Take the Lenox Avenue buses,
Taxis, subways,
And for your love song tone their rumble
   down.
Take Harlem's heartbeat,
Make a drumbeat,
Put it on a record, let it whirl,

From Langston Hughes, *The Langston Hughes Reader* (New York: Braziller, 1958). Reprinted by permission of Harold Ober Associates.

And while we listen to it play,
Dance with you till day—
Dance with you, my sweet brown Harlem
girl.

I saw him with my own eyes in those days
The God of stickball
Disappearing down the street
Skinny and shining in the nightfall light.

Of Kings and Things

Lillian Morrison

*Lillian Morrison was born in Jersey City,
New Jersey, where many of her poems,
including this one, are set. Here, she
captures the elusive and fleeting spirit of
childhood that exists everywhere, city or
country.*

What happened to Joey on our block
Who could hit a spaldeen four sewers
And wore his invisible crown
With easy grace, leaning, body-haloed
In the steet-lamp night?

He was better than Babe Ruth
Because we could actually see him hit
Every Saturday morning,
With a mop handle thinner than any
baseball bat,
That small ball which flew forever.
Whack! straight out at first, then
Rising, rising unbelievably soaring in a
Tremendous heart-bursting trajectory
To come down finally, blocks away,
Bouncing off a parked car's
Fender, eluding the lone outfielder.

Did he get a good job?
Is he married now, with kids?
Is he famous in another constellation?

From Lillian Morrison, *The Ghosts of Jersey City and
Other Poems* (New York: Crowell, 1967).

Rain

Frank Marshall Davis

*In "Rain," Frank Marshall Davis gives us
an unusual glimpse of rain in the city,
stressing in free verse the sounds of rain, as
well as its visual images. Children delight in
hearing different sounds, and this poem
enables them to conjure up the different
sounds of rain as personified by the "aged
man" with his harp.*

Today the rain
is an aged man
a gray old man
in a music store.

Today houses
are strings of a harp
soprano harp strings
bass harp strings
in a music store

The ancient man
strums the harp
with thin long fingers
attentively picking
a weary jingle
a soft jazzy jingle
then dodders away
before the boss comes 'round. . . .

From Frank Marshall David, "Rain," in *I Think I Saw a
Snail*, Lee Bennett Hopkins, ed. (New York: Crown,
1969).

FICTION

From the Mixed-up Files of Mrs. Basil E. Frankweiler

E. L. Konigsburg

E. L. Konigsburg's books deal with the problems and joys of suburban children. In this book, for which she received the Newbery Award, Kronigsburg chronicles the adventures of two such children, Claudia and her brother, Jamie, who run away from home and take up residence in the Metropolitan Museum of Art in New York City. There, Claudia becomes intrigued by a statue of an angel that is so beautiful that she refuses to go home until she discovers its sculptor. Claudia and Jamie adjust amusingly to their strange surroundings and to city life, as this chapter illustrates.

They had been gone from home for three days now. Claudia insisted on a fresh change of underwear every day. That was the way she had been brought up. She insisted for Jamie, too. No question about it; their laundry was becoming a problem. They had to get to a laundromat. That night they removed all their dirty clothes from their instrument cases and stuffed those that would fit into various pockets. Those that didn't fit, they wore. A double layer of clothes never hurts anyone in winter, as long as the clean ones are worn closest to the skin.

Saturday seemed a good day for house-keeping chores. There would be no school groups for them to join. Claudia suggested that they eat both meals outside the museum. Jamie agreed. Claudia next suggested a real sit-down restaurant with tablecloths on the tables and waiters to serve you. Jamie said ''NO'' with such force that Claudia didn't try to persuade him.

From breakfast at the automat they went to laundry at the laundromat. They emptied their pockets of underwear and removed the layer of soiled socks. No one stared. Someone before them had probably done the same thing some time that week. They bought soap from a machine for ten cents and deposited a quarter into the slot in the washer. Through the glass in the door they watched their assorted clothing spill and splash over and over and around and around. Drying cost ten cents for ten minutes, but it took twenty cents worth of minutes to dry everything. When all was done, they were disappointed; all of it looked dismally gray. Very unelegant. Claudia had thought that their white underwear should not have been washed with the red and navy blue socks, but she would not have considered asking for more money for anything as unglamorous as dirty socks.

''Oh, well,'' she moaned, ''at least they smell clean.''

Jamie said, ''Let's go to the TV department of Bloomingdale's and watch TV.''

''Not today. We've got to work on the mystery of the statue all morning tomorrow, because tomorrow the museum doesn't open until one o'clock. Today we must learn all about the Renaissance and Michelangelo to prepare ourselves. We'll do research at the big library at 42nd Street.''

''How about the TV department of Macy's instead?''

From E. L. Konisgburg, *From the Mixed-up Files of Mrs. Basil E. Frankweiler* (New York: Atheneum, 1970). Illustrations by E. L. Konigsburg.

"To the library, Sir James."

"Gimbels?"

"Library."

They packed their gray-looking laundry back into their pockets and walked to the door of the laundromat. At the door Claudia turned to Jamie and asked, "Can we . . .?"

Jamie didn't let her finish, "No, dear Lady Claudia. We have not the funds for taxis, buses, or subways. "Shall we walk?" He extended his arm. Claudia placed her gloved fingertips on top of Jamie's mittened ones. Thus they began their long walk to the library.

Once there, they asked the lady at the information booth where they could find books on Michelangelo. She directed them first to the children's room, but when the librarian there found out what they wanted to know, she advised them to go to the Donnell Branch Library on Fifty-third Street. Jamie hoped this would discourage Claudia, but it didn't. She didn't even seem to mind backtracking up Fifth Avenue. Her determination convinced Jamie that Saturday should be spent just this way. Once at the library, they examined the directory which told what was available where and when the library was open. In the downstairs Art Room the librarian helped them find the books which Claudia selected from the card catalogue. She even brought them some others. Claudia liked that part. She always enjoyed being waited on.

Claudia began her studies never doubting that she could become an authority that morning. She had neither pencil nor paper to make notes. And she knew she wouldn't have a lot of time to read. So she decided that she would simply remember everything, absolutely everything she read. Her net profit, therefore, would be as great as that of someone who read a great deal but remembered very little.

Claudia showed the executive ability of a corporation president. She assigned to Jamie the task of looking through the books of photographs of Michelangelo's work to find pictures of Angel. She would do the reading. She glanced through several thick books with thin pages and tiny print. After reading twelve pages, she looked to the end to see

how many more pages there were to go: more than two hundred. The book also had footnotes. She read a few more pages and then busied herself with studying some of Jamie's picture books.

"You're supposed to do the reading!"

"I'm just using these pictures for relief," Claudia whispered. "I have to rest my eyes sometime."

"Well, I don't see any pictures that look like that statue," Jamie sighed.

"Keep looking. I'll do some more reading."

A few minutes later Jamie interrupted her. "Here he is," he said.

"That doesn't look anything like the statue. That's not even a girl," Claudia said.

"Of course not. That's Michelangelo himself."

Claudia replied, "I knew that."

"Two minutes ago you didn't. You thought I was showing you a picture of the statue."

"Oh, I meant . . . I meant. Well . . . there's his broken nose." She pointed to the nose in the picture. "He got in a fight and had his nose broken when he was a teenager.''

"Was he a juvenile delinquent? Maybe they do have his fingerprints on file.''

"No, silly,'' Claudia said.''He was a hot-tempered genius. Did you know he was famous even when he was alive?''

"Is that so? I thought that artists don't become famous until after they're dead. Like mummies.''

They studied a while longer before Jamie's next interruption. "You know, a lot of his works were lost. They say *lost* in parentheses under the picture.''

"How can that be? A statue isn't something like an umbrella that you leave in a taxi and lose. That is, those people who actually ride taxis; something you wouldn't know about.''

"Well, they weren't lost in taxis. They were lost track of.''

"What kind of a sentence is that? Lost track of?''

"Oh, boloney! There are whole long books about the lost works of Michelangelo. Picture books and sculptor works that people lost track of.''

Claudia softened. "Is the little angel one of them?''

"What's the difference between an angel and a cupid?'' Jamie inquired.

"Why?'' Claudia asked.

"Because there's a lost cupid for sure.''

"Angels wear clothes and wings and are Christian. Cupids wear bows and arrows; they are naked and pagan.''

"What's pagan?'' Jamie asked. "Boy or girl?''

"How would I know?'' Claudia answered.

"You said they are naked.''

"Well, pagan has nothing to do with that. It means worshipping idols instead of God.''

"Oh,'' Jamie nodded. "The statue in the museum is an angel. It's dressed in its altogether. I don't know yet if an angel was lost . . . '' Then he glanced over at his sister and muttered, "track of.''

Claudia had begun her research confident that a morning's study would make her completely an expert; but Michelangelo had humbled her, and humility was not an emotion

with which she felt comfortable; she was irritable. Jamie ended his research where Claudia had begun: very confident and happy. He felt that his morning had been well spent; he had seen a lot of pictures and he had learned about pagan. He leaned back and yawned; he was becoming bored with pictures of David and Moses and the Sistine Ceiling; he wanted to find clues. Already he knew enough to tell if Michelangelo had sculptured the little angel. All he needed was a chance to investigate. Without the guards hurrying him. He would know, but would his opinion be accepted by the experts?

"I think we should find out how the experts decide whether or not the statue belongs to Michelangelo. That will be better than finding out about Michelangelo himself,'' Jamie said.

"I know how they find out. They gather evidence like sketches he did and diaries and records of sales. And they examine the statue to see what kind of tools were used and how they were used. Like no one living in the fifteenth century would use an electric drill. How come you didn't take art appreciation lessons with me?''

"The summer before last?''

"Yes. Before school started.''

"Well, the summer before last, I had just finished the second half of first grade.''

"So what?''

"So boloney! It was all I could do to sound out the name of Dick and Jane's dog.''

Claudia had no answer for Jamie's logic. Besides, Jamie agreed with her, "I guess it is better to look for clues. After all, we're doing something that none of the experts can do.''

Claudia's impatience surfaced. She had to pick a fight with Jamie. "Don't be silly. They can read all this stuff, too. There's certainly plenty of it.''

"Oh, I don't mean that. I mean that we're living with the statue. You know what they always say: The only two ways to get to know someone are to live with him or play cards with him.''

"Well, at least the little statue can't cheat at cards like someone else I know.''

"Claudia, dear, I'm no angel. Statue or otherwise."

Claudia sighed, "O.K. Sir James, let's go." And they did.

As they were walking up the steps, Jamie spied a Hershey's almond bar still in its wrapper lying in the corner of the landing. He picked it up and tore open one corner.

"Was it bitten into?" asked Claudia.

"No," Jamie smiled. "Want half?"

"You better not touch it," Claudia warned. "It's probably poisoned or filled with marijuana, so you'll eat it and become either dead or a dope addict."

Jamie was irritated. "Couldn't it just happen that someone dropped it?"

"I doubt that. Who would drop a whole candy bar and not know it? That's like leaving a statue in a taxi. Someone put it there on purpose. Someone who pushes dope. I read once that they feed dope in chocolates to little kids, and then the kids become dope addicts, then these people sell them dope at very high prices which they just can't help but buy because when you're addicted you have to have your dope. High prices and all. And Jamie, we don't have that kind of money."

Jamie said, "Oh, well, bottoms up." He took a big bite of the candy, chewed and swallowed. Then he closed his eyes, leaned against the wall and slid to the floor. Claudia stood with her mouth open, stunned. She was on the verge of screaming for help when Jamie opened his eyes and smiled. "It's delicious. Want a bite?"

Claudia not only refused the bite, she also refused to talk to Jamie until they got to the restaurant. Lunch cheered her. She suggested that they play in Central Park for a while, and they did. They bought peanuts, chestnuts, and pretzels from the vendor outside the museum. They knew that since the museum opened late on Sunday, they would accumulate a lot of hunger before they got out. Their bulging pockets were now full of the staples of life: food and clothing.

Jamie entered the men's room. He had arrived, as was his custom, shortly before the first bell rang, the bell that warned everyone that the museum would close in five minutes.

He waited; the bell rang. He got into a booth. First bell, second bell, it was routine just as boarding the school bus had once been routine. After the first day, they had learned that the staff worked from nine A.M. until five P.M., a work schedule just like their father's. Routine, routine. The wait from nine when the staff came until ten when the public came seemed long. Claudia and Jamie had decided that the washrooms were good for the shorter evening wait when the help left at the same time as the visitors, but the washrooms were less satisfactory for the long morning wait . . . especially after Jamie's close call that first morning. So time from eight forty-five until some safe time after ten in the mornings was spent under various beds. They always checked for dust under the beds first. And for once Claudia's fussiness was not the reason. Reason was the reason. A dustless floor meant that it had been cleaned very recently, and they stood less chance of being caught by a mop.

Jamie stood on the toilet seat waiting. He leaned his head against the wall of the booth and braced himself for what would happen next. The guard would come in and make a quick check of his station. Jamie still felt a ping during that short inspection; that was the only part that still wasn't quite routine, and that's why he braced himself. Then the lights would be turned out. Jamie would wait twelve minutes (lag time, Claudia called it) and emerge from hiding.

Except.

Except the guard didn't come, and Jamie couldn't relax until he felt that final ping. And the lights stayed on, stayed on. Jamie checked his watch ten times within five minutes; he shook his arm and held the watch up to his ear. It was ticking slower than his heart and much more softly. What was wrong? They had caught Claudia! Now they would look for him! He'd pretend he didn't speak English. He wouldn't answer any questions.

Then he heard the door open. Footsteps. More footsteps than usual. What was happening? The hardest part was that every corpuscle of Jamie's nine-year-old self was throbbing with readiness to run, and he had to bind up all that energy into a quiet lump. It was like trying to wrap a loose peck of potatoes into a neat four-cornered package. But he managed to freeze. He heard the voices of two men talking over the sound of water running in the sink.

"I guess they expect even more people tomorrow."

"Yeah. Sundays are always jammed up anyway."

"It'll be easier to move the people in and out of the Great Hall."

"Yeah. Two feet of marble. What do you figure it weighs?"

"I dunno. Whatever it weighs, it has to be handled delicate. Like it was a real angel."

"C'mon. They probably have the new pedestal ready. We can start."

"Do you think they'll have as many people as they had for the Mona Lisa?"

"Naw! The Mona Lisa was here for a short time only. Besides it was the real McCoy."

"I think this one's . . ."

The men left, turning off the lights as they did so. Jamie heard the door close before he melted. Legs first. He sat down on the seat as he allowed the familiar darkness as well as new realization to fill him.

They were moving Angel. Did Claudia know? They wouldn't have women moving the statue. There would be no one in the ladies' room washing up. Who would give her the information? He would. By mental telepathy. He would think a message to Claudia. He folded his hands across his forehead and concentrated. "Stay put, Claudia, stay put. Stay put. Stay put. Claudia, stay put." He thought that Claudia would not approve of the grammar in his mental telegram; she would want him to think *stay in place*. But he didn't want to weaken his message by varying it one bit. He continued thinking STAY PUT.

He must have thought STAY PUT exactly hard enough, for Claudia did just that. They never knew exactly why she did, but she did. Perhaps she sensed some sounds that told her that the museum was not yet empty. Maybe she was just too tired from running around in Central Park. Maybe they were not meant to

get caught. Maybe they were meant to make the discovery they made.

They waited for miles and miles of time before they came out of hiding. At last they met in their bedroom. Claudia was sorting the laundry when Jamie got there. In the dark, mostly by feel. Although there is no real difference between boys' stretch socks and girls', neither ever considered wearing the other's. Children who have always had separate bedrooms don't.

Claudia turned when she heard Jamie come up and said, "They moved the statue."

"How did you know? Did you get my message?"

"Message? I saw the statue on my way here. They have a dim light on it. I guess so that the night guard won't trip over it."

Jamie replied, "We're lucky we didn't get caught."

Claudia never thought very hard about the plus-luck she had; she concentrated on the minus-luck. "But they held us up terribly. I planned on our taking baths tonight. I really can't stand one night more without a bath."

"I don't mind," Jamie said.

"Come along, Sir James. To our bath. Bring your most elegant pajamas. The ones embroidered in gold with silver tassels will do."

"Where, dear Lady Claudia, dost thou expect to bathe?"

"In the fountain, Sir James. In the fountain."

Jamie extended his arm, which was draped with his striped flannel pajamas, and said, "Lady Claudia, I knew that sooner or later you would get me to that restaurant."

(It makes me furious to think that I must explain that restaurant to you, Saxonberg. I'm going to make you take me to lunch in there one day soon. I just this minute became determined to get you into the museum. You'll see later how I'm going to do it. Now about the restaurant. It is built around a gigantic fountain. Water in the fountain is sprayed from dolphins sculptured in bronze. The dolphins appear to be leaping out of the water. On their backs are figures representing the arts, figures that look like water sprites. It is a joy to sit around that wonderful fountain and to snack petit fours and sip espresso coffee. I'll bet that you'd even forget your blasted ulcer while you ate there.)

Lady Claudia and Sir James quietly walked to the entrance of the restaurant. They easily climbed under the velvet rope that meant that the restaurant was closed to the public. Of course they were not the public. They shed their clothes and waded into the fountain. Claudia had taken powdered soap from the restroom. She had ground it out into a paper towel that morning. Even though it was freezing cold, she enjoyed her bath. Jamie, too enjoyed his bath. For a different reason.

When he got into the pool, he found bumps on the bottom; smooth bumps. When he reached down to feel one, he found that it moved! He could even pick it up. He felt its cool roundness and splashed his way over to Claudia. "Income, Claudia, income!" he whispered.

Claudia understood immediately and began to scoop up bumps she had felt on the bottom of the fountain. The bumps were pennies and nickels people had pitched into the fountain to make a wish. At least four people had thrown in dimes and one had tossed in a quarter.

"Some one very rich must have tossed in this quarter," Jamie whispered.

"Some one very poor," Claudia corrected. "Rich people have only penny wishes."

Together they collected $2.87. They couldn't hold more in their hands. They were shivering when they got out. Drying themselves as best they could with paper towels (also taken from the restroom), they hurried into their pajamas and shoes.

They finished their preparations for the night, took a small snack and decided it was safe to wander back into the Great Hall to look again at their Angel.

"I wish I could hug her," Claudia whispered.

"They probably bugged her already. Maybe that light is part of the alarm. Better not touch. You'll set it off."

"I said, 'hug' not 'bug!' Why would I want to bug her?"

"That makes more sense than to hug her!"

"Silly. Shows how much you know. When you hug someone, you learn something else about them. An important something else."

Jamie shrugged his shoulders.

Both looked at Angel a long time. "What do you think?" Jamie asked. "Did he or didn't he?"

Claudia answered, "A scientist doesn't make up his mind until he's examined all the evidence."

"You sure don't sound like a scientist. What kind of scientist would want to hug a statue?"

Claudia was embarrassed, so she spoke sternly, "We'll go to bed now, and we'll think about the statue very hard. Don't fall asleep until you've really thought about the statue and Michelangelo and the entire Italian Renaissance."

And so they went to bed. But lying in bed just before going to sleep is the worst time for *organized* thinking; it is the best time for free thinking. Ideas drift like clouds in an undecided breeze, taking first this direction and then that. It was very difficult for Jamie to control his thoughts when he was tired, sleepy, and lying on his back. He never liked to get involved just before falling asleep. But Claudia had planned on their thinking, and she was good at planning. So think he did. Clouds bearing thoughts of the Italian Renaissance drifted away. Thoughts of home, and more thoughts of home settled down.

"Do you miss home?" he asked Claudia.

"Not too much," she confessed. "I haven't thought about it much."

Jamie was quiet for a minute, then he said. "We probably have no conscience. I think we ought to be homesick. Do you think Mom and Dad raised us wrong? They're not very mean, you know; don't you think that should make us miss them?"

Claudia was silent. Jamie waited. "Did you hear my question, Claude?"

"Yes. I heard your question. I'm thinking." She was quiet a while longer. Then she asked, "Have you ever been homesick?"

"Sure."

"When was the last time?"

"That day Dad dropped us off at Aunt Zell's when he took Mom to the hospital to get Kevin."

"Me, too. That day," Claudia admitted. "But, of course, I was much younger then."

"Why do you suppose we were homesick that day? We've been gone much longer than that now."

Claudia thought. "I guess we were worried. Boy, had I known then that she was going to end up with Kevin, I would have known why we were worried. I remember you sucked your thumb and carried around that old blanket the whole day. Aunt Zell kept trying to get the blanket away from you so that she could wash it. It stank."

Jamie giggled, "Yeah, I guess homesickness is like sucking your thumb. It's what happens when you're not very sure of yourself."

"Or not very well trained," Claudia added. "Heaven knows, we're well trained. Just look how nicely we've managed. It's really their fault if we're not homesick."

Jamie was satisfied. Claudia was more. "I'm glad you asked that about homesickness, Jamie. Somehow, I feel older now. But, of course, that's mostly because I've been the oldest child forever. And I'm extremely well adjusted."

They went to sleep then. Michelangelo, Angel, and the entire Italian Renaissance waited for them until morning.

FANTASY

Paddington Goes to Town

Michael Bond

*Paddington is a little Peruvian bear who was adopted by the Brown family when
they found him at Paddington railway station in London. In this book,
Paddington goes to London with the Browns. If one is unaccustomed to a city and
its inhabitants, havoc can ensue, as it does, humorously, for Paddington.*

Mr. Brown lowered his evening paper and
looked around the room at the rest of the
family. "Do you realise something?" he
said. "It's nearly Christmas and we haven't
been up to Town to see the decorations yet!"

Paddington pricked up his ears at Mr.
Brown's words. "I don't think I've *ever*
been to see them, Mr. Brown," he said.
"Not the Christmas ones."

The Browns stopped what they were doing
and stared at him in wide-eyed amazement.
Paddington had been with them for so long,
and was so much a part of their lives, they'd
somehow taken it for granted that he'd seen
the Christmas decorations at some time or
another and it didn't seem possible for such
an important matter to have been overlooked.

"Mercy me, I do believe that bear's
right," said Mrs. Bird. "We've seen the ordinary lights several times, and we've seen
the decorations during daylight when we've
been doing our Christmas shopping, but
we've never been up specially. Not at
night."

"Gosh, Dad," exclaimed Jonathan. "Can
we go tonight? It's years since we went."

Mr. Brown looked first at his watch and
then at his wife and Mrs. Bird. "I'm game,"
he said. "How about you?"

Mrs. Brown looked at Mrs. Bird. "I've
done everything I want to do," said their
housekeeper. "I'm very well advanced this
year. I only have to take my mince pies out
of the oven and I shall be ready."

"May we go, Daddy?" implored Judy.
"*Please?*"

Mr. Brown glanced round the room with a
twinkle in his eye. "What do you say, Paddington?" he asked. "Would you like to?"

"*Yes, please,* Mr. Brown," exclaimed
Paddington eagerly. "I should like that very
much indeed."

Paddington was always keen on trips,
especially unexpected ones with the whole
family, and when Mr. Brown announced that
he would call in on the way and pick up Mr.
Gruber into the bargain he grew more and
more excited.

For the next half an hour there was great
pandemonium in number thirty-two Windsor
Gardens as everyone rushed around getting
ready for the big event and even Paddington
himself went so far as to rub a flannel over
his whiskers while Judy gave his fur a brush
down.

It was a very gay party of Browns that
eventually set off in Mr. Brown's car and
shortly afterwards the hilarity was increased

From Michael Bond, *Paddington Goes to Town* (Boston: Houghton Mifflin, 1968). Illustrations by Peggy Fortnum.

still further as Mr. Gruber emerged from his shop carrying a camera and some flashbulbs, several of which he used in order to take photographs of the assembly.

"You're not the only one who hasn't been to see the Christmas decorations, Mr. Brown," he said, addressing Paddington as he squeezed into the back seat alongside Mrs. Bird, Jonathan and Judy. "I've never been either and I want to make the most of it."

If the Browns had been surprised to discover that Paddington had never seen the lights they were even more astonished at this latest piece of information and Paddington himself was so taken aback he quite forgot to give his usual paw signal as they swung out of the Portobello Road.

Mr. Gruber chuckled at the effect of his words. "People never do see things that are on their own doorstep," he said wisely. "I must say it'll be a great treat. I've heard they're particularly good this year."

As they drove along Mr. Gruber went on to explain to Paddington how each year all the big shops in London got together in order to festoon the streets with huge decorations made up of hundreds of coloured lights, and also how each year an enormous Christmas tree was sent from Norway as a gift to the people of London, and how it was always placed in a position of honour in Trafalgar Square.

It all sounded most interesting and the excitement mounted as they drew nearer and nearer to the centre of London.

Mr. Gruber coughed as Paddington jumped up in his seat and began waving his paws in the direction of a cluster of green lights some distance ahead.

"I have a feeling those are traffic lights, Mr. Brown," he said tactfully, as they changed to amber. "But just you wait until you see the real thing."

At that moment the lights suddenly changed again, this time to red, and the car screeched to a halt. "I'm not surprised he mistook them," grumbled Mr. Brown. "It's a wonder he could see anything at all. If we're not careful we shall have a nasty accident." Rather pointedly he picked up a

duster and began wiping the glass in front of him. "Bear's steam all over my windscreen! People will begin to think we're boiling a kettle in here or something."

"It's always worse when he's excited, Henry," said Mrs. Brown, coming to Paddington's rescue as he sank back into his seat looking most offended.

"If I were you," she continued, "I'd stop somewhere. We shall see much more if we walk."

Mrs. Brown's suggestion met with wholehearted approval from the rest of the family. They were beginning to feel a bit cramped, and some while later, having disentangled the car from the maze of traffic and found somewhere to park, even Mr. Brown had to agree that it was a good idea as they climbed out and set off on foot down one of the busy London thoroughfares.

It was a crisp, clear night and the pavement on either side of the street was thronged with people gazing into shop windows, staring up at the decorations which seemed to hang overhead like a million golden stars in the sky, or simply, like the Browns, strolling leisurely along drinking it all in.

Near by, on the Browns' side of the street, a long queue of people were waiting to go into a cinema, and somewhere in the background there was the sound of a man's voice raised in song—a song punctuated every now and then by a rhythmic clicking like that of castanets.

"I do believe it's someone playing the spoons, Mr. Brown," exclaimed Mr. Gruber. "I haven't seen that for years."

Paddington, who'd never even heard of anyone playing the spoons before let alone seen it happen, peered around with interest while Mr. Gruber explained how some people, who called themselves "buskers", earned their living by entertaining the theatre and cinema queues every evening while they were waiting to go in.

To his disappointment the owner of the spoons appeared to be somewhere out of sight round a corner and so rather reluctantly he turned his attention back to the lights.

There were so many different things to see it was difficult to know which to investigate first and he didn't want to run the risk of missing anything, but the Christmas lights themselves seemed very good value indeed. After considering the matter for a moment or two he took off his hat so that the brim wouldn't get in the way and then, holding it out in front of him, he hurried along the pavement after the others with his neck craned back so that he would have a better view.

A little way along the street he was suddenly brought back to earth when he bumped into Mr. Gruber, who'd stopped outside the entrance to the cinema in order to set up his camera on a tripod and make a record of the scene.

Paddington was just staggering back after his collision when to his surprise a man in the front of the near-by queue leaned over and dropped a small, round shiny object into his hat.

"There you are," he said warmly. "Merry Christmas."

"Thank you very much," exclaimed Paddington, looking most surprised. "Merry Christmas to you."

Peering into his hat to see what the man had given him he nearly fell over backwards on to the pavement in astonishment and his eyes grew rounder and rounder as they took in the sight before them.

For inside his hat was not just one, but a whole pile of coins. There were so many, in fact, that the latest addition—whatever it had been—was lost for all time amongst a vast assortment of pennies, threepenny pieces, sixpences; coins of so many different shapes, sizes and values that Paddington soon gave up trying to count them all.

"Is anything the matter, dear?" asked Mrs. Brown, catching sight of the expression on his face. "You look quite . . . " her voice broke off as she too caught a glimpse of the inside of Paddington's hat. "Good gracious!" She put a hand to her mouth. "What *have* you been up to?"

"I haven't been *up* to anything," said Paddington truthfully. Still hardly able to believe his good fortune he gave his hat a shake and several sixpences and a halfpenny fell out through some holes in the side.

"Crikey!" exclaimed Jonathan. "Don't

say you've been collecting money from the queue!"

"They must have thought you were with the man playing the spoons," said Judy in alarm.

"Look here," said the man who'd just made the latest contribution to Paddington's collection. "I thought you were a busker."

"A busker!" exclaimed Paddington, giving him a hard stare. "I'm not a busker—I'm a bear!"

"In that case I'd like my sixpence back," said the man sternly. "Collecting money under false pretences."

"'Ear, 'ear," said a man with a muffler as he pushed his way to the front. "Came round with 'is 'at 'e did. What about my fourpence?"

Mrs. Brown looked round desperately as the murmurings in the front of the queue began to grow and several people farther down the street began pointing in their direction. "Do something, Henry!" she exclaimed.

"*Do something!*" repeated Mr. Brown. "I don't see what I can do."

"Well, it was your idea to come up and see the lights in the first place," said Mrs. Brown. "I knew something like this would happen."

"I like that!" exclaimed Mr. Brown indignantly. "It's not my fault." He turned to the queue. "People ought to make sure they know what they are giving their money to before they part with it," he added in a loud voice.

"Came round with 'is 'at 'e did," repeated the man who was wearing the muffler.

"Nonsense!" said Mrs. Bird. "He only happened to be holding it in his paw. It's coming to something if a bear can't walk along a London street with his hat in his paw when he wants to."

"Oh, dear," said Judy. "Look!" She pointed towards the tail end of the queue where another argument appeared to be developing. It was centered around a man dressed in an old raincoat. He was holding an obviously empty hat in one hand while shaking his other fist at a group of people who, in turn, were pointing back up the street towards the Browns.

"Crikey! We're for it now," breathed

Jonathan, as the man, having been joined by two stalwart policemen who'd been drawn to the scene by all the noise, turned and began heading in their direction.

"That's 'im! That's 'im!" cried the busker, pointing an accusing finger at Paddington. "Trying to earn an honest bob to buy meself a loaf of bread for Christmas day I was . . . and what 'appens? 'E comes round with 'is 'at and robs me of all me takings!"

The first policeman took out his notebook. "Where do you come from, bear?" he asked sternly.

"Peru," said Paddington promptly. "*Darkest* Peru!"

"Number thirty-two Windsor Gardens," replied Mrs. Brown at the same time.

The policeman looked from one to the other. "No fixed abode," he said ponderously as he licked his pencil.

"No fixed abode!" repeated Mrs. Bird. She took a firm grip of her umbrella and glared at the speaker. "I'll have you know that young bear's abode's been fixed ever since he arrived in this country."

The second policeman viewed Mrs. Bird's umbrella out of the corner of his eye and then glanced round at the rest of the Browns. "I must say they don't look as if they've been working the queues," he said, addressing his colleague.

"Working the queues!" said Mr. Brown indignantly. "We most certainly have been doing nothing of the sort. We came up to show this young bear the lights."

"What about my takings then," interrupted the busker. " 'Ow do they come to be in 'is 'at?"

"Deliberate it was," shouted the man with the muffler. "Took my fourpence 'e did."

"It certainly wasn't deliberate," said Mr. Gruber, stepping into the breach. "I saw the whole thing through my viewfinder.

"I happened to be taking a photograph at the time, officer," he continued, turning to the first policeman in order to explain the matter, "and I'm quite sure that when it's developed you'll see this young bear is in no way to blame."

Mr. Gruber looked as if he would like to have said a good deal more on the subject but at that moment to everyone's relief a commissionaire appeared at the cinema doors and the queue began to move.

"That's all very well," said the busker. "But what about my takings?"

"Two choruses of *Rudolph the Red Nosed Reindeer* I gave 'em on me spoons," he continued plaintively, "and all for nothing."

As the last of the queue disappeared into the cinema and the rest of the crowd began to disperse the first policeman put his notebook away. "It seems to me," he said, turning to his colleague as they made to leave, "if this young bear here gives up his collection everyone'll be happy and we can call it a night. Only look slippy, mind," he continued, addressing himself to Paddington. "Otherwise if certain people are still here when we get back they may find themselves in trouble for causing an obstruction."

Thanking the policeman very much for his advice Paddington began hastily emptying the contents of his hat into the one belonging to the busker.

As the pile of coins cascaded down in a shower of bronze and silver he began to look more and more disappointed. It was difficult to tell exactly how much was in the collection but he felt sure it would have been more than enough to enable Jonathan, Judy and himself to reach their target for the Children's Christmas Party Fund.

"I don't know about no bear's targets," said the busker as Paddington explained what he'd been hoping to do with the money. "I've got me own targets to worry about."

"Never mind, Paddington," said Judy, squeezing his paw. "We've done very well. You never know—something may turn up."

"Tell you what," said the busker, catching sight of the expression on Paddington's face. "I'll give you a tune on me spoons to cheer you up before you go."

Lifting up his hand he was about to break into the opening bars when to everyone's surprise Mr. Gruber, who had been listening to the conversation with a great deal of interest, suddenly stepped forward. "May I see those spoons a moment?" he asked.

"Certainly, guv'," said the busker, handing them over. "Don't tell me you play 'em as well."

Mr. Gruber shook his head as he took a

small spyglass from his pocket and held the spoons up to a near-by lamp so that he could examine them more closely. "You know," he said, "these could be quite valuable. They may even be very rare Georgian silver. . . ."

"What!" began the busker, staring open-mouthed at Mr. Gruber. "*My* spoons . . . ."

"I have an idea," said Mr. Gruber briskly, silencing the busker with a wave of his hand before he had time to say any more. "If I give you five pounds for this pair of spoons will you let young Mr. Brown keep the collection? After all, he did make it in a way, even if it was an accident."

"Five pounds!" exclaimed the busker, eyeing Mr. Gruber's wallet. "For them spoons? Lor' bless you, sir. Why, 'e can 'ave me 'at as well for that!"

"No, thank you," broke in Mrs. Brown hastily. Paddington's own hat was bad enough at the best of times but from where she was standing it looked as if the busker's might well have matched up to it, give or take a few marmalade stains.

"Tell you what, guv'," said the busker hopefully, as he took Mr. Gruber's five-pound note in exchange for the spoons and began transferring the money back into Paddington's hat. "There's some more where them two came from. 'Ow about . . . ."

Mr. Gruber gave him a hard look. "No," he said firmly. "I think these two will do admirably, thank you."

A few mintues later, bidding a rather dazed-looking busker good-bye, the Browns resumed their stroll, with Paddington keeping very much to the outside this time.

"Well," said Mr. Brown, "I'm not quite sure what all that was about, but it seems to have worked out all right in the end."

"Thirty-seven shillings and fourpence halfpenny," exclaimed Jonathan a few minutes later as he finished counting the money. "That's more than enough to reach our target. I bet they'll be jolly pleased at the hospital."

"I didn't know you were collecting for a children's party," said Mrs. Brown. "You should have said. We could have given you some towards it."

"It was really Paddington's idea," said Judy, giving the paw by her side another squeeze. "Besides, it wouldn't have been the same if you'd given it to us. Not the same at all."

Mr. Brown turned to Mr. Gruber. "Fancy you noticing those spoons," he said. "Isn't it strange how things work out."

"Very strange," agreed Mr. Gruber, taking a sudden interest in some decorations just overhead.

Only Mrs. Bird caught a faint twinkle in his eye—a twinkle not unlike the one she'd noticed when he'd been conducting his deal with the busker, and one moreover which caused her to have certain suspicions on the matter—but wisely she decided it was high time the subject was changed.

"Look," she said, pointing ahead. "There's the Christmas tree in Trafalgar Square. If we hurry we may be in time for the carols."

Mr. Brown gave a sniff. "I'll tell you something else," he said. "I can smell hot chestnuts."

Paddington licked his lips. Although it wasn't long since he'd had his tea all the excitement was beginning to make him feel hungry again. "Hot chestnuts, Mr. Brown," he exclaimed with interest. "I don't think I've ever had any of those before."

The Browns stopped in their tracks and for the second time that day stared at Paddington in amazement.

"You've never had any hot chestnuts?" repeated Mr. Brown.

Paddington shook his head. "Never," he said firmly.

"Well, we can soon alter that," said Mr. Brown, leading the way towards a coke brazier at the side of the road. "Seven large bags, please," he announced to the man who was serving.

"What a good thing I brought my camera," exclaimed Mr. Gruber. "Two firsts in one evening," he continued, as he set up his tripod. "The decorations and now this. I shall have to make some extra copies for your Aunt Lucy in Peru, Mr. Brown. I expect she'll find them most interesting."

Paddington thanked his friend happily

through a mouthful of hot chestnuts. In the distance he could still see some decorations in the busy shopping part of London, whilst in front the biggest tree he'd ever seen in his life rose up into the night supporting a myriad of brightly coloured fairy lights, and from somewhere near by the sound of a Christmas carol filled the air. All in all, he thought it had been a lovely evening out and it was nice, not only to think that Christmas Day itself was still to come, but to round things off in such a tasty manner.

"Are you having trouble with your exposures, Mr. Gruber?" he asked hopefully, as he came to the end of his chestnuts.

Mr. Gruber looked up in some surprise. "I only wondered," said Paddington hastily, eyeing the brazier before his friend had time to reply, "because if you are I thought perhaps you'd like me to have another bag just to make sure!"

"There's one thing about bears," said Mrs. Bird, joining in the laughter which followed Paddington's last remark. "They certainly don't believe in taking any chances!"

Mr. Brown reached into his pocket. "And for once," he said, amid general agreement, "I'm entirely on their side. Seven more bags, please!"

The Country

FABLES, MYTHS, AND LEGENDS

The Farmer and His Sons

Aesop

Much can be learned from the land and sea, and fables often draw on nature and the birds and beasts to teach lessons. These two fables of Greek origin stress the necessity of hard work if one is to prosper. Aesop is said to have lived sometime in the sixth century B.C. In "The Farmer and His Sons," he tells us that, in the countryside, a person's wealth lies in nature and the abundance it can produce if the person works hard. Often, however, those who depend on nature are faced with scarcity. Then, as Aesop illustrates in "The Fisherman and the Little Fish," it is better to have a little for one's work than nothing at all.

A rich old farmer, who felt that he had not many more days to live, called his sons to his bedside.

"My sons," he said, "heed what I have to say to you. Do not on any account part with the estate that has belonged to our family for so many generations. Somewhere on it is hidden a rich treasure. I do not know the exact spot, but it is there, and you will surely find it. Spare no energy and leave no spot unturned in your search."

The father died, and no sooner was he in his grave than the sons set to work digging with all their might, turning up every foot of ground with their spades, and going over the whole farm two or three times.

No hidden gold did they find; but at harvest time when they had settled their accounts and had pocketed a rich profit far greater than that of any of their neighbors, they understood that the treasure their father had told them about was the wealth of a bountiful crop, and that in their industry had they found the treasure.

INDUSTRY IS ITSELF A TREASURE.

From *The Aesop for Children* (Chicago: Rand McNally, 1919).

The Fisherman and the Little Fish*

Aesop

A poor Fisherman, who lived on the fish he caught, had bad luck one day and caught nothing but a very small fry. The Fisherman was about to put it in his basket when the little Fish said:

"Please spare me, Mr. Fisherman! I am so small it is not worth while to carry me home. When I am bigger, I shall make you a much better meal."

But the Fisherman quickly put the fish into his basket.

"How foolish I should be," he said, "to throw you back. However small you may be, you are better than nothing at all."

A SMALL GAIN IS WORTH MORE
THAN A LARGE PROMISE.

The Raven and the Cattle†

Adapted by P. V. Ramaswami Raju

"The Raven and the Cattle" is a modern adaptation of an old Indian fable. As in Greek fables, animals and the countryside figure prominently. This fable points out humorously that people—or birds—often take credit for work they have not done.

One evening, as some cattle were wending their way home, a raven rode on the horns of a bull in the herd; and as he approached the cottage, cried to the farmer, "Friend, my work for the day is over; you may now take charge of your cattle."

"What was your work?" asked the farmer.

"Why," said the raven, "the arduous task of watching these cattle and bringing them home."

"Am I to understand you have been doing all the work for me?" said the farmer.

"Certainly," said the raven, and flew away with a laugh.

Quoth the farmer with surprise, *"How many there are that take credit for things which they have never done!"*

Telipinu‡

Theodor H. Gaster

Children are curious about the seasons and find it interesting to learn how earlier peoples explained nature. How did people in early farming communities view the seasons, for example? This ancient Hittite tale is a good example of a "why"

---

*From *The Aesop for Children* (Chicago: Rand McNally, 1919).

†From Eva March Tappan, ed., *Folk Stories and Fables* (Boston: Houghton Mifflin, 1907).

‡From Theodor H. Gaster, "Telipinu," *The Oldest Stories in the World* (New York: Viking Press, 1952).

tale, a tale that explains some natural occurrence. In this story, the god Telipinu becomes angry and disappears and the earth becomes barren. As in the Greek legend of Demeter and her daughter, Persephone—who spends six months in the Underworld—Telipinu's return brings a rebirth of nature. Interestingly, Telipinu is symbolized by the newborn lamb, linking this tale with later Christian stories. Perhaps this is also one source of the tradition of spring cleaning.

Thereupon the goddess [Kamrusepa] summoned an eagle and told it to go forth along with the bee and bring Telipinu back.

"But that," she added, "is only the first step. He is still furious and in a temper, and it will need high magic both in heaven and on earth to drive out his wrath!"

Across the hills and over the dales flew the eagle and the bee, while the gods clustered about the ramparts of heaven, waiting with bated breath for the moment of their return.

It was a long and anxious wait, but at last what seemed like a small black cloud rolled up on the horizon; and even as it appeared there was a rumble of thunder and a flash of lightning, and the air was rent with loud and angry cries.

The gods huddled together.

Louder and louder grew the thunder, more strident the cries, more dazzling and more frequent the lightning, until it seemed as though heaven and earth were locked in combat.

Suddenly, above the din and clamor, came the steady drone of a bee in flight, and the black cloud began to take on a familiar shape. When the gods looked closer, there, winging toward them, was the eagle, with Telipinu poised upon its pinion, and the little bee buzzing and humming around it, partly in triumph, partly in fear.

In a few moments the bird had alighted, and immediately a train of servants moved forward, bearing in their hands goblets of nectar, jars of cream and honey, and baskets of fruit; and as they set them before Telipinu the great goddess Kamrusepa stood beside them and made sweet music, crooning over each a little snatch of song.

Over the figs she sang:

"Bitter figs turn sweet with age.
Be turn'd to sweet thy bitter rage!"

And over the grapes and olives:

"As the olive's with oil, the grape's with wine,
With grace be fill'd that heart of thine!"

And over the cream and honey:

"Be smooth as cream, as honey sweet.
Now from thine angry mood retreat!"

Although they sounded to Telipinu like prayers and petitions, these words were really magic spells—for Kamrusepa was the mistress of the black art—and so no sooner had the angry god tasted a few bites of the food and quaffed a few sips of the drink then he was instantly bewitched. All the rage and fury which had been seething within him seemed of a sudden to vanish, and in its place there stole over him a warm and gentle glow of benevolence. The more he ate and the more he drank, the more kindly he became, for every time the enchanted fare touched his lips grace abounding entered his soul.

At length, when the gods saw that his anger had altogether departed and that he was filled with love and tenderness toward them, they redecked the tables and replaced the benches and resumed the banquet which had been so rudely interrupted. There they sat as before, feasting and carousing—the gods of field, crop, and grain, and the goddesses of birth and of fate—but now, in the center, sat Telipinu himself, gaily receiving and returning their toasts.

Meanwhile, down on earth, mortals too were bestirring themselves to remove the god's displeasure, but because of the blight and the famine they could not offer him food and drink, as did his brothers and sisters in heaven. So in every house they flung open the doors and windows and chanted in chorus:

"Out of the house and thro' the window,
Out of the window and thro' the yard,
Out of the yard and thro' the gate,
Out of the gate and down the path
Go the fury, the rage, the wrath!

Down the path and straight ahead,
Nor turn aside to garden-bed
Or field or orchard-close, but hie
To where the earth doth meet the sky,
And, like the setting sun at night,
Sink and disappear from sight!"

Then they went out into the yard and emptied into large bins all the ashes and garbage which had gathered during the winter months, and as they did so they again chanted in chorus:

"Ash and trash and rag and clout,
In it goes and never out!
Toss thy temper in the bin;
Let it stay and rot therein!

Finally they washed and scoured the insides of their houses and then tossed the pails of sullied water upon the stones, while they sang:

"Water pour'd upon the floor
To the pail returns no more.
Pour the temper from thy heart,
Likewise let it now depart!

Now although they sounded to Telipinu like prayers and petitions, the words they chanted were also really magic spells, and suddenly the cold winter winds seemed to abate, and through the open doors and windows stole the first breezes of spring. On the branches of the trees and in the hedgerows a promise of green began to appear and, as if in a moment, field and woodland were alive with a thousand sounds—the purling of brooks, the scampering of tiny feet, the first hesitant notes of fledgling birds.

A few days later a tall pole was set up in the courtyard of the temple, and from it was hung, in honor of Telipinu, the snow-white fleece of a newborn lamb.

Earth and Its Seeds

Carleton Beals

For those who live close to the earth and depend on nature, the land and nature itself can assume mystical qualities. Most mythologies contain tales of why crops grow and the seasons change. Like "Telipinu," "Earth and Its Seeds" is such a tale. It explains the various deities the Aztecs held responsible for the seasons and crops, and it also describes the festivals held to honor those gods.

After having made the waters, the gods created the fish called Cipactli, which was converted into Earth. The hieroglyph of this birth of continents was Tlaltecutli, God of Earth, riding on the back of Earth-Woman-Thalcíhuatl—the chief Earth Goddess, the Holy Dweller. Most beloved was Xochiquétzal, Precious Flower Feather, the Goddess of Flowers, of Artists and of Love, also the benefactress of weaving and embroidery.

Those who went hunting for wild honey prayed to her for good luck. So did those who hunted deer with lariats. The shooters of arrows, the cutters of canebrakes for fish traps, all fishermen using traps, hooks, nooses and spears paid her special court.

She wore gold pendants and nose-ring. Her diadem was a band of red leather, from which waved long green quétzal feathers. Her elaborate blue dress was embroidered

From Carleton Beals, *Stories Told by the Aztecs before the Spaniards Came* (New York: Abelard-Schuman, 1979).

with flowers and feathers in sophisticated designs, and with red and gold bands about the flounce. She carried in her outstretched hands bunches of feather flowers, bound with gold ribbons. Her small shrine, erected within the large holy compound, was lavishly hung with tapestries and featherwork, well filled with jewels and gold ornaments.

Precious Flower lived in the ninth heaven, a delectable place of fountains, rivers and flowers. There grew the marvelous tree, Xochitlicán; its sweet potent flowers, if merely touched, converted one into a happy and faithful lover. She was waited upon by many female genii, dwarfs, hunchbacks and buffoons, who prevented any man from seeing her.

Originally Flower Feather had been the wife of Centéotl, God of Corn, then of Tlaloc, *i.e.,* Flowers married to Rain. But Tezcatlipoca, the cunning deceiver, fell in love with her and stole her from Tlaloc. He shut her up in that flowery and delectable abode. Tlaloc, scorned and sad, sought consolation in the arms of beautiful Emerald-Skirt-of-the-Lakes.

Flower Feather's farewell festival, just before the arrival of cold weather, in the Month-When-the-Fruit-Falls, ran over into the next two months. Branches and flowers were twined about all the temples, houses and streets, and people decked themselves with vines and flowers. The faithful gathered in the temple, especially painters, artists, silver-workers, feather-workers and weavers. A girl dressed as Flower Feather presided.

All danced gaily, masquerading as monkeys, cats, dogs, foxes, mountain lions and coyotes. While performing the steps they carried the various work tools. They ate honey bread painted to represent dolls, flowers and birds.

Flower Feather, also Seven Flower (Chicomexochitl), were honored in the second movable fiesta by the Brotherhood of Painters and Weavers. After a forty-day fast, blood drawn from the fingers and the eyelids was offered by the men to Seven Flower, the inventor of the artist's brush; by the women, to Flower Feather, who invented weaving. Many quail were sacrificed.

Maciuxóchitl, God-of-Five-Flowers, and of Fire, was worshiped chiefly in the homes of nobility. This was the major flower festival of the year. Before it was celebrated everyone fasted for four days. If any man or woman sinned, the god punished them with diseases. Many savory foods on painted wooden plates were brought as offerings.

Another earth goddess was called Chicomecóatl, Seven Serpents, because of the seven racimes (sprays of flowers) of the corn plant and the writhing corn silk. Also, seven corn plants were always set out in each hill. Seven Snakes was a beautiful young girl wearing a red crown; her dress and sandals were of the same color—she was red from head to foot. Gold earrings glistened in her ears and a necklace of golden ears of corn, strung on a blue ribbon, hung about her neck. She carried cornstalks with double ears made from gold and feathers. To insure good crops, when the first blades of corn appeared people went out at night and lit an *ocotli* torch in the center of the field, where they sacrificed a fowl and offered bread, tamales and sweet copal. As Goddess of Cookery, Seven Snakes had been the first to make bread, tortillas and other toothsome dishes, and on her feast day the housewife carried to her altar a basket of provisions surmounted by a cooked frog, bearing on his back a cornstalk stuffed with pounded corn and boiled vegetables.

The festival in her honor and the corn god Centéotl was celebrated with feasting, dancing and music. The altars were lavishly decorated with green boughs, herbs and flowers. Girls in capes carried seed corn to the temple to be blessed—six ears each, wrapped in paper sprinkled with holy rubber sap. The arms and legs of these girls were adorned with rich plumage of many colors; their faces were stained with pine resin or tar called *chapopoctli*. They went in procession, surrounded by the crowd. No one was supposed to talk to them. If some young blood did speak, he was rebuked by one of the old women chaperoning the girls: "You speak, coward, greenhorn? Do you have to open your mouth? You had better be thinking of some exploit to rid yourself of the long hair on your neck, sign of cowardice and lack of manhood. Chicken-heart, you don't need to pipe up here. You are just as much a woman as I am. You have never left the fireside.''

One of the youths would respond: "Very well said, madam . . . Never worry, I shall do something that will cause the girls to consider me a man. I care more for two cacao beans than for you and all your lineage. Put mud on your belly, scratch yourself, cross your legs and go roll in the dust. Here is a sharp stone, cut yourself in the face and the nose till blood comes; and if that doesn't satisfy you, swallow chalk and spit. I beg you to be still and leave us in peace.''

When the corn had been blessed, it was brought back to the house, and the rest of the day was spent in revelry.

The male equivalent of Flower Feather was Xochipilli, Lord of Flowers, of dances, song and games. He wore a high *cocoxtli,* or pheasant crest; and in his mouth a white butterfly. His body was patterned with painted flowers. He sat on a flower throne, adorned with symbols of fertility, rain, water and the sun, and his hands and his painted face were always lifted up in rhapsodic awe. In his role as Macuilxochitl, Five-Flower, he was the god of gambling. Aztec dice were made of five different colored beans.

Many earth divinities were worshiped by the decapitation of victims, to symbolize the reaping of the corn. In the codices these victims are represented with their heads half-severed, with two writhing snakes about the neck to represent streams of blood, rain, corn floss and other things.

Woman Snake, called Tlillán, *i.e.* Blackness, had a temple called Tlillán, the Black House, beside that of the Plumed Serpent in the great temple square. Only priests of her cult might enter there. The door was so small it was necessary for them to crawl in on all fours, and the passageway was so arranged that the interior remained pitch black, with not a ray of light. Her stone image had a large mouth and teeth bared ready to devour. Her hair hung free down her back. Near this temple the priests kept an eternal fire lit, and they presented themselves once a week to the emperor for food for the goddess.

If the goddess did not receive her weekly ration the priests placed a sacrificial knife in a cradle, and a woman carried it to the market place (the *tiánquiz*) where she left it in the care of a seller, to be kept until she returned.

When the woman did not return, the market woman, wondering why the child did not cry, would discover the knife. This was a sign that Woman Snake had been among them and was hungry. The market woman cried out the bad news, and the priests gathered weeping, reverently taking the knife off with them. The emperor, the nobles and all the people, thus publicly shamed, hastened to provide the goddess with her usual repast.

FOLKTALES—
INHERITED AND LITERARY

The Little Farmer

Jacob and Wilhelm Grimm

The folktales collected by Jakob (1785–1863) and Wilhelm (1789–1859) Grimm illustrate the timelessness and universality of the genre. These tales, as the Brothers Grimm discovered, are preserved longer among country folk than among city dwellers, largely because the tales often deal with rural people and events and change occurs more slowly in the country. In many folktales, the person from the country is hoodwinked. In this tale, sometimes also called "Farmer Little," it is the farmer who is tricking others.

There was a certain village where lived many rich farmers and only one poor one, whom they called the Little Farmer. He had not even a cow, and still less had he money to buy one; and he and his wife greatly wished for such a thing. One day he said to her,—

"Listen, I have a good idea; it is that your godfather the joiner shall make us a calf of wood, and paint it brown, so as to look just like any other; and then in time perhaps it will grow big and become a cow."

This notion pleased the wife; the godfather joiner set to work to saw and plane, and soon turned out a calf complete, with its head down and neck stretched out as if it were grazing.

The next morning, as the cows were driven to pasture, the Little Farmer called out to the drover,—

"Look here, I have got a little calf to go; but it is still young and must be carried."

"All right!" said the drover, and tucked it under his arm, carried it into the meadows, and stood it in the grass. So the calf stayed where it was put, and seemed to be eating all the time; and the drover thought to himself,—

"It will soon be able to run alone, if it grazes at that rate!"

In the evening, when the herds had to be driven home, he said to the calf, "If you can stand there eating like that, you can just walk off on your own four legs; I am not going to lug you under my arm again!"

But the Little Farmer was standing by his house door, waiting for his calf; and when he saw the cowherd coming through the village without it, he asked what it meant. The cowherd answered, "It is still out there eating away, and never attended to the call, and would not come with the rest."

Then the Little Farmer said,—

"I will tell you what, I must have my beast brought home."

And they went together through the fields in quest of it; but some one had stolen it, and it was gone. And the drover said,—

"Most likely it has run away."

But the Little Farmer said, "Not it!" and

From The Brothers Grimm, *Household Stories by the Brothers Grimm,* trans. by Lucy Crane (New York: Crowell, c. 1915).

brought the cowherd before the bailiff, who ordered him for his carelessness to give the Little Farmer a cow for the missing calf.

So now the little Farmer and his wife possessed their long-wished-for cow: they rejoiced with all their hearts; but unfortunately they had no fodder for it, and could give it nothing to eat, so that before long they had to kill it. Its flesh they salted down; and the Little Farmer went to the town to sell the skin, and buy a new calf with what he got for it. On the way he came to a mill, where a raven was sitting with broken wings; and he took it up out of pity, and wrapped it in the skin. The weather was very stormy, and it blew and rained; so he turned into the mill and asked for shelter. The miller's wife was alone in the house; and she said to the Little Farmer,

"Well, come in and lay thee down in the straw;" and she gave him a piece of bread and cheese. So the Little Farmer ate, and then lay down with his skin near him, and the miller's wife thought he was sleeping with fatigue. After a while in came another man; and the miller's wife received him very well, saying,—

"My husband is out; we will make good cheer."

The Little farmer listened to what they said, and when he heard good cheer spoken of, he grew angry to think he had been put off with bread and cheese. For the miller's wife presently brought out roast meat, salad, cakes, and wine.

Now, as the pair were sitting down to their feast, there came a knock at the door.

"Oh, dear!" cried the woman, "it is my husband!" In a twinkling she popped the roast meat into the oven, the wine under the pillow, the salad in the bed, the cakes under the bed, and the man in the linen closet. Then she opened the door to her husband, saying,—

"Thank goodness, you are here! what weather it is, as if the world were coming to an end!"

When the miller saw the Little Farmer lying in the straw, he said,—

"What fellow have you got there?"

"Oh!" said the wife, "the poor chap came in the midst of the wind and rain and asked for shelter, and I gave him some bread and cheese and spread some straw for him."

The husband answered, "Oh, well, I have no objection, only get me something to eat at once."

But the wife said, "There is nothing but bread and cheese."

"Anything will do for me," answered the miller; "bread and cheese forever!" and catching sight of the Little Farmer, he cried,—

"Come along, and keep me company!" The Little Farmer did not wait to be asked twice, but sat down and ate. After a while the miller noticed the skin lying on the ground with the raven wrapped up in it, and he said, "What have you got there?"

The Little Farmer answered, "A fortune-teller."

And the miller asked, "Can he tell my fortune?"

"Why not?" answered the Little Farmer. "He will tell four things, and the fifth he keeps to himself." Now the miller became very curious, and said, "Ask him to say something."

And the Little Farmer pinched the raven, so that it croaked, "Crr, crr."—"What does he say?" asked the miller. And the Little Farmer answered,—

"First he says that there is wine under the pillow."

"That would be jolly!" cried the miller; and he went to look, and found the wine, and then asked, "What next?"

So the Little Farmer made the raven croak again, and then said,—

"He says, secondly, that there is roast meat in the oven."

"That would be jolly!" cried the miller; and he went and looked, and found the roast meat. The Little Farmer made the fortune-teller speak again, and then said,—

"He said, thirdly, that there is salad in the bed."

"That would be jolly!" cried the miller; and went and looked, and found the salad. Once more the Little Farmer pinched the raven so that he croaked, and said,—

"He says, fourthly and lastly, that there are cakes under the bed."

"That would be jolly!" cried the miller;

and he went and looked, and found the cakes.

And now the two sat down to table; and the miller's wife felt very uncomfortable, and she went to bed and took all the keys with her. The miller was eager to know what the fifth thing could be; but the Little Farmer said,—

'Suppose we eat the four things in peace first, for the fifth thing is a great deal worse.''

So they sat and ate, and while they ate they bargained together as to how much the miller would give for knowing the fifth thing; and at last they agreed upon three hundred dollars. Then the Little Farmer pinched the raven, so that he croaked aloud. And the miller asked what he said; and the Little Farmer answered,—

"He says that there is a demon in the linen closet."

"Then," said the miller, "that demon must out of the linen closet;" and he unbarred the house door, while the Little Farmer got the key of the linen closet from the miller's wife, and opened it. Then the man rushed forth, and out of the house; and the miller said,—

"I saw the black rogue with my own eyes; so that is a good riddance."

And the Little Farmer took himself off by daybreak next morning with the three hundred dollars.

And after this the Little Farmer by degrees got on in the world, and built himself a good house; and the other farmers said,—

"Surely the Little Farmer has been where it rains gold pieces, and has brought home money by the bushel."

And he was summoned before the bailiff to say whence his riches came. And all he said was,—

"I sold my calf's skin for three hundred dollars."

When the other farmers heard this they wished to share such good luck, and ran home, killed all their cows, skinned them, in order to sell them also for the same high price as the Little Farmer. And the bailiff said, "I must be beforehand with them." So he sent his servant into the town to the skin-buyer, and he only gave her three dollars for the skin; and that was faring better than the others, for when they came, they did not get as much as that, for the skin-buyer said,—

"What am I to do with all these skins?"

Now the other farmers were very angry with the Little Farmer for misleading them; and they vowed vengeance against him, and went to complain of his deceit to the bailiff. The poor Little Farmer was with one voice sentenced to death, and to be put into a cask with holes in it, and rolled into the water. So he was led to execution; and a priest was fetched to say a mass for him, and the rest of the people had to stand at a distance. As soon as the Little Farmer caught sight of the priest he knew him for the man who was hid in the linen closet at the miller's. And he said to him,—

"As I let you out of the cupboard, you must let me out of the cask."

At that moment a shepherd passed with a flock of sheep; and the Little Farmer, knowing him to have a great wish to become bailiff himself, called out with all his might,—

"No, I will not; and if all the world asked me, I would not!"

The shepherd, hearing him, came up and asked what it was he would not do. The Little Farmer answered,—

"They want to make me bailiff, if I sit in this cask; but I will not do it!"

The shepherd said,—

"If that is all there is to do in order to become bailiff, I will sit in the cask and welcome." And the Little Farmer answered,—

"Yes, that is all; just get into the cask, and you will become bailiff." So the shepherd agreed, and got in, and the Little Farmer fastened on the top; then he collected the herd of sheep and drove them away. The priest went back to the parish assembly, and told them the mass had been said. Then they came and began to roll the cask into the water; and as it went the shepherd inside called out, "I consent to be bailiff!"

They thought that it was the Little Farmer who spoke, and they answered,—

"All right; but first you must go down below and look about you a little;" and they rolled the cask into the water.

Upon that the farmers went home; and when they reached the village there they met the Little Farmer driving a flock of sheep and looking quite calm and contented. The farmers were astonished and cried,—

"Little Farmer, whence come you? how did you get out of the water?"

"Oh, easily," answered he; "I sank and sank until I came to the bottom; then I broke through the cask and came out of it, and there were beautiful meadows and plenty of sheep feeding, so I brought away this flock with me."

Then said the farmers, "Are there any left?"

"Oh, yes," answered the Little Farmer; "more than you can possibly need."

Then the farmers agreed that they would go and fetch some sheep also, each man a flock for himself; and the bailiff said, "Me first." And they all went together; and in the blue sky there were little fleecy clouds like lambkins, and they were reflected in the water; and the farmers cried out,—

"There are the sheep down there at the bottom."

When the bailiff heard that he pressed forward and said,—

"I will go first and look about me, and if things look well, I will call to you."

And he jumped plump into the water, and they all thought that the noise he made meant "Come;" so the whole company jumped in one after the other. So perished all the proprietors of the village, and the Little Farmer, as sole heir, became a rich man.

The Boggart and the Farmer

Retold by Eileen Colwell

This folktale comes from Lincolnshire, a county on the east coast of England. The boggart was a type of mischievous brownie of English country tales who delighted in tormenting those whose farms he decided to inhabit. Many tales dealing with boggarts tell of vain attempts to get rid of them. In this tale, however, the farmer succeeds because of his intelligence and guile.

There was once a farmer who lived at Mumby, near Alford, in Lincolnshire. He had a good enough farm but he thought he would like to add a field or two. So he bought a piece of land and was pleased with his bargain for the soil was good and the land level.

The next day he went to look at the field and to plan what crop he would sow there first. Suddenly a Boggart appeared from nowhere; a thick-set hairy thing he was with arms as long again as the farmer's.

"Clear off!" he says to the farmer. "This is my land."

"That it ain't!" says the farmer. "I've just bought it."

From Eileen Colwell, *Round About and Long Ago: Tales from the English Counties* (Boston: Houghton Mifflin, 1972). Illustrations by Anthony Colbert.

"'Tis mine!" yells the Boggart, clenching his fists and looking as though he would throttle the farmer.

Now the farmer was afraid to argue with such a strong, ugly creature, but he didn't see why he should give up land he had paid for fairly. So he said, trying to look pleasant, "Mebbe we could strike a bargain?"

"I'll tell you what," says the Boggart grinning, "we'll *share* the crops. You'll have to do the work of course."

"Agreed," says the farmer. "When I've grown the crops, which will you have, Tops or Bottoms? What grows above ground or under ground?"

"Tops!" says the Boggart, thinking he was getting the better of the farmer.

The cunning farmer set potatoes on his land. When the Boggart came to collect his share at harvest time, only the shrivelled tops were left, but the farmer had a ton or two of fine potatoes for his share.

Well, there was nothing the Boggart could do about it, for the farmer had given him what he had promised. However, when the Boggart was asked what he would have the second year, he said he would have Bottoms.

"Ah-ha," he thought. "He'll not trick me a second time. I'm clever, I am."

He was not as clever as he thought, for the farmer planted barley. The Boggart came along several times to see how the crop looked, but he suspected nothing for he did not know barley from any other crop.

When the barley was ready, the farmer cut it and stored away many bushels in his barns. When the Boggart came to collect his share, the field was bare and there were only the roots and stubble of the barley left. He had been outwitted again.

How angry he was! But a bargain's a bargain—he had asked for Bottoms and the farmer had given him Bottoms.

Then the Boggart had what he thought was a clever idea. "This year you'll sow wheat," he said, for he knew what wheat was. "We'll share what comes up and then we'll each mow and *keep* what we mow." The Boggart knew that his arms were twice as strong as the farmer's and he reckoned he could mow a great deal faster than the farmer could.

Well, there was nothing for it, the farmer had to sow wheat, but he was very worried about how much of it would be his. He went to look at the field every week and he saw that it was going to produce a fine crop. It vexed him to think that the ugly Boggart was going to get most of it.

The Wise Man of the village heard about it and suggested a plan. The farmer rubbed his hands with glee and went straight to the village smith and asked him to make some iron rods. These he took to the field and scattered them amongst the wheat on the side the Boggart was to mow.

On the day of the harvest the sun shone and the wheat was at its best. The Boggart arrived grinning, his scythe over his shoulder. "I'll start one end and you can start t'other," he said.

They began to mow. The farmer moved steadily forward, swinging his scythe, but the Boggart kept striking iron rods and blunting his scythe. He thought the rods were tough weeds, docks maybe.

"These are mortal tough docks!" he grumbled, stopping to sharpen his scythe.

Crash! He struck another iron rod. "Plague take it! Another one!" he growled angrily, stopping again. By midday the farmer has mowed half the field but the Boggart had only cut one corner.

The sun blazed down and the Boggart got crosser and crosser. At last he yelled, "Ain't you got any docks your side?"

"Ne'er a one," answered the farmer mowing steadily.

At last, when he had to stop for the twentieth time, the Boggart gave up. He flung down his blunt scythe and screamed, "Keep the land! I won't have no more to do with it." He gave a tremendous stamp on the ground, a hole opened in the earth, and the Boggart popped down it. The last the farmer saw of him was his shock of black hair disappearing with an angry flourish.

The Boggart never came back to claim the land, but even today he sometimes pops up suddenly to frighten people, nasty creature that he is. Men say, too, that when their tools are lost it is the Boggart who has taken them.

The Winning of Kwelanga

Retold by Verna Aardema

This folktale of Zulu origin stresses again the universality of the genre. There are many versions of this tale, and they come from every country. The poor man who wins the hand of the princess is a common theme in folk literature, perhaps because it can be a source of hope for those who have less than others.

Near the Mountains of the Dragon, there once lived a great chief named Ngazulu. He had a daughter who was so beautiful and gentle that she was called Kwelanga, which means sunrise.

It was the chief's desire that Kwelanga be married to a man worthy of her. So all suitors were put to impossible tests. Naturally all failed to win her.

One day a young man named Zamo heard about this. At once he decided to try his luck. His father tried to dissuade him. He said, "We are poor people. How dare you think of marrying the daughter of the chief?"

His mother said, "Oh, Zamo! Every man who has tried has lost his life. Do you think you would fare any better?"

But Zamo said, "I can't whistle with another man's mouth. I must try it myelf."

So one day Zamo went to Chief Ngazulu and said, "Greetings, *Nkosi*." Then he waited for the chief to speak.

The chief said, "Young man, what are you doing here? Have you lost your way?"

"No, *Nkosi*," said Zamo. "This is the end of my journey. I have come to propose marriage with your daughter."

"*You* come, with no attendants, to propose marriage?" cried the chief.

"*Nkosi*," said Zamo humbly, "it is the custom of my people to act alone."

"Proposer-of-marriage," said the chief, "you are prepared to do the tasks we will set for you?"

"I am here to try," said Zamo.

Ngazulu said, "Well then, look yonder. Do you see that cultivated field? Kaffir corn has been sown there. Before sundown you must gather all the grain that has been scattered. Then you may speak to me of marriage."

At that moment Kwelanga passed by on her way to the stream to draw water. She swayed gracefully beneath the earthen pot

From Verna Aardema, *Behind the Back of the Mountain; Black Folktales from Southern Africa* (New York: Dial Press, 1973). Illustrations by Leo and Diane Dillon.

said, "You did well, young man. But that task was too easy. Tomorrow we shall talk again."

Zamo was given food and a hut in which to sleep. Very early the following morning he went to sit near the chief's door.

When Ngazulu came out, he said, "Young man, what do you want with me?"

Zamo said, *"Nkosi,* I have come to propose marriage at this *kraal."*

The chief said, "See that forest in the valley? If you are able to chop down all the trees before sunset, then come to me and talk of marriage."

Zamo fetched an axe and went to the forest. He set to work with all speed. Many trees fell before his axe. But the forest was large, and though he worked all day without resting, most of the trees were still left. As the sun was slipping behind the hill, he heard a sweet voice singing:

"Trees of the forest,
In the sun's red glow,
Fall before Zamo—
Bow yourselves low."

At that, the trees crashed down on every side. Not one was left standing. Just then the sun set. Zamo went to the chief and said, *"Nkosi,* have I not finished the task you gave me?"

The chief was very much surprised. He called his counselor and said, "Think of something really hard for this man to do. The tasks I have given him have been too easy."

The counselor put his hand over his mouth, as is the way with people in deep thought. Then he said, "Let Zamo come to us in the morning. We will think of something that is not so easy."

The chief and his counselor sat up all night discussing what trial to give the young man. Just as the sun was rising they came to a decision.

When Zamo appeared, the counselor said, "Young man, do you see that thorn tree growing out from the edge of the cliff—the one way up high on the mountainside? You are to climb out on it and pluck the topmost thorn."

Zamo saw the scraggly tree growing out

balanced on her head. When she saw the handsome suitor talking with her father, she began humming a little tune.

When the young man saw Kwelanga he thought she was as pretty as a sunbird. He said, "Let me begin at once."

Zamo went straight to the field. Finding a huge basket nearby, he took it and began picking up the kernels of kaffir corn. He worked all day without resting. When the sun was about to disappear in the west, he still hadn't finished half the field.

Just then he heard someone singing from the hillside above him:

"Red grains of kaffir corn
Scattered by our mothers,
Fly back from whence you came,
Gather with the others."

Suddenly the basket was heaped with grain. Zamo looked about and saw that the field was clean. He knew that every kernel had returned to the basket, and he carried the grain to Ngazulu.

When the chief saw the filled basket, he

from a crag high up on the mountain. No one could climb out on that, he thought. But he said nothing and set off up a steep mountain path.

The chief and his counselor watched him go. They were sure that Zamo would not be able to climb the tree because of the thorns. Even if he should manage to crawl out on it, the tree would bend with his weight and surely throw him off into the gorge. In any event, they thought they had seen the last of him.

When Zamo reached the edge of the cliff, he looked down to see what lay beneath the thorn tree. Far, far down he saw nothing but gray rubble—the rocks of all sizes that had rolled down the mountain. He knew that to fall would mean certain death.

The trunk of the thorn tree angled outward and upward from the edge of the cliff. Zamo began to creep out on it, picking his way between big thorns. As he neared the twisted umbrella of branches, the thorns were so close together that there was no place even for fingertips. Then the tree began to bend. Zamo stopped breathing, and with great difficulty made his way back to the foot of the tree.

Just then he heard a voice singing behind him:

"Thorn tree, thorn tree,
Wind and weather worn tree,
Your topmost thorn, please
Pluck for Zamo and me."

Suddenly a small gray thorn came twirling through the air. It landed beside Zamo. He picked it up and, turning quickly, he saw Kwelanga coming toward him with outstretched hands. He knew at once that it was she who had sung the magic songs that had helped him every time.

Zamo took Kwelanga's hand, and together they went to her father.

"*Nkosi,*" said Zamo, "here is the topmost thorn. I have finished the tasks. Kwelanga is willing, and I have come to propose marriage at this *kraal.*"

When Ngazulu saw the look of happiness on the face of his daughter, he knew that Zamo truly was worthy of her. For he knew that the best husband for a woman is the man who can make her happy.

The Kingdom of the Lazy People

Edited by Dov Noy

*Dov Noy, the editor of the anthology from which this tale comes, comments,
"The name Oved [the character in the tale] . . . is a common name in the Bible,*

From Dov Noy, ed., *Folktales of Israel,* trans. by Gene Baharav (Chicago: University of Chicago Press, 1963).

and in Hebrew it retains the meaning of Laborer." Jewish tradition emphasizes working the land for a living and there are many tales about this. For the Jewish people, Noah is the culture-hero who taught people how to till the land. Note the similarity betwen this tale and Aesop's fable "The Farmer and His Sons."

In a certain far-off land there was a kingdom of idlers. All day long the people dug the ground for gold, hoping to become rich. For years and years they went on digging, but they did not find anything. They were sad, and their king became angry and bad-tempered. But they still disdained honest work.

One day a young man happened to pass by. He was cheerful and good-humored. He walked in a carefree way, and on his lips was a merry song. When the diggers saw him, they asked him to stop whistling: "Our king is very angry and bad-tempered. He may even kill you," they warned him. The young man laughed, "Be it so; just bring me to him."

The diggers stopped their work and took the young man to the king's palace. On the way they asked him, "What is your name?"

"Oved (worker)," answered the young man.

"And why do you whistle?"

"Because I am cheerful and content."

"And why are you cheerful and content?"

"Because I have a lot of gold."

Hearing this they were filled with joy and told the king about the gold. The king asked Oved, "Is it true that you have a hoard of gold?"

"Yes!" was the answer. "I have seven sacks full of gold."

The king became very excited, and he immediately called his people and ordered them to bring the sacks. But Oved explained, "It will take time to get the gold, my king. It is kept in a cave, guarded by a seven-headed ogre. Only I myself can take it out from there. Give me all your people for one year, and during that time we will free the gold from the monster."

The king had no alternative. He put horses, oxen, and men at Oved's disposal and commanded the people to carry out the young man's instructions.

Oved ordered his men to bring plows and to plow the rich and fertile land of the country. Then, after plowing, they sowed, and at harvest season they collected seven wagons full of the finest wheat.

All the while the king warned Oved that if he did not bring him the sacks of gold at the end of the year, he would be beheaded. Whereon Oved smiled and explained, "We need wheat to block up the mouth of the monster," and he continued to be cheerful and to sing merry songs.

For seven days Oved wandered with his seven wagons until he reached a large town whose land had no vegetation. When the merchants of the town saw the wagons of ripe wheat, they paid a large sum of money in exchange—seven sacks full of gold. After seven more days had passed, Oved once again came before the king, who asked him, "Have you succeeded in overcoming the monster?"

Oved answered with a smile, "I sold the wheat to people whose soil is barren, and in return I was given seven sacks of gold."

When the king heard Oved's story, he said to him in excitement, "He who tills the earth provides the bread. Indeed, we can get out of our good earth even more than seven sacks of gold each year." And he asked Oved to stay in his kingdom and rule his citizens.

Oved, however, refused, saying "There are many men in this world who do not know the secret of labor. One can dig gold from the earth by tilling it, sowing golden wheat, and turning it into bread. It is my duty to reveal this secret to others too."

Cheerfully and happily Oved set off on his wanderings.

The Great Big Enormous Turnip*

Leo Tolstoy

This simple cumulative tale of Russian origin stresses working together cooperatively. A cumulative rhyme or story is one in which a new character or element is added to the old to build to a resolution. The Great Big Enormous Turnip is reminiscent of such rhymes as "The House That Jack Built," which is descended from an old Hebrew chant.

Once upon a time an old man planted a little turnip and said, "Grow, grow, little turnip, grow sweet. Grow, grow, little turnip, grow strong." And the turnip grew up sweet and strong, and big and enormous. Then, one day, the old man went to pull it up. He pulled and pulled again, but he could not pull it up. He called the old woman. The old woman pulled the old man. The old man pulled the turnip. And they pulled and pulled again, but they could not pull it up. So the old woman called her granddaughter. The granddaughter pulled the old woman, The old woman pulled the old man, The old man pulled the turnip. And they pulled and pulled again, but they could not pull it up. The granddaughter called the black dog. The black dog pulled the granddaughter, The granddaughter pulled the old woman, The old woman pulled the old man, The old man pulled the turnip. And they pulled and pulled again, but they could not pull it up. The black dog called the cat. The cat pulled the dog, The dog pulled the granddaughter, The granddaughter pulled the old woman, The old woman pulled the old man, The old man pulled the turnip. And they pulled and pulled again, but still they could not pull it up. The cat called the mouse. The mouse pulled the cat, The cat pulled the dog, The dog pulled the granddaughter, The granddaughter pulled the old woman, The old woman pulled the old man, The old man pulled the turnip. They pulled and pulled again, and up came the turnip at last.

FOLK RHYMES AND POETRY

Mother Goose Rhymes

A proverb condenses the wisdom of experience to produce a homely illustration of a general truth. Many proverbs draw from nature and country life to teach children.

*Leo Tolstoy and Helen Oxenbury, *The Great Big Enormous Turnip* (New York: Franklin Watts, 1968).

Birds of a feather flock together,
And so will pigs and swine.
Rats and mice will have their choice,
And so will I have mine.

This rhyme was used to entertain infants and may have had a connection with a boys' game played at Christmastime in the seventeenth century.

Shoe the colt,
Shoe the colt,
Shoe the wild mare.
But for the little foal,
Let her run bare.

Katherine Elwes Thomas identified Little Boy Blue as Thomas Cardinal Wolsey, adviser to Henry VIII. Although the rhyme has lost its political connotations for children (if it ever had any), it remains a rollicking part of childhood lore.

Little Boy Blue, come, blow me your
horn;
The sheep's in the meadow, the cow's
in the corn.
Where's the little boy that looks after
the sheep?
He's under the haycock, fast asleep.

This chant describes a common problem associated with milking a cow.

A-milking, a-milking, my maid,
"Cow, take care of your heels," she
said;

"And you shall have some
nice new hay,
If you'll quietly let me milk
away."

This short rhyme teaches a child where rolls come from; it is interesting to compare this rhyme with Maurice Sendak's In the Night Kitchen.

Blow, wind, blow! and go, mill, go!
That the miller may grind his corn;
That the baker may take it,
And into rolls make it,
And send us some hot in the morn.

Hens to Sell

Olive Beaupré Miller (trans.)

This simple French rhyme takes the chant of the street vendor and uses it to create a children's game.

I have hens to sell you!
Red or white, I tell you!
Four sous here,
Four sous here,—
Mary, Mary, turn, my dear!

From Olive Beaupré Miller, trans., *Nursery Friends from France* (Chicago, Ill: Book House for Children, 1927).

Klumperty and His Wifie

Olive Beaupré Miller (trans.)

This lively Dutch rhyme gives a humorous view of a farmer and his rather vain wife.

Klumperty and his wifie
Rose early one fine day,
And with their butter and eggs, eggs, eggs,
To market off went they!

From Olive Beaupré Miller, trans., *Tales Told in Holland* (Chicago, Ill.: Book House for Children, 1926).

They'd gone half way to market,
Half down the dike when thud!
They dropped and broke their eggs, eggs,
   eggs,
The butter it fell in the mud!
She wept but not for the eggs, eggs, eggs;
'Twas for her shawl, perchance,
Which she had made the day before
Out of Klumperty's Sunday pants.

Bim, Bam, Beggs

Olive Beaupré Miller (trans.)

*This Dutch rhyme is very similar to rhymes
from other countries, such as the English
"Jack Sprat."*

Bim, bam, beggs.
The farmer won't eat eggs;
He'll eat, if he can,
Ham in the pan,
And that makes fat our farmer man!

From Olive Beaupré Miller, trans., *Tales Told in Holland* (Chicago, Ill.: Book House for Children, 1926).

The Farmer's Lament

Mrs. Eliza Gutch and
Mabel Peacock (collectors)

*A farmer's lot is not always an idyllic one,
as "The Farmer's Lament" readily shows.
According to the collectors of this poem, it
was "recited in January, 1888, by an old
gentleman, a native of Louth, on his 87th
birthday; he remembered [its] being
commonly sung by children in the year
1804. . . ." "The Lincolnshire Farmer,"
a poem from the same period, paints a
brighter picture of a farmer's life.*

From Mrs. Eliza Gutch and Mabel Peacock, collectors,
County Folklore (London: David Nutt, 1908), vol. 5.

Times are hard and very cold
  And all of us well know
Our creditors we cannot meet,
  The corn it sells so low.

Our wheelwright and knacker is unpaid,
  So is the blacksmith too;
Our butcher, also, he must trust,
  The corn it sells so low.

Last year we could wear black-strap boots,
  When times so well did go,
But now we scarce get shoes to wear.
  The corn it sells so low.

Then the grooms would bring our horse
  Around the farm to view,
But all of us must walk it now,
  The corn it sells so low.

Miss Kitty must the parlour quit,
  So must Miss Nancy too,
And round the milk-yard they must trot,
  The corn it sells so low.

The Lincolnshire Farmer

Mrs. Eliza Gutch and
Mabel Peacock (collectors)

The doctor his medical man doth tend,
  The parson doth with him pray;
And the farmer doth to the market ride
  Upon the market day.

The farmer doth to the market go
  To sell his barley and wheat;
His wife on a pilloring seat rides behind,
  Dressed up so clean and neat.

With a basket of butter and eggs she rides
  So merrily on I'll vow;
There's none so rare that can compare
  With the lads that follow the plough.

And when from the market they do return
  That is the best comfort of all;
We have a lusty black pudding in the pot
  And a good piece of beef and all.

From Mrs. Eliza Gutch and Mabel Peacock, collectors,
County Folklore (London: David Nutt, 1908), vol. 5.

And then after supper a jug of brown beer
  Is brought to the table I'll vow;
And there's none so rare that can compare
  With the lads that follow the plough.

Paper Boats

Rabindranath Tagore

*Sir Rabindranath Tagore (1861–1941) was
an Indian poet, born in Calcutta. His works
are infused with a strong sense of the beauty
of the earth and sky in his native land and
with a love of childhood.*

Day by day I float my paper boats one by
  one down the running stream.
In big black letters I write my name on them
  and the name of the village where I live.
I hope that someone in some strange land
  will find them and know who I am.
I load my little boats with *shuili* flowers from
  our garden, and hope that these blooms of
  dawn will be carried safely to land in the
  night.
I launch my paper boats and look up into the
  sky and see the little clouds setting their
  white bulging sails.
I know not what playmate of mine in the sky
  sends them down the air to race with my
  boats!
When night comes I bury my face in my
  arms and dream that my paper boats float
  on and on under the midnight stars.
The fairies of sleep are sailing in them, and
  the lading is their baskets full of dreams.

From Rabindranath Tagore, *Collected Poems and Plays*
(New York: Macmillan, 1941).

The Pasture

Robert Frost

*The poetry of Robert Frost (1874–1963) is
restrained in both emotion and language.*

From Robert Frost, *The Poetry of Robert Frost*, ed. by
Edward Connery Lathem (New York: Holt, Rinehart &
Winston, 1969).

*One critic has pointed out that Frost
demanded that his verse "be as simple and
honest as an axe or hoe." Frost himself
said, "To me, the thing that art does for life
is to clean it, to strip it to form." This
philosophy is reflected in both the form of his
verses and his choice of subjects—the
simple, natural things of life that have
meaning within themselves.*

I'm going out to clean the pasture spring;
I'll only stop to rake the leaves away
(And wait to watch the water clear, I may):
I sha'n't be gone long.—You come too.

I'm going out to fetch the little calf
That's standing by the mother. It's so young
It totters when she licks it with her tongue.
I sha'n't be gone long.—You come too.

Haiku

Kenneth Rexroth

*Japanese poetry intensifies and exalts
experience; it is less distracted by nonpoetic
considerations than is poetry from other
countries. The poet X. J. Kennedy notes, in
his* Literature, an Introduction to Fiction,
Poetry and Drama, *that traditionally, "haiku
in Japanese is rimeless, its seventeen
syllables usually arranged in three lines,
often following a pattern of five, seven, and
five syllables. Haiku written in English
[however] frequently ignores such a
pattern."*

  *As in the following poem, Japanese haiku
tends to be seasonal in subject and, as
Kennedy further states, "assumes a view of
the universe in which observer and nature
are not separated."*

From Kenneth Rexroth, *100 Poems from the Japanese*
(New York: New Directions, 1964).

When I went out
In the Spring meadows
To gather violets,
I enjoyed myself
So much that I stayed all night.

After Snow

GRAZ, AUSTRIA

Walter Clark

*There is a strong reminder of the Greek myth
of Demeter in this poem. The reader is led to
wonder who the woman is and whether
something is happening that is of greater
significance than the mere brushing away of
snow.*

After snow a lady is out in our garden
Cleaning the trees.
She carries a long, light pole.
First she rattles the bamboo
And the low bushy still-green plants.
Now she is chastising a fir tree,
Now the ivy along the wall.
She has covered her footprints
With helpings of snow.

And now she has gone.

From Walter Clark, *View from Mt. Paugus.*

He Was

Richard Wilbur

*Richard Wilbur's poetry shows the influence
of Marianne Moore, Wallace Stevens, and
the French symbolists. In this particular
poem death and rebirth, spring and fall
combine to paint a portrait of the almost
symbiotic relationship that can exist between
a man and the land he tills.*

From Richard Wilbur, *Ceremony and Other Poems* (Orlando, Fla.: Harcourt Brace Jovanovich, 1950).

a brown old man with a green thumb:
I can remember the screak on stones of his
    hoe,
The chug, choke, and high madrigal wheeze
Of the spray-cart bumping below
The sputtery leaves of the apple trees,
But he was all but dumb

Who filled some quarter of the day with
    sound
All of my childhood long. For all I heard
Of all his labors, I can now recall
Never a single word
Until he went in the dead of fall
To the drowsy underground,

Having planted a young orchard with so
    great care
In that last year that none was lost, and May
Aroused them all, the leaves saying the
    land's
Praise for the livening clay,
And the found voice of his buried hands
Rose in the sparrowy air.

The Farm

Vassar Miller

*With its simplicity of thought and action and
its expressive language, this rich poem
brings forth in modern form the full strength
of the pastoral tradition. Since ancient times,
pastoral poets have depicted life in the
country as unsullied and therefore superior
to urban life. In ''The Farm,'' Vassar Miller
sketches the things of the country that are to
be valued.*

Where peace goes whispering by,
creaks in the turning windmill,
lows in the cattle;
where the hot light stretches over the fields
like a lazy cat;

From Vassar Miller, *Onions and Roses* (Middletown, Conn.: Wesleyan University Press, 1968).

where the clouds scatter
and graze like sheep on the barren skies,
but gather no rain;
where the darkness opens its fist
spilling stars and the wind;
where love has grown quiet,
assuming the shapes
of the soil and the rock and the tree—
here in this land
let me rest, rest, rest, oh, filling my heart
full of a sweet emptiness!

I Never Saw a Moor

Emily Dickinson

*Emily Dickinson (1830–1886) often used
images from nature in her writings to convey*

From Thomas H. Johnson, ed., *The Poems of Emily
Dickinson* (Cambridge, Mass.: The Belknap Press of
Harvard University Press, 1983).

*larger meanings. The impression of a
delicacy of style and content that a first
reading of her poetry suggests is misleading.
Closer reading reveals a poetry that is
powerful and charged with meaning. In this
poem, for example, she plays on the
association between nature and the divine.*

I never saw a moor,
I never saw the sea;
Yet know I how the heather looks,
And what a wave must be.

I never spoke with God,
Nor visited in heaven;
Yet certain am I of the spot
As if the chart were given.

FICTION

Farmer Boy
The Turn of the Year

Laura Ingalls Wilder

*The frontier books of Laura Ingalls Wilder (1867–1957) illustrate the bravery,
hardships, and joys of pioneer family life.* Farmer Boy *details the childhood of
her husband, Almanzo Wilder, on his parents' farm in New York state. It depicts
a childhood that built character, a childhood filled with hard work in every
season but work that was fun for young Almanzo and his brother and sister. In
1954, the Children's Library Association established the Laura Ingalls Wilder*

From Laura Ingalls Wilder, *Farmer Boy* (New York: Harper & Row, 1953). Illustrated by Garth Williams.

Award to be given for "a lasting contribution to literature for children." Wilder herself was the first recipient of this award.

The days were growing longer, but the cold was more intense. Father said:

"When the days begin to lengthen
The cold begins to strengthen."

At last the snow softened a little on the south and west slopes. At noon the icicles dripped. Sap was rising in the trees, and it was time to make sugar.

In the cold mornings just before sunrise, Almanzo and Father set out to the maple grove. Father had a big wooden yoke on his shoulders and Almanzo had a little yoke. From the ends of the yokes hung strips of moosewood bark, with large iron hooks on them, and a big wooden bucket swung from each hook.

In every maple tree Father had bored a small hole, and fitted a little wooden spout into it. Sweet maple sap was dripping from the spouts into small pails.

Going from tree to tree, Almanzo emptied the sap into his big buckets. The weight hung from his shoulders, but he steadied the buckets with his hands to keep them from swinging. When they were full, he went to the great caldron and emptied them into it.

The huge caldron hung from a pole set between two trees. Father kept a bonfire blazing under it, to boil the sap.

Almanzo loved trudging through the frozen wild woods. He walked on snow that had never been walked on before, and only his own tracks followed behind him. Busily he emptied the little pails into the buckets, and whenever he was thirsty he drank some of the thin, sweet, icy-cold sap.

He liked to go back to the roaring fire. He poked it and saw the sparks fly. He warmed his face and hands in the scorching heat and smelled the sap boiling. Then he went into the woods again.

At noon all the sap was boiling in the caldron. Father opened the lunch-pail, and Almanzo sat on the log beside him. They ate and talked. Their feet were stretched out to the fire, and a pile of logs was at their backs.

All around them were snow and ice and wild woods, but they were snug and cosy.

After they had eaten, Father stayed by the fire to watch the sap, but Almanzo hunted wintergreen berries.

Under the snow on the south slopes the bright-red berries were ripe among their thick green leaves. Almanzo took off his mittens and pawed away the snow with his bare hands. He found the red clusters and filled his mouth full. The cold berries crunched between his teeth, gushing out their aromatic juice.

Nothing else was ever so good as wintergreen berries dug out of the snow.

Almanzo's clothes were covered with snow, his fingers were stiff and red with cold, but he never left a south slope until he had pawed it all over.

When the sun was low behind the mapletrunks, Father threw snow on the fire and it died in sizzles and steam. Then Father dipped the hot syrup into the buckets. He and Almanzo set their shoulders under the yokes again, and carried the buckets home.

They poured the syrup into Mother's big brass kettle on the cook-stove. Then Almanzo began the chores while Father fetched the rest of the syrup from the woods.

After supper, the syrup was ready to sugar off. Mother ladled it into six-quart milk-pans and left it to cool. In the morning every pan held a big cake of solid maple-sugar. Mother dumped out the round, golden-brown cakes and stored them on the top pantry shelves.

Day after day the sap was running, and every morning Almanzo went with Father to gather and boil it; every night Mother sugared it off. They made all the sugar they could use next year. Then the last boiling of syrup was not sugared off; it was stored in jugs down cellar, and that was the year's syrup.

When Alice came home from school she smelled Almanzo, and she cried out, "Oh, you've been eating wintergreen berries!"

She thought it wasn't fair that she had to

go to school while Almanzo gathered sap and ate wintergreen berries. She said:

"Boys have all the fun."

She made Almanzo promise that he wouldn't touch the south slopes along Trout River, beyond the sheep pasture.

So on Saturdays they went together to paw over those slopes. When Almanzo found a red cluster he yelled, and when Alice found one she squealed, and sometimes they divided, and sometimes they didn't. But they went on their hands and knees all over those south slopes, and they ate wintergreen berries all afternoon.

Almanzo brought home a pailful of the thick, green leaves, and Alice crammed them into a big bottle. Mother filled the bottle with whisky and set it away. That was her wintergreen flavoring for cakes and cookies.

Every day the snow was melting a little. The cedars and spruces shook it off, and it fell in blobs from the bare branches of oaks and maples and beeches. All along the walls of barns and house the snow was pitted with water falling from the icicles, and finally the icicles fell crashing.

The earth showed in wet, dark patches here and there. The patches spread. Only the trodden paths were still white, and a little snow remained on the north sides of buildings and woodpiles. Then the winter term of school ended and spring had come.

One morning Father drove to Malone. Before noon he came hurrying home, and shouted the news from the buggy. The New York potato-buyers were in town!

Royal ran to help hitch the team to the wagon, Alice and Almanzo ran to get bushel baskets from the woodshed. They rolled them bumpity-bump down the cellar stairs, and began filling them with potatoes as fast as they could. They filled two baskets before Father drove the wagon to the kitchen porch.

Then the race began. Father and Royal hurried the baskets upstairs and dumped them into the wagon, and Almanzo and Alice hurried to fill more baskets faster than they were carried away.

Almanzo tried to fill more baskets than Alice, but he couldn't. She worked so fast that she was turning back to the bin while her hoopskirts were still whirling the other way. When she pushed back her curls, her hands left smudges on her cheeks. Almanzo laughed at her dirty face, and she laughed at him.

"Look at yourself in the glass! You're dirtier than I be!"

They kept the baskets full; Father and Royal never had to wait. When the wagon was full, Father drove away in a hurry.

It was mid-afternoon before he came back, but Royal and Almanzo and Alice filled the wagon again while he ate some cold dinner, and he hauled another load away. That night Alice helped Royal and Almanzo do the chores. Father was not there for supper; he did not come before bedtime. Royal sat up to wait for him. Late in the night Almanzo heard the wagon, and Royal went out to help Father curry and brush the tired horses who had done twenty miles of hauling that day.

The next morning, and the next, they all began loading potatoes by candlelight, and Father was gone with the first load before sunrise. On the third day the potato-train left for New York city. But all Father's potatoes were on it.

"Five hundred bushels at a dollar a bushel," he said to Mother at supper. "I told you when potatoes were cheap last fall that they'd be high in the spring."

That was five hundred dollars in the bank. They were all proud of Father, who raised such good potatoes and knew so well when to store them and when to sell them.

"That's pretty good," Mother said, beaming. They all felt happy. But later Mother said,

"Well, now that's off our hands, we'll start house-cleaning tomorrow, bright and early."

Almanzo hated house-cleaning. He had to pull up carpet tacks, all around the edges of miles of carpet. Then the carpets were hung on clotheslines outdoors, and he had to beat them with a long stick. When he was little he had run under the carpets, playing they were tents. But now he was nine years old, he had to beat those carpets without stopping, till no more dust would come out of them.

Everything in the house was moved,

everything was scrubbed and scoured and polished. All the curtains were down, all the feather-beds were outdoors, airing, all the blankets and quilts were washed. From dawn to dark Almanzo was running, pumping water, fetching wood, spreading clean straw on the scrubbed floors and then helping to stretch the carpets over it, and then tacking all those edges down again.

Days and days he spent in the cellar. He helped Royal empty the vegetable-bins. They sorted out every spoiled apple and carrot and turnip, and put back the good ones into a few bins that Mother had scrubbed. They took down the other bins and stored them in the woodshed. They carried out crocks and jars and jugs, till the cellar was almost empty. Then Mother scrubbed the walls and floor. Royal poured water into pails of lime, and

Almanzo stirred the lime till it stopped boiling and was whitewash. Then they whitewashed the whole cellar. That was fun.

"Mercy on us!" Mother said when they came upstairs. "Did you get as much whitewash on the cellar as you got on yourselves?"

The whole cellar was fresh and clean and snow-white when it dried. Mother moved her milk-pans down to the scrubbed shelves. The butter-tubs were scoured white with sand and dried in the sun, and Almanzo set them in a row on the clean cellar floor, to be filled with the summer's butter.

Outdoors the lilacs and the snowball bushes were in bloom. Violets and buttercups were blossoming in the green pastures, birds were building their nests, and it was time to work in the fields.

Stairstep Farm: Anna Rose's Story
The Gander Bites

Anne Pellowski

Stairstep Farm *is one of four books that trace four generations of a Polish-American family in Wisconsin. These books convey the strong sense of continuity provided by the values and traditions that are passed on from generation to generation within a close-knit country family.*

After the anniversary, Mama had to start doing all her own chores again. When the morning milking was done, Lawrence, Francis, Angie, and Millie went off to school in the buggy.

"I want to go to school, too," begged Anna Rose.

"You have to wait until you're old enough," said Mama with a sigh.

"How come Laura can go to kindergarten? I'm as old as she is," insisted Anna Rose.

"They don't have kindergarten at the school in Pine Creek," answered Mama.

"But if you really want to go, I suppose you could live in Winona with Uncle John and Aunt Laura, like Francis did."

Anna Rose was silent. She wanted very badly to go to school, but she didn't want to leave her family. So she stayed at home and helped Mama with the work, or played with her younger sisters.

After breakfast, while Daddy cleaned the barn or did other work, Mama went to the cellar and separated the cream from the milk. Usually Anna Rose, Janie, and Mary Elizabeth went with her, while Virgie slept. They

From Anne Pellowski, *Stairstep Farm: Anna Rose's Story* (New York: Philomel Books, 1981).

had to walk outside and around to the back of the house to get to their cellar. It had two flat doors, sloping down from the side of the house and out toward the backyard. The doors were covered with slippery metal and in spring and summer they could slide down them as though they were in a playground.

Now it was winter and the doors had a thin covering of ice and snow. Sometimes Mama had to chop through it with a small hatchet, in order to get the doors to lift up and open out.

The front cellar room was the separating room. The walls were of thick stone and the floor was concrete. Along one side was a built-in trough. It was partly filled with water and there was a constant trickle of more water coming out from a pipe at one side. In winter and in summer the water was icy cold because it came from a spring deep underground. In the water in the trough they kept the cans of cream that Daddy took to the creamery twice a week.

Jutting out into the room from one wall was the shiny black separating machine, with its long-handled crank hanging down at one side. At the top was a wide, round bowl. Into this, Mama poured the milk. She began to turn the crank at a steady pace.

"I want to turn it," said Anna Rose one morning.

"Well, then, you have to count as you turn it. You must make it go around thirty times in one minute. If you go like this: One . . . two . . . three . . . four . . . five . . .," Mama counted slowly, "that will make the right speed. Can you count up to thirty?"

Anna Rose turned the crank and counted slowly out loud, from one to thirty, with a pause between each number. When the crank was going smoothly, Mama turned the small handle of a spigot at the bottom of the bowl. Now it was harder to turn at the same speed. Before long, separate streams of cream and skim milk began to flow out. The cream went into a tall can and the milk dropped into the larger milk can. But it wasn't long before Anna Rose's arms got tired and Mama had to turn the crank once more.

When the skim milk and cream were separated, Mama took off the top bowl, pulled out the rod with the steel disks, and washed everything in hot soapy water. From a kettle, she poured boiling water over the bowl and disks, so that they would dry quickly and be free of germs.

All through February and March, Mama and the three girls started out their mornings down in the separating room of the cellar. Afterward, Mama had to do all her other work. Twice a week she wheeled out the washing machine to wash the diapers and other clothes. Virgie made a lot of diapers dirty. They didn't have electricity on their farm, so the washing machine had to run on a gasoline motor. It made a lot of rackety noise.

Three times a week Mama baked bread. She would let the dough rise, punch it down, then let it rise again. Finally, she would shape it into eight fat loaves and put each into a pan. Once more the dough had to rise and at last the loaves were ready to go into the oven. After an hour, Mama took them out, crispy and golden brown. Somehow, the bread always got done about a half-hour before the older children came home from school. They wanted to eat some before starting their chores.

"I get the crust!" yelled Lawrence.

"No fair! You had it last time," argued Angie. They each wanted the end piece because it was so crunchy and tasty. When the bread was a day or more old, they didn't argue so much over the end crust, but when it was fresh out of the oven, Mama made them take turns cutting off the first slice.

Saturday bread baking was the best. Before the dough got kneaded into a round, satiny ball, Mama took part of it and put it into another large bowl. She added sugar and raisins and a little milk and more flour before she kneaded it and set it to rise, next to the big bowl of bread dough.

"Punch the bread down for me, Angeline," Mama would say if she was busy doing something else. Angie would rub her hands with a light coating of lard and punch down the bread dough and the sweet dough.

She had learned how to knead it with the palms of her hands and how to turn it over again so it made a smooth, round shape.

"Can't I do that?" asked Anna Rose. She thought it would be fun, and it looked easy.

"You have to watch for a long time, and then practice a lot before you get it just right," said Mama. "Pretty soon I'll let you try with your own little loaf."

After the bread loaves were shaped, Mama took her rolling pin and rolled out the sweet dough in two big rectangles. Over these she spread more raisins, and sugar and cinnamon. Then she folded over one long edge of the rectangle and began to curl it up, as though it were a small carpet being rolled up. She cut the plump coil into slices, lined them up on baking sheets, almost touching each other, and brushed them with butter. The sheets were set aside for the dough to rise once more, but not as long as the dough for the bread loaves. Finally, into the oven they went, and when they came out they were covered with fat, puffy coils of golden brown. Here and there a raisin had popped out, making a splotch of dark brown.

Mama called them snails, because they looked like the coiled shell of a snail. As soon as they cooled off for a few minutes, she slathered vanilla frosting over the tops, so much that it dripped down the sides. One batch they saved to eat for breakfast on Sunday, but the other they could eat on Saturday afternoon, after all the cleaning and chores were done. They sighed with satisfaction, gulping down mugs of cold milk in between bites of sweet snails.

In early April, Mama was busier than ever. In one corner of the garden she planted the first rows of lettuce, onions, and radishes.

"I don't care if I am taking a risk that a hard frost will kill them," she said. "I'm so hungry for fresh vegetables that I can't wait."

The weather stayed mild, and in two weeks there were rows of tiny green shoots in the garden. The grass and hay started coming up, too, and that meant the geese and gander could be let out of the shed where they spent the winter. Every day after school, Angie and Millie had to go looking for the secret hiding places where the geese chose to lay their eggs.

"Those darn geese," complained Angie. "Why can't they lay their eggs where they are supposed to?" Then she had an idea. "Anna Rose, can you watch out during the day, and tell me where the geese go? Then I'll know where to look for the eggs. But don't get too near that gander. He's a mean one and he'll bite you."

Every day after that, while Mama worked in the garden and Janie and Mary Elizabeth puddled around making mud pies, Anna Rose tried to watch carefully where the geese went. She never walked too close behind them because as soon as she came within a few yards of them, Hissssssss!, the gander would turn toward her, neck stretched out and beak wide open, ready to bite. Anna Rose ran as fast as she could, to the safety of the house or the garden. In the late afternoon, she told Angie where to look for the eggs.

Soon, there were three broody hens and two geese sitting on nests of eggs. Mama made a mark on the calendar hanging on the kitchen wall.

"We have to watch carefully after thirty days to see that the eggs hatch out all right. We should have about forty goslings, if we're lucky." Mama was happy about that.

Angie still had to watch out for the geese in the afternoon, spreading mash in their feeders and making sure there was enough water in their trough. The gander hissed a bit when she did that, but it was just for show. He didn't come after her.

On May 20th, when she went to give the geese their usual food, Angie heard a funny "Whit, whit!" Sticking out from one of the nests was the head of a gosling. Back she ran to the house.

"They're starting to hatch!" she said excitedly to Anna Rose. Then she turned to Mama. "Should I make some of the special mash?"

"Yes," answered Mama. "Bring some skim milk from the cellar and I'll show you how to mix it with the mash.'' They stirred the mixture until it was like a thick porridge. After spreading it in small, low pans, Angie returned to the nests where the goslings were hatching. She poked the beak of a gosling into the mash and then into the water. Soon, the gosling knew how to eat by itself.

Within seven days, all the eggs were hatched but one.

''It's probably rotten and won't hatch out,'' Mama explained. ''You'll have to throw it away, Angeline. Take it out from the nest when the goose isn't looking and throw it far down in the big ditch, where we can't smell it.''

Anna Rose watched as Angie skillfully sneaked the egg away when the geese and gander were busy gobbling up mash. Gingerly, she carried the large egg in her cupped hands, all the way to the big ditch, where she threw it down as far as she could. Plock! The egg landed far down, but even so, the smell began to rise up in penetrating fumes.

''Phew! Let's get out of here,'' cried Angie, holding her nose.

By the end of May when school was out for the summer, the goslings were covered with a soft, white down.

''Now you have to start feeding them nettles,'' Mama told Angie and Millie. ''Remember to chop them up fine, like I showed you last year. Anna Rose can help you pick the leaves. It's time she started learning how.''

Angie and Millie both groaned. That was just about the worst job they could think of. Nettles had something on their leaves that made your skin itch. They called the nettles by their Polish name, which sounded like *pokshee-vas.*

''That makes me think of something that pokes and prickles,'' thought Anna Rose, and that was what the leaves seemed to do.

''Why do we have to cut up those *pok-shee-vas* for the geese?'' she asked. ''Can't they eat them off the plants where they are growing?''

''The big geese can do that because they have strong beaks, but the goslings can't tear or chew for a while yet, so we have to cut things up for them,'' explained Mama.

''Goslings need to eat green things to grow; *pok-shee-vas* happen to have a flavor that geese like. My grandma once told me that in Poland they used to boil up the young *pok-shee-vas* and eat them as vegetables, so they must be tasty. Shall I make some for supper?'' asked Mama with a laugh.

''Ugh! I would never in my life eat boiled *pok-shee-vas,*'' said Millie in a disgusted voice. Anna Rose firmly shook her head ''No'' and closed her mouth tight. No one would *ever* get her to eat such a thing! Nettles were quite different from Brown Betty. She didn't have to see them cooked to know she would not like them.

''I'm only teasing,'' said Mama. ''I'm not going to boil any *pok-shee-vas.*'' But they still had to pick them every day for Angie to chop up. If they put on their mittens, they couldn't tear off the leaves properly. When they used old cloth gloves or wrapped their hands in a dishcloth, the nettles still stung their skin, right through the cloth. There was nothing to do except pick them as fast as they could, then run into the house and wash their hands and arms with lots of soap and water. That seemed to stop the stinging.

One morning Mama announced that she and Daddy had to go to Winona on some business.

''I think this time Angeline and Mildred may go along. They have not had a turn for quite a while,'' said Mama. ''That means you have to take care of the little ones, Francis, and you'll have to do all the barn work by yourself, Lawrence.''

''Gee whiz,'' complained Francis. ''Can't one of them stay home?'' He had had to take care of Millie when she was little, but now that she and Angie were old enough, he didn't see why he should have to take his turn again. ''Besides, I don't know how to change diapers any more,'' Francis stated flatly, sure that this excuse would be a good one.

''You won't have to. I'll take Virginia with me because she is still nursing, and she's no trouble. She sleeps most of the time. You only have to watch out for Mary Elizabeth and Jane and Anna Rose. Weed at least ten rows of potatoes in the garden and be sure to do the *pok-shee-vas* for the geese."

"And watch out that the gander doesn't get near the girls," added Daddy. "He's been acting so fierce of late, he'll bite anyone who comes his way."

Lawrence ducked out of the house and headed for the barn as fast as he could. He didn't want to be given any extra jobs. All morning, Francis grumbled but he stayed close to the house, watching his sisters.

"Aren't you going to feed the geese?" asked Anna Rose, when it was almost time to eat. She wanted to see how he did it.

"I'm going to wait until Mary Elizabeth takes her nap. Then she won't be following me around," Francis replied.

Mama had left some sausage meat on the table, and there were eggs in a bowl that Francis had to scramble and cook on the stove. He sliced a loaf of bread, and buttered a slice for each of his sisters. There was also a quart jar of raspberries that Mama had left as a special treat. Lawrence opened it and spooned the red berries and juice into five bowls. He gave himself and Francis the most, but they all had second helpings. Soon the whole jar was empty.

After they had put the dishes in the sink, Lawrence went out to the machine shed to hitch up the cultivator, and Francis put Mary Elizabeth on the small cot in the spare bedroom off the front room. That was where she always took her nap.

They went out to the potato patch above the garden where row after row of new plants were struggling to hold their own against the weeds. Francis showed the two girls how to grab hold of the crabgrass and weeds close to the ground and pull hard without tearing out any of the potato plants. Janie started on the first row, but before long she was playing in the dirt, forgetting all about the weeds. Anna Rose worked slowly and methodically on her row.

"She should weed, too," protested Anna Rose.

"Let her be," answered Francis. "She would pull up too many plants anyway."

They weeded for more than an hour. It was hot and Anna Rose was tired of leaning over and stooping down. There were still so many rows left to do.

"Let's stop," she pleaded. "Isn't it time to feed the geese?"

"All right," agreed Francis. He was tired of weeding, too.

"I'll help you pick the *pok-shee-vas*," offered Anna Rose.

Carrying a big pan, they set off for the back part of the orchard where many nettles grew in clumps. Janie followed them, clutching two fistfuls of dirt. As fast as they could, Francis and Anna Rose plucked leaves from the stinging plants until the pan was full.

"That should be enough," said Francis. Anna Rose tore back to the house and washed her arms and hands in soap and water. When she came outside again, Francis was already chopping up the nettles, using a long, sharp knife and a flat board. Janie watched for a while and then wandered off. Just then, they heard Mary Elizabeth crying and calling out.

"Go and get her up," Francis ordered Anna Rose. She went into the house and back to the spare room. Mary Elizabeth stopped crying the moment she saw her.

"Drink!" she demanded.

Anna Rose took her by the hand and led her to the kitchen sink. She ran water into a glass and gave it to Mary Elizabeth. Above the sink and just off to the side was a big window that looked out on the backyard and orchard. Standing on the little stool, Anna Rose could see Francis, chop-chopping at the nettles. Behind him a few yards to the right was Janie. She was stretching out her hands to one of the goslings that had wandered away from the rest. It must have smelled the nettles, and was coming to get some to eat. Closer and closer came the gosling. Janie reached down to catch it so she could pet it.

All of a sudden, Anna Rose gasped. There, half flying across the backyard, was the mean gander, headed straight for Janie! Janie couldn't see the gander coming because she was bent down over the gosling. Francis had his back turned as he busily chopped the nettles.

"Stop him!" shrieked Anna Rose, but, of course, Francis could not hear. She reached for a spoon to bang on the window and just as she did, Francis looked up and saw the gander.

Too late! The gander had snapped his beak right into Janie's bottom.

"Ow! Ow! Ow!" howled Janie.

"Get away from here!" yelled Francis as he swatted the knife and board at the gander, sending the chopped nettles flying in all directions. The gander let go of Janie. Francis dropped the knife and board, picked her up and ran with her into the house. Janie was sobbing and screaming.

Francis sat down on a chair and lay Janie across his knees, on her stomach. He lifted up her dress and pushed aside her panties. There, on one of Janie's buttocks, was a big round bite mark, all red and swollen and bleeding a little. The two girls stared at it while Janie continued to cry.

"Ow! Ow! Ow!"

Francis took her to the front room and laid her on the couch. Anna Rose and Mary Elizabeth followed silently.

"Watch her for a minute," Francis said in a shaky voice. He went back to the sink, rinsed out a clean cloth in cold water, and took the small bottle of iodine from the medicine chest. Gently he washed the gander bite and held the cold cloth against the wound. Janie only whimpered now.

"I'm going to put some iodine on it. It will sting for a while but then it will feel better," Francis assured Janie, but Anna Rose could see he looked scared. Would Janie get sick from the gander bite? She had heard of people getting sick or dying from a dog bite. That was why Mama told them to stay away from any strange dogs that wandered on to the farm by accident.

"Hold on to her legs," whispered Francis. Anna Rose grabbed hold of Janie's feet. As fast as he could, Francis swabbed the iodine over the bite mark, but still Janie screamed.

"It pinches! It pinches!" Janie kicked her legs so hard she almost hit Anna Rose in the jaw. At last she calmed down and lay still.

"You stay with her while I go finish feeding the geese and start my other chores," said Francis.

Janie lay quietly and Anna Rose took out one of the reading books from the shelf. She pretended to read it aloud. She knew a lot of the pages by heart because Angie had read them to her so many times. "If I could only go to school, then I'd really know how to read," thought Anna Rose.

The dogs began to bark. Anna Rose ran to the front porch.

"Mama and Daddy are back!"

Janie slid off the couch and ran out of the house toward her mother, who was just getting out of the car.

"Mama, Mama!" she cried. "The gander bit me in the *dupa!*"

Anna Rose gasped. *Dupa* was a naughty word in Polish. They weren't supposed to use it at all.

Mama didn't know what to say or do. She looked as though she wanted to laugh and scold at the same time. Without a word, she put her arm around Janie, and then examined the gander bite.

"I thought you were supposed to be minding the girls," Daddy scolded Francis angrily.

"I *was* minding them," protested Francis, trying to explain.

"If you had been paying attention, Janie would not have got bitten. Bring me my strap from the kitchen. If you can't learn to mind when we tell you to do something, then I'll have to teach you another way!" Daddy's voice was hard and angry.

Francis hung his head and went to the kitchen for the razor strap. Daddy took him behind the woodpile.

Whack! Whack! Whack! They heard three loud smacks.

Anna Rose felt sorry for Francis. It was not his fault that the gander came up so suddenly. Janie shouldn't have been playing with the gosling anyway.

That night, at the supper table, Janie sat on a soft feather pillow because her bottom still hurt if she sat on something hard.

"Let that be a lesson to all of you," Mama spoke seriously. "You have to learn to obey, or you'll get hurt."

When Francis came in, he sat down slowly and stiffly.

"Does your *dupa* hurt, too?" Janie asked him.

Everyone at the table started laughing, even Francis and Daddy.

"Don't you be saying words like that. It's not nice," Mama scolded Janie, but they could see she was holding back a laugh.

FANTASY

***

Rabbit Hill
There Is Enough for All

Robert Lawson

Robert Lawson, perhaps more than any other fantasy writer for children, captures the sense of the pastoral in his work. His gentle, whimsical writing shows the peaceful coexistence of human beings and nature; he presents an ideal to be reached for. Most stories that deal with country life portray people combating nature—hacking a living from the wilderness and trying to conquer nature. Rabbit Hill *shows that if one keeps nature in mind, there is, indeed, "enough for all" when planting a garden.*

The sun had set, and the gold of the west slowly faded to a cool clear green. Venus, hanging low over the Pine Wood, burned brilliantly, all alone at first, but as the sky deepened the smaller stars began to show themselves. High up the new moon swam like a silver sickle.

As the dusk thickened the whole Hill began to whisper with the soft rustle of small bodies passing through the grass, with the swish of tiny feet, all making their way toward the garden, for this was Midsummer's Eve and the Little Animals were gathering.

On the edge of the small circular lawn the Folks sat silently. It was dark and shadowy here under the big pine. All that could be seen was the dim whiteness of the stone benches, the regular glowing and dying of the Man's pipe, and the tent-like, gray tarpaulin. The top of this glowed in the moon's pale light like a beacon, and like a beacon it seemed to beckon all the Animals, for instead of gathering at the garden they were all pressing closer and closer to the little round lawn. Slowly, silently, one step at a time, they moved through the deep grass and the shrub shadows until the clearing was entirely surrounded by an audience of small, tense Animals, waiting for—they knew not what.

The moonlight was brighter now; the little lawn was like a small, lighted stage. They could make out the Lady sitting motionless

From Robert Lawson, *Rabbit Hill* (New York: Viking Press, 1944). Illustrations by Robert Lawson.

on the bench, beside her the drowsing bulk of Mr. Muldoon. It was so still that they could hear his wheezy breathing.

Suddenly the silence was rudely shattered by Uncle Analdas' harsh cry as he stepped shakily into the open. His sunken eyes were staring, his ears cocked at crazy angles.

"Where is he?" he croaked wildly. "Where is he? Where's that dingblasted old Cat? Leave me at him! They're not a-goin' to hang our Little Georgie!"

Mother sprang from the shadows, calling, "Analdas, come back. Oh, stop him, someone, stop him!"

There was a sudden stir in the Lady's lap; then, clear and joyous, Little Georgie's voice rang out. "Mother," it cried. A small form sprang to the ground and sped across the clearing. "Mother, Father, it's me, Little Georgie, I'm all well—look at me—look—"

In the bright moonlight he leaped and cavorted on the lawn, around and across, up and down, over and over. He jumped high over Uncle Analdas and turned a double handspring. He sprang to the bench and kicked Mr. Muldoon playfully in the stomach. The old Cat lazily caught him round the waist and they wrestled happily, finally falling to the ground with a thump. Remembering his age and dignity, Muldoon clambered back onto the bench, where his purr rumbled like a far-off gristmill.

A joyous chattering broke out among the Animals, but stilled when the Man quietly rose and approached the tarpaulin. Very deliberately he loosed its fastenings and flung it clear. In the deep silence that followed it was almost possible to hear the sound of a hundred little breaths caught and released in a sigh of awe.

The Mole grasped Willie Fieldmouse's elbow. "Willie, what is it?" he whispered. "What is it? *Willie, be eyes for me.*"

Willie's voice was hushed and breathless. "Oh, Mole," he said. "Oh, Mole, it's so beautiful. It's him, Mole, it's *him*—the Good Saint!"

"Him—of Assisi?" asked the Mole.

"Yes, Mole, *our* Saint. The good St. Francis of Assisi—him that's loved us and protected us Little Animals time out of mind—and, oh, Mole, it's so beautiful! He's all out of stone, Mole, and his face is so kind and so sad. He's got a long robe on, old and poor like, you can see the patches on it.

"And all around his feet are the Little Animals. They're *us*, Mole, all out of stone. There's you and me and there's all the Birds and there's Little Georgie and Porkey and the Fox—even old Lumpy the Hop Toad. And the Saint's hands are held out in front of him sort of kind—like blessing things. And from his hands there's water dropping, Mole, clear, cool water. It drops into a pool there in front of him."

"I can hear it splashing," the Mole whispered, "and I can smell the good clear pool and feel its coolness. Go on, Willie, be eyes for me."

"It's a fine pool for drinking of, Mole, and at each end it's shallow like, so the Birds can bathe there. And, oh, Mole, all around the pool is broad flat stones, a sort of rim, like a shelf or something, and it's all set out with things to eat, like a banquet feast. And there's letters, there's words onto it, Mole, cut in the stones."

"What does it say, Willie, the printing?"

Willie spelled it out slowly, carefully. "It says—'There—is—enough—for—all.' There's enough for all, Mole. And there *is*.

"There's grain—corn and wheat and rye for us—and there's a big cake of salt for the Red Buck, and there's vegetables, all kinds of vegetables out of the garden, all fresh and washed clean, no dirt on *them*, and there's clover and there's bluegrass and buckwheat. There's even nuts for the squirrels and chipmunks—and they're all starting in to eat them now, Mole, and if you don't mind—if you'll excuse me—I think I'll sort of join in."

Willie joined in with his cousins, who were fairly wallowing in grain. Near by, Uncle Analdas, looking slightly bewildered, was gulping alternate mouthfuls of clover and carrots. Porkey was working determinedly on a pile of buckwheat, unconscious that a sprig of it, draped over one ear, gave him a most rakish appearance.

There was a steady sound of chewing and munching and champing. The Folks sat silent, the glow of the Man's pipe rising and falling with slow regularity, the Lady gently rubbing Mr. Muldoon's jowls. The Red Buck licked salt till his lips were thick with foam, took a long drink from the pool, and then, tossing his head, snorted loudly. The eating stopped and Willie eased his belt a hole or two; his softly furred little stomach seemed to have suddenly swollen alarmingly.

With slow and stately tread the Red Buck began a circuit of the garden. The Doe and their Fawn walked behind him. Obediently all the other Animals fell into line. There came Phewie and the Gray Fox, side by side, waddling Porkey and Uncle Analdas, Mother and Father with Little Georgie between them, his arms around their necks, the Pheasant and his wife, with their mincing, rocking-chair walk, feathers glimmering bronze-gold in the moonlight. There came all the Fieldmouse tribe, the Raccoon and the Opossum, the Chipmunks and the Squirrels, gray and red. And alongside them, on the very edge of the garden, the quivering and humping of the earth showed the progress of the Mole and his three stout brothers.

Slowly, solemnly the procession circled the garden until they had all returned to the little lawn where the Good Saint stood. The Red Buck snorted again, and all gave attention as he spoke.

"We have eaten their food." His voice rang out impressively. "We have tasted their salt, we have drunk their water, and all are good." He tossed his proud head in the direction of the garden. "From now on this is forbidden ground." His chisel-sharp hoof rapped the earth. "Does anyone dispute me?"

None did, and there was a silence, broken at last by the voice of Uncle Analdas. "Haow 'bout them dingblasted Cutworms?" he called. "They don't know no laws or decent regulations."

The Mole, who had been a little slower than the rest, leaned his elbows on the earth as he reared up from his just-completed tunnel and turned his blind face toward the sound. "We'll patrol," he said, smiling, "me and my brothers, night and day, turn and turn about. Good hunting too; got six on that trip."

As the Animals resumed their dining, Phewie and the Gray Fox suddenly pricked up their ears at a clatter from the grape arbor back of the house. Sulphronia's mellow voice echoed up the Hill. "Hi, Mr. Skunk," she called, "come and get it." Eagerly they trotted away into the darkness.

The moon was dipping behind the Pine Wood before the last trace of the feast was cleaned up and the well-stuffed Little Animals took their way down the Hill. They scattered to their respective homes with gay but sleepy farewells. Mother carried a small market basket on either arm. "Soup tomorrow," she cried happily. "Peavine and lettuce soup, tomorrow and every day from now on."

Uncle Analdas cleared his throat. "If there ain't nobody occupying that there guest room," he announced a little sheepishly, "I might sorta try it out again fer a spell. Porkey's a good feller and all that, but that there burrow of his is mighty musty, yes *sir,* mighty musty, and as fer his cookin'—"

"Of course you shall, Uncle Analdas." Mother smiled. "Your room is just as you left it. I've dusted it every day."

Little Georgie, running in gay circles, called to Father. "Any new Dogs around?"

"I understand there is a newly arrived pair of Setters up on Good Hill Road," Father answered. "Said to be very highly bred and quite capable. When you have had a few more days of rest and recuperation we must give them a workout."

"I'm ready any time." laughed Little Georgie gaily. "Any time at all." He leaped high in the air, rapping his heels together three times, soared clear over Father, Mother, *and* Uncle Analdas. "I'm *fine!*"

Each evening throughout the summer the kindly Saint's ledge was spread with a banquet; each morning it was clean and neatly swept. Each night the Red Buck, Phewie, and the Gray Fox patrolled the premises against wandering marauders, the Mole and his stout brothers made their faithful rounds.

All summer Mother and the other womenfolk preserved, packed, and put away winter stores. Once again there were parties and merrymaking, laughter and dancing. Good days had come back to the Hill.

Tim McGrath surveyed the flourishing garden and lifted his voice in wonderment. "Louie," he said, "I just can't understand it. Here's these new folks with their garden and not a sign of a fence around it, no traps, no poison, no nothing; and not a thing touched, not a thing. Not a footprint onto it, not even a cutworm. Now me, I've got all them things, fences, traps, poisons; even sat up some nights with a shotgun—and what happens? All my carrots gone and half my beets, cabbages et into, tomatoes tromp down, lawn all tore up with moles. Fat-Man-down-to-the-Crossroads, he keeps dogs even and he ain't got a stalk of corn left standing, all his lettuce gone, most of his turnips. I can't understand it. Must just be Beginner's Luck."

"Must be," agreed Louie. "Must be that—or something."

City versus Country

FABLES, MYTHS, AND LEGENDS

The Town Mouse and the Country Mouse

Aesop

In many ways this fable epitomizes the tension that can exist between country and city. The country mouse is made to feel that the city must be very fine and that the things of the city are better than those of the country. However, despite the glorification of cities as works of art, as seen in the myths and legends of now-vanished civilizations such as Troy and Atlantis, people still yearn for the simple, uncomplicated country life idealized in pastoral literature. Hence the country mouse returns to the country "knowing" that country life is better.

A Town Mouse once visited a relative who lived in the country. For lunch the Country Mouse served wheat stalks, roots, and acorns, with a dash of cold water for drink. The Town Mouse ate very sparingly, nibbling a little of this and a little of that, and by her manner making it very plain that she ate the simple food only to be polite.

After the meal the friends had a long talk, or rather the Town Mouse talked about her life in the city while the Country Mouse listened. They then went to bed in a cozy nest in the hedgerow and slept in quiet and comfort until morning. In her sleep the Country Mouse dreamed she was a Town Mouse with all the luxuries and delights of city life that her friend had described for her. So the next day when the Town Mouse asked the Country Mouse to go home with her to the city, she gladly said yes.

When they reached the mansion in which the Town Mouse lived, they found on the table in the dining room the leavings of a very fine banquet. There were sweetmeats and jellies, pastries, delicious cheeses, indeed, the most tempting foods that a Mouse can imagine. But just as the Country Mouse was about to nibble a dainty bit of pastry, she heard a Cat mew loudly and scratch at the door. In great fear the Mice scurried to a hiding place, where they lay quite still for a long time, hardly daring to breathe. When at last they ventured back to the feast, the door opened suddenly and in came the servants to clear the table, followed by the House Dog.

From *The Aesop for Children* (Chicago: Rand McNally, 1919). Illustrated by Milo Winter.

The Country Mouse stopped in the Town Mouse's den only long enough to pick up her carpet bag and umbrella.

"You may have luxuries and dainties that I have not," she said as she hurried away, "but I prefer my plain food and simple life in the country with the peace and security that go with it."

POVERTY WITH SECURITY IS BETTER THAN PLENTY IN THE MIDST OF FEAR AND UNCERTAINTY.

FOLKTALES— INHERITED AND LITERARY

The Shepherd at Court

Retold by Italo Calvino

Folk literature abounds with trickster tales. This tale—from Italy—and "The Shepherd Who Laughed Last" (p. 219)—from Spain—feature shepherds who are supposed by others to be simple fellows but who triumph through cleverness. Often, country people are portrayed as being a bit slower than those from the city; these two tales reverse the stereotype.

A boy was tending the flock, when a lamb fell into a ravine and perished. The shepherd went home, and his parents, who had little love for him to begin with, screamed at him and beat him, then turned him out of the house into the night. Weeping, he wandered about over the mountain and found a hollow rock, which he lined with dry leaves and nestled in the best he could, stiff from the cold air. But he was unable to sleep.

Through the darkness, a man made his way to the rock and said, "You had the nerve to take my bed! What are you doing here at this time of night?"

Shaking with fright, the boy told how he had been turned out of the house, and begged the man to let him stay there the rest of the night.

The man said, "You were very clever to bring in dry leaves. The idea never occurred to me. Go on and stay here." And he lay down beside him.

The lad made himself as small as possible so as not to disturb him, keeping perfectly still to give the impression he was sleeping: but he couldn't shut his eyes for watching the man. Nor was the man sleeping, but mumbling to himself under the illusion the boy was asleep. "What present can I make this boy who lined the stone for me with leaves

From Italo Calvino, ed., *Italian Folktales*, trans. by George Martin (New York: Harcourt Brace Jovanovich, 1980).

and who's thoughtful enough to stay on his side and not disturb me? I can give him a linen napkin which, unfolded, produces dinner for everybody present. I can give him a little box which, opened, produces a gold coin. I can give him a harmonica which, played, sets everyone within earshot to dancing.''

This mumbling slowly put the boy to sleep. He awakened at dawn, thinking he had been dreaming. But there beside him on the bed of leaves lay the napkin, the little box, and the harmonica. The man was gone and the boy had not even seen his face.

After walking some distance he came to a crowded city that was getting ready for a big tournament. The king of that city had staked his daughter's hand, together with the entire treasure of the state. The lad thought, Now I can test the little box. If it gives me the money needed, I too can line up to joust. He began opening and closing the box and, every time, it produced a shiny new gold piece. He took all the money and purchased horses, armor, princely clothes, engaged squires and servants, and passed himself off as the son of the king of Portugal. He won every match, and the king was bound to declare him his daughter's bridegroom.

But at court, the lad, having been raised with sheep, was as uncouth as could be: all his food he picked up in his hands, then wiped them on the curtains, and he was constantly slapping the ladies on the back. The king became suspicious. He dispatched ambassadors to Portugal and found out that the king's son, having dropsy, had never set foot outside the palace. So he ordered the lying lad imprisoned at once.

The palace prison was right under the banquet hall. When the boy walked in, the nineteen prisoners already there greeted him with a chorus of jeers, knowing he'd had the impudence to become the king's son-in-law. He let them jeer all they liked. At noon, the jailer brought the prisoners the usual pot of beans. The lad rushed up and kicked the pot over on the floor.

"Have you lost your mind? What will we now eat? You'll pay for this!"

"Shhhhhhh! Just wait," he replied. Pull-

ing the napkin out of his pocket, he said, "For twenty," and unfolded it. Dinner for twenty appeared, including soup, many tasty dishes, and excellent wine. At that, they all hailed the lad as a hero.

Every day the jailer found the pot of beans overturned on the floor and the prisoners better fed and livelier than ever. So he went and told the king. Curious, the king went down into the prison and asked for an explanation. The lad stepped forward. "Listen, Majesty, I am the one providing my companions with food and drink far better than what's on the royal table. So if you'll accept, I invite you to dine with us and promise you'll go away happy."

"I accept," said the king.

The lad unfolded the napkin and said, "For twenty-one, and fit for a king." Out came the most wonderful dinner you ever saw and the king, delighted with the sight, took a seat in the midst of the prisoners and ate and ate.

When dinner was over, the king said, "Will you sell me the napkin?"

"Why not, Majesty? But on condition you let me sleep one whole night with your daughter, my rightful betrothed."

"Why not, prisoner?" replied the king. "But on condition you keep perfectly still and quiet on the edge of the bed, with the windows open, a lamp lit, and eight guards in the room. If that suits you, well and good. Otherwise you get nothing at all."

"Why not, Majesty? That's settled."

So the king got the napkin, and the boy slept an entire night with the princess, but with no possibility of talking to her or touching her. And in the morning he was taken back to prison.

Seeing him back, the prisoners all raised their voices in mockery.

"Hey, stupid! What a blockhead you are! Now we'll be back on our daily beans! A fine bargain you made with the king!"

But the lad didn't lose countenance. "Why can't we buy our dinner from now on with perfectly good money?"

"Who has any of that?"

"Take heart," he said, and started pulling gold pieces out of his purse. So they had grand dinners sent in from the inn next door, and continued to kick over the pot of beans on the floor.

The jailer went to the king again, and the king came down to investigate. As soon as he found out about the box, he asked, "Will you sell it to me?"

"Why not, Majesty?" he replied, making the same bargain as before. He gave the king the box, and slept with the princess another time without being able to touch her or talk to her.

Seeing him back, the prisoners resumed their taunts. "Well, here we are on beans once more, hurrah!"

"Joy is a good thing indeed. Whether we eat or not, we will dance."

"What!"

The lad pulled out the harmonica and began to play. The prisoners started dancing around him, with their ankle-chains clanking loudly. They broke into minuets, gavottes, and waltzes, and couldn't stop. The jailer rushed in, and he too started dancing, with all his keys jingling at his side.

In the meantime the king had just sat down to a banquet with his guests. Hearing the notes of the harmonica float up from the prison, they all jumped to their feet and began dancing. They looked like so many bewitched souls, and nobody knew what was going on: the ladies danced with the butlers, and the gentlemen with the cooks. Even the furniture danced. The crockery and crystal were smashed to smithereens; the roasted chickens flew off; and people butted the walls and ceiling beams. The king himself danced while yelling for everyone to stop. All of a sudden the lad stopped playing, and everyone fell to the floor at once with heads spinning and legs collapsing.

Out of breath, the king went down to the prison. "Just who is being so funny?" he began.

"It's me, Majesty," answered the lad, stepping forward. "Would you like to see?" He blew a note, and the king took a dance step.

"Stop! Stop this instant!" he said, frightened, then asked, "Will you sell it to me?"

"Why not, Majesty? But under what conditions this time?"

"The same as before."

"Well, Majesty, here we're going to have to make a new bargain, or I'll play more music."

"No, no, please! Tell me your terms."

"Tonight I'll be satisfied with talking to the princess and having her answer me."

The king thought it over and ended up agreeing. "But I'm doubling the number of guards, and there'll be two lamps lit."

"As you like."

Then the king called his daughter to him in secret and said to her, "Listen carefully: you are to say no, and only no, to every question which that rascal asks you tonight." The princess promised she would.

Night fell, and the lad went to the bedchamber—which was brightly lit and full of guards—and stretched out on the edge of the bed at some distance from the princess. Then he said, "My bride, do you think that in this chilly night air we ought to keep the windows open?"

"No."

"Did you hear that, guards?" cried the lad. "By express orders of the princess, the windows are to be closed." The guards obeyed.

A quarter of an hour passed, and the lad said, "My bride, do you think it is quite right for us to be in bed and have all these guards around us?"

"No."

"Guards!" cried the lad. "Did you hear? By express orders of the princess, be gone and don't show your faces here any more." So the guards went off to bed, which struck them as almost too good to be true.

Letting another quarter of an hour pass, he said, "My bride, do you think it right to be in bed with two lamps lit?"

"No."

So he put out the lamps, making the room pitch-dark.

He came back and took his place on the edge of the bed, then said, "Dear, we are lawfully married, and yet we are as far apart as if we had a thornbush hedge between us. Do you like that?"

"No."

At that, he took her in his arms and kissed her.

When day dawned and the king appeared in his daughter's room, she said to him, "I obeyed your orders. Let bygones be bygones. This young man is my lawful husband. Pardon us."

Having no alternative, the king ordered sumptuous wedding festivities, balls, and tournaments. The lad became the king's son-in-law and then king himself, and there you have the tale of a shepherd boy lucky enough to plop down on a royal throne for life.

The Shepherd Who Laughed Last

Ralph Steele Boggs
Mary Gould Davis

The landlord of the little roadside Inn near La Granja loved a good laugh.

He and his special cronies among the men who came often to the Inn never tired of repeating a funny story, or of playing a practical joke upon those who came their way. The Inn became famous for its good cheer, and it was well known that it needed a sharp wit to get the best of old Tomás, the landlord.

One night there came to the Inn a shepherd. He was a simple looking fellow, with mild gray eyes and a face as smooth and innocent as a babe's. And how was Tomás to know that behind those mild eyes there was a quick brain?

After he had served the shepherd, Tomás winked at his cronies.

"Here is one who will be easy to fool," he whispered.

The others watched delightedly as Tomás, settling himself comfortably before the charcoal fire and lighting his pipe, said to the stranger:

"Here in La Granja, you know, we have different names for things. You had best learn them before you go any farther."

The shepherd took another sip of his *valdepeñas*.

"Yes," he said stupidly.

Tomás nodded. "Yes," he answered. "Here in La Granja we call a bottle, for example, a Fat Boy. The blood pudding we call Johnny. The rooster we call the Singer, the hen the Woman, the cat Our Neighbor, the chimney chain Forbearance. We call the bed St. Sebastian, the fire Happiness, and the master of the house Holy Lord."

The shepherd began earnestly to repeat the new names over and over, while the men rocked with silent laughter over his gullibility.

They were still laughing and the shepherd was still gravely conning over the names when the Inn closed for the night. Tomás went upstairs to bed, and the shepherd laid himself down beside the fire to sleep. He kept one eye open, however, and when the black cat came in he watched her. She went over to the fire for warmth and, getting too near it, set fire to the end of her tail. The

From Ralph Steele Boggs and Mary Gould Davis, *Three Golden Oranges and Other Spanish Folktales* (New York: McKay, 1936).

pain maddened her, and yowling loudly, she began to climb up the chain into the chimney.

The shepherd rose, took a bottle or two of *valdepeñas* and the blood pudding from the cupboard, the hen and the rooster from their corner, and thrust them into his pouch.

Then he lifted up his voice and called out: "Arise, Holy Lord, from the heights of St. Sebastian. For there goes Our Neighbor up Forbearance pursued by Happiness. As for the Fat Boys, Johnny, the Singer, and the Woman, they go along the road with me!"

"What can the simpleton be saying?" Tomás thought. Then he turned over and went to sleep again.

And the shepherd unlatched the door and went off along the road, laughing.

The Mermaid of Edam

Olive Beaupré Miller (trans.)

This interesting Dutch tale tells of a mermaid who is taken to the city and made to follow its ways. Unlike most such tales, which would have her returning happily to the sea, the mermaid in this story is made to stay in the city but exacts revenge from the burgomaster for keeping her there.

It happened once that a mighty storm broke the great dykes, those giant walls which hold back the Zuyder Zee. Plunging and rolling, the angry waters rushed in over the flat green meadows of North Holland that lie lower than the sea. The tall windmills waved their arms in vain,—they stood knee-deep in water. The little toy villages poked up their red roofs in huge astonishment above the flood, and the cowbells on the scattered cattle rang out a wild tonkatonka, discordant in alarm.

When the waves began to recede somewhat, and the green meadows showed themselves again, smiling in the sunlight, certain young lassies from the city of Edam set out to carry fresh water to the cows in the distant pastures, for the poor things had had nothing to drink for hours, with only salt-water about them. The girls were merrily splashing along through the puddles in their wooden shoes, carrying their pails on wooden yokes slung over their shoulders, when all of a sudden one of them cried:

"Look there! Look there!"

At that the lassies all stood still, and what should they see in a shallow pool before them, but a gleaming silver-green tail, floundering helplessly and churning up a shining shower of water.

"It's a great fish," cried one of the maids, "a fish, carried in by the flood!"

"It will never get back," said another, "for this pool is standing alone with no outlet to the sea!"

But just as they spoke, the third lass gave a shriek.

"O look, look! It's a mermaid!"

There, as sure as butter and cheese, rising from the water, appeared the dripping head and shoulders of a woman,—a beautiful woman with sea-green hair and the glistening tail of a fish!

The girls stood open-mouthed.

"What a curious thing!" whispered one. "Let's take her to the city."

All this time, the poor mermaid was struggling sadly with her arms to get out of the mud, hoping to reach a place where she could float and make her way back to the sea. It was beautiful where she lived far out

From Olive Beaupré Miller, trans., *Tales Told in Holland* (Chicago: Book House for Children, 1926).

on the sapphire waters. Her friends and loved ones were there, sporting with the waves. She must return. She must. But the bevy of Edam lassies surrounded her. Though she protested with all her might, they lifted her in their arms and carried her off to the town.

Past quiet, shady canals, by the huge towering Gothic Church, as solid as a fortress, they bore her struggling and straining, to the great Town Hall. And when the Burgomaster heard that a mermaid had been found you may well believe that he came to the Town Hall in a hurry, in as much of a hurry, that is, as his dignity would permit him. And the town-councillors came likewise, and crowds and crowds of people—for Edam was a great city in those days, the water gate to Amsterdam, with twenty-five thousand burghers; and as many of that twenty-five thousand as could walk or run or hobble, came clumping and clattering to see the marvelous wonder cast up for them by the sea.

First they fed the mermaid and treated her very kindly, till they stopped her wild struggling and put her at her ease. Then they set about in proper manner debating what they should do with her. The Burgomaster was of opinion that a mermaid could not be permitted to remain a mermaid in Edam. A mermaid was a wild, fantastical creature, savoring too much of Fairyland. She had no place in a sober, substantial city like Edam.

Now, you must know that the burghers of Edam have little to do with mermaids and giants and fairies. They live in a placid and beautiful country and are content with the world as it is. What need have they to go building castles in the air, or riding the horses of fancy to the moon? Leave it to the poor folk of the barren heath or fen-country to the northward and eastward, in Drente or thereabouts, to run off to Fairyland and have dealings with elves and earthmen and giants. Their own land is poor enough. No wonder at times they must needs run away on the fluttering wings of fancy. Not so with North Holland, ah, no, indeed! North Holland is rich and green and satisfying as it is. No need to fly away from North Holland on a wild goose chase into the clouds! So say the people of Edam. North Holland is the Land-of-Reality, the Land-of-things-as-they-are, the country of markets and black and white cows! And Edam, ah, Edam is the city of cheese, famed to the uttermost ends of the earth for the glories of its cheese. In such a place, pray tell, what room was there for a mermaid?

The Burgomaster gazed upon the coat-of-arms of Edam, hanging on the wall before him, and he was well pleased that it was adorned with no griffin or dragon or suchlike fantastical monster. It bore the figure of a fine, sleek, fighting steer, with no nonsense whatever about him, and as the Burgomaster looked, he exclaimed with great solemnity:

"We cannot let a mermaid remain a mermaid in Edam. There is only one thing to do. We must make her over into a useful Edam housewife!"

"But,—" cried a very young town-councillor, with a flash of inspiration, "why not take her back and put her in the sea?"

The Burgomaster was shocked. Impressively, he replied:

"Nay, that would be shirking our bounden duty. If we put her in the sea, the poor thing will remain always a mermaid and never be anything better. Since she has been brought to us, we must civilize her and make her like ourselves. We must turn her into a good burgher-vrouw with no absurd nonsense about her."

"But," objected the young town-councillor. "Maybe she wasn't meant to be a good burgher-vrouw. Perhaps it isn't in her nature to be a burgher-vrouw. Perhaps she was meant to be a mermaid and sport in the water. Who are we, that we should try to make her like ourselves? Would it not be best to put her back in the sea?"

But the Burgomaster and the older men frowned sternly on the young fellow and thought him a silly booby who was greatly in need of years and gray hair to bring him wisdom. If he did not know that to be like the burghers of Edam was the height of desirable glories, then he had a great deal to learn, the poor, unfortuante simpleton! Who were they, indeed!

So it was agreed by the city council,—

they would make the mermaid over into a proper Edam housewife.

Well, they didn't ask permission of the mermaid, but they dressed her up in robes of the finest fashion then in vogue in the city, and they did their best to cover her long green tail from sight. Every now and then, however, the outlandish thing would show itself below her voluminous petticoats. As to her tell-tale hair with the sea-green sheen like waves flung up by the west-wind, why they hid that beneath a white lace cap. All was of the very best style and quality, you may be sure of that.

And when the mermaid was installed in a good substantial townhouse, the women of the city came by turns to teach her to sew and to spin, and to churn the cheese which is the pride of Edam. They taught her to work, work, work, to save, save, save, and to take such pride in cleanliness, that she could not endure so much as the smallest speck of dirt. They provided her too, with a stout and buxom servant lass, who scrubbed from morning till night,—pots, pans, windows, hearth, doorstep, sidewalk, housefront,—yes, even the neat red bricks of the street before the door,—scrub, scrub, scrub! And what would you have? With teaching like this, the mermaid was quite made over. She sewed, she spun, she churned, she looked after her servant lass, and kept her eternally scrubbing.

But sometimes there came memories and a longing upon the mermaid. She longed for the water again. She longed to play with wind and wave, to fly with the flying-fish, leap with the dolphins. She longed for her little home of shells amid a forest of seaweed. She longed to lie lazily and sun herself on the rocks. She longed for her old free life among mermen and mermaidens,—that happy, carefree life that had nothing to do with scrubbing, nothing to do with saving, nothing to do with cheese.

Then she would tear off her clothes and wriggle away toward the sea. Aye, at such times it took two strong men to keep her from jumping into the water! It took two strong men to bring her back to the city.

They were very patient with her, very courteous, very kindly, the sturdy burghers of Edam, but they kept unswervingly to their purpose, plodding on and on and on. So, bye-and-bye, they accomplished their end, and crushed all the nonsense out of her. She no longer tried to run away. She became a proper burgher-vrouw, who sewed and spun and churned. Then all the good folk of Edam congratulated themselves.

"We have done a fine work," said they, "to make a mermaid over into a housewife like ourselves." Only sometimes a child, a very young child, would come and sit before the strange woman with a question in his eyes. She knew something he wanted to know, something the burghers of Edam could not tell him. Ah, if she would only speak, she could carry him off to a beautiful land, a free, a glorious, a golden land, where dreams are the only truth.

But alack! the mermaid never spoke. This one thing the burghers of Edam could not accomplish. They could not make her speak Dutch! No, that they could not bring about. They could not make her speak Dutch! And so she never told her secrets to the children.

But one day the Burgomaster came, in condescending glory, to pay an afternoon call and delight his eyes with a sight of the good work done by the burghers, for which he took no small amount of credit to himself. Important, pompous, proud, he stood on the mermaid's threshold.

"Now," he thought, "I shall see how greatly we have improved this poor, silly, flighty creature!"

With that, the servant lass opened the door, and the Burgomaster requested her to lead him to her mistress. And now, from an inner room, the mermaid saw the visitor. Her servant had just scrubbed the floor, which was white as driven snow, and had the mermaid not become a proper Edam housewife? Would any Edam housewife permit a Burgomaster to soil the fresh-scoured planks by trampling them with his boots? She waved a sign to her servant, who straightway picked the Burgomaster up bodily in her arms. Ah, the poor old fellow! How painfully he was astounded! How helplessly he kicked his legs! How wounded was his dignity! She bore him to a chair on the opposite side of the hall. Then, without aye, yes, or no, she set him down, kerplunk, as though he had been a baby; she took off his boots; she put a pair of slippers on his feet; and when she had thus prepared him, she led him across to her mistress. Thus was the Burgomaster rewarded for civilizing a mermaid.

Elsie Piddock Skips in Her Sleep

Eleanor Farjeon

The Industrial Revolution, which brought towns, factories, and manufacturing to the countryside, is epitomized in this captivating story. Eleanor Farjeon (1881–1965) received numerous awards for her books and poetry. In the 1950s, the Children's Book Circle in England instituted the Eleanor Farjeon Award, to be given annually for distinguished contributions to children's literature. Farjeon's stories reflect her British background and the county of Sussex, where she lived.

Elsie Piddock lived in Glynde under Caburn, where lots of other little girls lived too. They lived mostly on bread-and-butter, because their mothers were too poor to buy cake. As soon as Elsie began to hear, she heard the other little girls skipping every evening after school in the lane outside her mother's cottage. *Swish-swish!* went the rope through the air. *Tappity-tap!* went the little girls' feet on the ground. *Mumble-umble-umble!* went the children's voices, saying a rhyme that the skipper could skip to. In course of time, Elsie not only heard the sounds, but understood what they were all about, and then the *mumble-umble* turned itself into words like this:

'*Andy*
*Spand*y
*Sugard*y
Candy,
French
Almond
ROCK!
Breadandbutterforyoursupper's
allyourmother'sGOT!'

The second bit went twice as fast as the first bit, and when the little girls said it

Elsie Piddock, munching her supper, always munched her mouthful of bread-and-butter in double-quick time. She wished she had some Sugardy-Candy-French-Almond-Rock to suck during the first bit, but she never had.

When Elsie Piddock was three years old, she asked her mother for a skipping-rope.

'You're too little,' said her mother. 'Bide a bit till you're a bigger girl, then you shall have one.'

Elsie pouted, and said no more. But in the middle of the night her parents were wakened by something going *Slap-slap!* on the floor, and there was Elsie in her nightgown skipping with her father's braces. She skipped till her feet caught in the tail of them, and she tumbled down and cried. But she had skipped ten times running fast.

'Bless my buttons, mother!' said Mr. Piddock. 'The child's a born skipper.'

And Mrs. Piddock jumped out of bed full of pride, rubbed Elsie's elbows for her, and said: 'There-a-there now! dry your tears, and tomorrow you shall have a skip-rope all of your own.'

So Elsie dried her eyes on the hem of her nightgown; and in the morning, before he went to work, Mr. Piddock got a little cord,

Eleanor Farjeon, *Martin Pippin in the Daisy Field* (Philadelphia: Lippincott, 1965).

just the right length, and made two little wooden handles to go on the ends. With this Elsie skipped all day, scarcely stopping to eat her breakfast of bread-and-butter, and her dinner of butter-and-bread. And in the evening, when the schoolchildren were gathered in the lane, Elsie went out among them, and began to skip with the best.

'Oh!' cried Joan Challon, who was the champion skipper of them all, 'just look at little Elsie Piddock skipping as never so!'

All the skippers stopped to look, and then to wonder. Elsie Piddock certainly *did* skip as never so, and they called to their mothers to come and see. And the mothers in the lane came to their doors, and threw up their hands, and cried: 'Little Elsie Piddock is a born skipper!'

By the time she was five she could outskip any of them: whether in 'Andy-Spandy,' 'Lady, Lady, drop your Purse,' 'Charley Parley Stole some Barley,' or whichever of the games it might be. By the time she was six her name and fame were known to all the villages in the county. And by the time she was seven, the fairies heard of her. They were fond of skipping themselves, and they had a special Skipping-Master who taught them new skips every month at the new moon. As they skipped they chanted:

'The High Skip,
The Sly Skip,
The Skip like a Feather,
The Long Skip,
The Strong Skip,
And the Skip All Together!

The Slow Skip,
The Toe Skip,
The Skip Double-Double,
The Fast Skip,
The Last Skip,
And the Skip Against Trouble!'

All these skips had their own meanings, and were made up by the Skipping-Master, whose name was Andy-Spandy. He was very proud of his fairies, because they skipped better than the fairies of any other county; but he was also very severe with them if they did not please him. One night he scolded

Fairy Heels-o'-Lead for skipping badly, and praised Fairy Flea-Foot for skipping well. Then Fairy Heels-o'-Lead sniffed and snuffed, and said: 'Hhm-hhm-hhm! there's a little girl in Glynde who could skip Flea-Foot round the moon and back again. A born skipper she is, and she skips as never so.'

'What is her name?' asked Andy-Spandy.

'Her name is Elsie Piddock, and she has skipped down every village far and near, from Didling to Wannock.'

'Go and fetch her here!' commanded Andy-Spandy.

Off went Heels-o'-Lead, and poked her head through Elsie's little window under the eaves, crying: 'Elsie Piddock! Elsie Piddock! there's a Skipping-Match on Caburn, and Fairy Flea-Foot says she can skip better than you.'

Elsie Piddock was fast asleep, but the words got into her dream, so she hopped out of bed with her eyes closed, took her skipping-rope, and followed Heels-o'-Lead to the top of Mount Caburn, where Andy-Spandy and the fairies were waiting for them.

'Skip, Elsie Piddock!' said Andy-Spandy, 'and show us what you're worth!'

Elsie twirled her rope and skipped in her sleep, and as she skipped she murmured:

'Andy
Spandy
Sugardy
Candy,
French
Almond
Rock!
Breadandbutterforyoursupper's allyourmother'sGOT!'

Andy-Spandy watched her skipping with his eyes as sharp as needles, but he could find no fault with it, nor could the fairies.

'Very Good, as far as it goes!' said Andy-Spandy. 'Now let us see how far it *does* go. Stand forth, Elsie and Flea-Foot, for the Long Skip.'

Elsie had never done the Long Skip, and if she had had all her wits about her she wouldn't have known what Andy-Spandy meant; but as she was dreaming, she understood him perfectly. So she twirled her rope, and as it came over jumped as far along the ground as she could, about twelve feet from where she had started. Then Flea-Foot did the Long Skip, and skipped clean out of sight.

'Hum!' said Andy-Spandy. 'Now, Elsie Piddock, let us see you do the Strong Skip.'

Once more Elsie understood what was wanted of her; she put both feet together, jumped her rope and came down with all her strength, so that her heels sank into the ground. Then Flea-Foot did the Strong Skip, and sank into the ground as deep as her waist.

'Hum!' said Andy-Spandy. 'And now, Elsie Piddock, let us see you do the Skip All Together.'

At his words, all the fairies leaped to their ropes, and began skipping as lively as they could, and Elsie with them. An hour went by, two hours, and three hours; one by one the fairies fell down exhausted, and Elsie Piddock skipped on. Just before morning she was skipping all by herself.

Then Andy-Spandy wagged his head and said: 'Elsie Piddock, you are a born skipper. There's no tiring you at all. And for that you shall come once a month to Caburn when the moon is new, and I will teach you to skip till a year is up. And after that I'll wager there won't be mortal or fairy to touch you.'

Andy-Spandy was as good as his word. Twelve times during the next year Elsie Piddock rose up in her sleep with the new moon, and went to the top of Mount Caburn. There she took her place among the fairies, and learned to do all the tricks of the skipping-rope, until she did them better than any. At the end of the year she did the High Skip so well, that she skipped right over the moon.

In the Sly Skip not a fairy could catch her, or know where she would skip to next; so artful was she, that she could skip through the lattice of a skeleton leaf, and never break it.

She redoubled the Skip Double-Double, in which you only had to double yourself up twice round the skipping-rope before it came down. Elsie Piddock did it four times.

In the Fast Skip, she skipped so fast that you couldn't see her, though she stood on the same spot all the time.

In the Last Skip, when all the fairies skipped over the same rope in turn, running round and round till they made a mistake from giddiness, Elsie never got giddy, and never made a mistake, and was always left in last.

In the Slow Skip, she skipped so slow that a mole had time to throw up his hill under her rope before she came down.

In the Toe Skip, when all the others skipped on their tip-toes, Elsie never touched a grassblade with more than the edge of her toe-nail.

In the Skip Against Trouble, she skipped so joyously that Andy-Spandy himself chuckled with delight.

In the Long Skip she skipped from Caburn to the other end of Sussex, and had to be fetched back by the wind.

In the Strong Skip, she went right under the earth, as a diver goes under the sea, and the rabbits, whose burrows she had disturbed, handed her up again.

But in the Skip like a Feather she came down like gossamer, so that she could alight on a spider-thread and never shake the dewdrop off.

And in the Skip All Together, she could skip down the whole tribe of fairies, and remain as fresh as a daisy. Nobody had ever found out how long Elsie Piddock could skip without getting tired, for everybody else got tired first. Even Andy-Spandy didn't know.

At the end of the year he said to her: 'Elsie Piddock, I have taught you all. Bring me your skipping-rope, and you shall have a prize.'

Elsie gave her rope to Andy-Spandy, and he licked the two little wooden handles, first the one and then the other. When he handed the rope back to her, one of the handles was made of Sugar Candy, and the other of French Almond Rock.

'There!' said Andy-Spandy. 'Though you suck them never so, they will never grow less, and you shall therefore suck sweet all your life. And as long as you are little enough to skip with this rope, you shall skip as I have taught you. But when you are too big for this rope, and must get a new one, you will no longer be able to do all the fairy skips that you have learned, although you will still skip better in the mortal way than any other girl that ever was born. Good-bye, Elsie Piddock.'

'Aren't I ever going to skip for you again?' asked Elsie Piddock in her sleep.

But Andy-Spandy didn't answer. For morning had come over the Downs, and the fairies disappeared, and Elsie Piddock went back to bed.

If Elsie had been famous for her skipping before this fairy year, you can imagine what she became after it. She created so much wonder, that she hardly dared to show all she could do. Nevertheless, for another year she did such incredible things, that people came from far and near to see her skip over the church spire, or through the split oak-tree in the Lord's Park, or across the river at its widest point. When there was trouble in her mother's house, or in any house in the village, Elsie Piddock skipped so gaily that the trouble was forgotten in laughter. And when she skipped all the old games in Glynde, along with the little girls, and they sang:

'Andy
Spandy
Sugardy
Candy,
French
Almond
Rock!
Breadandbutterforyoursupper's
allyourmother'sGOT!'—

Elsie Piddock said: 'It aren't all *I've* got!' and gave them a suck of her skipping-rope handles all round. And on the night of the new moon, she always led the children up Mount Caburn, where she skipped more marvellously than ever. In fact, it was Elsie Piddock who established the custom of New-Moon-Skipping on Caburn.

But at the end of another year she had grown too big to skip with her little rope. She laid it away in a box, and went on skipping with a longer one. She still skipped as never so, but her fairy tricks were laid by

with the rope, and though her friends teased her to do the marvelous things she used to do, Elsie Piddock only laughed, and shook her head, and never told why. In time, when she was still the pride and wonder of her village, people would say: 'Ah, but you should ha' seen her when she was a littling! Why, she could skip through her mother's keyhole!' And in more time, these stories became a legend that nobody believed. And in still more time, Elsie grew up (though never very much), and became a little woman, and gave up skipping, because skipping-time was over. After fifty years or so, nobody remembered that she had ever skipped at all. Only Elsie knew. For when times were hard, and they often were, she sat by the hearth with her dry crust and no butter, and sucked the Sugar Candy that Andy-Spandy had given her for life.

It was ever and ever so long afterwards. Three new Lords had walked in the Park since the day when Elsie Piddock had skipped through the split oak. Changes had come in the village; old families had died out, new families had arrived; others had moved away to distant parts, the Piddocks among them. Farms had changed hands, cottages had been pulled down, and new ones had been built. But Mount Caburn was as it always had been, and as the people came to think it always would be. And still the children kept the custom of going there each new moon to skip. Nobody remembered how this custom had come about, it was too far back in the years. But customs are customs, and the child who could not skip the new moon in on Caburn stayed at home and cried.

Then a new Lord came to the Park; one not born a Lord, who had grown rich in trade, and bought the old estate. Soon after his coming, changes began to take place more violent than the pulling down of cottages. The new Lord began to shut up footpaths and destroy rights of way. He stole the Common rights here and there, as he could. In his greed for more than he had got, he raised rents and pressed the people harder than they could bear. But bad as the high rents were to them, they did not mind these so much as the loss of their old rights. They fought the new Lord, trying to keep what had been theirs for centuries, and sometimes they won the fight, but oftener lost it. The constant quarrels bred a spirit of anger between them and the Lord, and out of hate he was prepared to do whatever he could to spite them.

Amongst the lands over which he exercised a certain power was Caburn. This had been always open to the people, and the Lord determined if he could to close it. Looking up the old deeds, he discovered that, though the Down was his, he was obliged to leave a way upon it by which the people could go from one village to another. For hundreds of years they had made a short cut of it over the top.

The Lord's Lawyer told him that, by the wording of the deeds, he could never stop the people from travelling by way of the Downs.

'Can't I!' snorted the Lord. 'Then at least I will make them travel a long way round!'

And he had plans drawn up to enclose the whole of the top of Caburn, so that nobody could walk on it. This meant that the people must trudge miles round the base, as they passed from place to place. The Lord gave out that he needed Mount Caburn to build great factories on.

The village was up in arms to defend its rights.

'Can he do it?' they asked those who knew; and they were told: 'It is not quite certain, but we fear he can.' The Lord himself was not quite certain either but he went on with his plans, and each new move was watched with anger and anxiety by the villagers. And not only by the villagers; for the fairies saw that their own skipping-ground was threatened. How could they ever skip there again when the grass was turned to cinders, and the new moon blackened by chimney-smoke?

The Lawyer said to the Lord: 'The people will fight you tooth and nail.'

'Let 'em!' blustered the Lord; and he asked uneasily: 'Have they a leg to stand on?'

'Just half a leg,' said the Lawyer. 'It would be as well not to begin building yet,

and if you can come to terms with them you'd better.'

The Lord sent word to the villagers that, though he undoubtedly could do what he pleased, he would, out of his good heart, restore to them a footpath he had blocked, if they would give up all pretensions to Caburn.

'Footpath, indeed!' cried stout John Maltman, among his cronies at the Inn. 'What's a footpath to Caburn? Why, our mothers skipped there as children, and our children skip there now. And we hope to see our children's children skip there. If Caburn top be built over, 'twill fair break my little Ellen's heart.'

'Ay, and my Margery's,' said another.

'And my Mary's and Kitty's!' cried a third. Others spoke up, for nearly all had daughters whose joy it was to skip on Caburn at the new moon.

John Maltman turned to their best adviser, who had studied the matter closely, and asked: 'What think ye? Have we a leg to stand on?'

'Only half a one,' said the other. 'I doubt if you can stop him. It might be as well to come to terms.'

'None of his footpaths for us,' swore stout John Maltman. 'We'll fight the matter out.'

So things were left for a little, and each side wondered what the next move would be. Only the people knew in their hearts that they must be beaten in the end, and the Lord was sure of his victory. So sure, that he had great loads of bricks ordered; but he did not begin building for fear the people might grow violent, and perhaps burn his ricks and destroy his property. The only thing he did was to put a wire fence round the top of Caburn, and set a keeper there to send the people round it. The people broke the fence in many places, and jumped it, and crawled under it; and as the keeper could not be everywhere at once, many of them crossed the Down almost under his nose.

One evening, just before the new moon was due, Ellen Maltman went into the woods to cry. For she was the best skipper under Mount Caburn, and the thought that she would never skip there again made her more unhappy than she had ever thought she could be. While she was crying in the dark, she felt a hand on her shoulder, and a voice said to her: 'Crying for trouble, my dear? That'll never do!'

The voice might have been the voice of a withered leaf, it was so light and dry; but it was also kind, so Ellen checked her sobs and said: 'It's a big trouble, ma'am, there's no remedy against it *but* to cry.'

'Why yes, there is,' said the withered voice. 'Ye should skip against trouble, my dear.'

At this Ellen's sobs burst forth anew. 'I'll never skip no more!' she wailed. 'If I can't skip the new moon in on Caburn, I'll never skip no more.'

'And why can't you skip the new moon in on Caburn?' asked the voice.

Then Ellen told her.

After a little pause the voice spoke quietly out of the darkness. 'It's more than you will break their hearts, if they cannot skip on Caburn. And it must not be, it must not be. Tell me your name.'

'Ellen Maltman, ma'am, and I do love skipping, I can skip down anybody, ma'am, and they say I skip as never so!'

'They do, do they?' said the withered voice. 'Well, Ellen, run you home and tell them this. They are to go to this Lord and tell him he shall have his way and build on Caburn, if he will first take down the fence and let all who have ever skipped there skip there once more by turns, at the new moon. *All*, mind you, Ellen. And when the last skipper skips the last skip, he may lay his first brick. And let it be written out on paper, and signed and sealed.'

'But ma'am!' said Ellen, wondering.

'No words, child. Do as I tell you.' And the withered voice sounded so compelling that Ellen resisted no more. She ran straight to the village, and told her story to everybody.

At first they could hardly swallow it; and even when they had swallowed it, they said: 'But what's the sense of it?' But Ellen persisted and persisted; something of the spirit of the old voice got into her words, and against their reason the people began to think it was the thing to do. To cut a long story short they sent the message to the Lord next day.

The Lord could scarcely believe his ears. He rubbed his hands, and chortled at the people for fools.

'They've come to terms!' he sneered. 'I shall have the Down, and keep my footpath too. Well, they shall have their Skipping-Party; and the moment it is ended, up go my factories!'

The paper was drawn out, signed by both parties in the presence of witnesses, and duly sealed; and on the night of the new moon, the Lord invited a party of his friends to go with him to Caburn to see the sight.

And what a sight it was for them to see; every little girl in the village was there with her skipping-rope, from the toddlers to those who had just turned up their hair. Nay, even the grown maidens and the young mothers were there; and the very matrons too had come with ropes. Had not they once as children skipped on Caburn? And the message had said 'All.' Yes, and others were there, others they could not see: Andy-Spandy and his fairy team. Heels-o'-Lead, Flea-Foot, and all of the rest, were gathered round to watch with bright fierce eyes the last great skipping on their precious ground.

The skipping began. The toddlers first, a skip or so apiece, a stumble, and they fell out. The Lord and his party laughed aloud at the comical mites, and at another time the villagers would have laughed too. But there was no laughter in them tonight. Their eyes were bright and fierce like those of the fairies. After the toddlers the little girls skipped in the order of their ages, and as they got older, the skipping got better. In the thick of the schoolchildren, 'This will take some time,' said the Lord impatiently. And when Ellen Maltman's turn came, and she went into her thousands, he grew restive. But even she, who could skip as never so, tired at last; her foot tripped, and she fell on the ground with a little sob. None lasted even half her time; of those who followed some were better, some were worse, than others; and in the small hours the older women were beginning to take their turn. Few of them kept it up for half a minute; they hopped and puffed bravely, but their skipping days were done. As they had laughed at the babies, so now the Lord's friends jibed at the babies' grandmothers.

'Soon over now,' said the Lord, as the oldest of the women who had come to skip, a fat old dame of sixty-seven, stepped out and twirled her rope. Her foot caught in it; she staggered, dropped the rope, and hid her face in her hands.

'Done!' shouted the Lord; and he brandished at the crowd a trowel and a brick which he had brought with him. 'Clear out, the lot of you! I am going to lay the first brick. The skipping's ended!'

'No, if you please,' said a gentle withered voice, 'it is *my* turn now.' And out of the crowd stepped a tiny woman, so very old, so very bent and fragile, that she seemed to be no bigger than a little child.

'You!' cried the Lord. 'Who are *you?*'

'My name is Elsie Piddock, if you please, and I am a hundred and nine years old. For the last seventy-nine years I have lived over the border, but I was born in Glynde, and I skipped on Caburn as a child.' She spoke like one in a dream, and her eyes were closed.

'Elsie Piddock! Elsie Piddock!' the name ran in a whisper round the crowd.

'Elsie Piddock!' murmured Ellen Maltman. 'Why, mum, I thought Elsie Piddock was just a tale.'

'Nay, Elsie Piddock was no tale!' said the fat woman who had skipped last. 'My mother Joan skipped with her many a time, and told me tales you never would believe.'

'Elsie Piddock!' they all breathed again; and a wind seemed to fly round Mount Caburn, shrilling the name with glee. But it was no wind, it was Andy-Spandy and his fairy team, for they had seen the skipping-rope in the tiny woman's hand. One of the handles was made of Sugar Candy, and the other was made of French Almond Rock.

But the new Lord had never even heard of Elsie Piddock as a story; so laughing coarsely once again, he said: 'One more bump for an old woman's bones! Skip, Elsie Piddock, and show us what you're worth.'

'Yes, skip, Elsie Piddock,' cried Andy-Spandy and the fairies, 'and show them what you're worth!'

Then Elsie Piddock stepped into the middle of the onlookers, twirled her baby rope over her little shrunken body, and began to skip. And she skipped as NEVER SO!

First of all she skipped:

'*An*dy
*Span*dy
*Sugar*dy
*Can*dy,
French
*Al*mond
ROCK!
Breadandbutterforyoursupper's
allyourmother'sGOT!'

And nobody could find fault with her skipping. Even the Lord gasped: 'Wonderful! wonderful for an old woman!' But Ellen Maltman, who *knew*, whispered: 'Oh, mum! 'tis wonderful for *any*body! And oh mum, do but see—she's skipping in her sleep!'

It was true. Elsie Piddock, shrunk to the size of seven years old, was sound asleep, skipping the new moon in with her baby rope that was up to all the tricks. An hour went by, two hours, three hours. There was no stopping her, and no tiring her. The people gasped, the Lord fumed, and the fairies turned head-over-heels for joy. When morning broke the Lord cried: 'That's enough!'

But Elsie Piddock went on skipping.

'Time's up!' cried the Lord.

'When I skip my last skip, you shall lay your first brick,' said Elsie Piddock.

The villagers broke into a cheer.

'Signed and sealed, my lord, signed and sealed,' said Elsie Piddock.

'But hang it, old woman, you can't go on for ever!' cried the Lord.

'Oh yes, I can,' said Elsie Piddock. And on she went.

At midday the Lord shouted: 'Will the woman never stop?'

'No, she won't,' said Elsie Piddock. And she didn't.

'Then I'll stop you!' stormed the Lord, and made a grab at her.

'Now for a Sly Skip,' said Elsie Piddock, and skipped right through his thumb and forefinger.

'Hold her, you!' yelled the Lord to his Lawyer.

'Now for a High Skip,' said Elsie Piddock, and as the Lawyer darted at her, she skipped right over the highest lark singing in the sun.

The villagers shouted for glee, and the Lord and his friends were furious. Forgotten was the compact signed and sealed—their one thought now was to seize the maddening old woman, and stop her skipping by sheer force. But they couldn't. She played all her tricks on them: High Skip, Slow Skip, Sly Skip, Toe Skip, Long Skip, Fast Skip, Strong Skip, but never Last Skip. On and on and on she went. When the sun began to set, she was still skipping.

'Can we never rid the Down of the old thing?' cried the Lord desperately.

'No,' answered Elsie Piddock in her sleep, 'the Down will never be rid of me more. It's the children of Glynde I'm skipping for, to hold the Down for them and theirs for ever; it's Andy-Spandy I'm skipping for once again, for through him I've sucked sweet all my life. Oh, Andy, even you never knew how long Elsie Piddock could go on skipping!'

'The woman's mad!' cried the Lord. 'Signed and sealed doesn't hold with a madwoman. Skip or no skip, I shall lay the first brick!'

He plunged his trowel into the ground, and forced his brick down into the hole as a token of his possession of the land.

'Now,' said Elsie Piddock, 'for a Strong Skip!'

Right on the top of the brick she skipped, and down underground she sank out of sight, bearing the brick beneath her. Wild with rage, the Lord dived after her. Up came Elsie Piddock skipping blither than ever—but the Lord never came up again. The Lawyer ran to look down the hole; but there was no sign of him. The Lawyer reached his arm down the hole; but there was no reaching him. The Lawyer dropped a pebble down the hole; and no one heard it fall. So strong had Elsie Piddock skipped the Strong Skip.

The Lawyer shrugged his shoulders, and he and the Lord's friends left Mount Caburn for good and all. Oh, how joyously Elsie Piddock skipped then!

'Skip Against Trouble!' cried she, and skipped so that everyone present burst into happy laughter. To the tune of it she skipped the Long Skip, clean out of sight. And the people went home to tea. Caburn was saved for their children, and for the fairies, for ever.

But that wasn't the end of Elsie Piddock; she has never stopped skipping on Caburn since, for Signed and Sealed is Signed and Sealed. Not many have seen her, because she knows all the tricks; but if you go to Caburn at the new moon, you may catch a glimpse of a tiny bent figure, no bigger than a child, skipping all by itself in its sleep, and hear a gay little voice, like the voice of a dancing yellow leaf, singing:

'Andy
Spandy
Sugardy
Candy,
French
Almond
Rock!
Breadandbutterforyoursupper's
allyourmother'sGOT!'

The Two Skyscrapers Who Decided to Have a Child

Carl Sandburg

Although best known for his poetry, Carl Sandburg also wrote literary folktales that are not to be missed. They incorporate a wit, poignancy, and uniqueness of story not often seen in the genre. This story vividly depicts the loneliness of the city.

From Carl Sandburg, *Rootabaga Stories* (Orlando, Fla.: Harcourt Brace Jovanovich, 1951).

Two skyscrapers stood across the street from each other in the Village of Liver-and-Onions. In the daylight when the street poured full of people buying and selling, these two skyscrapers talked with each other the same as mountains talk.

In the night time when all the people buying and selling were gone home and there were only policemen and taxicab drivers on the streets, in the night when a mist crept up the streets and threw a purple and gray wrapper over everything, in the night when the stars and the sky shook out sheets of purple and gray mist down over the town, then the two skyscrapers leaned toward each other and whispered.

Whether they whispered secrets to each other or whether they whispered simple things that you and I know and everybody knows, that is their secret. One thing is sure: they often were seen leaning toward each other and whispering in the night the same as mountains lean and whisper in the night.

High on the roof of one of the skyscrapers was a tin brass goat looking out across prairies, and silver blue lakes shining like blue porcelain breakfast plates, and out across silver snakes of winding rivers in the morning sun. And high on the roof of the other skyscraper was a tin brass goose looking out across prairies, and silver blue lakes shining like blue porcelain breakfast plates, and out across silver snakes of winding rivers in the morning sun.

Now the Northwest Wind was a friend of the two skyscrapers. Coming so far, coming five hundred miles in a few hours, coming so fast always while the skyscrapers were standing still, standing always on the same old street corners always, the Northwest Wind was a bringer of news.

"Well, I see the city is here yet," the Northwest Wind would whistle to the skyscrapers.

And they would answer, "Yes, and are the mountains standing yet way out yonder where you come from, Wind?"

"Yes, the mountains are there yonder, and farther yonder is the sea, and the railroads are still going, still running across the prairie to the mountains, to the sea," the Northwest Wind would answer.

And now there was a pledge made by the Northwest Wind to the two skyscrapers. Often the Northwest Wind shook the tin brass goat and shook the tin brass goose on top of the skyscrapers.

"Are you going to blow loose the tin brass goat on my roof?" one asked.

"Are you going to blow loose the tin brass goose on my roof?" the other asked.

"Oh, no," the Northwest Wind laughed, first to one and then to the other, "if I ever blow loose your tin brass goat and if I ever blow loose your tin brass goose, it will be when I am sorry for you because you are up against hard luck and there is somebody's funeral."

So time passed on and the two skyscrapers stood with their feet among the policemen and the taxicabs, the people buying and selling,—the customers with parcels, packages and bundles—while away high on their roofs stood the goat and the goose looking out on silver blue lakes like blue porcelain breakfast plates and silver snakes of rivers winding in the morning sun.

So time passed on and the Northwest Wind kept coming, telling the news and making promises.

So time passed on. And the two skyscrapers decided to have a child.

And they decided when their child came it should be a *free* child.

"It must be a free child," they said to each other. "It must not be a child standing still all its life on a street corner. Yes, if we have a child she must be free to run across the prairie, to the mountains, to the sea. Yes, it must be a free child."

So time passed on. Their child came. It was a railroad train, the Golden Spike Limited, the fastest long distance train in the Rootabaga Country. It ran across the prairie, to the mountains, to the sea.

They were glad, the two skyscrapers were, glad to have a free child running away from the big city, far away to the mountains, far away to the sea, running as far as the farthest mountains and sea coasts touched by the Northwest Wind.

They were glad their child was useful, the two skyscrapers were, glad their child was carrying a thousand people a thousand miles a day, so when people spoke of the Golden Spike Limited, they spoke of it as a strong, lovely child.

The time passed on. There came a day when the newsies yelled as though they were crazy. "Yah yah, blah blah, yoh yoh," was what it sounded like to the two skyscrapers who never bothered much about what the newsies were yelling.

"Yah yah, blah blah, yoh yoh," was the cry of the newsies that came up again to the tops of the skyscrapers.

At last the yelling of the newsies came so strong the skyscrapers listened and heard the newsies yammering, "All about the great train wreck! All about the Golden Spike disaster! Many lives lost! Many lives lost!"

And the Northwest Wind came howling a slow sad song. And late that afternoon, taxi-cab drivers, newsies and customers with bundles, all stood around talking and wondering about two things next to each other on the street car track in the middle of the street. One was a tin brass goat. The other was a tin brass goose. And they lay next to each other.

FOLK RHYMES AND POETRY

Mother Goose Rhymes

The first of these rhymes is the one with which we are most familiar. The queen mentioned in this rhyme is, according to William and Cecil Baring-Gould, often thought to be Elizabeth. The two rhymes that follow are variants of the first. It is interesting to note that the third rhyme reflects country life rather than city life.

Pussy cat, pussy cat, where have you
    been?
I've been to London to look at the
    queen.
Pussy cat, pussy cat, what did you
    there?
I frightened a little mouse under her
    chair.

Little girl, little girl, where have you been?

Little girl, little girl, where have you
  been?
Gathering roses to take to the queen.
Little girl, little girl, what gave she
  you?
She gave me a diamond as big as my
  shoe.

Pussycat, Pussycat, where have you
  been?
I've been to see grandmother over the
  green!
What did she give you? Milk in a can.
What did you say for it? Thank you,
  Grandam!

Within any community, whether rural or
urban, problems arise in relationships.

Whose little pigs are these, these, these?
  Whose little pigs are these?
They are Roger the Cook's, I know by
  their looks;
  I found them among my peas.
Go pound them, go pound them.
  I dare not on my life.
For though I love not Roger the Cook.
  I dearly love his wife.

This rhyme is said to relate to an actual
historical event, the invasion of Scotland by
the Earl of Hertford (Hector Protector) on
behalf of Henry VIII.

Hector Protector was dressed all in green;
Hector Protector was sent to the Queen.
  The Queen did not like him.
  No more did the King;
So Hector Protector was sent back again.

In Mother Goose's Melody, *the editor*
added this maxim: "Provide against the
worst, and hope for the best."

The Rats, and the Mice.
They made such a strife.
I was forc'd to go to
London, to buy me a Wife.

The Streets were so
Broad, and the Lanes
Were so narrow,

I was forc'd to bring
My Wife home,
In a Wheelbarrow.

The Wheelbarrow broke.
And give my Wife a fall.
The duce take
Wheelbarrow, Wife & all.

Market days in small towns were often the
high point of rural social life.

At Islington a fair they hold,
Where cakes and ale are to be sold,
At High Gate and at Holloway
The like is kept from day to day;
At Totnam and at Kentish Town.
And all those places up and down.

The Story
of the Little Market Woman

On market day, both men and women often
had a few drinks. This may be why the old
woman fell asleep by the road.

There was a little woman,
  As I have heard tell,
She went to market
  Her eggs for to sell,
She went to market
  All on a market day,
And she fell asleep
  On the King's highway.

There came by a pedlar
  His name was Stout,
He cut her petticoats
  All round about;
He cut her petticoats
  Up to her knees,
Which made the poor woman
  To shiver and sneeze.

From Iona and Peter Opie, *The Oxford Nursery Rhyme
Book* (New York: Oxford University Press, 1964). Re-
printed by permission of Oxford University Press. Illus-
trations by Pauline Baynes, in Iona and Peter Opie, *The
Puffin Book of Nursery Rhymes* (New York: Penguin
Books, 1963).

When the little woman
  Began to awake,
She began to shiver,
  And she began to shake;
She began to shake,
  And she began to cry,
Goodness mercy on me,
  This is none of I!

If it be not I,
  As I suppose it be,
I have a little dog at home,
  And he knows me;
If it be I,
  He'll wag his little tail,
And if it be not I,
  He'll loudly bark and wail.

Home went the little woman,
  All in the dark,
Up jumped the little dog,
  And he began to bark,
He began to bark,
  And she began to cry,
Goodness mercy on me,
  I see I be Not I!

The Tropics in New York

Claude McKay

Claude McKay (1890–1948) emigrated from his native Jamaica to the United States in 1912. In this poem, he captures his yearnings for the land of his birth and childhood.

From Claude McKay, *The Selected Poems of Claude McKay* (Boston: Twayne Publishers, 1953).

Bananas ripe and green, and gingerroot,
  Cocoa in pods' and alligator pears,
And tangerines and mangoes and grapefruit,
  Fit for the highest prize at parish fairs,

Set in the window, bringing memories
  Of fruit trees laden by low-swinging
    rills,
And dewy dawns, and mystical blue skies
  In benediction over nunlike hills.

My eyes grew dim, and I could no more
    gaze;
  A wave of longing through my body
    swept,
And, hungry for the old, familiar ways,
  I turned aside and bowed my head and
    wept.

In the City

Lois Lenski

There may be many drawbacks to city life, but, as Lois Lenski points out, those who like the city do so despite its disadvantages. Lois Lenski is perhaps best known for her "small" books such as Cowboy Small, Policeman Small, *and others. Her poetry, like her books, captures the feeling of childhood and speaks of things that interest children.*

The buildings are tall,
The people are small
In the city, in the city.

The noises are loud,
There's always a crowd
In the city, in the city.

The cars move fast,
The trucks jolt past;
Up in the sky the pigeons fly.

From Lois Lenski, *City Poems* (Silver Springs, MD: Henry Z. Walck, 1971). Reprinted by permission of the Lois Lenski Covy Foundation.

East or West,
I like it best
In the city, in the city.

Rudolph Is Tired of the City

Gwendolyn Brooks

*Here, the negative side of the city is not
ignored and there is a yearning for the space
and freedom of the countryside. Gwendolyn
Brooks writes from experience, having
grown up in Chicago.*

These buildings are too close to me.
I'd like to PUSH away.
I'd like to live in the country,
And spread my arms all day.

I'd like to spread my breath out, too—
As farmers' sons and daughters do.

I'd tend the cows and chickens.
I'd do the other chores.
Then, all the hours left I'd go
A-SPREADING out-of-doors.

From Gwendolyn Brooks, "Rudolph Is Tired of the
City," *Selected Poems* (New York: Harper & Row,
1960). Reprinted by permission of Gwendolyn Brooks.

Little park that I pass through,
I carry off a piece of you
Every morning hurrying down
To my work-day in the town;
Carry you for country there
To make the city ways more fair.
I take your trees,
And your breeze,
Your greenness,
Your cleanness,
Some of your shade, some of your sky,
Some of your calm as I go by;
Your flowers to trim
The pavements grim;
Your space for room in the jostled street
And grass for carpet to my feet.
Your fountains take and sweet bird calls
To sing me from my office walls.

All that I can see
I carry off with me.
But you never miss my theft,
So much treasure you have left.
As I find you, fresh at morning,
So I find you, home returning—
Nothing lacking from your grace.
All your riches wait in place
For me to borrow
On the morrow.

Do you hear this praise of you,
Little park that I pass through?

Ellis Park

Helen Hoyt

*In the conflict between city and country,
there are compromises that can be made.
"Ellis Park" speaks of that little patch of
country within the city—the park. City
people need that reminder of country and of
nature; perhaps it is a reminder of their
collective past.*

From *Poetry* (The Modern Poetry Association, 1913).

Afternoon on a Hill

Edna St. Vincent Millay

*Edna St. Vincent Millay (1892-1950) is
marked by a lyrical brightness underlaid by
a tone of sadness. "Afternoon on a Hill"
displays a melancholic wish for the things of
the country but also a certain satisfaction on
the part of the speaker with having a place
that belongs to her, even though it is in the
city. Regardless where a person lives—the*

From Edna St. Vincent Millay, *Collected Poems of Edna
St. Vincent Millay* (New York: Harper & Row, 1945).

city or the country—each one needs a spot to call his or her own.

I will be the gladdest thing
  Under the sun!
I will touch a hundred flowers
  And not pick one.

I will look at cliffs and clouds
  With quiet eyes,
Watch the wind bow down the grass,
  And the grass rise.

And when lights begin to show
  Up from the town,
I will mark which must be mine,
  And then start down!

Population Drifts

Carl Sandburg

This very powerful poem eloquently expresses the idea that there is something life-defeating about the city, a common theme in literature.

New-mown hay smell and wind of the plain
  made her a woman whose ribs had the
  power of the hills in them and her hands
  were tough for work and there was passion
  for life in her womb.
She and her man crossed the ocean and the
  years that marked their faces saw them
  haggling with landlords and grocers while
  six children played on the stones and
  prowled in the garbage cans.
One child coughed its lungs away, two more
  have adenoids and can neither talk nor run
  like their mother, one is in jail, two have
  jobs in a box factory
And as they fold the pasteboard, they wonder
  what the wishing is and the wistful glory
  in them that flutters faintly when the
  glimmer of spring comes on the air or the
  green of summer turns brown:

They do not know it is the new-mown hay
  smell calling and the wind of the plain
  praying for them to come back and take
  hold of life again with tough hands and
  with passion.

The Lake Isle of Innisfree

William Butler Yeats

William Butler Yeats (1865–1939) was born in Dublin but spent much of his childhood on the western coast of Ireland with his maternal grandfather. He was an avid reader of folktales, and his poetry is imbued with the same sense of mystery that we often see in folk literature. For Yeats, the countryside had a special quality that was revitalizing and filled with renewal.

I will arise and go now, and go to Innisfree,
  And a small cabin build there, of clay and
    wattles made;
Nine bean rows will I have there, a hive for
  the honey bee,
  And live alone in the bee-loud glade.

And I shall have some peace there, for peace
  comes dropping slow,
Dropping from the veils of the morning to
  where the cricket sings;
There midnight's all a-glimmer, and noon a
  purple glow,
  And evening full of the linnet's wings.

I will arise and go now, for always night and
  day
I hear lake water lapping with low sounds by
  the shore;
While I stand on the roadway, or on the
  pavements gray,
  I hear it in the deep heart's core.

From Carl Sandburg, *Chicago Poems* (Orlando, Fla.: Harcourt Brace Jovanovich, 1944).

From William Butler Yeats, *Collected Poems of W. B. Yeats* (New York: Macmillian, 1956).

The World

William Wordsworth

The belief that religion, even superstition, is preferable to rationalism flows throughout William Wordsworth's poetry. For Wordsworth, nature and country life have a healing effect on people; he refers to nature as a "kindly nurse" and idealizes the humble life in his poetry. It is interesting to compare this poem with the sonnet "Upon Westminster Bridge," on page 165.

The world is too much with us; late and
   soon,
  Getting and spending, we lay waste our
   powers:

Little we see in Nature that is ours;
We have given our hearts away, a sordid
  boon!
This sea that bares her bosom to the moon;
  The winds that will be howling at all
  hours,
  And are up-gather'd now like sleeping
  flowers;
For this, for everything, we are out of tune;
It moves us not.—Great God! I'd rather be
  A Pagan suckled in a creed outworn;
So might I, standing on this pleasant lea,
  Have glimpses that would make me less
  forlorn;
Have sight of Proteus rising from the sea;
  Or hear old Triton blow his wreathèd
  horn.

From William Wordsworth, *The Poetical Works of Wordsworth* (New York: Crowell, 1877).

FICTION

Snowbound in Hidden Valley
In the Hidden Valley

Holly Wilson

Jo lived in town and had heard terrible stories about the Indians, who lived in the country. When she was hit on the head by a falling brick during a fire, wound up in the back of a truck belonging to the Indians, and had to stay with them during a blizzard, she was uncertain and fearful. Jo found, however, that the stories she had heard were wrong. The Indian family was different from the people in town, but those differences were not bad. Holly Wilson (1907–1980) grew up in the Upper Peninsula of Michigan and wrote from her own childhood experiences.

The floor on which Jo was lying would not stay still. It heaved from side to side and jolted up and down, throwing her around like popcorn in a popper. She opened her eyes

From Holly Wilson, *Snowbound in Hidden Valley* (New York: Julian Messner, 1957). Illustration by Dorothy Bayley Morse.

and tried to look around, but everything was black. She could hear the roaring of the engine and the clanking of tire chains on spinning wheels underneath her, and she realized she was still in the truck where the policeman had shoved her. But the truck was moving!

"Hey!" cried Jo loudly and tried to get up. But she was still too dizzy and her head hurt too much. She slumped down again and leaned her head against a big, lumpy sack of something that had a dry, sandy smell of potatoes. Her cry was lost in the noise of the truck engine and the howling of the snowstorm. Whoever the driver was, he had not heard her.

She could understand what had happened. The policeman had shoved her in here, after she got hit, and she remembered hearing the doors slam at the back of the truck. In the excitement of the fire, no one had remembered her, and now the owner of the truck was on his way home. He didn't even know she was there.

Her head was heavy and a sharp pain shot through it at every bounce and bump, but she made a great effort and yelled again. It was no use. The driver was racing the motor, the wheels were spinning madly and the tire chains were beating and clanking against the fenders. Her voice was lost in all that noise.

Jo threshed around blindly, got hold of something at the side of the truck and hung on. Sometimes the truck tilted steeply to the right and sometimes to the left, as it got off the road and back on again. But still it crept forward through the storm. After a long, long time, while Jo grew colder and colder and her teeth began to chatter, the truck dove headfirst into a snowbank and died.

There was a deep silence. Outside the truck the wind howled. Then Jo could hear voices but she could not understand what they were saying. After a moment, the back door of the truck creaked open, someone set a flashlight inside and began to reach for the boxes and bags of groceries. Jo sat up and found herself staring into the dark face of the Indian, Charlie Leroy, and just back of his shoulder peered his son. They both began to talk at once, and Jo's heart dropped with a

sickening thud. They weren't even talking English!

The next moment the thin, excited face of Onota poked around the edge of the truck door.

"Jo Shannon!" she cried, her dark eyes widening. "What are you doing here?"

Jo's lip trembled and tears started to her eyes.

"I got hurt at the fire," she wailed, "and I don't know where *here* is!"

"We're at the bottom of the gully in front of my father's house," said Onota. "That's our home up there where the light is."

Jo gasped. She was way out in the woods, back of Mount Menard, alone with the Indians! The thought made her head ache worse than ever.

"I've got to go home," she said feverishly. "I've got to go home!"

Mr. Leroy spoke up at last and this time, to Jo's relief, he spoke in English.

"We'll see," he said gently. "Come into the house, little girl, and we will talk it over. We'll freeze if we stay here much longer."

He pushed the door open wider and braced himself against it to keep the wind from slamming it. Jo crawled out and sank, floundering, in the deep snow that came above her waist. But Mr. Leroy and Jim were helpful. They pulled her out of it. Then Onota's father lifted her and carried her through the deep drifts. Jim dragged the gunny sack of potatoes out of the truck and slung it on his back. With great effort, he got a box of groceries balanced on his hip and struggled after them through the snow. Onota followed, carrying more bundles.

They reached the house at last, staggered through the door and slammed it after them. They were in a narrow, chilly hallway, lighted by a single electric-light bulb in the ceiling, and there was nothing to be seen except the bare, worn and splintered treads of an old walnut staircase. Mr. Leroy set Jo down. Then he opened a door to the left and pushed her ahead of him into her own great-grandmother's parlor.

The warm air in the room had a strong but rather pleasant smell, like wood smoke and furs and sweet grass, all combined. It seemed to Jo that the room was bursting with dark, strange people, bright lights, noise and warmth and laughter. Then the noise and laughter died down and everyone was staring curiously at her. A black and white dog, lying under the table, lifted his lip and snarled at her. Another dog, a shaggy, yellow mongrel, was asleep in front of the fire and seemed to be dreaming about something. He growled in his sleep and gave little muttering barks, but he did not wake up.

Jo swallowed hard and rubbed her snowy mittens together. A pool of water from the melting snow on her boots began to spread around her feet. Onota's father put his hand on her shoulder and began to talk in the foreign language again. Three boys, who were about as big as Jo herself, were playing a game with beans on the floor. They looked at her out of the sides of their eyes and then looked away again.

When Onota's father finished speaking, everyone burst into chatter that Jo could not understand, although once in a while she thought she heard a word of French. She knew a few words of French from some of her friends in town who were French Canadians. But everyone here talked so fast it made her head whirl.

Onota, who had gone out somewhere to the back of the house to leave her packages, now came into the room and Jo grabbed her by the arm.

"Onota!" she cried. "What are they saying? What are they going to do with me?"

Onota slipped her arm around Jo comfortingly. "It's all right, Jo," she said. "They want you to take off your things and get warm."

"But I want to go home!" wailed Jo. "My mother doesn't know where I am. I want to go home to my mother!"

She could hear the French words more clearly now, because they were repeated so often in the flood of Indian talk.

"Pauvre petite!" they were saying, over and over again, sympathetically. That meant "Poor little thing!" and Jo had a frightened feeling that they meant she could not go home. Onota confirmed it.

"You can't go home tonight, Jo," she was saying. "The storm is too bad and, anyway, you know our truck broke down. We almost didn't get here ourselves."

Jo held her head and sobbed. What was she going to do? She couldn't stay here with these Indians—Father and Mother would be worried and Aunt Maggie would be furious! And what if Boyd Lacey should hear about it? Then she looked up and met Onota's dark, sympathetic glance, and she was ashamed of herself for bothering about what Boyd would think. Onota was really her friend. When she looked around the room at the rest of the family, she suddenly saw the same bright, dark eyes smiling everywhere. These people wanted to be friendly. Jo made an effort and gave them a watery little smile in return. The three boys ducked their heads bashfully, picked up their bean game and moved to the other side of the room, leaving a place for her in front of the warm fire.

Onota's father gave her a push toward the wood fire that was crackling and glowing in a small marble fireplace, whose mantel had once been white but was now stained black with years of soot.

"Here," he said gruffly, "you girls get those wet clothes off. Do you want to die of pneumonia?"

A tall woman, whose soft black eyes were like Onota's, got up from where she had been doing some work at the big center table and came to them.

"This is my mother," said Onota proudly. "Mother, this is my friend Jo Shannon."

"Onota's friend," repeated Mrs. Leroy gravely. "You are my friend, too."

It seemed so queer that, for a minute, Jo did not know what to say. Then she remembered her manners and said politely, "How do you do?"

She fumbled with the zipper of her jacket, then she and Onota began to shed their wet outer clothes, dropping them on the floor where they stood by the fire. When Jo pulled off her wool hood and her bright hair fluffed out, glowing in the light, there was a sudden silence in the room. Mrs Leroy reached out and gently felt Jo's hair, while several of the other Indians crowded around. Other hands began to touch her head and an excited hum of talking arose. Jo began to get alarmed again.

"What's the matter?" she whispered to Onota. "What are they saying?"

Onota smiled.

"It's your red hair," she explained. "We don't often see anyone with red hair like yours, and it brings good luck to touch it."

Jo felt a little better, but she was still uneasy and moved closer to Onota.

"Don't they talk English?" she asked under her breath.

"Oh, yes," said Onota. "We all know how to speak English and French, but the older people don't like it. They think it is not dignified. They would—what do you call it?—lose face, if they did not speak in Chippewa."

"Oh." Jo did not exactly understand this, but she thought she had better not ask any more questions.

At that moment Mrs. Leroy's exploring fingers touched the swelling on the side of her head, and Jo gave a little gasp of pain. Onota's mother felt it again, looking kind and concerned.

"What happened to your head?" she asked.

"I got hit by a brick at the fire," said Jo.

Mr. Leroy and Jim began to talk rapidly in Chippewa, explaining about the fire, and the Indians turned away from Jo to listen. Onota's mother bent over Jo.

"I'll tie it up for you—with some herbs to take down the swelling," she murmured.

"Now you and Onota sit here by the fire. I'll take care of your head and then get you something to eat. There's some stew on the stove."

"Gee, thanks," breathed Jo earnestly. "I'm starved!"

She was starved, she realized. Her supper at home seemed to have been eaten in another lifetime, and at the mention of food her stomach squeaked. She could hardly wait while Mrs. Leroy spread some sweet-smelling ointment through her hair, rubbing it gently on the bump, and then bandaging her head, round and round, with a long white cloth. It felt good. Then Onota's mother gathered up their wet coats and boots and carried them out to the kitchen to dry, when she went out to get the stew.

Onota shoved at the sleeping yellow dog in front of the fire.

"Move over, Rusty," she said firmly.

Rusty woke up, gave her a reproachful glance and reluctantly got up and padded away.

There was a big pile of thick mats and fur robes and blankets stacked up in one corner of the room. Onota dragged one of the mats over in front of the fire. Then she brought over some of the biggest, softest rabbitskin blankets that Jo had ever seen. She spread some of them on the mat and helped Jo wrap up in one.

"Take your shoes off," she suggested. "I'll get some moccasins for us."

Half an hour later, snuggled in the heap of blankets and furs before the fire, with her feet toasting in a pair of sheepskin moccasins (woolly side in), Jo finished eating her stew and leaned back. She felt recovered enough to look around the parlor.

It was not a very big room and it was crowded with Onota's family. They all looked alike to Jo—black hair, black eyes and copper-colored faces. Even the women and children looked secretive to her. Yet, queerly enough, she could tell that they liked her. When one of them happened to glance around and catch her eyes, there was a friendly feeling in the air. She could almost feel it.

Most of them were seated in straight chairs

around a huge, square golden oak table, and at first she thought they were playing games. Then she saw that everyone was working. Some of the women were making pretty baskets of white birchbark laced with twigs, while others were working on furs and pelts of small animals. Even the small children had jobs and were importantly sorting scraps that dropped off the table, putting them into paper bags. One of the older men was writing a letter on the corner of the table, and the others were cleaning hunting equipment, sharpening knives or oiling guns.

Over their heads, above the center of the table, a large brass chandelier spread its four stiff arms, at the end of which were curved brass acanthus leaves holding big hundred-watt bulbs. The brilliant light was bright enough for a searchlight, but no one seemed to mind, and it made the most minute and careful work possible. Jo, who was used to the charm of shaded lamps, suddenly began to understand the use of a good, bright light.

From one of the acanthus leaves dangled a long, black extension cord, attached to a big radio in the center of the table. From time to time, someone tried to turn on the radio, but the storm was causing so much static that they could not hear much more than noise.

The rest of the room was bare, except for the heaps of mats and blankets and furs in the corner. The old hardwood floor was dull and scarred by heavy boots, but still solid; and in spots where the yellowed damask wallpaper was peeling, Jo could see that the plaster was still holding up. When Great-grandfather Shannon built this house for his bride, nearly a hundred years ago, he had built well.

Of course, it wasn't perfect, like a house that had been kept up. It was drafty and it leaked air from somewhere around the baseboards. An icy draft of wind chilled Jo's back and she pulled her rabbitskin blanket closer around her shoulders. There was a thin, powdery drift of snow sifting in under the windows. The Indians had nailed blankets over the windows to keep out the cold, and their brightly colored designs gave the room a warm, cheerful appearance, but every now and then, when the wind blew strongly, the blankets billowed out.

However, here by the fire it was snug and warm. Jo was so comfortable and so sleepy that when she suddenly thought of a way to get home, she almost hated to say so. But of course she had to. She wanted to go home, even if it meant going out in the cold storm again. Mother and Father were probably frantic with worry by now.

FANTASY

Tucker's Countryside
Connecticut

George Selden

In this sequel to The Cricket in Times Square, *Tucker Mouse and Harry Cat have been called to the country to help Chester Cricket solve a problem. Houses are taking over his meadow; the city is encroaching upon the country. In this excerpt,*

From George Selden, *Tucker's Countryside* (New York: Farrar, Straus & Giroux, 1969). Illustration by Garth Williams.

Tucker and Harry, two inveterate denizens of the city, find it difficult to adjust to the country.

Late that night the cat, the mouse, and the robin were almost ready to leave for Connecticut. John Robin was hopping back and forth impatiently. "Don't you think we ought to get going?" he said. "We don't want to miss the train."

"Tucker, what are you doing?" called Harry Cat.

Tucker Mouse was over in his pantry, making a great stir about something. He came back to the others carrying a big package neatly wrapped in wax paper retrieved from the Nedick's lunch counter and tied with string from the Loft's Candy Store. "This is one thing I *am* taking," he said.

"What is it?" said Harry.

"Never mind." Tucker held the bundle out of the cat's reach. "It's something for Chester."

"Gee, let's *go!*" In his impatience John Robin hopped up so high that he hit his head on the drainpipe ceiling.

"All right, all right," said Tucker. "Take it easy. I don't want you braining yourself in my living room." He sighed and took a last look around the drain pipe. "My nice home—I wonder if I'll ever see it again."

"Of course you will," said Harry Cat. "Now come on."

They began the climb up through the labyrinth of pipes to the street. Harry went first, Tucker last, and John Robin stayed in the middle so he wouldn't get lost down any of the dozens of openings they passed. In a few minutes they were on the sidewalk. Times Square stretched up above and all around them. Most of the moviegoers and crowds from the theaters had gone home, but the huge neon signs were still spilling their torrents of color over the Square.

"Goodbye, Times Square," said Tucker Mouse. "The soul who loves you most is going away."

"For goodness' sakes!" said Harry Cat. "You sound like the last act of an Italian Opera!" Harry liked opera very much and had sneaked into the Metropolitan Opera House many times.

The three of them went down Forty-second Street toward Grand Central Station. John Robin flew on ahead—it was easier for him than hopping—and then waited on the curb until the cat and the mouse came creeping along under the cars that lined the street.

They reached Bryant Park, the neat little patch of grass and trees behind the Public Library on the corner of Fifth Avenue. "That's the only countryside I've ever seem." said Tucker to the robin.

John flew up, circled once over the park, and came back. "Why, that's nothing!" he said. "Most of the houses near the Meadow have *lawns* that are bigger than that!"

They continued on. While Harry and Tucker were padding silently under a big Cadillac, the mouse suddenly said, "Harry, if even the houses have lawns that are bigger than Bryant Park, there must be a lot of open space in Connecticut."

"I guess so," said Harry Cat.

"Do they have wild animals in Connecticut, Harry?"

"Most likely."

"What kind of wild animals?"

"Oh—lions, tigers. Elephants, maybe."

"Harry, if you wouldn't mind—be serious, please!"

"Don't worry, Mousiekins," said Harry. "I'll protect you!" He sometimes called Tucker "Mousiekins" when he wanted to tease him.

But Tucker was not amused. He trudged along behind, muttering, "Bears. I'll bet they have bears anyway."

And at last they reached Grand Central Station. Down they went, through the same series of pipes and deserted corridors and drafty back rooms that Tucker and Harry had passed last September. But then Chester Cricket had been clinging tightly to the fur on Harry's back. The Late Local Express was still leaving from track 18. This time of night there were very few passengers, so the animals had no trouble slipping into a shady corner in one of the compartments between the cars. And they didn't have long to wait either. In a few minutes there was a lurch and a screech of iron wheels, and the train began to move.

"We're going!" shouted Tucker Mouse. "I feel it—we're really moving, Harry! Our first trip anywhere! Oh! oh! oh!"

"Now, take it easy," said Harry Cat, and lifted his right front paw.

"You wouldn't squash me, please, Harry," said Tucker indignantly. "That's no way to begin a trip!"

"Then don't get too excited," said Harry, and lowered his paw.

"A fine thing!" sniffled Tucker Mouse. "I couldn't even get excited on my very first journey!"

"You can get excited, Mousiekins. But *not* hysterical!"

They all settled back to enjoy the ride.

Three and a half hours later the three friends were wondering about the name of the train they were on. They understood the "Late" and the "Local" part, but they couldn't imagine why anyone would call it an "Express." It seemed to stop at every crossroads, and when it did stop, it waited—and waited—and *waited!* "We've been on this thing long enough to get to Canada!" complained Harry Cat. He was a very curious cat, Harry was, and he enjoyed looking at the maps that sometimes appeared in the newspapers he and Tucker used to furnish their home. So he knew the direction in which they were traveling: northwest and then due north.

"I think we're almost there," said John Robin. He flew up and took a look out of the window in the compartment where they were. In the black night heavens, the moon, which was just a few days past the full, was shining brightly. It looked as if some great sky monster had begun to nibble away at it. "I was right—we're here!" said John, and flew down again. "I recognize the houses outside."

"Thank goodness!" said Tucker Mouse. He stood up and stretched his limbs. They were sore from the pounding of the wheels below. "We should have stowed away on a Greyhound bus instead."

The train rattled to a halt. "Everybody off!" said the robin. Since no one was getting out at this station, the conductor didn't bother to open the door, and the animals had to scramble down through an opening between two cars. "Welcome to *Hedley!*" said John when they were on the platform.

"Is that the name of the town?" said Harry.

"Yes." The robin pointed with one wing. Down on the wall of the station house a sign lit up by an electric bulb said HEDLEY CONNECTICUT. "Hedley was the name of the man who settled this whole part of the state."

Tucker Mouse looked around: "Where's Chester?"

"Oh, it was too far for him to come all the way to the station," said John. "I'm afraid we have a long walk ahead of us."

"I don't care *how* long it is!" said Harry Cat. "As long as we're off that train!"

They set off, with John Robin sometimes fluttering, sometimes hopping along in the lead. Tucker had a hard time with his package. He tried to carry it first in his right front paw, then in his left front, then switching often from one to the other. It seemed to get heavier and heavier, and he kept falling farther and farther behind. He wouldn't think of abandoning it, though. When Harry saw what was happening, he went up to Tucker without a word and hooked the string around the package under one of his sharp lower teeth. It was no weight at all for a big cat like Harry.

They went on walking. At first they passed stores, offices, a movie theater—the kind of buildings you would find in the center of a town. There was almost no one on the streets. The store fronts were dark, and only the high street lights cast patches of brightness down where the animals scurried along. Then, when they got to the parts of Hedley were people lived, there were apartment houses, and two-family houses, and finally single-family homes. Tucker had never seen one before in his life, and even Harry had only seen the town houses of the upper East Side in New York, and they were all connected.

"I couldn't believe it!" said Tucker Mouse. "Look at the size of that lawn over there! John was right—it's bigger than Bryant Park!"

"I like it here!" said Harry enthusiastically. "It's beau'i'ful in 'onne'i'uh—'onnekikuk—" He gave up trying to say "Connecticut" with Tucker's package dangling from his mouth.

And on they padded. Until, on their left, a vast darkness appeared. No houses or lawns were there. But the moon, which was dropping toward the morning, silvered the branches of trees and bushes. And a sound of running water came rustling up to them. "The meadow starts here," said John Robin. "Do you hear the brook?"

"It looks more like a jungle to me!" said Tucker Mouse.

"This is one of the woodsy parts," said John. "The flat part, with grass and everything, is down at the other end. That's where Chester lives. Can you make it?"

"Of 'ourse!" said Harry. In a minute, though, he suddenly dropped the package and said, "Did you hear anything?"

"Like what?" said Tucker.

From the dark ahead came a single chirp. Then another. And another.

"It's Chester!" shouted Harry. He grabbed up the bundle and dashed on into the night. Tucker Mouse scuttled after him, and John Robin took off and flew over them both.

A fence ran beside the road. With each post that Harry went past, the chirps sounded nearer and nearer. They seemed to be coming from one certain post. Harry stopped in front of it. "Chester!" he called up. "Is that you?"

And down, in one jump, from the top of the fencepost came Chester Cricket. "Harry!" he said. "I'm so *glad* to see you!" The cat gave him such a big lick on the head that it knocked him right over.

"Watch it, Harry," said Tucker Mouse, who came puffing up just then. "With a kiss like that, you could knock the cricket unconscious."

"Tucker!" exclaimed Chester Cricket. "Oh, isn't that wonderful!"

Then, naturally, everybody started hugging everybody. It isn't so easy to hug a cricket, either. And they all talked at once— exclaiming and laughing the way old friends

do when they haven't seen each other for months and months.

"I've been waiting on that fencepost for hours!" said Chester.

"We've been *traveling* for hours!" said John Robin.

For no good reason everyone burst out laughing again. But gradually the laughter subsided into a few final chuckles. The robin began hopping around nervously. "I guess I'd better get back to my nest, Chester," he said. "It's almost light, and I'd like to get a little sleep at least. I have a big morning of worming planned for tomorrow."

"All right, John," said Chester. "And thanks for showing Tucker and Harry the way."

The cat and the mouse thanked him, too. Then the little bird flew off into the night. As he disappeared, they heard him saying, "Whee-*ooo!* Down to New York and back in one day! What a flight!"

"Come on," said Chester to Harry and Tucker. "I'll show you the way to my stump."

He led them under the lowest wire of the fence and out into the Old Meadow. There was a path worn through the grass, and the moon, although it was riding low on the horizon, still shed enough light for them to see where they were going. "Be careful you don't go too far off to the right,'' said Chester. ''The bank drops right down to the brook. Can you both swim, by the way?''

''I can, but I hate it,'' said Harry Cat.

''I don't know if I can or not,'' said Tucker, ''And I don't want to find out tonight.'' He moved a little over to the left.

Even before they reached his home, Chester insisted on hearing all about New York—and expecially the Bellini family. So, as they walked, and Chester hopped, Harry and Tucker told him the news. Mario was studying violin at the Juilliard School of Music. He had become so interested in music during Chester's stay in New York that he had decided to make it his career. ''And I heard him tell Mr. Smedley that he chose the violin because it sounded more like a cricket's chirp than any other instrument,'' said Harry. As for Mr. Smedley, whose letter to the *The New York Times* had launched Chester on his famous career, he had become one of the most successful piano teachers in the city. ''Mostly because he keeps telling everybody that he was the one who discovered you,'' said Tucker. ''And it was really me!'' And Mama and Papa Bellini were doing very well, too. Most of the people who began coming to the newsstand while Chester was giving his concerts there kept buying their papers and magazines from the Bellinis even after the cricket had left. ''And you know what,'' said Harry Cat. ''After all those years of complaining about how old and rickety the newsstand was, when they *could* afford to have a new one made—they decided they didn't want to! Mama said it was too much like an old friend to have it changed. So there it stands—the same as always!''

''I'm glad,'' said Chester. ''I like to think of everything just the way it was.''

Their walk through the meadow had brought them at last to Chester's stump. ''This is just the way I imagined it,'' said Tucker Mouse. It was on a bank, not too high, not too low, just at the point where the brook made a turn. So it had the water bubbling on two sides. And a big willow tree dropped lacy branches over it.

''I hope there's room enough for Harry in-side,'' said Chester as he hopped through an opening into the stump. ''I had some field mice gnaw out some more space this afternoon.''

''You have *mice* here?'' said Tucker, following Chester in.

''Lots of them,'' said the cricket. ''You'll meet everybody tomorrow.''

''Plenty of room.'' said Harry. He stretched out on the spongy wooden floor of the stump.

Chester pointed at something above their heads. ''Do you recognize that?'' The moonlight, reflected from the brook, picked out a spark of silver.

''It's your bell!'' said Tucker.

''My bell.'' The cricket nodded. ''I found some string beside the road and tied it to the ceiling.''

''Well, I have something else to remind you of New York,'' said the mouse. He began carefully untying the package, which he had carried himself since they left the road.

''At last we see what it is!'' said Harry. ''We've lugged that thing all the way from Times Square.''

''*Liverwurst!*'' exclaimed Chester. For Tucker Mouse had undone the wax paper to reveal a big chunk of the meat.

''Stolen only this morning from the Nedick's lunch counter,'' said Tucker. ''Remember your first night in the city, when we had the liverwurst together? I thought it would be nice again.''

''Oh, that *is* nice of you!'' said Chester. ''I haven't had any since I left New York.''

So the three friends sat down to a delicious, late-night snack of liverwurst. And they talked and reminisced about Chester's adventures in the city, as always happens when old friends meet. And outside the tree stump the night wore away.

A lull came in the conversation, and Harry Cat said, ''Now what's this big problem about the meadow, Chester?''

The cricket shook his head. ''It's something very serious. Come on—I'll show you. It's almost sunrise—you'll be able to see.'' He jumped out the opening in the stump, then up on top of it. Harry and Tucker scrambled after him. Above them, a pale lavender light, the color of lilacs, seemed to lift the sky up-wards. The heavens stood high. "Now look all around," said Chester, "all around the meadow, and tell me what you see."

Tucker and Harry did as they were told. They could see the flat, grassy land around Chester's stump, and farther off the woodsy part where the meadow began, and still far-ther, toward the west, a ridge of hills that were also covered with trees. Here and there, through the brush, through the reeds, they caught a glitter of the brook in its course. In the dawn the meadow looked so fresh, and everything in it, that it seemed as if it had just been created today.

"Beautiful!" said Harry Cat.

"But look *outside* the meadow!" said Chester. "Look all around outside."

Everywhere, on all sides—beyond the hills, beyond the woodsy parts—there were houses. To the east, where the sun was just coming up, two new ones were being built. "I only see houses," said Harry Cat.

"That's just it," said Chester. "Houses!"

Tucker Mouse scratched his head. "I don't get it, Chester. What's wrong with houses?"

"It's too long to go into now," said the cricket. "I'll explain it when we wake up. Let's get some sleep while we can."

The Wind in the Willows
The Open Road

Kenneth Grahame

The Wind in the Willows *portrays an idyllic countryside as the setting for the lively, whimsical adventures of three animal friends, Ratty, Mole, and Toad. As Cornelia Meigs, author of* A Critical History of Children's Literature, *has pointed out, "It is a book which has one motif, but plays that motif in many different keys. The motif is the 'spirit of divine discontent and longing . . . .' " In "The Open Road," Ratty and Mole long for a life of adventure and go with Toad in his Gypsy Cart. Toad himself longs for speed and progress. Critic Peter Green writes, "Into that chapter Grahame packed a whole social revolution, focused and scaled down into an episode at once fabulous and familiar." The progress of the city intrudes into the pastoral countryside of the three animals in the form of a motorcar—a social revolution has occurred.*

'Ratty,' said the Mole suddenly, one bright summer morning, 'if you please, I want to ask you a favour.'

The Rat was sitting on the river bank, singing a little song. He had just composed it himself, so he was very taken up with it, and would not pay proper attention to Mole or anything else. Since early morning he had been swimming in the river, in company with his friends the ducks. And when the ducks stood on their heads suddenly, as ducks will, he would dive down and tickle their necks, just under where their chins would be if ducks had chins, till they were forced to come to the surface again in a hur-ry, spluttering and angry and shaking their feathers at him. For it is impossible to say quite *all* you feel when your head is under water. At last they implored him to go away and attend to his own affairs and leave them to mind theirs. So the Rat went away, and sat on the river bank in the sun, and made up a song about them, which he called

From Kenneth Grahame, *The Wind in the Willows* (New York: Avon Books, 1965).

DUCKS' DITTY

All along the backwater,
Through the rushes tall,
Ducks are a-dabbling,
Up tails all!

Ducks' tails, drakes' tails,
Yellow feet a-quiver,
Yellow bills all out of sight
Busy in the river!

Slushy green undergrowth
Where the roach swim—
Here we keep our larder,
Cool and full and dim.

Everyone for what he likes!
We like to be
Heads down, tails up,
Dabbling free!

High in the blue above
Swifts whirl and call—
We are down a-dabbling
Up tails all!

'I don't know that I think so *very* much of that little song, Rat,' observed the Mole cautiously. He was no poet himself and didn't care who knew it; and he had a candid nature.

'Nor don't the ducks neither,' replied the Rat cheerfully. 'They say, "*Why* can't fellows be allowed to do what they like *when* they like and *as* they like, instead of other fellows sitting on banks and watching them all the time and making remarks and poetry and things about them? What *nonsense* it all is!" That's what the ducks say.'

'So it is, so it is,' said the Mole, with great heartiness.

'No, it isn't!' cried the Rat indignantly.

'Well then, it isn't, it isn't,' replied the Mole soothingly. 'But what I wanted to ask you was, won't you take me to call on Mr. Toad? I've heard so much about him, and I do so want to make his acquaintance.'

'Why, certainly,' said the good-natured Rat, jumping to his feet and dismissing poetry from his mind for the day. 'Get the boat out, and we'll paddle up there at once. It's never the wrong time to call on Toad. Early or late he's always the same fellow. Always good-tempered, always glad to see you, always sorry when you go!'

'He must be a very nice animal,' observed the Mole, as he got into the boat and took the sculls, while the Rat settled himself comfortably in the stern.

'He is indeed the best of animals,' replied Rat. 'So simple, so good-natured, and so affectionate. Perhaps he's not very clever—we can't all be geniuses; and it may be that he is both boastful and conceited. But he has got some great qualities, has Toady.'

Rounding a bend in the river, they came in sight of a handsome, dignified old house of mellowed red brick, with well-kept lawns reaching down to the water's edge.

'There's Toad Hall,' said the Rat; 'and that creek on the left, where the notice-board says, "Private. No landing allowed," leads to his boat-house, where we'll leave the boat. The stables are over there to the right. That's the banqueting-hall you're looking at now—very old, that is. Toad is rather rich, you know, and this is really one of the nicest houses in these parts, though we never admit as much to Toad.'

They glided up the creek, and the Mole shipped his sculls as they passed into the shadow of a large boat-house. Here they saw many handsome boats, slung from the crossbeams or hauled up on a slip, but none in the water; and the place had an unused and a deserted air.

The Rat looked around him. 'I understand,' said he. 'Boating is played out. He's tired of it, and done with it. I wonder what new fad he has taken up now? Come along and let's look him up. We shall hear all about it quite soon enough.'

They disembarked, and strolled across the gay flower-decked lawns in search of Toad, whom they presently happened upon resting in a wicker garden-chair, with a pre-occupied expression of face, and a large map spread out on his knees.

'Hooray!' he cried, jumping up on seeing them, 'this is splendid!' He shook the paws of both of them, warmly, never waiting for an introduction to the Mole. 'How *kind* of you!' he went on, dancing round them. 'I was just going to send a boat down the river for you, Ratty, with strict orders that you were to be fetched up here at once, whatever you were doing. I want you badly—both of you. Now what will you take? Come inside and have something! You don't know how lucky it is, your turning up just now!'

'Let's sit quiet a bit, Toady!' said the Rat, throwing himself into an easy chair, while the Mole took another by the side of him and made some civil remark about Toad's 'delightful residence.'

'Finest house on the whole river,' cried Toad boisterously. 'Or anywhere else, for that matter,' he could not help adding.

Here the Rat nudged the Mole. Unfortunately the Toad saw him do it, and turned very red. There was a moment's painful silence. Then Toad burst out laughing. 'All right, Ratty,' he said. 'It's only my way, you know. And it's not such a very bad house, is it? You know you rather like it yourself. Now, look here. Let's be sensible. You are the very animals I wanted. You've got to help me. It's most important!'

'It's about your rowing, I suppose,' said the Rat, with an innocent air. 'You're getting on fairly well, though you splash a good bit still. With a great deal of patience, and any quantity of coaching, you may—'

'O, pooh! boating!' interrupted the Toad, in great 'disgust. 'Silly boyish amusement. I've given that up *long* ago. Sheer waste of time, that's what it is. It makes me downright sorry to see you fellows, who ought to know better, spending all your energies in that aimless manner. No, I've discovered the real thing, the only genuine occupation for a lifetime. I propose to devote the remainder of mine to it, and can only regret the wasted years that lie behind me, squandered in trivialities. Come with me, dear Ratty, and your amiable friend also, if he will be so very good, just as far as the stable-yard, and you shall see what you shall see!'

He led the way to the stable-yard accordingly, the Rat following with a most mistrustful expression; and there, drawn out of the coach-house into the open, they saw a gipsy caravan, shining with newness, painted a canary-yellow picked out with green, and red wheels.

'There you are!' cried the Toad, straddling and expanding himself. 'There's real life for you, embodied in that little cart. The open road, the dusty highway, the heath, the common, the hedgerows, the rolling downs! Camps, villages, towns, cities! Here to-day, up and off to somewhere else to-morrow! Travel, change, interest, excitement! The whole world before you, and a horizon that's always changing! And mind! this is the very finest cart of its sort that was ever built, without any exception. Come inside and look at the arrangements. Planned 'em all myself, I did!'

The Mole was tremendously interested and excited, and followed him eagerly up the steps and into the interior of the caravan. The Rat only snorted and thrust his hands deep into his pockets, remaining where he was.

It was indeed very compact and comfortable. Little sleeping bunks—a little table that folded up against the wall—a cooking-stove, lockers, bookshelves, a bird-cage with a bird in it; and pots, pans, jugs and kettles of every size and variety.

'All complete!' said the Toad triumphantly, pulling open a locker. 'You see—biscuits, potted lobster, sardines—everything you can possibly want. Soda-water here—baccy there—letter-paper, bacon, jam, cards and dominoes—you'll find,' he continued, as they descended the steps again, 'you'll find that nothing whatever has been forgotten, when we make our start this afternoon.'

'I beg your pardon,' said the Rat slowly, as he chewed a straw, 'but did I overhear you say something about "*we*," and "*start*," and "*this afternoon*"?'

'Now, you dear good old Ratty,' said Toad, imploringly, 'don't begin talking in that stiff and sniffy sort of way, because you know you've *got* to come. I can't possibly manage without you, so please consider it settled, and don't argue—it's the one thing I can't stand. You surely don't mean to stick to your dull fusty old river all your life, and just live in a hole in a bank, and *boat*? I want to show you the world! I'm going to make an *animal* of you, my boy!'

'I don't care,' said the Rat, doggedly. 'I'm

not coming, and that's flat. And I *am* going to stick to my old river, *and* live in a hole, *and* boat, as I've always done. And what's more, Mole's going to stick to me and do as I do, aren't you, Mole?'

'Of course I am,' said the Mole, loyally. 'I'll always stick to you, Rat, and what you say is to be—has got to be. All the same, it sounds as if it might have been—well, rather fun, you know!' he added, wistfully. Poor Mole! The Life Adventurous was so new a thing to him, and so thrilling; and this fresh aspect of it was so tempting; and he had fallen in love at first sight with the canary-coloured cart and all its little fitments.

The Rat saw what was passing in his mind, and wavered. He hated disappointing people, and he was fond of the Mole, and would do almost anything to oblige him. Toad was watching both of them closely.

'Come along in, and have some lunch,' he said, diplomatically, 'and we'll talk it over. We needn't decide anything in a hurry. Of course, *I* don't really care. I only want to give pleasure to you fellows. "Live for others!" That's my motto in life.'

During luncheon—which was excellent, of course, as everything at Toad Hall always was— the Toad simply let himself go. Disregarding the Rat, he proceded to play upon the inexperienced Mole as on a harp. Naturally a voluble animal, and always mastered by his imagination, he painted the prospects of the trip and the joys of the open life and the roadside in such glowing colours that the Mole could hardly sit in his chair for excitement. Somehow, it soon seemed taken for granted by all three of them that the trip was a settled thing; and the Rat, though still unconvinced in his mind, allowed his good-nature to over-ride his personal objections. He could not bear to disappoint his two friends, who were already deep in schemes and anticipations, planning out each day's separate occupation for several weeks ahead.

When they were quite ready, the now triumphant Toad led his companions to the paddock and set them to capture the old grey horse, who, without having been consulted, and to his own extreme annoyance, had been told off by Toad for the dustiest job in this dusty expedition. He frankly preferred the paddock, and took a deal of catching. Meantime Toad packed the lockers still tighter with necessaries, and hung nosebags, nets of onions, bundles of hay, and baskets from the bottom of the cart. At last the horse was caught and harnessed, and they set off, all talking at once, each animal either trudging by the side of the cart or sitting on the shaft, as the humour took him. It was a golden afternoon. The smell of the dust they kicked up was rich and satisfying; out of thick orchards on either side the road, birds called and whistled to them cheerily; good-natured wayfarers, passing them, gave them 'Goodday,' or stopped to say nice things about their beautiful cart; and rabbits, sitting at their front doors in the hedgerows, held up their forepaws, and said, 'O my! O my! O my!'

Late in the evening, tired and happy and miles from home, they drew up on a remote common far from habitation, turned the horse loose to graze, and ate their simple supper sitting on the grass by the side of the cart. Toad talked big about all he was going to do in the days to come, while stars grew fuller and larger all around them, and a yellow moon, appearing suddenly and silently from nowhere in particular, came to keep them company and listen to their talk. At last they turned in to their little bunks in the cart; and Toad, kicking out his legs, sleepily said, 'Well, good night, you fellows! This is the real life for a gentleman! Talk about your old river!'

'I *don't* talk about my river,' replied the patient Rat. 'You *know* I don't, Toad. But I *think* about it,' he added pathetically, in a lower tone: 'I think about it—all the time!'

The Mole reached out from under his blanket, felt the Rat's paw in the darkness, and gave it a squeeze. "I'll do whatever you like, Ratty,' he whispered. 'Shall we run away to-morrow morning, quite early—*very* early—and go back to our dear old hole on the river?'

'No, no, we'll see it out,'' whispered back the Rat. 'Thanks awfully, but I ought to stick by Toad till this trip is ended. It wouldn't be safe for him to be left to himself. It won't take very long. His fads never do. Good night!'

The end was indeed nearer than the Rat suspected.

After so much open air and excitement the Toad slept very soundly, and no amount of shaking could rouse him out of bed next morning. So the Mole and Rat turned to, quietly and manfully, and while the Rat saw to the horse, and lit a fire, and cleaned last night's cups and platters, and got things ready for breakfast, the Mole trudged off to the nearest village, a long way off, for milk and eggs and various necessaries the Toad had, of course, forgotten to provide. The hard work had all been done, and the two animals were resting, thoroughly exhausted, by the time Toad appeared on the scene, fresh and gay, remarking what a pleasant easy life it was they were all leading now, after the cares and worries and fatigues of housekeeping at home.

They had a pleasant ramble that day over grassy downs and along narrow by-lanes, and camped as before, on a common, only this time the two guests took care that Toad should do his fair share of work. In consequence, when the time came for starting next morning, Toad was by no means so rapturous about the simplicity of the primitive life, and indeed attempted to resume his place in his bunk, whence he was hauled by force. Their way lay, as before, across country by narrow lanes, and it was not till the afternoon that they came out on the high-road, their first high-road; and there disaster, fleet and unforeseen, sprang out on them— disaster momentous indeed to their expedition, but simply overwhelming in its effect on the after-career of Toad.

They were strolling along the high-road easily, the Mole by the horse's head, talking to him, since the horse had complained that he was being frightfully left out of it, and nobody considered him in the least; the Toad and the Water Rat walking behind the cart talking together—at least Toad was talking, and Rat was saying at intervals, 'Yes, precisely; and what did *you* say to *him?*'—and thinking all the time of something very different, when far behind them they heard a faint warning hum, like the drone of a distant bee. Glancing back, they saw a small cloud of dust, with a dark centre of energy, advancing on them at incredible speed, while from out the dust a faint 'Poop-poop!' wailed like an uneasy animal in pain. Hardly regarding it, they turned to resume their conversation, when in an instant (as it seemed) the peaceful scene was changed, and with a blast of wind and a whirl of sound that made them jump for the nearest ditch, It was on them! The 'Poop-poop' rang with a brazen shout in their ears, they had a moment's glimpse of an interior of glittering plate-glass and rich morocco and the magnificent *motorcar*, immense, breath-snatching, passionate, with its pilot tense and hugging his wheel, possessed all earth and air for the fraction of a second, flung an enveloping cloud of dust that blinded and enwrapped them utterly, and then dwindled to a speck in the far distance, changed back into a droning bee once more.

The old grey horse, dreaming, as he plodded along, of his quiet paddock, in a new raw situation such as this simply abandoned himself to his natural emotions. Rearing, plunging, backing steadily, in spite of all the Mole's efforts at his head, and all the Mole's lively language directed at his better feelings, he drove the cart backwards towards the deep ditch at the side of the road. It wavered an instant—then there was a heartrending crash—and the canary-coloured cart, their pride and their joy, lay on its side in the ditch, an irredeemable wreck.

The Rat danced up and down in the road, simply transported with passion. 'You villains!' he shouted, shaking both fists, 'You scoundrels, you highwaymen, you—you— roadhogs!—I'll have the law on you! I'll report you! I'll take you through all the Courts!' His home-sickness had quite slipped away from him, and for the moment he was the skipper of a canary-coloured vessel driven on a shoal by the reckless jockeying of rival mariners, and he was trying to recollect all the fine and biting things he used to say to masters of steam-launches when their wash, as they drove too near the bank, used to flood his parlour-carpet at home.

Toad sat straight down in the middle of the dusty road, his legs stretched out before him, and stared fixedly in the direction of the disappearing motorcar. He breathed short, his face wore a placid satisfied expression, and at intervals he faintly murmured 'Poop-poop!'

The Mole was busy trying to quiet the horse, which he succeeded in doing after a time. Then he went to look at the cart, on its side in the ditch. It was indeed a sorry sight. Panels and windows mashed, axles hopelessly bent, one wheel off, sardine-tins scattered over the wide world, and the bird in the bird-cage sobbing pitifully and calling to be let out.

The Rat came to help him, but their united efforts were not sufficient to right the cart. 'Hi! Toad!' they cried. 'Come and bear a hand, can't you!'

The Toad never answered a word, or budged from his seat in the road; so they went to see what was the matter with him. They found him in a sort of a trance, a happy smile on his face, his eyes still fixed on the dusty wake of their destroyer. At intervals he was still heard to murmer 'Poop-poop!'

The Rat shook him by the shoulder. 'Are you coming to help us, Toad?' he demanded sternly.

'Glorious, stirring sight!' murmured Toad, never offering to move. 'The poetry of motion! The *real* way to travel! The *only* way to travel! Here to-day—in next week tomorrow! Villages skipped, towns and cities jumped—always somebody else's horizon! O bliss! O poop-poop! O my! O my!'

'O *stop* being an ass, Toad!' cried the Mole despairingly.

'And to think I never *knew!*' went on the Toad in a dreamy monotone. 'All those wasted years that lie behind me, I never knew, never even *dreamt!* But *now*—but now that I know, now that I fully realise! O what a flowery track lies spread before me, henceforth! What dust-clouds shall spring up behind me as I speed on my reckless way! What carts I shall fling carelessly into the ditch in the wake of my magnificent onset! Horrid little carts—common carts—canary-coloured carts!'

'What are we to do with him?' asked the Mole of the Water Rat.

'Nothing at all,' replied the Rat firmly.

'Because there is really nothing to be done. You see, I know him from of old. He is now possessed. He has got a new craze, and it always takes him that way, in its first stage. He'll continue like that for days now, like an animal walking in a happy dream, quite useless for all practical purposes. Never mind him. Let's go and see what there is to be done about the cart.'

A careful inspection showed them that, even if they succeeded in righting it by themselves, the cart would travel no longer. The axles were in a hopeless state, and the missing wheel was shattered into pieces.

The Rat knotted the horse's reins over his back and took him by the head, carrying the bird-cage and its hysterical occupant in the other hand. 'Come on!' he said grimly to the Mole. 'It's five or six miles to the nearest town, and we shall just have to walk it. The sooner we make the start the better.'

'But what about Toad?' asked the Mole anxiously, as they set off together. 'We can't leave him here, sitting in the middle of the road by himself, in the distracted state he's in! It's not safe. Supposing another Thing were to come along?'

'O, *bother* Toad,' said the Rat savagely; 'I've done with him!'

They had not proceeded very far on their way, however, when there was a pattering of feet behind them, and Toad caught them up and thrust a paw inside the elbow of each of them; still breathing short and staring into vacancy.

'Now, look here, Toad!' said the Rat sharply: 'as soon as we get to the town, you'll have to go straight to the police-station, and see if they know anything about that motor-car and who it belongs to, and lodge a complaint against it. And then you'll have to go to a blacksmith's or a wheelwright's and arrange for the cart to be fetched and mended and put to rights. It'll take time, but it's not quite a hopeless smash. Meanwhile, the Mole and I will go to an inn and find *comfortable* rooms where we can stay till the cart's ready, and till your nerves have recovered their shock.'

'Police-station! Complaint!' murmured Toad dreamily. 'Me *complain* of that beautiful, that heavenly vision that has been vouch-safed me! *Mend* the *cart!* I've done with carts for ever. I never want to see the cart, or to hear of it, again. O, Ratty! You can't think how obliged I am to you for consenting to come on this trip! I wouldn't have gone without you, and then I might never have seen that—that swan, that sunbeam, that thunderbolt! I might never have heard that entrancing sound, or smelt that bewitching smell! I owe it all to you, my best of friends!'

The Rat turned from him in despair. 'You see what it is?' he said to the Mole, address-ing him across Toad's head: 'He's quite hopeless. I give it up—when we get to the town we'll go to the railway station, and with luck we may pick up a train there that'll get us back to River Bank to-night. And if ever you catch me going a-pleasuring with this provoking animal again!'—He snorted, and during the rest of that weary trudge ad-dressed his remarks exclusively to Mole.

On reaching the town they went straight to the station and deposited Toad in the second-class waiting-room, giving a porter twopence to keep a strict eye on him. They then left the horse at an inn stable, and gave what directions they could about the cart and its contents. Eventually, a slow train having landed them at a station not very far from Toad Hall, they escorted the spell-bound, sleep-walking Toad to his door, put him in-side it, and instructed his housekeeper to feed him, undress him, and put him to bed. Then they got out their boat from the boat-house, sculled down the river home, and at a very late hour sat down to supper in their own cosy riverside parlour, to the Rat's great joy and contentment.

The following evening the Mole, who had risen late and taken things very easy all day, was sitting on the bank fishing, when the Rat, who had been looking up his friends and gossiping, came strolling along to find him. 'Heard the news?' he said. 'There's nothing else being talked about, all along the river bank. Toad went up to Town by an early train this morning. And he has ordered a large and very expensive motor-car.'

PICTURE BOOK

The Magic Fishbone

Charles Dickens
Illustrated by Hilary Knight

Picture books provide visual storytelling for the child who is too young to read and enhancement of the tale for the child who can read. When children set out to explore the world, picture books show them places near and far. Picture books

From Charles Dickens, *The Magic Fishbone* (1874). Illustrated by Hilary Knight, 1964.

enable children to travel immense distances without moving a step, to learn about
the world and appreciate it through the eyes of people (authors and artists) who
are familiar with it.

Charles Dickens (1812–1870), whom many critics regard as the greatest of
English writers, knew the bustling, busy London of the nineteenth century and
used it as the setting for many of his tales. In The Magic Fishbone, *Dickens's*
London provides the setting for a tale designed to delight children of all ages.
Dickens never forgot the time when his father was jailed for being in debt.
Although Charles was only 10 years old, he had to go to work to help his family.
That experience is reflected in The Magic Fishbone *and in many of Dickens's*
novels. The Magic Fishbone *tells a story about a "royal" family very much like*
Dickens's own, using a setting—the city—that is still familiar to us.

The accompanying illustrations, by Hilary Knight, have the same sprightliness
that Dickens communicates through his tale. These pictures reflect the gaiety and
ebullience readers have seen in Hilary Knight's illustrations in his five Eloise
books and many other picture books.

There was once a King, and he had a Queen; and he was the manliest of his sex, and she was the loveliest of hers. The King was, in his private profession, Under Government. The Queen's father had been a medical man out of town.

They had nineteen children, and were always having more. Seventeen of these children took care of the baby; and Alicia, the eldest, took care of them all. Their ages varied from seven years to seven months.

Let us now resume our story.

One day the King was going to the office, when he stopped at the fishmonger's to buy a pound and a half of salmon not too near the tail, which the Queen (who was a careful housekeeper) had requested him to send home. Mr. Pickles, the fishmonger, said, "Certainly, sir, is there any other article? Good morning."

The King went on towards the office in a melancholy mood, for quarter day was such a long way off, and several of the dear children were growing out of their clothes. He had not proceeded far, when Mr. Pickle's errand boy came running after him, and said, "Sir, you didn't notice the old lady in our shop."

"What old lady?" enquired the King. "I saw none."

Now, the King had not seen any old lady, because this old lady had been invisible to him, though visible to Mr. Pickles's boy.

Probably because he messed and splashed the water about to that degree, and flopped the pairs of soles down in that violent manner, that if she had not been visible to him, he would have spoilt her clothes.

Just then the old lady came trotting up. She was dressed in shot silk of the richest quality, smelling of dried lavender.

"King Watkins the First, I believe?" said the old lady.

"Watkins," replied the King, "is my name."

"Papa, if I am not mistaken, of the beautiful Princess Alicia?" said the old lady.

"And of eighteen other darlings," replied the King.

"Listen. You are going to the office," said the old lady.

It instantly flashed upon the King that she must be a Fairy, or how could she know that?

"You are right," said the old lady, answering his thoughts, "I am the Good Fairy Grandmarina. Attend. When you return home to dinner, politely invite the Princess Alicia to have some of the salmon you bought just now."

"It may disagree with her," said the King.

The old lady became so very angry at this absurd idea, that the King was quite alarmed, and humbly begged her pardon.

"We hear a great deal too much about this thing disagreeing, and that thing disagreeing," said the old lady, with the greatest contempt it was possible to express. "Don't be greedy. I think you want it all yourself."

The King hung his head under this reproof, and said he wouldn't talk about things disagreeing any more.

"Be good, then," said the Fairy Grandmarina, "and don't! When the beautiful Princess Alicia consents to partake of the salmon—as I think she will—you will find she will leave a fishbone on her plate. Tell her to dry it, and to rub it, and to polish it till it shines like mother-of-pearl, and to take care of it as a present from me."

"Is that all?" asked the King.

"Don't be impatient, sir," returned the Fairy Grandmarina, scolding him severely. "Don't catch people short, before they have done speaking. Just the way with you grown-up persons. You are always doing it."

The King again hung his head, and said he wouldn't do so any more.

"Be good then," said the Fairy Grandmarina, "and don't! Tell the Princess Alicia, with my love, that the fishbone is a magic present which can only be used once; but that it will bring her, that once, whatever she wishes for, PROVIDED SHE WISHES FOR IT AT THE RIGHT TIME. That is the message. Take care of it."

The King was beginning, "Might I ask the reason—?" when the Fairy became absolutely furious.

"*Will* you be good, sir?" she exclaimed, stamping her foot on the ground. "The reason for this, and the reason for that, indeed! You are always wanting the reason. No reason. There! Hoity toity me! I am sick of your grown-up reasons."

The King was extremely frightened by the old lady's flying into such a passion, and said he was very sorry to have offended her, and he wouldn't ask for reasons any more.

"Be good then," said the old lady, "and don't!"

With those words Grandmarina vanished, and the King went on and on and on, till he came to the office. There he wrote and wrote and wrote, till it was time to go home again. Then he politely invited the Princess Alicia, as the Fairy had directed him, to partake of the salmon. And when she had enjoyed it very much, he saw the fishbone on her plate, as the Fairy had told him he would, and he delivered the Fairy's message, and the Princess Alicia took care to dry the bone, and to rub it, and to polish it till it shone like mother-of-pearl.

And so when the Queen was going to get up in the morning, she said, "O, dear me, dear me; my head, my head!" and then she fainted away.

The Princess Alicia, who happened to be looking in at the chamber door, asking about breakfast, was very much alarmed when she saw her Royal Mama in this state, and she rang the bell for Peggy, which was the name of the Lord Chamberlain. But remembering where the smelling bottle was, she climbed on a chair and got it, and after that she climbed on another chair by the bedside and held the smelling bottle to the Queen's nose, and after that she jumped down and got some water, and after that she jumped up again and wetted the Queen's forehead, and, in short, when the Lord Chamberlain came in, that dear old woman said to the little Princess, "What a Trot you are! I couldn't have done it better myself!"

But that was not the worst of the good Queen's illness. O, no! She was very ill indeed, for a long time.

The Princess Alicia kept the seventeen young Princes and Princesses quiet, and dressed and undressed and danced the baby, and made the kettle boil, and heated the soup, and swept the hearth, and poured out the medicine, and nursed the Queen, and did all that ever she could, and was as busy busy busy, as busy could be. For there were not many servants at that Palace, for three reasons; because the King was short of money, because a rise in his office never seemed to come, and because quarter day was so far off that it looked almost as far off and as little as one of the stars.

But on the morning when the Queen fainted away, where was the magic fishbone?

Why, there it was in the Princess Alicia's pocket. She had almost taken it out to bring the Queen to life again, when she put it back, and looked for the smelling bottle.

After the Queen had come out of her swoon that morning, and was dozing, the Princess Alicia hurried upstairs to tell a most particular secret to a most particularly confidential friend of hers, who was a Duchess. People did suppose her to be a Doll; but she was really a Duchess, though nobody knew it except the Princess.

This most particular secret was a secret about the magic fishbone, the history of which was well known to the Duchess, because the Princess told her everything. The Princess kneeled down by the bed on which the Duchess was lying, full-dressed and wide-awake, and whispered the secret to her. The Duchess smiled and nodded. People might have supposed that she never smiled and nodded, but she often did, though nobody knew it except the Princess.

Then the Princess Alicia hurried downstairs again, to keep watch in the Queen's room. She often kept watch by herself in the Queen's room; but every evening, while the illness lasted, she sat there watching with the King. And every evening the King sat looking at her with a cross look, wondering why she never brought out the magic fishbone. As often as she noticed this, she ran upstairs, whispered the secret to the Duchess over again, and said to the Duchess besides, "They think we children never have a reason or a meaning!"

And the Duchess, though the most fashionable Duchess that ever was heard of, winked her eye.

"Alicia," said the King, one evening when she wished him good night.

"Yes, Papa."

"What is become of the magic fishbone?"

"In my pocket, Papa."

"I thought you had lost it?"

"O, no, Papa."

"Or forgotten it?"

"No, indeed, Papa."

And so another time the dreadful little snapping pug-dog next door made a rush at one of the young Princes as he stood on the steps coming home from school, and terrified him out of his wits, and he put his hand through a pane of glass, and bled bled bled. When the seventeen other young Princes and Princesses saw him bleed bleed bleed, they were terrified out of their wits too, and screamed themselves black in their seventeen faces all at once.

But the Princess Alicia put her hands over all their seventeen mouths, one after another, and persuaded them to be quiet because of the sick Queen. And then she put the wounded Prince's hand in a basin of fresh cold water, while they stared with their twice seventeen are thirty-four put down four and carry three eyes, and then she looked in the hand for bits of glass, and there were fortunately no bits of glass there. And then she said to two chubby-legged Princes who were sturdy though small, "Bring me in the Royal rag bag; I must snip and stitch and cut and contrive."

So those two young Princes tugged at the Royal rag bag and lugged it in, and the Princess Alicia sat down on the floor with a large pair of scissors and a needle and thread, and snipped and stitched and cut and contrived, and made a bandage and put it on, and it fitted beautifully, and so when it was all done she saw the King her Papa looking on by the door.

"Alicia."

"Yes, Papa."

"What have you been doing?"

"Snipping stitching cutting and contriving, Papa."

"Where is the magic fishbone?"

"In my pocket, Papa."

"I thought you had lost it?"

"O, no, Papa."

"Or forgotten it?"

"No, indeed, Papa."

After that, she ran upstairs to the Duchess and told her what had passed, and told her the secret over again, and the Duchess shook her flaxen curls and laughed with her rosy lips.

Well! and so another time the baby fell under the grate. The seventeen young Princes and Princesses were used to it, for they were almost always falling under the grate or down the stairs, but the baby was not used to it yet, and it gave him a swelled face and a black eye. The way the poor little darling came to tumble was that he slid out of the Princess Alicia's lap just as she was sitting in a great coarse apron that quite smothered her, in front of the kitchen fire, beginning to peel the turnips for the broth for dinner; and the way she came to be doing that was that the King's cook had run away that morning with her own true love, who was a very tall but very tipsy soldier.

Then the seventeen young Princes and Princesses, who cried at everything that happened, cried and roared. But the Princess Alicia (who couldn't help crying a little herself) quietly called to them to be still, on account of not throwing back the Queen upstairs, who was fast getting well, and said, "Hold your tongues, you wicked little monkeys, every one of you, while I examine baby!" Then she examined baby, and found that he hadn't broken anything, and she held cold iron to his poor dear eye, and smoothed his poor dear face, and he presently fell asleep in her arms.

Then she said to the seventeen Princes and Princesses, "I am afraid to lay him down yet, lest he should wake and feel pain. Be good, and you shall all be cooks." They jumped for joy when they heard that, and began making themselves cooks' caps out of old newspapers.

So to one she gave the salt box, and to one she gave the barley, and to one she gave the herbs, and to one she gave the turnips, and to one she gave the carrots, and to one she gave the onions, and to one she gave the spice box, till they were all cooks, and all running about at work, she sitting in the middle smothered in the great coarse apron, nursing baby.

By and by the broth was done, and the baby woke up smiling like an angel, and was trusted to the sedatest Princess to hold, while the other Princes and Princesses were squeezed into a far-off corner to look at the Princess Alicia turning out the saucepanful of broth, for fear (as they were always getting into trouble) they should get splashed and scalded.

When the broth came tumbling out, steaming beautifully, and smelling like a nosegay

good to eat, they clapped their hands. That made the baby clap his hands; and that, and his looking as if he had a comic toothache, made all the Princes and Princesses laugh.

So the Princess Alicia said, "Laugh and be good, and after dinner we will make him a nest on the floor in a corner, and he shall sit in his nest and see a dance of eighteen cooks."

That delighted the young Princes and Princesses, and they ate up all the broth, and washed up all the plates and dishes, and cleared away, and pushed the table into a corner, and then they in their cooks' caps, and the Princess Alicia in the smothering coarse apron that belonged to the cook that had run away with her own true love that was the very tall but very tipsy soldier, danced a dance of eighteen cooks before the angelic baby, who forgot his swelled face and his black eye, and crowed with joy.

And so then, once more, the Princess Alicia saw King Watkins the First, her father, standing in the doorway looking on, and he said: "What have you been doing, Alicia?"

"Cooking and contriving, Papa."

"What else have you been doing, Alicia?"

"Keeping the children lighthearted, Papa."

"Where is the magic fishbone, Alicia?"

"In my pocket, Papa."

"I thought you had lost it?"

"O, no, Papa."

"Or forgotten it?"

"No, indeed, Papa."

The King then sighed so heavily, and seemed so low-spirited, and sat down so miserably, leaning his head upon his hand, and his elbow upon the kitchen table pushed away in the corner, that the seventeen Princes and Princesses crept softly out of the kitchen, and left him alone with the Princess Alicia and the angelic baby.

"What is the matter, Papa?"

"I am dreadfully poor, my child."

"Have you no money at all, Papa?"

"None, my child."

"Is there no way left of getting any, Papa?"

"No way," said the King. "I have tried very hard, and I have tried all ways."

When she heard those last words, the Princess Alicia began to put her hand into the pocket where she kept the magic fishbone.

"Papa," said she, "when we have tried very hard, and tried all ways, we must have done our very very best?"

"No doubt, Alicia."

"When we have done our very very best, Papa, and that is not enough, then I think the right time must have come for asking help of others." This was the very secret connected with the magic fishbone, which she had found out for herself from the Good Fairy Grandmarina's words, and which she had so often whispered to her beautiful and fashionable friend the Duchess.

So she took out of her pocket the magic fishbone that had been dried and rubbed and polished till it shone like mother-of-pearl; and she gave it one little kiss and wished it was quarter day. And immediately it *was* quarter day; and the King's quarter's salary came rattling down the chimney, and bounced into the middle of the floor.

But this was not half of what happened, no not a quarter, for immediately afterwards the Good Fairy Grandmarina came riding in, in a carriage and four (Peacocks), with Mr. Pickles's boy up behind, dressed in silver and gold, with a cocked hat, powdered hair, pink silk stockings, a jeweled cane, and a nosegay. Down jumped Mr. Pickles's boy with his cocked hat in his hand and wonderfully polite (being entirely changed by enchantment), and handed Grandmarina out, and there she stood in her rich shot silk smelling of dried lavender, fanning herself with a sparkling fan.

"Alicia, my dear," said this charming old Fairy, "how do you do, I hope I see you pretty well, give me a kiss."

The Princess Alicia embraced her, and then Grandmarina turned to the King, and said rather sharply—"Are you good?"

The King said he hoped so.

"I suppose you know the reason, *now*, why my goddaughter here," kissing the Princess again, "did not apply to the fishbone sooner?" said the Fairy.

The King made her a shy bow.

"Ah! but you didn't *then!*" said the Fairy.

The King made her a shyer bow.

"Any more reasons to ask for?" said the Fairy.

The King said no, and he was very sorry.

"Be good then," said the Fairy, "and live happy ever afterwards."

Then Grandmarina waved her fan, and the Queen came in most splendidly dressed, and the seventeen young Princes and Princesses, no longer grown out of their clothes, came in newly fitted out from top to toe, with tucks in everything to admit of its being let out. After that, the Fairy tapped the Princess Alicia with her fan, and the smothering coarse apron flew away, and she appeared exquisitely dressed, like a little Bride, with a wreath of orange flowers and a silver veil. After that, the kitchen dresser changed of itself into a wardrobe, made of beautiful woods and gold and looking glass, which was full of dresses of all sorts, all for her and all exactly fitting her. After that, the angelic baby came in, running alone, with his face and eye not a bit the worse but much the better. Then Grandmarina begged to be introduced to the Duchess, and when the Duchess was brought down many compliments passed between them.

A little whispering took place between the Fairy and the Duchess, and then the Fairy said out loud, "Yes. I thought she would have told you." Grandmarina then turned to the King and Queen, and said, "We are going in search of Prince Certainpersonio. The pleasure of your company is requested at church in half an hour precisely." So she and the Princess Alicia got into the carriage, and Mr. Pickles's boy handed in the duchess who sat by herself on the opposite seat, and then Mr. Pickle's boy put up the steps and got up behind, and the Peacocks flew away with their tails spread.

Prince Certainpersonio was sitting by himself, eating barley sugar and waiting to be ninety.

When he saw the Peacocks followed by the carriage, coming in at the window, it immediately occurred to him that something uncommon was going to happen.

"Prince," said Grandmarina, "I bring you your Bride."

The moment the Fairy said those words, Prince Certainpersonio's face left off being sticky, and his jacket and corduroys changed to peachbloom velvet, and his hair curled, and a cap and feather flew in like a bird and settled on his head. He got into the carriage by the Fairy's invitation, and there he renewed his acquaintance with the Duchess, whom he had seen before.

In the church were the Prince's relations and friends, and the Princess Alicia's relations and friends, and the seventeen Princes and Princesses, and the baby, and a crowd of the neighbors. The marriage was beautiful beyond expression.

The Duchess was bridesmaid, and beheld the ceremony from the pulpit where she was supported by the cushion of the desk.

Grandmarina gave a magnificent wedding feast afterwards, in which there was everything and more to eat, and everything and more to drink. The wedding cake was delicately ornamented with white satin ribbons, frosted silver and white lilies, and was forty-two yards round.

When Grandmarina had drunk her love to the young couple, and Prince Certainpersonio had made a speech, and everybody had

cried "Hip hip hip hurrah!" Grandmarina announced to the King and Queen that in the future there would be eight quarter days in every year, except in leap year, when there would be ten.

She then turned to Certainpersonio and Alicia, and said, "My dears, you will have thirty-five children, and they will all be good and beautiful. Seventeen of your children will be boys, and eighteen will be girls. The hair of the whole of your children will curl naturally. They will never have the measles, and will have recovered from the whooping cough before being born."

On hearing such good news, everybody cried out "Hip hip hip hurrah!" again.

"It only remains," said Grandmarina in conclusion, "to make an end of the fishbone."

So she took it from the hand of the Princess Alicia, and it instantly flew down the throat of the dreadful little snapping pug-dog next door and choked him, and he expired in convulsions.

Explorations

1. The fable form is characterized by its brevity, the frequent use of animals as characters, and the fact that the action of the story is intended to point out a moral. Using the fables of Aesop as models, write your own fable or adapt a fable into a play that children might act out.

2. "The City of Troy" and "The Founding of Mexico City" are only two of the many legends that deal with cities. There are numerous legends of "lost" cities. Working as a class or in groups, reconstruct a lost city on paper using legends and your imagination.

3. Many of the folk rhymes dealing with the city today emerge in the art of "rapping," heard on city streets and on records. Listen to a "rap" record, and compare the rhymes and the issues being expressed with those in traditional folk rhymes.

4. Construct a board game children could play using *From The Mixed-Up Files of Mrs. Basil E. Frankweiler*. The game could take the players from "home," into and through the Metropolitan Museum of Art, Mrs. Basil E. Frankweiler's house, and back home again.

5. The essence of Pastoral poetry is simplicity of thought and action in a rustic setting. Discuss the pastoral tradition and attempt a short pastoral poem of your own.

6. The trickster is a common figure in folktales. Compare and discuss the role of the trickster in ''The Shepherd at Court'' and in ''The Shepherd Who Laughed Last.''

7. Using the selections from *Farmer Boy* and *Stairstep Farm,* make a list of chores that might have to be done on a farm during a typical day and that children might act out to gain a sense of what daily farm life used to involve. One child, for example, could be assigned the task of pretending to chop wood while another pretended to bake bread. Explain how you might carry out such a project with children.

8. Animals play an important part in country life and in literature about the country. Explore the symbolism surrounding animals and whether this symbolism is used in any of the stories about the country included in this section of the book.

9. Most books and stories for children present a somewhat biased view of either the city or the country. Try writing a short picturebook, drawing on your own background, that does not present biases or stereotypes.

10. Using children's books, pictures, and records, assume the role of a tour guide and conduct a ''tour'' of your favorite city or area of the country.

11. Using *Farmer Boy* and *Stairstep Farm* as guides, cook a country dinner for a group or cook such a dinner as a class with each member bringing one item (no instant mashed potatoes!).

References for Children

Anderson, Margaret. *In the Circle of Time,* New York: Knopf, 1979.

Anno, Mitsumasa. *Anno's Flea Market,* New York: Philomel, 1983.

Ayme, Marcel. *The Wonderful Farm.* Translated by Norman Denny. Illustrated by Maurice Sendak. New York: Harper & Row, 1951.

Babbit, Natalie, *KneeKnock Rise.* New York: Farrar, Straus, & Giroux, 1970.

Baylor, Byrd. *Best Town in the World.* Illustrated by Ronald Himler. New York: Scribner, 1983.

Beatty, Patricia. *Jonathan Down Under* New York: Morrow, 1982.

Bond, Michael. *A Bear Called Paddington.* Illustrated by Peggy Fortnum. Boston: Houghton Mifflin, 1960.

Bonham, Frank. *Durango Street.* New York: Dutton, 1965.

Boston, Lucy Maria. *The River at Green Knowe.* Illustrated by Peter Boston. Orlando, Fla.: Harcourt Brace Jovanovich, 1959.

Brett, Jan. *Fritz and the Beautiful Horses.* Boston: Houghton Mifflin, 1981.

Burton, Virginia Lee. *Katy and the Big Snow.* Illustrated by the author. Boston: Houghton Mifflin, 1943.

Christopher, John. *The City of Gold and Lead.* New York: Macmillan, 1967.

Clark, Ann Nolan. *In My Mother's House.* Illustrated by Veleno Herrera. New York: Viking Press, 1941.

Clarke, Arthur. *Dolphin Island*. New York: Holt, Rinehart & Winston, 1963.

Clifton, Lucille. *Everett Anderson's Christmas Coming*. Illustrated by Evaline Ness. New York: Holt, Rinehart & Winston, 1971.

Climo, Lindee. *Chester's Barn*. Montreal: Tundra Books, 1982.

De Angeli, Marguerite. *Yoni Wondernose*. New York: Doubleday, 1944.

Dewey, Ariane. *Febold Feboldson*. New York: Greenwillow, 1983.

Dickens, Charles. *A Christmas Carol*. Illustrated by Arthur Rackham. Philadelphia: Lippincott, 1956.

Druon, Maurice. *Tistou of the Green Thumbs*. Illustrated by Jacqueline Duhemé. New York: Scribner, 1958.

Duvoisin, Roger. *Petunia*. New York: Knopf, 1950.

Ellis, Anne Leo. *Dabble Duck*. Illustrated by Sue Truesdell. New York: Harper & Row, 1984.

Fatio, Louise. *The Happy Lion*. Illustrated by Roger Duvoisin. New York: McGraw-Hill, 1954.

Fitzhugh, Louise. *Harriet the Spy*. New York: Harper & Row, 1964.

Flora, James. *Grandpa's Farm*. Orlando, Fla.: Harcourt Brace Jovanovich, 1965.

Freeman, Don. *Fly High, Fly Low*. New York: Viking Press, 1957.

Gates, Doris. *Blue Willow*. Illustrated by Paul Lantz. New York: Viking Press, 1945.

Gibbons, Gail. *Department Store*. New York: Crowell, 1983.

———. *Fire! Fire!* New York: Crowell, 1984.

———. *The Seasons of Arnold's Apple Tree*. Orlando, Fla.: Harcourt Brace Jovanovich, 1985.

Hamilton, Virginia. *Junius Over Far*. New York: Harper & Row, 1984.

Heinlein, Robert. *Farmer in the Sky*. New York: Scribner, 1950.

Herriot, James. *Moses the Kitten*. Illustrated by Peter Barrett. New York: St. Martin's Press, 1984.

Highwater, Jamake. *The Ceremony of Innocence*. New York: Harper & Row, 1984.

Johnston, Tony. *The Quilt Story*. Illustrated by Tomie dePaola. New York: Putnam, 1984.

Kaye, Marilyn. *Will You Cross Me?* Illustrated by Ned Delaney. New York: Harper & Row, 1984.

Keats, Ezra Jack. *Apt. 3*. New York: Macmillan, 1971.

Kilgore, Kathleen. *The Wolfman of Beacon Hill*. Boston: Little, Brown, 1982.

Kroll, Steven. *The Biggest Pumpkin Ever*. Illustrated by Jeni Bassett. New York: Holiday, 1984.

Lamorisse, Albert. *The Red Balloon*. Illustrated with color photographs from the film of the same name. New York: Doubleday, 1957.

Lampman, Evelyn Sibley. *The City under the Back Steps*. Illustrated by Honoré Valincourt. New York: Doubleday, 1960.

Lindgren, Astrid. *The Runaway Sleigh Ride*. Illustrated by Ilon Wikland. New York: Viking Press, 1983.

Lord, Betty Bao. *The Year of the Boar and Jackie Robinson*. Illustrated by Marc Simont. New York: Harper & Row, 1984.

Macaulay, David. *Unbuilding*. Boston: Houghton Mifflin, 1980.

McDermott, Gerald. *Daughter of Earth, a Roman Myth*. New York: Dell (Delacorte Press), 1982.

McKillip, Patricia. *Moon-Flash*. New York: Atheneum, 1985.

Martin, Charles E. *Island Winter*. New York: Greenwillow, 1983.

Mills, Claudia. *Luisa's American Dream*. New York: Four Winds, 1981.

Moore, Elaine. *Grandma's House*. Illustrated by Elize Primavena. New York: Lothrop, 1984.

Nesbit, E. *The Magic City*. New York: Dover, 1985.

Obrist, Judith. *Fluffy: The Story of a Cat*. New York: Atheneum, 1981.

Rounds, Glen. *The Morning the Sun Refused to Shine*. New York: Holiday, 1983.

Roy, Ron. *Three Ducks Went Wandering*. Illustrated by Paul Galdone. New York: Clarion, 1979.

Schaaf, Peter. *An Apartment House Close Up*. New York: Four Winds, 1980.

Selden, George. *The Cricket in Times Square*. Illustrated by Garth Williams. New York: Farrar, Straus & Giroux, 1960.

Sendak, Maurice. *In The Night Kitchen*. New York: Harper & Row, 1970.

Spier, Peter. *People*. New York: Doubleday, 1978.

Stolz, Mary. *A Wonderful, Terrible Time*. Illustrated by Louis S. Glanzman. New York: Harper & Row, 1967.

Schick, Eleanor, *City in the Winter*. New York: Macmillan, 1980.

Travers, Pamela L. *Mary Poppins*. Illustrated by Mary Shepard. Orlando, Fla.: Harcourt Brace Jovanovich, 1934.

Watson, Clyde. *Father Fox's Pennyrhymes*. Illustrated by Wendy Watson. New York: Crowell, 1971.

Weiman, Eileen. *Which Way Courage?* New York: Atheneum, 1981.

Weiss, Nicki. *Weekend at Muskrat Lake*. New York: Greenwillow, 1984.

White, E. B. *Charlotte's Web*. Illustrated by Garth Williams. New York: Harper & Row, 1952.

––––––. *Stuart Little*. Illustrated by Garth Williams. New York: Harper & Row, 1945.

Yeoman, John. *The Young Performing Horse*. Illustrated by Quentin Blake. New York: Parent's Magazine Press, 1979.

Yep, Laurence. *The Serpent's Children*. New York: Harper & Row, 1982.

References for Adults

Adams, Bess Porter. *About Books and Children: An Historical Survey of Children's Literature*. New York: Holt, Rinehart & Winston, 1953.

Baker, Augusta. *The Black Experience in Children's Books*. New York: New York Public Library Office of Children's Services, 1970.

Bechtel, Louise S. *Books in Search of Children: Essays and Speeches*. Edited by Virginia Haviland. New York: Macmillan, 1969.

Blakelock, Denys. *Eleanor: Portrait of a Farjeon*. London: Gollancz, 1966.

Bredsdorff, Elias. "Hans Christian Andersen: A Bibliographic Guide to His Works," *Scandinavica 2* (November 1967):108–125

Brown, Ina Corinne. *Understanding Other Cultures*. Englewood Cliffs, N.J.: Prentice-Hall, 1963.

Cahn, Edgar S., ed. *Our Brother's Keeper: The Indian in White America*. New York: World Publishing, 1969.

Carlson, Ruth Kearney. *Emerging Humanity: Multi-ethnic Literature for Children and Adolescents*. Dubuque, Iowa: Brown, 1972.

Chalmers, Patrick R. *Kenneth Grahame: Life, Letters and Unpublished Work*. London: Methuen, 1933.

Colwell, Eileen H. "Eleanor Farjeon: A Centenary View." *Horn Book Magazine* 57(July 1981):280–287.

Commire, Anne, ed. *Something About the Author: Facts and Pictures About Authors and Illustrators of Books for Young People,* 30 vols. (Detroit, Mich.: Gale, 1971–).

Cott, Jonathan. *Pipers at the Gates of Dawn: The Wisdom of Children's Literature*. New York: Random House, 1983.

Crosby, Muriel. *An Adventure in Human Relations*. Chicago: Follett, 1965.

Egoff, Sheila A. "Beyond the Garden Wall: Some Observations on Current Trends in Children's Literature." May Hill Arbuthnot Lecture. *Top of the News* 35(Spring 1979):257–271.

Evans, Gwyneth. "Nothing Odd Ever Happens Here: Landscape in Canadian Fantasy." *Canadian Children's Literature* 15–16(1980):15–30.

Glancy, Barbara. *Children's Interracial Fiction*. Washington, D.C.: American Federation of Teachers, 1969.

Hopkins, Lee Bennett. *More Books by More People*. New York: Citation Press, 1974.

Hunter, Mollie. "One World" *Horn Book Magazine* 51(December 1975):557–563 and 52 (January 1976):32–38.

Jones, Cornelia, and Olivia R. Way. "Michael Bond." *British Children's Authors* (Chicago: American Library, 1976).

Karl, Jean. *From Childhood to Childhood*. New York: John Day, 1970.

Keating, Charlotte Matthews. *Building Bridges of Understanding*. Tucson, Ariz.: Palo Verde Publishing, 1967.

Kurth, Ruth Justine. "Realism in Children's Books of Fantasy." *California Librarian* 39(July 1978):39–40.

Kuznets, Lois R. "Toad Hall Revisited." *Children's Literature* 7 (1978): 115–128.

Leif, Irving P. *Children's Literature: A Historical and Contemporary Bibliography*. Troy, NY: Whitston, 1977.

Lynn, Joanne L. "Hyacinths and Biscuits in the Village of Liver and Onions: Sandburg's *Rootabaga Stories, Children's Literature* 8(1980):118–132.

Lynn, Ruth Nodelman. *Fantasy For Children: An Annotated Checklist and Reference Guide*. 2d ed. New York: Bowker, 1983.

Meigs, Cornelia, et al. *A Critical History of Children's Literature*. rev. ed. New York: Macmillan, 1969.

Rahn, Suzanne. *Children's Literature: An Annotated Bibliography of the History and Criticism*. New York: Garland, 1981.

Rosenblatt, Louise M. *Literature As Exploration*. Rev. ed. New York: Noble & Noble, 1968.

Sandburg, Carl. *Always the Young Strangers*. Orlando, Fla.: Harcourt Brace Jovanovich, 1952.

Shewar, Rodney. *Oscar Wilde: Art and Egotism*. New York: Harper & Row, 1977.

Singer, Isaac Bashevis. "Isaac Bashevis Singer on Writing for Children." *Children's Literature* 6(1977):9–16.

Slayton, R. "Love Story of Astrid Lindgren." *Scandinavian Review* 63(December 1975):44–53.

Spink, Reginald. *Hans Christian Andersen and His World*. New York: Putnam, 1972.

Steiner, Stan. *The New Indians*. New York: Harper & Row, 1969.

Taylor, S. Keith. "Universal Themes in Kenneth Grahame's *The Wind in the Willows*." Ph.D. diss., Temple University, 1967.

Thom, Douglas. *Everyday Problems of the Everyday Child*. Englewood Cliffs, N.J.: Prentice-Hall, 1929.

Townsend, John Rowe. *A Sense of Story: Essays on Contemporary Writers for Children*. Philadelphia: Lippincott, 1971.

Weston, Anette H. "Robert Lawson: Author and Illustrator." In *Authors and Illustrators of Children's Books,* by Miriam Hoffman and Eva Samuels. New York: Bowker, 1972.

THE NATURAL WORLD

Nature intrigues people, but we are often wary of it as well. On one hand, the earliest human societies developed in nature, maintaining a symbiotic harmony with forces beyond their control or comprehension. On the other hand, those same societies evolved by cultivating unique powers and talents that often relegated the natural order to "second place." Modern societies have distanced themselves from these natural surroundings. Literature can bridge this ever-widening gap.

Literature informs children and adults about the natural world while also reminding us of long-forgotten concepts. Perhaps we should reconsider the importance of nature to our daily lives. To this end, this section presents various literary perspectives, both literal and symbolic, of the natural world beyond human communities.

Water is the source of life for all living beings and appears frequently in literature as a powerful symbol. Many folktales tell of the magical "water of life" that can revive the dead or restore meaning to an otherwise arid and empty existence. In Christian symbolism, baptism, for example, is used to initiate a new life. Although in the natural order of things life arises out of water, water can take life away, as in a catastrophic flood or tidal wave. The stories of the Great Flood acknowledge the potential destructive force of water.

One of water's magical properties is its changeability. It can turn into vapor or ice or can take many liquid forms—river, lake, or sea. Of all its forms, the most awesome and mysterious is that of the sea, which ironically can be a home or a grave; one of the most haunting folktale motifs is that of the undersea city. All human beings share a fascination for this "world below the brine." Oceanographers have charted it, sounded it, and penetrated it, but most of it remains an enigma. Indeed, it is so mysterious that stories about it need not be fictitious. The simultaneously poetic and scientific descriptions of the sea by Rachel Carson and Jacques-Yves Cousteau have won enthusiastic audiences among all age groups.

Bodies of water can be a source of raw vitality, as in *Beowulf,* an ancient epic poem in an early form of the English language. Some Norse myths characterize the sea as gloomy, while in the German folktale "The Fisherman and His Wife," the sea becomes progressively angry as the fisherman's wife becomes progressively greedy. And the sea can present such a test to courage that the person facing it is transformed when the challenge is met. Whatever the context, water and the sea have diverse spiritual, psychological, and physical implications. When these implications are explored, the explorer comes closer to nature, including his or her own.

The aquatic landscape of corals and underwater caves has a counterpart on land in the world of trees and hills, which also bear symbolic significance in literature. Trees may represent security, the natural process of growth to maturity, psychic wholeness, the poetic imagination, or immortality. Like mountains, trees seem to connect heaven and earth, for they have roots in the earth, yet they soar toward the heavens. For this reason, trees and hills can be spiritual havens or bridges between people and their universe.

In folktales and myths, where metamorphoses are expected occurrences, people sometimes turn into trees, as in the Greek myth of Daphne and Apollo. In the forest of Meudon near Paris, France, one can still see garlands hung in trees by people who cling to the old druid worship of tree spirits. Trees also reputedly influence the course of human experience, as on the island of Cyprus, where even today, the cloth-laden branches of the "healing tree" near Paphos bear hopeful testament to its magical powers.

In the Norse myth "Yggdrasill the World Tree," a tree stands at the center of the mythic world of the Vikings. In the Buddha myth, a tree represents the spiritual essence of humanity, while in Hans Christian Andersen's tale "The Goblin and the Grocer," poetic imagination takes the form of a tree.

Like trees, hills can also be places of refuge and inspiration, as related in *My Side of the Mountain,* by Jean George. Since hills and mountains stand closer to the heavens, they are natural sites for revelation—to Moses, for instance—and they are something protective and permanent in an otherwise impermanent world, an observation noted by Hilda Conkling in the poem "Hills." And finally, a mountain is often the background, or impediment, to a quest in which a hero, after an arduous climb, gains some reward. The Scandinavian tale "The Princess of the Glass Hill" is a good case in point.

These landscapes and seascapes are inhabited by various creatures, of which human beings are but one form. Literature reveals our conceptions of the other inhabitants. Birds, for instance, are not earthbound like most creatures and therefore are often treated as creatures apart. In religion and folklore, birds often represent the human soul or the spiritual side of life. A powerful expression of this symbolism appears in the idea, prevalent in many cultures, that the soul leaves the body of a dying person in the shape of a bird. Because birds are inhabitants of the air, they are associated with the realm of wind or breath and therefore the universal *spiritus.* Many primitive peoples adorned themselves with feathers, as if to say that they are spiritual beings. Birds also symbolize intuition—secret hunches that later prove to be true—and are therefore often thought to have psychic powers. Because of their vantage point in the sky, for example, the birds in "The Water Lily" can forecast events and serve as prophets. This entire story is held together through the communication of birds, which prevents tragedy and makes possible the happy union of the lovers.

While birds in general symbolize the spiritual or intuitive, individual varieties of birds may carry their own particular meanings in folklore. The swan, which is said to sing before its impending death, is supposed to be able to foretell the future, and the dove is well known as a symbol of the Holy Spirit in Christian myth. Similarly the crow, the raven, the peacock, the duck, the nightingale, and the bluebird each has a symbolic meaning of its own.

Some people seek to imitate the birds. Icarus, in Greek mythology, flew higher and higher, until he went too near the sun and melted the glue that attached his wings to his body. Other people are turned into birds by enchantment, as in the case of the princes in "The Six Swans."

While birds are generally understood to represent the spiritual side of life, land animals represent instinctual nature, the unconscious energy that can be thought of as the flow of life. Individual types of animals express this energy in different ways, and each may carry a particular symbolism. Because of their positive relationship to mankind, dogs are seen as guardians or guides. Horses often represent powerful unconscious energy, while the lion is a symbol for the sun.

One of the most fascinating cases of animal symbolism is that of the wolf. This animal, like the raven, is associated with both strongly positive and strongly negative aspects of nature, depending on the mythological tradition one considers. In Roman mythology, Romulus and Remus were suckled by a she-wolf, which represents nature as a positive, life-giving force. In Norse mythology, however, the wolf is destructive and represents the principles of evil. This latter aspect may be based on reports of the wolf's voraciousness.

Animal stories are especially delightful for small children, who identify more freely with animal characters than adults do. Therefore, children particularly enjoy tales in which a physically inferior animal outwits a stronger opponent and prevails as the hero, much like Brer Rabbit in the *Uncle Remus* stories. In this way, children vicariously experience superiority to adults, baby-sitters, and even older siblings. Yet too often, stories for children distort the true qualities of animals or features in nature, interpreting literally the symbolic qualities man has given them. This can mislead the child regarding the "nature" of nature. For this reason, care has been taken in this section to include literature that tries to portray the natural world as it is, whether nurturing or hostile.

By examining nature through literature, we and our children may share our views of the all-encompassing natural world, which was once literally at our doorsteps. From this enlightened perspective, we may more perceptively observe what is before us and develop a lifelong appreciation of things natural, which will enable us to understand and enjoy more fully our particular significance within "the wide world all around."

Water and the Sea

FABLES, MYTHS, AND LEGENDS

The Great Flood

Retold by Olivia E. Coolidge

The myth of a great flood is an almost universal one, and controversy has raged over the factual basis for such an event. The version of the story most familiar to us is the Old Testament legend of Noah and the Ark, but many other tales also feature a good man and his wife who escape the Flood in a boat and who later become the parents of all succeeding generations. In this Greek myth, Deucalion and Pyrrha repeople the earth by scattering stones.

When evil first came among mankind, people became very wicked. War, robbery, treachery, and murder prevailed throughout the world. Even the worship of the gods, the laws of truth and honor, reverence for parents and brotherly love were neglected.

Finally, Zeus determined to destroy the race of men altogether, and the other gods agreed. All the winds were therefore shut up in a cave except the South Wind, the wet one. He raced over the earth with water streaming from his beard and long, white hair. Clouds gathered around his head, and dew dripped from his wings and the ends of his garments. With him went Iris, the rainbow goddess, while below Poseidon smote the earth with his trident until it shook and gaped open, so that the waters of the sea rushed up over the land.

Fields and farmhouses were buried. Fish swam in the tops of the trees. Sea beasts were quietly feeding where flocks and herds had grazed before. On the surface of the water, boats, stags, lions, and tigers struggled desperately to keep afloat. Wolves swam in the midst of flocks of sheep, but the sheep were not frightened by them, and the wolves never thought of their natural prey. Each fought for his own life and forgot the others. Over them wheeled countless birds, winging far and wide in the hope of finding something to rest upon. Eventually they too fell into the water and were drowned.

All over the water were men in small boats or makeshift rafts. Some even had oars which they tried to use, but the waters were fierce and stormy, and there was nowhere to go. In time all were drowned, until at last

From Olivia E. Coolidge, *Greek Myths* (Boston: Houghton Mifflin, 1949).

there was no one left but an old man and his wife, Deucalion and Pyrrha. These two people had lived in truth and justice, unlike the rest of mankind. They had been warned of the coming of the flood and had built a boat and stocked it. For nine days and nights they floated until Zeus took pity on them and they came to the top of Mount Parnassus, the sacred home of the Muses. There they found land and disembarked to wait while the gods recalled the water they had unloosed.

When the waters fell, Deucalion and Pyrrha looked over the land, despairing. Mud and sea slime covered the earth; all living things had been swept away. Slowly and sadly they made their way down the mountain until they came to a temple where there had been an oracle. Black seaweed dripped from the pillars now, and the mud was over all. Nevertheless the two knelt down and kissed the temple steps while Deucalion prayed to the goddess to tell them what they should do. All men were dead but themselves, and they were old. It was impossible that they should have children to people the earth again. Out of the temple a great voice was heard speaking strange words.

"Depart," it said, "with veiled heads and loosened robes, and throw behind you as you go the bones of your mother."

Pyrrha was in despair when she heard this saying. "The bones of our mother!" she cried. "How can we tell now where they lie? Even if we knew, we could never do such a dreadful thing as to disturb their resting place and scatter them over the earth like an armful of stones."

"Stones!" said Deucalion quickly. "That must be what the goddess means. After all Earth is our mother, and the other thing is too horrible for us to suppose that a goddess would ever command it."

Accordingly both picked up armfuls of stones, and as they went away from the temple with faces veiled, they cast the stones behind them. From each of those Deucalion cast sprang up a man, and from Pyrrha's stones sprang women. Thus the earth was repeopled, and in the course of time it brought forth again animals from itself, and all was as before. Only from that time men have been less sensitive and have found it easier to endure toil, and sorrow, and pain, since now they are descended from stones.

The Descent of Manu

Louis Renou

In this Hindu version of the Flood myth, Manu, the father of mankind, is saved by a fish (a variation of the helpful animal motif). The story is similar to that of Noah and the Ark.

In the morning they brought to Manu water for washing, just as now also they are wont to bring water for washing the hands. When he was washing himself, a fish came into his hands.

It spake to him the word, "Rear me, I will save thee!" "Wherefrom wilt thou save me?" "A flood will carry away all these creatures: from that I will save thee!" "How am I to rear thee?"

It said, "As long as we are small, there is great destruction for us: fish devours fish. Thou wilt first keep me in a jar. When I outgrow that, thou wilt dig a pit and keep me in it. When I outgrow that, thou wilt take me down to the sea, for then I shall be beyond destruction."

It soon became a large fish. Thereupon it said, "In such and such a year that flood will come. Thou shalt then attend to my advice

From Louis Renou, *Hinduism* (New York: Braziller, 1961).

by preparing a ship; and when the flood has risen thou shalt enter into the ship, and I will save thee from it.''

After he had reared it in this way, he took it down to the sea. And in the same year which the fish had indicated to him, he attended to the advice of the fish by preparing a ship; and when the flood had risen, he entered into the ship. The fish then swam up to him, and to its horn he tied the rope of the ship, and by that means he passed swiftly up to yonder northern mountain.

It then said, ''I have saved thee. Fasten the ship to a tree; but let not the water cut thee off, whilst thou art on the mountain. As the water subsides, thou mayest gradually descend!'' Accordingly he gradually descended, and hence that slope of the northern mountain is called "Manu's descent"! The flood then swept away all these creatures, and Manu alone remained here.

Why the Sun and Moon Live in the Sky

Kathleen Arnott

Water—a major source of life—is dangerous to life when unleashed, as this brief Nigerian tale clearly shows. In the story, the water indirectly cautions the sun that only a very big house will accommodate it, but the sun ignores the warning.

A long time ago the sun and the water both lived on the earth and were very friendly.

The sun often paid a visit to the house where the water lived and they would sit talking together for many hours. But the water never came to the sun's house, and one day the sun asked his friend:

"Why do you and your relations not come and visit me? My wife and I would be very pleased to welcome you into our compound.

The water laughed. 'I'm sorry not to have visited you before this,' he said, 'but the fact is that your house is too small. Were I to come with all my people, I'm afraid we would drive you and your wife away.'

'We are going to build a new compound soon,' replied the sun. 'If it is big enough, will you come and visit us then?'

'It would have to be very large indeed for me to come,' explained the water, 'as my people and I take up so much room I'm afraid we might damage your property.'

But the sun seemed so sad that his friend never visited him that the water said he would come when the new compound was ready, provided that it was a really big one.

The sun and his wife the moon set to work, and with the help of their friends, they built a magnificent compound.

'Come and visit us now,' begged the sun. 'For we are sure that our compound is large enough to hold any number of visitors.'

The water was still doubtful, but the sun begged so hard that the water began to come in. Through the door into the compound he flowed, bringing with him hundreds of fish, some water-rats, and even a few water-snakes.

When the water was knee-deep, he asked the sun:

'Do you still want my people and me to come into your compound?'

'Yes,' cried the foolish sun. 'Let them all come.'

From Kathleen Arnott, *African Myths and Legends* (New York: Henry Z. Walck, 1963).

So the water continued to flow into the compound and at last the sun and the moon had to climb on to the roof of their hut to keep dry.

'Do you still want my people and me to come into your compound?' asked the water again.

The sun did not like to go back on his word, so he replied:

'Yes. I told you I wanted them all. Let them all come.'

Soon the water reached the very top of the roof and the sun and the moon had to go up into the sky, where they have lived ever since.

Beowulf

Burton Raffel (trans.)

Beneath the surface of the water lies a deep and dark world rich in adventure and danger. In myths, attention is focused on the activities of the gods; in epics—of which Beowulf *is a supreme English-language example—attention is focused on the human hero.* Beowulf *is a warrior so brave and powerful that he is able to kill the water monsters of the dark lake, Grendel and Grendel's mother.*

Dating back to the eighth century A.D., Beowulf *is the chief literary work of the Old English period. Structurally, it is beautifully balanced and the flow of language is magnificent. It is enriched by* kennings—*expressions in place of the simple name of a thing—such as "whale road" for "sea." The setting is in Scandinavia.*

They sank into sleep. The price of that
    evening's
Rest was too high for the Dane who bought it
With his life, paying as others had paid
When Grendel inhabited Herot, the hall
His till his crimes pulled him into hell.
And now it was known that a monster had
    died
But a monster still lived, and meant revenge.
She'd brooded on her loss, misery had
    brewed
In her heart, that female horror, Grendel's
Mother, living in the murky cold lake
Assigned her since Cain had killed his only
Brother, slain his father's son
With an angry sword. God drove him off,
Outlawed him to the dry and barren desert,
And branded him with a murderer's mark.
    And he bore
A race of fiends accursed like their father;

So Grendel was drawn to Herot, an outcast
Come to meet the man who awaited him.
He'd snatched at Beowulf's arm, but that
    prince
Remembered God's grace and the strength
    He'd given him
And relied on the Lord for all the help,
The comfort and support he would need. He
    killed
The monster, as God had meant him to do,
Tore the fiend apart and forced him
To run as rapidly as he could toward death's
Cold waiting hands. His mother's sad heart,
And her greed, drove her from her den on the
    dangerous
Pathway of revenge.
              So she reached Herot,
Where the Danes slept as though already
    dead;
Her visit ended their good fortune, reversed

From Burton Raffel, trans., *Beowulf* (New York: New American Library, 1963).

The bright vane of their luck. No female, no
    matter
How fierce, could have come with a man's
    strength,
Fought with the power and courage men fight
    with,
Smashing their shining swords, their
    bloody,
Hammer-forged blades onto boar-headed
    helmets,
Slashing and stabbing with the sharpest of
    points.
The soldiers raised their shields and drew
Those gleaming swords, swung them above
The piled-up benches, leaving their mail
    shirts
And their helmets where they'd lain when
    the terror took hold of them.
To save her life she moved still faster,
Took a single victim and fled from the hall,
Running to the moors, discovered, but her
    supper
Assured, sheltered in her dripping claws.
She'd taken Hrothgar's closest friend,
The man he most loved of all men on earth;
She'd killed a glorious soldier, cut
A noble life short. No Geat could have
    stopped her:
Beowulf and his band had been given better
Beds; sleep had come to them in a different
Hall. Then all Herot burst into shouts:
She had carried off Grendel's claw. Sorrow
Had returned to Denmark. They'd traded
    deaths,
Danes and monsters, and no one had won,
Both had lost!
                    The wise old king
Trembled in anger and grief, his dearest
Friend and adviser dead. Beowulf
Was sent for at once: a messenger went
    swiftly
To his rooms and brought him. He came,
    his band
About him, as dawn was breaking through,
The best of all warriors, walking to where
    Hrothgar
Sat waiting, the gray-haired king wondering
If God would ever end this misery.
The Geats tramped quickly through the hall;
    their steps
Beat and echoed in the silence. Beowulf

Rehearsed the words he would want with
    Hrothgar;
He'd ask the Danes' great lord if all
Were at peace, if the night had passed
    quietly.
    Hrothgar answered him, protector of his
        people:
    "There's no happiness to ask about!
        Anguish has descended
On the Danes. Esher is dead, Ermlaf's
Older brother and my own most trusted
Counselor and friend, my comrade, when
    we went
Into battle, who'd beaten back enemy
    swords,
Standing at my side. All my soldiers
Should be as he was, their hearts as brave
And as wise! Another wandering fiend
Has found him in Herot, murdered him, fled
With his corpse: he'll be eaten, his flesh
    become
A horrible feast—and who knows where
The beast may be hiding, its belly stuffed
    full?
She's taking revenge for your victory over
    Grendel,
For your strength, your mighty grip, and
    that monster's
Death. For years he'd been preying on my
    people;
You came, he was dead in a single day,
And now there's another one, a second
    hungry
Fiend, determined to avenge the first,
A monster willing and more than able
To bring us more sorrow—or so it must
    seem
To the many men mourning that noble
Treasure-giver, for all men were treated
Nobly by those hands now forever closed.
    "I've heard that my people, peasants
        working
In the fields, have seen a pair of such fiends
Wandering in the moors and marshes, giant
Monsters living in those desert lands.
And they've said to my wise men that, as
    well as they could see,
One of the devils was a female creature.
The other, they say, walked through the
    wilderness
Like a man—but mightier than any man.

They were frightened, and they fled, hoping
    to find help
In Herot. They named the huge one
    Grendel:
If he had a father no one knew him,
Or whether there'd been others before these
    two,
Hidden evil before hidden evil.
They live in secret places, windy
Cliffs, wolf-dens where water pours
From the rocks, then runs underground,
    where mist
Steams like black clouds, and the groves of
    trees
Growing out over their lake are all covered
With frozen spray, and wind down snakelike
Roots that reach as far as the water
And help keep it dark. At night that lake
Burns like a torch. No one knows its
    bottom,
No wisdom reaches such depths. A deer,
Hunted through the woods by packs of
    hounds,
A stag with great horns, though driven
    through the forest
From faraway places, prefers to die
On those shores, refuses to save its life
In that water. It isn't far, nor is it
A pleasant spot! When the wind stirs
And storms, waves splash toward the sky,
As dark as the air, as black as the rain
That the heavens weep. Our only help,
Again, lies with you. Grendel's mother
Is hidden in her terrible home, in a place
You've not seen. Seek it, if you dare! Save
    us,
Once more, and again twisted gold,
Heaped-up ancient treasure, will reward you
For the battle you win!''
                  Beowulf spoke:
  ''Let your sorrow end! It is better for us
    all
To avenge our friends, not mourn them
    forever.
Each of us will come to the end of this life
On earth; he who can earn it should fight
For the glory of his name; fame after death
Is the noblest of goals. Arise, guardian
Of this kingdom, let us go, as quickly as we
    can,
And have a look at this lady monster.

I promise you this: she'll find no shelter,
No hole in the ground, no towering tree,
No deep bottom of a lake, where her sins
    can hide.
Be patient for one more day of misery;
I ask for no longer.''
                The old king leaped
To his feet, gave thanks to God for such
    words.
Then Hrothgar's horse was brought, saddled
And bridled. The Danes' wise ruler rode,
Stately and splendid; shield-bearing soldiers
Marched at his side. The monster's tracks
Led them through the forest; they followed
    her heavy
Feet, that had swept straight across
The shadowy waste land, her burden the
    lifeless
Body of the best of Hrothgar's men.
The trail took them up towering, rocky
Hills, and over narrow, winding
Paths they had never seen, down steep
And slippery cliffs where creatures from
    deep
In the earth hid in their holes. Hrothgar
Rode in front, with a few of his most
    knowing
Men, to find their way. Then suddenly,
Where clumps of trees bent across
Cold gray stones, they came to a dismal
Wood; below them was the lake, its water
Bloody and bubbling. And the Danes
    shivered,
Miserable, mighty men tormented
By grief, seeing, there on that cliff
Above the water, Esher's bloody
Head. They looked down at the lake, felt
How its heat rose up, watched the waves'
Blood-stained swirling. Their battle horns
    sounded,
Then sounded again. Then they set down
    their weapons.
They could see the water crawling with
    snakes,
Fantastic serpents swimming in the boiling
Lake, and sea beasts lying on the rocks
—The kind that infest the ocean, in the early
Dawn, often ending some ship's
Journey with their wild jaws. They rushed
Angrily out of sight, when the battle horns
    blew.

Beowulf aimed an arrow at one
Of the beasts, swimming sluggishly away,
And the point pierced its hide, stabbed
To its heart; its life leaked out, death
Swept it off. Quickly, before
The dying monster could escape, they
    hooked
Its thrashing body with their curved boar-
    spears,
Fought it to land, drew it up on the bluff,
Then stood and stared at the incredible
    wave-roamer,
Covered with strange scales and horrible.
    Then Beowulf
Began to fasten on his armor,
Not afraid for his life but knowing the
    woven
Mail, with its hammered links, could save
That life when he lowered himself into the
    lake,
Keep slimy monster's claws from snatching
    at
His heart, preserve him for the battle he was
    sent
To fight. Hrothgar's helmet would defend
    him;
That ancient, shining treasure, encircled
With hard-rolled metal, set there by some
    smith's
Long dead hand, would block all battle
Swords, stop all blades from cutting at him
When he'd swum toward the bottom, gone
    down in the surging
Water, deep toward the swirling sands.
And Unferth helped him, Hrothgar's courtier
Lent him a famous weapon, a fine,
Hilted old sword named Hrunting; it had
An iron blade, etched and shining
And hardened in blood. No one who'd worn
    it
Into battle, swung it in dangerous places,
Daring and brave, had ever been deserted—
Nor was Beowulf's journey the first time it
    was taken
To an enemy's camp, or asked to support
Some hero's courage and win him glory.
Unferth had tried to forget his greeting
To Beowulf, his drunken speech of
    welcome;
A mighty warrior, he lent his weapon
To a better one. Only Beowulf would risk

His life in that lake; Unferth was afraid,
Gave up that chance to work wonders, win
    glory
And a hero's fame. But Beowulf and fear
Were strangers; he stood ready to dive into
    battle.

Then Edgetho's brave son spoke:
                    "Remember,
Hrothgar, Oh knowing king, now
When my danger is near, the warm words
    we uttered,
And if your enemy should end my life
Then be, oh generous prince, forever
The father and protector of all whom I leave
Behind me, here in your hands, my beloved
Comrades left with no leader, their leader
Dead. And the precious gifts you gave me,
My friend, send them to Higlac. May he see
In their golden brightness, the Geats' great
    Lord
Gazing at your treasure, that here in
    Denmark
I found a noble protector, a giver
Of rings whose rewards I won and briefly
Relished. And you, Unferth, let
My famous old sword stay in your hands:
I shall shape glory with Hrunting, or death
Will hurry me from this earth!''
                    As his words ended
He leaped into the lake, would not wait for
    anyone's
Answer; the heaving water covered him
Over. For hours he sank through the waves;
At last he saw the mud of the bottom.
And all at once the greedy she-wolf
Who'd ruled those waters for half a hundred
Years discovered him, saw that a creature
From above had come to explore the bottom
Of her wet world. She welcomed him in
    her claws,
Clutched at him savagely but could not
    harm him,
Tried to work her fingers through the tight
Ring-woven mail on his breast, but tore
And scratched in vain. Then she carried
    him, armor
And sword and all, to her home; he
    struggled
To free his weapon, and failed. The fight
Brought other monsters swimming to see

Her catch, a host of sea beasts who beat at
His mail shirt, stabbing with tusks and teeth
As they followed along. Then he realized,
   suddenly,
That she'd brought him into someone's
   battle-hall,
And there the water's heat could not hurt
   him,
Nor anything in the lake attack him through
The building's high-arching roof. A brilliant
Light burned all around him, the lake
Itself like a fiery flame.
                Then he saw
The mighty water witch, and swung his
   sword,
His ring-marked blade, straight at her head;
The iron sang its fierce song,
Sang Beowulf's strength. But her guest
Discovered that no sword could slice her
   evil
Skin, that Hrunting could not hurt her, was
   useless
Now when he needed it. They wrestled, she
   ripped
And tore and clawed at him, bit holes in his
   helmet,
And that too failed him; for the first time in
   years
Of being worn to war it would earn no
   glory;
It was the last time anyone would wear it.
   But Beowulf
Longed only for fame, leaped back
Into battle. He tossed his sword aside,
Angry; the steel-edged blade lay where
He'd dropped it. If weapons were useless
   he'd use
His hands, the strength in his fingers. So
   fame
Comes to the men who mean to win it
And care about nothing else! He raised
His arms and seized her by the shoulder;
   anger
Doubled his strength, he threw her to the
   floor.
She fell, Grendel's fierce mother, and the
   Geats'
Proud prince was ready to leap on her. But
   she rose
At once and repaid him with her clutching
   claws,

Wildly tearing at him. He was weary, that
   best
And strongest of soldiers; his feet stumbled
And in an instant she had him down, held
   helpless.
Squatting with her weight on his stomach,
   she drew
A dagger, brown with dried blood, and
   prepared
To avenge her only son. But he was
   stretched
On his back, and her stabbing blade was
   blunted
By the woven mail shirt he wore on his
   chest.
The hammered links held; the point
Could not touch him. He'd have traveled to
   the bottom of the earth,
Edgetho's son, and died there, if that shining
Woven metal had not helped—and Holy
God, who sent him victory, gave judgment
For truth and right, Ruler of the Heavens,
Once Beowulf was back on his feet and
   fighting.

   Then he saw, hanging on the wall, a
   heavy
Sword, hammered by giants, strong
And blessed with their magic, the best of all
   weapons
But so massive that no ordinary man could
   lift
Its carved and decorated length. He drew it
From its scabbard, broke the chain on its
   hilt,
And then, savage, now angry
And desperate, lifted it high over his head
And struck with all the strength he had left,
Caught her in the neck and cut it through,
Broke bones and all. Her body fell
To the floor, lifeless, the sword was wet
With her blood, and Beowulf rejoiced at the
   sight.
   The brilliant light shone, suddenly,
As though burning in that hall, and as bright
   as Heaven's
Own candle, lit in the sky. He looked
At her home, then following along the wall
Went walking, his hands tight on the sword,
His heart still angry. He was hunting
   another

Dead monster, and took his weapon with
him
For final revenge against Grendel's vicious
Attacks, his nighttime raids, over
And over, coming to Herot when Hrothgar's
Men slept, killing them in their beds,
Eating some on the spot, fifteen
Or more, and running to his loathsome moor
With another such sickening meal waiting
In his pouch. But Beowulf repaid him for
those visits,
Found him lying dead in his corner,
Armless, exactly as that fierce fighter
Had sent him out from Herot, then struck
off
His head with a single swift blow. The body
Jerked for the last time, then lay still.
The wise old warriors who surrounded
Hrothgar,
Like him staring into the monsters' lake,
Saw the waves surging and blood
Spurting through. They spoke about
Beowulf,
All the graybeards, whispered together
And said that hope was gone, that the hero
Had lost fame and his life at once, and
would never
Return to the living, come back as
triumphant
As he had left; almost all agreed that
Grendel's
Mighty mother, the she-wolf, had killed
him.
The sun slid over past noon, went further
Down. The Danes gave up, left
The lake and went home, Hrothgar with
them.
The Geats stayed, sat sadly, watching,
Imagining they saw their lord but not
believing
They would ever see him again.
                —Then the sword
Melted, blood-soaked, dripping down
Like water, disappearing like ice when the
world's
Eternal Lord loosens invisible
Fetters and unwinds icicles and frost
As only He can, He who rules
Time and seasons, He who is truly
God. The monsters' hall was full of
Rich treasures, but all that Beowulf took

Was Grendel's head and the hilt of the
giants'
Jeweled sword; the rest of that ring-marked
Blade had dissolved in Grendel's steaming
Blood, boiling even after his death.
And then the battle's only survivor
Swam up and away from those silent
corpses;
The water was calm and clean, the whole
Huge lake peaceful once the demons who'd
lived in it
Were dead.
              Then that noble protector of all
seamen
Swam to land, rejoicing in the heavy
Burdens he was bringing with him. He
And all his glorious band of Geats
Thanked God that their leader had come
back unharmed;
They left the lake together. The Geats
Carried Beowulf's helmet, and his mail shirt.
Behind them the water slowly thickened
As the monsters' blood came seeping up.
They walked quickly, happily, across
Roads all of them remembered, left
The lake and the cliffs alongside it, brave
men
Staggering under the weight of Grendel's
skull,
Too heavy for fewer than four of them to
handle—
Two on each side of the spear jammed
through it—
Yet proud of their ugly load and determined
That the Danes, seated in Herot, should see
it.
Soon, fourteen Geats arrived
At the hall, bold and warlike, and with
Beowulf,
Their lord and leader, they walked on the
mead-hall
Green. Then the Geats' brave prince entered
Herot, covered with glory for the daring
Battles he had fought; he sought Hrothgar
To salute him and show Grendel's head.
He carried that terrible trophy by the hair,
Brought it straight to where the Danes sat,
Drinking, the queen among them. It was a
weird
And wonderful sight, and the warriors
stared.

FOLKTALES—
INHERITED AND LITERARY

The Well of Immortality

Retold by Ruth Q. Sun

Because water is necessary for life, it was represented in the earliest stories and myths as possessing magical properties, such as promoting eternal life. Water seemed to be a kind of divinity, and gods and goddesses often appeared in or near it. In this Vietnamese story, a god descends to the bottom of a well in order to lead people to immortality, but he is unsuccessful because the people are all too human.

Long, long ago, when the world was new and fresh and everything was just beginning, men lived an easy and comfortable life, without problems at all. As a natural consequence, men became insupportably lazy. So the time came when the Creator punished them by giving them a more limited lifetime. In other words, their life span became much, much shorter than in the good old days.

But up in the heavens there was a god named Nuoc who was extremely easygoing and kind. He thought it all over for some aeons, and finally decided he would like to do something so that human life need not be quite so curtailed.

So one late-winter day this god dropped down to earth and descended to the very bottom of a deep well with magic properties. When men became aware that there was a god down at the bottom of that well, they were very curious about the situation. Eventually a huge crowd of passers-by assembled at the edge of the well. While they were all standing there, peering intently into the dark shaft, the god Nuoc called up to them, saying that those who would follow him into the well could become immortal. After their deaths they could quickly be returned to life, he said.

Well, of course everyone who heard the god's words wanted immediately to descend and receive this promised gift of immortality, all the more so when they could finally perceive, far down in the water at the bottom of the well, the miraculous, sparkling, scintillating body of the god. How they wanted to join him—but my! the water was very cold indeed. They hesitated.

After much discussion among themselves, the people compromised by dipping only their fingertips, their toes, and the top of their heads in the icy water. They also drank a mouthful each. But, despite Nuoc's urgings, not one of them dared jump entirely into the well.

So from that time on, human beings have lived only one brief lifetime. But during that single lifetime their fingernails, toenails,

From Ruth Q. Sun, *Land of Seagull and Fox* (Rutland, Vt.: Charles E. Tuttle, 1967).

hair, and teeth keep growing out, growing out—and their nails and hair continue to grow even after death, it is said. This is the sustained life promised by the god Nuoc. Because of men's fear of ice-cold water, only these scattered parts of the body secured a form of immortality.

The Fisherman and His Wife

Jacob and Wilhelm Grimm

An enchanted fish-prince who can grant wishes, a power-mad fisherman's wife, and a weak husband who is their go-between are the three characters around whom the plot of this old folktale revolves. The atmosphere of the sea darkens as the greedy wife increases her demands for power and good fortune.

There was once a fisherman who lived with his wife in a ditch, close by the sea-side. The fisherman used to go out all day long a-fishing; and one day, as he sat on the shore with his rod, looking at the shining water and watching his line, all on a sudden his float was dragged away deep under the sea: and in drawing it up he pulled a great fish out of the water. The fish said to him, "Pray let me live: I am not a real fish; I am an enchanted prince, put me in the water again, and let me go." "Oh!" said the man, "you need not make so many words about the matter; I wish to have nothing to do with a fish that can talk; so swim away as soon as you please." Then he put him back into the water, and the fish darted straight down to the bottom, and left a long streak of blood behind him.

When the fisherman went home to his wife in the ditch, he told her how he had caught a great fish, and how it had told him it was an enchanted prince, and that on hearing it speak he had let it go again. "Did you not ask it for anything?" said the wife. "No," said the man, "what should I ask for?" "Ah!" said the wife, "we live very wretchedly here in this nasty stinking ditch;

do go back, and tell the fish we want a little cottage."

The fisherman did not much like the business: however, he went to the sea, and when he came there the water looked all yellow and green. And he stood at the water's edge, and said,

"O man of the sea!
Come listen to me,
For Alice my wife,
The plague of my life,
Hath sent me to beg a boon of thee!"

Then the fish came swimming to him, and said, "Well, what does she want?" "Ah!" answered the fisherman, "my wife says that when I had caught you, I ought to have asked you for something before I let you go again; she does not like living any longer in the ditch, and wants a little cottage." "Go home, then," said the fish, "she is in the cottage already." So the man went home, and saw his wife standing at the door of a cottage. "Come in, come in," said she; "is not this much better than the ditch?" And there was a parlour, a bed-chamber, and a kitchen; and behind the cottage there was a

From Jacob and Wilhelm Grimm, *German Popular Stories*, trans. Edgar Taylor (Menston, England: Scolar Press, 1971).

little garden with all sorts of flowers and fruits, and a court-yard full of ducks and chickens. "Ah!" said the fisherman, "how happily we shall live!" "We will try to do so at least," said his wife.

Every thing went right for a week or two, and then Dame Alice said, "Husband, there is not room enough in this cottage, the court-yard and garden are a great deal too small; I should like to have a large stone castle to live in; so go to the fish again, and tell him to give us a castle." "Wife," said the fisherman, "I don't like to go to him again, for perhaps he will be angry; we ought to be content with the cottage." "Nonsense!" said the wife; "he will do it very willingly; go along, and try."

The fisherman went; but his heart was very heavy: and when he came to the sea, it looked blue and gloomy, though it was quite calm, and he went close to it, and said,

"O man of the sea!
Come listen to me,
For Alice my wife,
The plague of my life,
Hath sent me to beg a boon of thee!"

"Well, what does she want now!" said the fish. "Ah!" said the man very sorrowfully, "my wife wants to live in a stone castle." "Go home then," said the fish, "she is standing at the door of it already." So away went the fisherman, and found his wife standing before a great castle. "See," said she, "is not this grand?" With that they went into the castle together, and found a great many servants there, and the rooms all richly furnished and full of golden chairs and tables; and behind the castle was a garden, and a wood half a mile long, full of sheep, and goats, and hares, and deer; and in the court-yard were stables and cow-houses. "Well!" said the man, "now will we live contented and happy in this beautiful castle for the rest of our lives." "Perhaps we may," said the wife; "but let us consider and sleep upon it before we make up our minds:" so they went to bed.

The next morning, when Dame Alice awoke, it was broad day-light, and she jogged the fisherman with her elbow, and said, "Get up, husband, and bestir yourself, for we must be king of all the land." "Wife, wife," said the man, "why should we wish to be king? I will not be king." "Then I will," said Alice. "But, wife," answered the fisherman, "how can you be king? the fish cannot make you a king." "Husband," said she, "say no more about it, but go and try; I will be king!" So the man went away, quite sorrowful to think that his wife should want to be king. The sea looked a dark grey colour, and was covered with foam as he cried out,

"O man of the sea!
Come listen to me,
For Alice my wife,
The plague of my life,
Hath sent me to beg a boon of thee!"

"Well, what would she have now!" said the fish. "Alas!" said the man, "my wife wants to be king." "Go home," said the fish; "she is king already."

Then the fisherman went home; and as he came close to the palace, he saw a troop of soldiers, and heard the sound of drums and trumpets; and when he entered in, he saw his wife sitting on a high throne of gold and diamonds, with a golden crown upon her head; and on each side of her stood six beautiful maidens, each a head taller than the other. "Well, wife," said the fisherman, "are you king?" "Yes," said she, "I am king." And when he had looked at her for a long time, he said, "Ah, wife! what a fine thing it is to be king! now we shall never have any thing more to wish for." "I don't know how that may be," said she; "never is a long time. I am king, 'tis true, but I begin to be tired of it, and I think I should like to be emperor." "Alas, wife! why should you wish to be emperor?" said the fisherman. "Husband," said she, "go to the fish; I say I will be emperor." "Ah, wife!" replied the fisherman, "the fish cannot make an emperor, and I should not like to ask for such a thing." "I am king," said Alice, "and you are my slave, so go directly!" So the fisherman was obliged to go; and he muttered as he went along, "This will come to no good, it is too much to ask, the fish will be tired at last, and then we shall repent of what we have done." He soon arrived at the sea, and the water was quite black and muddy, and a mighty whirlwind blew over it; but he went to the shore, and said,

"O man of the sea!
Come listen to me,
For Alice my wife,
The plague of my life,
Hath sent me to beg a boon of thee!"

"What would she have now?" said the fish. "Ah!" said the fisherman, "she wants to be emperor." "Go home," said the fish; "she is emperor already."

So he went home again; and as he came near he saw his wife sitting on a very lofty throne made of solid gold, with a great crown on her head full two yards high, and on each side of her stood her guards and attendants in a row, each one smaller than the other, from the tallest giant down to a little dwarf no bigger than my finger. And before her stood princes, and dukes, and earls: and the fisherman went up to her and said, "Wife, are you emperor?" "Yes," said she, "I am emperor." "Ah!" said the man as he gazed upon her, "what a fine thing it is to be emperor!" "Husband," said she, "why should we stay at being emperor; I will be pope next." "O wife, wife!" said he, "how can you be pope? There is but one pope at a time in Christendom." "Husband," said she, "I will be pope this very day." "But," replied the husband, "the fish cannot make you pope." "What nonsense!" said she, "if he can make an emperor, he can make a pope, go and try him." So the fisherman went. But when he came to the shore the wind was raging, and the sea was tossed up and down like boiling water, and the ships were in the greatest distress and danced upon the waves fearfully; in the middle of the sky there was a little blue but toward the south it was all red as if a dreadful storm was rising. At this the fisherman was terribly frightened, and trembled, so that his knees knocked together; but he went to the shore and said,

"O man of the sea!
Come listen to me,
For Alice my wife,
The plague of my life,
Hath sent me to beg a boon of thee!"

"What does she want now?" said the fish. "Ah!" said the fisherman, "My wife wants to be pope." "Go home," said the fish, "she is pope already."

Then the fisherman went home, and found his wife on a throne that was two miles high; and she had three great crowns on her head, and around stood all the pomp and power of the Church; and on each side were two rows of burning lights, of all sizes, the greatest as large as the highest and biggest tower in the world, and the least no larger than a small rushlight. "Wife," said the fisherman as he looked at all this grandeur, "Are you pope?" "Yes," said she, "I am pope." "Well, wife," replied he, "it is a grand thing to be pope; and now you must be content, for you can be nothing greater." "I will consider of that," said the wife. Then they went to bed: but Dame Alice could not sleep all night for thinking what she should be next. At last morning came, and the sun rose. "Ha!" thought she as she looked at it through the window, "cannot I prevent the sun rising?" At this she was very angry, and she wakened her husband, and said, "Husband, go to the fish and tell him I want to be lord of the sun and moon." The fisherman was half asleep, but the thought frightened him so much, that he started and fell out of bed. "Alas, wife!" said he, "cannot you be content to be pope?" "No," said she, "I am very uneasy, and cannot bear to see the sun and moon rise without my leave. Go to the fish directly."

Then the man went trembling for fear; and as he was going down to the shore a dreadful storm arose, so that the trees and the rocks shook; and the heavens became black, and the lightning played, and the thunder rolled; and you might have seen in the sea great black waves like mountains with a white crown of foam upon them; and the fisherman said,

"O man of the sea!
Come listen to me,
For Alice my wife,
The plague of my life,
Hath sent me to beg a boon of thee!"

"What does she want now?" said the fish. "Ah!" said he, "she wants to be lord of the sun and moon." "Go home," said the fish, "to your ditch again!" And there they live to this very day.

The City beneath the Sea

Retold by Francelia Butler

There are hundreds of stories about cities existing beneath the sea, rising from the sea, or being destroyed within the sea. Some of these stories may stem from Plato's account of the island and city of Atlantis in his dialogues Timaeus *and* Critias *(c. 355 B.C.). In* Timaeus, *Critias begins to tell the tale of Atlantis to Socrates—how in a single day and night it disappeared into the depths of the sea—and then adds something of interest to students of children's literature:*

> *Truly, as is often said, the lessons of our childhood make a wonderful impression on our memories, for I am not sure that I could remember all the discourse of yesterday, but I should be much surprised if I forgot any of these things which I have heard very long ago. I listened at the time with childlike interest to the old man's [Solon's] narrative: he was very ready to teach me, and I asked him again and again to repeat his words, so that, like an indelible picture, they were branded into my mind.**

The aged Critias explains that the story had been passed down through his family from Solon, the Greek lawmaker, who had heard it in Egypt.

One sunny afternoon, a little boy was stumbling his way through the sand along the shore of the ocean. Every once in a while, he stopped to pick up a bit of wood, twisted by the sea, or a bit of shining shell. Some bits he stuck in his pockets, but most he only glanced at and tossed into the sand. Once, thinking it might be tarnished gold, he picked up a coin. But when he saw it was only a penny, he tossed it contemptuously back into the sand. What could one buy with that?

Just then, he chanced to look out to sea and—was it a mirage? He saw a magnificent city rising out of the waves. A rainbow glistened behind its turrets of dull red and golden brown. The gates of the city were open and people in brilliant costumes were moving about inside. A causeway connected the city with the shore. Without pausing, the boy ran across it and into the city.

Inside the gates, in the marketplace, merchants were displaying beautiful goods—shimmering silks, lovely jewels in exquisite settings, and richly woven tapestries. And all of them seemed to be offering them to him.

---

*Plato, *Timaeus*, trans. by Benjamin Jowett, in Edith Hamilton and Huntington Cairns, ed., *The Collected Dialogues of Plato including the Letters* (New York: Pantheon Books, 1961), p. 1106.

"Please buy," they begged.

But he shook his head. "I have no money."

"But we will sell you anything, anything . . . even for a penny. Don't you have a penny?"

"No."

"Are you sure? Even a penny would save us. We are under a spell. We rise from the waves every five hundred years. We can be redeemed by one real coin, no matter how small."

"Just wait!" the boy shouted. "I know where there's a penny. I just saw a coin in the sand! I kicked it aside! I'll go back and look for it!"

The boy rushed back across the causeway, back to where he had seen the penny. He looked and looked, frantically sifting the sand through his fingers. He kept looking until the shadows of the setting sun crossed the sand. Then he looked out again toward the city. Slowly, it was sinking beneath the waves.

"I had the key to the mystery in my hands," he thought. "But I tossed it away."

FOLK RHYMES AND POETRY

Dr. Foster

Children enjoy playing in mud, but adults like Dr. Foster in the following rhyme have other feelings about rain and its results.

Dr. Foster
Went to Gloucester
In a shower of rain;
He stepped in a puddle
Up to his middle,
And never went there again.

From James O. Halliwell, *The Nursery Rhymes of England* (London: T. Richards, 1842).

There Were Three Children on the Seashore

The following rhyme from Italy tells the story of a girl at sea who has lost something precious. To the man who retrieves it from the sea, she will give something of value. The rhyme comes from Rome and was contributed by Litizia Maroni Lumbroso. Scraps of material from the unconscious seem to emerge, for this rhyme, like many folk rhymes, has a dreamlike quality—a way of expressing the inexpressible.

There were three children on the seashore.
Turnips, onions, five cents a bunch!

The prettiest and tiniest began to sail.
While she sailed, her ring fell in the sea.
She raised her eyes to the wave,
Turnips, onions, five cents a bunch!
She saw a fisherman.
"Oh, fisherman of the wave,
Come and fish over here."
"When I have caught turnips, onions, five
    cents a bunch,
"What will you give me?"
"Ten pieces of gold, an embroidered purse,
"Onions, turnips, five cents a bunch."

The Rains Began

*Alluding to a flood, as many myths do, this
Native American poem also notes the
cleansing, purifying nature of water. All
creatures rejoice as the rains rejuvenate the
land.*

The rains began and they did not stop.
They flooded the rivers, the streams;
The lakes ran over.

Water covered the land, rose
Over the mountain forest, drowned
The spruce and the larch and the limber pine,
Washed snow from the mountain peaks.

Frog floated in a basket.
Owl perched on its handle.
Pine Grosbeak and Mudhen
Rode on the rim of it.

Owl sang his magic song,
And the waters began to go down.

Frog sang his song,
Pine Grosbeak sang,
And Mudhen.

The floods drained from the forests,
Rushed down out of the canyons,
Fell off the mesas,
Went off through the creeks and the streams
To the sea

While Frog and Owl,
Pine Grosbeak and Mudhen
Sang.

The Negro Speaks of Rivers

Langston Hughes

*Water exemplifies the force of life, and
indeed of all nature. Rivers represent the
pulsing, flowing energy of this universal
power. In this poem by Langston Hughes,
mankind proudly associates with this silent
dignity.*

I've known rivers:
I've known rivers ancient as the world and
    older than the flow of human blood in
    human veins.

My soul has grown deep like the rivers.

I bathed in the Euphrates when dawns were
    young.
I built my hut near the Congo and it lulled
    me to sleep.
I looked upon the Nile and raised the
    pyramids above it.
I heard the singing of the Mississippi when
    Abe Lincoln went down to New Orleans,
    and I've seen its muddy bosom turn all
    golden in the sunset.
I've known rivers:
Ancient, dusky rivers.

My soul has grown deep like the rivers.

From Natalia Belting, *Our Fathers Had Powerful Songs*
(New York: Dutton, 1974).

From Langston Hughes, *Selected Poems* (New York:
Knopf, 1954).

The Sea

James Reeves

*Because of its variable nature, the sea elicits
various responses from people. The fury of a
storm at sea and the serenity of the sea on a
calm summer day, though apparent
opposites, are both admirable and
mysterious qualities.*

The sea is a hungry dog,
Giant and gray.
He rolls on the beach all day.
With his clashing teeth and shaggy jaws

Hour upon hour he gnaws
The rumbling, tumbling stones,
And "Bones, bones, bones, bones!"
The giant sea-dog moans,
Licking his greasy paws.

And when the night wind roars
And the moon rocks in the stormy cloud,
He bounds to his feet and snuffs and sniffs,
Shaking his wet sides over the cliffs,
And howls and hollos long and loud.

But on quiet days in May or June,
When even the grasses on the dune
Play no more their reedy tune,
With his head between his paws
He lies on the sand shores,
So quiet, so quiet, he scarcely snores.

From James Reeves, *The Wandering Moon* (New York:
Dutton, 1960).

The World below the Brine

Walt Whitman

*Human fascination with the ocean is in part
the result of our sense of alienation from an*
*"unnatural" world. But this other world is
merely the complement to our terrestrial
environment. It may seem a world apart, but
actually it bears considerable likeness to our
world on land.*

The world below the brine;
Forests at the bottom of the sea—the
    branches and leaves,
Sea lettuce, vast lichens, strange flowers and
    seeds—the thick tangle, the openings, and
    the pink turf,
Different colors, pale gray and green, purple,
    white, and gold—the play of light through
    the water,
Dumb swimmers there among the rocks—
    coral, gluten, grass, rushes—and the
    aliment of the swimmers,
Sluggish existences grazing there,
    suspended, or slowly crawling close to the
    bottom,
The sperm whale at the surface, blowing air
    and spray, or disporting with his flukes,
The leaden-eyed shark, the walrus, the turtle,
    the hairy sea leopard, and the sting ray;
Passions there—wars, pursuits, tribes—sight
    in those ocean depths—breathing that
    thick-breathing air, as so many do;
The change thence to the sight here, and to
    the subtle air breathed by beings like us,
    who walk this sphere;
The change onward from ours, to that of
    beings who walk other spheres.

Maggie and Milly and Molly and May

e. e. cummings

*For all its power and its potential for
calamity, the ocean provides knowledge in
many forms. The sea, within the vastness of
its horizons, inspires introspection and
humility, for there we encounter a world "as
large as alone."*

From Walt Whitman, *Leaves of Grass and Selected
Prose* (New York: Random House, 1950).

From e. e. cummings, *Complete Poems 1913–1962* (Orlando, Fla.: Harcourt Brace Jovanovich).

maggie and milly and molly and may
went down to the beach (to play one day)

and maggie discovered a shell that sang
so sweetly she couldn't remember her
    troubles, and

milly befriended a stranded star
whose rays five languid fingers were;

and molly was chased by a horrible thing
which raced sideways while blowing
    bubbles: and

may came home with a smooth round stone
as small as a world and as large as alone.

for whatever we lose (like a you or a me)
it's always ourselves we find in the sea

adults. In this poem, young Mary Yarmon
captures this sense of newness by the
personification of the sea.

The sea rushes up
To eat the muddy shore,
Slips back into the waves
To return once more.

Spluttering, foaming, frothing
Pulling at the land
Again it tries to eat
The dampened, salty sand.

But will it reach
Its destination soon?
Or must it always be
The slave of the moon?

Slave of the Moon

Mary Yarmon, age 11

The significance of a natural phenomenon is
enhanced when we understand it as a part of
an integrated system rather than as an entity
unto itself. This interrelationship should
increase our fascination with a world in
which we too are integral parts.
    Children often view nature with a
freshness that eludes the jaded eyes of

From Richard Lewis, *Miracles* (New York: Simon & Schuster, 1966).

See This Beautiful Rainy Day

Alliene Grover, age 7

The elements of nature influence each of us
in a personal way, as noted in the sincerity
and practicality of this poem.

See this beautiful rainy day
That waters the pretty flowers,
And washes away my hopscotch.

From Richard Lewis, *Miracles* (New York: Simon & Schuster, 1966).

FICTION

Call It Courage
The Sea

Armstrong Sperry

In Call It Courage, *the 1940 Newbery Medal winner, the ocean is a formidable natural force that demands courage from those who face it. Mafatu, a Polynesian chief's son, has been labeled a coward because of his fear of the sea. To prove himself, he sets sail alone in a canoe, hoping to find the courage to survive.*

Day broke over a gray and dismal world. The canoe lifted and fell idly on the glassy swells. Mafatu looked back over his shoulder, searching the horizon for a last glimpse of Hikueru; but the atoll had vanished, as if to hide itself forever from his concern.

The matting sail slatted uselessly. But there seemed to be no need of a sail: the little canoe was riding one of the mysterious ocean currents that flow in their courses through the length and breadth of the Pacific: the *Ara Moana,* Paths of the Sea, as the Ancients called them. They were the ocean currents that had carried the Polynesian navigators from island to island in the childhood of the world. Mafatu was drifting farther and farther away from his homeland.

With wide-flapping wings Kivi rose from the bow of the canoe. In ascending spirals the bird climbed higher and higher, until at last he was no more than a gray speck against the lighter gray of the sky. Mafatu watched his albatross disappear and felt a desolation flood in his heart. Now there was only Uri to keep him company in this hostile world of sky and sea. Uri. . . . The yellow dog lay curled up in the shadow of the bow, opening one eye from time to time to look at his master. Wherever Mafatu went, Uri, too, would go.

All around, as far as the eye could reach, were wastes of leaden water. The canoe was the moving center of a limitless circle of sea. The boy shuddered. His fingers gripped the paddle convulsively. He thought of Kana and the other boys—what would they say when they learned that he had disappeared? And Tavana Nui—would there be sorrow in his father's heart? Would he believe that Moana, the Sea God, had claimed his son at last?

It was an ominous, oppressive world at this season of storm. Half a mile distant a whale heaved its varnished hulk to the surface, to throw a jet of vapory mist high into the air; then it submerged, leaving scarcely a ripple to mark its passage. A shoal of flying fishes broke water, skimming away in a silver shimmer of flight. A dolphin sped after them, smooth-rolling in pursuit, so close that the boy could hear the sound of its breathing. This world of the sea was ruled by Nature's harsh law of survival. Mafatu knew the sea with an intimacy given to few. He had seen fleets of giant mantas whipping the lagoon of

From Armstrong Sperry, *Call It Courage* (New York: Macmillan, 1968). Illustrated by Armstrong Sperry.

Hikueru to a boiling fury; he had seen the mighty cachalot set upon by killer-whales and torn to ribbons almost in the blink of an eye; once he had seen an octopus as large as the trunk of a tamanu, with tentacles thirty feet long, rise from the mile-deep water beyond the barrier-reef. . . . *Ai*, this sea!

Mafatu opened one of the green drinking nuts and tilted back his head to let the cool liquid trickle down his parched throat; more refreshing than spring water, cool on the hottest days, and as sustaining as food. The boy scooped out the gelatinous meat for Uri and the dog ate it gratefully.

The ocean current which held the canoe in its grip seemed to have quickened. There was a wind rising, too, in little puffs and gusts. Now the canoe heeled over under the sudden attack, while Mafatu scrambled onto the outrigger to lend his weight for ballast; then the wind dropped as suddenly as it appeared, while the canoe righted itself and the boy breathed freely once again. He searched the skies for Kivi. His albatross might have been one of a thousand sea birds flying against the roof of the sky, or he might have vanished utterly, leaving his friends here in solitary space. The bird had led Mafatu out through the reef-passage at Hikueru into the open ocean, and now, it seemed, had deserted him.

A storm was making, moving in out of those mysterious belts which lie north and south of the equator, the home of hurricanes. The wind shifted a point, bringing with it a heavy squall. Mafatu lowered the sail on the run and gripped the steering paddle with hands that showed white at the knuckles. All around him now was a world of tumbling water, gray in the hollows, greenish on the slopes. The wind tore off the combing crests and flung the spray at the sky. Like advance scouts of an oncoming army, wind gusts moved down upon the canoe, struck at it savagely. So busy was Mafatu with the paddle that there was no time for thought. He called a prayer to Maui, God of the Fisherman:

"*Maui é! E matai tu!*"

Somehow the sound of his own voice reassured him. Uri lifted his head, cocked his ears, thumped his tail for a second. The

canoe rose to the swells as lightly as a gull and coasted like a sled down the frothing slopes. What skill had wrought this small canoe! This dugout, hewn from the mighty tamanu tree. It swooped and yielded, bucked and scudded, one with the fierce element whose back it rode.

The sky darkened. A burst of lightning lit up the sea with supernatural brilliance. An instantaneous crack of thunder shattered the world. Lightning again, striking at the hissing water. Mafatu watched it with fascinated eyes. Now it was all about him. It ran to the end of the boom in globes of fire that exploded and vanished, and in the awful moment of its being it revealed mountain shapes of dark water, heaving, shouldering. . . How long could this frail craft of wood and sennit resist? Under the combined attack of wind and sea it seemed that something must inevitably give way. The wind shrilled a fiercer note. Spray stung the boy's flesh, blinded his eyes, chilled his marrow.

The sail went first—with a split and a roar. Fragments swept off on the back of the wind. The cords that held the mast hummed like plucked wires. Then with a rending groan the mast cracked. Before Mafatu could leap to cut it clear, it snapped off and disappeared in a churn of black water. The boy clung to the paddle, fighting to keep his canoe from turning broadside. Water swept aboard and out again. Only the buoyancy of tamanu kept the craft afloat. Uri cowered in the bow, half submerged, his howls drowned by the roar of the elements. Mafatu gripped his paddle for very life, an unreasoning terror powering his arms. This sea that he had always feared was rising to claim him, just as it had claimed his mother. How rightly he had feared it! Moana, the Sea God, had been biding his time. . . . "Someday, Mafatu, I will claim you!"

The boy lost all sense of time's passage. Every nerve became dulled by tumult. The wind howled above his head and still Mafatu clung to the lashed steering paddle; clung fast long after strength had vanished and only the will to live locked his strong fingers about the shaft. Even death would not loose the grip of those fingers. He held his little craft true to the wind.

There was a wave lifting before the canoe. Many the boy had seen, but this was a giant—a monster livid and hungry. Higher, higher it rose, until it seemed that it must scrape at the low-hanging clouds. Its crest heaved over with a vast sigh. The boy saw it coming. He tried to cry out. No sound issued from his throat. Suddenly the wave was upon him. Down it crashed. *Chaos!* Mafatu felt the paddle torn from his hands. Thunder in his ears. Water strangling him. Terror in his soul. The canoe slewed round into the trough. The boy flung himself forward, wound his arms about the mid-thwart. It was the end of a world.

The wave passed. Stunned, gasping, Mafatu raised his head and looked about. For a second he could not believe that he still breathed and had being. He saw Uri wedged under the bow, choking for air. He pulled the dog free. Then he saw that his string of drinking nuts had vanished. His fish spear was gone. The knife that hung about his neck by a twist of bark had been torn away. Even his *pareu* of fiber tapa fell from his body as water soaked it through. He was naked, de-

fenseless, without food or weapon, hurled forward on the breath of the hurricane. Numb of all feeling, empty as a shell, still he clung to life, and the hours droned by. . . .

So gradual was the storm's easing that at first the boy was unaware of it. The wind was blowing itself out, moving off into the empty spaces of the world. Uri crept toward the prostrate boy, quailing beside him, whimpering softly.

Night came and passed.

There was no morning mist to dim the splendor of the sunburst across the swinging seas. Far away the wings of an albatross caught its gold as it wheeled and planed against the roof of heaven. The only hint of recent storm lay in the rough and tumbling waters. As the sun climbed through the hot hours of morning, it burned into the boy's body like the sacred fires of the great marae of Hikueru. Mafatu's skin blistered and cracked. His tongue swelled in his throat. He tried to call out a prayer to Maui, but his voice was thick; the sounds which came forth were no more than a hoarse cry. The canoe, stripped of sail and mast, without a paddle to guide it in the swift-racing current, twisted and shifted in the rushing waters.

As one hour merged into another there came moments of fitful, choking slumber, a growing agony of thirst for the boy and his dog. The sun burned into them like an inescapable eye. The current which held Mafatu's canoe fast in its grip was bearing it swiftly on toward its mysterious destination.

And thus the day passed, while night once more descended, bringing blessed release from the sun.

Now the air was luminous with promise of another day. Out of the sultry mists the sea emerged, blue and violent. With the coming of this new day terror raised its head. Mafatu tried to fight it back, to deny its existence; but it gripped his heart with clammy fingers, tightened his throat. He flung himself flat on the floor of the canoe and buried his face in his arms. He must have cried out then. His voice was but a hoarse croak, yet it stirred

Uri to life: the dog's ragged tail gave one feeble thump. With the ghost of a whimper the animal laid his hot nose against the boy's hand.

The brave thump of his dog's tail touched Mafatu profoundly. He caught the animal to him, while a new assurance, a new strength, flooded his being. If Uri could have courage to die, surely he, Mafatu, could not do less! In that instant he heard a whir and fury in the sky above, a beat of wide wings. . . .Looking upward, the boy's dulled eyes made out the widespread wings of an albatross, circling above the canoe.

"Kivi!" Mafatu cried hoarsely. "*Ai, Kivi!*"

Even as he spoke, the bird wheeled slowly, then flew off straight ahead for the distant horizon. The boy noticed then that the sea current was carrying him almost due southwest. Kivi's flight moved in exact parallel. Once more it seemed as if his albatross were leading him onward, just as he had led the canoe out of the passage of Hikueru.

Mafatu scanned the rim of the horizon; it looked as hard as the cut edge of a stone. But suddenly the boy's heart gave a great leap and he started forward. *It couldn't be!* It was a cloud. . . . But the sky was cloudless. Far off in the sea-shimmer lay something that was neither sea nor sky. The swells, lifting higher, now revealed, now concealed it. That shadow on the horizon—it was land! The boy flung himself forward, shaking uncontrollably.

He seized Uri in his arms and lifted him up, laughing, crying: "Uri! Uri! It's land. *Land!*"

The dog sniffed at the air and a little whimper broke from him.

What island could this be? Was it Tahiti, the golden island, whose language was akin to that of Hikueru? Or was it, perhaps, one of the terrible dark islands of the eaters-of-men?

Now the current had a westward drift, and it was to the west that the dark islands lay. . . .

All day, as the canoe drifted onward, the boy watched the distant shadow-shape of land, not daring to take his eyes from it lest it vanish into the sea. Hunger and thirst were lulled into forgetfulness. There was only this one reality, land—escape from the sea. Weak as he was, he still clung to the thwart, his lips whispering a silent prayer of gratitude. With waning afternoon, the island took more distinct form as the canoe drifted nearer. It was high and peaked, its valleys blue-shadowed against the paler tone of the sky. Hour by hour, with every lift of the swells, the island rose higher and higher, filling Mafatu's soul with wonder. Hikueru, the only land he had ever seen, was as flat as his hand; but a great single peak crowned this strange island. Trees rose green and fair, tier upon tier of them, from the shoreline into the foothills of the purple mountain. Uri had caught the scent of the land now and was quivering with delight.

Then from far off came the first muffled thunder of the reef: the boom of the surf high-bursting on the barrier coral. That sound—was it the voice of Moana? "Someday, Mafatu, someday." . . . Involuntarily the boy shuddered. Would his ears never be free of the Sea God's threat?

Mafatu was powerless to guide his craft. He sensed that the current had quickened. He could only watch helplessly as the little canoe, swift as the following gulls, rushed to meet the tides of the island where they met and churned in a cross sea of conflict. Now across the swells came a sound like a chorus of ghostly fishermen weary with their day's toil: sea birds, always complaining, never at rest; while softer, yet rising above it was another sound—the voice of the reef itself, quieting with sundown, like the reassuring hush of a mother to her child. . . .

Weak with thirst, the boy drifted now into a merciful sleep. He struggled against it, like a weary swimmer fighting a rip-tide, but his head drooped and his eyes closed.

He was aroused at midnight by a thunderous tumult in his ears. Of a sudden he felt the canoe under him lift and flung high into the air. Then down it crashed into splinters upon the reef. Boy and dog were hurled headlong into the boiling surf.

The shock of cold water brought Mafatu half back to consciousness. Blindly he struck out, fighting for survival. Uri—where was he? No sign of the dog. The boy was aware that the canoe must have been flung over the barrier-reef, for here the water was scarcely troubled by wind or tide. Now he was swimming, swimming. . . . Somewhere ahead a strip of beach, salt-white in the darkness, lured him onward. His muscles did it of themselves. Only a will to live. A strip of sand white in the night. . . . He caught the gleam of a shark's belly, close at hand, but on he swam. His unhampered limbs moved freely through the water.

Of a sudden there was something solid beneath his feet. Sand. Mafatu stumbled, staggered, fell to his knees in the shallows. His lips moved in dry, soundless speech. Lying there with the water rippling and breaking over him, he pulled himself half upright, swayed onward. The palms, trooping to the edge of the beach, were motionless in the night air. All the world seemed to hold its breath as this boy climbed up out of the sea.

He fell to the sand once more, then, guided by he knew not what impulse, he dragged himself to the edge of the jungle. A murmur of water reached his ears, soft as a chuckle of pleasant laughter. Water, sweet water. . . . Down the face of an age-worn rock a small cascade lost itself amid ferns and cool mosses. A ragged, strangling cry broke from Mafatu's throat. He stood upright to full height. Then he crashed to the mossy bank. One cheek lay in the cool water.

The moon lifted above the rim of the palms. It outlined in silver the form of a boy thin with hunger, naked as the daystar. It revealed a small wet dog, dragging himself across the beach to his master's side.

Mafatu lay without moving. Before Uri drank, he touched the boy's cheek with his hot muzzle.

NONFICTION

River Notes
Upriver

Barry Lopez

The imagery in this excerpt, provides a unique description of the creation of a river, and perhaps of all water. Apparent is the interrelation of wilderness phenomena often noted by naturalists.

From Barry Lopez, *River Notes* (Kansas City, Mo.: Andrews, McMeel & Parker, 1979).

The course of the river above the falls is largely unknown, for the climb is arduous and at that point the road passes near and provides a view to satisfy most. The country on up to the headwaters has been walked by government men looking for clues to mineral deposits and to complete maps, but it remains unknown nevertheless. The illusion has been sustained, if one asks around or consults a topographic map, that it is well known; but I know this to be false. And I cannot help but marvel at how little care has been taken in making certain distinctions. For example, at the headwaters itself, farther up than is shown, ravens are meditating, and it is from *them* that the river actually flows, for at night they break down and weep; the universal anguish of creatures, their wailing in desolation, the wrenching anger of betrayals—this seizes them and passes out of them and in that weeping the river takes its shape.

Any act of kindness of which they hear, no matter how filled with trepidation, brings up a single tear, and it, too, runs down the black bills, splashes on small stones and is absorbed in the trickle. Farther along the murmur of fish enters, and the sensation of your hands on sheets of cold steel, the impenetrable wall presented by certain deep shades of blue, the sound of a crack working its way through a plate of English china; this sound, the sound of quick drawn breath, the odor of humus, an image of the earth hurtling through space with thought ripped from its surface, left floating like shredded fabric in its wake, the loss of what is imagined but uncared for—all this is wound among the tears of bending pain and moments of complete vulnerability in each of us to form, finally, visible water, and farther on a creek, limpid and cool, of measurable dimension.

The Sea Around Us
Hidden Lands

Rachel Carson

This book by American scientist and author Rachel Carson won the National Book Award for nonfiction in 1951. It contains fascinating descriptions of the formation of oceans, the life found in the sea, the tides and their effect on sealife, and the beauty to be discovered in the depths of the ocean.

The continental shelf is of the sea, yet of all regions of the ocean it is most like the land. Sunlight penetrates to all but its deepest parts. Plants drift in the waters above it; seaweeds cling to its rocks and sway to the passage of the waves. Familiar fishes— unlike the weird monsters of the abyss— move over its plains like herds of cattle.

Much of its substance is derived from the land—the sand and the rock fragments and the rich topsoil carried by running water to the sea and gently deposited on the shelf. Its submerged valleys and hills, in appropriate parts of the world, have been carved by glaciers into a topography much like the northern landscapes we know and the terrain is strewn with rocks and gravel deposited by the moving ice sheets. Indeed many parts (or perhaps all) of the shelf have been dry land in the geologic past, for a comparatively slight fall of sea level has sufficed, time and again, to expose it to wind and sun and rain. The Grand Banks of Newfoundland rose above the ancient seas and were submerged again. The Dogger Bank of the North Sea shelf was once a forested land inhabited by prehistoric beasts; now its 'forest' are seaweeds and its 'beasts' are fishes.

Of all parts of the sea, the continental shelves are perhaps most directly important to man as a source of material things. The great fisheries of the world, with only a few exceptions, are confined to the relatively shallow waters over the continental shelves. Seaweeds are gathered from their submerged plains to make scores of substances used in foods, drugs, and articles of commerce. As the petroleum reserves left on continental areas by ancient seas become depleted, petroleum geologists look more and more to the oil that may lie, as yet unmapped and unexploited, under these bordering lands of the sea.

The shelves begin at the tidelines and extend seaward as gently sloping plains. The 100-fathom contour used to be taken as the boundary between the continental shelf and the slope: now it is customary to place the division wherever the gentle declivity of the shelf changes abruptly to a steeper descent toward abyssal depths. The world over, the average depth at which this change occurs is about 72 fathoms; the greatest depth of any shelf is probably 200 to 300 fathoms.

Nowhere off the Pacific coast of the United States is the continental shelf much more than 20 miles wide—a narrowness characteristic of coasts bordered by young mountains perhaps still in the process of formation. On the American east coast, however, north of Cape Hatteras the shelf is as much as 150 miles wide. But at Hatteras and off southern Florida it is merely the narrowest of thresholds to the sea. Here its scant development seems to be related to the press of that great and rapidly flowing river-in-the-sea, the

Gulf Stream, which at these places swings close inshore.

The widest shelves in all the world are those bordering the Arctic. The Barents Sea shelf is 750 miles across. It is also relatively deep, lying for the most part 100 to 200 fathoms below the surface, as though its floor had sagged and been down-warped under the load of glacial ice. It is scored by deep troughs between which banks and islands rise—further evidence of the work of the ice. The deepest shelves surround the Antarctic continent, where soundings in many areas show depths of several hundred fathoms near the coast and continuing out across the shelf.

Once beyond the edge of the shelf, as we visualize the steeper declivities of the continental slope, we begin to feel the mystery and the alien quality of the deep sea—the gathering darkness, the growing pressure, the starkness of a seascape in which all plant life has been left behind and there are only the unrelieved contours of rock and clay, of mud and sand.

Biologically the world of the continental slope, like that of the abyss, is a world of animals—a world of carnivors where each creature preys upon another. For no plants live here, and the only ones that drift down from above are the dead husks of the flora of the sunlit waters. Most of the slopes are below the zone of surface wave action, yet the moving water masses of the ocean currents press against them in their coastwise passage; the pulse of the tide beats against them; they feel the surge of the deep, internal waves.

Geographically, the slopes are the most imposing features of all the surface of the earth. They are the walls of the deep-sea basins. They are the farthermost bounds of the continents, the true place of beginning of the sea. The slopes are the longest and highest escarpments found anywhere on the earth; their average height is 12,000 feet, but in some places they reach the immense height of 30,000 feet. No continental mountain range has so great a difference of elevation between its foothills and its peaks.

Nor is the grandeur of the slope topography confined to steepness and height. The slopes are the site of one of the most mysterious features of the sea. These are the submarine canyons with their steep cliffs and winding valleys cutting back into the walls of the continents. The canyons have now been found in so many parts of the world that when soundings have been taken in presently unexplored areas we shall probably find that they are of worldwide occurrence. Geologists say that some of the canyons were formed well within the most recent division of geologic time, the Cenozoic, most of them probably within the Pleistocene, a million years ago, or less. But how and by what they were carved, no one can say. Their origin is one of the most hotly disputed problems of the ocean.

Only the fact that the canyons are deeply hidden in the darkness of the sea (many extending a mile or more below present sea level) prevents them from being classed with the world's most spectacular scenery. The comparison with the Grand Canyon of the Colorado is irresistible. Like rivercut land canyons, sea canyons are deep and winding valleys, V-shaped in cross section, their walls sloping down at a steep angle to a narrow floor. The location of many of the largest ones suggests a past connection with some of the great rivers of the earth of our time. Hudson Canyon, one of the largest on the Atlantic coast, is separated by only a shallow sill from a long valley that wanders for more than a hundred miles across the continental shelf, originating at the entrance of New York Harbor and the estuary of the Hudson River. There are large canyons off the Congo, the Indus, the Ganges, the Columbia, the São Francisco, and the Mississippi, according to Francis Shepard, one of the principal students of the canyon problem. Monterey Canyon in California, Professor Shepard points out, is located off an old mouth of the Salinas River; the Cap Breton Canyon in France appears to have no relation to an existing river but actually lies off an old fifteenth-century mouth of the Adour River.

Their shape and apparent relation to existing rivers have led Shepard to suggest that the submarine canyons were cut by rivers at some time when their gorges were above sea level. The relative youth of the canyons seems to relate them to some happenings in the world of the Ice Age. It is generally agreed that sea level was lowered during the existence of the great glaciers, for water was withdrawn from the sea and frozen in the ice sheet. But most geologists say that the sea was lowered only a few hundred feet—not the mile that would be necessary to account for the canyons. According to one theory, there were heavy submarine mud flows during the times when the glaciers were advancing and sea level fell the lowest; mud stirred up by waves poured down the continental slopes and scoured out the canyons. Since none of the present evidence is conclusive, however, we simply do not know how the canyons came into being, and their mystery remains.

The floor of the deep ocean basins is probably as old as the sea itself. In all the hundreds of million of years that have intervened since the formation of the abyss, these deeper depressions have never, as far as we can learn, been drained of their covering waters. While the bordering shelves of the continents have known, in alternating geologic ages, now the surge of waves and again in the eroding tools of rain and wind and frost, always the abyss has lain under the all-enveloping cover of miles-deep water.

But this does not mean that the contours of the abyss have remained unchanged since the day of its creation. The floor of the sea, like the stuff of the continents, is a thin crust over the plastic mantle of the earth. It is here thrust up into folds and wrinkles as the interior cools by imperceptible degrees and shrinks away from its covering layer; there it falls away into deep trenches in answer to the stresses and strains of crustal adjustment; and again it pushes up into the cone-like shapes of undersea mountains as volcanoes boil upward from fissures in the crust. . . .

As the hidden lands beneath the sea become better known, there recurs again and again the query: can the submerged masses of the undersea mountains be linked with the famed 'lost continents'? Shadowy and insubstantial as are the accounts of all such legendary lands—the fabled Lemuria of the Indian Ocean, St. Brendan's Island, the lost Atlantis—they persistently recur like some deeply rooted racial memory in the folklore of many parts of the world.

Best known is Atlantis, which according to Plato's account was a large island or continent beyond the Pillars of Hercules. Atlantis was the home of a warlike people ruled by powerful kings who made frequent attacks upon the mainlands of Africa and Europe, brought much of Libya under their power, roamed the Mediterranean coast of Europe, and finally attacked Athens. However, 'with great earthquakes and inundations, in a single day and one fatal night, all who had been warriors [against Greece] were swallowed up. The Island of Atlantis disappeared beneath the sea. Since that time the sea in these quarters has become unnavigable; vessels cannot press there because of the sands which extend over the site of the buried isle.'

The Atlantis legend has lived on through the centuries. As men became bold enough to sail out on the Atlantic, to cross it, and later to investigate its depths, they speculated about the locations of the lost land. Various Atlantic islands have been said to be the remains of a land mass once more extensive. The lonely wave-washed Rocks of St. Paul, perhaps more often than any other, have been identified as the remains of Atlantis. During the past century, as the extent of the Atlantic Ridge became better known, speculations were often centered upon this great mass, far below the surface of the ocean.

Unfortunately for these picturesque imaginings, if the Ridge was ever exposed, it must have been at a time long before there were men to populate such an Atlantis. Some of the cores taken from the Ridge show a continuous series of sediments typical of open oceans, far from land, running back to a period some 60 million years ago. And man, even the most primitive type, has appeared only within the past million years or so.

Like other legends deeply rooted in folklore, the Atlantis story may have in it an element of truth. In the shadowy beginnings of human life on earth, primitive men here and there must have had knowledge of the sinking of an island or a peninsula, perhaps not with the dramatic suddenness attributed to Atlantis, but well within the time one man could observe. The witnesses of such a happening would have described it to their neighbors and children, and so the legend of a sinking continent might have been born.

Such a lost land lies today beneath the waters of the North Sea. Only a few score of thousands of years ago, the Dogger Bank was dry land, but now the fishermen drag their nets over this famed fishing ground, catching cod and hake and flounders among its drowned tree trunks.

During the Pleistocene, when immense quantities of water were withdrawn from the ocean and locked up in the glaciers, the floor of the North Sea emerged and for a time became land. It was a low, wet land, covered with peat bogs; then little by little the forests from the neighboring high lands must have moved in, for there were willows and birches growing among the mosses and ferns. Animals moved down from the mainland and became established on this land recently won from the sea. There were bears and wolves and hyenas, the wild ox, the bison, the woolly rhinoceros, and the mammoth. Primitive men moved through the forests, carrying crude stone instruments; they stalked deer and other game and with their flints grubbed up the roots of the damp forest.

Then as the glaciers began to retreat and floods from the melting ice poured into the sea and raised its level, this land became an island. Probably the men escaped to the mainland before the intervening channel had become too wide, leaving their stone implements behind. But most of the animals remained, perforce, and little by little their island shrank, and food become more and more scarce, but there was no escape. Finally the sea covered the island, claiming the land and all its life.

As for the men who escaped, perhaps in their primitive way they communicated this story to other men, who passed it down to others through the ages, until it became fixed in the memory of the race.

None of these facts were part of recorded history until a generation ago. European fishermen moved out into the middle of the North Sea and began to trawl on the Dogger. They soon made out the contours of an irregular plateau nearly as large as Denmark, lying about 60 feet under water, but sloping off abruptly at its edges into much deeper water. Their trawls immediately began to bring up a great many things not found on any ordinary fishing bank. There were loose masses of peat, which the fishermen christened 'moorlog.' There were many bones, and, although the fishermen could not identify them, they seemed to belong to large land mammals. All of these objects damaged the nets and hindered fishing, so whenever possible the fishermen dragged them off the bank and sent them tumbling into deep water. But they brought back some of the bones, some of the moorlog and fragments of trees, and the crude stone implements; these specimens were turned over to scientists to identify. In this strange debris of the fishing nets the scientists recognized a whole Pleistocene fauna and flora, and the artifacts of Stone Age man. And remembering how once the North Sea had been dry land, they reconstructed the story of Dogger Bank, the lost island.

The Silent World

Jacques-Yves Cousteau, with Frédéric Dumas

Captain Jacques-Yves Cousteau of the French navy and the physiologist Frédéric Dumas began diving together in the summer of 1943, using the first aqualung, which Cousteau coinvented. Their account of this pioneer period in marine exploration has been praised for its fresh and vivid descriptions of the undersea world. Cousteau makes reference to the American classic Moby Dick, *by Herman Melville, of which there is a simple children's version published by Silver Burdett, Morristown, N.J. A film and a videocassette, starring Gregory Peck, John Huston, and Orson Welles, are also available. Adults will probably want to read the original version of the novel.*

The sea is a most silent world. I say this deliberately on long accumulated evidence and aware that wide publicity has recently been made on the noises of the sea. Hydrophones have recorded clamors that have been sold as phonographic curiosa, but the recordings have been grossly amplified. It is not the reality of the sea as we have known it with naked ears. There are noises under water, very interesting ones that the sea transmits exceptionally well, but a diver does not hear boiler factories.

An undersea sound is so rare that one attaches great importance to it. The creatures of the sea express fear, pain and joy without audible comment. The old round of life and death passes silently, save among the mammals—whales and porpoises. The sea is unaffected by man's occasional uproars of dynamite and ships' engines. It is a silent jungle, in which the diver's sounds are keenly heard—the soft roar of exhalations, the lisp of incoming air and the hoots of a comrade. One's hunting companion may be hun-

From Jacques-Yves Cousteau, with Frédéric Dumas, *The Silent World* (New York: Harper & Row, 1953).

dreds of yards away out of sight, but his missed harpoons may be clearly heard clanging on the rocks, and when he returns one may taunt him by holding up a finger for each shot he missed.

Attentive ears may occasionally perceive a remote creaking sound, especially if the breath is held for a moment. The hydrophone can, of course, swell this faint sound to a din, helpful for analysis, but not the way it sounds to the submerged ear. We have not been able to adduce a theory to explain the creaking sounds. Syrian fishermen select fishing grounds by putting their heads down into their boats to the focal point of the sound shell that is formed by the hull. Where they hear creaking sounds they cast nets. They believe that the sound somehow emanates from rocks below, and rocks mean fish pasturage. Some marine biologists suppose the creaking sound comes from thick thousands of tiny shrimps, scraping pincers in concert. Such a shrimp in a specimen jar will transmit audible snaps. But the Syrians net fish, not shrimps. When we have dived into creaking areas we have never found a single shrimp. The distant rustle seems stronger in calm seas after a storm, but this is not always the case. The more we experience the sea, the less certain we are of conclusions.

Some fish can croak like frogs. At Dakar I swam in a loud orchestration of these monotonous animals. Whales, porpoises, croakers and whatever makes the creaking noise are the only exceptions we know to the silence of the sea.

Some fish have internal ears with otoliths, or ear stones, which make attractive necklaces called "lucky stones." But fish show little or no reaction to noises. The evidence is that they are much more responsive to nonaudible vibrations. They have a sensitive lateral line along their flanks which is, in effect, the organ of a sixth sense. As a fish undulates, the lateral receiver probably establishes its main sense of being. We think the lateral line can detect pressure waves, such as those generated by a struggling creature at a great distance. We have noticed that hooting at fish does not perturb them, but pressure waves generated by rubber foot fins seem to have a distinct influence. To approach fish we move our legs in a liquid sluggish stroke, expressing a peaceful intention. A nervous or rapid kick will empty the area of fish, even those behind rocks which cannot see us. The alarm spreads in successive explosions; one small fleeing creature is enough to panic the others. The water trembles with emergency and fish far from sight receive the silent warning.

It has become second nature to swim unobtrusively among them. We will pass casually through a landscape where all sorts of fish are placidly enjoying life and showing us the full measure of acceptance. Then, without an untoward move on our part, the area will be deserted of all fish. What portent removes hundreds of creatures, silently and at once? Were porpoises beating up pressure waves out of sight, or were hungry dentex marauding off in the mists? All we know, hanging in the abandoned space, is that an unhearable raid siren has sent all but us to shelter. We feel like deaf men. With all senses attuned to the sea, we are still without the sixth sense, perhaps the most important of all in undersea existence.

At Dakar I was diving in water where sharks ranged peacefully among hundreds of tempting red porgies, unwary of the predators. I returned to the boat and threw in a fishing line and hooked several porgies. The sharks snapped them in two before I could boat them. I think perhaps the struggle of the hooked fish transmitted vibrations that told the sharks there was easy prey available, animals in distress. In tropical waters we have used dynamite to rally sharks. I doubt whether the explosion is anything more than a dull, insignificant noise to them, but they answer the pressure waves of the fluttering fish that have been injured near the burst.

On the Azure Coast there are vertical reefs two hundred feet deep. Going straight down one of these walls is an unusual excursion into the variety of the sea and its abrupt changes of environment. Mountain climbers, like our friend, Marcel Ichac, who have gone down the reefs with us, are surprised at the changes. Going up a mountain one struggles through miles of foothills, through extended zones of trees to the snow-line, to the tree-line, and into the thin air. On the reef the changes are rapid, almost bewildering, from one zone to another. The top ten fathoms, lighted by sunny lace from the surface, are populated with nervous darting fish. Then one enters a strange country upon which dusk has fallen at noon, an autumnal climb with insalubrious air that makes the head heavy, like that of a person doomed to live in a smoggy industrial town.

Gliding down the rock facade one looks back at the world where summer shines. Then one comes to the cold layer and grows tense for the leap into winter. Inside the dull dark cold one forgets the sun. One forgets a lot. The ears no longer announce pressure changes and the air tastes like pennies. An introspective calm rules there. The green mossy rocks are replaced by Gothic stones, pierced, cusped and enfinialed. Each vault and arcade of the bottom rocks is a little world with a sandy beach and a tableau of fish.

Deeper down are miniature blue trees with white blossoms. These are the real coral, the semiprecious *corallium rubrum* in brittle limestone fantasies of form. For centuries coral was commercially dredged in the Mediterranean with "coral crosses," a type of wooden drag that smashed down the trees and recovered a few branches. The once-thick trees on the floor that may have taken hundreds of years to grow, are no more. The surviving coral grow below twenty fathoms in protected recesses and grottoes, accumulating from the ceiling like stalactites. It may be gathered only by divers.

A diver entering a coral cave must be aware of its appearance in the sea's deceiving color filter. The coral branches appear blue-black. They are covered with pale blossoms that retract and disappear when disturbed. Red coral is out of fashion at the moment and sells for about ten dollars a pound.

In the zone of red coral black-striped lobster horns protrude from the lacunae of the reef. When a diver's hand comes near, the lobster stirs with a dry grating sound. On the rocks are living tumors and growths resem-

bling udders, long fleshy threads, chalice-shaped formations, and forms like mush-rooms. Objects may no longer be distinguished by color, although there are super-natural colors to them—the violet of wine dregs, blue-blacks, yellowish-green; all muted and grayed, but somehow vibrant.

Now at the base of the reef, the sand begins, bare and monotonously receding into the floor. There, on the border of life, nothing grows or crawls. One moves automatically without brain directives. In the recesses of the brain, one revives an old notion—return to the surface. The drugged state disappears on the rise along the wall, the departure from a discolored land, a country that has never shown its real face. . . .

A new day begins in the sea with the faintest of change in light. The predawn glow suffuses its light into the dark depths, but when the sun itself appears there is no burst of light, because the low sunbeams glance off the surface. The sun's direct rays do not strike into the gulf until it is riding overhead at noon. In the evening the sea light fades gradually and there is no sunset. Daylight dwindles down to starlight, or moonlight, and dark.

Sunlight penetrating the sea loses intensity as its energy is transformed to heat by absorption. Light is further diffused by particles suspended in the water, mud, sand and plankton and even by the water molecule itself. The particles are like motes in a sunbeam, reducing visibility and scattering the light supply before it can reach the great depths. The voids are black, like interplanetary space where no floating particles reflect the light of the sun.

In clear water it seems very dark a hundred feet down, but when the diver reaches the bottom it becomes half-bright again because the light reflects from the floor, the phenomenon we found in the aftercastle of the *Dalton*.

At the three-hundred-foot limit of aqua-lung diving there is usually enough light to work by and often to expose black-and-white photographs. Dr. William Beebe and others have measured light penetration to fifteen hundred feet.

Not only does water transparency vary from place to place, but from level to level. Once we made a dive to a submerged rock needle in the Mediterranean. The water was so turbid we could see only a few yards. Two fathoms down the water suddenly opened in a clear layer, going down some distance. Then came a fifteen-foot layer of milky water with about five-foot visibility. Under the milk was a clear world all the way to the bottom. The fish were lively and abundant in the shaded but very clear depths. Above us the foggy layer looked like a low overcast on a rainy day. Often on deep dives we pass through alternate layers of turbidity and clarity, puzzling in their dynamics.

Indeed, a given layer will sometimes change clarity before one's eyes. I have seen clear water grow dim, with no apparent current to shift the scenery, and have seen murk dissolve just as mysteriously. In the open sea our experience has been that the most turbid layer is on the surface in spring and fall, but again in those seasons we have found it deeper down under a thick layer of limpid water.

Turbidity near shore can be caused, of course, by silt particles emptied from rivers. But at sea, beyond this influence, opacity is mainly due to innumerable micro-organisms. In the late spring the water is saturated with algae, tiny one-celled and multi-celled animals, spores and eggs, minuscule crustaceans, larvae, living filaments and pulsating blobs of gelatin. These culture broths can reduce visibility to fifteen feet. Swimming through the soup may give the diver a germophobia. He does not like to have the multitudes of little creatures sliding along his skin. Indeed there is harm in the oceanic mites. One feels pin pricks and sharp burns in unexpected places, most painfully on the lips. It is just as well that one's eyes are behind glass.

People who describe the enchanting riot of color in tropical reef fairylands are talking about the environment down to perhaps twenty-five feet. Below that, even in sunflooded tropical shallows, one can see only about half the real color values. The sea is a bluing agent.

The color metamorphosis of the sea was studied by the Undersea Research Group. We took down color charts with squares of pure red, blue, yellow, green, purple and orange, together with a range of grays from white to black, and photographed the chart at various levels down to the twilight zone. At fifteen feet red turned pink, and at forty feet became virtually black. There also orange disappeared. At a hundred and twenty feet yellow began to turn green, and everything was expressed in almost monochromatic colors. Ultraviolet penetrated quite deeply, while infrared rays were totally absorbed in inches of water.

One time we were hunting under the isolated rocks of La Cassidaigne. Twenty fathoms down Didi shot an eighty-pound liche. The harpoon entered behind the head but missed the spinal column. The animal was well hooked but full of fight. It swam away, towing Didi on his thirty-foot line. When it went down, he held himself crosswise to cause a drag. When the fish climbed, Didi streamlined himself behind it and kicked his flippers to encourage ascent.

The liche fought on, untiringly. It was still struggling as we drew near the depletion of our air supply. Dumas hauled himself forward on the line. The fish circled him at a fast, wobbling speed, and Dumas spun with it to avoid being wound up in the line the way Tashtego was lashed to Moby Dick. Dumas hauled in the last feet of cord, and got a grip on the harpoon shaft. He flashed his belt dagger and plunged it into the heart of the big fish. A thick puff of blood stained the water.

The blood was green. Stupefied by the sight, I swam close and stared at the mortal stream pumping from the heart. It was the color of emeralds. Dumas and I looked at each other wildly. We had swum among the great liches as aqualungers and taken them on goggle dives, but we never knew there was a type with green blood. Flourishing his astounding trophy on the harpoon, Didi led the way to the surface. At fifty-five feet the blood turned dark brown. At twenty feet it was pink. On the surface it flowed red.

Once I cut my hand seriously one hundred

and fifty feet down and saw my own blood flow green. I was already feeling a slight attack of rapture. To my half-hallucinated brain, green blood seemed like a clever trick of the sea. I thought of the liche and managed to convince myself that my blood was really red.

In 1948 we took light into the twilight zone. At high noon in clear water Dumas went down with an electric lamp, as powerful as a movie "sunlight," with a cord to the surface. Although our eyes could well distinguish the blue forms of the twilight, we wanted to see the real colors of the place.

Didi trained his reflector on the reef wall one hundred and sixty feet down. He snapped the light on. What an explosion!

The beam exposed a dazzling harlequinade of color dominated by sensational reds and oranges, as opulent as a Matisse. The living hues of the twilight zone appeared for the first time since the creation of the world. We swam around hastily, feasting our eyes. The fish themselves could never have seen this before. Why were these rich colors placed where they could not be seen? Why were the colors of the deep the reds that were first to be filtered out in the top layer? What are the colors further down, where no light has ever penetrated?

It set us off in a technical drive to make color photography in the blue zone that begins roughly one hundred and fifty feet down. . . .

To add to our knowledge of light in the sea, I wanted to dive at night. I don't believe an undressed diver could honestly say that he was brave before a night dive. (*"I will have no man in my boat,"* says Starbuck in *Moby Dick, "who is not afraid of a whale."*) Some helmet divers are inured to working at night, because of their daytime familiarity with almost total darkness in dirty harbors and rivers, but I was scared of the sea at night.

I chose a ground I knew well, a rocky bottom twenty-five feet deep. It was a clear moonless summer night filled with bright stars. In the water billions of phosphorescent organisms vied with the stars and, as I put my mask under, the *noctiluca* redoubled their brightness, flashing on and off, like fireflies.

Overhead the hull of the launch was a trembling oval of silver.

I revolved slowly down into the submerged Milky Way. I came upon rocks, bumps of ugly reality, and the dream crumbled. I could distinguish faint rock shapes in a narrow orbit. My imagination ranged into the black beyond, to the unseen recesses where night hunters, such as the conger and the moray, writhed in the merciless chase for food. This notion, more than any conscious intent to do so, caused my flashlight to go on.

A blinding conical beam hung in the water, extinguishing the tiny lights in its path. The flashlight ray made a creamy circle on the rocks. The light had the effect of plunging outer space into profound darkness. I could no longer see rocks beyond the area struck by light. I felt that hidden creatures were watching me from behind. I spun around, flashing the beam in all directions. The maneuver succeeded only in making me the blinder and losing my sense of direction.

It took resolution to turn the light off. In total blackness I began to swim cautiously across the rocks, often turning my head to dispel anxieties. In a bit my eyes readjusted and morbid shapes reformed in the environs. A faint shape moved, threw off a luminous cloud and flashed away like a comet—some surprised fish, awakened by the intruder. More fish jumped and fled.

After a while I mastered the fear and even drew some comfort from the fact that I was not down at night in tropical waters, among sharks. Before I returned to the boat, I believe I was enjoying the experience. The dive produced no observations of value.

I made another night dive under a full moon. The white light filtered strongly into the rocks. The landscape was revealed as far as one could see in daylight. But what a difference in mood! The rocks were enlarged to otherworldly dimensions. I imagined spectral human shapes and faces on them. The *noctiluca* sparks were almost extinguished; few micro-organisms were powerful enough to glow in the moonbeams. Wherever I looked I saw no living creature apart from the feeble pinpoints exerting themselves against the lunar power. There were no fish in the sea. When the moon rises above the horizon fishermen know that the fish have deserted the sea.

Epilogue

"Why in the world do you want to go down into the sea?" is a riddle we are often asked by practical people. George Mallory was asked why he wanted to climb Mt. Everest, and his answer serves for us, too. "Because it is there," he said. We are obsessed with the incredible realm of oceanic life waiting to be known. The mean level of habitation on land, the home of all animals and plants, is a thin tissue shorter than a man. The living room of the oceans, which average twelve thousand feet in depth, is more than a thousand times the volume of the land habitat.

I have recounted how the first goggles led us underwater in simple and irresistible curiosity, and how that impulse entangled us in diving physiology and engineering, which produced the compressed-air lung. Our dives are now animated by the challenge of oceanography. We have tried to find the entrance to the great hydrosphere because we feel that the sea age is soon to come.

Since ancient times lonely men have tried to penetrate the sea. Sir Robert H. Davis has found records in each flourishing age of men who tried to make underwater breathing apparatus, most of them on swimming or free-walking principles. There are Assyrian bas-reliefs of men attempting impossible submersions while sucking on goatskin bellows. Leonardo da Vinci doodled several impractical ideas for diving lungs. Fevered Elizabethan craftsmen tinkered with leathern suits for diving. They failed because there was no popular economic movement to explore the sea, such as there was on land where Stephenson built the steam locomotive or when the Wrights took to the air.

Obviously man has to enter the sea. There is no choice in the matter. The human population is increasing so rapidly and land resources are being depleted at such a rate, that we must take sustenance from the great cornucopia. The flesh and vegetables of the sea are vital. The necessity for taking mineral and chemical resources from the sea is plainly indicated by the intense political and economic struggles over tidal oil fields and the "continental shelf," by no means confined to Texas and California.

Our best independent diving range is only halfway down to the border of the shelf. We are not yet able to occupy the ground claimed by the statesmen. When research centers and industrialists apply themselves to the problem we will advance to the six-hundred-foot "dropoff" line. It will require much better equipment than the aqualung. The lung is primitive and unworthy of contemporary levels of science. We believe, however, that the conquerors of the shelf will have to get wet.

FANTASY

The Light Princess

George MacDonald

George MacDonald uses water as a metaphor to comment on childhood. The Light Princess's weightlessness is not the problem in water that it is on land—she is at ease and can be herself, floating and playing freely. In this fantasy, water may have many meanings; one is that water represents the unconscious freedom and lightness of childhood, while land represents the burdensome qualities of the adult world. According to Glenn Sadler, editor of MacDonald's fairy tales, the water represents the relationship between the physical and spiritual worlds.

As in other fairy tales, when the princess was christened, a mean person, in this case, the king's sister, was accidentally not invited. For revenge, she placed a spell on the princess, depriving the princess of gravity.

Try a Drop of Water

Perhaps the best thing for the princess would have been to fall in love. But how a princess who had no gravity could fall into anything is a difficulty—perhaps *the* difficulty. As for her own feelings on the subject, she did not even know that there was such a beehive of honey and stings to be fallen into. But now I come to mention another curious fact about her.

The palace was built on the shores of the loveliest lake in the world; and the princess loved this lake more than father or mother. The root of this preference no doubt, although the princess did not recognise it as such, was, that the moment she got into it, she recovered the natural right of which she had been so wickedly deprived—namely, gravity. Whether this was owing to the fact that water had been employed as the means of conveying the injury, I do not know. But it is certain that she could swim and dive like the duck that her old nurse said she was. The manner in which this alleviation of her misfortune was discovered was as follows.

One summer evening, during the carnival of the country, she had been taken upon the lake by the king and queen, in the royal barge. They were accompanied by many of the courtiers in a fleet of little boats. In the middle of the lake she wanted to get into the lord chancellor's barge, for his daughter, who was a great favourite with her, was in it with her father. Now though the old king rarely condescended to make light of his misfortune, yet, happening on this occasion to be in a particularly good humour, as the barges approached each other, he caught up the princess to throw her into the chancellor's barge. He lost his balance, however, and dropping into the bottom of the barge, lost his hold of his daughter; not, however, before imparting to her the down-

From George MacDonald, *Adela Cathcart* (London: Hurst and Blackett, 1864).

301

ward tendency of his own person, though in a somewhat different direction; for, as the king fell into the boat, she fell into the water. With a burst of delighted laughter she disappeared in the lake. A cry of horror ascended from the boats. They had never seen the princess go down before. Half the men were under water in a moment; but they had all, one after another, come up to the surface again for breath, when—tinkle, tinkle, babble, and gush! came the princess's laugh over the water from far away. There she was, swimming like a swan. Nor would she come out for king or queen, chancellor or daughter. She was perfectly obstinate.

But at the same time she seemed more sedate than usual. Perhaps that was because a great pleasure spoils laughing. At all events, after this, the passion of her life was to get into the water, and she was always the better behaved and the more beautiful the more she had of it. Summer and winter it was quite the same; only she could not stay so long in the water when they had to break the ice to let her in. Any day, from morning till evening in summer, she might be descried—a streak of white in the blue water—lying as still as the shadow of a cloud, or shooting along like a dolphin; disappearing, and coming up again far off, just where one did not expect her. She would have been in the lake of a night too, if she could have had her way; for the balcony of her window overhung a deep pool in it; and through a shallow reedy passage she could have swum out into the wide wet water, and no one would have been any the wiser. Indeed, when she happened to wake in the moonlight, she could hardly resist the temptation. But there was the sad difficulty of getting into it. She had as great a dread of the air as some children have of the water. For the slightest gust of wind would blow her away; and a gust might arise in the stillest moment. And if she gave herself a push towards the water and just failed of reaching it, her situation would be dreadfully awkward, irrespective of the wind; for at best there she would have to remain, suspended in her night-gown, till she was seen and angled for by somebody from the window.

"Oh! if I had my gravity," thought she, contemplating the water, "I would flash off this balcony like a long white sea-bird, headlong into the darling wetness. Heigh-ho!"

This was the only consideration that made her wish to be like other people.

Another reason for her being fond of the water was that in it alone she enjoyed her freedom. For she could not walk out without a *cortège*, consisting in part of a troop of light-horse, for fear of the liberties which the wind might take with her. And the king grew more apprehensive with increasing years, till at last he would not allow her to walk abroad at all without some twenty silken cords fastened to as many parts of her dress, and held by twenty noblemen. Of course horseback was out of the question. But she bade good-by to all this ceremony when she got into the water.

And so remarkable were its effects upon her, especially in restoring her for the time to the ordinary human gravity, that Hum-Drum and Kopy-Keck agreed in recommending the king to bury her alive for three years; in the hope that, as the water did her so much good, the earth would do her yet more. But the king had some vulgar prejudices against the experiment, and would not give his consent. Foiled in this, they yet agreed in another recommendation; which, seeing that one imported his opinions from China and the other from Thibet, was very remarkable indeed. They argued that, if water of external origin and application could be so efficacious, water from a deeper source might work a perfect cure; in short, that if the poor afflicted princess could by any means be made to cry, she might recover her lost gravity.

But how was this to be brought about? Therein lay all the difficulty—to meet which the philosophers were not wise enough. To make the princess cry was as impossible as to make her weigh. They sent for a professional beggar; commanded him to prepare his most touching oracle of woe; helped him out of the court charade-box, to whatever he wanted for dressing up, and promised great rewards in the event of his success. But it was all in vain. She listened to the mendicant artist's story, and gazed at his marvellous make-up, till she could contain herself no longer, and went into the most undignified contortions for relief, shrieking, positively screeching with laughter.

When she had a little recovered herself, she ordered her attendants to drive him away, and not give him a single copper; whereupon his look of mortified discomfiture wrought her punishment and his revenge, for it sent her into violent hysterics, from which she was with difficulty recovered.

But so anxious was the king that the suggestion should have a fair trial, that he put himself in a rage one day, and, rushing up to her room, gave her an awful whipping. Yet not a tear would flow. She looked grave, and her laughing sounded uncommonly like screaming—that was all. The good old tyrant, though he put on his best gold spectacles to look, could not discover the smallest cloud in the serene blue of her eyes.

Put Me In Again

It must have been about this time that the son of a king, who lived a thousand miles from Lagobel, set out to look for the daughter of a queen. He travelled far and wide, but as sure as he found a princess, he found some fault in her. Of course he could not marry a mere woman, however beautiful; and there was no princess to be found worthy of him. Whether the prince was so near perfection that he had a right to demand perfection itself, I cannot pretend to say. All I know is, that he was a fine, handsome, brave, generous, well-bred, and well-behaved youth, as all princes are.

In his wandering he had come across some reports about our princess; but as everybody said she was bewitched, he never dreamed that she could bewitch him. For what indeed could a prince do with a princess that had lost her gravity? Who could tell what she might not lose next? She might lose her visibility, or her tangibility; or, in short, the power of making impressions upon the radical sensorium; so that he should never be able to tell whether she was dead or alive. Of

course he made no further inquiries about her.

One day he lost sight of his retinue in a great forest. These forests are very useful in delivering princes from their courtiers, like a sieve that keeps back the bran. Then the princes get away to follow their fortunes. In this they have the advantage of the princesses, who are forced to marry before they have had a bit of fun. I wish our princesses got lost in a forest sometimes.

One lovely evening, after wandering about for many days, he found that he was approaching the outskirts of this forest; for the trees had got so thin that he could see the sunset through them; and he soon came upon a kind of heath. Next he came upon signs of human neighbourhood; but by this time it was getting late, and there was nobody in the fields to direct him.

After travelling for another hour, his horse, quite worn out with long labour and lack of food, fell, and was unable to rise again. So he continued his journey on foot. At length he entered another wood—not a wild forest, but a civilized wood, through which a footpath led him to the side of a lake. Along this path the prince pursued his way through the gathering darkness. Suddenly he paused, and listened. Strange sounds came across the water. It was, in fact, the princess laughing. Now there was something odd in her laugh, as I have already hinted; for the hatching of a real hearty laugh requires the incubation of gravity; and perhaps this was how the prince mistook the laughter for screaming. Looking over the lake, he saw something white in the water; and, in an instant, he had torn off his tunic, kicked off his sandals, and plunged in. He soon reached the white object, and found that it was a woman. There was not light enough to show that she was a princess, but quite enough to show that she was a lady, for it does not want much light to see that.

Now I cannot tell how it came about,— whether she pretended to be drowning, or whether he frightened her, or caught her so as to embarrass her,—but certainly he brought her to shore in a fashion ignominious to a swimmer, and more nearly drowned than she had ever expected to be; for the water had got into her throat as often as she had tried to speak.

At the place to which he bore her, the bank was only a foot or two above the water; so he gave her a strong lift out of the water, to lay her on the bank. But, her gravitation ceasing the moment she left the water, away she went up into the air, scolding and screaming.

"You naughty, *naughty*, NAUGHTY, *NAUGHTY* man!" she cried.

No one had ever succeeded in putting her into a passion before.—When the prince saw her ascend, he thought he must have been bewitched, and have mistaken a great swan for a lady. But the princess caught hold of the topmost cone upon a lofty fir. This came off; but she caught at another; and, in fact, stopped herself by gathering cones, dropping them as the stalks gave way. The prince, meantime, stood in the water, staring and forgetting to get out. But the princess disappearing, he scrambled on shore, and went in the direction of the tree. There he found her climbing down one of the branches towards the stem. But in the darkness of the wood, the prince continued in some bewilderment as to what the phenomenon could be; until, reaching the ground, and seeing him standing there, she caught hold of him, and said,—

"I'll tell papa."

"Oh no, you won't!" returned the prince.

"Yes, I will," she persisted. "What business had you to pull me down out of the water, and throw me to the bottom of the air? I never did you any harm."

"Pardon me. I did not mean to hurt you."

"I don't believe you have any brains; and that is a worse loss than your wretched gravity. I pity you."

The prince now saw that he had come upon the bewitched princess, and had already offended her. But before he could think what to say next, she burst out angrily, giving a stamp with her foot that would have sent her aloft again but for the hold she had of his arm,—

"Put me up directly."

"Put you up where, you beauty?" asked the prince.

He had fallen in love with her almost, already; for her anger made her more charming than any one else had ever beheld her; and, as far as he could see, which certainly was not far, she had not a single fault about her, except, of course, that she had not any gravity. No prince, however, would judge of a princess by weight. The loveliness of her foot he would hardly estimate by the depth of the impression it could make in mud.

"Put you up where, you beauty?" asked the prince.

"In the water, you stupid!" answered the princess.

"Come, then," said the prince.

The condition of her dress, increasing her usual difficulty in walking, compelled her to cling to him; and he could hardly persuade himself that he was not in a delightful dream, notwithstanding the torrent of musical abuse with which she overwhelmed him. The prince being therefore in no hurry, they came upon the lake at quite another part, where the bank was twenty-five feet high at least; and when they had reached the edge, he turned towards the princess, and said,—

"How am I to put you in?"

"That is your business," she answered, quite snappishly. "You took me out—put me in again."

"Very well," said the prince; and, catching her up in his arms, he sprang with her from the rock. The princess had just time to give one delighted shriek of laughter before the water closed over them. When they came to the surface, she found that, for a moment or two, she could not even laugh, for she had gone down with such a rush, that it was with difficulty she recovered her breath. The instant they reached the surface—

"How do you like falling in?" said the prince.

After some effort the princess panted out,—

"Is that what you call *falling in?*"

"Yes," answered the prince, "I should think it a very tolerable specimen."

"It seemed to me like going up," rejoined she.

"My feeling was certainly one of elevation too," the prince conceded.

The princess did not appear to understand him, for she retorted his question:—

"How do *you* like falling in?" said the princess.

"Beyond everything," answered he; "for I have fallen in with the only perfect creature I ever saw."

"No more of that: I am tired of it," said the princess.

Perhaps she shared her father's aversion to punning.

"Don't you like falling in, then?" said the prince.

"It is the most delightful fun I ever had in my life," answered she. "I never fell before. I wish I could learn. To think I am the only person in my father's kingdom that can't fall!"

Here the poor princess looked almost sad.

"I shall be most happy to fall in with you any time you like," said the prince, devotedly.

"Thank you. I don't know. Perhaps it would not be proper. But I don't care. At all events, as we have fallen in, let us have a swim together."

"With all my heart," responded the prince.

And away they went, swimming, and diving, and floating, until at last they heard cries along the shore, and saw lights glancing in all directions. It was now quite late, and there was no moon.

"I must go home," said the princess. "I am very sorry, for this is delightful."

"So am I," returned the prince. "But I am glad I haven't a home to go to—at least, I don't exactly know where it is."

"I wish I hadn't one either," rejoined the princess, "it is so stupid! I have a great mind," she continued, "to play them all a trick. Why couldn't they leave me alone? They won't trust me in the lake for a single night!—You see where that green light is burning? That is the window of my room. Now if you would just swim there with me very quietly, and when we are all but under the balcony, give me such a push—*up* you call it—as you did a little while ago, I should

be able to catch hold of the balcony, and get in at the window; and then they may look for me till tomorrow morning!"

"With more obedience than pleasure," said the prince, gallantly; and away they swam, very gently.

"Will you be in the lake to-morrow night?" the prince ventured to ask.

"To be sure I will. I don't think so. Perhaps," was the princess's somewhat strange answer.

But the prince was intelligent enough not to press her further; and merely whispered, as he gave her the parting lift, "Don't tell." The only answer the princess returned was a roguish look. She was already a yard above his head. The look seemed to say, "Never fear. It is too good fun to spoil that way."

So perfectly like other people had she been in the water, that even yet the prince could scarcely believe his eyes when he saw her ascend slowly, grasp the balcony, and disappear through the window. He turned, almost expecting to see her still by his side. But he was alone in the water. So he swam away quietly, and watched the lights roving about the shore for hours after the princess was safe in her chamber. As soon as they disappeared, he landed in search of his tunic and sword, and, after some trouble, found them again. Then he made the best of his way round the lake to the other side. There the wood was wilder, and the shore steeper— rising more immediately towards the mountains which surrounded the lake on all sides, and kept sending it messages of silvery streams from morning to night, and all night long. He soon found a spot whence he could see the green light in the princess's room, and where, even in the broad daylight, he would be in no danger of being discovered from the opposite shore. It was a sort of cave in the rock, where he provided himself a bed of withered leaves, and lay down too tired for hunger to keep him awake. All night long he dreamed that he was swimming with the princess.

Where Is the Prince?

Never since the night when the princess left him so abruptly had the prince had a single interview with her. He had seen her once or twice in the lake; but as far as he could discover, she had not been in it anymore at night. He had sat and sung, and looked in vain for his Nereid; while she, like a true Nereid, was wasting away with her lake, sinking as it sank, withering as it dried. When at length he discovered the change that was taking place in the level of the water, he was in great alarm and perplexity. He could not tell whether the lake was dying because the lady had forsaken it; or whether the lady would not come because the lake had begun to sink. But he resolved to know so much at least.

He disguised himself, and, going to the palace, requested to see the lord chamberlain. His appearance at once gained his request; and the lord chamberlain, being a man of some insight, perceived that there was more in the prince's solicitation than met the ear. He felt likewise that no one could tell whence a solution of the present difficulties might arise. So he granted the prince's prayer to be made shoe-black to the princess. It was rather cunning in the prince to request such an easy post, for the princess could not possibly soil as many shoes as other princesses.

He soon learned all that could be told about the princess. He went nearly distracted; but after roaming about the lake for days, and diving in every depth that remained, all that he could do was to put an extra polish on the dainty pair of boots that was never called for.

For the princess kept her room, with the curtains drawn to shut out the dying lake. But could not shut it out of her mind for a moment. It haunted her imagination so that she felt as if the lake were her soul, drying up within her, first to mud, then to madness and death. She thus brooded over the change, with all its dreadful accompaniments, till she was nearly distracted. As for the prince, she had forgotten him. However much she had enjoyed his company in the water, she did not care for him without it. But she seemed to have forgotten her father and mother too.

The lake went on sinking. Small slimy spots began to appear, which glittered steadily amidst the changeful shine of the water.

These grew to broad patches of mud, which widened and spread, with rocks here and there, and floundering fishes and crawling eels swarming. The people went everywhere catching these, and looking for anything that might have dropped from the royal boats.

At length the lake was all but gone, only a few of the deepest pools remaining unexhausted.

It happened one day that a party of youngsters found themselves on the brink of one of these pools in the very centre of the lake. It was a rocky basin of considerable depth. Looking in, they saw at the bottom something that shone yellow in the sun. A little boy jumped in and dived for it. It was a plate of gold covered with writing. They carried it to the king.

On one side of it stood these words:—

"Death alone from death can save.
Love is death, and so is brave.
Love can fill the deepest grave.
Love loves on beneath the wave."

Now this was enigmatical enough to the king and courtiers. But the reverse of the plate explained it a little. Its writing amounted to this:—

"If the lake should disappear, they must find the hole through which the water ran. But it would be useless to try to stop it by any ordinary means. There was but one effectual mode.—The body of a living man should alone stanch the flow. The man must give himself of his own will; and the lake must take his life as it filled. Otherwise the offering would be of no avail. If the nation could not provide one hero, it was time it should perish."

• • •

[The prince leaps into the lake to plug the hole with his body. The princess, seeing that the prince is dying, leaps in to save him. Through this act of love, the spell is broken and the princess regains her gravity.]

• • •

Look at the Rain!

The princess burst into a passion of tears, and *fell* on the floor. There she lay for an hour, and her tears never ceased. All the pent-up crying of her life was spent now. And a rain came on, such as had never been seen in that country. The sun shone all the time, and the great drops, which fell straight to the earth, shone likewise. The palace was in the heart of a rainbow. It was a rain of rubies, and sapphires, and emeralds, and topazes. The torrents poured from the mountains like molten gold; and if it had not been for its subterraneous outlet, the lake would have overflowed and inundated the country. It was full from shore to shore.

But the princess did not heed the lake. She lay on the floor and wept. And this rain within doors was far more wonderful than the rain out of doors. For when it abated a little, and she proceeded to rise, she found to her astonishment, that she could not. At length, after many efforts, she succeeded in getting upon her feet. But she tumbled down again directly. Hearing her fall, her old nurse uttered a yell of delight, and ran to her, screaming,—

"My darling child! she's found her gravity!"

"Oh, that's it! is it?" said the princess, rubbing her shoulder and her knee alternately. "I consider it very unpleasant. I feel as if I should be crushed to pieces."

"Hurrah!" cried the prince from the bed. "If you've come round, princess, so have I. How's the lake?" "Brimful," answered the nurse.

"Then we're all happy."

"That we are indeed!" answered the princess, sobbing.

And there was rejoicing all over the country that rainy day. Even the babies forgot their past troubles, and danced and crowed amazingly. And the king told stories, and the queen listened to them. And he divided the money in his box, and she the honey in her pot, among all the children. And there was such jubilation as was never heard of before.

Of course the prince and princess were betrothed at once. But the princess had to learn to walk, before they could be married with any propriety. And this was not so easy at her time of life, for she could walk no more

than a baby. She was always falling down and hurting herself.

"Is this the gravity you used to make so much of?" said she one day to the prince, as he raised her from the floor. "For my part, I was a great deal more comfortable without it."

"No, no, that's not it. This is it," replied the prince, as he took her up, and carried her about like a baby, kissing her all the time. "This is gravity."

"That's better," said she. "I don't mind that so much."

And she smiled the sweetest, loveliest smile in the prince's face. And she gave him one little kiss in return for all his; and he thought them overpaid, for he was beside himself with delight. I fear she complained of her gravity more than once after this, notwithstanding.

It was a long time before she got reconciled to walking. But the pain of learning it was quite counterbalanced by two things, either of which would have been sufficient consolation. The first was, that the prince himself was her teacher; and the second, that she could tumble into the lake as often as she pleased. Still, she preferred to have the prince jump in with her; and the splash they made before was nothing to the splash they made now.

The lake never sank again. In process of time, it wore the roof of the cavern quite through, and was twice as deep as before.

The only revenge the princess took upon her aunt was to tread pretty hard on her gouty toe the next time she saw her. But she was sorry for it the next day, when she heard that the water had undermined her house, and that it had fallen in the night, burying her in its ruins; whence no one ever ventured to dig up her body. There she lies to this day.

So the prince and princess lived and were happy; and had crowns of gold, and clothes of cloth, and shoes of leather, and children of boys and girls, not one of whom was ever known, on the most critical occasion, to lose the smallest atom of his or her due proportion of gravity.

Trees and Hills

FABLES, MYTHS, AND LEGENDS

The Mountain and the Squirrel*

Ralph Waldo Emerson

Writers from LaFontaine to Ralph Waldo Emerson to Marianne Moore have often translated fables into poetry; both genres contain wisdom, very often in encapsulated form. The message of "The Mountain and the Squirrel" is that each of us has strengths and weaknesses and that, therefore, attempts to compare ourselves with others are frequently unjust. Emerson's poem on this theme is well known, but the fable on this subject has long been a favorite as well.

The mountain and the squirrel
Had a quarrel,
And the former called the latter 'Little Prig;'
Bun replied,
'You are doubtless very big;
But all sorts of things and weather
Must be taken in together,
To make up a year
And a sphere.
And I think it no disgrace
To occupy my place.
If I'm not so large as you,
You are not so small as I,
And not half so spry.
I'll not deny you make
A very pretty squirrel track;
Talents differ; all is well and wisely put;
If I cannot carry forests on my back,
Neither can you crack a nut.'

Yggdrasill the World Tree†

Retold by Roger Lancelyn Green

In the Norse myth of creation, the great tree Yggdrasill stands at the center of the universe, holding the world in place and supporting the sky. Asgard, the land of

*Ralph Waldo Emerson, *Poems* (Boston: Houghton Mifflin, 1932).

†From Roger Lancelyn Green, *Myths of the Norsemen* (New York: Viking Penguin, 1970). Copyright Roger Lancelyn Green, 1960.

the gods, is placed high in its branches. The tree is an important feature of Norse mythology, too, for as we are told here, the first man and the first woman were made from an ash and an elder. This selection also contains a "flood" story, like the Greek and Hindu tales in the previous section.

In the northern lands the summer is short and the winter long and cold. Life is a continual battle against the grim powers of nature: against the cold and the darkness—the snow and ice of winter, the bitter winds, the bare rocks where no green thing will grow, and against the terrors of dark mountains and wolf-haunted ravines.

The men and women who lived there in the early days needed to be strong and much-enduring to survive at all. They were tillers of the ground, but also warriors who did battle against the wolves, and against men even more savage who came down from the mountains or up from the deep sounds or fiords of the sea to burn their homes and steal away their treasures and their food, and often their wives and daughters as well.

Even when there were no wild beasts and wilder men to fight, it seemed that the very elements were giants who fought against them with wind, frost, and snow as weapons. It was a cruel world, offering little to hope for; yet there was love, and honour, courage and endurance. There were mighty deeds to be done and bards or skalds to sing of them, so that the names of the heroes did not die.

And, just as the deeds of men were remembered in song and story, tales were told of the gods, the Æsir, who must surely have fought even greater battles in the beginning of time against those Giants of Ice and Frost and Snow and Water who were still only kept at bay with difficulty.

In the very beginning of time, so the Norsemen believed, there was no Earth as we know it now: there was only Ginnungagap, the Yawning Void. In this moved strange mists which at length drew apart leaving an even deeper Gap, with Muspelheim, the Land of Fire, to the south of it, and Nifelheim, the Land of Mist, to the north of it.

Surtur the Demon of Fire sat at the world's southern end with his flaming sword, waiting for the Day of Doom, to go forth and destroy both gods and men.

Deep down in Ginnungagap lay the Well of Life, Hvergelmir, from which flowed rivers which the cruel breath of the north froze into grinding blocks of ice.

As the ages passed the grinding ice piled up mysteriously above the Well of Life and became Ymir, the greatest of all Giants, father of the terrible Frost Giants, and of all the Giant kin.

Ymir grew into life, and with him appeared the magic cow Audumla whose milk was his food. And very soon the ice of Ymir broke off in small pieces and each became a Rime Giant—a father of witches and warlocks, of ogres and trolls.

Audumla herself needed food, and she licked the ice about her and found in it the salt of life that welled up from Hvergelmir.

On the first day that she licked the ice there came forth in the evening the hair of a man; the second day she licked, and in the evening there was a man's head showing; and by the ending of the third day the whole man was there.

He was the first of the Æsir, and his name was Buri; he was tall and strong, and very fair to see. His son was called Borr, and this Borr married the giantess Bestla, and they were the mother and father of the Æsir who planted the World Tree, Yggdrasill, and made the Earth.

Borr had three sons called Odin, Vili, and Ve, and of these Odin, the Allfather, was the greatest and the most noble.

They fought against Ymir the great Ice Giant, and slew him, and the icy water gushed from his wounds and drowned most of the Rime Giants, except for one who was named Bergelmir. He was wise and clever, and for this reason Odin spared him.

For Bergelmir built himself a boat with a roof, and took shelter in it with his wife and

310 / THE NATURAL WORLD

children so that they escaped being drowned in the flood.

But Odin and his brothers thrust the dead Ymir down into the void of Ginnungagap and made of his body the world we live in. His ice-blood became the sea and the rivers; his flesh became the dry land and his bones the mountains, while the gravel and stones were his teeth.

Odin and his children set the sea in a ring round about the earth, and the World Tree, the Ash Yggdrasill, grew up to hold it in place, to overshadow it with its mighty branches, and to support the sky which was the ice-blue skull-top of Ymir.

They gathered the sparks that flew out of Muspelheim and made stars of them. They brought molten gold from the realm of Surtur, the Fire Demon, and fashioned the glorious Sun Chariot, drawn by the horses Earlywaker and All-strong, with the fair maiden, Sol, to drive it on its course. Before her went the bright boy, Mani, driving the Moon Chariot drawn by the horse All-swift.

The Sun and Moon move quickly, never pausing to rest. They dare not stop, even for a moment, for each of them is pursued through the sky by a fierce wolf panting to devour them—and that fate will befall them on the day of the Last Great Battle. These two wolves are the children of evil, for their mother was a wicked witch who lived in the Forest of Ironwood: her husband was a giant, and her children were werewolves and trolls.

When Odin had set the stars in their courses and had lit the earth with the Sun and Moon, he turned back to the new world which he had made. Already the Giants and other creatures of evil were stirring against him, so he took more of the bones of Ymir and spread the mountains as a wall against Giantland, or Jotunheim. Then he turned back to the land made for men, which he called Midgard or Middle Earth, and began to make it fruitful and fair to see.

Out of Ymir's curly hair he formed the trees, from his eyebrows the grass and flowers, and he set clouds to float in the sky above and sprinkle the earth with gentle showers.

Then for the making of Mankind, the All-father Odin took an ash tree and an elder upon the sea-shore and fashioned from them Ask and Embla, the first Man and the first Woman. Odin gave them souls, and his brother Vili gave them the power of thought and feeling, while Ve gave them speech, hearing and sight.

From these two came children enough to people Midgard: but sin and sorrow overtook them, for the Giants and other creatures of evil took on the shapes of men and women, and married with them, despite all that Odin could do.

The Dwarfs also had a hand in this for they taught men to love gold, and of the power that comes with riches. They were the little people who lived in Nifelheim, the region of mist, and in great caves under the earth. They had been made out of the dead flesh of Ymir, and the Æsir gave them the shape of men but a far greater cleverness in the arts and crafts of working with iron and gold and precious stones.

These Dwarfs, with Durin as their king, made rings and swords and priceless treasures, and mined gold out of the earth for the Æsir's use.

For after Midgard was made, wise Odin turned to the shaping of Asgard, his own strong and beautiful land, high in the branches of Yggdrasill the World Tree. The first palace was all of shining gold, and it was called Gladsheim, the Place of Joy: there Odin sat on his high seat, with beautiful Frigga his queen beside him.

Next they made palaces for their children, the great gods and goddesses who were so soon to play their part in the long struggle against the Powers of Evil: for Thor the Lord of Thunder and his wife Sif of the golden hair; for brave Tyr the young and battle-eager, guardian of the gods; for bright Baldur, fairest of all the Æsir, and sweet Nanna his wife; for Bragi and Iduna, who delighted in music and youth; for Uller of the Bow, and Vidar the Silent, and many another.

Round about Asgard stood great walls and towers, halls and palaces; and in the middle was the fair plain of Ida, where grew gardens of delight in front of Odin's palace of Gladsheim.

Every day Odin and the Æsir rode forth over the Bridge Bifrost, which appears to men on earth as the rainbow, and went down to the Well of Urd beneath one root of the Ash Yggdrasill—all, that is, except mighty Thor who dared not tread on that delicate arc for fear his weight might break it. He had instead to go round by the rough road over the mountains, and the Giants ran in terror whenever they saw him coming. Bifrost Bridge glows in the sky, for at its foot burns a bright fire to prevent the Giant kind from crossing it and so reaching Asgard.

Down in the shady gloom at the foot of the World Tree the Æsir held their council, to decide how they might bring help to mankind, and what must be done in the long war against the Giants. Down there under the Ash, beside the Well, stood a fair hall where dwelt the Norns, the three weird sisters Urd, Verlandi, and Skuld, who knew more even than Odin himself. For Urd could see all that had chanced in the past, while Verlandi had the power of knowing what was being done in all the worlds at the present; but Skuld was the wisest of all, for she could see into the future—and that not even Odin himself could do.

Often in time to come the Norns appeared at the birth of a hero to spin his web of fate and give him gifts of good and evil that should determine his future life.

They could tell Odin of the course of the world, and from them he knew, as well as from his own wisdom, of Ragnarok, the Last Great Battle, which must come at the end of the world when the Æsir and their Giant foes would fight out to the bitter end the great contest between Good and Evil.

The Norns also tended the Ash Yggdrasill, and watered the greatest of its roots daily from the Well of Urd. For the evil ones strove continually to destroy the World Tree: down in Nifelheim, where one root grew, the evil Nid Hog was for ever gnawing at it, while serpents twined and bit. Higher up four harts ran upon its branches and nibbled at the leaves, while at the top sat a wise eagle watching all that was done, and Ratatosk the mischievous red squirrel scampered up and down it, carrying news and gossip between Nid Hog and the Eagle.

In the midst of this strange and complicated world sat Odin the Allfather, like a kindly spider, in the centre of his web. His seat, high above Asgard, was called Lidskialf or Heaven's Crag, and there he sat and surveyed the world, with his two tame ravens Hugin and Munin perched on his shoulders. To them he owed much of his knowledge, for day by day they would fly forth through the world and return in the evening to tell what they had seen. . . .

Daphne and Apollo

Retold by Roger Lancelyn Green

This Greek myth is taken from Ovid's Metamorphoses. *Daphne, a wood nymph and huntress, is transformed into a laurel tree to escape Apollo, the god who loves her. But Apollo loves her even in her new tree form and declares that the laurel crown shall be used as a sign of victory forever. The action takes place in the mountains of the gods.*

From Roger Lancelyn Green, *Tales the Muses Told* (New York: Henry Z. Walck, 1965). Reproduced by permission of The Bodley Head, London.

Although the arrows of love were directed by Aphrodite, it was usually her son Eros (whom the Romans called Cupid) who actually discharged them.

Now Apollo was the god of the bow, and when he first saw Aphrodite's youthful son armed as an archer, he laughed scornfully.

"What has a child like you to do with the weapon of a warrior?" he asked. "It is only I who can shoot and never miss—whether it be man or beast that I slay with the swift arrows of sickness or pestilence. You should leave such things to your betters, and be content with the torch of love that excites desire."

"Your arrows may pierce all things mortal," answered Eros. "But mine strike to the hearts of even the gods themselves. So you see, I am a better archer than you are: and if you insult me again, I will prove it to you!"

As Apollo still could not believe that this pert boy could be a more deadly marksman than himself, he dared Eros to do his worst, and went angrily on his way to his shrine on Mount Parnassus—on the lower slopes of which he had recently slain with his arrows the terrible monster called Python who lived in the cave by Delphi.

But Eros made ready two arrows. One was as sharp as love itself, and this was for Apollo; the other was tipped with lead, and was the kind which kills desire and puts all love to flight.

Looking around to see some beautiful girl for Apollo to love in vain, Eros chose Daphne, the daughter of Amyclas, king of Sparta and struck her with the lead-tipped arrow.

Daphne was still too young to have done more than dream of a husband. Now her dreams changed and she thought only of the joys of maidenhood. Clad in a short tunic and with her hair tied back, she began to spend more and more time with a bow in her hand and a quiver of arrows at her side, hunting the deer over the lower slopes of Mount Taygetus above her Spartan home.

As she grew older she wandered farther, going north along the great range of Taygetus and into the wild mountain region of Arcadia where the goddess Artemis, twin-

sister of Apollo, hunted with her band of nymphs and maidens. Artemis and all who followed her were sworn never to marry, and no man was ever allowed to join in their hunt or witness their rites. So here Daphne found her true home and was as happy as could be.

Sometimes she returned to Sparta, and then her father, King Amyclas, would beg her to marry, with tears in his eyes:

"I am growing old," he would say. "Find a son-in-law for me soon! Grant my dearest wish—that I should see my grandchildren playing here in the palace of Sparta before I die!"

But Daphne would reply: "Kind father, let me enjoy this state of maiden bliss forever! The very thought of a husband or a child fills me with dismay. Great Zeus himself granted to his daughter Artemis that she should remain unwed and always be a maid: do not be less generous than Zeus—and grant me the same boon."

Amyclas loved his daughter so dearly that he could refuse her nothing; and he saw to it that she was troubled no more with suitors.

Yet Daphne was so beautiful that suitors came nonetheless. Many a young man who saw her for a moment as she sped among the trees in the forests of Arcadia, from the steep slopes of Taygetus in the south to Erymanthus and Cyllene in the north, lost his heart to her in that moment; yet she went ever on her way, and could not spare so much as a word for one of them.

But the day came at last when Apollo chanced to see her as he was walking on the slopes of Mount Cyllene. Eros had waited for this moment, and at once his sharp arrow of desire sped through Apollo's heart, and the god was a captive to love.

He realized at once the trick which Eros had played him, and for a long time he fought against his love and tried to keep away from Daphne.

But it was in vain. More and more of his time was given to watching her as he, being a god, could do from a great distance.

At last he could shun her no longer, and suddenly one day she met Apollo walking toward her under the trees where he shone like a golden sunbeam.

With a scream, she turned and fled down the mountainside, Apollo running after her and calling in vain for her to stop.

"Wait a moment, beautiful Daphne!" he cried. "I mean you no harm. I am Apollo, the god of the golden bow, the son of Zeus, the lord of music. Stay while I tell you that I have chosen you to be my bride! Daphne, I love you! I will give you sweet nectar to drink, the wine of the gods—and, if Zeus wills, you will become immortal even as I am. Daphne, wait!"

But Daphne sped on, scarcely heeding Apollo's words. Only one thought was in her mind, and that was to escape from him and from the terrible power of love.

Feeling certain that he could persuade her to accept him as her husband, and knowing nothing of the leaden arrow which Eros had lodged in her heart, Apollo gave chase to Daphne. Down and down and down the long hillsides they went; through great woods of pine and oak, and at last among the olive-groves that sloped down into the wide valley of the Alpheus.

Apollo was drawing nearer and nearer. Now he could see Daphne only a little way ahead of him, threading her way among the gnarled trunks of the olives and through the black shadows of their silvery leaves. She was so beautiful as she fled through the light and shadow with her golden hair streaming out behind her that Apollo could find no words. But he drew closer and closer, and almost could touch her with his outstretched hands.

Now they drew near to the steep bank of the Alpheus, and Daphne knew that she could run no farther.

"Help me, Artemis—help me, all you goddesses!" she prayed. "Turn this fatal beauty of mine into something that no man will run after!"

Not Artemis but Aphrodite heard her prayer; and she knew what Eros had done and that Daphne could never be moved by love, even for Apollo, the fairest of all the gods.

As his arms closed round her as she paused on the riverbank, Daphne turned suddenly into the tree which bears her name—the Daphne Laureola or laurel-tree. Apollo kissed the hard bark. Then he broke off a spray of leaves and twisted them into a crown.

"Daphne, I love you still!" he cried. "And since you can never be my bride, be at least my tree. I shall wear a crown of your leaves when I lead the Muses in song; and the laurel crown shall ever after be the victor's reward. All men shall seek to win you still—but only to crown themselves with your leaves, remembering you as they win honor from me. Surely you will grant me this much?"

And the laurel-tree bowed its new-made branches and nodded its leafy top as if consenting to Apollo's prayer.

The White Mountains

Retold by Marion E. Gridley

Mountains and hilltops were dwelling places for the deities of many cultures. Mount Olympus, for example, was a sacred site for the Greeks. Mountainsides provide food, shelter, and spiritual experiences, but they also represent hardship. The following legend, told by Native Americans of New Hampshire, addresses this duality.

Marion E. Gridley, *Indian Legends of American Scenes* (Chicago: M. A. Donohue, 1939).

A hunter roamed the country in search of game. He had come a long way from the lodges of his people, and was faint and weary from hunger. For game had been scarce, there was danger of famine, and he had been without food.

Exhausted from his fruitless search, he sank to the ground, crying aloud to the Great Spirit in his despair. His wife had no meat to cook. His child lay weeping and there was naught for it to eat. His parents walked with trembling limbs, though they made no complaint. They had known famine before.

Stretched helpless upon the earth, gradually his mind left his body. There came before his eyes the vision of a beautiful land, with game in plenty. He could hear the sound of laughter and singing—his wife singing, his child laughing. With a piece of flint he struck a spark and built a fire, so that he could roast the meat that he seemed to have. But with the building of the fire, the vision died away. Dense smoke arose, hiding all the land. Out of the smoke came a voice!

There was no other voice like it, nor so beautiful in all the world. Gentle with a gentleness that was beyond description. Deep with the depth of all the sounds of Nature. Sad, with the sorrow of all the troubled and heavy-laden. The voice of the Great Spirit!

At the command of the Voice, the rocks heaped themselves one upon the other, until they formed a mountain range. The mountains became thickly covered with forests. From the highest peak the Voice spoke again.

"In these mountains the Great Spirit shall dwell, that he may watch over His children and keep them from suffering. Game will always be found in these mountains of the Great Spirit, but the Indian shall take only what he needs and no more. None shall ever climb the heights to where the Great Spirit has His home, nor ever desire to do so, for punishment shall be theirs."

Famine came no more to the Indians. When food was scarce, they traveled to the mountains of the Great Spirit. If a hunter forgot the words that had been spoken from the lofty peak and wandered on, higher and higher, he never returned. He was doomed to wander on always over the highest summits and through the deepest chasms. The cries of these lost souls were heard in the wailing winds of the winter storms.

The bravest warrior trembled at the sound of these mournful cries, for this was a fate worse than death. Few there were that ventured far within the mountains of plenty.

Buddha the Tree-God

Retold by Ananda K. Coomaraswamy and Sister Nivedita

Jataka tales, originating in the East, tell of the various incarnations of the Buddha in the form of animals and plants and express compassion and reverence for life. In this tale, the Buddha, as tree-god, is the protector of the young trees that surround it.

Long ago, when Brahmadatta was king of Benāres, there came this thought into his mind: "Everywhere in India there are kings whose palaces have many columns; what if I build a palace supported by a single column only? Then shall I be the first and singular king among all other kings." So he summoned his craftsmen, and ordered them to

From Ananda K. Coomaraswamy and Sister Nivedita, *Myths of the Hindus and Buddhists* (New York: Dover, 1967).

build him a magnificent palace supported by a single pillar. "It shall be done," they said; and away they went into the forest.

There they found a tree, tall and straight, worthy to be the single pillar of such a palace. But the road was too rough and the distance too great for them to take the trunk to the city, so they returned to the king and asked him what was to be done. "Somehow or other," he said, "you must bring it, and that without delay." But they answered that neither somehow nor anyhow could it be done. "Then," said the king, "you must select a tree in my own park."

There they found a lordly sāl-tree, straight and beautiful, worshipped alike by village and town and royal family. They told the king, and he said to them: "Good, go and fell the tree at once." But they could not do this without making the customary offerings to the tree-god living there, and asking him to depart. So they made offerings of flowers and branches and lighted lamps, and said to the tree: "On the seventh day from this we shall fell the tree, by the king's command. Let any deva that may be dwelling in the tree depart elsewhere, and not unto us be the blame!" The god that dwelt in the tree heard what they said, and considered thus: "These craftsmen are agreed to fell my tree. I myself shall perish when my home is destroyed. All the young sāl-trees round me will be destroyed as well, in which many devas of my kith and kin are living. My own death touches me not so nearly as the destruction of my children, so let me, if possible, save their lives at least." So at the hour of midnight the tree-god, divinely radiant, entered the king's resplendent chamber, his glory lighting up the whole room. The king was startled, and stammered out: "What being art thou, so god-like and so full of grief?" The deva-prince replied: "I am called in thy realm, O king, the Lucky-tree; for sixty thousand years all men have loved and worshipped me. Many a house and many a town, many a palace, too, they made, yet never did me wrong; honour thou me, even as did they, O king!" But the king answered that such a tree was just what he needed for his palace, a trunk so fine and tall and straight; and in that palace, said he, "thou shalt long endure, admired of all who behold thee." The tree-god answered: "If it must be so, then I have one boon to ask: Cut first the top, the middle next, and then the root of me." The king protested that this was a more painful death than to be felled entire. "O forest lord," he said, "what gain is thine thus to be cut limb from limb and piece by piece?" To which the Lucky-tree replied: "There is a good reason for my wish: my kith and kin have grown up round me, beneath my shade, and I should crush them if I fall entire upon them, and they would grieve exceedingly."

At this the king was deeply moved, and wondered at the tree-god's noble thought, and lifting his hands in salutation, he said: "O Lucky-tree, O forest lord, as thou wouldst save thy kindred, so shall I spare thee; so fear nothing."

Then the tree-god gave the king good counsel and went his way; and the king next day gave generous alms, and ruled as became a king until the time came for his departure to the heavenly world.

FOLKTALES—
INHERITED AND LITERARY

The Princess on the Glass Hill

Andrew Lang

Katherine Briggs, in her Encyclopedia of Fairies, *notes that the Cinderella figure in tales is usually a princess or member of the nobility who has been cast down but that Cinderlads are just the opposite. They are portrayed as having "led a life of complete sloth, doing nothing to help towards the household expenses, idle, dirty, greedy, until suddenly they are roused into activity, and show great qualities of courage, resourcefulness and wit." In this tale by Andrew Lang, the traditional Cinderlad figure is seen rousing himself to rescue a beautiful princess who sits upon a hill of glass.*

Once upon a time there was a man who had a meadow which lay on the side of a mountain, and in the meadow there was a barn in which he stored hay. But there had not been much hay in the barn for the last two years, for every St. John's eve, when the grass was in the height of its vigour, it was all eaten clean up, just as if a whole flock of sheep had gnawed it down to the ground during the night. This happened once, and it happened twice, but then the man got tired of losing his crop, and said to his sons—he had three of them, and the third was called Cinderlad—that one of them must go and sleep in the barn on St. John's night, for it was absurd to let the grass be eaten up again, blade and stalk, as it had been the last two years, and the one who went to watch must keep a sharp look-out, the man said.

The eldest was quite willing to go to the meadow; he would watch the grass, he said, and he would do it so well that neither man, nor beast, nor even the devil himself should have any of it. So when evening came he went to the barn, and lay down to sleep, but when night was drawing near there was such a rumbling and such an earthquake that the walls and roof shook again, and the lad jumped up and took to his heels as fast as he could, and never even looked back, and the barn remained empty that year just as it had been for the last two.

Next St. John's eve the man again said that he could not go on in this way, losing all the grass in the outlying field year after year, and that one of his sons must just go there and watch it, and watch well too. So the next oldest son was willing to show what he could do. He went to the barn and lay down to sleep, as his brother had done; but when night was drawing near there was a great rumbling, and then an earthquake, which was even worse than that on the former St. John's night, and when the youth heard it he was terrified, and went off, running as if for a wager.

From Andrew Lang, *The Blue Fairy Book* (New York: Dover, 1965). Illustrated by H. J. Ford.

The year after, it was Cinderlad's turn, but when he made ready to go the others laughed at him, and mocked him. 'Well, you are just the right one to watch the hay, you who have never learnt anything but how to sit among the ashes and bake yourself!' said they. Cinderlad, however, did not trouble himself about what they said, but when evening drew near rambled away to the outlying field. When he got there he went into the barn and lay down, but in about an hour's time the rumbling and creaking began, and it was frightful to hear it. 'Well, if it gets no worse than that, I can manage to stand it,' thought Cinderlad. In a little time the creaking began again, and the earth quaked so that all the hay flew about the boy. 'Oh! if it gets no worse than that I can manage to stand it,' thought Cinderlad. But then came a third rumbling, and a third earthquake, so violent that the boy thought the walls and roof had fallen down, but when that was over everything suddenly grew as still as death around him. 'I am pretty sure that it will come again,' thought Cinderlad; but no, it did not. Everything was quiet, and everything stayed quiet, and when he had lain still a short time he heard something that sounded as if a horse were standing chewing just outside the barn door. He stole away to the door, which was ajar, to see what was there, and a horse was standing eating. It was so big, and fat, and fine a horse that Cinderlad had never seen one like it before, and a saddle and bridle lay upon it, and a complete suit of armour for a knight, and everything was of copper, and so bright that it shone again. 'Ha, ha! it is thou who eatest up our hay then,' thought the boy; 'but I will stop that.' So he made haste, and took out his steel for striking fire, and threw it over the horse, and then it had no power to stir from the spot, and became so tame that the boy could do what he liked with it. So he mounted it and rode away to a place which no one knew of but himself, and there he tied it up. When he went home again his brothers laughed and asked how he had got on.

'You didn't lie long in the barn, if even you have been so far as the field!' said they.

'I lay in the barn till the sun rose, but I saw nothing and heard nothing, not I,' said

the boy. 'God knows what there was to make you two so frightened.'

'Well, we shall soon see whether you have watched the meadow or not,' answered the brothers, but when they got there the grass was all standing just as long and as thick as it had been the night before.

The next St. John's eve it was the same thing once again: neither of the two brothers dared to go to the outlying field to watch the crop, but Cinderlad went, and everything happened exactly the same as on the previous St. John's eve: first there was a rumbling and an earthquake, and then there was another, and then a third; but all three earthquakes were much, very much more violent than they had been the year before. Then everything became still as death again, and the boy heard something chewing outside the barn door, so he stole as softly as he could to the door, which was slightly ajar, and again there was a horse standing close by the wall of the house, eating and chewing, and it was far larger and fatter than the first horse, and it had a saddle on its back, and a bridle was on it too, and a full suit of armour for a knight, all of bright silver, and as beautiful as anyone could wish to see. 'Ho, ho!' thought the boy, 'is it thou who eatest up our hay in the night? but I will put a stop to that.' So he took out his steel for striking fire, and threw it over the horse's mane, and the beast stood there as quiet as a lamb. Then the boy rode this horse, too, away to the place where he kept the other, and then went home again.

'I suppose you will tell us that you have watched well again this time,' said the brothers.

'Well, so I have,' said Cinderlad. So they went there again, and there the grass was, standing as high and as thick as it had been before, but that did not make them any kinder to Cinderlad.

When the third St. John's night came neither of the two elder brothers dared to lie in the outlying barn to watch the grass, for they had been so heartily frightened the night that they had slept there that they could not get over it, but Cinderlad dared to go, and everything happened just the same as on the two former nights. There were three earthquakes, each worse than the other, and the last flung the boy from one wall of the barn to the other, but then everything suddenly became still as death. When he had lain quietly a short time, he heard something chewing outside the barn door; then he once more stole to the door, which was slightly ajar, and behold, a horse was standing just outside it, which was much larger and fatter than the two others he had caught. 'Ho, ho! it is thou, then, who art eating up our hay this time,' thought the boy; 'but I will put a stop to that.' So he pulled out his steel for striking fire, and threw it over the horse, and it stood as still as if it had been nailed to the field, and the boy could do just what he liked with it. Then he mounted it and rode away to the place where he had the two others, and then he went home again. Then the two brothers mocked him just as they had done before, and told him that they could see that he must have watched the grass very carefully that night, for he looked just as if he were walking in his sleep; but Cinderlad did not trouble himself about that, but just bade them go to the field and see. They did go, and this time too the grass was standing looking as fine and as thick as ever.

The King of the country in which Cinderlad's father dwelt had a daughter whom he would give to no one who could not ride up to the top of the glass hill, for there was a high, high hill of glass, slippery as ice, and it was close to the King's palace. Upon the very top of this the King's daughter was to sit with three gold apples in her lap, and the man who could ride up and take the three golden apples should marry her, and have half the kingdom. The King had this proclaimed in every church in the whole kingdom, and in many other kingdoms too. The Princess was very beautiful, and all who saw her fell violently in love with her, even in spite of themselves. So it is needless to say that all the princes and knights were eager to win her, and half the kingdom besides, and that for this cause they came riding thither from the very end of the world, dressed so splendidly that their raiments gleamed in the sunshine, and riding on horses which seemed to dance as they went, and there was not one of these princes who did not think that he was sure to win the Princess.

When the day appointed by the King had come, there was such a host of knights and princes under the glass hill that they seemed to swarm, and everyone who could walk or even creep was there too, to see who won the King's daughter. Cinderlad's two brothers were there too, but they would not hear of letting him go with them, for he was so dirty and black with sleeping and grubbing among the ashes that they said everyone would laugh at them if they were seen in the company of such an oaf.

'Well, then, I will go all alone by myself,' said Cinderlad.

When the two brothers got to the glass hill, all the princes and knights were trying to ride up it, and their horses were in a foam; but it was all in vain, for no sooner did the horses set foot upon the hill than down they slipped, and there was not one which could get even so much as a couple of yards up. Nor was that strange, for the hill was as smooth as a glass window-pane, and as steep as the side of a house. But they were all eager to win the King's daughter and half the kingdom, so they rode and they slipped, and thus it went on. At length all the horses were so tired that they could do no more, and so hot that the foam dropped from them and the riders were forced to give up the attempt. The King was just thinking that he would cause it to be proclaimed that the riding should begin afresh on the following day, when perhaps it might go better, when suddenly a knight came riding up on so fine a horse that no one had ever seen the like of it before, and the knight had armour of copper, and his bridle was of copper too, and all his accoutrements were so bright that they shone again. The other knights all called out to him that he might just as well spare himself the trouble of trying to ride up the glass hill, for it was of no use to try; but he did not heed them, and rode straight off to it, and went up as if it were nothing at all. Thus he rode for a long way—it may have been a third part of the way up—but when he had got so far he

bridle of copper, and his armour and trappings were so bright that they shone to a great distance, and it was something like a sight to see him riding. He rode one-third of the way up the glass hill, and he could easily have ridden the whole of it if he had liked; but he had turned back, for he had made up his mind that that was enough for once. 'Oh! I should have liked to see him too, that I should,' said Cinderlad, who was as usual sitting by the chimney among the cinders. 'You indeed!' said the brothers, 'you look as if you were fit to be among such great lords, nasty beast that you are to sit there!'

Next day the brothers were for setting out again, and this time too Cinderlad begged them to let him go with them and see who rode; but no, they said he was not fit to do that, for he was much too ugly and dirty. 'Well, well, then I will go all alone by myself,' said Cinderlad. So the brothers went to the glass hill, and all the princes and knights began to ride again, and this time they had taken care to rough the shoes of their horses; but that did not help them: they rode and they slipped as they had done the day before, and not one of them could even get so far as a yard up the hill. When they had tired out their horses, so that they could do no more, they again had to stop altogether. But just as the King was thinking that it would be well to proclaim that the riding should take place next day for the last time, so that they might have one more chance, he suddenly bethought himself that it would be well to wait a little longer to see if the knight in copper armour would come on this day too. But nothing was to be seen of him. Just as they were still looking for him, however, came a knight riding on a steed that was much, much finer than that which the knight in copper armour had ridden, and this knight had silver armour and a silver saddle and bridle, and all were so bright that they shone and glistened when he was a long way off. Again the other knights called to him, and said that he might just as well give up the attempt to ride up the glass hill, for it was useless to try; but the knight paid no heed to that, but rode straight away to the glass hill, and went still farther up than the knight in

turned his horse round and rode down again. But the Princess thought that she had never yet seen so handsome a knight, and while he was riding up she was sitting thinking: 'Oh! how I hope he may be able to come up to the top!' And when she saw that he was turning his horse back she threw one of the golden apples down after him, and it rolled into his shoe. But when he had come down from off the hill he rode away, and that so fast that no one knew what had become of him.

So all the princes and knights were bidden to present themselves before the King that night, so that he who had ridden so far up the glass hill might show the golden apple which the King's daughter had thrown down. But no one had anything to show. One knight presented himself after the other, and none could show the apple.

At night, too, Cinderlad's brothers came home again and had a long story to tell about the riding up the glass hill. At first, they said, there was not one who was able to get even so much as one step up, but then came a knight who had armour of copper, and a copper armour had gone; but when he had ridden two-thirds of the way up he turned his horse round, and rode down again. The Princess liked this knight still better than she had liked the other, and sat longing that he might be able to get up above, and when she saw him turning back she threw the second apple after him, and it rolled into his shoe, and as soon as he had got down the glass hill he rode away so fast that no one could see what had become of him.

In the evening, when everyone was to appear before the King and Princess, in order that he who had the golden apple might show it, one knight went in after the other, but none of them had a golden apple to show.

At night the two brothers went home as they had done the night before, and told how things had gone, and how everyone had ridden, but no one had been able to get up the hill. 'But last of all,' they said, 'came one in silver armour, and he had a silver bridle on his horse, and a silver saddle, and oh, but he could ride! He took his horse two-thirds of the way up the hill, but then he turned back. He was a fine fellow,' said the brothers, 'and the Princess threw the second golden apple to him!'

'Oh, how I should have liked to see him too!' said Cinderlad.

'Oh, indeed! He was a little brighter than the ashes that you sit grubbing among, you dirty black creature!' said the brothers.

On the third day everything went just as on the former days. Cinderlad wanted to go with them to look at the riding, but the two brothers would not have him in their company, and when they got to the glass hill there was no one who could ride even so far as a yard up it, and everyone waited for the knight in silver armour, but he was neither to be seen nor heard of. At last, after a long time, came a knight riding upon a horse that was such a fine one, its equal had never yet been seen. The knight had golden armour, and the horse a golden saddle and bridle, and these were all so bright that they shone and dazzled everyone, even while the knight was still at a great distance. The other princes and knights were not able even to call to tell him how useless it was to try to ascend the hill,

so amazed were they at the sight of his magnificence. He rode straight away to the glass hill, and galloped up it as if it were no hill at all, so that the Princess had not even time to wish that he might get up the whole way. As soon as he had ridden to the top, he took the third golden apple from the lap of the Princess, and then turned his horse about and rode down again, and vanished from their sight before anyone was able to say a word to him.

When the two brothers came home again at night, they had much to tell of how the riding had gone off that day, and at last they told about the knight in the golden armour too. 'He was a fine fellow, that was! Such another splendid knight is not to be found on earth!' said the brothers.

'Oh, how I should have liked to see him too!' said Cinderlad.

'Well, he shone nearly as brightly as the coal-heaps that thou art always lying and raking amongst, dirty black creature that thou art!' said the brothers.

Next day all the knights and princes were to appear before the King and the Princess—it had been too late for them to do it the night before—in order that he who had the golden apple might produce it. They all went in turn, first princes, and then knights, but none of them had a golden apple.

'But somebody must have it,' said the King, 'for with our own eyes we all saw a man ride up and take it. So he commanded that everyone in the kingdom should come to the palace, and see if he could show the apple. And one after the other they all came, but no one had the golden apple, and after a long, long time Cinderlad's two brothers came likewise. They were the last of all, so the King inquired of them if there was no one else in the kingdom left to come.

'Oh! yes, we have a brother,' said the two, 'but he never got the golden apple! He never left the cinder-heap on any of the three days.'

'Never mind that,' said the King; 'as everyone else has come to the palace, let him come too.'

So Cinderlad was forced to go to the King's palace.

'Hast thou the golden apple?' asked the King.

'Yes, here is the first, and here is the second, and here is the third, too,' said Cinderlad, and he took all the three apples out of his pocket, and with that threw off his sooty rags, and appeared there before them in his bright golden armour, which gleamed as he stood.

'Thou shalt have my daughter, and the half of my kingdom, and thou hast well earned both!' said the King. So there was a wedding, and Cinderlad got the King's daughter, and everyone made merry at the wedding, for all of them could make merry, though they could not ride up the glass hill, and if they have not left off their merry-making they must be at it still.

The Three Robes

Andrew Lang

A common idea in folklore is that a tree can maintain or guard human life. This notion is expressed in the belief that a tree planted at the same time a person is born will die when he or she dies. In this Icelandic story, the shelter provided by two beautiful trees miraculously saves the lives of a prince and princess and is instrumental in restoring their birthright.

Long, long ago, a king and queen reigned over a large and powerful country. What their names were nobody knows, but their son was called Sigurd, and their daughter Lineik, and these young people were famed throughout the whole kingdom for their wisdom and beauty.

There was only a year between them, and they loved each other so much that they could do nothing apart. When they began to grow up the king gave them a house of their own to live in, with servants and carriages, and everything they could possibly want.

For many years they all lived happily together, and then the queen fell ill, and knew that she would never get better.

'Promise me two things,' she said one day to the king; 'one, that if you marry again, as indeed you must, you will not choose as your wife a woman from some small state or distant island, who knows nothing of the world, and will be taken up with thoughts of her grandeur. But rather seek out a princess of some great kingdom, who has been used to courts all her life, and holds them at their true worth. The other thing I have to ask is, that you will never cease to watch over our children, who will soon become your greatest joy.'

These were the queen's last words, and a few hours later she was dead. The king was so bowed down with sorrow that he would not attend even to the business of the kingdom, and at last his Prime Minister had to tell him that the people were complaining that they had nobody to right their wrongs. 'You must rouse yourself, sir,' went on the minister, 'and put aside your own sorrows for the sake of your country.'

'You do not spare me,' answered the king; 'but what you say is just, and your counsel is good. I have heard that men say, likewise,

From Andrew Lang, *The Crimson Fairy Book* (New York: Dover, 1967). Illustrated by H. J. Ford.

that it will be for the good of my kingdom for me to marry again, though my heart will never cease to be with my lost wife. But it was her wish also; therefore, to you I entrust the duty of finding a lady fitted to share my throne; only, see that she comes neither from a small town nor a remote island.'

So an embassy was prepared, with the minister at its head, to visit the greatest courts in the world, and to choose out a suitable princess. But the vessel which carried them had not been gone many days when a thick fog came on, and the captain could see neither to the right nor to the left. For a whole month the ship drifted about in darkness, till at length the fog lifted and they beheld a cliff jutting out just in front. On one side of the cliff lay a sheltered bay, in which the vessel was soon anchored, and though they did not know where they were, at any rate they felt sure of fresh fruit and water.

The minister left the rest of his followers on board the ship, and taking a small boat rowed himself to land, in order to look about him and to find out if the island was really as deserted as it seemed.

He had not gone far, when he heard the sound of music, and, turning in its direction, he saw a woman of marvellous beauty sitting on a low stool playing on a harp, while a girl beside her sang. The minister stopped and greeted the lady politely, and she replied with friendliness, asking him why he had come to such an out-of-the-way place. In answer he told her of the object of his journey.

'I am in the same state as your master,' replied the lady; 'I was married to a mighty king who ruled over this land, till Vikings [sea-robbers] came and slew him and put all the people to death. But I managed to escape, and hid myself here with my daughter.'

And the daughter listened, and said softly to her mother: 'Are you speaking the truth now?'

'Remember your promise,' answered the mother angrily, giving her a pinch which was unseen by the minister.

'What is your name, madam?' asked he, much touched by this sad story.

'Blauvor,' she replied, 'and my daughter is called Laufer'; and then she inquired the name of the minister, and of the king his master. After this they talked of many things, and the lady showed herself learned in all that a woman should know, and even in much that men only were commonly taught. 'What a wife she would make for the king,' thought the minister to himself, and before long he had begged the honour of her hand for his master. She declared at first that she was too unworthy to accept the position offered her, and that the minister would soon repent his choice; but this only made him the more eager, and in the end he gained her consent, and prevailed on her to return with him at once to his own country.

The minister then conducted the mother and daughter back to the ship; the anchor was raised, the sails spread, and a fair wind was behind them.

Now that the fog had lifted they could see as they looked back that, except just along the shore, the island was bare and deserted and not fit for men to live in; but about that nobody cared. They had a quick voyage, and in six days they reached the land, and at once set out for the capital, a messenger being sent on first by the minister to inform the king of what had happened.

When his Majesty's eyes fell on the two beautiful women, clad in dresses of gold and silver, he forgot his sorrows and ordered preparations for the wedding to be made without delay. In his joy he never remembered to inquire in what kind of country the future queen had been found. In fact his head was so turned by the beauty of the two ladies that when the invitations were sent by his orders to all the great people in the kingdom, he did not even recollect his two children, who remained shut up in their own house!

After the marriage the king ceased to have any will of his own and did nothing without consulting his wife. She was present at all his councils, and her opinion was asked before making peace or war. But when a few months had passed the king began to have doubts as to whether the minister's choice had really been a wise one, and he noticed that his children lived more and more in their palace and never came near their stepmother.

It always happens that if a person's eyes are once opened they see a great deal more than they ever expected; and soon it struck the king that the members of his court had a way of disappearing one after the other without any reason. At first he had not paid much attention to the fact, but merely appointed some fresh person to the vacant place. As, however, man after man vanished without leaving any trace, he began to grow uncomfortable and to wonder if the queen could have anything to do with it.

Things were in this state when, one day, his wife said to him that it was time for him to make a progress through his kingdom and see that his governors were not cheating him of the money that was his due. 'And you need not be anxious about going,' she added, 'for I will rule the country while you are away as carefully as you could yourself.'

The king had no great desire to undertake this journey, but the queen's will was stronger than his, and he was too lazy to make a fight for it. So he said nothing and set about his preparations, ordering his finest ship to be ready to carry him round the coast. Still his heart was heavy, and he felt uneasy, though he could not have told why; and the night before he was to start he went to the children's palace to take leave of his son and daughter.

He had not seen them for some time, and they gave him a warm welcome, for they loved him dearly and he had always been kind to them. They had much to tell him, but after a while he checked their merry talk and said:

'If I should never come back from this journey I fear that it may not be safe for you to stay here; so directly there are no more hopes of my return go instantly and take the road eastwards till you reach a high mountain, which you must cross. Once over the mountain keep along by the side of a little bay till you come to two trees, one green and the other red, standing in a thicket, and so far back from the road that without looking for them you would never see them. Hide

each in the trunk of one of the trees and there you will be safe from all your enemies.'

With these words the king bade them farewell and entered sadly into his ship. For a few days the wind was fair, and everything seemed going smoothly; then, suddenly, a gale sprang up, and a fearful storm of thunder and lightning, such as had never happened within the memory of man. In spite of the efforts of the frightened sailors the vessel was driven on the rocks, and not a man on board was saved.

That very night Prince Sigurd had a dream, in which he thought his father appeared to him in dripping clothes, and, taking the crown from his head, laid it at his son's feet, leaving the room as silently as he had entered it.

Hastily the prince awoke his sister Lineik, and they agreed that their father must be dead, and that they must lose no time in obeying his orders and putting themselves in safety. So they collected their jewels and a few clothes and left the house without being observed by anyone.

They hurried on till they arrived at the mountain without once looking back. Then Sigurd glanced round and saw that their stepmother was following them, with an expression on her face which made her uglier than the ugliest old witch. Between her and them lay a thick wood, and Sigurd stopped for a moment to set it on fire; then he and his sister hastened on more swiftly than before, till they reached the grove with the red and green trees, into which they jumped, and felt that at last they were safe.

Now, at that time there reigned over Greece a king who was very rich and powerful, although his name has somehow been forgotten. He had two children, a son and a daughter, who were more beautiful and accomplished than any Greeks had been before, and they were the pride of their father's heart.

The prince had no sooner grown out of boyhood than he prevailed on his father to make war during the summer months on a neighbouring nation, so as to give him a chance of making himself famous. In winter, however, when it was difficult to get food and horses in that wild country, the army was dispersed, and the prince returned home.

During one of these wars he had heard reports of the Princess Lineik's beauty, and he resolved to seek her out, and to ask for her hand in marriage. All this Blauvor, the queen, found out by means of her black arts, and when the prince drew near the capital she put a splendid dress on her own daughter and then went to meet her guest.

She bade him welcome to her palace, and when they had finished supper she told him of the loss of her husband, and how there was no one left to govern the kingdom but herself.

'But where is the Princess Lineik?' asked the prince when she had ended her tale.

'Here,' answered the queen, bringing forward the girl, whom she had hitherto kept in the background.

The prince looked at her and was rather disappointed. The Maiden was pretty enough, but not much out of the common.

'Oh, you must not wonder at her pale face and heavy eyes,' said the queen hastily, for she saw what was passing in his mind. 'She has never got over the loss of both father and mother.'

'That shows a good heart,' thought the prince; 'and when she is happy her beauty will soon come back.' And without any further delay he begged the queen to consent to their betrothal, for the marriage must take place in his own country.

The queen was enchanted. She had hardly expected to succeed so soon, and she at once set about her preparations. Indeed she wished to travel with the young couple, to make sure that nothing should go wrong; but here the prince was firm, that he would take no one with him but Laufer, whom he thought was Lineik.

They soon took leave of the queen, and set sail in a splendid ship; but in a short time a dense fog came on, and in the dark the captain steered out of his course, and they found themselves in a bay which was quite strange to all the crew. The prince ordered a boat to be lowered, and went on shore to look about

him, and it was not long before he noticed the two beautiful trees, quite different from any that grew in Greece. Calling one of the sailors, he bade him cut them down, and carry them on board the ship. This was done, and as the sky was now clear they put out to sea, and arrived in Greece without any more adventures.

The news that the prince had brought home a bride had gone before them, and they were greeted with flowery arches and crowns of coloured lights. The king and queen met them on the steps of the palace, and conducted the girl to the women's house, where she would have to remain until her marriage. The prince then went to his own rooms and ordered that the trees should be brought in to him.

The next morning the prince bade his attendants bring his future bride to his own apartments, and when she came he gave her silk which she was to weave into three robes—one red, one green, and one blue— and these must all be ready before the wedding. The blue one was to be done first and the green last, and this was to be the most splendid of all, 'for I will wear it at our marriage,' said he.

Left alone, Laufer sat and stared at the heap of shining silk before her. She did not know how to weave, and burst into tears as she thought that everything would be discovered, for Lineik's skill in weaving was as famous as her beauty. As she sat with her face hidden and her body shaken by sobs, Sigurd in his tree heard her and was moved to pity. 'Lineik, my sister,' he called, softly, 'Laufer is weeping; help her, I pray you.'

'Have you forgotten the wrongs her mother did to us?' answered Lineik, 'and that it is owing to her that we are banished from home?'

But she was not really unforgiving, and very soon she slid quietly out of her hiding-place, and taking the silk from Laufer's hands began to weave it. So quick and clever was she that the blue dress was not only woven but embroidered, and Lineik was safe back in her tree before the prince returned.

'It is the most beautiful work I have ever

seen,' said he, taking up a bit. 'And I am sure that the red one will be still better, because the stuff is richer,' and with a low bow he left the room.

Laufer had hoped secretly that when the prince had seen the blue dress finished he would have let her off the other two; but when she found she was expected to fulfil the whole task, her heart sank and she began to cry loudly. Again Sigurd heard her, and begged Lineik to come to her help, and Lineik, feeling sorry for her distress, wove and embroidered the second dress as she had done the first, mixing gold thread and precious stones till you could hardly see the red of the stuff. When it was done she glided into her tree just as the prince came in.

'You are as quick as you are clever,' said he, admiringly. 'This looks as if it had been embroidered by the fairies! But as the green robe must outshine the other two I will give you three days in which to finish it. After it is ready we will be married at once.'

Now, as he spoke, there rose up in Laufer's mind all the unkind things that she and her mother had done to Lineik. Could she hope that they would be forgotten, and that Lineik would come to her rescue for the third time? And perhaps Lineik, who had not forgotten the past either, might have left her alone, to get on as best she could, had not Sigurd, her brother, implored her to help just once more. So Lineik again slid out of her tree, and, to Laufer's great relief, set herself to work. When the shining green silk was ready she caught the sun's rays and the moon's beams on the point of her needle and wove them into a pattern such as no man had ever seen. But it took a long time, and on the third morning, just as she was putting the last stitches into the last flower the prince came in.

Lineik jumped up quickly, and tried to get past him back to her tree; but the folds of the silk were wrapped round her, and she would have fallen had not the prince caught her.

'I have thought for some time that all was not quite straight here,' said he. 'Tell me who you are, and where you come from?'

Lineik then told her name and her story.

LINEIK CAUGHT BY THE PRINCE

When she had ended the prince turned angrily to Laufer, and declared that, as a punishment for her wicked lies, she deserved to die a shameful death.

But Laufer fell at his feet and begged for mercy. It was her mother's fault, she said: 'It was she, and not I, who passed me off as the Princess Lineik. The only lie I have ever told you was about the robes, and I do not deserve death for that.'

She was still on her knees when Prince Sigurd entered the room. He prayed the Prince of Greece to forgive Laufer, which he did, on condition that Lineik would consent to marry him. 'Not till my stepmother is dead,' answered she, 'for she has brought misery to all that came near her.' Then Laufer told them that Blauvor was not the wife of a king, but an ogress who had stolen her from a neighbouring palace and had brought her up as her daughter. And besides being an ogress she was also a witch, and by her black arts had sunk the ship in which the father of Sigurd and Lineik had set sail. It was she who had caused the disappearance of the courtiers, for which no one could account, by eating them during the night, and she hoped to get rid of all the people in the country, and then to fill the land with ogres and ogresses like herself.

So Prince Sigurd and the Prince of Greece collected an army swiftly, and marched upon the town where Blauvor had her palace. They came so suddenly that no one knew of it, and if they had, Blauvor had eaten most of the strong men; and others, fearful of something they could not tell what, had secretly left the place. Therefore she was easily captured, and the next day was beheaded in the market-place. Afterwards the two princes marched back to Greece.

Lineik had no longer any reason for putting off her wedding, and married the Prince of Greece at the same time that Sigurd married the princess. And Laufer remained with Lineik as her friend and sister, till they found a husband for her in a great nobleman; and all three couples lived happily until they died.

FOLK RHYMES AND POETRY

Lady-Bug

In this rhyme, as in other forms of literature, mountains symbolize both freedom and security.

Lady-bug, lady-bug,
Fly away do,
Fly to the mountain
And feed upon dew.
Feed upon dew,
Feed upon dew,
And sleep on a rug,
And then fly away
Like a good little bug.

Let's Do Like the Olive Trees

The following dance rhyme comes from Portugal.

Let's do like the olive trees—
Swing and sway in the breeze.
When I put my foot on the ground,
Dust comes up all around.

Trees

Harry Behn

Trees frequently stand at the spiritual center of mythologies, perhaps because they are central to our daily lives as well. These silent, reliable companions offer simple comforts that too often go unnoticed.

Trees are the kindest things I know,
They do no harm, they simply grow

From Richard Lewis, ed., *Miracles* (New York: Simon & Schuster, 1966).

And spread a shade for sleepy cows,
And gather birds among their boughs.

They give us fruit in leaves above,
And wood to make our houses of,

And leaves to burn on Hallowe'en,
And in the Spring new buds of green.

They are the first when day's begun
To touch the beams of morning sun,

They are the last to hold the light
When evening changes into night,

And when a moon floats on the sky
They hum a drowsy lullaby

Of sleepy children long ago . . .
Trees are the kindest things I know.

Climbing

Aileen Fisher

*Climbing trees is a typical childhood
pastime. Though far removed from more
practical uses of trees, this use may be more
significant.*

The trunk of a tree
is the road for me
on a sunny summer day.

Up the bark
that is brown and dark
through tunnels of leaves that sway
and tickle my knees
in the trembly breeze,
that's where I make my way.

Leaves in my face
and twigs in my hair
in a squeeze of a place,
but I don't care!

From Aileen Fisher, *In the Woods, in the Meadow, in
the Sky* (New York: Scribner, 1965).

Some people talk
of a summer walk
through clover and weeds and hay.

Some people stride
where the hills are wide
and the rocks are speckled gray.

But the trunk of a tree
is the road for me
on a sunny summer day.

Hills

Hilda Conkling

*Hills, like trees, are reliable, stabilizing
phenomena in nature. Hills remain constant
throughout the changing seasons, supporting
life on and around them.*

*Hilda Conkling was between 7 and 9 years
of age when she wrote "Hills." Amy
Lowell, who wrote the preface to Conkling's*
Poems by a Little Girl, *considered Conkling
a gifted child, a genius, and "Hills" to be
one of her best poems. After childhood,
however, Conkling largely gave up writing
poetry. "I have lived my life in reverse," she
told us in her later years. She was admired
by many writers, including Harriet Monroe
of* Poetry *magazine, which published
some of Conkling's work as well as that of
Pound, Yeats, Tagore, Frost, Wallace
Stevens, T. S. Eliot, and Marianne
Moore.*

The hills are going somewhere;
They have been on the way a long time.
They are like camels in a line
But they move more slowly.
Sometimes at sunset they carry silks,
But most of the time silver birch trees,
Heavy rocks, heavy trees, gold leaves
On heavy branches till they are aching . . .
Birches like silver bars they can hardly lift

From Hilda Conkling, *Poems by a Little Girl* (New
York: Frederick A. Stokes, 1920).

With grass so thick about their feet to
   hinder . . .
They have not gone far
In the time I've watched them . . .

Strange Tree

Elizabeth Madox Roberts

*The shadow cast by a tree suggests a spirit
with outstretched limbs poised to ensnare
any passerby. Perhaps, as this poem seems
to suggest, trees routinely experience us
much as we experience them.*

Away beyond the Jarboe house
   I saw a different kind of tree.
Its trunk was old and large and bent,
   And I could feel it look at me.

The road was going on and on
   Beyond, to reach some other place.
I saw a tree that looked at me,
   And yet it did not have a face.

It looked at me with all its limbs;
   It looked at me with all its bark.
The yellow wrinkles on its sides
   Were bent and dark.

And then I ran to get away,
   But when I stopped and turned to see,
The tree was bending to the side
   And leaning out to look at me.

From Elizabeth Madox Roberts, *Under the Tree* (New
York: Viking Press, 1950).

Tree

John Hunter, age 12

*The desire to transcend mortality seems
inherent in human nature. But as this poem
suggests, nature teaches us a graceful,
gradual acceptance of our mortality.*

From Richard Lewis, ed., *Miracles* (New York: Simon
& Schuster, 1966).

Autumn has come and things begin
as the leaves fall off the tree.
Bare as can be and cold as can be
the trunk squiggles down.
Day by day, and night by night
the tree sways to and fro.
Morning begins, and things begin
as the tree trunk stays where it is.
It's nearly dead as it rots away
and nothing for it to care about.
It shrinks, twists, sways
as it's nearly ready to fall,
till at last its time has come
for it hits the mighty ground.
It's nearly daybreak
and the tree is still there
as it gradually crumbles away,
till at last it is gone
and nothing has begun
for that lonely tree.

Hills

Glennis Foster, age 10

*A universe of life and death plays out its
drama each day among the hills. The
players are often indifferent to the setting,
though without it, or each other, they could
not survive. Glennis Foster, like Hilda
Conkling, views hills with fresh eyes.*

Scrub hills,
      sheep-tongued, sheep-tramped hills
       mountain hills,
          rabbiter hills:
The brown patches blind my eyes;
      scrub pointed out, like rows of trains
        that drive along the rails.
Sheep happy,
     quietly eating.
     Starlings pick the ticks
       off the patchy
        green hills.
     Twitchy heads move
       up above the bluegum
        trees.

From Richard Lewis, ed., *Miracles* (New York: Simon
& Schuster, 1966).

Sheep rub on the
    bark trunks;
        dead gorse,
           live gorse,
                growing on the hills.

The Hills

Rachel Field

Hills harbor mystery in their silent and darkened caves, where mankind long ago sought refuge. We still admire hillsides, perhaps taking for granted the safety and comfort provided by the hills on which we have built our societies. In Field's "The

From Rachel Field, *Poems* (New York: Macmillan, 1957).

Hills," the strength of hills is seen as similar to the strength and eeriness of the dragons in myths and legends.

Sometimes I think the hills
That loom across the harbor
Lie there like sleeping dragons,
Crouched one above another,
With trees for tufts of fur
Growing all up and down
The ridges and humps of their backs,
And orange cliffs for claws
Dipped in the sea below.
Sometimes a wisp of smoke
Rises out of the hollows,
As if in their dragon sleep
They dreamed of strange old battles.

What if the hills should stir
Some day and stretch themselves,
Shake off the clinging trees
And all the clustered houses?

FICTION

My Side of the Mountain
In Which I Find a Real Live Man

Jean George

In this story mountains once again serve as a challenge to a youthful hero. Sam, a 14-year-old runaway from New York City, comes to the Catskill Mountains to live on his own for a year. Jean George's accurate account of Sam's finding food, making his own deerskin clothes, burning out the heart of a great tree to make a

From Jean George, *My Side of the Mountain* (New York: Dutton, 1959).

house, and taming Frightful the falcon is an example of good contemporary realistic fiction. It makes absorbing reading for adolescents, who naturally identify with the search for self-reliance.

One of the gasping joys of summer was my daily bath in the spring. It was cold water, I never stayed in long, but it woke me up and started me into the day with a vengeance.

I would tether Frightful to a hemlock bough above me and splash her from time to time. She would suck in her chest, look startled, and then shake. While I bathed and washed, she preened. Huddled down in the water between the ferns and moss. I scrubbed myself with the bark of the slippery elm. It gets soapy when you rub it.

The frogs would hop out and let me in, and the wood thrush would come to the edge of the pool to see what was happening. We were a gay gathering—me shouting, Frightful preening, the woodthrush cocking its pretty head. Occasionally The Baron Weasel would pop up and glance furtively at us. He didn't care for water. How he stayed glossy and clean was a mystery to me, until he came to the boulder beside our bath pool one day, wet with the dew from the ferns. He licked himself until he was polished.

One morning there was a rustle in the leaves above. Instantly, Frightful had it located. I had learned to look where Frightful looked when there were disturbances in the forest. She always saw life before I could focus my eyes. She was peering into the hemlock above us. Finally I too saw it. A young raccoon. It was chittering and now that all eyes were upon it, began coming down the tree.

And so Frightful and I met Jessie Coon James, the bandit of the Gribley farm.

He came headfirst down to our private bath, a scrabbly, skinny young raccoon. He must have been from a late litter, for he was not very big, and certainly not well fed. Whatever had been Jessie C. James's past, it was awful. Perhaps he was an orphan, perhaps he had been thrown out of his home by his mother, as his eyes were somewhat crossed and looked a little peculiar. In any event he had come to us for help, I thought, and so Frightful and I led him home and fed him.

In about a week he fattened up. His crumply hair smoothed out, and with a little ear scratching and back rubbing, Jessie C. James became a devoted friend. He also became useful. He slept somewhere in the dark tops of the hemlocks all day long, unless he saw us start for the stream. Then, tree by tree, limb by limb, Jessie followed us. At the stream he was the most useful mussel digger that any boy could have. Jessie could find mussels where three men could not. He would start to eat them and if he ate them, he got full and wouldn't dig any more, so I took them away from him until he found me all I wanted. Then I let him have some.

Mussels are good. Here are a few notes on how to fix them.

"Scrub mussels in spring water. Dump them into boiling water with salt. Boil five minutes. Remove and cool in the juice. Take out meat. Eat by dipping in acorn paste flavored with a smudge of garlic, and green apples."

Frightful took care of the small game supply, and now that she was an expert hunter, we had rabbit stew, pheasant potpie, and an occasional sparrow, which I generously gave to Frightful. As fast as we removed the rabbits and pheasants new ones replaced them.

Beverages during the hot summer became my chore, largely because no one else wanted them. I found some sassafras trees at the edge of the road one day, dug up a good supply of roots, peeled and dried them. Sassafras tea is about as good as anything you want to drink. Pennyroyal makes another good drink. I dried great bunches of this, and hung them from the roof of the tree room together with the leaves of winterberry. All these fragrant plants I also used in cooking to give a new taste to some not-so-good foods.

The room in the tree smelled of smoke and mint. It was the best-smelling tree in the Catskill Mountains.

Life was leisurely. I was warm, well fed. One day while I was down the mountain, I returned home by way of the old farmhouse site to check the apple crop. They were summer apples, and were about ready to be picked. I had gathered a pouchful and had sat down under the tree to eat a few and think about how I would dry them for use in the winter when Frightful dug her talons into my shoulder so hard I winced.

"Be gentle, bird!" I said to her.

I got her talons out and put her on a log, where I watched her with some alarm. She was as alert as a high tension wire, her head cocked so that her ears, just membranes under her feathers, were pointed east. She evidently heard a sound that pained her. She opened her beak. Whatever it was, I could hear nothing, though I strained my ears, cupped them, and wished she would speak.

Frightful was my ears as well as my eyes. She could hear things long before I. When she grew tense, I listened or looked. She was scared this time. She turned round and round on the log, looked up in the tree for a perch, lifted her wings to fly, and then stood still and listened.

Then I heard it. A police siren sounded far down the road. The sound grew louder and louder, and I grew afraid. Then I said, "No, Frightful, if they are after me there won't be a siren. They'll just slip up on me quietly."

No sooner had I said this than the siren wound down, and apparently stopped on the road at the foot of the mountain. I got up to run to my tree, but had not gotten past the walnut before the patrol cars started up and screamed away.

We started home although it was not late in the afternoon. However, it was hot, and thunderheads were building up. I decided to take a swim in the spring and work on the moccasins I had cut out several days ago.

With the squad car still on my mind, we slipped quietly into the hemlock forest. Once again Frightful almost sent me through the crown of the forest by digging her talons into my shoulder. I looked at her. She was staring at our home. I looked, too. Then I stopped, for I could make out the form of a man stretched between the sleeping house and the store tree.

Softly, tree by tree, Frightful and I approached him. The man was asleep. I could have left and camped in the gorge again, but my enormous desire to see another human being overcame my fear of being discovered.

We stood above the man. He did not move, so Frightful lost interest in my fellow being. She tried to hop to her stump and preen. I grabbed her leash however, as I wanted to think before awakening him. Frightful flapped. I held her wings to her body as her flapping was noisy to me. Apparently not so to the man. The man did not stir. It is hard to realize that the rustle of a falcon's wings is not much of a noise to a man from the city, because by now, one beat of her wings, and I would awaken from a sound sleep as if a shot had gone off. The stranger slept on. I realized how long I'd been in the mountains.

Right at that moment, as I looked into his unshaven face, his close-cropped hair, and his torn clothes, I thought of the police siren, and put two and two together.

"An outlaw!" I said to myself. "Wow!" I had to think what to do with an outlaw before I awoke him.

Would he be troublesome? Would he be mean? Should I go live in the gorge until he moved on? How I wanted to hear his voice, to tell him about The Baron and Jessie C. James, to say words out loud. I really did not want to hide from him; besides, he might be hungry, I thought. Finally I spoke.

"Hi!" I said. I was delighted to see him roll over, open his eyes, and look up. He seemed startled, so I reassured him. "It's all right, they've gone. If you don't tell on me I won't tell on you." When he heard this, he sat up and seemed to relax.

"Oh," he said. Then he leaned against the tree and added, "Thanks." He evidently was thinking this over, for he propped his head on his elbow and studied me closely.

"You're a sight for sore eyes," he said, and smiled. He had a nice smile—in fact, he looked nice and not like an outlaw at all. His eyes were very blue and, although tired, they did not look scared or hunted.

However, I talked quickly before he could get up and run away.

"I don't know anything about you, and I don't want to. You don't know anything about me and don't want to, but you may stay here if you like. No one is going to find you here. Would you like some supper?" It was still early, but he looked hungry.

"Do you have some?"

"Yes, venison or rabbit?" "Well . . . venison." His eyebrows puckered in question marks. I went to work.

He arose, turned around and around, and looked at his surroundings. He whistled softly when I kindled a spark with the flint and steel. I was now quite quick at this, and had a tidy fire blazing in a very few minutes. I was so used to myself doing this that it had not occurred to me that it would be interesting to a stranger.

"Desdemondia!" he said. I judged this to be some underworld phrase. At this moment Frightful, who had been sitting quietly on her stump, began to preen. The outlaw jumped back, then saw she was tied and said, "And who is this ferocious-looking character?"

"That is Frightful; don't be afraid. She's quite wonderful and gentle. She would be glad to catch you a rabbit for supper if you would prefer that to venison."

"Am I dreaming?" said the man. "I go to sleep by a campfire that looked like it was built by a boy scout, and I awaken in the middle of the eighteenth century."

I crawled into the store tree to get the smoked venison and some cattail tubers. When I came out again, he was speechless.

"My storehouse," I explained.

"I see," he answered. From that moment on he did not talk much. He just watched me. I was so busy cooking the best meal that I could possibly get together that I didn't say much either. Later I wrote down that menu, as it was excellent.

"Brown puffballs in deer fat with a little wild garlic, fill pot with water, put venison in, boil. Wrap tubers in leaves and stick in coals. Cut up apples and boil in can with dogtooth violet bulbs. Raspberries to finish meal."

When the meal was ready, I served it to the man in my nicest turtle shell. I had to whittle him a fork out of the crotch of a twig, as Jessie Coon James had gone off with the others. He ate and ate and ate, and when he was done he said. "May I call you Thoreau?"

"That will do nicely," I said. Then I paused—just to let him know that I knew a little bit about him too. I smiled and said. "I will call you Bando."

His eyebrows went up, he cocked his head, shrugged his shoulders and answered, "That's close enough."

With this he sat and thought. I felt I had offended him, so I spoke. "I will be glad to help. I will teach you how to live off the land. It is very easy. No one need find you."

His eyebrows gathered together again. This was characteristic of Bando when he was concerned, and so I was sorry I had mentioned his past. After all, outlaw or no outlaw, he was an adult, and I still felt unsure of myself around adults. I changed the subject.

"Let's get some sleep." I said.

"Where do you sleep?" he asked. All this time sitting and talking with me, and he had not seen the entrance to my tree. I was pleased. Then I beckoned, walked a few feet to the left, pushed back the deer-hide door, and showed Bando my secret.

"Thoreau," he said. "You are quite wonderful." He went in. I lit the turtle candle for him, he explored, tried the bed, came out and shook his head until I thought it would roll off.

We didn't say much more that night. I let him sleep on my bed. His feet hung off, but he was comfortable, he said. I stretched out by the fire. The ground was dry, the night warm, and I could sleep on anything now.

I got up early and had breakfast ready when Bando came stumbling out of the tree. We ate crayfish, and he really honestly seemed to like them. It takes a little time to acquire a taste for wild foods, so Bando surprised me the way he liked the menu. Of course he was hungry, and that helped.

That day we didn't talk much, just went over the mountain collecting foods. I wanted to dig up the tubers of the Solomon's-seal from a big garden of them on the other side of the gorge. We fished, we swam a little, and I told him I hoped to make a raft pretty soon, so I could float into deeper water and perhaps catch bigger fish.

When Bando heard this, he took my ax and immediately began to cut young trees for this purpose. I watched him and said, "You must have lived on a farm or something."

At that moment a bird sang.

"The wood peewee," said Bando, stopping his work. He stepped into the woods, seeking it. Now I was astonished.

"How would you know about a wood peewee in your business?" I grew bold enough to ask.

"And just what do you think my business is?" he said as I followed him.

"Well, you're not a minister."

"Right!"

"And you're not a doctor or a lawyer."

"Correct."

"You're not a businessman or a sailor."

"No, I am not."

"Nor do you dig ditches."

"I do not."

"Well . . ."

"Guess."

Suddenly I wanted to know for sure. So I said it.

"You are a murderer or a thief or a racketeer; and you are hiding out."

Bando stopped looking for the peewee. He turned and stared at me. At first I was frightened. A bandit might do anything. But he wasn't mad, he was laughing. He had a good deep laugh and it kept coming out of him. I smiled, then grinned and laughed with him.

"What's funny, Bando?" I asked.

"I like that," he finally said. "I like that a lot." The tickle deep inside him kept him chuckling. I had no more to say, so I ground my heel in the dirt while I waited for him to get over the fun and explain it all to me.

"Thoreau, my Friend, I am just a college English teacher lost in the Catskills. I came out to hike around the woods, got completely lost yesterday, found your fire and fell asleep beside it. I was hoping the scoutmaster and his troop would be back for supper and help me home."

"Oh, no." My comment. Then I laughed. "You see Bando, before I found you, I heard squad cars screaming up the road. Occasionally you read about bandits that hide out in the forest, and I was just so sure that you were someone they were looking for."

We gave up the peewee and went back to the raftmaking, talking very fast now, and laughing a lot. He was fun. Then something sad occurred to me.

"Well, if you're not a bandit, you will have to go home very soon, and there is no point in teaching you how to live on fish and bark and plants."

"I can stay a little while," he said. "This is summer vacation. I must admit I had not planned to eat crayfish on my vacation, but I am rather getting to like it.

"Maybe I can stay until your school opens," he went on. "That's after Labor Day, isn't it?"

I was very still, thinking how to answer that.

Bando sensed this. Then he turned to me with a big grin.

"You really mean you are going to try to winter it out here?"

"I think I can."

"Well!" He sat down, rubbed his forehead in his hands, and looked at me. "Thoreau, I have led a varied life— dishwasher, sax player, teacher. To me it has been an interesting life. Just now it seems very dull." He sat awhile with his head down, then looked up at the mountains and the rocks and trees. I heard him sigh.

"Let's go fish. We can finish this another day."

That is how I came to know Bando. We became very good friends in the week or ten days that he stayed with me, and he helped me a lot. We spent several days gathering white oak acorns and groundnuts, harvesting the blueberry crop and smoking fish.

We flew Frightful every day just for the pleasure of lying on our backs in the meadow and watching her mastery of the sky. I had lots of meat, so what she caught those days was all hers. It was a pleasant time, warm, with occasional thunder showers, some of which we stayed out in. We talked about books. He did know a lot of books, and could quote exciting things from them.

One day Bando went to town and came back with five pounds of sugar.

"I want to make blueberry jam," he announced. "All those excellent berries and no jam."

He worked two days at this. He knew how to make jam. He'd watched his Pa make it in Mississippi, but we got stuck on what to put it in.

I wrote this one night:

"August 29

"The raft is almost done. Bando has promised to stay until we can sail out into the deep fishing holes.

"Bando and I found some clay along the stream bank. It was as slick as ice. Bando thought it would make good pottery. He shaped some jars and lids. They look good—not Wedgwood, he said, but containers. We dried them on the rock in the meadow, and later Bando made a clay oven and baked them in it. He thinks they might hold the blueberry jam he has been making.

"Bando got the fire hot by blowing on it with some home-made bellows that he fashioned from one of my skins that he tied together like a balloon. A reed is the nozzle.

"August 30

"It was a terribly hot day for Bando to be firing clay jars, but he stuck with it. They look jam-worthy, as he says, and he filled three of them tonight. The jam is good, the pots remind me of crude flower pots without the hole in the bottom. Some of the lids don't fit. Bando says he will go home and read more about pottery-making so that he can do a better job next time.

"We like the jam. We eat it on hard acorn pancakes.

"Later, Bando met The Baron Weasel today for the first time. I don't know where The Baron has been this past week, but suddenly he appeared on the rock, and nearly jumped down Bando's shirt collar. Bando said he liked The Baron best when he was in his hole.

"September 3

"Bando taught me how to make willow whistles today. He and I went to the stream

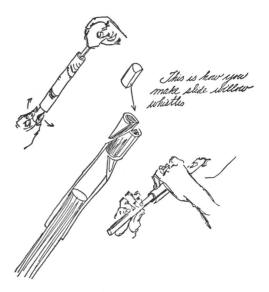

This is how you make slide willow whistles

Illustration by Jean George.

and cut two whistles about eight inches long. He slipped the bark on them. That means he pulled the wood out of the bark, leaving a tube. He made a mouthpiece at one end, cut a hole beneath it, and used the wood to slide up and down like a trombone.

"We played music until the moon came up. Bando could even play jazz on the willow whistles. They are wonderful instruments, sounding much like the wind in the top of the hemlocks. Sad tunes are best suited to willow whistles. When we played 'The Young Voyageur' tears came to our eyes, it was so sad."

There were no more notes for many days. Bando had left me saying: "Good-by, I'll see you at Christmas." I was so lonely that I kept sewing on my moccasins to keep myself busy. I sewed every free minute for four days, and when they were finished, I began a glove to protect my hand from Frightful's sharp talons.

One day when I was thinking very hard about being alone, Frightful gave her gentle call of love and contentment. I looked up.

"Bird," I said. "I had almost forgotten how we used to talk." She made tiny movements with her beak and fluffed her feathers. This was a language I had forgotten since Bando came. It meant she was glad to see me and hear me, that she was well fed, and content. I picked her up and squeaked into her neck feathers. She moved her beak, turned her bright head, and bit my nose very gently.

Jessie Coon James came down from the trees for the first time in ten days. He finished my fish dinner. Then just before dusk, The Baron came up on his boulder and scratched and cleaned and played with a fern leaf.

I had the feeling we were all back together again.

The Tree of Freedom
Lonesome Tilly

Rebecca Caudill

This story of pioneering Americans at the time of the Revolutionary War is an outstanding example of exciting historical fiction for children. Everyday details of life on the frontier are presented realistically and, along with strong characterizations, succeed in painting a living picture of the period. Stephanie's planting of an apple seed near her new home in Kentucky, one of a series of trees that symbolize her family's hope for freedom, is central to the meaning of the story.

Long before sunup the next morning the Venables rose from their pine bough pallets, stretched themselves, and set to work. Noel went to the edge of the clearing to call up the pigs and the chickens, to count the sheep, and unhobble the horse.

Some day they would fence in a pasture for the critters, said Jonathan. And after a year or two when they could raise enough corn to fatten pigs, they'd build a rail pen to keep the troublesome hogs in at night. Until the Venables got a shelter over their own heads, however, and vittles on their table, dumb animals would have to run free and forage through the woods. But their freedom was as studded with danger as a skunk cabbage was studded with spots.

As long as the wolves had plenty of deer for breakfast, dinner, and supper, and baby fawns for light snacks between meals, Jonathan reckoned the sheep would be safe. But nobody could tell when a bear might pounce on one of the pigs, wrap him in his forelegs and make off with him, running like a man, through the woods. The deputy said he once saw a bear running two-legged that way, toting a wriggling pig in his forelegs faster than a man could follow.

Stephanie untethered Brownie and milked her in a corner of the clearing. She sighed with relief as the last of the pigs came loping in answer to Noel's "Sho, pig! Sho, pig! Pig! Pig! Pig!" and turned her thoughts to other matters.

"I aim to plant my apple seed today," she told Noel.

"Whereabouts?" he asked.

"I haven't decided," Stephanie told him.

"Grandmammy's tree was planted right beside the door of their old house," Noel told her. "It was bloomin' when I left Charleston. Steppin' outside the door was like steppin' out into a perfumed cloud. And the bees were poppin' in and out of that tree like popcorn."

"My tree'll bloom that way, too," said Stephanie. "It sure will be a pretty sight, won't it, bloomin' here in the wilderness every springtime? But I don't aim to call it 'The Tree of St. Jean de Maurienne,'" she added. "I aim to call it 'The Tree of Freedom.' Your kind of freedom."

From Rebecca Caudill, *Tree of Freedom* (New York: Viking, 1974).

"A Tree of Freedom's apt to grow bitter fruit," Noel told her. "Sometimes mighty costly fruit."

"I know," said Stephanie.

All the Venable young uns knew from Bertha the story of the bitter, costly apples Marguerite de Monchard's tree had borne.

When the de Monchards fled their country and their biggety king, Bertha told the Venable young uns, because they refused to forsake their religion and make slaves of their consciences, they thought it mighty poor grace to begin enslaving others as soon as they found refuge in a new world, as many of the Huguenots who had fled France before them had done. The de Monchards looked on with sickening heart as broad rice fields turned the simple holdings of their Huguenot neighbors into estates, as fashionable country seats strutted up where simple Huguenot cottages had stood.

Had the liberty-loving Huguenots tended the rice and swept the mansion floors with their own hands, well and good Bertha said. But no, they bought black men and women off the auction block in Charleston. In time a Huguenot came to be known by the number of slaves he owned. Black gold, he called his slaves. The black men and women bent their backs in the hot, swampy rice fields, and swept the mansion floors, cooked the vittles, and shooed the flies off their Huguenot masters and mistresses, while the sting and the black sorrow of slavery seeped into them like a poison.

The de Monchards were a stubborn lot, Bertha told her young uns. Proud and stubborn. It was told of Marguerite that one day she and her pappy went walking through the Charleston market place, and heard an auctioneer's loud, raucous rigmarole, parading the salable qualities of a big Gambian Negro standing chained on the auction block. The Gambian was as strong as a brute ox for field labor, barked the auctioneer; he was docile; he had had the smallpox; he was already branded with two circles, one above the other, on his right buttock; he ought to bring not a shilling less than fifty pounds; if cash were offered, he might be had ten per cent cheaper, and rice and indigo might be used in place of specie.

Marguerite de Monchard was sixteen then. At that point in the transaction, it was told of her that she broke through the crowd of buyers and bystanders and standing before the auctioneer, screamed at him that he was no better than the tyrant who ruled France, and that wherever he went, deep, black shame ought to go with him that he could traffic in human beings as if they were cattle.

Annoyed men, who couldn't hear the auctioneer's description of the Gambian above her outburst, caught her and handed her, furious and outraged, to her pappy. Slowly the two of them made their way out of the tittering crowd and across the market square, Marguerite sobbing as she went.

That night the de Monchards made an agreement. They would go to the slave market themselves the next morning, they decided, and pay in cash for as many slaves as their money would buy, and give such slaves their freedom.

It was a long story Bertha told the Venable young uns of the slaves whose freedom was purchased by the de Monchards. But in the end, Bertha said, the de Monchards got licked for their pains. When their money was gone, they found most of their friends gone, too, while the dent they had made in the institution of slavery was so little a body couldn't see it even with a spyglass trained on it. Then they packed up their belongings and started north in the direction of the Tar River in North Carolina, where, they had heard, freedom-loving folks called Quakers had settled. They would seek asylum and new fields to cultivate among the Quakers, they decided.

Lucien, however, stayed in the old home because he was keeping a school for boys in Charleston, and he had a notion he might deal slavery a few blows in the school room. It was in the Quaker settlement on the Tar that Grandmammy Marguerite had married Grandpappy Linney.

"Grandmammy's tree cost her a sight, I reckon," said Stephanie, picturing the sunny, pleasant French village of St. Jean de Maurienne which the de Monchards had had to flee, and the spacious, broad-verandahed South Carolina houses, the broad, low-lying rice fields and the many black slaves on which they had turned their backs. "But Mammy's tree in the Back Country—it wasn't so costly."

Sometimes freedom's like a light you have to keep a-tendin', day in, day out," Noel said. "Nobody tries specially to blow it out. But it gets dimmer and dimmer if somebody ain't always tendin' the oil. That's what Mammy's done. She's tended the oil. And the wick. Why do you think she dinged at Pappy all summer to let me have a little schoolin' when Preacher Craig norated around that he'd teach a school on the Waxhaw fall before last? And why do you think she outtalked Pappy, and sent me to Uncle Lucien last winter? Know what Governor Jefferson's doin'?" he asked. "Uncle Lucien says he's talkin' up free education for everybody."

"What's free education?" asked Stephanie.

"Schools where the scholars don't have to pay."

"But somebody has to pay," said Stephanie, recollecting the goose feathers Bertha had traded to Preacher Craig in exchange for Noel's brief schooling.

"Oh, everybody'll pay all right," Noel told her.

"Everybody that has property, that is. Property owners'll be taxed for free schools."

"Taxed?" said Stephanie. "Well, Pappy sure ain't goin' to take to that."

After breakfast, Stephanie took the grubbing hoe, and on the east edge of the clearing turned up leaf mold, and crumbled it with her fingers to make a cool, black bed in which to lay her apple seed.

"What you plantin'?" asked Willie.

"A Tree of Freedom," Stephanie told him.

"What kind of tree's a Tree of Freedom?" asked Willie.

"A tree that grows sometimes sweet apples, sometimes bitter ones," said Stephanie.

"Humph!" sniffed Willie. "You're gullin'."

That morning Jonathan began cutting down trees for the Venable cabin.

"Shucks, now!" he said, as he picked up his ax. "If a body just had a passel of neigh-

bors, we'd get this cabin up in three shakes of a sheep's tail."

Every Venable knew, however, that Jonathan would be skittish if he had enough neighbors to help raise a cabin. A few neighbors he liked, and after a long spell of lonesomeness, he warmed toward folks the way a freezing man warms toward a fire. But if, on some winter morning when all the leaves were off the trees, a body, by standing on a rise of ground, could look a far piece up the river and down the river, and see blue smoke curling from half a dozen chimneys, then Jonathan would likely begin to complain that he felt crowded. Then his feet would begin to itch, and nothing would cure the itching except a week's hunt in the woods by his lonesome, and looking out over wild country where no white man had ever set foot.

The Venables working by themselves could raise a cabin in a couple of weeks, but not the sort of cabin Bertha wanted. A puncheon floor Bertha wanted, and a window, a cockloft, and a chimney made of rocks.

To all these fancy notions Jonathan raised objections. First of all, it was a piece of foolishness, he said, to build so fine a cabin unless he had a deed to the land on which he aimed to build it. Then, there wasn't time to raise a regular Tidewater mansion, he told Bertha. Time was short, considering all a body had to do before winter overtook them. It was enough to get four walls up and a roof over their heads.

"And, besides," he added, "a puncheon floor's a hotbed of splinters. The young uns'll be nussin' festered feet all winter."

"What are you aimin' to do with the skins from all the bears and buffaloes you aim to kill but lay 'em on the floor?" Bertha asked him.

"And a rock chimney!" Jonathan complained. "Mud and sticks are good enough for most chimneys around here, I notice."

"A rock chimney ain't tinder like a stick chimney," Bertha reminded him. "And anyway, it ain't as if the river bed wasn't choked with rocks to be had for the pickin' up."

Jonathan gave in grudgingly.

"You can leave the chinkin' out of the walls," Bertha said, thinking to lighten the labor of raising so fine a cabin with so few hands. "Fall will be time enough to daub the cracks, I reckon."

As long as they slept on the pine bough pallets and cooked their vittles in the clearing, it seemed to Stephanie they were only resting in their long, weary journey from the Back Country, and any morning they might reload Job and head west again. But the first log laid flush against the rectangle of earth which had been cleared of every kind of growth, and raked clean as a floor, was like a Venable taproot working its way down deep into the black Kentucky earth, and holding the Venables firmly in that spot.

With Jonathan and Noel taking turns, a *chop, chop, chop,* slow, but steady as the ticking of a clock, enlivened the words all day long, as the ax bit out of ancient tree butts great white chips smelling sweet of sap. Popple trees and oak trees Jonathan chose for the walls of the cabin, and oak for the floors, while he marked for shakes to cover the cabin a straight-grained oak whose bushy crown seemed to be brushing the clouds across the sky. Jonathan put Rob to work hacking the bark off the felled trees with a hatchet. Stephanie and Willie he sent to the river to hunt chimney rocks.

Willie wasn't a sight of help, but he filled out the letter of the wilderness law Jonathan and Bertha laid down for the Venable young uns. A young un under no circumstances was to go by his lonesome into the woods, Jonathan said. Never. Nor out of earshot of the clearing. Two must go together. There was no end of bears in the woods, and the wilderness could still hide red men. It didn't matter a piny woods Tory, said Bertha, how sure and certain a body was that the Indians had all been driven north of the Ohio, nor how much confidence the deputy placed in the man named George Rogers Clark. It paid to be cautious, at least as long as Clark was off traipsing about the Illinois country where the deputy said he was.

"Two sets of eyes are sharper than one," Bertha summed things up. "And two sets of ears are keener than one."

"But two sets of legs ain't faster than one, Mammy," Rob told her.

"What are your eyes and ears but leg-savin' devices?" she asked him.

Stephanie and Willie traipsed down the steep slope to the river and took a long look across to satisfy themselves that red men weren't hiding in the cane and the willows on the far bank.

"It's big, flat rocks we want, Willie," said Stephanie.

"You be the spy and hunt 'em out, and I'll come along and capture 'em."

Along the river northward they went, Willie in front, wading in the shallow water along the bank, pointing out likely chimney stones, Stephanie waded after him, lugging to dry land such of his findings as appeared likely for a chimney, and piling them in a heap. Rob and Noel would carry the rocks up the hill when Jonathan was ready to build the chimney.

"How about knockin' off for a rest, Willie?" Stephanie asked, when she had built six piles of rocks.

The notion suited Willie.

"Right back there in the woods is a big patch of wintergreen," he said. "Pappy and I found it the other day. I'm goin' to get some for us to eat."

"You can't go by your lonesome," Stephanie told him.

"But it's right through there," he pointed. "You can might' nigh see it from here."

"Well," said Stephanie grudgingly. "I reckon. As long as we can still hear the ax. But don't be gone long. And holler if you want me."

Hardly had the big trees closed around Willie when Stephanie began to wish he had not gone. A body never could tell what lay in wait for little shavers in the woods. A whole passel of things might happen to a young un besides having red men steal him and carry him off and keep him the rest of his days, and leave his pappy and his mammy and all his kinfolks wondering right down to their bury holes what had become of him. A rattlesnake with eyes like red-hot coals of fire and a body rising and falling like a gunsmith's bellows, or a sluggish copperhead out looking for frogs, might fang him. A bear or a slinking wolf or a painter might make off with him. Eagles, too, folks said, sometimes swooped down and picked up young uns and flew straight to their nests in the tiptop of craggy mountains. The deputy said a bald eagle once, clean as a whistle, stole a little baby belonging to some folks settling on Otter Creek near Boone's Fort.

The sun was climbing high, Stephanie noticed. She sat on a big bald rock near the edge of the river with her feet dangling in the cool stream. The sun felt hot on her bare head. It warmed her tired shoulders through her cottonade dress, and made her sleepy.

"Steffy!"

From deep in the woods came Willie's voice, so faint and smothered Stephanie could scarcely hear it. She stiffened with fear. Goose bumps broke out on her arms as she got to her feet.

"Steff-ee! Come a-runnin'!"

Through the woods she stumbled, afraid to go, afraid not to go.

A stone's throw from the river she spied Willie, making himself little behind a tree at the edge of a bed of May apples. It was plain to see that whatever was wrong, he wasn't scared of anything.

When he saw her peeping through the undergrowth, he made signs for her to come to him.

"Looky!" he whispered, pointing to a near-by sycamore that stood dying of old age. "Up in that there hole. See?"

Stephanie stared upward at the hole, twenty feet above the ground.

"I don't see anything," she told him. She was about to tell him, too, not to scare her that way again, ever, as long as he lived, but he put his finger across his mouth as a warning to her to be quiet.

"Keep a-lookin'," he whispered.

Stephanie fastened her eyes on the hole and waited.

"Look out! She's a-comin'!" whispered Willie, his voice smaller and more excited than ever.

"I don't see a thing!" grumbled Stephanie.

"Sh-h-h! Look 'way up!" whispered Willie.

Down through the trees to a limb of the sycamore plummeted a mammy wood duck, a slim, gray-brown bird with eyes bugged out with caution.

"She shot out of that hole a while ago like a bullet," whispered Willie. "She's hidin' somethin' in there, I bet."

"Babies," whispered Stephanie.

"How do you know?"

"Because it's baby time."

Cocking her head on one side, then on the other, the skittish duck rose from the limb, sailed straight for the tree trunk, and dropped out of sight into the hole. In a minute she was out again, and on the ground, prancing around in the May apple bed, persuading in her high-pitched, wary, duck voice.

"Pee, pee, pee, pee, pee!"

Over and over she begged. Then she waited. Begged and waited.

"That's the way she was behavin' when I called you," Willie whispered, so low that Stephanie could scarcely make out the words he said. "I scared her, I reckon."

Stephanie, motionless, pursed her mouth as a sign to him to keep quiet. As still as shadows they stood, their bodies pressed close against the tree, waiting.

Up flew the duck. Into the hollow of the sycamore she darted, then out again. Once more she dropped to the ground among the May apples and pranced nervously about.

"Pee, pee, pee, pee, pee!"

As they waited, her skittishness left her and she stopped her prancing. Standing shyly among the May apples, she began calling again, this time more plaintively.

Stephanie nudged Willie. "Look in the hole!" she whispered.

High on the edge of the hole balanced a little bitty ball of down, blackish and yellowish, blinking its eyes at the big, green, shady world.

Willie leaned forward, but Stephanie held him back.

"It can't get down, Steffy!" whispered Willie, anxiety in his voice.

"You wait and see," Stephanie told him. "Little wild things can always make out. Just you be still and don't scare the little mite."

The baby duckling perched on the edge of the hole a minute, listening to its mammy, turning its downy head first to one side, then to the other. Then, all of a sudden, it gave itself a shove into space, flapped its little bitty wings as hard as it could, hit the ground, bounced like an India rubber ball, righted itself, and tore in a waddling run on its brandnew feet through the May apple bed toward its mammy.

"I'm goin' to catch it," whispered Willie. "I can have it for a pet, 'stid of a kitten."

"You got nothin' to feed it," said Stephanie. "Look! Here comes another."

A long time they waited, watching the hole while thirteen ducklings, one after the other, clambered to the edge of the hole, screwed up their courage to leap the long leap to the ground, and waddled after their mammy in the direction of the river.

"Help me catch just one, Steffy!" begged Willie.

"The little tykes don't like to be caught," she told him, coming out from behind the tree. "They're too tender. You better just get a coon for a pet, like Mammy said. And we both better get back to our rocks."

She squatted to pick some leaves of wintergreen growing on the other side of the tree, but with the dark waxy leaves halfway to her mouth, she stopped short, her body taut as a bowstring as she noticed a slight movement among the bushes. Her feet froze to the gound with terror. Before she could leap through the May apple bed and run for her life, dragging Willie by the hand, a queer old man looking like some strange wild critter of the woods stepped out in full view.

Willie grabbed Stephanie around the knees and began to whimper.

"Hush!" she scolded, trying to think.

At least, she told herself above the wild thumping of her heart, the man wasn't an Indian. And he didn't carry a weapon—neither a knife, nor a rifle, nor a tomahawk.

As reason came slowly back to her, she noticed that the man wasn't a mite taller than Noel. His white hair that needed hackling fell about his shoulders, and his long dirtywhite beard straggled down his chest. His arms and his feet were bare, and the few clothes he wore looked not so much like hunting shirt and breeches as a queer assortment of patches and tatters of varmint skin he had grown on himself. He stood staring first at Stephanie, then at Willie, with eyes as soft as a heifer's in his rusty face—eyes, Stephanie noticed, that seemed to have

stayed young while the rest of him grew hoary.

Suddenly Stephanie remembered what Noel had told her: "When you meet up with Lonesome Tilly Balance, just say 'Howdy,' natural like."

She thought of the baby ducks screwing up their courage. Skittishly she screwed up her own.

"Howdy!" she managed to say, scarcely above a whisper.

The old man said never a word. He had his eyes fastened on Willie, and even when he turned and padded away, critter like, on his bare feet into the deep woods, he gazed over his shoulder at the young un until he was out of sight.

"Who was that, Steffy?" whimpered Willie, still clinging to her.

"That was Lonesome Tilly Balance," she told him, her voice quavery with fright.

Willie began to cry. "Will he hex us?" he asked.

"No. Don't you see you're not hexed?" she scolded.

"He—he was just watchin' the ducks. Same as you. He likes ducks, apt as not."

"Where's he gone?"

"Home, I reckon."

"Where's his home?"

"Over yonder on his claim somewhere."

"What's he doin' on Pappy's claim then?" asked Willie.

"These here are Pappy's trees. I don't want him to come here."

Leading Willie by the hand, Stephanie hurried toward the sound of the chopping, away from the river. She'd better tell her pappy about Lonesome Tilly, she decided. "He didn't hurt anything, did he?" she asked, feeling braver as the sound of the chopping grew nearer.

"He might have," said Willie in a tearful voice, crowding against Stephanie in his eagerness not to be left behind, and glancing fearfully over his shoulder now and then

"But he didn't," Stephanie told him. "Don't go out huntin' for trouble, Willie. You can plague yourself to death that way. Like as not, Lonesome Tilly's as genteel as—as a high-born Tidewater gentleman, if you're genteel to him."

NONFICTION

Mountains

Delia Goetz

Mountains *is a realistic blend of the natural and symbolic functions that mountains have for people. The scope of the book is international and considers theories of mountain formation as well as the religious beliefs they inspire. In the final line of this excerpt, the observation that "changes occur so slowly that they can scarcely be noticed" echoes the sentiment of Hilda Conkling's poem "Hills."*

Mountains are the highest lands on the face of the earth. They are also among the least known.

Long ago primitive peoples feared them. They believed that witches, wizards, dragons, giants, and other fearsome creatures had their homes in the high places. And when they were forced to travel through the mountains, many people were carried blindfolded to shut out the sight of them.

Throughout history some people have believed that mountains were sacred places, because the gods lived there. Each year long lines of pilgrims climbed the sacred mountains to pray before the shrines of their gods. Even today many people look at the heights with awe. The Mexican peasant stands with hat in hand to gaze at the peak of Popocatepetl. And each year people who still honor ancient gods climb the mountains sacred to them in Japan, Korea, and Burma.

Others avoided the sacred mountains, because they feared that the presence of human beings would disturb and anger the gods. Nepalese guides are still afraid to climb certain mountains for that reason.

Early traders and travelers had other motives for bypassing the mountains if possible. Travel was difficult over unmarked routes on rugged heights, which were lashed by harsh winds and frequent storms. Travelers had to look for lower passes, or take roundabout ways to get across. Usually they took guards on the trips too, for the lonely heights were often the haunts of bandits, who preyed on travelers.

But despite ancient fears and beliefs and the hardship of life, people do live in some parts of most mountains. Some of them sought refuge there to escape the tyranny of other tribes or nations. The Inca people, living in the Andes of Peru, retreated even higher into the mountains to escape the Spanish conquerors. Today the Berber tribes move higher and higher into the Atlas Mountains in Africa, so they can avoid their enemies.

Some people, like the early pioneers in the United States, settled in the mountains by accident. They set out for lands beyond the mountains, but stayed in the highlands, because they liked the life there. Other suffered illnesses or other bad luck, and got no farther.

And today, as in ancient times, many religious people live alone in the mountains to meditate and pray. In Tibet holy men turn their prayer wheels, as they have for centuries. And in mountains around the world other religious men live in monasteries.

Delia Goetz, *Mountains* (New York: Morrow, 1962).

Whatever people have felt about them and wherever they have lived, mountains have affected their lives in some way.

Look at the map and you will see that every continent has mountains. On some continents they are more continuous or more numerous than on others. High mountains sprawl over much of Asia. Australia, on the other hand, has only a small mountainous section. These high lands amount to about ten per cent of the earth's exposed surface. And great mountain ranges that rise from the floor of the sea may be even more extensive than those on land.

Among the great mountains of the world are those that ring the Pacific Ocean, broken here and there by valleys, plains, and high plateaus and interrupted by oceans and seas. They begin in Antarctica, and are found again in South America, where the Andes Mountains form a long and unbroken part of the ring. From the Strait of Magellan to the Caribbean Sea, the Andes make a continuous wall. The mountains of Central America, Mexico's Sierra Madres, the Coast Ranges, the Cascades, the Sierra Nevada, and the Coast Mountains of Alaska and British Columbia form more of the ring. Then it curves around to the western side of the Pacific, extending through the Aleutians, Japan, and other islands and rounding out the circle again in Antarctica.

The greatest mountainous area of the world lies in Asia. It includes such lofty ranges as the Himalayas, the Hindu Kush, the Caucasus, and others. The high mountains of southern Europe include the Alps, the Carpathians, the Pyrenees, and other mountains of Spain.

In addition to these massive ranges, mountains are scattered throughout the world—in Africa, in the eastern parts of North America and South America, in the islands of the Caribbean and the Pacific, and in northern Europe.

Some, like the Appalachian Highlands of the United States, are old mountains that were formed hundreds of millions of years ago. Through the years their peaks have been worn down, their slopes have become more gentle, and their valleys have broadened.

The sharp peaks and steep slopes of mountains like the Rockies and the Himalayas show that they are young mountains. But a young mountain may be millions of years old.

A mountain is formed by forces within the earth, which cause its crust to take different shapes. In some places, strain and pressure push it into large folds, much as a rug wrinkles when the ends are pushed toward the center. Some folds are high, with narrow spaces between them. Others are wide, with broad spaces between. Under great pressure some of the folds bend over across others. Sometime they give way and the rocks crack.

Moutains are also formed in other ways. Sometimes great cracks split far down and around a mass of rock. The rock pushes up, away from the cracks, like a huge block raised above the land around it. Unequal pressure underneath pushes one side of the block higher than the other and forms a steep slope.

Sometimes molten rocks, forced upward with tremendous pressure, form domes, like huge blisters, under the earth's crust. There they harden. In time, the softer rock lying above them wears away, leaving the domes exposed high above their surroundings.

Often hot lava forces itself against the earth's crust and strikes a weak spot. The crust gives way, and then the hot lava flows out and around the opening, cools, and becomes solid. This happens again and again, building higher and higher, to form a mountain. Other times lava is forced from a pipe-like opening, and builds a high cone.

Many mountains are formed by combinations of these different forces.

As mountains are formed by action under the earth's crust, they are also shaped by action from the outside. Rapid changes in temperature, from the heat of day to the cold of night, cause rocks to crack. Bits of rock and sand, blown against sharp peaks, smooth them and wear away soft rock. Rain freezes in cracks, widens them, and loosens pieces of rock. Flowing water carries away the loosened rocks and carves gullies and gorges into the mountainside. Masses of moving ice and snow scoop soil off the slopes and gouge valleys.

And so, although mountains may seem permanent, they are always changing, wearing down bit by bit, while new ones are being built. Old mountains, long since worn down, may rise again, and form highlands just as they did before. But these changes occur so slowly that they can scarcely be noticed in the lifetime of one person.

The Secret Life of the Forest

Richard M. Ketchum

This book documents the life cycle of individual trees and notes their significance to the forest community, which does not cease with the death of the tree. Falling to earth, the tree provides food and shelter for innumerable creatures, underscoring natural interrelationships as well as the balance between life and death. Older children can read the piece themselves; adults can explain it to young children before they take a walk in the woods together.

A mature natural forest is not unlike a human community, in which individuals of all ages, sizes, shapes, and differing characteristics go about the business of living and growing old and dying in a myriad of ways. In these wooded lands a rich diversity of plants is struggling to root and grow toward the light, while great numbers are dead or dying, breaking up in various forms of decay. And the forest floor is the best indication of this perpetual waxing and waning of life; it is a mass of rotten branches and tree trunks, strewn with fallen leaves, through which new seedlings and saplings are beginning to emerge.

In such a forest there is an excess of growth; over the years twigs, leaves, flower parts, pollen, fruit, seed pods, buds, and bits of bark have fallen to the earth, covering the forest floor with a thickening litter that gradually becomes part of the humus beneath the trees. Giant hulks of trees killed or split in two lean against others or lie on the ground. Trees that have somehow lagged behind in the struggle for light maintain a tenuous foothold, riddled with insects and rot, ready to topple over at the slightest push. Ancient decaying stumps are mute evidence of forest giants whose trunks and branches have long since disintegrated; huge hollows, in which the remnants of roots persist, mark the site of a fallen tree whose root ball was torn from the soil in the violence of its crash to earth.

There are many reasons for a tree's death, almost all traceable to some external force— fire, drought, insect damage, extreme cold, disease, or simply lack of food or light. Lightning, attracted to the tallest specimens, fells some; ice storms coat the trunk and branches and bend trees to the snapping point; high winds tear off branches and blow down trees; hurricanes and gales take down whole swaths of growth, leaving a desolate, twisted mass of wreckage in their wake. Some trees become topheavy and tumble over from their own weight, or are blown down, knocking apart neighboring trees and smashing branches all around, leaving wounds and broken surfaces that attract insects and invite disease. Healthy specimens are able to resist most invasions of insects or disease, but insect borers, woodpeckers, and tiny creatures work away at every damaged tree, making "sawdust" of the supporting

Richard M. Ketchum, *The Secret Life of the Forest* (New York: McGraw-Hill, 1970).

heartwood, and fungi hollow it out so that it becomes an easy victim of windstorms. Fire, of course, is the forest's worst enemy. Even if a tree is not consumed by a forest fire, the intense heat may kill it or make it an easy prey for insects.

As it does to all living organisms, old age come to trees. Like animals, certain kinds of trees have fairly predictable life spans: a gray birch is considered old when it is forty, whereas a sugar maple may live to be five hundred, and some giant sequoias are estimated to be more than three thousand years old. Unlike animals however, trees do not age uniformly; as we have noted, the inner cells of a tree trunk may be dead for years while the growing extremities continue to push out into the environment, until they reach the outer limit to which water can be brought to the leaves and food to the roots. When they are old, trees have difficulty respiring, their new growth is not as vigorous as it once was, and the activity of the cambium cells is much reduced. This breakdown in the tree's vitality has visible effects: the leaves become smaller, more and more dead branches are evident, and damage to the bark or limbs is not so easily repaired, since an old tree lacks the recuperative powers of a more vigorous plant. The annual rings of an old tree are narrower, partly because the cambium layer is less active, but also because the tree finds it ever more difficult to provide moisture for its various parts.

But the death of a tree in the forest community is not the end; it is part of a marvelous cycle that prepares riches for the future.

One of the most remarkable characteristics of the flowering forest is its capacity to maintain itself. It is distinguished by the fact that it provides a rich food source for various forms of animal and plant life and by the fact that its remains do not accumulate permanently. There is an inevitable piling up of materials on the forest floor; in an acre of woodland as much as two tons of waste, including dead insects and animal droppings, as well as the debris of branches and leaves from trees and other plants, falls to the ground every year. But these great quantities of refuse are slowly broken down to form organic material through the work of hordes of soil creatures that attack it. This is the environment of the fungi, which can exist in darkness and which, with bacteria and an almost infinite variety of invertebrate animals, live in and exploit the remains of vegetation, eventually reducing it to fine humus. All the minerals that have been absorbed through the roots of the living tree and used in the building of plant tissues are discarded into the wastebasket of the forest floor and transformed so that they can be absorbed by the roots of other plants.

The forest community is a fantastic complex of organisms that live together in the same environment, all of them dependent upon and interacting with the others in some fashion. When the debris from trees falls to the ground, it is attacked first by shallow-boring grubs, which begin to work into it, eating as they go. Then termites and deeper borers appear on the scene, cutting up the dead material into minuscule pieces. They are assisted in the task by small armies of beetles, ants, grubs, centipedes, snails, slugs, and other creatures. Water seeps into the crevices, and fungi of all sorts attach themselves to the tree's remains and hasten decomposition. The wood becomes softer as a result and is soon a place where bacteria can thrive.

Earthworms work away at tiny pieces, taking them into their network of tunnels below ground, where they soften them by bacterial action and excrete the remains. Their importance as an agent of decomposition can be seen in the fact that the earthworm population of one acre of forest floor is capable of eating eighteen tons of debris in a year's time, mixing it with the soil and leaving tunnels into which water, air, seeds, and bacteria can penetrate. There may be millions of worms to an acre of forest land, and they crush and dissolve leaves and woody fragments in their digestive tracts, mixing those remains with tiny mineral particles they have picked up from the soil itself.

Fungi grow on the dead material, reducing even the bark of trees to a consistency that animals can eat. The excretion and slime from this process become the stuff on which bacteria grow and multiply. Tiny parasitic worms—the nematodes—propagate in the forest trash, consume minute bits of it, and add their excretions to the humus. Predator insects—spiders, scorpions, centipedes, and others—devour the minute soil creatures and add their waste products to the growing humus. The untiring little shrew, only two or three inches long, which must eat at least once an hour to maintain its incredible activity, runs about searching for insects and worms. The mole, in quest of the same prey, burrows through the upper layers of soil, working its path through as much as three hundred feet of tunnels a day.

But the chief agents in transforming litter into the dark, spongy material known as humus are the fungi. These nongreen plants, or plants without chloroplasts, do not photosynthesize like the green plants. They are capable of living in darkness, and they are scavengers that exist on the remains of green plants. They are able to decompose lignin, which is bacteria-resistant, and they reduce the fallen giants of the forest to smaller pieces, making them more susceptible to attack by insects. The fungi—which most of us recognize in their fruiting form as mushrooms or toadstools—decompose the substance on which they are growing by secreting enzymes through their walls. At the same time, they absorb water through their walls for their own growth. The mycelium, or vegetative part, of a fungus grows in rich, deep humus, and it requires a great deal of rain or ample water in the soil. The fungi are most likely to be seen, in fact, after a heavy rain that follows a prolonged dry spell; typically, one finds thriving colonies of toadstools in dark, moist corners of the woods, particularly after the autumn rains have ended a dry summer.

In the deciduous forests of the East, where there is adequate moisture and a generally moderate climate, the leaves that fall in the autumn are decomposed rather rapidly by the small organisms that inhabit the woods—sometimes within a month of the time the leaves have come off the trees. Indeed, autumn is a period of intense activity on the part of all small animals, which are laying in supplies of food for the long winter of hibernation.

The surface of the forest floor may appear to be a lifeless carpet of refuse and dead leaves, but immediately below the top layer are the decaying remains of other seasons, occupied by a busy community of tiny organisms. Deeper still, the humus is honeycombed with the passageways and burrows of insects, worms, moles, and the roots of plants, which make it a protective, insulating cover for the soil and a heavy sponge to check and absorb moisture, preventing rain from running off too quickly.

Growth and decay is the eternal cycle of life in the forest; neither is possible without the other. All the organic matter that has been locked up within a mature tree for dozens or even hundreds of years is released and returned to the soil intact when the tree dies and decomposes. These chemicals are neither reduced in quantity nor is their quality impaired, so the process of growth and decay is one of complete rejuvenation. How that rejuvenation is accomplished is largely the work of the lowly fungi and the unseen bacteria, which break down foliage and wood from trees, and muscle and bone and flesh from animals. The decay bacteria perform one of the most essential functions in our environment by making possible what is known as the carbon cycle. Carbon dioxide exists in the atmosphere, from which, as noted earlier, it is drawn into the leaves of plants as part of the process of photosynthesis. The oxygen molecules are released, and the carbon is converted into the body tissues of the trunk, roots, leaves, fruit, and seeds. When the tree dies, it is decomposed by decay bacteria and fungi and consumed by the millions of forest animals. In the latter process the carbon is absorbed directly into the animals' tissues. In other words, carbon that was originally removed from the atmosphere by photosynthesis is not returned to the atmosphere; instead, it is deposited in the bodies of a multitude of tiny animals. When these creatures die, decay bacteria will feed upon their remains. If they are eaten by predators, which may in turn be devoured by larger animals or birds, the residue of carbon from the tree is passed along intact to each successive predator, adding its bulk to the carbon already in the predator's system. Not until the last link in this food chain dies do the bacteria go to work on the remains. Then they bring about a remarkable chemical transformation by which the complex protoplasmic substances of the animal's body is once again reduced, or broken down, to inorganic, simple forms. By working on the remains of plants or animals, the decay bacteria return the carbon to the air, completing the cycle and making it possible for other plants to draw upon it again for a new round of growth.

Our atmosphere, it is believed, contains only enough carbon dioxide at any one time to support the earth's plant population for forty years. So the part played by bacteria in returning carbon to the air is crucial; without it, all the carbon dioxide would be withdrawn from the air, and vegetation would disappear from the planet.

FANTASY

The Goblin and the Grocer

Hans Christian Andersen

In this fantasy about the value of poetry in human life, poetry is symbolized as a wonderful tree of light that bears fruit of glittering stars. The goblin of the story, who is very human, is torn between the spiritual beauty of the tree and the material delights of jam and butter.

There was once a hard-working student who lived in an attic, and he had nothing in the world of his own. There was also a hard-working grocer who lived on the first floor, and he had the whole house for his own.

The Goblin belonged to him, for every Christmas Eve there was waiting for him at the grocer's a dish of jam with a large lump of butter in the middle.

The grocer could afford this, so the Goblin stayed in the grocer's shop; and this teaches us a good deal. One evening the student came in by the back door to buy a candle and some cheese; he had no one to send, so he came himself.

He got what he wanted, paid for it, and nodded a good evening to the grocer and his wife (she was a woman who could do more than nod; she could talk).

When the student had said good night he

From Andrew Lang, *The Pink Fairy Book* (New York: Dover, 1966). Translated by Alma Alleyne. Illustrated by H. J. Ford.

suddenly stood still, reading the sheet of paper in which the cheese had been wrapped.

It was a leaf torn out of an old book—a book of poetry.

'There's more of that over there!' said the grocer. 'I gave an old woman some coffee for the book. If you like to give me twopence you can have the rest.'

'Yes,' said the student, 'give me the book instead of the cheese. I can eat my bread without cheese. It would be a shame to leave the book to be torn up. You are a clever and practical man, but about poetry you understand as much as that old tub over there!'

And that sounded rude as far as the tub was concerned, but the grocer laughed, and so did the student. It was only said in fun.

But the Goblin was angry that anyone should dare to say such a thing to a grocer who owned the house and sold the best butter.

When it was night and the shop was shut, and everyone was in bed except the student, the Goblin went upstairs and took the grocer's wife's tongue. She did not use it when she was asleep, and on whatever object in the room he put it that thing began to speak, and spoke out its thoughts and feelings just as well as the lady to whom it belonged. But only one thing at a time could use it, and that was a good thing, or they would have all spoken together.

The Goblin laid the tongue on the tub in which were the old newspapers.

'Is it true,' he asked, 'that you know nothing about poetry?'

'Certainly not!' answered the tub. 'Poetry is something that is in the papers, and that is frequently cut out. I have a great deal more in me than the student has, and yet I am only a small tub in the grocer's shop.'

And the Goblin put the tongue on the coffee-mill, and how it began to grind! He put it on the butter-cask, and on the till, and all were of the same opinion as the waste-paper tub, and one must believe the majority.

'Now I will tell the student!' and with these words he crept softly up the stairs to the attic where the student lived.

There was a light burning, and the Goblin peeped through the key-hole and saw that he was reading the torn book that he had bought in the shop.

But how bright it was! Out of the book shot a streak of light which grew into a large tree and spread its branches far above the student. Every leaf was alive, and every flower was a beautiful girl's head, some with dark and shining eyes, others with wonderful blue ones. Every fruit was a glittering star, and there was a marvellous music in the student's room. The little Goblin had never even dreamt of such a splendid sight much less seen it.

He stood on tiptoe gazing and gazing, till the candle in the attic was put out; the student had blown it out and had gone to bed, but the Goblin remained standing outside listening to the music, which very softly and sweetly was now singing the student a lullaby.

'I have never seen anything like this!' said the Goblin. 'I never expected this! I must stay with the student.'

What the GOBLIN said in the Student's room

The little fellow thought it over, for he was a sensible Goblin. Then he sighed, 'The student has no jam!'

And on that he went down to the grocer again. And it was a good thing that he did go back, for the tub had nearly worn out the tongue. It had read everything that was inside it, on the one side, and was just going to turn itself round and read from the other side when the Goblin came in and returned the tongue to its owner.

But the whole shop, from the till down to the shavings, from that night changed their opinion of the tub, and they looked up to it, and had such faith in it that they were under the impression that when the grocer read the art and drama critiques out of the paper in the evenings, it all came from the tub.

But the Goblin could no longer sit quietly listening to the wisdom and intellect downstairs. No, as soon as the light shone in the evening from the attic it seemed to him as though its beams were strong ropes dragging him up, and he had to go and peep through the key-hole. There he felt the sort of feeling we have looking at the great rolling sea in a storm, and he burst into tears. He could not himself say why he wept, but in spite of his tears he felt quite happy. How beautiful it must be to sit under that tree with the student, but that he could not do; he had to content himself with the key-hole and be happy there!

There he stood out on the cold landing, the autumn wind blowing through the cracks of the floor. It was cold—very cold, but he first found it out when the light in the attic was put out and the music in the wood died away. Ah! then it froze him, and he crept down again into his warm corner; there it was comfortable and cosy.

When Christmas came, and with it the jam with the large lump of butter, ah! then the grocer was first with him.

But in the middle of the night the Goblin awoke, hearing a great noise and knocking against the shutters—people hammering from outside. The watchman was blowing his horn: a great fire had broken out; the whole town was in flames.

Was it in the house? or was it at a neighbour's? Where was it?

The alarm increased. The grocer's wife was so terrified that she took her gold earrings out of her ears and put them in her pocket in order to save something. The grocer seized his account books, and the maid her black silk dress.

Everyone wanted to save his most valuable possession; so did the Goblin, and in a few leaps he was up the stairs and in the student's room. He was standing quietly by the open window looking at the fire that was burning in the neighbour's house just opposite. The Goblin seized the book lying on the table, put it in his red cap, and clasped it with both hands. The best treasure in the house was saved, and he climbed out on to the roof with it—on to the chimney. There he sat, lighted up by the flames from the burning house opposite, both hands holding tightly on his red cap, in which lay the treasure; and now he knew what his heart really valued most—to whom he really belonged. But when the fire was put out, and the Goblin thought it over—then—

'I will divide myself between the two,' he said. 'I cannot *quite* give up the grocer, because of the jam!'

And it is just the same with us. We also cannot quite give up the grocer—because of the jam.

Birds and Other Animals

FABLES, MYTHS, AND LEGENDS

The Fox Bit by Mosquitoes

Aesop

This fable is believed to have been told by Aesop. It is a veiled reference to the ancient Greek tyrants, who, if replaced, would be followed by ever worse scoundrels.

A fox was running along through the reeds when an entire swarm of mosquitoes attacked him. They infested his fur to such an extent that his whole body was covered with insects who were sucking his blood. He squirmed on the ground, rubbing his back against the earth in agony.

A crow watched from a tree. ''Why don't you wade in a pond and rid yourself of them?'' the crow asked.

''Because if I did, it would be much worse,'' the fox replied. ''These mosquitoes, once they have been glutted with my blood, will leave me. A new swarm would come to me empty and finish me off.''

How Raven Created the World

Retold by Ronald Melzack

In Germanic mythology, the raven generally appears as a symbol of sadness or melancholy. It is therefore thought of as embodying destructiveness. In Eskimo and North American mythologies, however, the symbolism is just the opposite; as in this tale, the raven is a creator and a bearer of light.

From Ronald Melzack, *Raven: Creator of the World* (Toronto: McClelland & Stewart, 1970). Illustrated by Laszlo Gol.

In the beginning, there was only Raven and the falling snowflakes. Raven sailed through the soft silvery glow of the universe which stretched endlessly around him. Sparkling snowflakes swirled past him and tumbled around in circles as his wings swayed ever so slightly.

Once, Raven caught some snowflakes on his outstretched wings. He lowered one wing, and the snowflakes trickled down to his wingtip and made a little snowball. He amused himself as he flew, gently lowering and raising his wing, and watched the little snowball grow as it rolled back and forth. Then, with a great sweep of his wing, he hurled the snowball through the air.

Raven watched, fascinated, as his snowball soared across the sky, picking up more snowflakes as it hurtled along. It grew larger and larger until it was immense. Raven flew after it, sailed above it, and then lowered himself gently onto it. He stretched out his legs and realized that he had never before stood on solid ground. He had been flying for as long as he could remember, and it felt good to rest his wings.

Raven felt an itch near his beak. He scratched it and, to his astonishment, his beak moved! He pushed it up so that it sat on his forehead. His wings felt strange, and, as he moved them, his wing-cape slipped off his shoulders. He stood upright on two legs and moved his hands slowly over his face. He felt his eyes, his nose, his mouth. His fingers examined the beak on his forehead.

The soft, white snow-hills sparkled in the pale, silvery light. Raven kicked away at the snow with his foot, and soon he saw rich brown clay. He picked up the clay and moulded little seeds out of it. Then Raven swept his wing-cape across his shoulders, lowered his beak, and flew from place to place and planted the seeds. Wherever he planted them a forest grew up—tree after tree, with herbs and plants around their roots. Raven thought this new land was beautiful and he called it Earth. The place he came from he called the Sky.

Raven liked Earth and each day he flew to see all the things he had created. He wandered through the forests and tended the plants and flowers, especially the tiny shoots that sprang out of the earth and grew slowly upward.

One plant grew quickly, so quickly that Raven could actually see it grow. Leaves sprouted out of the plant, and little buds near the leaves grew into pea-pods.

As he watched, he saw a pea-pod move and jiggle, yet there was no wind. It shook and quivered and then it split open, and a little living creature popped out. It jumped around and kicked the snow. The creature was cold, and, as it jumped up and down, its teeth chattered.

Raven went up to the newcomer and smiled. ''Who are you?'' he asked.

''I came from that pod,'' said the creature. ''I was tired of lying there, so I kicked out a hole and jumped through!''

Raven laughed heartily. ''You're a funny fellow! You look a little familiar, though I've never seen you before!'' And he laughed again. ''I created that pod plant myself, but I had no idea that you would jump out.''

''And where did *you* come from?'' asked the little creature.

''I have always been here,'' said Raven. ''Come to think of it, you look a lot like me,

except that you don't have a beak on your forehead. I will call you Man and I will be your friend.'' Raven plucked feathers from his wing-cape and made a little parka for Man to wear and keep his body warm.

That was how the first man was created, and Raven watched many more men, and women too, hop out of the pea-pod plant.

Raven fed the people with berries from the plants that he had grown. But the people needed more food. And so Raven made the animals and he made them of clay. After he had fashioned them in the shapes that delighted him, he set the clay creatures out to dry in the cool air. And when they had dried out, Raven called the people to behold what he had made. The people thought they were beautiful. Then Raven told the people to close their eyes. He pulled his beak down over his mouth, and waved his wings five times over the shapes. Soon they started to breathe and move. They were alive. Raven raised his mask and told the people to look. When they saw the animals moving, full of life, they cried out with pleasure. Raven experimented with these creatures until they looked just right to him. And that is how he learned to make every kind of animal, fish, and bird, and he taught each kind to live on the earth, in the sea, or in the air.

Raven showed the animals to the people and said that some animals would be their food as soon as people learned to hunt. But that would not be easy, because the pale, silvery glow of the sky was just enough for people to see things close at hand. When men wanted to walk to distant places, they had to grope about with their hands and find things out by listening.

Men heard the howling of the wolves, the grunting of the bears, and the growling of the foxes. In the sea the seals snorted, the walruses wheezed, the whales blew. Birds whistled and sang, insects hummed. Men heard, too, the whispering of the winds, the rustle and murmur of the leaves, and the surging of the surf against the shore.

Raven loved all the creatures he had created, but there were none that he respected or admired more than the sparrows. One day, he called a little sparrow and said to her,

''Far off in the universe lies the source of all light. Even though you are small and plain, you are the hardiest and bravest creature of all. Therefore I command you to fly out into the universe and bring back Light so that people may see the world, the animals, and one another.''

The little sparrow flew off and stayed away in the darkness until Raven thought she would never come back. At last, he heard the whirr of her wings and felt her floating down and settling on his hand. The sparrow carried three little packets in her beak, each wrapped in a leaf. She gave them to Raven.

Raven opened one of the leaves and saw a ball of brilliant, dazzling gold. He called it the Sun. He threw it into the air, and immediately a great radiance filled the earth and dazzled everyone. For the first time, people could see the earth on which they lived. They saw the woods, the animals on land and in the sea, and the birds in the air. They rejoiced at all the beauty around them. Life became a new and greater thing for all of them. When the sun set, Raven opened another leaf, and in it was a ball of iron. Raven threw it up into the air and called it the Moon. Raven called the light of the sun Day and the light of the moon Night, and both the sun and the moon have gracefully shared the sky with each other ever since.

Now people were happy. Raven taught them to build igloos and tents to shelter themselves from the wind and the storms. He taught them to make kayaks and big boats so that they could sail on the sea and hunt the sea-creatures. He taught them to make spears and other weapons to hunt the animals that roam the land. And he showed them how to build a fire to warm themselves when they were cold, and to cook the meat when it was too tough to eat.

Men and animals flourished on earth and their numbers kept increasing. But the land was too small to hold them all. One day, Raven said to the people, ''So that there may be food and space enough for all, the old must henceforth make way for the young.'' And for the first time, the oldest of all living things—people and animals, plants and trees—weakened and died. Yet men and animals continued to flourish, and their numbers kept increasing.

One day, Raven moulded clay to make new kinds of animals for his people. The clay was too wet, and when he set it out to dry, it all ran together and made a huge serpent unlike any other animal. The serpent slithered down to the sea, and swam around near shore, waiting to pounce on the men in their boats. Men rode up to it in their kayaks and tried to harpoon it, but all the harpoons bounced off its sides.

Raven saw the hopeless struggle and said to the little sparrow, who followed him everywhere, "Fly out and hover above the serpent while I hunt it from my kayak." Then Raven followed the sparrow to the serpent.

The sparrow glided above the serpent and inspected it intently. Soon she pointed to its soft belly, and Raven threw his harpoon. The serpent exploded with a tremendous roar. The men shouted with joy as they watched bits of serpent fly up into the air and then come crashing down into the sea, where they turned into islands. Land shot up near land,

and the whole became a wide and spacious coast. In this way, new land was created and there was enough room on earth for everybody, men and animals too.

One day, just after the sun had gone down and the sky was a deep, rich blue, Raven gathered all the people and said to them, "I am your Creator. To me you owe your lives and your land, and you must never forget me."

Raven drew his beak down over his mouth and swept his wing-cape across his shoulders. He spread his wings wide and sailed up to the sky, where it was dark. In one wing he held the last of the leaves that the sparrow had given him. He shook open the leaf, and in it were little pieces of silver. He threw the silver pieces into the air, and they scattered across the whole sky. Raven called them the Stars. The people were enchanted by the tiny, glittering lights, and they sang out in awe and delight.

And this was the way Raven made the earth, the men, and the animals, and the sun, the moon, and the stars.

The Fenris Wolf

Retold by Olivia E. Coolidge

The wolf in this Norse myth is seen as dangerous and destructive. With teeth "as large as the trunks of oak trees and as sharply pointed as knives," he seeks to devour the world. The wolf is held in check temporarily by a magic chain woven by dwarf people under the earth. But according to the myth, when the end of the world comes, the Fenris wolf will break loose and devour the sun and the moon.

Though Loki, the fire God, was handsome and ready-witted, his nature was really evil. He was, indeed, the cause of most of the misfortunes which befell the gods. He was constantly in trouble, yet often forgiven because the gods valued his cleverness. It was

he who found ways out of difficulty for them, so that for a long time they felt that they could not do without him.

In the early days Loki, though a god, had wedded a monstrous giantess, and the union of these two evil beings produced a fearful

From Olivia E. Coolidge, *Legends of the North* (Boston: Houghton Mifflin, 1979).

brood. The first was the great world serpent, whom Odin cast into the sea, and who became so large that he completely encircled the earth, his tail touching his mouth. The second was Hel, the grisly goddess of the underworld, who reigned in the horrible land of the dead. The third was the most dreadful of all, a huge monster called the Fenris Wolf.

When the gods first saw the Fenris Wolf, he was so young that they thought they could tame him. They took him to Asgard, therefore, and brave Tyr undertook to feed and train him. Presently, however, the black monster grew so enormous that his open jaws would stretch from heaven to earth, showing teeth as large as the trunks of oak trees and as sharply pointed as knives. The howls of the beast were so dreadful as he tore his vast meals of raw meat that the gods, save for Tyr, dared not go near him, lest he devour them.

At last all were agreed that the Fenris Wolf must be fettered if they were to save their very lives, for the monster grew more ferocious towards them every day. They forged a huge chain, but since none was strong enough to bind him, they challenged him to a trial of strength. "Let us tie you with this to see if you can snap the links," said they.

The Fenris Wolf took a look at the chain and showed all his huge white teeth in a dreadful grin. "Bind me if you wish," he growled, and he actually shut his eyes as he lay down at ease to let them put it on.

The gods stepped back, and the wolf gave a little shake. There was a loud cracking sound, and the heavy links lay scattered around him in pieces. The wolf howled in triumph until the sun and moon in heaven trembled at the noise.

Thor, the smith, called other gods to his aid, and they labored day and night at a second chain. This was half as strong again as the first, and so heavy that no one of the gods could drag it across the ground. "This is by far the largest chain that was ever made," said they. "Even the Fenris Wolf will not be able to snap fetters such as these."

Once more they brought the chain to the wolf, and he let them put it on, though this time it was clear that he somewhat doubted his strength. When they had chained him, he shook himself violently, but the fetters held. His great, red eyes burned with fury, the black hair bristled on his back, and he gnashed his teeth until the foam flew. He strained heavily against the iron until the vast links flattened and lengthened, but did not break. Finally with a great bound and a howl he dashed himself against the ground, and suddenly the chain sprang apart so violently that broken pieces were hurled about the heads of the watching gods.

Now the gods realized in despair that all their strength and skill would not avail to bind the wolf. Therefore Odin sent a messenger to the dwarf people under the earth, bidding them forge him a chain. The messenger returned with a little rope, smooth and soft as a silken string, which was hammered on dwarfish anvils out of strange materials which have never been seen or heard. The sound of a cat's footfall, the breath of a fish, the flowing beard of a woman, and the roots of a mountain made the metal from which it was forged.

The gods took the little rope to the Fenris Wolf. "See what an easy task we have for you this time," they said.

"Why should I bother myself with a silken string?" asked the wolf sullenly. "I have broken your mightiest chain. What use is this foolish thing?"

"The rope is stronger than it looks," answered they. "We are not able to break it, but it will be a small matter to you."

"If this rope is strong by enchantment," said the wolf in slow suspicion, "how can I tell that you will loosen me if I cannot snap it after all? On one condition you may bind me: you must give me a hostage from among yourselves."

"How can we do this?" they asked.

The Fenris Wolf stretched himself and yawned until the sun hid behind clouds at the sight of his great, red throat. "I will let you bind me with this rope," he said, "If one of you gods will hold his hand between my teeth while I do it."

The gods looked at one another in silence.

The wolf grinned from ear to ear. Without a word Tyr walked forward and laid his bare hand inside the open mouth.

The gods bound the great wolf, and he stretched himself and heaved as before. This time, however, he did not break his bounds. He gnashed his jaws together, and Tyr cried out in pain as he lost his hand. Nevertheless, the great black wolf lay howling and writhing and helplessly biting the ground. There he lay in the bonds of the silken rope as long as the reign of Odin endured. The Fates declared, however, that in the last days, when the demons of ice and fire should come marching against the gods to the battlefield, the great sea would give up the serpent, and the Fenris Wolf would break his bonds. The wolf would swallow Odin, and the gods would go down in defeat. Sun and moon would be devoured and the whole earth would perish utterly.

FOLKTALES—
INHERITED AND LITERARY

The Golden Phoenix

Marius Barbeau

The theme of this French-Canadian folktale is similar to that of "The Firebird"
(p. 92), but many symbolic images in the action are different. They include a
glass mountain, a unicorn, a lion, a serpent, and a Great Sultan who is able to
change shape. Once again, though, a magic bird, the Golden Phoenix—who
carries in its voice the blessing of eternal youth—is at the heart of the story.

There was once a King renowned for his wisdom. And how did he come to be so wise? Well, in his garden there grew a magic tree; and every night that tree bore one silver apple—the apple of wisdom. Each morning the King would take it from the tree and eat it while the trumpets blew. As a result he governed wisely and well, and all his people lived happily.

Then a strange thing happened. One morning, when the King came to pick the apple, it was gone. No one saw it go; and no one admitted to taking it.

"Someone has stolen the silver apple,"

From Marius Barbeau, *The Golden Phoenix and Other Fairy Tales from Quebec,* retold by Michael Hornyansky. Illustrated by Arthur Price. Copyright © Oxford University Press, 1980. Reprinted by permission of the publisher.

said the King grimly. The next night he set his royal guards about the tree to keep watch.

But to no avail. In the evening the silver apple was there, ripening on its branch; in the morning it had gone. The guards swore that no one had passed them during the night.

The King called his three sons to him.

"This is a serious matter," he said. "Someone is stealing the silver apple during the night, and not even my royal guards can catch him. My sons, I put the task in your hands. Whichever one of you succeeds in catching the thief will be rewarded with my crown and my kingdom."

"I will stand guard tonight," promised the eldest prince.

That evening he went into the garden and prepared to spend the night at the foot of the tree. He took a bottle of wine to keep himself company. From time to time he poured himself a cupful and gulped it down. Then as midnight drew near, he began to yawn.

"I must not fall asleep," he told himself. And he got up and marched around the tree. He could see the silver apple gleaming in the moonlight.

But soon he was too tired to go on walking. Surely it would do no harm to sit down for a moment? He sat down. Pop! He fell asleep.

When he woke, the damage was done. The silver apple had vanished.

"Well," he said, "good-bye to the crown!"

Next morning the King asked for news of the thief, and of course there was no news. The eldest prince had gone to sleep at his post.

"Leave it to me, Father," said the second prince. "I'll catch your thief."

The King shook his head doubtfully. But next evening the second prince went into the garden and prepared to spend the night at the foot of the tree. He took a platter of food to keep himself company. He felt sure that cold chicken and potato salad would keep him awake. But as midnight drew near he began to yawn.

"No one is going to bewitch me into falling asleep," he told himself. And he got up and marched around the tree. The apple was still there, gleaming in the moonlight.

But soon he was too tired to go on walking. Surely it would do no harm to sit down for a moment? He sat down. Pop! He fell asleep.

When he woke an hour later he jumped to his feet. But the damage was done. The silver apple had vanished.

"Well, that's that," he said. "I too have lost the crown."

Next morning the King asked if he had had better luck than his brother.

"No, Father," said the second prince, ashamed. "I stayed awake till midnight. But when midnight struck, I was sleeping like a badger."

Petit Jean, the youngest prince, burst out laughing. "A fine pair of sentries you are!"

"It's easy for you to talk," said his brother crossly. "You were sound asleep in your bed."

"All the same, if the King my father sends me to stand guard, I will bring back news of how the apple disappears."

"My dear son," said the King. "This is no ordinary thief. How can you be so sure you'll do better than your brothers?"

"Well," said Petit Jean, "I'm sure I can do no worse."

And so next evening he went into the garden and prepared to spend the night there. He looked up at the silver apple, gleaming by the light of the moon. Then he sat down to wait. When he felt himself growing sleepy, he got up and marched around the tree. But as midnight drew near, he began to yawn.

"This will never do," he told himself. "If I fall asleep, the apple will disappear as usual—and how my brothers will laugh!"

He climbed up into the tree and settled himself in a forked branch near the magic fruit. Then he put out his hand to the apple. It was as smooth as ivory, and cool as the night.

"Suppose I picked it now," he thought. "Then no one would be able to steal it without my noticing."

He plucked the apple from the branch and put it inside his shirt. Then he tucked in his shirt and buttoned it right up to the neck. Not a moment too soon. Pop! His eyes closed and he fell sound asleep.

But he was waked almost at once by something pulling at his shirt. Seeing a bright shadow in front of him, he reached out to grapple with the thief. He hung on with all his strength, but the thief broke free, leaving his hands full of shining feathers.

He felt in his shirt. The apple was gone.

"Oh, well," he said, "at least I have some evidence."

He tucked the feathers in his shirt and went to bed. Next morning, when the King asked for news of the thief, Petit Jean spread the feathers on the table.

"I couldn't hold him," he said. "But he left these behind in my hands."

"A fine thing," sneered his brothers, who were jealous of his success. "To have the thief in your hands and let him go!"

"Hush!" said the King, staring at the bright feathers. "I know this bird—it is the Golden Phoenix. No man can hold him against his will. Petit Jean, do you know in which direction he flew?"

"He left a fiery trail behind him, like a shooting star," said Petit Jean. "I saw him go over the top of the Glass Mountain."

"Good," said the King. "We shall be able to follow his trail."

And they all set off toward the Glass Mountain. Along the path from time to time they found a shining feather. But at the top of the Glass Mountain they stopped. They could see the shining feathers leading down into the Great Sultan's country. But they could not follow, for on this side the mountain fell away in a sheer cliff, a thousand feet straight down.

"We can go no farther," said the King.

"Father, look," said Petit Jean. "I've found a trap-door."

"A trap-door in a mountain?" scoffed his brothers. "Ridiculous!"

"Please, Father, come and see," repeated Petit Jean. "Perhaps it leads down into the Great Sultan's country."

The King came over to see the trap-door and decided it was worth looking into. All of them heaved together, and at last they managed to pull it open. Underneath they found a well going down into darkness.

"The sides are as smooth as ice," said the elder princes. "There is no way to climb down."

"We need a good long rope," said the King, "and a stout basket on the end of it."

These things were brought from the castle. To the end of the rope the princes tied a basket big enough for a man to sit in. On the King's advice they also attached a string to the basket, fastened at the other end to a bell.

"So if there is danger," he explained, "whoever is in the basket can signal us here at the top. Now, who is going down?"

The eldest prince turned white. "Not I," he said. "I can't stand heights."

The second prince turned green. "Not I," he said. "I don't like the dark."

Petit Jean laughed. "Then it's my adventure," he said. "Wish me luck, Father."

"Good luck, my boy," said the King. "And take with you this sword. Use it well, and it will keep you from harm. We shall keep watch here. When you come back and ring the bell, we will pull you up.''

Petit Jean said good-bye and climbed into the basket. Down, down, down he went, with the sword in one hand and the bell-rope in the other. For a long time he heard nothing and saw nothing. Then at last the basket stopped with a bump. He climbed out and gave two quick tugs on the bell-rope. Then he groped his way along a tunnel towards a faint light.

"Just as I thought," he said. "It leads into the Great Sultan's country."

The light grew stronger, and the tunnel widened into a cavern. But here Petit Jean found his way barred. In the middle of the cavern stood a fierce beast with one long horn in the middle of its forehead. When it saw him it bellowed.

"I am the Unicorn of the Cave," it said. "You may not pass!"

"But I must pass," said the prince. "I am on my way to see the Sultan."

"Then prepare for combat!" said the Unicorn.

And without another word it charged at him, the long sharp horn pointing straight at his heart. Petit Jean had no time to use his sword. At the last moment he dodged to one side, and the Unicorn thundered past. There was a terrific crash. The Unicorn had stuck fast in the wall of the cavern.

"Now may I pass?" asked Petit Jean.

"Yes, as far as I'm concerned," grunted the Unicorn as it tried to work its horn free.

But Petit Jean could not pass. This time his way was barred by a great Lion, waving his tail menacingly.

"I am the Lion of the Cave," he roared. "Prepare for combat!"

And without another word he sprang straight at Petit Jean. The prince stood firm, and at the last moment swung his sword. *Snick!* He shaved the whiskers off the Lion's left cheek. With a fierce roar the Lion sprang again. Petit Jean swung his sword on the other side—*snick!*—and shaved the whiskers off the Lion's right cheek.

At this the Lion gave a deafening roar. He gathered himself for one more leap, and came down on Petit Jean with his paws out

and his mouth open. This time the prince judged his moment very carefully. *Snick, snack!* And the Lion's head tumbled to the ground.

"Ouch!" said the Lion. Petit Jean was amazed to see him pick up his head with his front paws and set it on his neck again, as good as new.

"Now may I pass?" asked Petit Jean. "Or must I do it again?"

"Oh, no," said the Lion wearily. "Once is enough for me."

But Petit Jean still could not pass. The cavern was suddenly filled with a slithery hissing noise, and he found his way barred by a terrible beast with seven heads.

"I am the Serpent of the Cave," hissed the beast. "Prepare for combat!"

Petit Jean took a deep breath. This one looked very dangerous indeed. But it did not spring at him. It just waited in his path. Wherever he tried to strike with his sword, he found a head snapping at him with fierce jaws and a forked tongue.

Then the young prince had a bright idea. He began running around the Serpent, striking with his sword; and the seven heads began to twist round each other trying to keep up with him. When the seven necks were twisted tight as a rope, he took a wide swing with his sword and—*snock!*—he cut off all the seven heads at once. There was a roar of applause from the Unicorn and the Lion.

"Now may I pass?" asked Petit Jean again.

"You may pass," sighed the Serpent, trying to find its seven heads and get them back on the right necks.

And so Petit Jean walked out into the realm of the Great Sultan. Just outside the cavern he found a glittering feather, so he knew he was still on the trail of the Golden Phoenix.

Before he had gone very far he was met by the Sultan himself riding on a white elephant. The Sultan had a long black moustache, and he stroked it as he looked down at his visitor.

"Who are you that have passed the Glass Mountain?" he asked. "And what do you seek in my realm?"

"I am the son of your neighbour, the wise King," replied Petit Jean. "And I am looking for a bird that has been raiding our apple tree."

The Sultan nodded thoughtfully. He invited Petit Jean to climb up on to the elephant behind him, and they rode back to the Sultan's palace. All along the road the prince kept his eyes open for the feathers that the Golden Phoenix had dropped in its flight.

When they reached the palace, the Sultan invited Petit Jean to dine with him in the garden. They were joined at table by the Sultan's daughter, who was more beautiful than the moon and stars combined. Petit Jean could hardly take his eyes off her.

They sat down beneath a jasmine tree, and as they began the feast a bird sang above their heads, filling the evening air with beautiful music. Petit Jean caught a glimpse of gold among the leaves.

"May I ask what bird is singing, your highness?" he said.

The Sultan stroked his moustache. "There are many birds in my realm," he said. "This one is probably a nightingale."

Petit Jean thought it was probably something else; but he said no more about it. He complimented the Sultan on the food, which was delicious, and on his daughter, who looked more beautiful every moment.

When they had finished, the Sultan spoke to him again.

"It is the custom of this country," he said, "that every stranger passing through must play a game of hide-and-seek with me. Tomorrow morning it will be your turn. If you should win, you shall have the hand of my daughter in marriage. How does that appeal to you?"

"It appeals to me more than anything else in the world," said Petit Jean. "But what if I should lose?"

The Sultan stroked his long black moustache and smiled. "Ah," he said. "Then you will lose the dearest thing you own."

"I see," said Petit Jean. "But I am a stranger here. How can I be expected to play hide-and-seek in a place I do not know?"

The Sultan nodded. "This evening my daughter will show you round the garden. Take care to notice all the places where I might hide, for tomorrow morning you must find me three times. And now I shall wish you good night."

When the Sultan had gone, the Princess began showing Petit Jean round the garden. But she noticed that he was not really paying attention.

"I think you do not wish to win my hand," she said sadly, "for you are not looking at anything I show you."

"Dear Princess," said Petit Jean, "I would much rather look at you."

The Princess could not help smiling. But suddenly she looked so sad that Petit Jean asked her what was the matter.

"I am thinking of what must happen to you tomorrow," she said. "I will tell you the truth: no matter how well you knew this garden, you would not be able to find my father. For he has the power to change his shape so that not even I can recognize him. So you see, nobody can win his game of hide-and-seek."

"Then only luck can save me," said Petit Jean cheerfully. "Well, let us have no more sad talk. Tell me of yourself, Princess, and of the bird that sings over your banquet table."

"The bird?" said the Princess. "Oh, that is the Golden Phoenix. Whoever lives within the sound of its voice will never grow old."

"A very useful bird," said Petit Jean. "And how do you make sure it doesn't fly away?"

The Princess told him that the Phoenix did fly free during the night. But at sunrise he always came back to his golden cage. So whoever owned the cage could be sure of owning the Golden Phoenix.

They walked in the garden, talking of many things, until the moon rose. Then Petit Jean went to bed and slept soundly till morning.

Next day the Sultan was very cheerful, for he expected to win his game of hide-and-seek. He could hardly wait for Petit Jean to finish his breakfast.

"Now here are the rules of the game," he said. "I shall hide three times in the garden, and you must find me. And just to prove I am a fair man, I will offer you three prizes. If you find me once, you shall escape with your life. If you find me twice, you shall have your life and my daughter. If you find me three times, you shall have your life, my daughter, and whatever you choose as a dowry.''

''Agreed,'' said Petit Jean.

The Sultan rushed off to hide, and Petit Jean invited the Princess to walk in the garden with him. She grew very pale and nervous, because he seemed to be making no effort to find her father.

At the Sultan's fish-pond they stopped and looked down. There were fishes of all colours and sizes swimming in it. Petit Jean looked at them closely and burst out laughing. One of the fishes had a long black moustache.

''Princess,'' he said, ''I should like to borrow a net.''

''A net?'' said the Princess. ''How can you think of fishing at a time like this?''

But she went and found him a net. Petit Jean leaned down and scooped out the fish with the moustache. There was a puff of white smoke, and the fish vanished. In its place was the Sultan, breathing hard.

''Humph!'' growled the Sultan, climbing out of the net. ''And how did you happen to find me, young man?''

''Beginner's luck,'' said Petit Jean. ''Well, have I earned my life?''

''Yes,'' said the Sultan angrily. ''Do you want to stop there, or go on with the game?''

Petit Jean looked at the Princess. ''Oh,'' he said, ''I shall go on.''

The Sultan rushed off to hide again. Petit Jean took the Princess's arm and they walked round the garden together. When she asked him where he would look this time, he shook his head.

''I don't know,'' he said. ''I don't think your father will forget about his moustache again.''

They looked everywhere, but found nothing that turned out to be the Sultan. At last Petit Jean stopped beside a rose-bush and sighed.

''Well,'' he said, ''if I am never to see you again, I would like to give you something to remember me by.''

And he leaned down to pluck the reddest rose on the bush. Pop! The rose disappeared

in a puff of red smoke, and in its place stood the Sultan, red with anger.

''Oh!'' exclaimed Petit Jean. ''I thought you were a rose.''

''You are too lucky for words,'' snarled the Sultan. ''Well, you've won your life and my daughter. I suppose you want to stop there?''

''Oh, no,'' said Petit Jean. ''That wouldn't be fair to you. I shall try my luck once more.''

And so the Sultan rushed off to hide for the last time. The Princess and Petit Jean went on walking in the garden, wondering where he might be. No matter where they tried, they could not find him.

At last Petit Jean stopped beneath a pear-tree.

''All this exercise is making me hungry,'' he said. And reaching up, he plucked the ripest, roundest pear he could see.

Bang! There was a puff of black smoke, and in place of the pear stood the Sultan, black with fury.

''Oh,'' said Petit Jean. ''I thought you were a pear.''

''You are too lucky to live!'' roared the Sultan.

''But I have already won my life,'' Petit Jean reminded him. ''And now I have won my choice of dowry.''

The Sultan grumbled, but finally asked what dowry Petit Jean would choose.

''A little thing which you'll hardly miss,'' said Petit Jean. ''I choose the old gold cage which hangs in your daughter's chamber.''

The Sultan leaped into the air. ''The old gold cage!'' he shouted. Then he pretended to be calm. ''Oh, you wouldn't want that old thing,'' he said. ''Let me offer you three chests of treasure instead.''

''I couldn't possibly take your treasure,'' said Petit Jean. ''The cage is quite enough.''

The Sultan turned purple with rage. But at last he agreed that Petit Jean had won the cage fair and square. He even promised to give them an escort as far as the Glass Mountain next day.

Meanwhile there was a banquet to celebrate Petit Jean's success, and above their heads the Golden Phoenix sang in the jasmine tree. But all through the meal the

Sultan kept pulling his moustache and glancing angrily at Petit Jean. It was easy to see that he was not at all happy.

The Princess noticed her father's mood, and as she had by now fallen in love with Petit Jean, she felt nervous. When they were alone together she told him her fears.

"I do not believe my father will keep his word," she said. "He is so angry at losing the Golden Phoenix that he will try to kill you while you sleep."

"Then we had better leave during the night," said Petit Jean.

The Princess agreed. "Bring two horses from the stable, and muffle their hooves," she said. "Meanwhile I will fetch my travelling cloak and the golden cage."

Petit Jean tiptoed to the stable and chose two horses. He tied pieces of blanket around their hooves and led them back to the kitchen door. There he met the Princess, wearing her cloak and carrying the cage.

"My father is suspicious," she said. "But as long as he hears voices talking he will not stir from his room."

She put two beans into a frying-pan on the stove. As soon as they felt the heat the beans began to croak. One of them said "Nevertheless" in a high voice; the other said "Notwithstanding" in a deep voice. When they were both croaking they sounded just like a man and woman talking together.

Petit Jean and the Princess mounted their horses and rode softly away, carrying the golden cage, while upstairs the Sultan listened to the conversation in the kitchen. He had a sleepless night, for the two beans went on saying "Nevertheless-notwithstanding" until morning. And by the time he found out what had happened, Petit Jean and the Princess had reached the Glass Mountain.

The Unicorn, the Lion, and the Serpent were there in the cavern, but they did not bar the way. Petit Jean placed his Princess in the basket and pulled on the bell-rope. His father and brothers were waiting at the top, and when they heard the bell they pulled the basket up the well.

They were astonished to see the Princess. The two princes would have stopped and gazed at her, but she told them to let down the basket again before it was too late. Presently they pulled up Petit Jean with the golden cage in his arms.

"Welcome home, my boy," said the King. "And welcome to your lady, too. But where is the bird you set off to find? This cage is empty."

Petit Jean pointed to the Great Sultan's country, and they saw a dazzling radiance moving toward them through the sky, with a beating of golden wings: for it was near daybreak, and the Phoenix was looking for his cage. And after him on the road below came the Sultan himself, riding his white elephant and shaking his fist at the sky.

The three princes rolled a big stone over the trap-door so that the Sultan could never follow them. Then, with the Golden Phoenix safe in his cage, they set off homewards.

Petit Jean and his Princess were married, and the King gave them his crown and kingdom as he had promised. And with the Golden Phoenix singing every night in the tree where the silver apple of wisdom grew, they lived wisely and happily ever afterwards.

The Wonderful Tar-Baby Story

Retold by Joel Chandler Harris

The American slaves created a rich body of folklore—songs, rhymes, and tales—but it was not until after the Civil War that collectors like Joel Chandler Harris put them into print. Black metaphors are rich and highly imaginative, and black

Joel Chandler Harris, "The Wonderful Tar-Baby Story," from *Uncle Remus: His Songs and His Sayings* (New York: Dutton, 1963).

folk literature has the lilt of spirituals or blues songs. Harris preserved some of this for us at a time when blacks were denied the freedom to preserve their culture in written form.

Harris's talking-animal tales were published in 1880 as Uncle Remus: His Songs and His Sayings. *Brer Rabbit is the prankster hero who overcomes adversity with intelligence. The slaves saw themselves outwitting their masters whenever Brer Rabbit outwitted another animal. So these stories, though amusing, carried a much deeper meaning. Because of the rich dialect of the tales, they should be read aloud to children, if possible.*

"Didn't the fox *never* catch the rabbit, Uncle Remus?'' asked the little boy the next evening.

"He come mighty nigh it, honey, sho's you born—Brer Fox did. One day atter Brer Rabbit fool 'im wid dat calamus root, Brer Fox went ter wuk en got 'im some tar, en mix it wid some turkentime, en fix up a contrapshun wat he call a Tar-Baby, en he tuck dish yer Tar-Baby en he sot 'er in de big road, en den he lay off in de bushes fer to see what de news wuz gwineter be. En he didn't hatter wait long, nudder, kaze bimeby here come Brer Rabbit pacin' down de road—lippity-clippity, clippity-lippity—dez ez sassy ez a jay-bird. Brer Fox, he lay low. Brer Rabbit come prancin' 'long twel he spy de Tar-Baby, en den he fotch up on his behime legs like he wus 'stonished. De Tar-Baby, she sot dar, she did, en Brer Fox, he lay low.

"Mawnin'!' sez Brer Rabbit, sezee—'nice wedder dis mawnin',' sezee.

"Tar-Baby ain't sayin' nothin', en Brer Fox, he lay low.

" 'How duz yo' sym'tums seem ter segashuate?' sez Brer Rabbit, sezee.

"Brer Fox, he wink his eye slow, en lay low, en de Tar-Baby, she ain't sayin' nothin'.

" 'How you come on, den? Is you deaf?' sez Brer Rabbit, sezee. 'Kaze if you is, I kin holler louder,' sezee.

"Tar-Baby stay still, en Brer Fox, he lay low.

" 'Youer stuck up, dat's w'at you is,' says Brer Rabbit, sezee, 'en I'm gwineter kyore you, dat's w'at I'm a gwineter do,' sezee.

"Brer Fox, he sorter chuckle in his stummick, he did, but Tar-Baby ain't sayin' nothin'.

" 'I'm gwineter larn you howter talk ter 'spect-tubble fokes ef hit's de las' ack,' sez Brer Rabbit, sezee. 'Ef you don't take off dat hat en tell me howdy, I'm gwineter bus' you wide open,' sezee.

"Tar-Baby stay still, en Brer Fox, he lay low.

"Brer Rabbit keep on axin' 'im, en de Tar-Baby, she keep on sayin' nothin', twel present'y Brer Rabbit draw back wid his fis', he did, en blip he tuck'er side er de head. Right dar's whar he broke his merlasses jug. His fis' stuck, en he can't pull loose. De tar hilt 'im. But Tar-Baby, she stay still, en Brer Fox, he lay low.

" 'Ef you don't lemme loose, I'll knock you agin,' sez Brer Rabbit, sezee, en wid dat he fotch 'er a wipe wid de udder han', en dat stuck. Tar-Baby, she ain't sayin' nothin', en Brer Fox, he lay low.

" 'Tu'n me loose, fo' I kick de natal stuffin' outen you,' sez Brer Rabbit, sezee, but de Tar-Baby, she ain't sayin' nothin'. She des hilt on, en den Brer Rabbit lose de use er his feet in de same way. Brer Fox, he lay low. Den Brer Rabbit squall out dat ef de Tar-Baby don't tu'n 'im loose he butt 'er cranksided. En den he butted, en his head got stuck. Den Brer Fox, he sa'ntered fort', lookin' des ez innercent ez one er yo' mammy's mockin'-birds.

" 'Howdy, Brer Rabbit,' sez Brer Fox, sezee. 'You look sorter stuck up dis mawnin',' sezee, en den he rolled on de groun', en laughed en laughed twel he couldn't laugh no mo'. 'I speck you'll take dinner wid me dis time, Brer Rabbit. I done laid in some calamus root, en I ain't gwineter take no skuse,' sez Brer Fox, sezee.''

Here Uncle Remus paused, and drew a two-pound yam out of the ashes.

"Did the fox eat the rabbit?" asked the little boy to whom the story had been told.

"Dat's all de fur de tale goes," replied the old man. "He mout, en den again he moutent. Some say Jedge B'ar come long en loosed 'im—some say he didn't. I hear Miss Sally callin'. You better run 'long.''

The Water Lily

Birds—creatures of the air, the medium of the spirit world—often symbolize intuition, thoughts that are later found to be true. In this sense, one who can understand the "language of the birds" is in touch with the intuitive knowledge that may be needed as a protection from danger. In this folk tale, also known as "The Gold Spinners," only the youngest of the three gold spinners is able to understand the speech of the birds at first. Later, the wind wizard's son develops this power (the wind being associated too with spirit or intuition). But it is not until the prince hero is fed a cake of magic herbs and comes to understand the birds that the evils of the story can be undone.

Once upon a time, in a large forest, there lived an old woman and three maidens. They were all three beautiful, but the youngest was the fairest. Their hut was quite hidden by trees, and none saw their beauty but the sun by day, the moon by night, and the eyes of the stars. The old woman kept the girls hard at work, from morning till night, spinning gold flax into yarn, and when one distaff was empty another was given them, so they had no rest. The thread had to be fine and even, and when done was locked up in a secret chamber by the old woman, who twice or thrice every summer went on a journey. Before she went she gave out work for each day of her absence, and always returned in the night, so that the girls never saw what she brought back with her, neither would she tell them whence the gold flax came, nor what it was to be used for.

Now, when the time came round for the old woman to set out on one of these journeys, she gave each maiden work for six days, with the usual warning: 'Children, don't let your eyes wander, and on no account speak to a man, for, if you do, your thread will lose it brightness, and misfortunes of all kinds will follow.' They laughed at this oft-repeated caution, saying to each other: 'How can our gold thread lose its brightness, and have we any chance of speaking to a man?'

On the third day after the old woman's departure a young prince, hunting in the forest, got separated from his companions, and completely lost. Weary of seeking his way, he flung himself down under a tree, leaving his horse to browse at will, and fell asleep.

The sun had set when he awoke and began once more to try and find his way out of the forest. At last he perceived a narrow footpath, which he eagerly followed and found that it led him to a small hut. The maidens, who were sitting at the door of their hut for coolness, saw him approaching, and the two elder were much alarmed, for they remembered the old woman's warning; but the

From Andrew Lang, *The Blue Fairy Book* (New York: Dover, 1965).

youngest said: 'Never before have I seen anyone like him; let me have one look.' They entreated her to come in, but, seeing that she would not, left her, and the Prince, coming up, courteously greeted the maiden, and told her he had lost his way in the forest and was both hungry and weary. She set food before him, and was so delighted with his conversation that she forgot the old woman's caution, and lingered for hours. In the meantime the Prince's companions sought him far and wide, but to no purpose, so they sent two messengers to tell the sad news to the King, who immediately ordered a regiment of cavalry and one of infantry to go and look for him.

After three days' search, they found the hut. The Prince was still sitting by the door and had been so happy in the maiden's company that the time had seemed like a single hour. Before leaving he promised to return and fetch her to his father's court, where he would make her his bride. When he had gone, she sat down to her wheel to make up for lost time, but was dismayed to find that her thread had lost all its brightness. Her heart beat fast and she wept bitterly, for she remembered the old woman's warning and knew not what misfortune might now befall her.

The old woman returned in the night and knew by the tarnished thread what had happened in her absence. She was furiously angry and told the maiden that she had brought down misery both on herself and on the Prince. The maiden could not rest for thinking of this. At last she could bear it no longer, and resolved to seek help from the Prince.

As a child she had learnt to understand the speech of birds, and this was now of great use to her, for, seeing a raven pluming itself on a pine bough, she cried softly to it: 'Dear bird, cleverest of all birds, as well as swiftest of wing, wilt thou help me?' 'How can I help thee?' asked the raven. She answered: 'Fly away, until thou comest to a splendid town, where stands a king's palace; seek out the king's son and tell him that a great misfortune has befallen me.' Then she told the raven how her thread had lost its brightness,

how terribly angry the old woman was, and how she feared some great disaster. The raven promised faithfully to do her bidding, and, spreading its wings, flew away. The maiden now went home and worked hard all day at winding up the yarn her elder sisters had spun, for the old woman would let her spin no longer. Towards evening she heard the raven's 'craa, craa' from the pine tree and eagerly hastened thither to hear the answer.

By great good fortune the raven had found a wind wizard's son in the palace garden, who understood the speech of birds, and to him he had entrusted the message. When the Prince heard it, he was very sorrowful, and took counsel with his friends how to free the maiden. Then he said to the wind wizard's son: 'Beg the raven to fly quickly back to the maiden and tell her to be ready on the ninth night, for then will I come and fetch her away.' The wind wizard's son did this, and the raven flew so swiftly that it reached the hut that same evening. The maiden thanked the bird heartily and went home, telling no one what she had heard.

As the ninth night drew near she became very unhappy, for she feared lest some terrible mischance should arise and ruin all. On the night she crept quietly out of the house and waited trembling at some little distance from the hut. Presently she heard the muffled tramp of horses, and soon the armed troop appeared, led by the Prince, who had prudently marked all the trees beforehand, in order to know the way. When he saw the maiden he sprang from his horse, lifted her into the saddle, and then, mounting behind, rode homewards. The moon shone so brightly that they had no difficulty in seeing the marked trees.

By-and-by the coming dawn loosened the tongues of all the birds, and, had the Prince only known what they were saying, or the maiden been listening, they might have been spared much sorrow, but they were thinking only of each other, and when they came out of the forest the sun was high in the heavens.

Next morning, when the youngest girl did not come to her work, the old woman asked where she was. The sisters pretended not to know, but the old woman easily guessed what had happened, and, as she was in reality a wicked witch, determined to punish the fugitives. Accordingly, she collected nine different kinds of enchanters' night shade, added some salt, which she first bewitched, and, doing all up in a cloth into the shape of a fluffy ball, sent it after them on the wings of the wind, saying:

> Whirlwind!-mother of the wind!
> Lend thy aid 'gainst her who sinned!
> Carry with thee this magic ball.
> Cast her from his arms for ever,
> Bury her in the rippling river.

At midday the Prince and his men came to a deep river, spanned by so narrow a bridge that only one rider could cross at a time. The horse on which the Prince and the maiden were riding had just reached the middle when the magic ball flew by. The horse in its fright suddenly reared, and before anyone could stop it flung the maiden into the swift current below. The Prince tried to jump in after her, but his men held him back, and in spite of his struggles led him home, where for six weeks he shut himself up in a secret chamber, and would neither eat nor drink, so great was his grief. At last he became so ill his life was despaired of, and in great alarm the King caused all the wizards of his country to be summoned. But none could cure him. At last the wind wizard's son said to the King: 'Send for the old wizard from Finland, he knows more than all the wizards of your kingdom put together.' A messenger was at once sent to Finland, and a week later the old wizard himself arrived on the wings of the wind. 'Honoured King,' said the wizard, 'the wind has blown this illness upon your son, and a magic ball has snatched away his beloved. This it is which makes him grieve so constantly. Let the wind blow upon him that it may blow away his sorrow.' Then the King made his son go out into the wind, and he gradually recovered and told his father all. 'Forget the maiden,' said the King, 'and take another bride;' but the Prince said he could never love another.

A year afterwards he came suddenly upon the bridge where his beloved had met her death. As he recalled the misfortune he wept bitterly, and would have given all he possessed to have her once more alive. In the midst of his grief he thought he heard a voice singing, and looked round, but could see no one. Then he heard the voice again, and it said:

> Alas ! bewitched and all forsaken,
> 'Tis I must lie for ever here!
> My beloved no thought has taken
> To free his bride, that was so dear.

He was greatly astonished, sprang from his horse, and looked everywhere to see if no one were hidden under the bridge; but no one was there. Then he noticed a yellow water-lily floating on the surface of the water, half hidden by its broad leaves; but flowers do not sing, and in great surprise he waited, hoping to hear more. Then again the voice sang:

> Alas ! bewitched and all forsaken.
> 'Tis I must lie for ever here!
> My beloved no thought has taken
> To free his bride, that was so dear.

The Prince suddenly remembered the gold-spinners, and said to himself: 'If I ride thither, who knows but that they could explain this to me?' He at once rode to the hut, and found the two maidens at the fountain. He told them what had befallen their sister the year before, and how he had twice heard a strange song, but yet could see no singer. They said that the yellow water-lily could be none other than their sister, who was not dead, but transformed by the magic ball. Before he went to bed, the eldest made a cake of magic herbs, which she gave him to eat. In the night he dreamt that he was living in the forest and could understand all that the birds said to each other. Next morning he told this to the maidens, and they said that the charmed cake had caused it, and advised him to listen well to the birds, and see what they could tell him, and when he had recovered his bride they begged him to return and deliver them from their wretched bondage.

Having promised this, he joyfully returned home, and as he was riding through the forest he could perfectly understand all that the birds said. He heard a thrush say to a magpie: 'How stupid men are! they cannot understand the simplest thing. It is now quite a year since the maiden was transformed into a water-lily, and, though she sings so sadly that anyone going over the bridge must hear her, yet no one comes to her aid. Her former bridegroom rode over it a few days ago and heard her singing, but was no wiser than the rest.'

'And he is to blame for all her misfortunes,' added the magpie. 'If he heeds only the words of men she will remain a flower for ever. She were soon delivered were the matter only laid before the old wizard of Finland.'

After hearing this, the Prince wondered how he could get a message conveyed to Finland. He heard one swallow say to another: 'Come, let us fly to Finland: we can build better nests there.'

'Stop, kind friends!' cried the Prince. 'Will ye do something for me?' The birds consented, and he said: 'Take a thousand greetings from me to the wizard of Finland, and ask him how I may restore a maiden transformed into a flower to her own form.'

The swallows flew away, and the Prince rode on to the bridge. There he waited, hoping to hear the song. But he heard nothing but the rushing of the water and the moaning of the wind, and, disappointed, rode home.

Shortly after, he was sitting in the garden, thinking that the swallows must have forgotten his message, when he saw an eagle flying above him. The bird gradually descended until it perched on a tree close to the Prince and said: 'The wizard of Finland greets thee and bids me say that thou mayst free the maiden thus: Go to the river and smear thyself all over with mud; then say: "From a man into a crab," and thou wilt become a crab. Plunge boldly into the water, swim as close as thou canst to the water-lily's roots, and loosen them from the mud and reeds. This done, fasten thy claws into the roots and rise with them to the surface. Let the water flow all over the flower, and drift with the current until thou comest to a mountain ash tree on the left bank. There is near it a large stone. Stop there and say: "From a crab into a man,

from a water-lily into a maiden," and ye will both be restored to your own forms.'

Full of doubt and fear, the Prince let some time pass before he was bold enough to attempt to rescue the maiden. Then a crow said to him: 'Why dost thou hesitate? The old wizard has not told thee wrong, neither have the birds deceived thee; hasten and dry the maiden's tears.'

'Nothing worse than death can befall me,' thought the Prince, 'and death is better than endless sorrow.' So he mounted his horse and went to the bridge. Again he heard the water-lily's lament, and, hesitating no longer, smeared himself all over with mud, and, saying: 'From a man into a crab,' plunged into the river. For one moment the water hissed in his ears, and then all was silent. He swam up to the plant and began to loosen its roots, but so firmly were they fixed in the mud and reeds that this took him a long time. He then grasped them and rose to the surface, letting the water flow over the flower. The current carried them down the stream, but nowhere could he see the mountain ash. At last he saw it, and close by the large stone. Here he stopped and said: 'From a crab into a man, from a water-lily into a maiden,' and to his delight found himself once more a prince, and the maiden was by his side. She was ten times more beautiful than before, and wore a magnificent pale yellow robe, sparkling with jewels. She thanked him for having freed her from the cruel witch's power, and willingly consented to marry him.

But when they came to the bridge where he had left his horse it was nowhere to be seen, for, though the Prince thought he had been a crab only a few hours, he had in reality been under the water for more than ten days. While they were wondering how they should reach his father's court, they saw a splendid coach driven by six gaily caparisoned horses coming along the bank. In this they drove to the palace. The King and Queen were at church, weeping for their son, whom they had long mourned for dead. Great was their delight and astonishment when the Prince entered, leading the beautiful maiden by the hand. The wedding was at once celebrated, and there was feasting and merry-making throughout the kingdom for six weeks.

Some time afterwards the Prince and his bride were sitting in the garden, when a crow said to them: 'Ungrateful creatures! Have ye forgotten the two poor maidens who helped ye in your distress? Must they spin gold flax for ever? Have no pity on the old witch. The three maidens are princesses, whom she stole away when they were children together, with all the silver utensils, which she turned into gold flax. Poison were her fittest punishment.'

The Prince was ashamed of having forgotten his promise and set out at once, and by great good fortune reached the hut when the old woman was away. The maidens had dreamt that he was coming, and were ready to go with him, but first they made a cake in which they put poison, and left it on a table where the old woman was likely to see it when she returned. She *did* see it, and thought it looked so tempting that she greedily ate it up and at once died.

In the secret chamber were found fifty waggon-loads of gold flax, and as much more was discovered buried. The hut was razed to the ground, and the Prince and his bride and her two sisters lived happily ever after.

FOLK RHYMES AND POETRY

Poor Robin

In the following old rhyme, the narrator is taking it upon himself to interpret the bird's feelings. Actually, the bird may be quite comfortable out in the barn.

The North Wind doth blow
And we shall have snow,
And what will poor Robin do then,
    Poor thing:
He'll sit in the barn
To keep himself warm,
And hide his head under his wing,
    Poor thing.

If I Had a Donkey That Wouldn't Go

The importance of allowing and appreciating diversity of character among creatures is explicit in this rhyme about a donkey and his owner.

If I had a donkey that wouldn't go,
Would I beat him? Oh no, no.
I'd put him in the barn and give him some corn,
The best little donkey that ever was born.

From Iona and Peter Opie, *Oxford Dictionary of Nursery Rhymes* (New York: Oxford University Press, 1951).

The Bird of Night

Randall Jarrell

Some societies believed that owls are bewitched, since they appear at night but are seldom seen during the day. Silent flight is essential to this stealthy, spectral predator.

A shadow is floating through the moonlight.
Its wings don't make a sound.
Its claws are long, its back is bright.
Its eyes try all the corners of the night.

It calls and calls: all the air swells and heaves
And washes up and down like water.
The ear that listens to the owl believes
in death. The bat beneath the eaves,

The mouse beside the stone are still as death.
The owl's air washes them like water.
The owl goes back and forth inside the night,
And the night holds its breath.

From Randall Jarrell, *The Bat-Poet* (New York: Macmillan, 1963).

Something Told the Wild Geese

Rachel Field

Many creatures, including migratory geese, exhibit a fascinating capacity to respond to natural cycles. This sensitivity to environmental rhythms remains largely unexplained.

Something told the wild geese
It was time to go.
Though the fields lay golden.
Something whispered, "Snow."
Leaves were green and stirring
Berries, luster-glossed,
But beneath warm feathers
Something cautioned, "Frost."
All the sagging orchards
Steamed with amber spice,
But each wild breast stiffened
At remembered ice.
Something told the wild geese
It was time to fly—
Summer sun was on their wings,
Winter in their cry.

From Rachel Field, *Branches Green* (New York: Macmillan, 1962).

Mice

Rose Fyleman

Vermin are an essential component in any ecosystem. Though generally regarded as pests, mice are described here in an alternative, and possibly more accurate, way.

I think mice
Are rather nice.

Their tails are long,
Their faces small,
They haven't any
Chins at all.
Their ears are pink,
Their teeth are white,
They run about
The house at night.
They nibble things
They shouldn't touch
And no one seems
To like them much.

But *I* think mice
Are nice.

From Rose Fyleman, *Fifty-One New Nursery Rhymes* (New York: Doubleday, 1932).

Cat

Mary Britton Miller

Cats may be among nature's more aloof creatures, and it is this enigmatic quality that many people find appealing.

The black cat yawns,
Opens her jaws,
Stretches her legs,
And shows her claws.

Then she gets up
And stands on four
Long stiff legs
And yawns some more.

She shows her sharp teeth,
She stretches her lip,
Her slice of a tongue
Turns up at the tip.

Lifting herself
On her delicate toes,
She arches her back
As high as it goes.

She lets herself down
With particular care,
And pads away
With her tail in the air.

From Mary Britton Miller, *Menagerie*. Copyright estate of Mary Britton Miller.

Deer

Harry Behn

Deer are exceptionally wary animals, which partially explains their ability to survive in vast numbers near human populations.

From Harry Behn, *Sombra*. Copyright 1961 by Harry Behn. Reprinted by permission of Marian Reiner.

Proud in a cloud of sun
Stands deer,
His head held high
As petals fall
Over his quivering flanks.

Under a tree
Brighter than sun
Stands deer
Rubbing moss
From his polished weapons.

Wild Horse

Hillary Allen, age 9

Horses embody power and grace, but they also represent a mythological nobility that may be linked to our romanticized ideal of unharnessed freedom. This 9-year-old poet captures this feeling.

With shiny skin
    And fiercest eye
Clattering hoof
    Will never die.

From memory of mine,
    The horse (if wild)
A creature fine
    Who's always bright

Yet man took horse
    To call his own
And broke him in
    With reins and such.

Man used a whip
    'Twas very coarse
And took the life
    From wild horse

That proud creature
    Jumping free!
Is now a sad and gloomy one
    Oh, think! of what the man has done

From Richard Lewis, ed., *Miracles* (New York: Simon & Schuster, 1966).

Wild, free
>Full of glee
That was
>The wild one!

Shame on man
>To do what's done
Took spirit, soul, all joy as well
>Oh—! wild horse!

Dance of the Animals

It is common among human societies to identify with birds and animals. The following poem from Africa expresses the unity, and potential for elation, of all creatures, including people.

I throw myself to the left,
I turn myself to the right
I am the fish
Who glides in the water, who glides.
Who twists himself, who leaps.
Everything lives, everything dances,
>everything sings.

The bird flies,
Flies, flies, flies,
Goes, comes back, passes,
Mounts, hovers, and drops down.
I am the bird.
Everything lives, everything dances,
>everything sings.

The monkey, from bough to bough,
Runs, leaps, and jumps,
With his wife, with his little one,
His mouth full, his tail in the air:
This is the monkey, this is the monkey.
Everything lives, everything dances,
>everything sings.

From Blaise Cendrars, ed., *The African Saga* (Orlando, Fla.: Harcourt Brace Jovanovich, 1927).

Wild Spurs

Owen, age 12

Children attribute regal airs to the most common of creatures. The elegance of barnyard stock should not be discounted.

My rooster comes to me
On big eagle's feet
And goes away
On little horse's spurs
Guarding and watching
The strutting hens
That tear the ground
And get the worms.

From Richard Lewis, ed., *Miracles* (New York: Simon & Schuster, 1966).

Sea Gull

Elizabeth Coatsworth

There is a balance within nature, as represented by various phenomena. Though all creatures struggle to avoid death, it plays as important a role in the natural cycle as birth does.

The sea gull curves his wings,
the sea gull turns his eyes.
Get down into the water, fish!
(if you are wise.)

The sea gull slants his wings,
the sea gull turns his head.
Get deep into the water, fish!
(or you'll be dead.)

From Elizabeth Coatsworth, *Summer Green* (New York: Macmillan, 1947).

FICTION

Sounder

William H. Armstrong

This is a somber story of a sharecropper who has been jailed for stealing some food for his wife and children. The big hunting dog, Sounder, after whom the story is named, is the central symbol of the story, for he represents the mute endurance of the family. Sounder is shot and gravely wounded when trying to save his master, but he manages to survive, even though badly crippled. The fictional treatment of the animal is natural and unsentimentalized. Sounder *received the 1970 Newbery Award.*

The road which passed the cabin lay like a thread dropped on a patchwork quilt. Stalk land, fallow fields, and brushland, all appeared to be sewn together by wide fencerow stitches of trees. Their bare branches spread out to join together the separate patches of land. Weeds grew on either side of the road in summer, and a thin strip of green clung to life between the dusty tracks. In summer a horse and wagon made almost no noise in the soft earth. In winter when the ground was frozen, the rattle of wheels and each distinct hoofbeat punctuated the winter quiet. When the wind blew, little clouds of dust would rise in the road and follow the wind tracks across the fields.

The boy was allowed to go as far as he wanted to on the road. But the younger children couldn't go past the pine clump toward the big house and the town, or the bramble patch where they picked blackberries in summer in the other direction. Almost no one passed on the road in winter except to buy flour at the store far down the road or to go to the town of a Saturday. Even in summer a speck on the horizon was a curiosity. People sitting on cabin porches would wonder whether the speck would take the form of man, woman, or child.

The third day after the boy had awakened to the smell of ham bone and pork sausage, it was still cold and the wind still blew. But the cabin still smelled good, and there was plenty to eat. Just as dark was gathering, the boy started to go to the woodpile to bring in wood for the night. The dim light of the lamp ran past the boy as he stood motionless in the open cabin door.

"Shut the door," the boy's father called from where he sat near the stove. But the boy did not move.

Just past the edge of the porch three white men stood in the dim light. Their heavy boots rattled the porch floor, and the boy backed quickly into the cabin as they pushed their way in.

"There are two things I can smell a mile," the first man said in a loud voice. "One's a ham cookin' and the other's a thievin' nigger."

"Get up," the second man ordered. The warm, but frozen circle of man, woman, and three small children around the stove jumped to their feet. A stool on which a child had

From William H. Armstrong, *Sounder* (New York: Harper & Row, 1969). Illustrations by James Barkley. Text copyright © 1969 by William H. Armstrong. Illustrations copyright © 1969 by James Barkley.

been sitting fell backward and made a loud noise. One of the men kicked it across the room. The boy did not move from his place just inside the door.

"Here's the evidence," said the first man. He jerked at the grease-spotted cloth on the tin-topped table. The oak slab and the half-eaten ham fell to the floor with a great thud and slid against the wall.

"You know who I am," said the first man as he unbuttoned his heavy brown coat and pulled it back to show a shiny metal star pinned to his vest. "These are my deputies." The stranger nearest the door kicked it shut and swore about the cold.

"Stick out your hands, boy," ordered the second man. The boy started to raise his hands, but the man was already reaching over the stove, snapping handcuffs on the outstretched wrists of his father.

The click of the handcuffs was like the click of a gate latch at the big house where the boy had once gone with his father to work. He had swung on the gate and played with the latch until someone had called out from the house, "If you want to swing on a gate, boy, swing on the one behind the house. Get away from the front."

The third stranger, who had not spoken, turned toward the door. "I'll bring up the wagon." But he did not open the door.

Suddenly the voice of the great dog shattered the heavy, seemingly endless silence that came between the gruff words of the sheriff and those of his men. Sounder was racing toward the cabin from the fields. He had grown restless from waiting to go hunting with his master and had wandered away to hunt alone. That's why he hadn't warned them. He always barked and sometimes, even in daytime, he would start from under the porch, the hair on his back straightening before anyone had sighted a moving speck at the far end of the road. "Somebody's comin' or a creature's movin'," the boy's mother would say.

Now he was growling and scratching at the door. The noise seemed to undo the fearful shock that had held the smaller children ashen and motionless. The youngest child began to cry and hid behind his mother. He

tugged at her apron, but the woman did not move.

The men were speaking roughly to Sounder's master. "That tear in your overalls where the striped ticking is—that's where you tore them on the door hook of the smokehouse. We found threads of torn cloth in the hook. You gonna wear nothing but stripes pretty soon. Big, wide black and white stripes. Easy to hit with a shotgun."

The deputy who had started out to bring up the wagon kicked the closed door and swore at the dog on the other side.

"Go out and hold that mongrel if you don't want him shot." He held the door ajar the width of the boy's body and thrust him out. The boy fell on the back of the dog, whose snarling jaws had pushed into the light between the boy's legs. A heavy boot half pushed, half kicked the entangled feet of the sprawled boy and the nose of the dog and slammed the door. "Get that dog out of the way and hold him if you don't want him dead."

The boy, regaining his balance, dragged Sounder off the porch and to the corner of the cabin. Then the deputy, hearing the barking move back from the door, opened it and came out. He walked out of the circle of light but returned soon leading a horse hitched to a spring wagon. A saddled horse followed behind the wagon.

The appearance of the horses and the added confusion of people coming from the cabin roused Sounder to new fury. The boy felt his knees give. His arms ached, and his grip on the dog's collar was beginning to feel clammy and wet. But he held on.

"Chain him up," said the sheriff.

The boy thought they were telling him to chain up Sounder, but then he saw that one of the men had snapped a long chain on the handcuffs on his father's wrists. As the men pushed his father into the back of the wagon his overalls caught on the end of the tail-gate bolt, and he tore a long hole in his overalls. The bolt took one side of the ticking patch with it. The man holding the chain jerked it, and the boy's father fell backward into the wagon. The man swung the loose end of the chain, and it struck the boy's father across

the face. One of the deputies pulled the chain tight and tied it to the wagon seat. The two deputies climbed on the wagon seat; the sheriff mounted the saddled horse. The cabin door was open; the boy's mother was standing in the doorway. He did not see his brother and sisters.

Sounder was making an awful noise, a half-strangled mixture of growl and bark. The boy spoke to him, but the great paws only dug harder to grip the frozen earth. Inch by inch the boy was losing his footing. Numbness was beginning to creep up his arms and legs, and he was being dragged away from the corner of the house.

The wagon started, and the sheriff rode behind it on his horse. Sounder made a great lunge forward, and the boy fell against the corner of the porch. Sounder raced after the wagon. No one yelled after him. The mother stood still in the doorway. The deputy who wasn't holding the reins turned on the seat, aimed his shotgun at the dog jumping at the side of the wagon, and fired. Sounder fell in the road, and the sheriff rode around him.

Sounder's master was still on his back in the wagon, but he did not raise his head to look back.

The boy struggled to his feet. His head hurt where he had hit it against the corner of the porch. Now his mother spoke for the first time since he had opened the door to bring in wood. "Come in, child, and bring some wood."

Sounder lay still in the road. The boy wanted to cry; he wanted to run to Sounder. His stomach felt sick; he didn't want to see Sounder. He sank to his knees at the woodpile. His foot hurt where the door had been slammed on it. He thought he would carry in two chunk-sticks. Maybe his mother would drag Sounder out of the road. Maybe she would drag him across the fields and bury him. Maybe if she laid him on the porch and put some soft rags under him tonight, he might rise from the dead, like Lazarus did in a meetin'-house story. Maybe his father didn't know Sounder was dead. Maybe his father was dead in the back of the sheriff's wagon now. Maybe his father had said it hurt to bounce over the rough road on his back, and the deputy had turned around on the seat and shot him.

The second chunk-stick was too big. It slipped out of the boy's arms. Two of his fingers were bruised under the falling wood.

Suddenly a sharp yelp came from the road. Just like when a bee stung Sounder under the porch or a brier caught his ear in the bramble, the boy thought. In an instant the boy was on his feet. Bruised foot and fingers, throbbing head were forgotten. He raced into the dark. Sounder tried to rise but fell again. There was another yelp, this one constrained and plaintive. The boy, trained in night-sight when the lantern was dimmed so as not to alert the wood's creatures, picked out a blurred shape in the dark.

Sounder was running, falling, floundering, rising. The hind part of his body stayed up and moved from side to side, trying to lift the front part from the earth. He twisted, fell, and heaved his great shoulders. His hind paws dug into the earth. He pushed himself up. He staggered forward, sideways, then fell again. One front leg did not touch the ground. A trail of blood, smeared and blotted, followed him. There was a large spot of mingled blood, hair, and naked flesh on one shoulder. His head swung from side to side. He fell again and pushed his body along with his hind legs. One side of his head was a mass of blood. The blast had torn off the whole side of his head and shoulder.

The boy was crying and calling Sounder's name. He ran backward in front of Sounder. He held out his hand. Sounder did not make a sign to stop. The boy followed the coon dog under the porch, but he went far back under the cabin. The boy was on his knees, crying and calling, "Sounder, Sounder, Sound . . ." His voice trailed off into a pleading whisper.

The cabin door opened, and the boy's mother stood in the door. The pale light of the lamp inside ran past the woman, over the edge of the porch, and picked out the figure of the boy on his hands and knees. "Come in, child," the woman said. "He is only dying."

Inside the cabin the younger children sat huddled together near the stove. The boy rubbed his hands together near the stovepipe to warm them. His bruised fingers began to throb again. His foot and his head hurt, and he felt a lump rising on the side of his head. If Sounder would whimper or yelp, I would know, the boy thought. But there was no sound, no thump, thump, thump of a paw scratching fleas and hitting the floor underneath.

"Creatures like to die alone," the mother said after a long time. "They like to crawl away where nobody can find them dead, especially dogs. He didn't want to be shot down like a dog in the road. Some creatures are like people."

The road, the boy thought. What would it be like? Did the shotgun blast a hole in the road?

"I ain't got the wood," the boy said at last. "I'll light the lantern and get it."

"You know where the wood is. You won't need the lantern," the woman said.

The boy paused in the doorway. Then he took the lantern from the nail where it hung beside the possum sack. He took the lantern to the stove, lit a splinter of kindling through the open door-draft, and held it to the lantern wick the way his father always did. His mother said nothing to him. She spoke to the younger children instead. "I ain't fed you yet."

When he got outside, the boy did not go to the woodpile. He followed the trail of blood in its zigzag path along the road. At the end of it there was a great wide spot, dark on the frozen ground. Little clumps of Sounder's hair lay in the blood. There was no hole where the shotgun had blasted. At the edge of the dark stain, the boy touched his finger to something. It was more than half of Sounder's long thin ear. The boy shivered and moved his finger away. He had seen dead lizards and possums and raccoons, but he'd never seen a human animal, like Sounder, dead.

It wouldn't work, he thought. But people always said to put things under your pillow when you go to bed, and if you make a wish, it will come true. He touched Sounder's ear again. It was cold. He picked it up. One edge of it was bloody, and jagged like the edge of a broken windowpane. He followed the zigzag trail back along the road, but he could scarcely see it now. He was crying again. At the corner of the porch he took the possum sack from the nail where it hung and wiped the ear. It gave him the shivers. He jumped down quickly, and holding the lantern near the ground, tried to see under the porch. He called Sounder. There was no sound. He went back to wiping the ear. His throat hurt. He put the ear in the pocket of his overall jacket. He was going to put it under his pillow and wish that Sounder wasn't dead.

The wind had stopped blowing. This would have been a good hunting night, he thought. Far away, a single lantern was moving into the foothills. The boy was still crying. He had not forgotten the wood. Now he put out the lantern and hung it against the wall. He went to the woodpile, picked up two chunk-sticks, and went into the cabin.

The loneliness that was always in the cabin, except when his mother was singing or telling a story about the Lord, was heavier than ever now. It made the boy's tongue heavy. It pressed against his eyes, and they burned. It rolled against his ears. His head seemed to be squeezed inward, and it hurt. He noticed grease spots on the floor where the oak slab and the ham had fallen. He knew his mother had picked them up. His father would be cold, he thought, with that great rip in his overalls.

His mother sat by the stove. "You must eat," the woman said. The boy had been outside a long time. His mother had fed the other children, and they were already in bed. She did not take down her walnut basket to begin the slow filling of her apron with fat kernels. She did not sing or even hum. "Child . . . child" she would say with long spaces between. Sometimes she would murmur to herself with her eyes closed. His little brother would murmur and be addled in his sleep tonight, the boy thought. He would set as long as his mother would let him. Maybe his mother would let him set and listen all night.

The boy listened for a yelp, a whine, a thump, thump, thump under the floor. There was no sound. His mother's rocker did not even move enough to squeak. One chunk-stick burning atop another in the stove rolled against the stove door with a slight thump. The boy started toward the cabin door.

"You know it was the stove," the mother said as she reached for the poker to push the wood back from the door.

"It sounded outside," the boy said as he pulled the door closed after him.

Soon he returned carrying the lantern. "I want to look more," he said. "I keep hearin' things." He lit the lantern from the stove as he had done before. His mother said nothing. He had thought she might say "Hang it back, child" as she often did when he wanted to go along the fencerows and hunt with Sounder after dark.

Outside, he murmured to himself, "That was the stove, I reckon." He put the lantern on the ground and tried to see under the cabin. Nothing moved in the dim light. He wished the light would shine in Sounder's eyes and he would see them in the dark, but it didn't. Backing from under the porch on his hands and knees, he touched the lantern and tipped it over. He grabbed it by the wire rim that held the top of the globe and burned his hand. "Don't let it fall over; it'll explode" his father had said to him so many times when they hunted together. He sucked his burned fingers to draw out the fire. Sounder's pan was on the ground, and someone had stepped on it. The mean man who had kicked him with his big boot, the boy thought. He straightened it as best he could with his hurt fingers and put it on the porch.

He blew out the lantern and hung it by the possum sack. He stood on the porch and listened to the faraway. The lantern he had seen going into the foothills had disappeared. There were gravestones behind the meetin' house. Some were almost hidden in the brambles. If the deputy sheriff had turned around on the seat of the wagon and shot his father, the visiting preacher and somebody would bring him back and bury him behind the meetin' house, the boy thought. And if Sounder dies, I won't drag him over the hard earth. I'll carry him. I know I can carry him if I try hard enough, and I will bury him across the field, near the fencerow, under the big jack oak tree.

The boy picked up Sounder's bent tin pan and carried it into the cabin. The woman pushed back in her chair for a brief second in surprise and half opened her mouth. But, seeing the boy's face in the lamplight, she closed her mouth, and the rocker came slowly back to its standing position—her head tilted forward again, her eyes fixed on the boy's uneaten supper, still warming on the back of the stove.

In the corner of the room next to the dish cupboard, the boy filled Sounder's tin with cold hamboiling from the possum kettle. "What's that for, child?" asked the mother slowly, as though she were sorry she had asked and would like to take it back.

"For if he comes out."

"You're hungry, child. Feed yourself."

The boy put Sounder's tin under the porch, closed the door, pushed the night latch, sat down behind the stove, and began to eat his supper.

Pigeon, Fly Home!

Thomas Liggett

*Racing pigeons are the subject of this story about a courageous, coffee-colored
starveling pigeon named Leyden, who survives the rejection and pecking attacks
of his fellow birds to become a strong homer—the finest bird in Chad's flock. The
unabashedly positive emphasis on nurturant values in Chad, the young owner,
and accurate details about pigeon racing make this an interesting story for young
readers. This selection shows Leyden, in his first homing flight, successfully
eluding the attack of a falcon hawk.*

Early the next Saturday morning Chad put
Leyden in a large brown paper sack. He fold-
ed over the top of the sack and ripped little
V's in the creases to make vent holes.

With the sack in one hand, he rode on his
bicycle across town to Charlie Wilson's. It
was a long trip, but it would be worth while
if Mr. Wilson could tell him what really was
wrong with the pigeon and what to do about
it.

Chad was the first person there that morning.

The black stubble on the pigeon dealer's
face stood out against a ruddy background.
He asked Chad into the kitchen—a
bachelor's. That was a surprise—and an
honor, a sign that Mr. Wilson was interested
in a person, anyway.

With the sack still clutched in his hands,
Chad sat down while Mr. Wilson finished his
coffee. Through the doorway into the dining
room, Chad could see a sideboard with a
disorderly collection of trophies and cups,
medals and ribbons piled on top. Mr. Wilson
had raced and shown pigeons before he'd become a pigeon dealer.

Smiling his usual amused, unhurried
smile, he lighted his pipe and stretched his
legs out full under the table. "What's on
your mind today? Want to sell the bird in the
sack?"

"Well," said Chad, uncertainly, "I want

to buy about twenty pounds of grit. I'm just
about out of grit. Eggs take a lot . . ."

He didn't know how to start explaining
about Leyden, and that made him unsure of
what to say. How was a fellow going to explain about sadism among pigeons?

"What've you got in the sack?"

"Oh, the bird in here," Chad said, moving the sack up and forward a little, "is that
coffee-colored youngster I've had nothing
but trouble from, and I don't know if I can
keep the rest of the birds from pecking him
to death. I never heard of anything like this
before. Maybe he's not getting enough of the
right kind of grain with the right kind of vita-
mins to eat or something."

"Let's see the bird." Mr. Wilson reached
out his hands.

Chad fumbled around with the sack and
fished out the pigeon, which managed to lash
free with one wing before it was subdued.

"It's not sick, anyway," Mr. Wilson said,
finding it amusing that the problem pigeon
was in such vigorous shape.

He became serious again. "Sometimes it's
a bird's being sick that sets it off wrong with
the rest."

He carefully looked at the pigeon's head,
now partly covered over with a rough mat of
pin feathers. He looked into the glistening
eyes and at the crust just barely beginning to
form on the back part of its beak.

From Thomas Liggett, *Pigeon, Fly Home!* (New York: Holiday House, 1956). Illustrated by Marc Simont.

"This bird's taken some nasty pecking, all right."

"Yeah, and I'm wondering why."

Charlie Wilson sighed faintly and said in a kind of tired way, "Hard to tell what sets animals beating up on each other. Fools, just like people, I guess. They have bossy ones and scapegoats, same as people. Especially when you keep the same bunch of pigeons together for a time and they get to know the looks of one another. This little gal looks like she's been way at the bottom of everybody's list."

"You think it's a she?"

"Shape of the bones. Shape of the beak."

Charlie Wilson knew a lot about pigeons—in a sort of mysterious, wise way that made Chad somber and respectful.

"She's flown around some?" There was that curious, amused smile on the ruddy face again.

"Some," Chad said. "She was a slow learner. She'd just sit on a corner of the roof when I'd let her out and act—not afraid—but just sort of apart, you know. She's been flying around some, though."

Charlie Wilson sucked on his pipe and then, as though finished with his private speculations, he said, "Maybe now she can go back with the others. Maybe they won't bother her. Why don't you let her loose and see if she can find her way home?"

"What!? From here!?"

This place of Mr. Wilson's, way at the west end of town at the edge of the Great Marsh, was a lot farther away than Chad had figured on taking any of his pigeons on their first homing flight. And this messed-up little hen, at that!

"I don't know, Mr. Wilson," Chad said, carefully and a little plaintively. "You see, I've been kind of putting off training them to home until I'd be pretty sure they'd be good and ready."

Mr. Wilson bent forward to argue, good-naturedly. "What do you think ready is? If this bird can find her way home, then you'll know she's worth fooling with. And *that's* the question. Is she or isn't she worth fooling with? Ain't it?"

Chad hesitated. He felt if he let Leyden go now, he'd never see her again. But then Charlie Wilson knew more than he about what could be expected.

"All right." The two words sounded faint in his own ears, and for a moment he wished he could take them back.

He and Mr. Wilson stepped out of the kitchen into the yard. The morning sun had risen well off the horizon toward the center of the city. The day was clear. A brisk, cold wind pushed in from the direction of the Great Marsh.

Mr. Wilson let Leyden flap out of his hands. She flew to the top of the shingled roof of the house and perched there.

"Taking her bearings," Mr. Wilson said.

He and Chad casually swept the sky in all directions with their eyes.

The pigeon, seemingly on an impulse, took off with an abrupt clatter. Around and around the Wilson place she circled, gaining altitude. Then she started out over the Great Marsh. But soon she came swooping back. It was, of course, impossible to tell what, if anything, was in her mind. Since she already had been fed that morning she was in no big hurry to get home to eat. Maybe she was just glad to be away from home and stretching her wings and alone.

"Uh-oh." Mr. Wilson said. "Look."

Far up in the direction of the Great Marsh, a large bird was approaching. It flapped its wings three or four times, then glided before flapping its wings again. Its slow up-and-down motion distinguished it from pigeons and smaller birds.

"A hawk?" Chad asked, trying not to sound anxious.

"Maybe."

"What kind?"

"I'm not sure exactly what you would call it," Mr. Wilson said, shading his eyes and squinting at the bird, which was still a long way off. "I think it sees the pigeon."

Chad could feel a dull pain growing in his throat. The muscles in his face tightened. Waves of electricity seemed to pass over his skin.

"Is it a vulture or a buzzard—or an eagle?"

"Wish it was," Mr. Wilson said, unemotionally. "Then we'd have nothing to worry about. They eat carrion—dead cattle and things, mostly. Things on the ground. A very big hawk, the soaring kind, couldn't catch a pigeon.''

"Oh.''

There was a moment's silence as the short-necked bird came closer to Leyden.

Being on the ground, helpless, gave Chad a regretful feeling, but he didn't want to blame Charlie Wilson, who stood near with eyes fixed on the sky.

"It's a hawk, is what it is,'' Mr. Wilson said slowly. "A falcon-hawk, I guess you could call it. A duck hawk is really what it is, unless I miss my guess. Really part of the falcon family.''

Leyden was circling higher and higher, apparently unaware of what was going on.

"I wish I had a shotgun,'' Chad said.

Mr. Wilson smiled. "No shotgun I know of could hit that far up.''

Leyden was beginning a long arc which would bring her almost directly overhead. The hawk was coming up fast and high. It started to dive on her, but then it changed its course, ballooning way up behind her.

Leyden now apparently saw the hawk, because she began to fly in a straight line in the opposite direction. The hawk, making a diving turn, began to head her off.

"Fear,'' Mr. Wilson said. "It's just one of those things that fear makes you do the wrong way. That pigeon could stay and dive around that hawk until the cows come home and never lose a feather, but as soon as she starts to run, she's in trouble.''

"She's heading home anyway,'' Chad almost shouted as he moved around restlessly. He hopped a step as he said, "Maybe she'll make it.''

"Maybe she will,'' Mr. Wilson said.

"Well, I'm going to see,'' Chad shouted as he grabbed the handles of his bicycle and started to wheel it down the walk. He vaulted onto the seat and started pushing fiercely on the pedals.

The young pigeon looked at the hawk, looked through eyes much sharper than human eyes.

Although she had never seen a hawk close up before, she knew the big, short-necked bird hovering above her was an enemy. No bird had ever before hovered above her like that.

An urgent feeling of alarm churned within her. It became panic as the short-necked bird folded its wings close to its body and tipped over in a dive. As the hawk's speed increased, it tucked its wings in closer and closer until, finally, they formed little fins that were just barely capable of holding it on course. It was falling like a rocket shot from above. It was diving straight at the pigeon.

Then the hawk swerved a little from its course, probably testing its flight control and the fight-wariness of the young pigeon.

The pigeon continued her flight in a straight line, too overwhelmed by stark fear to plan escape.

Gradually banking on course again, the hawk bore directly down on the pigeon. Talons—curved, sharp, hooked knives—were held rigid and ready to mesh into the pigeon's hot body.

Her wings felt heavy and stiff and slow. It seemed almost as though she couldn't move. But in a convulsive impulse of final terror, she darted toward and then under the big bird.

The hawk threw out its great wings at the last fraction of a moment as it tried to change

its path, but it was going too fast. Now fully open, its wings bent like taut bows as they broke the downward fall.

The pigeon fled.

The hawk turned and began to climb again with tremendous sweeps of its wings. It quickly gained a new vantage position high above the pigeon.

The hawk dove again. And again, this time more deliberately, the pigeon turned into and under the hawk, making it miss. The hawk flapped high for still another attack on her.

She saw that the hawk had been slow in starting to climb, just as it had been slow to check its downward plummet and just as it had been slow to turn. She felt safer, and her body seemed light again. Her wings now carried her precisely where she wanted to go.

The big bird was fast, fast as another pigeon, after it had got well started. But it was clumsy and slow to maneuver. It couldn't catch her now if she kept steady.

Free of fear, she was almost back to her loft. She could see the bunch of houses and streets where she lived. The roofs and the things sticking up out of them and the patches of green and brown were all familiar from the few flights she had already had close at home. Nearby, in the direction of the sun when it rises, was the big green place near the city. Off far in the same direction, far beyond the city, was the ocean— something the pigeon had never investigated, something big, flat and blue-black reaching far to the north and far to the south.

She could soon have swooped down to the loft without a bit of trouble, and just sit there outside the trap bars for a moment and catch her breath.

She felt satisfied with herself . . .

The hawk!

In the excess of her confidence, the pigeon had taken her eyes off the hawk for a mo-

ment. And now it was upon her. Frantically she started to duck and turn.

The hawk, which had been planning to strike the pigeon from the rear with clenched fists, now quickly opened its fists into fans of sharp, grasping hooks.

The tip of one of the hooks cut a straight, clean gash down her breast.

For an instant she felt no pain. She had escaped easily and her fear was over. The big bird was far below, its large, lumbering wings asprawl in the air.

Then pain came.

It was more frightening to her than the pain she had felt when the pigeons in the flock pecked her—though it was the same sort of thing. It was pain. Her crop felt cold and wet. Her wings were no longer light and free. Anxiety and panic came again.

The pigeon could not dive, because the hawk was down there. It had completed its turn and was beginning to climb. Its motions were faster, more precise than they had been. When it got to the pigeon's level, it abruptly turned toward her instead of climbing above her as it had done before. It came flying straight at its prey.

Using all her lessening strength in a crucial flip of her wings, she darted under the big bird, ducking to avoid the talons overhead.

She dove almost straight down.

The hawk started to change direction with a gigantic, coordinated swish of its tail and wings. Then it took a huge bite out of the air with its massive wings. But, in spite of its blazing power, it could not get started down in time to catch the wounded pigeon.

She landed with a plop on the tar-paper roof of the loft. She dashed through the one-way bars and into the loft. This was the first time in weeks that she was in with the rest of the flock.

She was tired and hurt—but she felt exhilarated.

NONFICTION

The Secrets of the Dolphin
A Mermaid on a Dolphin's Back

Helen Kay

Because of their intelligence and their playful, curious nature, dolphins have fascinated human beings for centuries. The people of Crete, an island in the Mediterranean, revered dolphins 3500 years ago. The sun god Apollo was thought to have changed himself into a dolphin to guide sailors safely across the Mediterranean. Modern-day interest in dolphins is equally strong, as shown in The Secrets of the Dolphin, *a collection of observations and stories about this remarkable animal of the sea.*

. . . once I sat upon a promontory,
And heard a mermaid on a dolphin's back
Uttering such dulcet and harmonious breath
That the rude sea grew civil at her song
And certain stars shot madly from their spheres,
To hear the sea-maid's music.

WILLIAM SHAKESPEARE,
A Midsummer Night's Dream

Suddenly one day Jill Baker of Opononi, New Zealand, aged twelve, was turned into a mermaid—not by the wave of a magic wand, but by an odd and beautiful circumstance.

Jill Baker was a powerful swimmer. She couldn't help being one, for she lived right on the sea. Opononi Beach at Hokianga Harbor on the western side of northern New Zealand was a seaside resort. Jill needed only to cross the main road, pass a strip of sandy beach, and step into the water.

One day as she bathed in the harbor with the pink sand hills all around, she was startled by a large animal that rose out of the sea in front of her. Face to face with her, it seemed to grin. It was even staring curiously at her out of large brown eyes.

Jill was frightened . . . frightened by its size and the many teeth in its open mouth. Turning quickly about, she began to swim to safety.

The dolphin followed her—raced her, in fact. It popped up in front, then swam alongside. It leaped out of the water and circled her. Jill swam faster, but she could not outswim it. She realized the dolphin wanted to play. This, then, was the friendly dolphin she had heard about.

Jill slowed her pace, and together they glided side by side.

Measuring the animal by the length of her own body, she saw that "when swimming along beside, it did not seem very large . . . probably because the back half was nearly always under water," she said.

By the time Jill reached shallow water, they had become good friends. When she stood up, the dolphin swam between her legs, lifted her gently and carried her out again, playfully dumped her and raced back to shore.

From that moment on, Opononi Beach was on the map of the world. Jill Baker was no

From Helen Kay, *The Secrets of the Dolphin* (New York: Macmillan, 1964).

longer just a New Zealand schoolgirl in a sleepy vacation town. She had been turned into a "mermaid on a dolphin's back."

The dolphin, too, was given a name, "Opo," shortened from Opononi Beach, the seaside resort that was its home for six months during the winter of 1955–1956, which is summer "down under" in New Zealand.

Beyond the beach lived the farmers and fishermen—many of them Maori, the original inhabitants of New Zealand.

One farmer, Piwai Toi, described how he had met the friendly dolphin for the first time: "There was a splash and a boiling swirl, and a large fish was streaking for my boat just under the surface. I really thought it was going to hit us, when about ten yards away it dived and surfaced on the other side. It played round and round the boat. I was afraid she would be hit by my outboards, so I went inshore. . . . When I looked back . . . she was about three feet out of the water, standing literally on her tail, and looking at me from a distance of about fifty yards. . . ."*

Opo continued to look at the people at Opononi Beach, and the people on the beach looked back.

They came by hundreds and they came by the thousands. By Christmas of 1955, the weekends saw as many as two thousand people looking for Jill Baker's friend, Opo. They filled the one hotel and overflowed the pine-tree motor camp. Then they slept in their cars or on the beach. They came on foot, by bicycle, motor scooter, boat, car, bus, van, truck, any way they could—"to see the friendly fish."

Mothers with children—whole families—arrived to picnic and look for Opo. Up and down the shore they waited.

If Opo was not there yet, boatmen called her from her fishing coves by starting their motors. The "putt putt putt" of the motors brought her with a swish and a swirl, a dive and a leap full of the sheer joy of living.

* *Te Ao Hou,* The Maori Magazine, Wellington, New Zealand.

That season Opo was the star of Opononi Beach. Even the experts came to see.

A zoologist announced that Opo of Opononi was indeed a Bottlenose Dolphin, *Tursiops truncatus,* and was almost fully grown. "This is no fish," he said, "but an aquatic mammal."

What sex?

No one was sure. Most thought Opo must be female since she was so gentle with children. Opo would swim right among them to join their games. "Ketch and fetch" was her favorite; next came water polo, and "ring-around-a-porpoise."

From the very first moment Opo was thrown a ball, she showed she was a champion. She couldn't catch with her stubby flippers. They were too short, equivalent only to a mittened hand without the stretch of an arm behind it. But her mouth was large and fine for grasping. With the ball in her mouth, she began to play. She dribbled it in the water; carefully she balanced it on her blunt snout. Then she sent it spinning twenty feet in the air. Before it reached the sea again, Opo was under it for the catch. All alone, she was an all-star team.

"And," said Jill Baker, "she was never *taught* any of these tricks."

The people were excited by the daring dolphin. Some ran into the sea, still wearing all their clothes. They were like the children: they wanted to get close; touch her; pinch her. "Is she real?" They needed to make sure.

As the season reached its peak, Opo showed even greater talent. She rolled the ball down her back, then hit it sideways like a bat with her dorsal fin or tail. Sometimes she would turn upside down, showing a round white belly, clutching a big red ball between those stubby flippers.

"Opo loved to play best of all in the evening when most of the crowds had gone home. One of her favorite tricks was to find an empty bottle at the bottom of the sea and toss it into the air, then catch it with her tail. She would get quite excited and start snorting like a pig," Jill Baker said.

"Sometimes while playing with the peo-

A dolphin is not a fish, but an aquatic mammal that requires air to live.

ple, she would follow them right into the edge of the beach, and would of course get stranded. She would then have to be helped out again into deeper water.''

Opo enjoyed those games, but she liked Jill even better than ball playing.

Jill thought it was because she was so gentle with her. She touched Opo kindly, lightly. She understood that Opo had a tender skin. She learned that Opo liked to be tickled and scratched like a kitten. She scratched her on the top of her head or under her throat. She would put her arms around Opo and marvel at her skin's smooth coolness.

How did it feel to ride Opo?

Jill Baker answered: ''Riding Opo felt like riding a rolling piece of floating wood, because you wouldn't know when you were going to fall off.''

When Opo did not see her friend on the shore, or was suddenly bored with ball playing or became hungry, she would splash all with a flip of her tail and swim off to fish in the quiet bays on the other side of the harbor. Opo had to eat, and she had to catch her own food. She never took food from her human friends, though she spent whole days playing with them.

There were some who hit Opo too hard, in their enthusiasm, yet Opo never hit back. No one was ever hurt by Opo. She did butt some on the shins; she did dig curiously under wiggling toes with her snout, but she did not bite a single adult or child. She had the teeth to do it with—there were one hundred in her mouth. And she had the strength to hurt— Opo already weighed two hundred pounds. She also had the provocation.

''Opo did not like being grabbed by the dorsal fin or her tail, as I think they were both very tender,'' Jill Baker said.

Once a boat hurt Opo. The propellers from a fishing smack scraped her side. The bleeding dolphin raced out to sea, and all Opononi worried. Would she come back?

That was an anxious night at Opononi Beach.

Next morning a reassuring shout went up as Opo returned with a leap and a dive: ''She's all right!''

And the people kept coming. They came from nearby towns and villages. They came from the big cities, too.

Little children mispronounced ''dolphin'' and coined a new name for Opo. They called her ''Golphin.'' So a sign was posted on the road, a plea to visitors: ''Welcome to Opononi, but don't try to shoot our Gay Golphin.''

The newspaper photographers found Opo

photogenic, but a fine way to waste film. They complained Opo liked to nuzzle so closely they couldn't shoot a good picture. One photographer thought Opo was in love with his bright blue swimming trunks. He couldn't get her away from them.

"She was a lovely creature, very gentle with children," Jill said, remembering how patiently the dolphin waited as Jill mounted small children on her back.

One day a teacher brought the whole class to the beach for a picnic. Twelve small schoolchildren went into two feet of water and formed a circle. The dolphin swam into the middle; the children threw the bright red ball and Opo tossed it high.

She stayed in the center of that ring as though she had been trained to do so. Never had there been such a picnic. Where in all the oceans had a wild dolphin joined a school of children?

One afternoon Opo did not return from fishing.

The people of Opononi Beach did not worry at first. Perhaps she needed to fish longer? Some fishermen thought the dolphin was already spending too much time playing and not enough time eating. If Opo played with them for as long as six hours a day, she could not eat during that time. While all eyes were looking for Opo, they thought: "Perhaps she is catching her supper, making up for a lost eating time?"

But she was missing all the next day, too.

Jill Baker watched the horizon with the others.

The fishermen started up their motors. The "putt putt putt" did not bring Opo back.

On the third day, Don Boyce, a farmer, was out collecting mussels, and he found her. She was jammed between large rocks on the southern side of the harbor about three miles from the village. Opo was dead. Everyone thought he knew how it had happened.

She had been catching fish when the tide went out. Suddenly a prisoner in a rocky crevice, she struggled to escape. But she had no hands or feet to maneuver, and without water to hold her up, she thrashed her body against the rough rock edges and cut herself

to shreds. Perhaps she bled to death trying to free herself? Or she drowned, when the tide came in, imprisoned by the rocks, too exhausted to hold her blowhole above water?

Drowned? You might wonder: can a dolphin drown?

On Saturday, as the weekend crowds were coming, a boat brought Opo's body back to Opononi Beach. All on shore seemed to know. It was a gloomy day, though the sun still shone when she was brought onto the beach and laid gently in the sand.

The flag on the Memorial Hall was lowered. The postmistress of Opononi said "This is a sad, sad place," as she read a telegram from the Auckland War Memorial Museum. They wanted a plaster cast of Opo, and were sending a staff member to determine Opo's sex, species, and other scientific data.

When the man from the Museum arrived, he said that Opo was a female dolphin, a *Tursiops truncatus,* about a year and a half in age. She was a young dolphin, a playful puppy still.

They made the plaster cast to take to the Auckland Museum, and only then was Opo buried near the Memorial Hall.

The children came with bouquets for her grave, covering it with wild flowers from the pink sand hills.

"I was home at the time she died, and couldn't really believe it at first," Jill said. "I think she was almost too good to be true."

The editor of the Maori magazine *Te Ao Hou* has given me the true facts about Opo's death. Three young boys had accidentally killed the dolphin when they were dynamiting for fish in the middle of Hokianga Harbor. Horrified at what they had done, they put Opo's body in the rocky crevice, to be found later by Don Boyce. They were just as tearful as the rest of Opononi Beach—knowing their foolishness had killed Opononi's prize.

Sculptor Russell Clark was so moved by Opo's death that he carved a statue out of fawn-colored Hinuera stone in her memory. With Opo, the friendly dolphin, stands a small Maori boy.

Jill Baker described it: "The stone carving of Opo is about six feet long. The boy has his arm resting on Opo. The boy represents the children who played with her. They are both in the water with waves all around. At the moment the statue is standing on her grave in front of the Memorial Hall, but it is only in a temporary position."

To the question "Why did Opo choose you, Jill Baker, among all the others at Opo-noni Beach as a friend?" Jill answered that she thought she knew the secret of her popularity with Opo:

"Opo was always nearby when I went in for a swim. I used to wear blue flippers, and I think she took a fancy to them."

Jill Baker has grown to womanhood, but she will never forget the dolphin who made her a mermaid in the twentieth century.

FANTASY

The Adventures of Reddy Fox
Granny Shows Reddy a Trick

Thornton Burgess

This brief tale is another example of stories in which animals talk but successfully portray themselves as animals rather than as human beings in animal skins. Thornton Burgess, once an exceptionally popular children's writer, is now somewhat out of fashion. Although his writing has been criticized for sentimentality and coyness, his tales still have broad appeal and children as well as adults enjoy his books. His home in Hampden, Massachusetts, now one of the headquarters of the Audubon Society of Massachusetts, resembles the setting of his stories and the natural world in which he lived.

Every day Granny Fox led Reddy Fox over to the long railroad bridge and made him run back and forth across it until he had no fear of it whatever. At first it had made him dizzy, but now he could run across at the top of his speed and not mind it in the least.

"I don't see what good it does to be able to run across a bridge; any one can do that!" exclaimed Reddy one day.

Granny Fox smiled. "Do you remember the first time you tried to do it?" she asked.

Reddy hung his head. Of course he remembered—remembered that Granny had had to scare him into crossing that first time.

From Thornton Burgess, *The Adventures of Reddy Fox* (Boston: Little, Brown, 1915).

Suddenly Granny Fox lifted her head.

"Hark!" she exclaimed.

Reddy pricked up his sharp, pointed ears. Way off back, in the direction from which they had come, they heard the baying of a dog. It wasn't the voice of Bowser the Hound but of a younger dog. Granny listened for a few minutes. The voice of the dog grew louder as it drew nearer.

"He certainly is following our track," said Granny Fox. "Now, Reddy, you run across the bridge and watch from the top of the little hill over there. Perhaps I can show you a trick that will teach you why I have made you learn to run across the bridge."

Reddy trotted across the long bridge and up to the top of the hill, as Granny had told him to. Then he sat down to watch. Granny trotted out in the middle of a field and sat down. Pretty soon a young hound broke out of the bushes, his nose in Granny's track. Then he looked up and saw her, and his voice grew still more savage and eager. Granny Fox started to run as soon as she was sure that the hound had seen her, but she did not run very fast. Reddy did not know what to make of it, for Granny seemed to be simply playing with the hound and not really trying to get away from him at all. Pretty soon Reddy heard another sound. It was a long, low rumble. Then there was a distant whistle. It was a train.

Granny heard it, too. As she ran, she began to work back towards the long bridge. The train was in sight now. Suddenly Granny Fox started across the bridge so fast that she looked like a little red streak. The dog was close at her heels when she started and he was so eager to catch her that he didn't see either the bridge or the train. But he couldn't begin to run as fast as Granny Fox. Oh, my, no! When she had reached the other side, he wasn't half way across and right behind him, whistling for him to get out of the way, was the train.

The hound gave one frightened yelp and then he did the only thing he could do; he leaped down, down into the swift water below, and the last Reddy saw of him he was frantically trying to swim ashore.

"Now you know why I wanted you to learn to cross a bridge; it's a very nice way of getting rid of dogs," said Granny Fox, as she climbed up beside Reddy.

The Six Swans

Andrew Lang

There are many versions of this beautiful folktale in both the inherited and the literary tradition. Hans Christian Andersen's version is called "The Wild Swans," and Asbjornsen's is "The Twelve Wild Ducks." In this retelling by Andrew Lang, the swans (who are really enchanted princes) are beautifully characterized and are convincing in their bird form.

Like the raven, the swan was considered to be imbued with powers of divination and so was thought to be a holy bird. This is important to the climax of the story, for it explains why, when the swans descend to the stake where their little sister is to be burned alive, the spell is broken, the good are rewarded, and the wicked stepmother comes "to no good end."

From Andrew Lang, *The Yellow Fairy Book* (New York: Dover, 1966. Originally published by Longmans, Green & Co., London, 1894). Illustrated by H. J. Ford.

A King was once hunting in a great wood, and he hunted the game so eagerly that none of his courtiers could follow him. When evening came on he stood still and looked around him, and he saw that he had quite lost himself. He sought a way out, but could find none. Then he saw an old woman with a shaking head coming towards him; but she was a witch.

'Good woman,' he said to her, 'can you not show me the way out of the wood?'

'Oh, certainly, Sir King,' she replied, 'I can quite well do that, but on one condition, which if you do not fulfil you will never get out of the wood, and will die of hunger.'

'What is the condition?' asked the King.

'I have a daughter,' said the old woman, 'who is so beautiful that she has not her equal in the world, and is well fitted to be your wife; if you will make her lady-queen I will show you the way out of the wood.'

The King in his anguish of mind consented, and the old woman led him to her little house where her daughter was sitting by the fire. She received the King as if she were expecting him, and he saw that she was certainly very beautiful; but she did not please him, and he could not look at her without a secret feeling of horror. As soon as he had lifted the maiden on to his horse the old woman showed him the way, and the King reached his palace, where the wedding was celebrated.

The King had already been married once, and had by his first wife seven children, six boys and one girl, whom he loved more than anything in the world. And now, because he was afraid that their stepmother might not treat them well and might do them harm, he put them in a lonely castle that stood in the middle of a wood. It lay so hidden, and the way to it was so hard to find, that he himself could not have found it out had not a wisewoman given him a reel of thread which possessed a marvellous property: when he threw it before him it unwound itself and showed him the way. But the King went so often to his dear children that the Queen was offended at his absence. She grew curious, and wanted to know what he had to do quite alone in the wood. She gave his servants a great deal of money, and they betrayed the secret to her, and also told her of the reel which alone could point out the way. She had no rest now till she had found out where the King guarded the reel, and then she made some little white shirts, and, as she had learnt from her witch-mother, sewed an enchantment in each of them.

And when the King had ridden off she took the little shirts and went into the wood, and the reel showed her the way. The children, who saw someone coming in the distance, thought it was their dear father coming to them, and sprang to meet him very joyfully. Then she threw over each one a little shirt, which when it had touched their bodies changed them into swans, and they flew away over the forest. The Queen went home quite satisfied, and thought she had got rid of her step-children; but the girl had not run to meet her with her brothers, and she knew nothing of her.

The Six Brothers Changed Into Swans by their Stepmother.

The next day the King came to visit his children, but he found no one but the girl.

'Where are your brothers?' asked the King.

'Alas! dear father,' she answered, 'they have gone away and left me alone.' And she told him that looking out of her little window she had seen her brothers flying over the wood in the shape of swans, and she showed him the feathers which they had let fall in the yard, and which she had collected. The King mourned, but he did not think that the Queen had done the wicked deed, and as he was afraid the maiden would also be taken from him, he wanted to take her with him. But she was afraid of the stepmother, and begged the King to let her stay just one night more in the castle in the wood. The poor maiden thought, 'My home is no longer here; I will go and seek my brothers.' And when night came she fled away into the forest. She ran all through the night and the next day, till she could go no farther for weariness. Then she saw a little hut, went in, and found a room with six little beds. She was afraid to lie down on one, so she crept under one of them, lay on the hard floor, and was going to spend the night there. But when the sun had set she heard a noise, and saw six swans flying in at the window. They stood on the floor and blew at one another, and blew all their feathers off, and their swan-skin came off like a shirt. Then the maiden recognised her brothers, and overjoyed she crept out from under the bed. Her brothers were not less delighted than she to see their little sister again, but their joy did not last long.

'You cannot stay here,' they said to her. 'This is a den of robbers; if they were to come here and find you they would kill you.'

'Could you not protect me?' asked the little sister.

'No,' they answered, 'for we can only lay aside our swan skins for a quarter of an hour every evening. For this time we regain our human forms, but then we are changed into swans again.'

Then the little sister cried and said, 'Can you not be freed?'

'Oh, no,' they said, 'the conditions are too hard. You must not speak or laugh for six years, and must make in that time six shirts for us out of star-flowers. If a single word comes out of your mouth, all your labour is vain.' And when the brothers had said this the quarter of an hour came to an end, and they flew away out of the window as swans.

But the maiden had determined to free her brothers even if it should cost her her life. She left the hut, went into the forest, climbed a tree, and spent the night there. The next morning she went out, collected star-flowers, and began to sew. She could speak to no one, and she had no wish to laugh, so she sat there, looking only at her work.

When she had lived there some time, it happened that the King of the country was hunting in the forest, and his hunters came to the tree on which the maiden sat. They called to her and said 'Who are you?'

But she gave no answer.

'Come down to us,' they said, 'we will do you no harm.'

But she shook her head silently. As they pressed her further with questions, she threw them the golden chain from her neck. But they did not leave off, and she threw them her girdle, and when this was no use, her garters, and then her dress. The huntsmen would not leave her alone, but climbed the tree, lifted the maiden down, and led her to the King. The King asked, 'Who are you? What are you doing up that tree?'

But she answered nothing.

He asked her in all the languages he knew, but she remained as dumb as a fish. Because she was so beautiful, however, the King's heart was touched, and he was seized with a great love for her. He wrapped her up in his cloak, placed her before him on his horse, and brought her to his castle. There he had her dressed in rich clothes, and her beauty shone out as bright as day, but not a word could be drawn from her. He set her at table by his side, and her modest ways and behaviour pleased him so much that he said, 'I will marry this maiden and none other in the world,' and after some days he married her. But the King had a wicked mother who was displeased with the marriage, and said shirts and troubling herself about nothing. The next time she had a child the wicked mother did the same thing, but the King could not make up his mind to believe her. He said, 'She is too sweet and good to do such a thing as that. If she were not dumb and could defend herself, her innocence would be proved.' But when the third child was taken away, and the Queen was again accused, and could not utter a word in her own defence, the King was obliged to give her over to the law, which decreed that she must be burnt to death. When the day came on which the sentence was to be executed, it was the last day of the six years in which she must not speak or laugh, and now she had freed her dear brothers from the power of the enchantment. The six shirts were done; there was only the left sleeve wanting to the last.

When she was led to the stake, she laid the shirts on her arm, and as she stood on the pile and the fire was about to be lighted, she looked around her and saw six swans flying through the air. Then she knew that her release was at hand and her heart danced for joy. The swans fluttered round her, and hovered low so that she could throw the shirts over them. When they had touched them the swan-skins fell off, and her brothers stood before her living, well and beautiful. Only the youngest had a swan's wing instead of his left arm. They embraced and kissed each other, and the Queen went to the King, who was standing by in great astonishment, and began to speak to him, saying, 'Dearest husband, now I can speak and tell you openly that I am innocent and have been falsely accused.'

She told him of the old woman's deceit, and how she had taken the three children away and hidden them. Then they were fetched, to the great joy of the King, and the wicked mother came to no good end.

But the King and the Queen with their six brothers lived many years in happiness and peace.

'And then her dress.'

wicked things of the young Queen. 'Who knows who this girl is?' she said: 'she cannot speak, and is not worthy of a king.'

After a year, when the Queen had her first child, the old mother took it away from her. Then she went to the King and said that the Queen had killed it. The King would not believe it, and would not allow any harm to be done her. But she sat quietly sewing at the

PICTURE BOOKS

A Prairie Boy's Winter

William Kurelek

William Kurelek was a Canadian author and illustrator. In A Prairie Boy's
Winter *and* A Prairie Boy's Summer, *Kurelek documented unromanticized
recollections of his youth on the Canadian prairie. The texts and illustrations,
which are simple and direct, reveal one boy's perspective on natural phenomena
and his relationship with his environment.*

Spring was on its way when most of the
snow had gone from the schoolyard and the
little that remained lay in drifts along the
fences. The ice on the rink became too "rub-
bery" for skating, but the hockey enthusiasts
played on in their boots. It was a time of
year when William liked to go off by himself
to explore the water holes. He was fascinated
by spring run-off water. He never knew from
day to day how deep it was, so he had to test
it— just as mountains have to be climbed.

Testing was risky, but that was part of the
thrill. Ice or snow beneath the surface of the
water might suddenly give, and then he had a
rubber boot full of icy cold water. Out he
would scramble, for even one dry foot was
better than none. He emptied the boot,
tugged off the soaking sock, and wrung it
out. The trouser leg could be wrung a little
against the leg, or slipped down over the outside of the boot.

William had early experiences of wet-
tings—against his will. Older boys would
bully the youngest during recess to test the
spring ice on the ditch in front of the school.

Testing the depth of spring run-off.

They would break through, of course, and
the teacher would have to dry out their
clothes behind the school stove. Now
that William was growing older, he
remembered—and got no one wet except
sometimes himself.

William Kurelek, *A Prairie Boy's Winter* (Montreal, Canada: Tundra Books; Boston: Houghton Mifflin, 1973).

A Prairie Boy's Winter

William Kurelek

Before his father got prosperous enough to put an electric fence around temporary pastures, William often had to pasture cows all day. This wasn't a bad job if the cows were satisfied, for then he could read the pulpy western novels Steve had lent him at school and daydream that he was one of the heroes of the American frontier.

But faraway fields always look greener to a cow, and sometimes, even when William was sure the pasture offered them enough to eat, the herd grew pesky. He'd have sworn they even plotted escape, for they seemed to be only pretending to graze as they moved right up to a grain or corn field. Then, even before William could read another line of the western to find out if his hero had escaped an ambush, the "ornery critters" had crossed the forbidden line and were reveling in "the real thing." If the farm dog stayed with him, his help was appreciated.

Sometimes William tried ambushing the cows to teach them a lesson. He'd hide at the edge of the cornfield, and as soon as he could hear the clicking of ankles and snort-like heavy breathing of a grazing herd, he knew he was close enough to let fly with his slingshot. Sometimes the lead cow, which he'd struck in the forehead with a pebble,

Pasturing cows.

would raise her head in the air and shake it about as if dazed. William would fall into a brief panic. "Had he permanently injured her? What would his parents say?" But no, she soon rejoined the rest of the retreating herd and he'd have peace for half an hour or so before "the lesson" had worn off. Then the herd once more pretended to be in grazing formation and headed for the forbidden field.

William Kurelek, *A Prairie Boy's Summer* (Montreal, Canada: Tundra Books; Boston: Houghton Mifflin, 1975).

Explorations

1. List as many symbolic meanings as you can that are associated with water and the sea. Then try to find these meanings in the stories and poems in the first part of this section. Can you think of any other stories or poems that reveal symbolic meanings of water?

2. On a field trip to a seashore, lakeside, or river bank, examine forms of aquatic life, such as shellfish and marine plants, to determine what relationship, if any, they have to terrestrial life. Is the "world beneath the brine" truly a world apart?

3. Compare the Dutch folktale "The City beneath the Sea" with Rachel Carson's explanation of the various "lost continent" stories in the selection from *The Sea Around Us*. Are Atlantis myths the result of memories deeply rooted in folklore, as Carson suggests? What other explanations may there be?

4. When you visit aquatic areas, observe the surrounding environment and consider why certain species are represented there and why many are not.

5. Read some material about tree spirits as represented by totems and druids, and write a story about them. Consider primitive ancestor-worship carvings in this regard.

6. Compile a scrapbook of leaves, noting variations in their shape and vein patterns that aid in species identification. Also consider the various bark patterns of the trees from which the leaves come. Be sure to include the coniferous (evergreen) trees and their curious "needle" leaves.

7. How were the hills in your region formed? Are they an accumulation, such as a glacial deposit? Or are they the remains of lands once swept away by a flood?

8. The top of a mountain is often the culmination of a long quest. This is true in real life as well as fiction, as mountain climbers will attest. Mountains, such as Everest, and rock cliffs offer the potential for triumph. Prepare a brief list of books that use this as their theme.

9. Collect stray bird feathers and compile a feather scrapbook. Zoo attendants and farm workers can be helpful in your search. Create stories about the birds represented in your collection, highlighting the particular characteristics of the feathers, such as size, shape, and coloration. What purposes do these qualities serve for the bird, as well as for your story?

10. Choose a story—"The Firebird" or "The Water Lily," for instance—and stage a puppet show or shadow play about birds. One effective device is to make the bird puppets out of luminous paper and to perform the show with a black light in a darkened room.

11. Go on nature walks and make drawings of animal tracks in a notebook. Research these tracks to determine the type of animal that made them. Consider the surrounding environment and that animal's adaptability to it. You may even make plaster of paris castings of the tracks that larger animals have left.

12. The African Pygmy song "Dance of the Animals" was originally a song-dance that was acted out by a dancer. Choreograph such a dance for an entire class, imitating the movements of various fishes, birds, and other animals.

13. Choose a wild or domestic animal that you can observe directly yourself or read a naturalist's observation of that animal. Then write a story or poem that describes that animal in an accurate, unsentimentalized way. Or act out an animal pantomime, as represented in "Dance of the Animals."

References for Children

Adler, Irving and Ruth. *Irrigation*. New York: John Day, 1964.

Aiken, Conrad. *Cats and Bats and Things with Wings*. New York: Atheneum, 1965.

Ardizzone, Edward. *Little Tim and the Brave Sea Captain*. New York: Walck, 1955.

Asimov, Isaac. *ABC's of the Ocean*. New York: Walker, 1970.

Bellamy, David. *The Life-Giving Sea*. New York: Crown, 1975.

Buehr, Walter. *Timber!* New York: Morrow, 1960.

Credle, Ellis. *Down, Down the Mountain*. New York: Thomas Nelson, 1934.

Donovan, John. *Wild in the World*. New York: Harper & Row, 1971.

Evans, Eva Knox. *The Dirt Book*. Illustrated by Robert Quackenbush. Boston: Little, Brown, 1969.

Farmer, Penelope. *The Summer Birds*. Illustrated by James Spanfeller. Orlando, Fla.: Harcourt Brace Jovanovich, 1962.

Fisher, Aileen. *Feathered Ones and Furry*. Illustrated by Eric Carle. New York: Crowell, 1971.

Fisher, Ronald. *A Day in the Woods*. Photographs by Gordon W. Gahan. Washington: National Geographic Society, 1975.

French, Fiona. *King Tree*. New York: Walck, 1973.

George, Jean. *Julie of the Wolves*. Illustrated by John Schoenherr. New York: Harper & Row, 1972.

Goetz, Delia. *Tropical Rain Forests*. Illustrated by Louis Darling. New York: Morrow, 1957.

Holl, Adelaide. *The Wonderful Tree*. Racine, Wisc.: Western, 1974.

Holling, Holling C. *Paddle-to-the-Sea*. Boston: Houghton Mifflin, 1941.

Kingsley, Charles. *The Water-Babies*. Illustrated with photographs and maps and drawings by Pippa Brand. New York: Walck, 1974.

Lampman, Evelyn Sibley. *Treasure Mountain*. Illustrated by Richard Bennett. Garden City, N.Y.: Doubleday, 1949

Lasky, Kathryn. *Sugaring Time*. Photographs by Christopher G. Knight. New York: Macmillan, 1983.

Lavine, Sigmund A. *Wonders of the Peacock*. New York: Dodd, Mead, 1982.

Lewis, C. S. *The Voyage of the Dawn Treader*. Illustrated by Pauline Baynes. Harmondsworth, England: Penguin, 1968.

McCord, David. *Every Time I Climb A Tree*. Illustrated by Marc Simont. Boston: Little, Brown, 1967.

Mowat, Farley. *Owls in the Family*. Boston: Little, Brown, 1961.

Pringle, Laurence P. *Discovering the Outdoors*. New York: Natural History Press, 1969.

Rawlings, Marjorie Kinnan. *The Yearling*. Illustrated by N. C. Wyeth. New York: Scribner, 1939.

Sage, Michael. *The Tree and Me*. Illustrated by Arnold Spilka. New York: Walck, 1970.

Shaw, Evelyn. *Sea Otters*. New York: Harper & Row, 1980.

Silverstein, Shel. *The Giving Tree*. New York: Harper & Row, 1964.

Tresselt, Alvin. *Rain Drop Splash*. Illustrated by Leonard Weisgard. New York: Lothrop, Lee & Shepard, 1946.

Weiss, Renée Karol, ed. *A Paper Zoo: A Collection of Animal Poems*. Illustrated by Ellen Raskin. New York: Macmillan, 1968.

Wier, Ester. *The Straggler: Adventures of a Sea Bird*. New York: McKay, 1970.

Yahsima, Taro. *Seashore Story*. New York: Viking Press, 1967.

References for Adults

Armstrong, Edward A. *The Folklore of Birds: An Enquiry into the Origin and Distribution of Some Magico-Religious Traditions*. 2d ed. New York: Dover, 1970.

Auden, Wystan Hugh. *The Enchafed Flood; or the Romantic Iconography of the Sea*. London: Faber & Faber, 1951.

Cirlot, J. E. *A Dictionary of Symbols*. Translated by Jack Sage. New York: Philosophical Library, 1962. See entries for ''Tree'' and ''Mountain.''

DeCamp, Lyon Sprague. *Lost Continents: The Atlantis Theme in History, Science, and Literature*. New York: Dover, 1970.

Frazier, Sir James George. *The Golden Bough: A Study in Magic and Religion*. New York: Macmillan, 1958.

Jung, C. G. *Man and His Symbols*. Garden City, N.Y.: Doubleday, 1964.

Mattiessen, Peter. *The Tree Where Man Was Born*. New York: Dutton, 1972.

Rowland, Beryl. *Animal with Human Faces: A Guide to Animal Symbolism*. Knoxville, Tenn.: University of Tennessee Press, 1973.

Wolff, Robert Lee. *The Golden Key: A Study of the Fiction of George MacDonald*. New Haven, Conn.: Yale University Press, 1961. See criticism of *The Light Princess*.

Acknowledgments (continued)

Poems, copyright 1916 by Holt, Rinehart and Winston; renewed 1944 by Carl Sandburg. Reprinted by permission of Harcourt Brace Jovanovich, Inc.

p. 236: "The Lake Isle of Innisfree," from W. B. Yeats, *The Collected Poems of W. B. Yeats,* by permission A. P. Watt Ltd. on behalf of Michael B. Yeats and Macmillan London Ltd.

p. 237: "Snowbound in a Hidden Valley," copyright © 1957 by Helen Finnegan Wilson. Reprinted by permission of Julian Messner, a division of Simon & Schuster, Inc.

p. 241: "Connecticut," from *Tucker's Countryside,* by George Selden. Copyright © 1969 by George Selden. Illustration copyright © by Garth Williams. Reprinted by permission of Farrar, Straus and Giroux, Inc.

p. 252: "The Magic Fishbone," illustrated and copyrighted by Hilary Knight.

p. 268: "The Great Flood," from *Greek Myths,* by Olivia Coolidge. Copyright 1949 and copyright © renewed 1977 by Olivia E. Coolidge. Reprinted by permission of Houghton Mifflin Company.

p. 269: "The Descent of Manu," by Louis Renou. Reprinted by permission of George Braziller Inc.

p. 270: "Why the Sun and Moon Live in the Sky," by Kathleen Arnott. Reprinted by permission.

p. 271: "Grendel's Mother," from *Beowolf,* translated by Burton Raffel. Copyright © 1963 by Burton Raffel. Reprinted by arrangement with New American Library, New York, New York.

p. 277: "The Well of Immortality," from *Land of Seagull and Fox,* by Ruth Q. Sun. Charles E. Tuttle Co., Inc., Tokyo, Japan.

p. 283: "The Rains Began," from *Our Fathers Had Powerful Songs,* by Natalia Belting. Text copyright © 1974 by Natalia Belting. Reprinted by permission of the publisher, E. P. Dutton, a division of New American Library.

p. 283: "The Negro Speaks of Rivers," by Langston Hughes. Copyright 1926 by Alfred A. Knopf, Inc., and renewed 1954 by Langston Hughes. Reprinted from *Selected Poems of Langston Hughes,* by Langston Hughes, by permission of Alfred A. Knopf, Inc.

p. 284: "The Sea," by James Reeves. © James Reeves Estate. Reprinted by permission of the James Reeves Estate.

p. 284: "Maggie and Millie and Molly and May," copyright 1956 by e.e. cummings. Reprinted from his volume *Complete Poems 1913–1962,* by permission of Harcourt Brace Jovanovich, Inc.

p. 285: "Slave of the Moon," and "See This Beautiful Rainy Day," from *Miracles,* edited by Richard Lewis. Copyright © 1966 by Richard Lewis. Reprinted by permission of Simon & Schuster, Inc.

p. 286: "The Sea," by Armstrong Sperry. Reprinted with permission of Macmillan Publishing Company from *Call It Courage,* by Armstrong Sperry. Copyright 1940 by Macmillan Publishing Company, renewed by Armstrong Sperry.

p. 290: "Upriver," from *River Notes,* by Barry Lopez. © 1976, reprinted with permission of Andrews, McMeel & Parker. All rights reserved.

p. 291: "Hidden Lands," from *The Sea Around Us,* by Rachel L. Carson. © 1961 by Rachel L. Carson. Reprinted by permission of Oxford University Press.

p. 295: Specified excerpts from pgs. 242–247, 253–257, 262–264, 265–266, in *The Silent World,* by Captain J. Y. Cousteau, with

Frederic Dumas. Copyright, 1953, by Harper & Row, Publishers, Inc. Copyright, 1950, by Time Inc. Reprinted by permission of Harper & Row, Publishers, Inc.

p. 308: "Yggdrasill the World Tree," from *Myths of the Norseman,* by Roger Lancelyn Green (Puffin Books, 1970) pp. 15–21, copyright © Roger Lancelyn Green, 1960.

p. 311: "Daphne and Apollo," from *Tales the Muses Told,* by Roger Lancelyn Green, reproduced by permission of The Bodley Head, London.

p. 313: "White Mountains," from *Indian Legends of American Scenes,* by Marion E. Gridley. Reprinted by permission of Rand McNally & Company.

p. 314: "Buddha the Tree-God," from *Myths of the Hindus and Buddhists,* by Ananda K. Coomaraswamy and Sister Nivedita. Reprinted by permission of Dover Publications.

p. 316: "Princess on the Glass Hill," from *The Blue Fairy Book,* by Andrew Lang. Illustrated by H. J. Ford. Reprinted by permission of Dover Publications, Inc.

p. 321: "The Three Robes, " from *The Crimson Fairy Book,* by Andrew Lang. Illustrated by H. J. Ford. Reprinted by permission of Dover Publications, Inc.

p. 326: "Trees," from *The Little Hill,* by Harry Behn. Copyright 1949 by Harry Behn, © renewed 1977 by Alice L. Behn. All rights reserved. Reprinted by permission of Marian Reiner.

p. 327: "Climbing," from *In the Woods, in the Meadow, in the Sky,* by Aileen Fisher. Reprinted by permission of the author.

p. 327: "Hills," from *Poems by a Little Girl,* by Hilda Conkling. Reprinted by permission of the author.

p. 328: "Strange Tree," from *Under the Tree,* by Elizabeth Madox Roberts. Copyright 1922 by B. W. Huebsch. Copyright renewed 1950 by Ivor S. Roberts. Copyright 1930 by The Viking Press, Inc. Copyright renewed © 1958 by Ivor S. Roberts and Viking Penguin Inc. Reprinted by permission of Viking Penguin, Inc.

p. 328: "Tree" and "Hills," from *Miracles,* edited by Richard Lewis. Copyright © 1966 by Richard Lewis. Reprinted by permission of Simon & Schuster, Inc.

p. 329: "The Hills," by Rachel Field. Reprinted with permission of Macmillan Publishing Company from *Poems,* by Rachel Field (New York: Macmillan, 1957).

p. 329: "In Which I Find a Real Live Man," from *My Side of the Mountain,* by Jean George. Copyright © 1959 by Jean George. Reprinted by permission of the publisher, E. P. Dutton, a division of New American Library.

p. 335: From *Tree of Freedom,* by Rebecca Caudill. Copyright 1947, renewed © 1974 by Rebecca Caudill. Reprinted by permission of Viking Penguin Inc.

p. 341: From pp. 5–22 "Mountains are . . . of one person," in *Mountains,* by Delia Goetz. Copyright © 1962 by Delia Goetz. By permission of William Morrow & Company.

p. 343: From *The Secret Life of the Forest,* by Richard M. Ketchum. Reproduced by permission of the McGraw-Hill Book Company.

p. 346: "The Goblin and the Grocer," from *The Pink Fairy Book,* by Andrew Lang. Illustrated by H. J. Ford. Reprinted by permission of Dover Publications, Inc.

p. 349: "How Raven Created the World," from *Raven: Creator of the World,* by Ronald Melzack. Reprinted by permission of McClelland and Stewart, Ltd.

p. 352: "Fenris Wolf," from *Legends of the North,* by Olivia E. Coolidge, copyright 1951 by Olivia E. Coolidge. Copyright © renewed 1979 by Olivia E. Coolidge. Reprinted by permission of Houghton Mifflin Company.

p. 354: "The Golden Phoenix," from *The Golden Phoenix and Other Fairy Tales from Quebec,* by Marius Barbeau, retold by Michael Hornyansky. Illustration by Arthur Price. Copyright © Oxford University Press 1980. Reprinted by permission of the publisher.

p. 360: "The Wonderful Tar-Baby Story," from *Uncle Remus: His Songs and His Sayings,* by Joel Chandler Harris. Copyright 1908, 1921, 1935, 1963 by Esther La Rose Harris. A Hawthorn book. Reprinted by permission of E. P. Dutton, a division of New American Library.

p. 362: "The Water Lily," from *The Blue Fairy Book,* by Andrew Lang. Reprinted by permission of Dover Publications, Inc.

p. 367: "The Bird of Night," by Randall Jarrell. Reprinted by permission of Macmillan Publishing Company from *The Bat-Poet,* by Randall Jarrell. Copyright © Macmillan Publishing Company 1963, 1964.

p. 367: "Something Told the Wild Geese," by Rachel Field. Reprinted with permission of Macmillan Publishing Company from *Branches Green,* by Rachel Field. Copyright 1934 by Macmillan Publishing Company, renewed 1962 by Arthur S. Pederson.

p. 367: "Mice," by Rose Fyleman, from *Fifty-One New Nursery Rhymes,* by Rose Fyleman. Copyright 1931, 1932, by Doubleday & Company, Inc. Reprinted by permission of the publisher.

p. 368: "Cat," by Mary Britton Miller. Copyright estate of Mary Britton Miller.

p. 368: "Deer," by Harry Behn. From *Sombra,* by Harry Behn. Copyright 1961 by Harry Behn. Reprinted by permission of Marian Reiner.

pp. 368, 369: "Wild Horse" and "Wild Spurs," from *Miracles,* edited by Richard Lewis. Copyright © 1966 by Richard Lewis. Reprinted by permission of Simon & Schuster, Inc.

p. 369: "Dance of the Animals," from *The African Saga,* by Blaise Cendrars, translated by Francesco and Margery Bianco, copyright 1927 by Payson & Clark, Ltd. Reprinted by permission of Harcourt Brace Jovanovich, Inc.

p. 369: "Sea Gull," by Elizabeth Coatsworth. Reprinted with permission of Macmillan Publishing Company from *Summer Green* by Elizabeth Coatsworth. Copyright 1947 by Macmillan Publishing Company, renewed 1975 by Elizabeth Coatsworth Beston.

p. 370: Chapter 2 (pp 19–34) and illustration on p. 25 from *Sounder,* by William H. Armstrong. Illustrations by James Barkley. Text copyright © 1969 by William H. Armstrong. Illustrations copyright © 1969 by James Barkley. Reprinted by permission of Harper & Row, Publishers, Inc.

p. 375: From *Pigeon, Fly Home!* by Thomas Liggett. Illustrated by Marc Simont. Holiday House, Inc. Reprinted by permission.

p. 379: "A Mermaid on a Dolphin," from *The Secrets of the Dolphin,* by Helen Kay. Copyright © 1964. Reprinted by permission of the author.

p. 383: From *The Adventures of Reddy Fox,* by Thornton Burgess. Copyright 1915 by Thornton Burgess. By permission of Little, Brown and Company.

p. 388: From *A Prairie Boy's Winter,* by William Kurelek. Copyright © 1973 by William Kurelek. Reprinted by permission of Houghton Mifflin Company and Tundra Books (Canada).

p. 389: From *A Prairie Boy's Summer,* by William Kurelek. Copyright © 1975 by William Kurelek. Reprinted by permission of Houghton Mifflin Company and Tundra Books (Canada).

Index